Building Corporate Portals with XML

Building Corporate Portals with XML

Clive Finkelstein and
Peter H. Aiken

McGraw-Hill
New York San Francisco Washington, D.C.
Auckland Bogotá Caracas Lisbon London
Madrid Mexico City Milan Montreal New Delhi
San Juan Singapore Sydney Tokyo Toronto

Library of Congress Cataloging-in-Publication Date

Finkelstein, Clive.
Building corporate portals with XML / Clive Finkelstein and Peter H. Aiken.
p. cm.
ISBN 0-07-913705-9
1. XML (Document markup language) 2. Data warehousing.
I. Aiken, Peter. H. II. Title.
QA76.76.H94F56 1999
658′.05572–dc21 99-35910
CIP

3 4 5 6 7 8 9 0 DOC/DOC 0 4 3 2 1 0

ISBN 0-07-913705-9

The sponsoring editor for this book was Simon Yates and the production supervisor was Claire Stanley. It was set in New Century Schoolbook by Keyword Publishing Services Ltd.

Printed and bound by R. R. Donnelley & Sons Company.

Permissions are notified on page xvii.

This book is printed on recycled, acid-free paper containing a minimum of 50% recycled de-inked fiber.

To Jill, Kristi, and Megan—*Clive Finkelstein*

To Jasmine, and all of those who are reversing and reengineering their systems from a data-centric perspective—*Peter Aiken*

CONTENTS

FOREWORD

Clearly, by its very name, *Building Corporate Portals with XML*, is a "how to do it" book for implementing modern technology for information professionals. By definition, Clive and Peter get into the detail about how to reverse engineer the logical data models from the existing legacy data. That is an obvious requirement if you are ever to derive value for an Information Age business from its existing accumulation of data.

Further, there is a detailed discussion of XML that conveys both the power of XML but also its simplicity; that is, the ease of understanding of the logic of the language. It is their contention (and I would agree) that Data Reverse Engineering and XML are the foundational technological tools required for building a Corporate Portal.

However, I love this book, not for its technical explanations or for the rigor of the methodological permutations, but because hiding between its covers is a gem . . . the clearest explanation I have ever seen for navigating an Enterprise into the dangerous straits of the sea changes of the Information Age.

Alvin Toffler says in *The Third Wave*:

> The question now is not, who controls the last days of the industrial society, but who shapes the new civilization rising rapidly to replace it?

It is my observation that if you are going to shape the new Information Age Enterprise rising rapidly to replace the prevalent Industrial Age Enterprises, you are going to have to do the following four things.

Enterprise Strategy

First, you are going to have to become far more rigorous in defining who you are as an Enterprise and what value you are contributing to your maketplace. Business (Public Sector or Private Sector) is no longer as simple as, "while keeping your costs in line, develop a good product or service and find a bunch of customers to sell it to." No!! In the Information Age, where everybody has access to the same information at the same time, the power shifts outboard. In fact, if the customer has access to the same information that the Enterprise has access to, the power will shift outboard into the customer environment. It will become a "buyer's market." Now the name of the game is becoming, "find a good customer and identify and integrate the products and services required to keep them a good customer." This will cause wrenching changes in the Enterprise and will drive the complexity up by orders of magnitude, because the burden of integration falls now on the Enterprise, not on the customer.

Building Corporate Portals has as lucid a discussion of the process of identifying the Enterprise mission and goals, and so on, and transforming them into rigorous models that are fundamental to engineering a modern Enterprise as I have seen. If you read no more, this discussion alone would justify the price of the book.

Enterprise Models

Second, you are not only going to have to build Enterprise models, you are going to have to manage them as well in order to have the capability to continuously re-shape the Enterprise to respond to the dramatically changing environment around it. Not many people take issue with Alvin Toffler's proposition in *Future Shock* that

> knowledge is change ... and the ever-increasing body of knowledge feeding the great engine of technology creates ever-increasing change.

We are only now beginning to actually experience future shock. The question is, how do you intend to accommodate orders of magnitude increases in the rate of change? Any serious research on change management will reveal that change management starts with the drawings, the functional specs, the bills of material of the object you are trying to change. Drawings, functional specs and bills of material translate into logistics models, process models and semantic models in Enterprise terms. If you find that you have to change the Enterprise and you have no logistics models, process models and semantic models, you have three alternatives. You can either: spend the time to reverse engineer the models out of the operating Enterprise and then change them, or change by trial and error ... at the risk of possibly causing the Enterprise to fail, or don't change.

In *Building Corporate Portals* the process for deriving models from the Enterprise Mission and Strategy and transforming them into the operating Enterprise is described in detail. In fact, I have heard Clive Finkelstein describe this process dozens of times but he knows it so well and normally is describing it so quickly that he makes you dizzy!! In the book, however, he takes you through the process step-by-step and shows you how to derive the build sequence that allows you to build the Enterprise piece-by-piece without introducing the discontinuity that renders the data of the Enterprise useless and/or unavailable.

Technology Change

Third, you are going to have to understand the technological changes as they start coming faster and faster and, more importantly, you are going to have to understand how you are going to have to reengineer your Enterprise at best to leverage these new technologies and at worst to prevent other Enterprises from supplanting you in your own marketplace! This presumes that you have the models already available to understand the impact of the changes and to reeingeer and then to affect the changes into the actual reality of the Enterprise itself.

Building Corporate Portals not only describes the process of building the models but it also succinctly defines the next wave of technological change and provides samples of how you might reengineer the Enterprise to capitalize on the new technologies. In fact, this is as concise a description of the next wave of technology and the Enterprise reconceptualization as I have seen. It has all of the positive (exploitative) as well as negative (defensive) implications I have alluded to above.

Decision Early Warning

The fourth thing you are going to have to do is to continuously and dynamically monitor your Enterprise performance as well as the external environment to anticipate the changes you are going to have to make. This is what the whole idea of "portals" is all about; that is, how to access the performance data within the Enterprise, how to access the environmental data outside the Enterprise, and how to analyze the inside and outside data and decide what to do . . . and to do all of this dynamically. Of course, this all presumes you have the models (the "architecture") to understand and to affect the change.

Building Enterprise Portals has an extensive discussion of Decision Early Warning and the bulk of the book describes the process of developing the Portals in support of Decision Early Warning in depth.

Summary

In summary, when I look at the Information Age with orders of magnitude increases in complexity and orders of magnitude increases in the rate of change, it is obvious to me that you are going to have to do the following:

- *Develop* a rigorous and explicit definition of your Enterprise, your mission, goals, objectives, the value you intend to contribute and then to translate them into definitive models.
- *Build* the models required to transform your intentions into the reality of your Enterprise and further to manage these models to serve as a baseline for managing change.
- *Anticipate* the next wave of technology and begin the reengineering process to ensure your survival as one of the remaining players in the changing game.
- *Develop* a Decision Early Warning system to evaluate the internal performance and external changes to give you a modicum of time to respond to the changing environment.

How else would you be able to accommodate orders of magnitude increases in complexity and orders of magnitude increases in the rate of change???

This is a GREAT book!! Hiding inside the covers of this book about *Building Corporate Portals with XML* (which is a very significant issue in itself) lies some real gems about how to steer your Enterprise into a profitable/viable experience in the Information Age. How long do you think you have? I would suggest, not as long as you need!!!

Thank you Clive and Peter for giving us this road map and some short cuts!!

—JOHN A. ZACHMAN
July 1999
Glendale, California

ACKNOWLEDGMENTS

This book would not have been possible without the efforts of many people. I acknowledge the hard work, dedication, and intellect of past and present staff of Information Engineering Service Pty Ltd (IES) in Australia and New Zealand. From the late 1970s with the original work carried out in developing Information Engineering (IE), to its further refinement in the early 1980s and its acceptance throughout the world, IE has evolved into a powerful methodology.

I acknowledge also the innovative approaches adopted by staff of Information Engineering Systems Corporation (IESC) in the USA in the late 1980s and early 1990s, to translate the IE methodology into software as IE: Advantage—and the further evolution of IE into Enterpise Engineering (EE). And with the merger of IESC and Visible in 1997, I also acknowledge staff of Visible Systems Corporation as they evolved IE: Advantage into Visible Advantage. The power of IE and EE, and effectiveness of Visible Advantage, are all testament to the intellect and capabilities of these dedicated people.

But above all, I acknowledge the contributions of my very good friend, John Zachman. John and I have known and respected each other for more than 20 years. The insight and perception that John applied to create the *Zachman Framework for Information Systems Architecture* has made the IT world a less confusing place. Its evolution into the *Zachman Framework for Enterprise Architecture* has introduced clarity and encouraged easier communication and understanding between business and IT.

Above and beyond all of these good people, this book only exists because of the support, encouragement, and love of Jill, my wife. Being with her means that everything is possible and achievable. I love my wife, and I am delighted to tell the world. Together we can enjoy life, our daughter Kristi, and our granddaughter, Megan. But when we are apart, life loses all meaning.

—CLIVE FINKELSTEIN
Perth, Western Australia
March 1999
cfink@ies.aust.com
http://www.ies.aust.com/~ieinfo/

As I said in the acknowledgements of *Data Reverse Engineering* (for which Clive wrote the foreword), writing a book is very much an opportunity. It has been a privilege and a pleasure to become more closely associated with Clive Finkelstein and John Zachman—two pioneers in the world of systems-thinking as these materials have evolved. In addition, I acknowledge the support and contributions of my colleagues at the many organizations with whom my students and I have worked as we have researched and developed these methods. In particular: Marie Freeman (Director of Marketing Research/Mattel Incorporated); Bill Girling (Manager of Systems for the Department of Personnel and Training/Commonwealth of Virginia); Joe Cipolla (VP MIS/Circuit City Stores); Lewis Broome (Director of University Relations/Innovative Business Solutions, Inc.); Aaron Shapiro (Director of New Business Development/Evoke Software); and finally, Martin Yates and Diana Elman (Managing Director and VP of Architecture Development/ Deutsche Bank New York Center of Competence) have been instrumental in supporting these efforts. In addition, Elliot Chikofsky's (Meta Group) research and other activities have done much to motivate the continued interest in reverse engineering. A bit closer to home, my colleagues John Sutherland, Robert Mann, and E. G. Miller in the School of Business at Virginia Commonwealth University have provided ongoing support and/or acted as excellent sounding boards for some of these ideas. Professor Youngohc Yoon (also at VCU) co-developed the data quality approach described in Chapter 9 and Wendy Wood (Data Quality Manager/PacBell) synthesized the data quality engineering approach described in Chapter 14. There have literally been dozens of students who have helped out on these projects—performing the majority of the work. Finally, at home, my partner Jasmine Jaslow has continued to show me that it is all possible, and has continued to help me to make it so!

—Peter H. Aiken
Richmond, Virginia
paiken@acm.org
http://fast.to/peteraiken

PERMISSIONS

The authors acknowledge the following copyright owners of material used in this book. We would like to thank them for permission to include or reference their material. We thank Microsoft for permission to include material and reference the XML Scenarios on the Microsoft XML web site. Portions have been reprinted with permission from Microsoft Corporation. These XML applications are discussed in Chapters 12 and 15. We also thank Visible Systems Corporation for permission to use Visible Advantage throughout the book to illustrate many of the concepts we discuss. In particular, this modeling tool is used in Chapters 4, 5, 6, 7, 8, 11 and 12. We thank Evoke Software for the use of Mitigation Architect in Chapter 14. Database Associates articles by Colin White, from the Decision Processing web site, are referenced in Chapter 15. IDC have given us permission to reference and quote from an article by Gerry Murray in Chapter 15. We thank Object Design for permission to use material in Chapter 15 from their web site on the eXcelon XML database. We also thank Viador for permission to use material in Chapter 15 from their web site on the Viador E-Portal Suite. We thank Richard Hackathorn and his publishers for permission to use material in Chapter 15 from his WebFarming book and from the WebFarming web site. We acknowledge the material used in Chapter 15 on DSS Broadcaster, obtained from the MicroStrategy web site. We acknowledge the Merrill Lynch report on Nov 16, 1998 on Enterprise Information Portals (EIP), which identified the emerging interest in EIPs. InfoWorld reported this in a front-page article Jan 25, 1999. These are both referenced in Chapters 1 and 15. We acknowledge the previous books by Clive Finkelstein published by Addison-Wesley. For all copyright owners not explicitly mentioned above, but whose material we have included or referenced in the book, we also acknowledge their copyright ownership.

—Clive Finkelstein
—Peter H. Aiken
July 1999

INTRODUCTION

The profoundest thought or passion sleeps as in a mine, until an equal mind and heart finds and publishes it.

—Ralph Waldo Emerson

The *profound thoughts* and *passions* referred to by Emerson are the organizational resources that have unleashed the current technological revolution and the countless start-up ventures that have fueled the Information Age. If organizations do not provide the tools for their employees to publish and subsequently make use of these organizational resources, these thoughts and passions might as well remain securely locked in a vault.

This book is about the design, development, and deployment of *Corporate Portals;* also called *Enterprise Information Portals* or *Enterprise Portals*. The term "Enterprise Information Portal" (EIP) we believe was first used in a report published by Merrill Lynch on November 16, 1998—further reported in a Front Page article by *InfoWorld* in the January 25, 1999 issue—and defined as follows:

> Enterprise Information Portals are applications that enable companies to unlock internally and externally stored information, and provide users a single gateway to personalized information needed to make informed business decisions.
>
> Enterprise Information Portals (EP) are an emerging market opportunity; an amalgamation of software applications that consolidate, manage, analyze and distribute information across and outside of an enterprise (including Business Intelligence, Content Management, Data Warehouse and Mart, and Data Management applications.
>
> *Merrill Lynch: November 16, 1998*

Merrill Lynch were interested in the potential of the emerging EIP market: "*We have conservatively estimated the 1998 total market opportunity of the EIP market at $4.4 billion. We anticipate that revenues could top $14.8 billion by 2002, approximately 36% CAGR* (Compound Annual Growth Rate) *for this sector.*"

In many articles that have appeared since publication of the Merrill Lynch report and the InfoWorld article, the terms *Enterprise Information Portal* (EIP), *Corporate Portal* (CP), and *Enterprise Portal* (EP) have been variously used. This is a new field and the terminology has not settled yet. So we use all three terms interchangeably in this book to refer to portals for all enterprises: large Corporations; Small or

Medium Enterprises (SMEs); Federal, State or Local Government departments; and Defense departments.

As we move into the next century, Corporate or Enterprise Portals will be the primary methods used by organizations to publish and access Business Intelligence and Knowledge Management resources. These portals will evolve from today's Data Warehouses to provide the common technology for implementing Executive Information System (EIS), Decision Support System (DSS), Online Analytical Processing (OLAP), and Decision Early Warning (DEW) tools. We refer to all of these as Knowledge Management Tools (KMTs). Four characteristics shared by all Corporate Portal solutions are that:

1. Corporate Portals will be delivered via the Internet, intranets or extranets;
2. Corporate Portals will be inherently metadata and XML-based;
3. Corporate Portals will occur in Data Warehouse or Data Mart formats; and
4. Users won't know or really care about any of the above, because they will finally have access to the data that they need when they need it!

In the late 1990s we saw an explosion of interest in the Internet and its application to business. We saw Internet technologies applied to build corporate intranets and also extranets between customers, suppliers, and business partners. These opened up heterogeneous access to knowledge resources for business intelligence and knowledge management.

We also saw the emergence of new metadata management practices and standards. As we moved into the twenty first century, the World Wide Web Consortium (W3C) published recommendations for new standards that could provide access to and integration of dissimilar resources. These included the Extensible Markup Language (XML) and its related Extensible Style Language (XSL) and Extensible Linking Language (XLL). The W3C also published recommendations for the Document Object Model (DOM), a language-independent program interface standard to create, access, process, and modify these resources dynamically using XML. Emerging XML standards will be incorporated into Data Warehousing efforts and used by Corporate Portals to provide access to the knowledge resources within all parts of an organization, and outside via the Internet, intranets, and extranets.

But without modern and flexible data delivery systems such as provided by Data Warehouse and Data Mart technologies, a Corporate Portal cannot be effective. Corporate Portals provide vital access to both structured and unstructured data in enterprises residing in old and new systems and databases. Ninety percent of the knowledge resources in most organizations do not reside as structured data. They exist as unstructured data that comprise textual documents, reports, graphics and images, or audio and video resources. Business intelligence and knowledge management tools have not been able to access these resources effectively until now.

The Merrill Lynch report also affected ourselves—your authors. We had been writing a book on Data Warehousing. Our purpose was to publish a book that would help enterprises move their Data Warehouses and Data Marts to the Internet, intranet, and extranet. We felt that this would provide benefit to the enterprises, their employees, customers, suppliers, and business partners.

This was a difficult task to do, as another author whom we respected had found. Richard Hackathorn had published *Web Farming for the Data Warehouse*. He wrote this around the time when the groundswell of support for XML had begun to build following its acceptance as a recommended standard by the W3C Committee in February 1998.

We saw XML also as an important component to move Data Warehouses and Data Marts to The Web. The Merrill Lynch report identified the market potential that justified what was, until then, just a "gut feel" for us. It highlighted a glaring omission: the absence of clear technical direction on how to build for this new environment. As authors, we do not pretend to have all of the answers. But this certainly is our field of expertise, having been involved in many projects and having built many Data Warehouses, Data Marts, Web Sites, and Electronic Commerce applications as consultants, instructors, and webmasters over many years.

We will share our knowledge with you in this book. We will discuss problems and solutions. And there will be others after us who will add more, based on their experience. They will also write, or consult, or teach: this new discipline will further evolve—that is the nature of the Information Technology industry.

This book is therefore about the design, development, and deployment of Corporate Portals using a technology that successfully enables organizations to deliver valuable data assets to those requiring them. But success in this endeavor is not measured solely by technical excellence. A Corporate Portal that cannot provide the information needed by its end users is a failure, no matter how well it is delivered from a technical perspective. Corporate Portal success depends on a number of factors and methods that are covered extensively by this book.

The first factor is a clear understanding of the information that should be provided by the portal. A number of methods can be used to identify these information needs. These are the focus of Part I, addressing *Enterprise Portal Design* and methods for knowledge management tool development. While the focus of Part I is mainly on structured data, many of the principles can also be applied to unstructured data. This part of the book applies equally to the design of Data Warehouses as well as Corporate Portals.

The second factor is the identification of data sources to be loaded into the Corporate Portal, so it can provide that information. Part II addresses methods for *Enterprise Portal Development*. These methods are used to identify source data, typically from legacy files and relational databases—or from external sources—then extract, transform, and load that data into the warehouse. Part II thus focuses on structured data, but many of these methods also apply to unstructured data. It equally addresses the development of Data Warehouses and Corporate Portals.

The third factor addresses the utilization of Corporate Portals and the dissemination of information. As the focus of Part III, *Enterprise Portal Deployment* uses the latest technologies for delivery of information via the Internet or corporate intranets for knowledge management and decision support. It shows how to integrate structured and unstructured data to build effective and flexible Corporate Portals. Part III brings together all methods in the book, discussing how Data Warehouses evolve into Corporate Portals—implemented with these technologies—that lead to significant business reengineering, systems reeengineering, and quality improvements.

The methods in this book define a methodology to design, develop, and deploy Corporate Portals, Enterprise Portals, or Enterprise Information Portals. This methodology is called *Engineering Enterprise Portals*. Accordingly it is abbreviated to *EEP*. It is a refinement and an outgrowth of a number of methodologies that came before it. EEP is built on a firm foundation based on Information Engineering (IE), Software and Systems Engineering (SSE), and Enterprise Engineering (EE). One author is the originator and "Father" of Information Engineering and is a major contributor to Systems and Enterprise Engineering—the other pioneered the extraction of structured data and metadata from legacy systems and in reverse engineering and systems reengineering projects; both have been major contributors to the development and evolution of other aspects of the Data Administration profession. Clive Finkelstein and Peter Aiken are joint developers of the *Engineering Enterprise Portals* (EEP) methodology discussed in this book.

The process of Engineering Enterprise Portals follows the sequence laid out in this book. A discussion of the chapters in each Part will therefore provide an introduction to the book, as well as an overview of EEP.

An Overview of the Book

Each chapter is described next. All chapters are intended to be read in sequence; they progressively introduce the methodology for Engineering Enterprise Portals (EEP). Some chapters may contain material that you feel you already know. However, we strongly recommend that you at least skim-read them; they illustrate some familiar concepts applied in different ways. EEP brings together IE, EE, and SE and modifies the results specifically to build EPs. To get the full benefit from the book, it is safest therefore not to make any assumptions. The reference to Enterprise Portals in the EEP methodology below applies equally to Corporate Portals.

Chapter	Summary
Part I	**Enterprise Portal Design** *The relationship between EEP and development, implementation, and refinement of organizational strategy is addressed. The goal of any Enterprise Portal effort is to develop effective knowledge management capabilities that provide quality data to users so they can develop, implement, and refine organizational strategies. Part I describes strategic planning, data modeling, strategic modeling, and decision support methods to capture strategic, tactical, and operational knowledge as structured data in support of Data Warehouse design and Enterprise Portal design.*
1	***Enterprise Portal Concepts*** This chapter introduces the concepts of Corporate Portals, Enterprise Portals, and Enterprise Information Portals and the engineering disciplines that are used in the EEP methodology. It discusses the roles of data models and metadata and briefly introduces how XML uses metadata. It introduces the basic principles of the Zachman Framework

for Enterprise Architecture as the basis for integration of the information and knowledge assets that exist throughout enterprises.

2 ***Strategic Business Planning: Designing Tomorrow, Today***

A starting point for Enterprise Portals is to understand the information needs of managers and their staff. This is indicated, directly or indirectly, by business plans defined at various management levels. This chapter introduces *Goal Analysis*, an easy-to-apply strategic planning methodology used at the strategic, tactical, and operational levels of an organization to identify EP-based information needs. Using goal analysis, planning statements documenting policies, goals, objectives, strategies, and key performance indicators are defined for each management level. These are called performance measures. Goal analysis is also used to document the planning statements that focus on a project, such as a data warehousing or EP project. The performance measures so identified represent a major component of the information to be delivered by the EP.

3 ***Data Modeling: A Window into the Enterprise***

Data Modeling is a critical method essential for success in data warehousing and EPs. The principles of data modeling are first introduced for the development of data models and data maps that represent data and information of interest. The chapter uses data modeling concepts to capture expert knowledge for knowledge management purposes in "structure" entities, as used by Information Engineering (IE) and Enterprise Engineering (EE). Even if you are already familiar with data modeling concepts, we recommend that you at least skim-read this chapter. For example, structure entities take tacit knowledge held by individual business experts and make it explicit. Structure entities therefore offer great potential to capture and manage expert knowledge in Enterprise Portals.

4 ***Strategic Modeling: A Map for the Future***

This chapter uses *Strategic Modeling* and an integrated CASE tool to develop a high-level data model—a strategic model—from the planning statements defined in Chapter 2. The specific information needed, based on the performance measures identified in that chapter, are added to the strategic model. The strategic model is analysed by the I-CASE tool to derive project plans from the data model, identifying business activities and processes that represent structured and unstructured data sources for the required information. The strategic model is also analyzed to develop project maps for Enterprise Portal implementation priority and progressive delivery of enterprise-wide data. These project maps and project plans are used for more detailed tactical and operational modeling—to define detailed source data, from which can be derived the required information.

5 ***EEP Framework: Implementing Decision Early Warning***

Knowledge Management Tools (KMTs) require not only the right information needed to support decision making, but also that it be delivered in a timely fashion. *Decision Early Warning* (DEW) is a performance monitoring method that enables managers to define upper and lower boundaries of acceptable performance. These are based on the performance measures incorporated in strategic, tactical, and operational models. Performance can then be monitored periodically and automatically within these bounds. Unacceptable performance is immediately notified to the responsible manager for action. Trends towards unacceptable performance can be notified on an early warning basis via email, fax, pager, phone, intranet, or Internet so that a decision can be taken early, to avoid later poor performance. Decision Early Warning concepts are used extensively in Enterprise Information Portals. The chapter concludes with the EEP Framework, describing the EEP phases of EP Design, EP Development, and EP Deployment, discussed further in Parts II and III.

Part II **Enterprise Portal Development**

Part II describes our approach to defining quality metadata, quickly and accurately, that is required to develop Enterprise Portals. This specifies the precise data requirements to develop, implement, and refine EP-based organizational strategies. EP development provides the required structured data in specific formats or environment combinations to develop and implement organizational strategies. Much source data exists as structured data in legacy systems. We therefore describe a method to reverse engineer legacy system metadata, in order to extract the system metadata required to develop your Data Warehouse or Enterprise Portal. Too many warehouse and EP efforts skip over or only informally carry out these activities.

6 ***Metadata Analysis Dimensions***

This chapter discusses metadata analysis dimensions, describing why it is necessary to first develop and analyze metadata in order to accurately engineer a Data Warehouse or an Enterprise Portal. Understanding these dimensions is a key prerequisite to their effective development.

7 ***Metadata Engineering Activities***

This chapter illlustrates the key role that metadata engineering plays in integrating data warehouse and EP development with the implementation of organizational strategy. Unless you understand possible dimensions of system metadata and metadata engineering it is not possible to specify what components will be able to help you solve your problem. We illustrate how to match the development of appropriate system metadata subsets with specific requirements for developing a Data Warehouse or an Enterprise Portal.

8 ***Metadata Types***

Understanding the system metadata types and how they are interrelated will enable you to identify and obtain the metadata relevant to your EEP efforts.

9 ***Metadata Quality***

This chapter describes the process of engineering quality into your organizational metadata engineering practice, so that a Data Warehouse or Enterprise Portal has quality engineered into it from the beginning. This avoids having to "bolt quality on" after your warehouse or Enterprise Portal is up and running. Not only will this save you embarrassment when you go live but it will also reduce your overall development costs.

10 ***Metadata Project Example***

The methods described in previous chapters of Part II are applied to examples that illustrate the metadata methods of EEP. Typical contents of a Request for Information (RFI) from vendors are considered. Project budgets and metadata capture approaches are discussed to establish a business case for a metadata project. Real-life projects using this approach are discussed and examined to determine the lessons learned.

Part III **Enterprise Portal Deployment**

Technologies that can be used for deployment of Enterprise Portals are examined. Part III introduces use of the Internet and intranets to access external knowledge using XML. XML enables both structured and unstructured data to be integrated seamlessly within an enterprise. Part III describes how the EEP methodology and XML are used for business reengineering, systems reengineering, and data quality. It discusses the evolution of Data Warehouses into Enterprise Portals. Future applications and directions that these and other technologies will take for EP-based knowledge management are also discussed.

11 ***The Internet and XML: The Future of Metadata***

This chapter briefly discusses HTML as used by the Internet and corporate intranets. It introduces concepts used by Extensible Markup Language (XML) and its impact on metadata. XML presents a powerful approach for using metadata: not just for structured data as discussed in Parts I and II, but also for unstructured textual documents, graphics, images, audio, video, and other sources of organizational knowledge. XML can be used to define metadata languages and methods for different industries and applications, using the Internet and intranets for data interchange and to capture external knowledge. XML provides a vital technology for the development and deployment of Enterprise Portals.

12 ***Using XML as a Business Reengineering Technology***

Part I incorporated business plans in data models, identifying the information needed to implement those plans using structured data. Analysis of these data models derived project plans and project maps for development of EPs. These project plans and maps also identify business processes that cross functional boundaries. Cross-functional processes can indicate business reengineering opportunities that utilize Internet technologies for direct and immediate access to customers, suppliers, and business partners for competitive advantage. XML is a significant enabler to translate these business reengineering opportunities into fact.

13 ***Using XML as a Systems Reengineering Technology***

The reverse engineering carried out with structured data in Part II to capture metadata as part of metadata engineering also establishes an environment for forward engineering to different platforms, DBMS, or operating systems environments. This is called systems reengineering. EEP can play an important role in the reengineering of legacy systems and databases. Further, it can be integrated with existing or planned business reengineering efforts using EPs to leverage enterprise integration activities.

14 ***Implementing Organizational Quality Initiatives***
The quality of business plans and data models was discussed in Part I. The problems of data quality were addressed in Part II. This chapter draws on the lessons learned to provide useful direction and guidance for deploying quality data at all organizational levels. It describes an EEP method used to establish and maintain high quality data throughout an enterprise.

15 ***The Central Role of Enterprise Portals***
A number of XML applications are discussed. These are potentially all Enterprise Portal applications. *Pull* technologies are used today with Data Warehouses that enable users to request information via Knowledge Management Tools. These KMTs include Executive Information Systems (EIS); Decision Support Systems (DSS); Online Analytical Processing (OLAP); and Decision Early Warning (DEW). These tools can also deliver their results via the Internet and intranets. Methods are also emerging for *Web Farming,* using the Internet to discover unstructured and structured data, information, and knowledge of interest, and acquire it. New tools are emerging that use *Push* technologies to deliver results directly to users based on registered information needs or early warning interests. Push tools can deliver this information via the Internet, intranet, email, fax, pager, or voice for immediate notification. Methods are described to structure this information and knowledge for incorporation in, and dissemination via, Enterprise Portals. The chapter closes by discussing the role that Enterprise Architecture and Enterprise Portals will take in transforming enterprises—helping them to operate and complete effectively into the twenty first century.

PART 1

Enterprise Portal Design

CHAPTER 1

Enterprise Portal Concepts

I know the data is there, but I can't get the information I need.
—Anonymous Manager

How many times have you heard this cry from management? But you are not alone; the same cry has been expressed in most languages around the world. It is a common problem: the data is in the computer, but cannot be located readily; or it is not in a format that is suitable for use by management. So what do you do?

You have taken an important first step: you are reading this book. Between the three of us—Clive Finkelstein, Peter Aiken and yourself—we will discuss approaches that can help you resolve this problem. The solution is based on Corporate Portals (also called Enterprise Portals or Enterprise Information Portals). It is also based on *Engineering Enterprise Portals* (EEP)—a methodology used for the design, development, and deployment of *Enterprise Portals* (EPs). We will discuss the basic concepts of Corporate Portals, Enterprise Portals and the Engineering Enterprise Portals methodology later in this chapter.

Enterprise Portals are based on Data Warehousing technologies, using *Metadata* and the *Extensible Markup Language* (XML) to integrate both structured and unstructured data throughout an enterprise. Metadata, XML, and EPs will be vital elements of the twenty-first century enterprise. We will briefly introduce the basic concepts of metadata, XML, and Enterprise Portals below, covering them in more detail in later chapters.

Structured data exists in databases and data files that are used by current and older operational systems in an enterprise. We call these older systems *legacy systems;* we call the data they use *legacy data*. In most enterprises, structured data comprises only 10 percent of the data, information, and knowledge resources of the business; the other 90 percent exists as *unstructured data* in textual documents, or as graphics and images, or in audio or video formats. These unstructured data sources are not easily accessible to Data Warehouses, but EPs use metadata and XML to integrate both structured and unstructured data seamlessly, for easy access throughout the enterprise.

What Is Metadata?

IT staff in most enterprises have a common problem. How can they convince managers to plan, budget, and apply resources for metadata management? What is metadata and why is it important? What technologies are involved? Internet and intranet technologies are part of the answer and will get the immediate attention of management. XML is the other technology. The following analogy may help you outline to management the important role that metadata takes in an enterprise.

Every country is now interconnected in a vast, global telephone network. We are now able to telephone anywhere in the world. We can phone a number, and the telephone assigned to that number would ring in Russia, or China, or in Outer Mongolia. But when it is answered, we may not understand the person at the other end. They may speak a different language. So we can be connected, but what is said has no meaning. We cannot share information.

Today, we also use a computer and the World Wide Web. We enter a Web site address into a browser on our desktop machine—a unique address in words that is analogous to a telephone number. We can then be connected immediately to a computer assigned to that address and attached to the Internet anywhere in the world. That computer sends a Web page based on the address we have supplied, to be displayed in our browser. This is typically in English, but may be in another language. We are connected, but like the telephone analogy—if it is in another language, what is said has no meaning. We cannot share information.

Now consider the reason why it is difficult for some of the systems used in an organization to communicate with and share information with other systems. Technically, the programs in each system are able to be interconnected and so can communicate with other programs. But they use different terms to refer to the same data that needs to be shared. For example, an accounting system may use the term "customer" to refer to a person or organization that buys products or services. Another system may refer to the same person or organization as a "client." Sales may use the term "prospect." They all use different terminology—different language—to refer to the same data and information. But if they use the wrong language, again they cannot share information.

The problem is even worse. Consider terminology used in different parts of the business. Accountants use a "jargon"—a technical language—which is difficult for non-accountants to understand. So also the jargon used by engineers, or production people, or sales and marketing people, or managers is difficult for others to understand. They all speak a different "language." What is said has no meaning. They cannot easily share common information. In fact in some enterprises it is a miracle that people manage to communicate meaning at all!

Each organization has its own internal language, its own jargon, which has evolved over time so similar people can communicate meaning. As we saw above, there can be more than one language or jargon used in an organization. Metadata identifies an organization's own "language." Where different terms refer to the same thing, a common term is agreed for all to use. Then people can communicate more clearly. And systems and programs can intercommunicate with meaning. But without a clear definition and without common use of an organization's metadata, information cannot be shared effectively throughout the enterprise.

Previously each part of the business maintained its own version of "customer," or "client" or "prospect." They defined processes—and assigned staff—to add new customers, clients, or prospects to their own files and databases. When common details about customers, clients, or prospects changed, each redundant version of that data also had to be changed. It requires staff to make these changes. Yet these are all redundant processes making the same changes to redundant data versions. This is enormously expensive in time and people. It is also quite unnecessary.

The importance of metadata can now be seen. *Metadata defines the common language used within an enterprise so that all people, systems, and programs can communicate precisely.* Confusion disappears. Common data is shared. And enormous cost savings are made. For it means that redundant processes (used to maintain redundant data versions up to date) are eliminated, as the redundant data versions are integrated into a common data version for all to share.

What Is XML?

Much effort has earlier gone into the definition and implementation of *Electronic Data Interchange* (EDI) standards to address the problem of intercommunication between dissimilar systems and databases. EDI has now been widely used for business-to-business commerce for many years. It works well, but it is quite complex and very expensive. As a result, it is cost-justifiable generally only for large corporations.

Once an organization's metadata is defined and documented, all programs can use it to communicate. EDI was the mechanism that was used previously. But now this intercommunication has become much easier.

Extensible Markup Language (XML) is a new Internet technology that has been developed to address this problem. XML can be used to document the metadata used by one system so that it can be integrated with the metadata used by other systems. This is analogous to language dictionaries which are used throughout the world, so that people from different countries can communicate. Legacy files and other databases can now be integrated more readily. Systems throughout the business can now coordinate their activities more effectively as a direct result of XML and management support for metadata.

XML now provides the capability that was previously only available to large organizations through the use of EDI. XML allows the metadata used by each program and database to be published as the language to be used for this intercommunication. But distinct from EDI, XML is simple to use and inexpensive to implement for both small and large organizations. Because of this simplicity, we like to think of XML as:

XML is EDI for the Rest of Us

XML will become a major part of the application development mainstream. It provides a bridge between structured and unstructured data, delivered via XML then converted to HTML for display in Web browsers. Together with metadata, XML is a key component in the design, development, and deployment of Enterprise Portals.

How Is Metadata Used with XML?

Metadata is used to define the structure of an XML document or file. Metadata is published in a *Document Type Definition* (DTD) file for reference by other systems. A DTD file defines the structure of an XML file or document. It is analogous to the *Database Definition Language* (DDL) file that is used to define the structure of a database, but with a different syntax.

An example of an XML document identifying data retrieved from a PERSON database is illustrated in Figure 1-1. This includes metadata markup tags (surrounded by < ... >, such as `<person_name>`) that provide various details about a person. From this, we can see that it is easy to find specific contact information in `<contact_details>`, such as `<email>`, `<phone>`, `<fax>`, and `<mobile>` (cell phone) numbers. Although we have not shown it here, the DTD also specifies

Figure 1-1 An example of an XML document with metadata tags (surrounded by <. . . >) identifying the meaning of following data.

```
<PERSON person_id="p1100" sex="M">
  <person_name>
    <given_name>Clive</given_name>
    <surname>Finkelstein</surname>
  </person_name>
  <company>
    Information Engineering Services Pty Ltd
  </company>
  <country>Australia</country>
  <contact_details>
    <email>cfink@ies.aust.com</email>
    <phone>+61-8-9309-6163</phone>
    <phone>(08) 9309-6163</phone>
    <fax>+61-8-9309-6165</fax>
    <mobile>+61-411-472-375</mobile>
    <mobile>0411-472-375</mobile>
  </contact_details>
</PERSON>
```

whether certain tags must exist or are optional, and whether some tags can exist more than once—such as multiple <phone> and <mobile> tags below. XML is introduced in more detail in Chapter 11.

Metadata that is used by various industries, communities, or bodies can be used with XML to define markup vocabularies. The World Wide Web Consortium (W3C) has developed a standard framework that can be used to define these vocabularies. This is called the *Resource Description Framework* (RDF). It is a model for metadata applications that support XML. RDF was initiated by the W3C to build standards for XML applications so that they can interoperate and intercommunicate more easily, avoiding the communication problems that we discussed earlier.

With XML, many applications that were difficult to implement before—often due to metadata differences—now become possible. For example, an organization can define the unique metadata used by each supplier's legacy inventory systems. This enables the organization to place orders via the Internet directly with those suppliers' systems, for automatic fulfillment of product orders. We will see an example of this in Chapter 12.

XML is enabling technology to integrate structured and unstructured data for next-generation E-Commerce and EDI applications. Web sites will evolve to use XML, with far greater power and flexibility than offered by HTML. Netscape Communicator 5.0 and Microsoft Internet Explorer 5.0 browsers both support XML. Most productivity tools and office suites (such as Microsoft Office 2000) support XML. Business Intelligence and Knowledge Management tools will support XML. XML development tools are also being released so that XML applications can be developed more easily.

The acceptance of XML is progressing rapidly, as it offers a very simple—yet extremely powerful—way to intercommunicate between different databases and systems, both within and outside an organization. How well an organization accesses and uses its knowledge resources can determine its competitive advantage and future prosperity. Use and application of knowledge will become even more important in the competitive Armageddon of the Internet, in which we will all participate.

The tools are coming, but a greater task still remains to be completed. This is the definition of your own metadata, your common enterprise language for intercommunication, so that you can use these tools effectively. The definition of metadata depends on knowledge of data modeling, previously carried out by IT people. But this is not just a task for IT. As it is vitally dependent on business knowledge, it also requires the involvement of business experts. Not by interview, but by their active participation. While data modeling has until now been a technical IT discipline, business data modeling is not. It can be learned by business people as well as IT staff. This was one of our motivations for the development of the Engineering Enterprise Portals methodology.

The Impact of Technology

One thing we are not short of today, is information. We are swimming in it! Our information comes from traditional printed sources such as books, magazines, newspapers, subscription reports and newsletters; from audio sources such as radio; from video sources such as free-to-air television or cable TV; from email and from word-of-mouth. The saving grace with these information sources—apart from radio and free-to-air TV—is that they are limited only to those who have subscribed to receive that information.

Not any more. Even today, and certainly more so in the future, each of these sources is moving to the Internet. They are offered as free services, where the cost of preparation is paid not by subscription but by advertising. Even word-of-mouth, previously a reliable source of information from people you knew personally and whose opinion you respected, has moved to the Internet in newsgroups and chat rooms—but with opinions offered by people, perhaps in another country, who are totally unknown to you. Both accurate and inaccurate comment now circle the globe not at word-of-mouth speed, but at electronic speed.

Email is the killer application of the Internet; even more so of the corporate intranet. Enormous knowledge is retained in corporate email archives—much to the chagrin of Microsoft, with certain email messages used by government prosecutors in the Microsoft Antitrust trial as smoking guns to illustrate alleged abuses of monopoly power. Corporate email is a knowledge resource that is of great value, yet until now it has been largely inaccessible.

Text searches on the Internet by traditional search engines are largely ineffective; a simple query can return thousands of links containing the entered keywords or search phrase. Only a small fraction of these may be relevant, yet each link must be manually investigated to assess its content—if relevancy ratings are not also provided.

The problem is no less severe with enterprises. We are inundated with information. To the credit of the Information Technology (IT) industry, at least this information is being organized and made more readily available through Data Warehouses. We discuss the building of Data Warehouses extensively in this book.

Most information in Data Warehouses is based on structured data sources as operational databases used by older legacy systems and relational databases. Data Warehouse products are also now becoming available that use Internet technologies. These valuable information tools can now be used within an exterprise across the corporate intranet. The information is thus more readily available.

We discussed earlier that structured data represents only 10 percent of the information and knowledge resource in most enterprises. The remaining 90 percent exists as unstructured data that has been largely inaccessible to Data Warehouses. Text documents, email messages, reports, graphics, images, audio and video files all are valuable sources of data, information, and knowledge that have been untapped. They exist in physical formats that have been difficult to access by computer—as if they were behind locked doors.

The technologies are now available to open these doors. XML is one technology, as we have briefly seen. XML enables structured and unstructured data sources to be integrated easily, where this was extremely difficult before. Organizations will develop new business processes and systems based on this integration, using Business Reengineering and Systems Reengineering methods. They will at last be able to break away from the business process constraints that have inhibited change in the past.

Process Technologies in the Industrial Age

Most organizations today still use processes based on principles that are no longer effective. They were designed using the process engineering "bible." Here is a short quiz: which book are we referring to? Who was the author? When was it published?

Was the process engineering bible written by Michael Hammer, acknowledged by many as the "Father" of Business Process Reengineering [Hammer 1990]? Was it [Hammer and Champy 1993]? No, it was before them ...

Was it written by Ed Yourdon, Tom deMarco, Ken Orr or Gane and Sarson—all giants of the Structured Software Engineering era, which was process-driven? No to all of these ...

Was it written by Edwards Deming, regarded by many as the "Father" of the quality movement? No, not him ...

What about Peter Drucker, considered the "Father" of management gurus? Not him, either ...

Was it Henry Ford, the "Father" of the assembly line? No, not him ...

Yet each of these giants has contributed in their separate ways to improve the design, operation, and functioning of enterprises and of information systems. We owe them all our thanks; we are in their debt. They contributed greatly to the theory and practice of management, of organization and process design, of systems design and development. We draw on their works many times throughout this book.

No, the process engineering bible was written long before each of these esteemed gentlemen.

We are in fact referring to *The Wealth of Nations* by Adam Smith, written around 1776, published most recently in [Smith 1910]. This has been the basis of most business processes used in enterprises today!

Expressing what he wrote, but in today's terminology, Adam Smith took complex processes and broke them down into simple steps. These were then carried out using the technology of his day—a workforce that was largely illiterate. He showed that people could be trained to carry out these simple process steps, which they repeated endlessly. He then combined each of these steps in different ways to build complex processes. While we have greatly simplified what he wrote and translated it into today's environment, essentially this was its impact. For these became the processes that fueled the Industrial Age.

Organizations grew as complex processes were built in this way. Manual technologies also used other technologies to supplement them. Mechanical technologies, electrical, electronic, and other technologies led to corresponding engineering disciplines: mechanical engineering, electrical engineering, etc. Yet the basic principle behind all of these processes was the work done by Adam Smith.

Henry Ford made a great contribution, with the assembly line. But still essentially the same approach was being used to design processes. And as these processes were automated, they were implemented on computer in much the same way as the processes were carried out in the enterprise. The computer was used basically to do the same tasks, yet faster and more accurately.

The processes referred to relevant data. Each part of the enterprise maintained its own copy of the data that was required. As the processes were automated, the data was also automated. The same data was implemented often in different versions, redundantly. The Information Engineering (IE) methodology, developed from 1976, was designed to address this problem—evolving in the mid-1980s into Enterprise Engineering (EE) [Finkelstein 1981a, 1981b, 1989, 1992].

By the late 1980s, the inhibiting factor in the effectiveness and operation of processes in many enterprises was seen to be due to this evolutionary approach to business process design. The Business Process Reengineering (BPR) revolution of the early 1990s began to address these problems. This was largely started by Michael Hammer in his landmark paper, provocatively titled: *Reengineering Work: Don't Automate, Obliterate*! [Hammer 1990].

XML and Enterprise Portals offer technologies that will progress these methods further. We will discuss their impact on Business Reengineering and on Systems Reengineering in Chapters 12 and 13.

Data Technologies in the Information Age

Our focus in this book is on Data Warehouses and Enterprise Portals. Data Warehouses provide access to structured data as discussed earlier. We will discuss data, warehouses, and engineering later in this chapter. We introduce Enterprise Portals here.

The term "Enterprise Information Portal" (EIP) we believe was first used in a report published by Merrill Lynch on November 16, 1998. A summary of this report is available from the [SageMaker] Web site. The full report can be downloaded as an Adobe Acrobat Portable Document Format (PDF) file from this same Web site. The Merrill Lynch summary and report define EIPs as:

> Enterprise Information Portals are applications that enable companies to unlock internally and externally stored information, and provide users a single gateway to personalized information needed to make informed business decisions.
>
> Enterprise Information Portals (EIP) are an emerging market opportunity; an amalgamation of software applications that consolidate, manage, analyze and distribute information across and outside of an enterprise (including Business Intelligence, Content Management, Data Warehouse and Mart, and Data Management applications.
>
> *[Merrill Lynch: November 16, 1998 [SageMaker] Web site]*

The Merrill Lynch report and summary highlight the emergence of Enterprise Information Portals as an investment opportunity for their clients and others. *InfoWorld* presented a summary of the report as a Front Page article of the January 25, 1999 issue. A copy of that article is available from the [InfoWorld Electric] Web site. A financial summary of the potential of the EIP market from the Merrill Lynch report was provided in the *InfoWorld* article. This is reproduced here as Figure 1-2.

The summary states: *We have conservatively estimated the 1998 total market opportunity of the EIP market at $4.4 billion. We anticipate that revenues could top $14.8 billion by 2002, approximately 36 percent CAGR* (Compound Annual Growth Rate) *for this sector.*

As Figure 1-2 illustrates, software is required for Content Management, which is projected to grow from a market worth $1.2 billion in 1998 to one worth $4.7 billion in 2002. Products in the Business Intelligence EIP market are expected to grow from $2.0 billion to $7.2 billion. The Data Warehouse and Data Mart EIP market is projected to grow from nearly $1 billion to $2.5 billion, while the Data Management market will grow from $184 million to $360 million. The total EIP market therefore was projected in the Merrill Lynch report to grow from $4.4 billion to $14.8 billion over the period 1998 to 2002.

Discussing the potential of the EIP market, the authors of the Merrill Lynch report believe it will *eventually reach or exceed the investment opportunities provided by the Enterprise Resource Planning (ERP) market.* They give three main reasons why:

> Enterprise Information Portals will emerge from a consolidation within and between the Business Intelligence, Content Management, Data Warehouse, Data Mart and Data Management markets:
>
> 1. *EIP systems provide companies with a competitive advantage:* Corporate management is just realizing the competitive potential

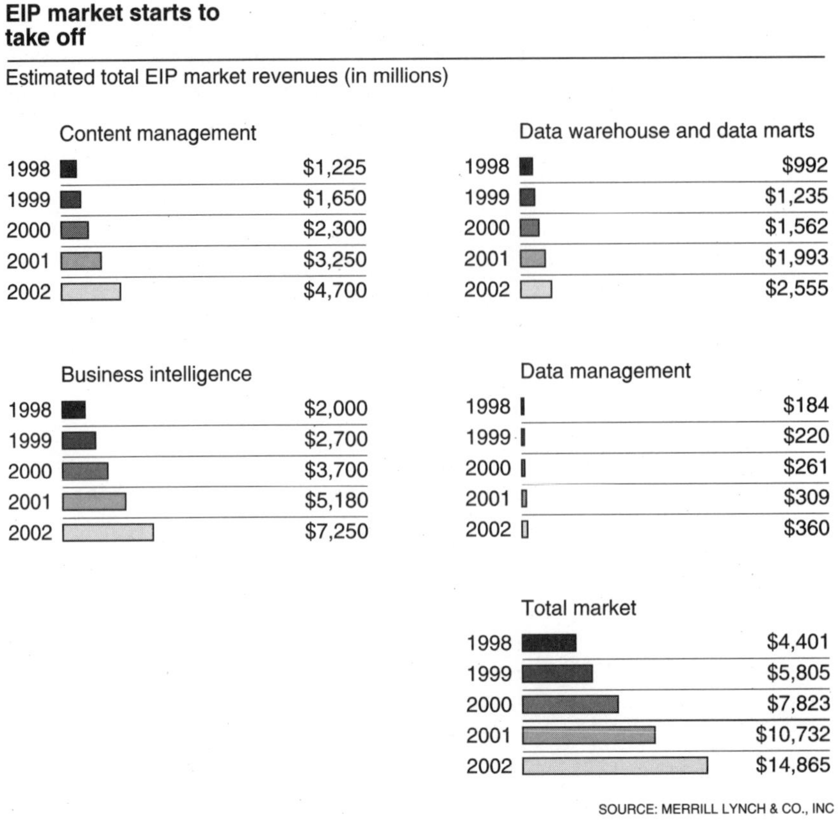

Figure 1-2 Enterprise Information Portal Market. *Source*: [InfoWorld] Web Site and Merrill Lynch.

EIP market starts to take off

Estimated total EIP market revenues (in millions)

Content management

1998	$1,225
1999	$1,650
2000	$2,300
2001	$3,250
2002	$4,700

Data warehouse and data marts

1998	$992
1999	$1,235
2000	$1,562
2001	$1,993
2002	$2,555

Business intelligence

1998	$2,000
1999	$2,700
2000	$3,700
2001	$5,180
2002	$7,250

Data management

1998	$184
1999	$220
2000	$261
2001	$309
2002	$360

Total market

1998	$4,401
1999	$5,805
2000	$7,823
2001	$10,732
2002	$14,865

SOURCE: MERRILL LYNCH & CO., INC

lying dormant in the information stored in its enterprise systems. . . . EIP applications combine, standardize, index, analyze and distribute targeted, relevant information that end users need to do their day-to-day jobs more efficiently and productively. The benefits include lowered costs, increased sales and better deployment of resources.

2. *EIP systems provide companies with a high return on investment (ROI):* The emergence of "packaged" EIP Applications are more attractive to customers because they are less expensive than customized systems, contain functionality that caters to specific industries, are easier to maintain and faster to deploy. . . . EIP products help companies cut costs *and* generate revenues.

3. *EIP systems provide access to all:* The Internet provides the crucial inexpensive and reliable distribution channel that enables companies to make the power of information systems available to all users

> (employees, customers, suppliers). Distribution channels include the Internet, Intranet and Broadcasting. ... Companies will need to use both "publish" (pull) and "subscribe" (push) mediums to ensure the right information is available or distributed to the right people at the right time.

They go on to say that they: *envision the Enterprise Information Portal as a Browser-based system providing ubiquitous access to business related information in the same way that Internet content portals are the gateway to the wealth of content on the Web.*

The Merrill Lynch report and the *InfoWorld* Front Page article triggered a flurry of articles in other publications. Software companies in these markets scrambled to refocus their software development plans to deliver products for the new emerging market that had been identified.

Enterprise Information Portal Directions

The market potential had been identified, the software vendors had begun to develop products, but there was no clear definition of the EIP market apart from general directions in the Merrill Lynch report. And there was no technical guidance that would help software vendors and their enterprise customers to build these Enterprise Information Portals.

The report also affected ourselves: your authors. We had been writing a book on Data Warehousing. Our purpose was to publish a book that would help enterprises move their Data Warehouses and Data Marts to the Internet, intranet, and extranet. We felt that this would provide benefit to the enterprises, their employees, customers, suppliers, and business partners.

This was a difficult task to do, as another author whom we respected had found. Richard Hackathorn had published *Web Farming for the Data Warehouse* [Hackathorn 1999]. He was writing this around the time when the groundswell of support for XML had begun to build up following its acceptance as a recommended standard by the W3C Committee in February 1998 [W3C].

As discussed earlier in this chapter, XML is a technology that enables many applications and databases to overcome the great constraints of legacy systems and databases that had evolved as redundant data versions. It is also an important component to move Data Warehouses and Data Marts to Corporate Intranets or to the Internet. The Merrill Lynch report identified the market potential that justified what was, until then, just a "gut feel" for us. It highlighted a glaring omission: the absence of clear technical direction on how to build for this new environment. As authors, we do not pretend to have all of the answers. But this is our field, having built many Data Warehouses, Data Marts, Web Sites, and Electronic Commerce applications as consultants, instructors, and webmasters over many years.

We will share our knowledge with you in this book. The three of us, together, will discuss problems and solutions. And there will be others after us who will add more, based on their experience. They will also write, or consult, or teach: this new discipline will further evolve—that is the nature of the Information Technology industry.

Enterprise Portal Terminology

A number of terms have emerged along with the growing interest in Enterprise Information Portals. Internet Content Portals such as NetCenter (Netscape), MyYahoo (Yahoo), MSN (Microsoft), and AOL became popular in 1998 as a central point that could be visited by millions on the Internet—as a gateway or jumping-off point to other locations on the World Wide Web. Some of these are content providers; others are search engines. The terminology differs, but we feel a general term describing all of these is *Internet Portal.* This is the term we will use in this book for reference to WWW consumer portals.

In the many articles that have appeared since publication of the Merrill Lynch report and the InfoWorld article, the terms "Enterprise Information Portal" (EIP), "Corporate Portal" (CP), and "Enterprise Portal" (EP) have been variously used.

"Enterprise Information Portal," being the first used, is the obvious term. But we find many articles are using *Enterprise Portal* and *Corporate Portal* as equivalent terms to refer to an EIP. This is a new field and the terminology has not settled yet. So we will use all three terms interchangeably in this book to refer to portals for all enterprises: large Corporations; Small or Medium Enterprises (SMEs); Federal, State or Local Government departments; and Defense departments.

Enterprise Portal Concepts

We will introduce some of the basic concepts of an Enterprise Portal in this section, with related concepts covered later in this chapter. The remainder of the book will progressively introduce you to the concepts and methods that can be used to build Enterprise Portals.

In *Part 1: Enterprise Portal Design*, there is a great parallel with Data Warehouse design. *Part 2: Enterprise Portal Development* also parallels Data Warehouse development. Our focus in these two parts is therefore mainly on Data Warehouses and Data Marts.

In *Part 3: Enterprise Portal Deployment* we cover XML in Chapter 11. XML is an enabling technology that offers great benefit for Business Reengineering and Systems Reengineering. These are covered in Chapters 12 and 13. Many enterprises are struggling to move out from under the weight of legacy systems and processes that are not appropriate or responsive enough for the Information Age. Enterprise Portals and XML will enable these enterprises to transform themselves more effectively, without first having to throw all those legacy systems away and develop new systems at great cost. Chapter 14 addresses quality in these transformed enterprises.

Finally, in Chapter 15 we will return to discuss the central role of Enterprise Portals, summarizing the main points from the book.

The main concepts of Enterprise Portals are illustrated in Figure 1-3, from the *InfoWorld* article on the [InfoWorld Electric] Web site. The focus of Data Warehouses is *Structured Data*, shown in the top part of Figure 1-3. Source data is drawn from *online transactional databases* such as *ERP applications*, legacy files, or other relational databases. Source data may also be *point of sale data*. This source data is first extracted, transformed, and loaded by *ETL and data quality* tools into *Relational OLAP* databases and/or the *Data Warehouse*. *Data marts* take subject area subsets from the *Data Warehouse* for *query and reporting*. *Analytical applications* carry out *OLAP analysis* using OLAP tools. Business Intelligence tools also provide analytical processing, such as EIS and DSS products. *Data mining* tools are used to drill down and analyze data in the warehouse. *Warehouse management* operates to manage the *ETL and data quality* stage, the *Relational OLAP* databases and *Data Warehouse*, and the *analytical applications*.

The bottom part of Figure 1-3 lists *Unstructured Data* sources that are used by Enterprise Portals. In Chapter 11 we see how XML can use metadata tags to integrate unstructured data sources with the *Structured Data* sources above. These unstructured data sources are

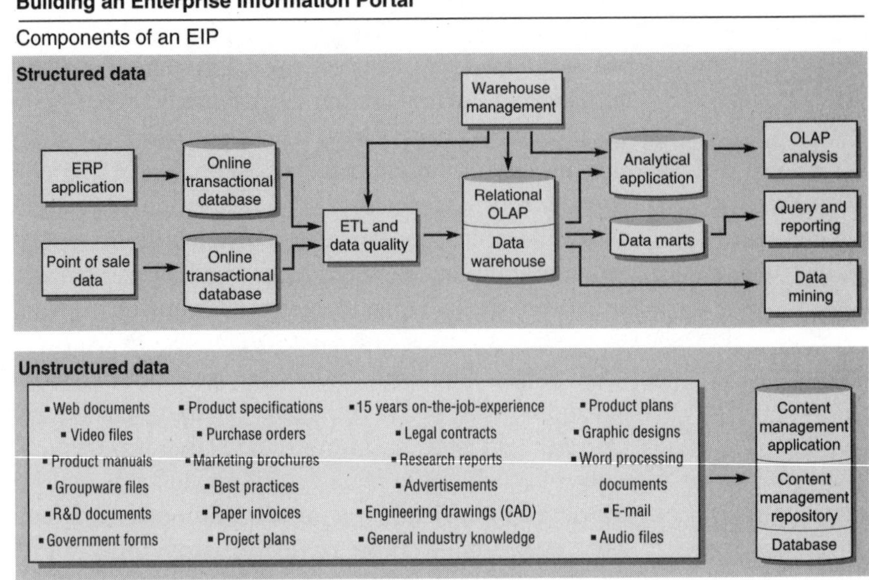

Figure 1-3 Enterprise Portal concepts. *Source:* [InfoWorld Electric] Web site.

managed by a *Content Management Repository* as *Content Management Applications* and *Database*. While they are conceptual in Figure 1-3, we will see these referenced as XML databases later in the book. Enterprise Portals extend Data Warehouses to the intranet and Internet. But unlike Data Warehouses which are data-driven, Enterprise Portals are also process-driven. They enable organizations to change their business processes and workflow practices in dramatic ways. We introduce some of these ways when we discuss reengineering in Chapters 12 and 13. We cover many more changes and opportunities in Chapter 15.

A Methodology for Building Enterprise Portals

To provide guidance in building Enterprise Portals, we developed a methodology that we will use throughout the book. We call it the *Engineering Enterprise Portals* (EEP) methodology. EEP is based on concepts that are combined into an organizational approach to large-scale information management, in direct support of management information needs. By applying data warehousing and engineering concepts to the design, development, and deployment of Enterprise Portals, we will see how organizations can achieve a fundamental goal of identifying the information that is needed by management to achieve strategic business plans and corporate goals. This is a fundamental goal of organizations, which is called *information alignment*. Once identified, this information can be implemented in a variety of ways, as we will shortly discuss.

A second fundamental goal is *information leveraging*. This is defined as accurately and effectively maintaining a relatively large amount of information by automated management of a significantly smaller volume of metadata. Information leverage is typically achieved by maintaining dense and intricate data structures consisting of interconnected or interwoven data arraignment.

Metadata comprise data definitions that describe data. Although the term "metadata" is widely used, there is no accepted formal definition of it. Metadata is typically defined as "data about data," consistent with ISO description 11179 as *the information and documentation which makes data sets understandable and sharable for users* [ISO 1996]. Metadata are descriptions of various characteristics of different components of an information system—for example, specifying the precise entity, attribute, and relationship facts that must be maintained by a data warehouse in order to supply the information required by the user community.

The third fundamental goal combines these concepts—data warehousing and engineering—to achieve effective and accurate *metadata management*. In this manner a relatively small number of metadata are combined into orders of magnitude greater amounts of information [Moriarty 1992]. We will now introduce each of these concepts further, focusing on Engineering Enterprise Portals. We will contrast EEP with data architecting and specifically address the development of metadata. Part 2 will then cover metadata in more detail.

Fundamental Concepts

Data

Many have adopted Appleton's [1984] useful description of data as at least one fact paired with at least one meaning. Each unique combination of facts and meanings defines an individual piece of data. When data is supplied in response to a request, it becomes information. Different facts and meanings can be combined into data and supplied as information in response to different queries.

DEFINITIONS

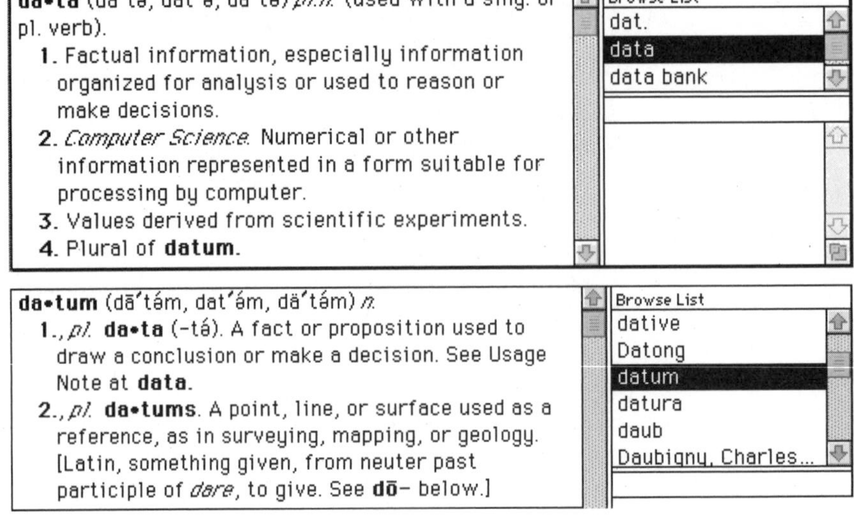

da•ta (dā'tə, dat'ə, dä'tə) *pl.n.* (used with a sing. or pl. verb).
1. Factual information, especially information organized for analysis or used to reason or make decisions.
2. *Computer Science.* Numerical or other information represented in a form suitable for processing by computer.
3. Values derived from scientific experiments.
4. Plural of **datum**.
Browse List
dat.
data
data bank
da•tum (dā'təm, dat'əm, dä'təm) *n.*
1., *pl.* **da•ta** (-tə). A fact or proposition used to draw a conclusion or make a decision. See Usage Note at **data**.
2., *pl.* **da•tums**. A point, line, or surface used as a reference, as in surveying, mapping, or geology. [Latin, something given, from neuter past participle of *dare*, to give. See **dō-** below.]
Browse List
dative
Datong
datum
datura
daub
Daubigny, Charles...

Figure 1-4 illustrates this concept. An association requested by an inventory manager links a fact—230 (units)—with a specific meaning: a reduction in the inventory. It is provided in response to a standing request from a sales manager, for example. The same fact—reduction in the inventory—can also be combined with a different meaning: sales for a given time period. The sales manager can now use this information to determine total commissions for the period. (Other useful meanings for "230" could include such measures as advertising effectiveness, perceived product quality, or market penetration.)

Organizations can afford to develop and maintain information systems because of the leverage achieved by this economy of scale. If technology didn't permit association of individual facts with multiple meanings, the cost of maintaining data comprising the required information would be much larger. Over the years, organizations have permitted the number of applications and types of information systems to increase. Simultaneously, while architectural and engineering advances have increased the possible range of integration that organizations can achieve, the overall level of integration has decreased. Integration of the data is a prerequisite to enterprise integration. The data architect is concerned with maintaining the organizational data assets in forms

Figure 1-4
Facts, meaning, data, and information. The fact "230" is associated with the meaning "inventory reduction." This is an example of data, which may be supplied as information in response to a query from a manager.

manager

Fact	Fact	Meaning	Meaning
230	Fact	Meaning	Meaning
Fact	Fact	Meaning	Meaning
Fact	Fact	Meaning	Meaning
Fact	Fact	Meaning	**Inventory Reduction**

Data Warehouse

that are of most use to the organization, implemented as an organizational data architecture.

Warehouse

While most consider a warehouse as a place to put things, there is still room for definition variations. The term "warehouse" actually represents a continuum. A range of data warehousing options includes various data precision, detail, scope, context, view, and other user requested classification dimensions.

Consider the process of storing retail packages in a regional warehouse, while awaiting distribution to the stores. A warehouse might also function as an interim stop where the retail goods are logged in, tagged with an organizational label, and physically sorted and reorganized for transport to their next destination. This warehouse variation functions as a middleware buffer between the outside vendors and the organization's internal distribution system.

Another warehouse variation occurs as products are accumulated for permanent storage because they are read infrequently, such as the proverbial government storage warehouse (where the alien body parts are stored, in *The X Files* TV program). Warehousing solutions serve a variety of needs.

DEFINITIONS

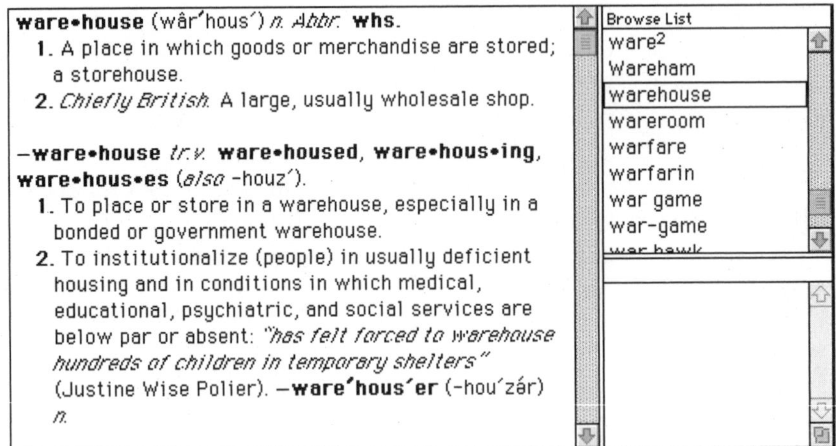

ware•house (wâr′hous′) *n. Abbr.* **whs.**
1. A place in which goods or merchandise are stored; a storehouse.
2. *Chiefly British.* A large, usually wholesale shop.

–**ware•house** *tr.v.* **ware•housed, ware•hous•ing, ware•hous•es** (*also* -houz′).
1. To place or store in a warehouse, especially in a bonded or government warehouse.
2. To institutionalize (people) in usually deficient housing and in conditions in which medical, educational, psychiatric, and social services are below par or absent: *"has felt forced to warehouse hundreds of children in temporary shelters"* (Justine Wise Polier). –**ware′hous′er** (-hou′zər) *n.*

Browse List
ware2
Wareham
warehouse
wareroom
warfare
warfarin
war game
war-game

Data Warehouse

Combining data and warehouse, the term data warehouse represents an approach to data management, sharing a number of characteristics with Enterprise Portals. It is through the active use of metadata, XML, and Internet/intranet technologies that data warehouses evolve into EPs. Many of the methods used by the EEP methodology apply to the design, development, and deployment of both Data Warehouses and EPs. We will therefore use the terms Data Warehouse (DW) and Enterprise Portal (EP) interchangeably unless an approach or technology applies to one and not the other, when we will indicate the differences.

The concept of decision support is extended to incorporate *multi-dimensional* databases—data accessed from different perspectives or dimensions, such as region, product group, market, etc. The data contents of data warehouses are most effective when they are the direct, time-based output of operational systems. Data warehouse data contents tend to be organized by various subject areas to facilitate navigation and reporting. For example, customer information is summarized in a single table in one conceptual warehouse location. Equipped with easy-to-use interfaces, users can navigate the warehouse contents via an electronic map. Quickly moving among locations, users examine various data—adding items to their collection and maintaining bookmarks so they can easily go back later to specific information of interest.

While operational data is a "snapshot" taken at the time of an inquiry, data warehouse data is *time-variant* for trend analysis. The warehouse contains a series of non-volatile snapshots over time for historical reference. Since the data warehouse contains multidimensional, time-varying information derived over a period of time [Inmon 1993], it is a better data source for time-dependent trend analysis.

Warehouse updating loads additional snapshots from the operational systems. The warehouse information is read-only, never deleted or modified. The snapshots are integrated into a consistent structure containing varying levels of detail ranging from highly to lightly summarized, and from current to historical detail. The snapshots are integrated using a non-redundant representation.

Typically, staff with great knowledge of operational data define the data warehouse, which typically provides information needed by operational and middle-level managers. These users are given the capability to slice and dice the warehouse data using a variety of criteria. This is shown as Figure 1-5.

The primary benefit is derived when the organization treats the data warehouse as a single, authoritative source of organizational data. Other benefits of data warehousing, introduced below and discussed in more detail later in this chapter, include:

- Ease of use in obtaining timely information
- Reduction of inflexible, hard copy reports

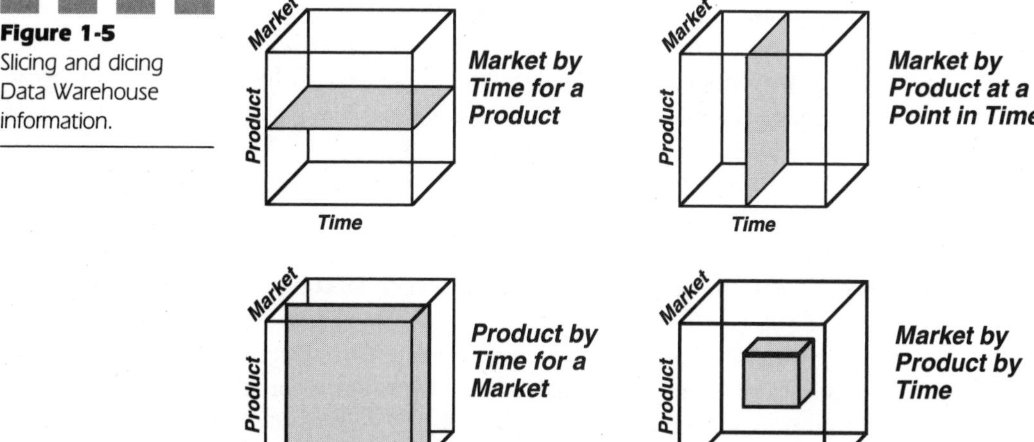

Figure 1-5 Slicing and dicing Data Warehouse information.

- Saving in ad-hoc programming costs and time
- Reduction of duplication of effort in reporting
- Centralized site processing for data integrity
- Trend analysis and "What if" scenarios
- Directory defining meaning of information metadata (data about data) in a repository
- Access to data to satisfy immediate information needs of management

Queries, reports, and analyses provide analysis of trend changes over time such as demographic, population, etc. In addition, software packages are available for purchase that provide plug and play capabilities supporting Executive Information Systems (EIS), Decision Support Systems (DSS), and Online Analytical Processing (OLAP).

However, what cannot be purchased is the organizational data to be analyzed by this software, and also software packages for Decision Early Warning (DEW). We will discuss the identification of organizational data later in this chapter; the rest of the book provides further detail. We will discuss decision early warning concepts in Chapter 5.

Much of what has been written about data warehousing has focused on success stories. Some examples of data warehousing projects are discussed later in this book. Other examples can readily be found by using search engines on the Internet.

The fact is that in today's business environment, to be viable, a successful data warehouse or EP project must achieve positive return on investment by replacing non-integrated reporting and transaction processing system components. These savings alone must justify the cost of data warehouse planning and ongoing operation by releasing the responsibility to support user interaction with the systems that the data warehouse was designed to replace.

Extract, Transform, and Load

Figure 1-6 illustrates the process of data extraction and loading from operational databases into a data warehouse or EP. The structure of the data so loaded into the data warehouse is defined as metadata by the development of data models. This metadata can be defined by using reverse engineering or forward engineering methodologies, or both—as

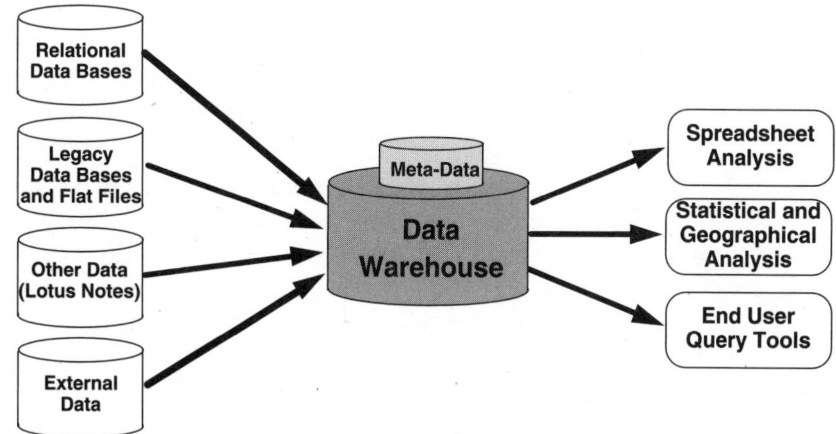

Figure 1-6 Metadata for the Warehouse.

we will later discuss in this chapter. The resulting organizational metadata is then used in the context of organizational Enterprise Portals. Development of data models and metadata is a *mandatory* prerequisite to designing, developing, and deploying data warehouses and EPs. We will discuss this in Chapters 3 and 4.

Engineering

DEFINITIONS

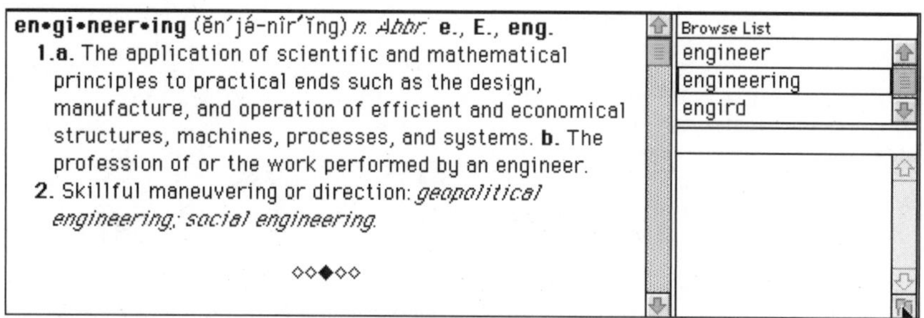

en•gi•neer•ing (ĕn′jə-nîr′ĭng) n. Abbr. e., E., eng.
1.a. The application of scientific and mathematical principles to practical ends such as the design, manufacture, and operation of efficient and economical structures, machines, processes, and systems. b. The profession of or the work performed by an engineer.
2. Skillful maneuvering or direction: geopolitical engineering; social engineering.
Browse List
engineer
engineering
engird

In the Summer of 1997 Peter Aiken was asked to present a synthesis of the definition of engineering [Aiken 1997]. The definition derived is also useful for describing the engineering of data warehouses and EPs. The term engineering originally meant "the art of managing engines." A modern, extended definition includes "elements of the arts and sciences used to make the mechanical properties of matter more useful as systems."

Engineering is fundamentally concerned with the design and manufacture of complex products using calculated manipulation or direction. Engineering was originally divided into military engineering, which is the art of designing and constructing offensive and defensive works, and civil engineering—in a broad sense—as relating to other kinds of public works, machinery, etc. It was further divided into steam engineering, gas engineering, agricultural engineering, topographical engineering, electrical engineering. Today the list of occupations recognized as separate engineering disciplines includes civil, mechanical, chemical, electronic, electrical, aerospace, software, and systems.

The term "architecture" is applied to each of these terms as all can be, and typically are, architected. The process of architecting is defined as the process of implementing an architecture. A more useful understanding can be gained by examining Rechtin and Maier's distinction between *architecture* and *engineering*.

> Generally speaking, engineering deals almost entirely with measurable—using analytic tools derived from mathematics and the hard sciences; that is, engineering is a *de*ductive process. Architecting deals largely with un-measurable—using non-quantitative tools and guidelines based on practical lessons learned; that is, architecting is an *in*ductive process. ... By definition and practice both, from time to time an architect may perform engineering and an engineer may perform architecting—whatever it takes to get the job done.
>
> [*Rechtin and Maier 1996, from the preface*].

The Engineering Enterprise Portals (EEP) Methodology

In this context, *Engineering Enterprise Portals* is defined as *the process of designing, developing, and deploying data warehouses and enterprise portals that provide homogeneous access to vast amounts of facts using metadata, XML, Internet, and intranet technologies.* These facts are formally related with organizationally understood meanings, making the potential amount of data that can be managed more accessible and meaningful to end users and making useful combinations of data more useful to business operations and management. We will introduce and apply the EEP methodology throughout this book to design, develop, and deploy Data Warehouses and Enterprise Portals. We will refer to people who use the EEP methodology as *Enterprise Portal engineers*.

Three particular challenges face EP engineers: (1) designing the EP; (2) planning, developing, and implementing initial extract/load operations required to populate the EP; and (3) the size of the dimensions of each of the first two tasks introduces further potentially significant characteristics. Thus the goal of Engineering Enterprise Portals is the improvement of organizational EP efforts.

The direct results of EPs should be seen in improvements in the organizational decision-making process. This is accomplished by increasing comprehensiveness, precision, and accuracy, and decreasing data redundancy and data imprecision.

The Role of Data Models and Metadata in EEP

Engineering Enterprise Portals is accomplished by managing organizational metadata. Data models are used to represent metadata; these models therefore become valuable organizational assets. We will be better able to understand the roles of metadata and data models by considering the following example, drawn from town planning and architecture.

A town plan is a plan for construction of a city—it represents a strategic model of the city. For suburbs that are needed first, the major roads in the town plan are designed in detail and constructed before others so that initial buildings and houses can be built.

We will use the term *strategic model* to represent the "town plan" needed for construction of an organization's databases and systems. As a town plan shows the high-level layout of a city, so also a strategic model shows the high-level layout of an organization's databases and systems. A strategic model is used also for construction of data warehouses and EPs.

As the layout of streets in a suburb is documented using a street map and a street directory, so also data definitions are documented using a data map and a data directory. Together these comprise a *data model*. Data map diagrams and data details in a data directory in fact document data about data. A data model therefore represents metadata. A data directory that is used to store metadata is typically called a *repository*.

A strategic model is sometimes called a *strategic data model*. For information that managers need, the data from which that information is derived must be defined in detail at the tactical or middle management levels, or at the operational or lower management levels. These are respectively defined in *tactical data models* and in *operational data models*.

When streets are in place, the design of buildings by architects can begin, for those buildings that will be occupied first. This is followed by construction of those buildings by builders (using available raw materials).

So also, once detail data is documented in tactical data models for priority tactical areas of interest to management, the source of that data can be determined from operational data models. This data is the raw material that will be used for derivation of the information needed by management.

Some data may be stored in existing operational databases. Other data may exist in databases outside the enterprise, accessible via extranets for customers, suppliers, and business partners, or accessible more widely via the Internet. Once located, that data must be processed: so transforming the raw data into the information needed by management—analogous to constructing a building. As data changes over time, this processing is carried out at regular intervals. The information that is derived from this regular processing can be stored on a historical basis in a data warehouse.

As a street directory enables people to find their way about a city, so a repository is a directory of information in the databases and systems. It contains the metadata that helps managers find the information they need. A strategic data model, together with more detailed data models at the tactical and operational levels, provide the metadata to be stored in the organization's repository.

An architect first designs a building to define its structure and the layout of all aspects of the building. This design is documented as floor plan maps that indicate *where* various rooms and other components are located. Specifications document *what* materials are to be used for construction, together with relevant dimensions. Only then is construction defined in detail—this specifies *how* construction is to be carried out.

So also, an EP is first designed by developing data models that document *what* data and information are required and their relationships with other data and information. Only then is it appropriate to define *how* the data and information will be processed or analyzed. These data models, when later defined as physical databases, are used to indicate *where* the data resides physically. Thus the EEP methodology focuses first on identifying what data and information is required. Only later does EEP define how that data and information is processed and where it will be located.

The Zachman Framework

The *Zachman Framework for Information Systems Architecture* [Zachman 1987, 1991, 1992] and the *Zachman Framework for Enterprise Architecture* [Zachman 1996] are based on similar concepts. John Zachman observed how the disciplines of architecture and manufacturing have evolved to manage the design, construction, and maintenance of buildings and complex manufactured products such as airplanes. He saw that experience from these disciplines could also be applied to management of the design, construction, and maintenance of similarly complex systems such as information systems and the enterprises that they support.

He saw that columns representing the interrogatives of *what* (for data), *how* (for process), and *where* (for location) could be considered from different perspectives, represented as rows in Figure 1-7:

- Row 1 considers *objectives* and *scope* from the perspective of the *planner*.
- Row 2 considers the conceptual *enterprise model* from the perspective of the *owner*.
- Row 3 considers the logical *system model* from the perspective of the *designer*.
- Row 4 considers the physical *technology model* from the perspective of the *builder*.
- Row 5 considers the *detailed representations* from the perspective of the *subcontractor*.

Different documentation or representations may be utilized in each cell of the Zachman Framework. For Data Warehouses we focus mainly on data—the *Data* column of Figure 1-7. For Enterprise Portals we also focus on the *Process* column. For example, the cell formed by intersection of the *Objectives/Scope* row (of interest to the *Planner)* and the *Data* column shows that a *List of Things* is appropriate for this cell. The intersection with the *Process* column shows a *List of Processes.* We will discuss goals, objectives, and key performance indicators in strategic business plans in Chapter 2. This will help us to identify information "things" to be deliv-

Figure 1-7 Concepts of the Zachman Framework for Enterprise Architecture.

	WHAT *Data*	HOW *Process*	WHERE *Network*
Objectives/ Scope *Planner*	List of Things	List of Processes	List of Locations
Enterprise Model *Owner*	Conceptual Enterprise Model	Business Process Model	Business Logistics System
System Model *Designer*	Logical Data Model	Application Architecture	Distributed System Architecture
Technology Model *Builder*	Physical Data Model	System Design	System Architecture
Detailed Rep-resentations *Subcontractor*	Data Definition	Program	Network Architecture
Functioning Enterprise	Data	Function	Network

ered by a data warehouse. We will also discuss strategies and tactics in Chapter 2 to identify processes for an Enterprise Portal.

The cell for the *Designer* row and the *Data* column shows that *Logical Data Model* documentation is appropriate for this cell. We discuss the concepts of logical data models in Chapter 3. The *Owner* row and *Data* column cell contains *Conceptual Enterprise Model*—called the *strategic model* in EEP. We discuss strategic models in Chapter 4. The *Builder* row and *Data* column contains *Physical Data Model.* We cover reverse engineering of databases to develop physical data models for implementation as *Data Definitions* by Subcontractors in Part 2.

The *Business Process Model, Application Architecture*, *Systems Design*, and *Program* representations at the intersection of the *Process* column and the *Owner, Designer*, *Builder*, and *Subcontractor* rows, respectively, are discussed in Part 3 in relation to Enterprise Portal Deployment.

The Zachman Framework thus is a useful way to discuss complex activities, such as the design, implementation, and maintenance of Data Warehouses and Enterprise Portals. As a complete Framework, it has three additional interrogatives for a total of six columns—*who* (people), *when* (time), and *why* (motivation). Chapter 2, covering Strategic Business Planning, describes methods that can be used for the "why" column. Workflow and events—which are used extensively with Enterprise Portals in Part 3—relate to the *who* and *when* columns. The six-column Framework for Enterprise Architecture is discussed in Chapter 8 and illustrated in Figure 8-18 in relation to Reverse Engineering. It is discussed further in the context of Enterprise Portals in Chapter 15.

Benefits of Data Models and Metadata

The development of data models and definition of metadata in an organization can be summarized to achieve the following purposes:

- Data models provide a framework for development of databases and systems that provide timely and accurate information—accessed, manipulated, and presented in different ways to support the changing information requirements of management.
- Data models define the layout and structure of databases to be developed for a data warehouse or EP, as well as for tactical and operational databases and systems used for day-to-day processing.
- Metadata defines the meaning of data, its current and historical context, and the relationship of that data to other data.
- EEP uses metadata stored in a repository for the design, development, and deployment of data warehouses and EPs.

The use of data models and metadata realizes the following benefits for data warehouses and EPs:

- Data integration to remove data inconsistencies—reducing situations where different versions of the same data can exist in an organization at different stages of update. Information derived from out-of-step data versions would otherwise be inconsistent or incorrect.
- A data warehouse or EP offers ease of use in obtaining information from operational databases, where that information is currently very difficult to obtain.
- Reduction of inflexible, hardcopy reports that are not responsive to changing business needs.
- A saving in ad-hoc programming costs and time—desktop tools enable managers and their staff to obtain information without having to wait for IT systems analysts and programmers.

- Instant access to data to satisfy immediate information needs of management, so removing the delays caused by multiple interactions between managers and IT staff—with intrinsic possibilities for misunderstanding.
- Timeliness—delays in access to information incur considerable costs for an organization, owing to an inability to respond promptly, and wasted resources, both human and material.
- Data Analysis Capabilities—sophisticated end-user tools for user-friendly access with a capability to "drill down" through different levels of data summarization and aggregation in a data warehouse, from the big picture to fine detail. These capabilities are provided by EIS, DSS, OLAP, and DEW software. A manager can examine the result of an information request and decide to seek additional information, which can then be provided immediately.
- Trend analysis—the opportunity to examine trends over time and respond where needed to achieve outcomes.
- "What if" scenarios—the ability to create hypothetical situations and assess their effect on the organization. For example, *if staffing in an area was to change in a defined way, how would this affect costs and product delivery?*

Related Term: Systems Engineering

The Engineering Enterprise Portals methodology evolved from Systems and Software Engineering (SSE), Information Engineering (IE), and Enterprise Engineering (EE) methodologies. Systems Engineering (SE) is defined as the engineering of systems. Rechtin and Maier describe systems as *collections of different things which produce results unachievable by the elements alone* [1996 p. 10]. Systems engineering therefore is the attempt to construct systems which by virtue of their construction produce more than the components could produce individually. Another definition states that:

> Systems engineering is an appropriate combination of mathematical, behavioral, and management theories in a useful setting appropriate for the resolution of complex real-world issues of large scale and scope. As such, systems engineering consists of the use of mathematical, behavioral, and management constructs to identify, structure, analyze, evaluate, and

interpret generally incomplete information. A central problem of systems engineering is to select methods that are explicit, rational, and compatible with the policy implementation framework extant such that decision making and the resulting policies become as efficient, effective, equitable, explicable as possible

[*Sage 1985*].

Related Term: Information Engineering

Information Engineering (IE) was first developed by Clive Finkelstein (the "Father" of IE) and Information Engineering Services Pty Ltd (IES) in Australia from 1976. It evolved rapidly through its use in many projects across a wide range of industries over the period 1976–1980. It was further refined in public and inhouse education courses that were presented in Australia and New Zealand during this period. The history of IE is documented in [Finkelstein 1989]. IE first appeared outside Australia and NZ as six InDepth articles in *US ComputerWorld* in May–June, 1981 [Finkelstein 1981a]. IE was published as a co-authored report by Savant Institute in November, 1981 [Finkelstein 1981b]. It was popularized worldwide in the 1980s by James Martin and so gained wide acceptance.

IE was originally designed as a business-driven methodology, to be used actively by business experts and IT experts working together in a design partnership. Both business experts and IT experts were trained together in joint classes in Australia and NZ. But as IE became more widely used in the USA and Europe through the 1980s, it began to be used mainly as a methodology for IT experts, who used it only to interview business experts—rather than train them in IE so that these business people could actively participate in projects. Two distinct variants emerged: referred to as "Martin IE" [Martin 1986] and "Finkelstein IE" [Finkelstein 1989, 1992], but more accurately described as "IT-driven IE" and "business-driven IE."

Related Term: Enterprise Engineering

Recognizing that IT-driven IE was not working effectively, techniques called *Joint Application Design* (JAD) and *Rapid Application Development* (RAD) were introduced in the late 1980s. With these changes, business experts could become more actively involved in their projects, with the result that business quality improved dramatically and development time decreased. IT-driven IE projects then had greater success. However, the principles of JAD and RAD had always been an integral part of business-driven IE—although these terms were not used in the late 1970s or early 1980s.

To distinguish between the two IE variants—and before the introduction of JAD and RAD—"business-driven IE" evolved in 1986 into Enterprise Engineering (EE). It actively used both business experts and IT experts, who learned Enterprise Engineering in joint classes and then actively worked together in projects: *the business experts knew the business, while IT experts knew computers.*

We found that these EE projects resulted in systems and databases that were developed much faster, and were of higher business quality, than those developed using SSE or IT-driven IE. Although Enterprise Engineering was still called "business-driven IE" at the time, EE was fully documented in [Finkelstein 1992].

With an emphasis on metadata, XML, and Internet/intranet technologies, in the late 1990s the "business-driven IE" and Enterprise Engineering methodologies provided the foundation for the development of the Engineering Enterprise Portals (EEP) methodology. If you are familiar with these two business-driven methodologies, you will see the strong influence that they have had on EEP when we cover strategic business planning (in Chapter 2), data modeling (in Chapter 3), and strategic modeling (in Chapter 4).

SE, IE, and EE Principles used in EEP

Some of the principles of SE, IE, and EE that are also applicable to Engineering Enterprise Portals include the following:

- *Iterative Top-down* (or hierarchical) design—a complex system is designed by breaking a system down into its component subsystems, then repeating the process on each subsystem until off-the-shelf or easily designable components are all that remain.
- *Forward Engineering* – a methodology used for iterative top-down design. This analyzes strategic, tactical, and operational business plans to identify the information needed by managers to achieve those plans. This analysis is used to develop strategic, tactical,

and operational data models that define the metadata for that information. Forward engineering will be used later in Part 1 to develop data models and identify information needs.

- *Bottom-up Integration*—large systems are built by taking the lowest-level components and putting them together one level at a time. Between each level's integration, the result of the previous level is tested to make sure it works.
- *Reverse Engineering*—a methodology that is used for bottom-up integration. This derives data models from the existing databases that are used in an organization. These reverse-engineered data models can be compared with forward-engineered data models that identify information needed by management. From this, the location of source data to be used to derive that information is identified—then extracted and loaded into a data warehouse or EP. Reverse engineering is a major focus of Part 2.
- *Systems Development Life Cycle*—an understanding of the progression of a system from inception, to design, to construction, implementation, operation, maintenance, and eventually to its shutdown, disassembly, and disposal. This aids in the understanding of "what needs to be done when and where," "how each small piece fits in the big picture," and aids in breaking large conceptual procedures or processes into smaller, more easily manageable chunks.
- *User Perspective*—building systems to take into account what the user wants, needs, prefers, is happy with, and is capable of. Every type of user of a potential system (operator, maintenance, management, etc.) must be involved in the design of that system.

Data Architecture Development and EEP

Engineering Enterprise Portals is one half of a dyad, the other half being *data architecture development* (DAD). EEP and DAD must be coordinated, but DAD is also typically accomplished as one part of overall information framework development [Zachman 1987, 1991, 1992].

As an architect defines an architectural framework for construction of a building, so also DAD provides an architectural framework for EEP development. EEP is a disciplined approach or framework to develop organizational data warehousing and EP capabilities. The EEP framework provides a template that organizations can use to guide their data warehousing or EP initiatives.

Other related terms include:

- *Data Marts*—which are subject-oriented data and information subsets of interest to a specific function or business unit of an organization.
- *Information Warehouses*—which are top-down representations of information, summarized or derived from mid-level and operational data that is of interest to management based on strategic and tactical business plans.

A Data Warehouse or Enterprise Portal plan is required to support the development of a data mart, and a data warehouse is required to support the development of an information warehouse. The definitions of data marts and information warehouses above will suffice at this stage: we will discuss these terms in more detail in later chapters.

REFERENCES

Aiken, P. (1997) "Some (Incomplete) Thoughts on the Role of Maintenance in Systems Engineering," in Joint Logistics Commanders/Joint Group on Systems Engineering Workshop, Functional Working Group on Systems Engineering Life-Cycle Process, July 28–August 1, 1997, San Diego, CA.

Aiken, P., Ngwenyama, O. and Broome, L. (1999) "Reverse Engineering New Systems," IEEE Software (March/April).

Appleton, D. (1984) "Business Rules: The Missing Link," *Datamation* (October 1984), 30(16):145–150.

Finkelstein, C. (1981) "Information Engineering," a series of six InDepth articles published in *US Computerworld* (May–June), Framingham, MA: IDG Communications.

Finkelstein, C. and Martin, J. (1981) *Information Engineering*, two-volume Technical Report, Savant Institute (November), Carnforth, Lancs, UK.

Finkelstein, C. (1989) *An Introduction to Information Engineering*, Sydney, Australia: Addison-Wesley.

Finkelstein, C. (1992) *Information Engineering: Strategic Systems Development*, Sydney, Australia: Addison-Wesley.

Hackathorn, R. (1999) *Web Farming for the Data Warehouse*, Morgan Kaufman, ISBN: 1-55860-503-7. Includes use of XML for data sources from Internet (368 pages).

Hammer, M. (1990) "Reengineering Work: Don't Automate, Obliterate," *Harvard Business Review*, Cambridge, MA (Jul–Aug).

Hammer, M. and Champy, J. (1993) *Reengineering the Corporation: A Manifesto for Business Revolution*, HarperBusiness.

InfoWorld Electric Web Site—http://www.infoworld.com/cgi-bin/displayStory.pl?/features/990125eip.htm

Inmon, B. (1993) *Data Architecture: The Information Paradigm*, QED Technical Publishing Group.

ISO 11179:195-1996 *Information Technology—Specification and Standardization of Data Elements.*

Martin, J. (1986) *Information Engineering*, Englewood Cliffs, NJ: Prentice Hall.

Moriarty, T. (1992) "Migrating the Legacy: as the Industry Migrates to the PC, don't give up your Mainframe Products yet," *Database Programming & Design*, Dec. 5(12):73(2).

Rechtin, E. and Maier, M. (1996) *The Art of Systems Architecting* (November 1996), CRC Press, ISBN: 0849378362.

Sage, A. (1977) "Introduction to Systems Engineering: Methodology and Applications—Part 1," *IEEE Transactions on Systems, Man, and Cybernetics*, July, SMC-7(7):499–504.

SageMaker Web site—http://www.sagemaker.com/company/lynch.htm

Smith, A. (1910) *The Wealth of Nations*, London: Dent.

WWW Consortium: XML, XSL and XLL specifications—http://www.w3.org/

Zachman, J.A. (1987) "A Framework for Information Systems Architecture," *IBM Systems Journal*, 26(3):276–292, IBM Publication G321-5298.

Zachman, J.A. (1991) "Zachman Framework Extensions: An Update," *Data Base Newsletter,* July/August, 19(4):1–16.

Zachman, J.A. and Sowa, J.F. (1992) "Extending and Formalizing the Framework for Information Systems Architecture," *IBM Systems Journal*, 31, IBM Publication G321-5488.

Zachman, J.A. (1996) *Concepts of the Framework for Enterprise Architecture*, Los Angeles, CA: Zachman International.

CHAPTER 2

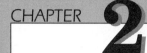

Strategic Business Planning

Designing Tomorrow, Today

> Most corporate planning is like a ritual rain dance: it has no effect on the weather that follows, but it makes those who engage in it feel that they are in control. Most discussions of the role of models in planning are directed at improving the dancing, not the weather.
>
> —[Ackoff 1981]

To provide information to management from a data warehouse, we first must be aware of their information needs. Most corporate planning, Ackoff states above [1981], is *directed at improving the dancing, not the weather*. He worries that many corporate planning experts are more concerned with the techniques they use for planning (the "dancing") rather than the results they achieve (the "weather").

Our focus in this chapter is to learn how to use a strategic business planning method that delivers results rapidly. This will help us identify information to be delivered by a Data Warehouse or an Enterprise Portal (EP).

The planning method we will use is called *Goal Analysis*. It can be used at the corporate, business unit, and business function levels of an organization to define clear, concise strategic business plans, tactical business plans, and also operational business plans, respectively. It is used to analyze goals and objectives and define business plans at all management levels of an organization, so that the management information needs are clearly apparent. It is part of the engineering enterprise portals (EEP) methodology and is very effective when used for information needs at any management level, to build data warehouses or EPs. Goal Analysis is used to:

- Define business goals, issues and strategies
- Address identified problems and opportunities
- Establish strategy and technology requirements
- Define functional responsibility and accountability

Goal Analysis in Business Planning

At the corporate level, strategic business plans provide guidance for the whole organization, which comprises many business units. At this level, tactical business plans are used to manage each (tactical) business unit. Each business unit carries out many business functions, managed according to operational business plans. Goal analysis can be used to define these plans so that the needs of managers at each level are clearly understood and expressed. Figure 2-1 shows the hierarchical nature of these business plans.

Plans documented at one level provide input to define plans at the next lower level. At this level, there may be problems or opportunities identified that need clarification or resolution from the higher-level managers. We call these *Issues*.

By examining these issues, we will see that goal analysis helps us identify strategies that address problems or opportunities. There may be many alternative strategies. The proposed strategies are presented with the issues to management, for their direction or resolution. For example, the resolution of an issue associated with a business function may require the introduction and use of new technologies. This feedback obtains management agreement for directions to be taken by the organization and the resources needed for implementation.

The managers who will participate in goal analysis are decision makers at all organizational levels, as well as staff who develop recommendations for them. It is their responsibility to ensure that business plans are well defined and clearly understood. By participating in goal analysis they use their organizational knowledge to develop business plans which incorporate that knowledge.

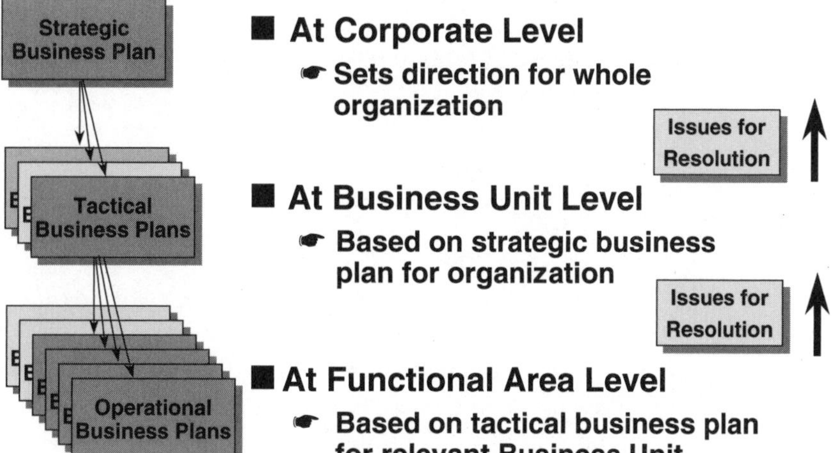

Figure 2-1
Hierarchical nature of business plans.

Goal analysis can be used to develop a formal business plan rapidly, if no documented plan presently exists. It defines the Vision, Mission, Core Values, Goals, Objectives, Strategies, and Key Performance Indicators of the organization, and defines business functions and business function accountabilities. It will establish directions and priorities for later development in Chapter 4 of a strategic model. It can be easily applied at all business levels.

We will see later in this chapter that goal analysis can also be used to define Project Specifications for building a Data Warehouse or Enterprise Portal, or for any other project. It identifies business and project goals, with clear business reasons for the project. It determines business functions that the project will support after implementation. It identifies technology strategies, showing how technology can assist those functions. It identifies business system requirements and obtains higher management agreement that those requirements are valid. These are expressed as project goals.

An Example of Goal Analysis

We will use an example to illustrate the application of goal analysis. Goal analysis was first described in [Finkelstein 1992] as a reactive planning method. The following example shows its use also as a proactive planning method.

We will examine the strategic plan of a hypothetical company, XYZ Corporation. This is documented as a Mission statement and associated *Critical Success Factors* (CSFs) in Figure 2-2. These typically are major factors that managers determine are important for the success of an organization. We will later use this strategic plan to decide the directions that XYZ should take for the future, and goals and strategies that XYZ should establish to help it to achieve that plan.

The mission statement in Figure 2-2 indicates that XYZ can potentially operate in any industry or market that enables it to achieve a Return On Investment (ROI) of 20 percent. However, a problem exists with the present CSFs: they are not clearly stated. As one or two words, they are subject to misinterpretation.

You can demonstrate this quickly yourself by asking two or three people what "market analysis" means to them. You will find that each person will have a slightly different idea of its meaning, and how XYZ can use market analysis in planning its future directions.

Figure 2-2
Initial Strategic Plan of XYZ Corporation.

XYZ Mission and Purpose

Develop, deliver, and support products and services that satisfy the needs of customers in markets where we can achieve a return on investment of at least 20 percent pa within two years of market entry.

XYZ Critical Success Factors

- Market Analysis
- Market Share
- Innovation
- Customer Satisfaction
- Product Quality
- Product Development
- Staff Productivity
- Asset Growth
- Profitability

The Quality of Planning Statements

To be effective, a strategic plan must be clear and unambiguous. We can test this as follows. Does the XYZ strategic plan:

- Provide sufficient guidance for XYZ?
- State clearly what is to be done in XYZ?
- Constitute an effective strategic plan for XYZ?

Each of these questions, when applied to the plan expressed in Figure 2-2, leads to an answer of NO. The plan in its present form is confusing. Its quality is low. We will examine planning statements so we understand them better, for their later use in goal analysis.

A Mission statement is also called a *Mission and Purpose*. To provide clear guidance it should answer Drucker's questions [1974]:

- What is our business?
- Who is the customer?
- Where is the customer located?

- What products or services does the customer want from us?
- What does the customer consider as value?
- What is the customer prepared to "pay"?
- What will the business be?
- What should the business be?
- What is the key strategic thrust?

The *Mission* statement must clearly answer these questions. Most organizations focus on business processes—on "how" they operate, rather than "what" are their reasons for existence. Few ask themselves "what is our business?" Fewer still ask the related questions: "what will our business be?"—if we make no changes—and "what should our business be?" This latter question helps us decide on the changes that should be made, if we are to succeed in the future. It helps us determine the key strategic thrusts.

Many organizations focus on the products and services that they deliver to their customers, rather than first finding out the needs of those customers. By understanding those needs, a better appreciation of existing (or new) products and services that satisfy the needs can be gained. By knowing what our customers consider value, we can better decide whether price is important, or quality, or service. Some are internal customers who will "pay" not by price, but in other ways—such as by "political" or other support.

When these questions are used in conjunction with a data warehouse project, each manager who will use the warehouse becomes an internal customer. Their needs must be understood, so that information "products and services" can be designed and delivered to satisfy those needs. The answers to all of these questions must be known.

From a clear expression of the mission, there may be many statements of goals that indicate WHAT the organization must achieve, to realize the mission. This "many" is shown by a three-pronged symbol (called a "crow's foot") on the line from Mission to Goals in Figure 2-3.

There may be many Concerns or Issues (perhaps expressed by CSFs) that are associated with these goals. These indicate problems that impede, or opportunities that enhance, the achievement of the goals. Understanding these will help us to define relevant strategies. These strategies specify WHAT we must DO to achieve the goals, and so realize the mission. A goal may have many strategies; these represent alternative strategies from which the best strategies to achieve the goals must be selected.

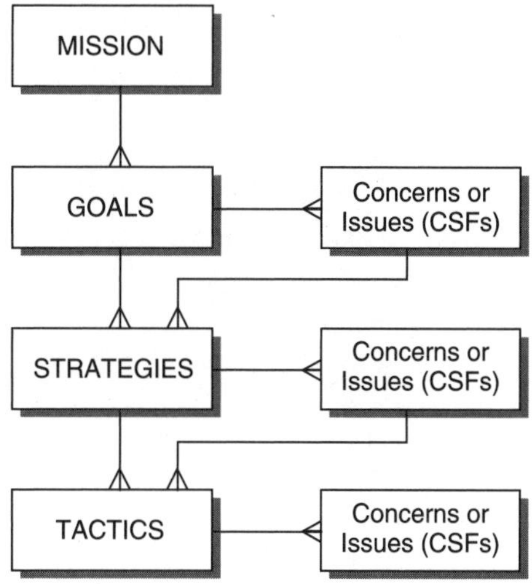

Figure 2-3 Relationship between Planning Statements.

An understanding of the many concerns and issues associated with these strategies will help us also to decide relevant tactics. Tactics and tasks are defined that specify HOW we will carry out the strategies to achieve the goals. These tactics or tasks will later be implemented as business processes.

Goal analysis comprises a series of steps that progressively develop these statements. In the following section we will see how clear, unambiguous tactical business planning statements are developed from the XYZ Strategic Plan in Figure 2-2. Irrespective of the quality of the initial planning statements, those statements are catalysts for the definition of refined statements at the next planning level. We will use these planning statements in Chapter 4. In that chapter we will develop a strategic model that will help us to identify the information needs that are to be satisfied by a Data Warehouse or an Enterprise Portal.

The Steps of Goal Analysis

Goal Analysis has nine steps, listed in Figure 2-4. We will carry out each of these steps using the XYZ example, to understand their application to goal analysis when used for business planning.

Figure 2-4
The steps of Goal Analysis.

1. Understand the mission and purpose
2. Identify the major business areas
3. What has to be achieved to realize the mission?
4. What opportunities or problems exist?
5. What will achieve or resolve the issues?
6. What are the quantitative results?
7. What are the current functions?
8. Who will implement the strategies?
9. Define job responsibilities

Step 1: Understand the Mission and Purpose

To understand the mission and purpose, we must be aware of the environment in which the organization operates now, and how that environment will change in the future. This is shown in Figure 2-5.

Geography, industry, markets, legislation, the economy, and technology all affect the environment. They affect also the public and private sector organizations that operate in that environment as partners, customers, suppliers, and competitors. These all influence the mission statement. According to Drucker: *clear definition of mission and purpose makes possible clear and realistic business objectives. It is the foundation for priorities, strategies, plans and work assignments* [Drucker 1974].

The *Vision* statement defines where the organization is going and how it will get there. It is the organizing force behind every corporate decision. *Core Values* are factors or beliefs that are important drivers of decisions or activities. These can be incorporated in the mission statement. Two examples of typical mission statements follow:

Figure 2-5
The Mission reflects the Environment, Vision and Core Values.

A Corporate Mission for a Private Sector Company

We are the leading provider of electronic and fiber optic connections and accessories. We bring the benefits of modern products and their technologies from the world's leading suppliers. We will create and satisfy the needs of professional users to achieve physical connections for communications or control purposes.

We are skilled and dedicated people working in partnership with our customers to satisfy their needs and their expectations for our long-term mutual benefit. Our major focus is to provide exceptional service and value so that we will be their first choice.

We will increase the value of our Company, and improve the economic well-being and quality of life of our customers, suppliers, staff, and other stakeholders.

A Document Management Unit Mission for Local Government

To provide any individual or organization who is located predominantly within our local government area, or anywhere in the country or overseas, document-based information:

- about the activities for which our authority has responsibility, either as prescribed by legislation or on an elective basis, or
- that enhances decision making by elected members and/or our employees.

Our primary focus is the efficient and effective provision of timely, accurate, and complete document-based information consistent with the recipient's security classification and the document-based information's release status.

Each statement can be tested by the questions discussed earlier in *The Quality of Planning Statements.* These mission statements are not perfect, but they certainly provide better guidance than the mission of XYZ in Figure 2-2.

The objective of this step has been to understand the mission and purpose. An ideal mission should be timeless—it should identify directions now and into the future. It should clearly express: (1) What the business is doing now; (2) What is happening in the environment; and (3) What the business should be doing in the future. It should broadly indicate markets, customers, products, and services.

Corporate and business unit mission statements, as we saw above, are expressed at a very high level. They can be difficult to use as information catalysts for engineering enterprise portals. We will see that goal analysis helps us to define business plans at the next lower level that become excellent information catalysts for data warehouses.

Step 2: Identify the Major Business Areas

From the understanding of the mission gained from step 1, we will now analyze its focus further to identify major business areas that should be involved. Business experts from these areas will be invited to participate in later goal analysis steps.

We will use the XYZ statements in Figure 2-2. We will start by examining the mission and purpose statement, looking for explicit and implicit nouns in the statement. There will typically be 6–10 major nouns. These nouns should enable us to determine what parts of the business are involved. For example:

> Develop, deliver and support *products* and *services* which satisfy the *needs* of *customers* in *markets* where we can achieve a return on *investment* of at least 20 percent pa within two years of market entry.

The underlined nouns in the mission statement above suggest the following major business areas in XYZ Corporation:

Noun	Business Area
Product (or Service)	Production/Service Delivery
Customer	Sales and Distribution
Need	Product Development, R&D
Market	Marketing
Investment (or Performance)	Finance

Managers from each of the business areas listed above are invited to participate in the remaining goal analysis steps. They may attend alone—or they may prefer to bring along business experts from their areas, to participate with them.

Step 3: What has to be Achieved to Realize the Mission?

Step 3 focuses on identifying and refining goals. This depends on the policies set by management, which define "the rules of the game."

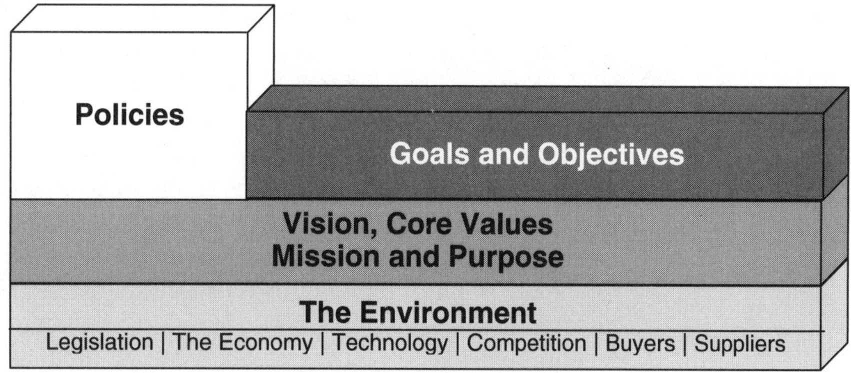

Figure 2-6
Relationship of Policies and Goals to the Mission.

Policies are defined as qualitative guidelines that are based on the mission. They are the internal rules (as company policies) or external rules (as legislation, laws etc.) that the business follows to achieve its goals. They define boundaries of responsibility in the organization and must be known if valid goals are to be defined based on those policies. The relationship of policies and goals to the mission is shown in Figure 2-6.

Goals are typically layered hierarchically, made up of principal goals and contributing Key Performance Indicators (KPIs) or CSFs. In most organizations there are 3–6 major CSFs (typically 6) whose achievement is critical to realize the mission. The number of CSFs that are identified decides the duration of goal analysis. Six CSFs typically take two to three days for managers to discuss all relevant factors, as they complete the steps of goal analysis. More CSFs than this will require greater time for discussion in planning sessions.

Goals and objectives are measurable targets. To be measured, they must be quantitative. They have three characteristics: *measure*, *level*, and *time*. The *measure* defines what performance indicator will be used for measurement. The *level* indicates what result value must be achieved. The *time* specifies when that result should be achieved. If only two of the three characteristics are defined, goals and objectives are meaningless; all three must be known for quantitative targets.

Notice that measure, level, and time focus on what and when, not *how*. Only when we know what result is to be achieved and the timeframe can we determine the most appropriate strategies or tactics—which indicate how.

Typically goals are long-term targets while objectives are generally short-term. Some industries reverse these. We will use "goals" for the rest of this chapter to refer to both goals and objectives.

In one industry, long-term may be two years; for another industry in a rapid-change environment, long-term might only be six months. The rate of change in an industry or in the environment affects the focus of goals. Technology can also affect the rate of change. For example, owing to rapid technological progress, sometimes more change occurs in one month on the Internet than in one year in real-time. This rate of change is expressed by the term "Internet time."

We do not have clear statements of goals for XYZ. In Figure 2-2 we only have poorly defined Critical Success Factors. We will ask managers and business experts from XYZ, drawn from the business areas identified in step 2, to define relevant statements in a planning session. We will ask them to identify the goals that they believe will realize the mission.

In the format of this book it is difficult to achieve the interactivity of a real-life planning session. Because of this, we will instead evaluate the wording of each goal that the managers and business experts define, to assess whether their goals are clearly defined. The statements they developed for the Asset Growth, Profitability, Market Share, and Market Analysis CSFs in Figure 2-2 are documented in Figure 2-7.

The first statement in Figure 2-7 on *Asset Growth* is not quantitative. It does not include measure, level, and time and so is not expressed as a goal statement. Neither does it communicate qualitative guidelines or boundaries of responsibility; it is therefore not a policy. Instead it describes WHAT to DO and so is a potential strategy statement.

The same arguments can be made for the statements of *Profitability* and *Market Analysis* in Figure 2-7. They are not quantitative and so are

Figure 2-7
Statements from XYZ managers and business experts.

Asset Growth

"Monitor performance of all aspects of our business so that each activity has a favorable effect, directly or indirectly, on our mission ROI."

Profitability

"Monitor financial performance of all activities to ensure that profit and cash flow projections are achieved according to, or ahead of, plan."

Market Share

"Achieve the targeted annual market share (expressed as ...) for the chosen market segments of XYZ."

Market Analysis

"Analyze existing and emerging markets on a regular basis, to assess market growth, potential market size, and potential market competition."

not goals. They do not provide qualitative guidelines and so are not policies. But they also describe WHAT to DO and so are potential strategy statements.

The third statement, however, on *Market Share*, is almost a quantitative target. Market share is a measure, but the level and time have not yet been defined. The statement is almost complete; when level and time are defined it will potentially be a goal statement. We will refine this statement later in this chapter.

Only one out of the four statements in Figure 2-7 was found to be a potential goal. This is not unusual. Statements often specify what to do, rather than define what is to be achieved. Only when we understand *what* has to be achieved (goals) can we determine *what* we should *do* (strategies) and *how* we should implement them (tactics).

We could ask the managers and business experts to change the other three statements of strategy so that they are quantitative goals. They may define better statements next time. But we will defer this refinement until we have completed more of the steps of goal analysis. We will find that these later steps give us a better appreciation of what is to be achieved, so that then we can later come back to refine the statements above. We can still make good use of them in their present form for the next goal analysis step.

Step 4: What Opportunities or Problems Exist?

When we know of the *problems* or *threats* that are barriers to, or that impede, the achievement of goals—or when we are aware of the *opportunities* or *technologies* that enhance or facilitate their achievement—we can then determine the most relevant strategies to follow for those goals. In the following discussion we will refer to these collectively as *issues*. These issues can be internal or external to the organization.

As well as defining issues in this step, we can also list the organization's strengths and weaknesses. With our understanding of opportunities, and threats, we can analyze strengths, weaknesses, opportunities, and threats in a *SWOT analysis*, sometimes renamed using a more memorable acronym "WOTS up?" [Rowe et al 1990].

In Figure 2-8 we will examine the issues that the XYZ managers and their staff define for the statements in Figure 2-7, focusing on Asset Growth, Profitability, and Market Share. We will ask them to consider the potential barriers or problems that impede, and the opportunities or technologies that facilitate or enhance the statements—considering both internal and external factors. We will encourage them also to identify strengths and weaknesses. They begin their discussion. Sometime later, after much heated debate, the Chief Financial Officer (CFO) describes the factors they identified. From this, we learn a little about XYZ Corporation.

> XYZ experienced major asset growth in the late 1980s, when our industry expanded rapidly due to the ready availability of funding. At that time we entered some markets that had only a short life. These markets are now in decline. It is hard to extract ourselves from those markets and sell our investments in them. Other markets were not researched well before entry, resulting in high market entry costs and low profitability. These are also difficult to leave. And much debt was assumed for sunset markets at the end of their useful life. This is fixed interest debt which must be serviced and is very costly today.

The three bullet points under Asset Growth in Figure 2-8 summarize this statement of issues. As spokesperson, the CFO then moves on to the issues that the XYZ managers identified relating to Profitability.

> In the first few months following my recent appointment as CFO, I found that I had inherited a sorry situation. We have been very profitable, but our products were of poor quality and we provided very poor service to our customers. As an organization we became fat and lazy. We were a monopoly in our industry. And we became more and more arrogant as our customers had nowhere else to go.
>
> But because of poor quality products, high prices and poor service, we were embarrassed to report our high profits. Each year our annual report was a public relations nightmare. It was a media disaster.

The CFO then told us how XYZ had resolved this problem. He spoke of the decisions taken by previous incumbents of his position, as they acted to reduce the source of the embarrassment.

> We were so profitable we could afford to delay financial reporting and operate with poor financial controls. We carried high interest costs and we had poor cash flow management. We were doing all we could to reduce those profits. In fact, while our group listed "poor budget control" as one issue from our planning session, I should emphasize that this is really "no budget control." That certainly had an impact on our bottom line; we spent money like water, with absolutely no controls.

Figure 2-8
Issues identified by the XYZ managers and business experts.

Asset Growth

"Monitor performance of all aspects of our business so that each activity has a favorable effect, directly or indirectly, on our mission ROI."

Issues

- Many investments in declining markets
- High market entry cost into marginal markets
- High debt levels for assets in sunset markets

Profitability

"Monitor financial performance of all activities to ensure that profit and cash flow projections are achieved according to, or ahead of, plan."

Issues

- Delayed financial reporting; poor financial control
- High interest costs; poor cash flow management
- Poor budget control

Market Share

"Achieve the targeted annual market share (expressed as . . .) for the chosen market segments of XYZ."

Issues

- No market share information (unavailable or inaccurate)
- Competitor activity (analysis not available)
- Market definition (growth rates and size not known)
- Corporate image (poor)
- Product Range Definition (limited)
- Product Pricing Policy (high and inflexible)

Strengths

- Large, cash-rich organization
- Established market position
- Experienced, capable staff

Weaknesses

- Poor financial control and management
- Arrogant, reactive corporate culture
- Poor customer service and products
- Limited experience in a competitive environment

> Our profitability was not because of the excellence of XYZ, it was in spite of XYZ. Our position of monopoly was a license to print money. Now that our industry is deregulated, those days have long gone. We now have many competitors who view our historical poor performance as a golden market opportunity. We are rapidly losing market share. Our bottom line is a blood bath. And we are now losing money when we can ill afford to.

Wow! The CFO certainly pulled no punches! Interestingly, in many planning sessions the identification of problems or threats leads to a similar outpouring of issues. Sometimes identifying opportunities is equally productive. We will not look yet at how we can address these issues. That will be done in the next goal analysis step. Instead we list them as bullet points in Figure 2-8. Let us now hear from the Marketing Manager who picks up the same theme.

> In those days we had no market share information as we had 100 percent of the market. We were a government monopoly. We had no competitors. Any competitors were legally prevented from entering our industry by legislation that was enacted to protect us.
>
> We had all of the market and we were very profitable, so we did not act to expand the market. We would only have had to explain more profits! And our corporate image was very poor because of our lousy service and poor products.
>
> We had only a limited product range, so our customers had to buy what we sold, not what they needed. Our pricing policy for these products was high, and inflexible. We did not try to satisfy our customers' needs; if they did not like what we offered them, bad luck!
>
> Yes, we were arrogant. Now we are paying the cost. Our competitors designed products that corrected our product deficiencies and now they are making a fortune. They sell those products way under our prices; we can't even match them because our costs are so high. They will even change their products and tailor them to the customer's exact needs. How about that! And their service is outstanding. I confess that whenever I have had to use their products I have been amazed that they can do so much at such a low price compared to us.

These comments were also summarized as bullet points. The issues identified in their planning session are listed in Figure 2-8, together with bullet points of strengths and weaknesses identified by the managers and included in the comments above.

By examining the issues, strengths, and weaknesses in Figure 2-8, we have learned a lot about XYZ. Problems or threats are readily identified in a planning session that focuses on issues; most managers are well aware of them. Opportunities will also be well known. Potential technologies that can help are also identified by the IT staff who participate in these planning sessions.

The participants also know their strengths and weaknesses. Sometimes similar points appear in each; for example, staff are capable and have good product knowledge (a strength), but are arrogant (a weakness).

An identification of strengths and weaknesses can be carried out more formally than discussed above, using an *Internal Appraisal*. A number of useful techniques for internal appraisal are described in Chapter 10 of [Finkelstein 1992]. Similarly, we can analyze our competitors by "wearing their hat." An internal appraisal can be carried out for each competitor in turn—particularly those that represent threats—so that we understand them better. This analysis uncovers weaknesses that we can attack, or identifies strengths that we must be aware of.

From an internal appraisal of our competitors, and ourselves, we can identify areas of *Comparative Advantage*. We know where we are strong and where they are weak. And we also know where they are strong and we are weak. An understanding of respective comparative advantages allows us to identify vulnerabilities in our competitors that can be attacked.

When comparative advantages are used in this way, the attacker is using *Competitive Advantage*. It therefore is imperative that we take the initiative if we are to succeed. An understanding of comparative advantage and competitive advantage principles will help us identify the information that should be provided by a data warehouse, to enable managers to make the best competitive decisions. Further detail on these subjects can be found in [Porter 1980] and [Rowe et al 1990].

Competitive advantage applies to commercial organizations in the private sector. But does this mean it has no relevance for public sector, government organizations? Absolutely not: every type of organization competes with others. In the public sector, however, this competition is indirect: government organizations compete with others for resources—the funding and budgets that enable them to operate. One government department may gain funding at the expense of others. Competition therefore applies to all organizations: Private Sector, Public Sector, and Defense.

It is not appropriate in this book to address these subjects in more detail. During goal analysis, after identifying our own strengths and weaknesses we can informally "wear the hat" of our major competitors—especially those that threaten us—to identify their strengths and weaknesses. Formal techniques for deciding comparative advantage and competitive advantage are discussed for Internal Appraisal and External Appraisal in Chapters 10–12 of [Finkelstein 1992].

The next step decides what to do about these issues, strengths, and weaknesses.

Step 5: What Will Achieve or Resolve the Issues?

With this knowledge of issues (problems or threats, opportunities or technologies) we have an agenda. We know what has to be corrected or protected. This is reactive. We know where we should focus attention to achieve opportunities or take advantage of technologies. This is proactive. And our understanding of comparative advantage helps us to use our strengths as weapons for competitive advantage to resolve the issues, while being aware of our weaknesses. We will use this new understanding to identify relevant strategies in this step.

The natural tendency of most organizations is to focus on resolving their problems, protect themselves against their threats and correct their weaknesses. This reactive approach places the organization at a disadvantage: at best it will equal its competitors, not better them.

Instead the emphasis should be to identify strategies that will realize the opportunities, using technologies and strengths as competitive weapons. This proactive approach will enable the organization to gain the initiative. It can diminish the impact of problems, threats, or weaknesses so that they are less important. It leads to aggressive strategies that focus on competitive advantage.

Aggressive strategies that use our strengths or technologies to attack competitors where they are vulnerable can divert their attention. They require that XYZ takes the initiative to *do unto them before they do it unto us!*

We will now ask the XYZ managers to review each issue listed in Figure 2-8. They should ask the following questions for each bullet point:

- What should we do to take advantage of the opportunities?
- What technologies are available to assist us?
- What strengths can we use to help us?
- What has to be done to resolve the problems?

- What should we do to protect ourselves from the threats?
- What should we do to correct our weaknesses?

The focus of these questions is "what should we do," not "how." Only when we know what we should do can we select the best strategies. Only then can we decide how to carry them out. Only then can we define relevant tactics and processes to implement the strategies.

The role of strategies and tactics is illustrated in Figure 2-9. These statements focus on concerns and issues to achieve goals and objectives, within boundaries defined by policies and the mission.

The XYZ managers identify many alternative strategies that they feel will address the issues and achieve the goals. They discuss each major goal in turn, starting with the issues listed under Asset Growth in Figure 2-8. According to the CFO:

> The issues we identified for Asset Growth suggested that we need to establish criteria for minimum return on investment of assets. Obviously, investments that we already have that do not meet the criteria should be sold. We also need strategies to assess the profitability of markets, which will enable us to exit those markets that are unprofitable. Further, these strategies will allow us to assess new potential markets before entry.

Based on these comments, the XYZ managers defined the following strategies for Asset Disposal and Market Exit.

Asset Disposal Strategy:

> Identify assets that cannot provide a return within two years consistent with the mission ROI, and dispose of them at the best possible price.

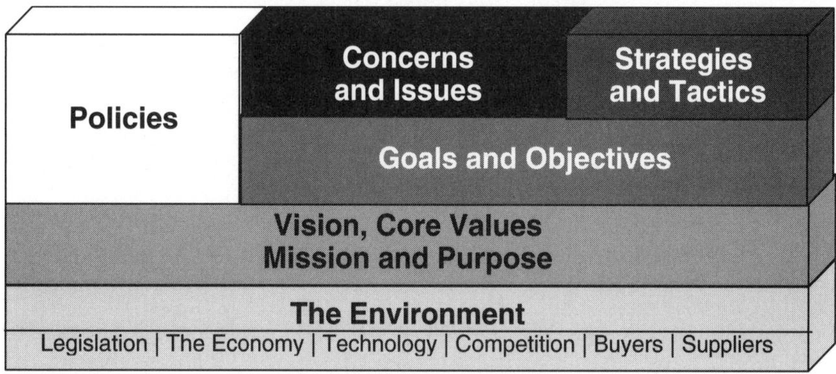

Figure 2-9 Strategies and Tactics address Issues to achieve Goals and Objectives.

Market Exit Strategy:

Identify markets which are unprofitable and in decline, and exit those markets at the lowest possible cost.

The CFO then continued with the managers' assessment of the Profitability issues in Figure 2-8.

These issues suggest that we need strategies to improve our financial reporting and financial control. We also need strategies to improve our budgeting and cash flow management.

The XYZ managers defined profitability and budget control strategies to address these issues.

Financial Reporting Strategy:

Implement flexible financial reporting systems able to be introduced at any organizational level, and which can provide profit and loss statements for any defined reporting frequency, with associated balance sheet statements.

Budget Control Strategy:

Establish and maintain strong budgetary controls for all expenditure, linked directly to revenue achievement. All financial statements must clearly show actual revenue and expenditure against budget, and indicate percentage change from the previous reporting level.

These strategies were easy to define, once the issues were understood and the managers knew what had to be done. The Marketing Manager then addressed the Market Share issues in Figure 2-8.

If we are going to measure market share, we also must know market size and growth. We need all of these. A market share strategy is only effective when it helps us to increase market share faster than the market is growing. If not, we are losing market share. We also must know how our competitors are performing, as their total share helps us assess ours. And associated with all of this, we must define strategies that enable us to decide product ranges and pricing for different markets.

As we saw earlier, XYZ has historically operated as a monopoly. It had no competitors. As a result, today it has no market analysis or competitive analysis information. This information must be obtained from somewhere. It suggests that strategies are needed to survey existing and potential markets to determine potential market size, growth rates, potential for competition, identification of competitors and their market share. These surveys should also identify the needs of current and new customers in those markets.

Information from market surveys will permit analysis of existing and potential markets. Decisions can then be made of products to satisfy those needs, product ranges, and pricing for each market. After discussion, the managers suggested the following strategies.

Market Survey Strategy:

Ensure regular surveys are undertaken to determine market size and our market share, and to understand the needs and the expectation characteristics of our chosen and potential market segments.

Product Range Strategy:

Establish and maintain a product range definition that recognizes the strength of our products and technology, and the capabilities for bundling products into innovative packages.

Product Pricing Strategy:

Establish and maintain a pricing policy which will sustain long-term achievement of market share targets by market segment, that is consistent with achieving profitability targets.

In deciding on these strategies, the managers relied on two strengths of XYZ: it still had a large (but shrinking) market share; it was cash-rich. In contrast, they knew their competitors were small and financially vulnerable. They also knew that XYZ had no inhouse market survey, market analysis, or competitive analysis expertise. But it had deep pockets, and it could buy this expertise from outside market analysis consulting organizations.

So far in goal analysis we have discussed three of the CSFs in Figure 2-2—Asset Growth, Profitability, and Market Share. Discussion of the other CSFs will lead to an agreement on wording for relevant statements, identification of issues, and definition of potential strategies. They are all discussed in more detail in [Finkelstein 1992]. Steps 3–5 are repeated as shown in Figure 2-10, until all have been considered.

At this point, we have agreed (in step 3) on the wording of statements that define the intent of the CSFs in Figure 2-2. Other statements may have been added to these in later planning sessions. We considered any

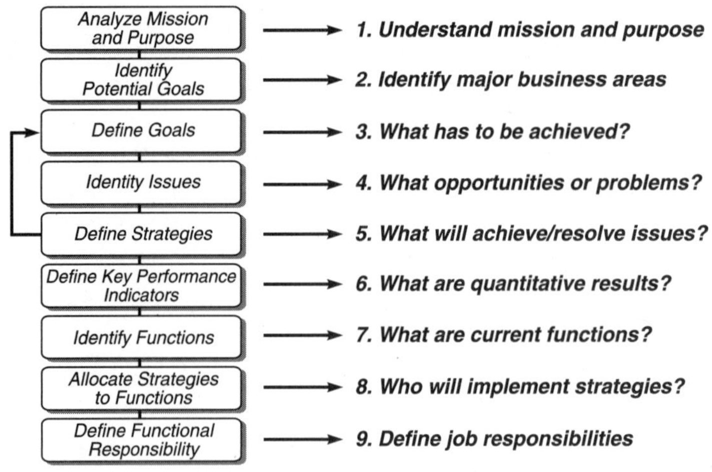

Figure 2-10 The steps of Goal Analysis.

issues (step 4) that indicate problems or threats, opportunities or technologies. We carried out an informal SWOT analysis by including strengths and weaknesses. We defined strategies (step 5) to address these issues based on identified SWOTs. We repeated these three steps as shown in Figure 2-10 until all statements, issues, and strategies had been covered.

We are now ready to move on to the next goal analysis step. This identifies quantitative measures that will enable managers to assess the effectiveness of these strategies, once implemented. This is where our earlier work starts to pay dividends. We will identify information and performance measures that will later be delivered by the Data Warehouse or EP to the managers.

Step 6: What Are the Quantitative Results?

We saw that performance measures are quantitative—they must clearly express the measure, the result level to be achieved, and the time for that achievement. We defined goals and objectives as quantitative targets where goals are long-term and objectives are short-term. We refer to both, collectively, as goals. But targets change over time; typically in the level to be achieved, or the time for achievement. We will see how to express goals that accommodate change.

The relevant goal or objective statement must define the performance measure clearly. But rather than change the wording of level or time for each change, we will instead cross-reference the statement to Key Performance Indicators (KPIs). We will use KPIs to express the level and time. Changes in either or both of these then only need to be made to the relevant KPI. We will discuss the principles for definition of KPIs in some detail in the following pages. We will use these KPIs in later chapters also, to identify information needs using strategic models and to illustrate other Data Warehousing and EP concepts.

KPIs can be used not only to define goal achievement, but also to monitor the effectiveness of strategies. For example, you will remember that the Product Pricing strategy was defined earlier as:

Product Pricing Strategy:

Establish and maintain a pricing policy which will sustain long-term achievement of market share targets by market segment, that is consistent with achieving profitability targets.

We can achieve market share targets in particular market segments by reducing sales price. But there is no point in setting attractive prices to achieve market share if potential customers are not aware of them. Market share is dependent not only on pricing, but also on advertising. Advertising costs money; a manager must decide what proportion of funding should be allocated to advertising.

We now come to the role of a manager. In fact, let us ask—how would you define the job of "manager"? Is it to manage people? Yes, but it is more than that. Is it to manage funds, or equipment, or other resources? Yes, but it is more than that. A manager certainly must manage each of these resources, but still do more. In fact, we now see that resources are a manager's "tools of trade." A manager's job is easy to define, but very difficult to do because it depends on information feedback. We shall define the job of a manager as:

Allocate resources optimally, to achieve defined objectives.

Unless goals or objectives are set—with measure, level, and time—a manager cannot determine which and how many resources to allocate to achieve a desired result. And there must be an element of feedback to the manager, to assess whether the resources have been allocated optimally to produce the best result possible. To allocate too few relevant resources may not have the desired effect. To allocate too many may waste resources that could be used elsewhere. And if objectives are not defined, there is no way to assess if resources are allocated optimally.

Information feedback to the manager on the effect of resource allocation decisions is essential for good management. Otherwise later decisions are made "in the dark." We will see in Chapter 5 how information feedback is provided for performance monitoring, so the manager can assess the effectiveness of earlier decisions and so make future resource allocation decisions with that knowledge. KPIs enable target result levels to be set for future time periods. As each of those time periods complete, the actual result level that was achieved can be measured and compared with the target that was set. This comparison feeds valuable information back to management. A Data Warehouse or EP can provide this information feedback.

Furthermore, a series of levels can be defined over a number of periods for a KPI, to achieve progressive changes in the performance results of a goal. These changes may arise from a decision by management to allocate additional resources for achievement of that goal. We will see in Chapter 5 that KPI series used this way lead to decision early warning and automatic monitoring within pre-defined performance boundaries.

We will now use the Product Pricing and Market Share strategies in Figure 2-8 to discuss how such KPIs are defined. We reviewed the Product Pricing strategy above. The Market Share strategy was earlier defined as:

Market Share:

Achieve the targeted annual market share (expressed as . . .) for the chosen market segments of XYZ.

When we examined this statement we considered it was a potential goal; we said that the level and time needed definition before it could express a quantitative target. We will refine this strategy now, by cross-referencing it to one or more KPIs.

Many things affect the market share of each product. Some factors include product sales price, product quality, customer service, and advertising. We will use sales price and advertising to illustrate the development of suitable KPIs. We ask the XYZ managers to examine Product Pricing. Their initial results follow.

Pricing by Market Segment	Pricing by Product Group
Target gross margin	Target gross margin
Actual gross margin	Actual gross margin

They have identified two potential factors that affect market share: Pricing by Market Segment, and Pricing by Product Group. Of course, the price of products can be set unrealistically low to gain market share, but this may be at the expense of profit. Market share gained this way can be disastrous. Controls should be defined to avoid this. The Product Pricing strategy acknowledges this by adding *consistent with achieving profitability targets.*

By monitoring gross margin—the difference between sales price and cost price—a manager can ensure that products or services are priced above their cost to XYZ so that a profit can be made. We now see that gross margin, typically set as a percentage of cost price, can be used to control profit. A manager can decide to maintain a fixed margin, or may vary that margin for different market segments or product groups to arrive at a sales price.

To reduce sales price without sacrificing profit, a manager must reduce product or service cost. This will likely require resources: funds, people, equipment, technology, etc. These resources all cost money. We will monitor the funds allocated to reduce product cost. The product or service cost and gross margin control the ability to reduce sales price and gain market share. Advertising is another factor that affects market share.

The managers felt that the target gross margin for each market segment or product group can later be compared with the actual gross margin achieved in each period. The effectiveness of funding decisions in those periods for advertising and product or service cost (which affects sales price) can be assessed. The impact of these decisions on market share can be monitored to protect gross margin and profit.

We discussed earlier that monitoring market share alone, without also monitoring market size and growth, is pointless. A Market Size and Market Growth strategy follows, with appropriate measures.

Market Size and Market Growth:

Monitor market size and growth rates in chosen markets.

Market Size by Total Units	Market Size by Total Value
Target total units Actual total units	Target total value Actual total value

Market size is measured in total units, and in total value. By tracking these historically, market growth can be calculated as the annual change in market size, or the quarterly change or monthly change in size depending on the volatility of each market.

From historical results, planned market size and growth targets in total units and total value can be projected into the future. The actual market size and growth achieved in future periods enable the effect of product cost and advertising funding decisions on the size and growth of each market, and on the market share realized, to be assessed. The sensitivity of market size, growth, and market share on these funding decisions can be evaluated, as we will see shortly.

It is difficult to determine exactly how much funding is required to achieve specific market size and market share results. It is easier instead to assess the effect of funding on growth rates. For example, different technologies can achieve efficiencies in production that may lead to product or service cost reductions. This can permit sales price reductions while maintaining gross margin. Funds allocated in a period to technology and advertising should therefore lead to changes in market size, market growth, and market share.

The managers evaluate technology funding to achieve product or service cost reductions, projected for the next four quarters—numbered Q1–Q4. They call this "Product Cost Funding." Funding is also allocated to advertising. The Marketing Manager presents the results of their deliberations based on the Unit Market Share KPI Spreadsheet shown as Figure 2-11.

Figure 2-11
Unit Market Share KPI Spreadsheet of Projected Funding and Targets for Market Growth and XYZ Unit Sales Growth.

Key Performance Indicator	Q1	Q2	Q3	Q4
Product Cost Funding (in $000s)	350	300	250	200
Advertising Funding (in $000s)	400	450	500	550
Total Funding (in $000s)	750	750	750	750
Market Growth in Total Units (%)	0.0%	2.5%	2.8%	3.2%
Market Size in Total Units (000s)	200	205	211	217
XYZ Unit Sales Growth (%)	0.0%	7.0%	8.5%	9.0%
XYZ Unit Sales (in 000s)	120	128	139	152
XYZ Unit Market Share Growth (%)	0.0%	4.2%	5.3%	5.3%
XYZ Unit Market Share (%)	60.0%	62.6%	66.1%	69.8%

They decided that technology funding had to be high in early periods to achieve product cost reductions, but they felt this funding could be reduced progressively as the technology took effect. In contrast, they decided that advertising funding should increase progressively as the technology funding decreased, maintaining the same total funding in each period as shown by Figure 2-11.

To evaluate these funding decisions, they decided that the most effective measure was Total Units Sold. They projected sales of 200,000 units as the Total Market Size for the first quarter (Q1), with XYZ Unit Sales of 120,000. For later quarters, they estimated quarterly Market Growth Rates between 2.5 and 3.2 percent. The Total Market Size will then grow to 217,000 units in Q4, as illustrated in Figure 2-12.

They felt that their funding decisions would lead to XYZ Unit Sales Growth of 7.0 percent, 8.5 percent, and 9.0 percent in each of Q2–Q4 respectively. This growth would give the Total XYZ Unit Sales in those periods as shown in Figure 2-11 and illustrated in Figure 2-12.

Figure 2-11 shows that the XYZ Market Share in Q1 was 60 percent. Taking into account the market growth and resulting market size in each of those periods and the growth in XYZ unit sales, they calculated in Figure 2-11 that XYZ Market Share should increase to almost 70 percent by Q4. These growth rates are illustrated in Figure 2-13.

This allocation of funding to technology and advertising, and its impact on total market growth and XYZ unit sales growth, provides results that can be monitored over quarterly periods. In Chapter 5 we

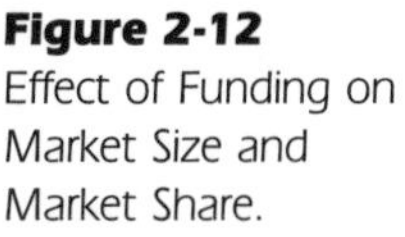

Figure 2-12
Effect of Funding on Market Size and Market Share.

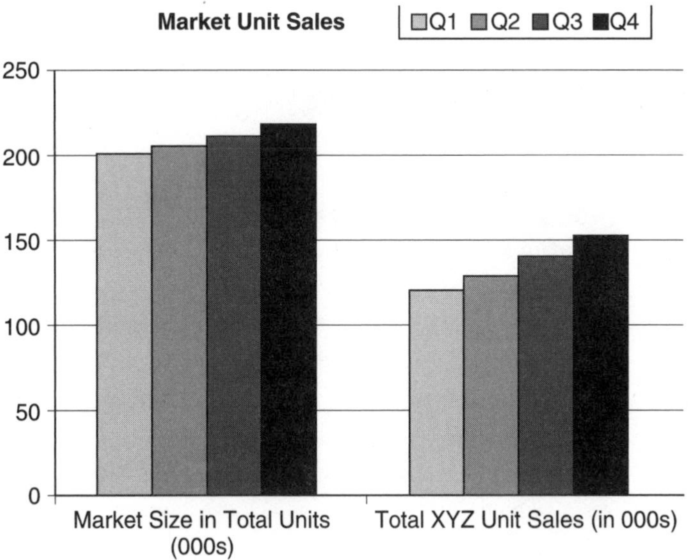

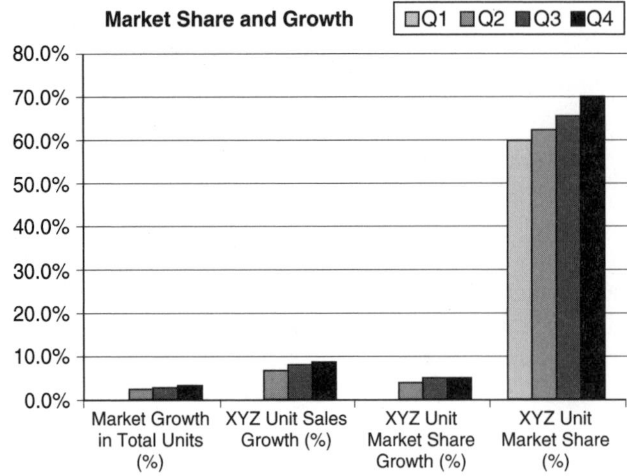

Figure 2-13 Effect of Projected Funding on Market Growth and Market Share Growth.

will see how information feedback can be provided for decision early warning, so that decisions on total funding and its proportional distribution to technology and to advertising can be varied in later periods to achieve the desired market share targets in Figure 2-13.

From this insight, the managers refined the Market Share strategy (while observing the Product Pricing strategy) and defined the KPI as follows:

Market Share:

Achieve the targeted annual market share based on *Unit Market Share KPI* for the chosen market segments of XYZ.

The earlier Market Share strategy has changed to cross-reference the *Unit Market Share KPI* (shown in italic above). This KPI is defined and cross-referenced to the *Unit Market Share KPI Spreadsheet* that was earlier presented as Figure 2-11. That spreadsheet defines the calculations of Market Size, XYZ Unit Sales, and XYZ Market Share based on relevant growth rates.

Unit Market Share KPI:

The Unit Market Share KPI monitors Market Growth in Total Units and Unit Sales Growth targets by quarter. These targets are managed by varying total and proportional funding for advertising and product cost reduction technologies, to achieve decreases in sales price with consistent gross margins. The Unit Market Share KPI Spreadsheet (in Figure 2-11) defines each of these targets.

Finally, we will check the statements against the Product Pricing strategy to satisfy ourselves that it has not been violated.

Product Pricing Strategy:

Establish and maintain a pricing policy which will sustain long-term achievement of market share targets by market segment, that is consistent with achieving profitability targets.

We validly observed the Product Pricing strategy, using technologies to bring about product or service cost reductions while maintaining consistent gross margins and hence profitability. We have refined the Market Share strategy and defined a new Unit Market Share KPI and spreadsheet. We are now ready to move on to the next goal analysis step.

Step 7: What Are the Current Functions?

The refined strategic plans for XYZ are now taking shape. But these plans are pointless unless their implementation is managed. Specific managers must be given this responsibility. The final steps of goal analysis focus on assigning implementation responsibility for these planning statements to relevant parts of the business.

We first must be aware of the current functions. This is easy to determine. A *Function* is defined as a group of related activities. Some managers are responsible for more than one function (and therefore activities), which may not be apparent from their job title. We group related activities (and the strategies they support) into functions. Some business activities may be shared across more than one function. We need to identify or define function responsibilities independently of how the organization is currently structured. The managers provide us with a list of the current functions of XYZ.

- Corporate
- Finance
- Forecasting
- Marketing
- Sales

- Research & Development
- Production
- Purchasing
- Personnel

For each strategy, we can identify the principal business activities. We may have to derive new functions and activities that are needed for some strategies in addition to the current functions above. The next goal analysis step helps us do this.

Step 8: Who Will Implement the Strategies?

This step helps us to establish action plans for strategy implementation. It allocates responsibility for achieving goals and KPIs. A matrix is developed, with each strategy on a separate row and each function listed as a column heading.

For each strategy in turn, the managers decide which function has primary responsibility for managing implementation of that strategy. A solid bullet in the cell for the function column signifies this primary responsibility; there can therefore only be one solid bullet in a row.

Other functions may also need to be involved; they have secondary responsibility for implementation. An open bullet in a cell for a function shows it has secondary responsibility. The primary function is responsible for coordinating each secondary function for implementation of the strategy.

The result is the *Business Function–Strategy Matrix* illustrated in Figure 2-14. There are more strategies listed in that figure than we have discussed in this chapter. A full discussion of all of these strategies is provided in Chapter 9 of [Finkelstein 1992].

Notice that arrows highlight some columns in Figure 2-14. These indicate new functions that XYZ will need to support. For example, the managers defined Market Data and Market Analysis strategies to implement the Market Survey strategy. These are part of a Market Research function that XYZ does not currently have, so a new column was added to the matrix for this function. This does not imply that XYZ has to establish a new Market Research Department. Instead it can contract with an external Market Research firm to carry out the function on its behalf. But XYZ may need to appoint a Market Research Manager to liaise with this firm, and receive their market analysis results from the market data they obtain through market surveys.

A Sales, Support, and Customer Training strategy was also defined by the managers in Figure 2-14. The Education function is given primary responsibility for implementing this strategy. As XYZ does not currently have this function, it should appoint an Education Manager to select and liaise with external education firms to carry out this training on its behalf.

Finally, the Product Review strategy has been allocated to a Product Management function. Again, an arrow highlights this new function in Figure 2-14. We earlier discussed that XYZ had entered many markets at high cost, where those markets did not give a satisfactory return. This was found to be due to a lack of coordination between the functions of R&D, Product Development, Production, and Marketing. The managers decided a new Product Management function should be established to coordinate these other functions for new products and

Figure 2-14 Business Function–Strategy Matrix. Arrows identify new Functions.

LEGEND
● Primary resp.
○ Shared resp.

Strategy	Corporate	Finance	Mkt Research	Forecasting	Marketing	Sales	R & D	Product Mgt	Production	Purchasing	Education	Personnel		
Asset Disposal	○	●												
Market Exit		○	○	○	●									
Financial Reporting		●		○	○	○								
Budget Control		●		○	○	○								
Market Data		○	●	○	○	○								
Market Analysis		○	●	○	○	○								
Market Needs Analysis		○	○	○	●									
Technology Monitoring			○	○	○	○	●							
R & D			○	○	○		●							
R & D Funding		●	○	○	○									
Customer Satisfaction Survey			○	○	○	●		○						
Sales, Support & Customer Training					○	○		○			●			
Quality Control								○	●	○	○			
Product Maintenance Improvement								○	●	○	○			
Product Review								●	○	○	○			
Product Release						●		○	○	○	○			
Career Planning	○	○	○	○	○	○	○	○	○	○	○	●		
Staff Incentives	○	○										●		

markets. The Product Management function is responsible for Product Review, and for the Product Range and Product Pricing strategies discussed earlier.

The *Business Function–Strategy Matrix* in Figure 2-14 enables primary and secondary implementation responsibility to be allocated for each strategy. It leads to proactive management of strategy implementation. Each strategy is allocated to at least one function, with new functions identified and added as required.

Step 9: Define Job Responsibilities

The Business Function–Strategy Matrix allows the responsibilities of each function now to be identified. This is used to document the job responsibilities for each manager appointed to manage each function.

For example, in Figure 2-15 an arrow highlights the Finance column. Reading down, we see solid bullets that identify each strategy where the

Figure 2-15
Job responsibilities can be read down each Function column.

LEGEND
● Primary resp.
○ Shared resp.

Strategy	Function													
	Corporate	Finance	Mkt Research	Forecasting	Marketing	Sales	R & D	Product Mgt	Production	Purchasing	Education	Personnel		
Asset Disposal	○	●												
Market Exit		○	○	○	●									
Financial Reporting		●		○	○	○								
Budget Control		●		○	○	○								
Market Data		○	●	○	○	○								
Market Analysis		○	●	○	○	○								
Market Needs Analysis		○	○	○	●									
Technology Monitoring			○	○	○	○	●							
R & D			○	○	○		●							
R & D Funding		●	○	○	○									
Customer Satisfaction Survey			○	○	○	●		○						
Sales, Support & Customer Training					○	○		○			●			
Quality Control								○	●	○	○			
Product Maintenance Improvement								○	●	○	○			
Product Review								●	○	○	○			
Product Release						●		○	○	○	○			
Career Planning	○	○	○	○	○	○	○	○	○	○	○	●		
Staff Incentives	○	○										●		

Chief Financial Officer has primary responsibility, as the manager of the Finance Department. We also see open bullets that identify strategies where Finance has secondary responsibility to participate with other functions.

We will now use Figure 2-15 to focus on Asset Disposal, Financial Reporting, and Budget Control, which we defined earlier in step 3. This will incorporate the strategies and their KPIs or objectives as action plans for the CFO job description. The result for the CFO is documented in Figure 2-16. We will see that this job description also becomes the Tactical Business Plan for the Finance Department.

DEFENSE NOTE *While commercial and government enterprises (and this book) use strategic business plans—with tactical business plans at a lower level and operational business plans at the lowest level—most Defense Departments reverse their use of the terms "tactical" and "operational". In contrast, they use strategic, then operational, with tactical at the lowest level. Apart from this terminology difference, Goal Analysis is also used by Defense Departments exactly as described in this book.*

These strategies, with identified issues, strengths, and weaknesses from step 4 (see Figure 2-8) and KPIs or objectives defined in step 5, can now be consolidated as a Position Statement for the role of CFO. This is documented in Figure 2-16.

We see in Figure 2-16 that the CFO has defined objectives for the Asset Disposal, Financial Reporting, and Budget Control strategies, using the same names. These are definitely quantitative, as they define measure, level, and time quite clearly.

For example, the Asset Disposal objective defines the measure as *following Board approval, dispose of non-performing assets;* the level is *all* (100 percent) and the time is *within 12 months.* The Financial Reporting objective defines the measure as *implement financial reporting systems that provide profit and loss, balance sheet, and cash flow reporting;* the level is *within 1 day of the close of any defined financial period* and the time is *within 6 months.*

By progressively applying the steps of goal analysis we have developed a precise job description for the CFO. But it is more than that. We see that Figure 2-16 also becomes the Tactical Business Plan for the Finance Department (see Defense Note above).

Goal analysis can be applied at each lower management level, to ensure that this tactical business plan is implemented correctly. The objectives defined at this level become "goals" for achievement at the

Figure 2-16 CFO Position Statement, from Business Strategy–Function Matrix.

Position:	Chief Financial Officer
Reports to:	President and CEO
Asset Growth	*Monitor performance of all aspects of our business so that each activity has a favorable effect, directly or indirectly, on our mission ROI.*
Issues	■ Many investments in declining markets ■ High market entry cost into marginal markets ■ High debt levels for assets in sunset markets
Asset Disposal Strategy	*Identify assets that cannot provide a return within two years consistent with the mission ROI, and dispose of them at the best possible price.*
Asset Disposal Objective	*Following Board approval, dispose of all non-performing assets within 12 months.*
Profitability	*Monitor financial performance of all activities to ensure that profit and cash flow projections are achieved according to, or ahead of, plan.*
Issues	■ Delayed financial reporting ■ High interest costs ■ Poor cash flow management
Strengths	■ Profitable ■ Cash-rich
Weaknesses	■ Poor financial reporting ■ Poor budget control
Financial Reporting Strategy	*Implement flexible financial reporting systems able to be introduced at any organizational level, and which can provide profit and loss statements for any defined reporting frequency, with associated balance sheet statements.*
Financial Reporting Objective	*Implement financial reporting systems within 6 months that provide profit and loss, balance sheet, and cash flow reporting within 1 day of the close of any defined financial period.*
Budget Control Strategy	*Establish and maintain strong budgetary controls for all expenditure, linked directly to revenue achievement. All financial statements must clearly show actual revenue and expenditure against budget, and indicate percentage change from the previous reporting level.*
Budget Control Objective	*Implement budget control systems directly linked to financial reports according to the budget control strategy, within 6 months.*

next lower level. The Finance managers and the staff who report to the CFO identify issues associated with the achievement of these objectives. They define "strategies" that address these issues. These in fact become tactics for implementing strategies defined by the CFO.

Benefits of Goal Analysis

Goal analysis is easy to learn and use, yet it is quite rigorous. It normally requires 3–5 days of group planning sessions by managers to develop Tactical Business Plans from the starting point of six typical CSFs in an organization. Goal analysis delivers a number of benefits:

- Produces clear, performance-based statements of policies, goals, objectives, strategies, KPIs, and action plans (tactics)
- Implements business plans at all management levels
- Produces clear definition of quantitative goals and objectives
- Defines KPIs for performance measurement of changing goals
- Defines strategies to address opportunities and resolve issues
- Defines objectives or KPIs so that strategies can be implemented correctly and in a timely fashion
- Defines tactics for implementation of plans at lower levels

We have discussed the use of goal analysis to develop, or refine, business plans at all management levels of an organization. Goal analysis can also be used to develop project specifications for data warehouse or EP projects, or for any other projects of interest. In the final pages of this chapter we will briefly review how goal analysis is used for this purpose.

Goal Analysis for Project Specifications

Goal analysis is also used to define specifications for projects where none presently exist, or to refine current specifications so that the business requirements and project focus are clearly expressed. It defines project goals, and identifies issues. These are problems that are to be resolved by the project, opportunities to be realized, or technologies to be used. These issues, with strengths and weaknesses, are all used to define project strategies and project objectives for implementation, as well as KPIs and performance criteria.

Changes are made to the steps of goal analysis for this project focus. These changes are briefly discussed in the following paragraphs.

Step 1: Examine the Business and Project Mission Statements

This step identifies the business areas to be addressed by the project. These areas may be in specific business units, or could be in certain functions of the organization. Typically, this step examines existing business and project mission statements to understand the business purpose of each area.

Where they are missing, a mission statement should be defined for each involved business area. Ideally, a manager or experienced staff member from each area should define these statements. They are intended for use by the project team to define project specifications, and so should first be reviewed (and corrected where necessary) by other managers of each business area.

Where statements do exist, this step clarifies those existing statements as required. It ensures that the purpose of each business area is clearly documented. From this greater business understanding, a project mission statement can then be defined.

Step 2: Identify Preliminary Project Goals and Performance Criteria

From the project mission, preliminary project goals are defined and performance criteria are established. For example, a project goal may be defined to design and build a data warehouse. A performance criterion may be to complete implementation of the warehouse by a certain date. But to build the data warehouse on time, without first ensuring its ability to deliver required information needed by management, is pointless. These preliminary project goals and performance criteria must be expanded into more detailed goals and criteria.

Step 3: Define Clear Business and Project Goals

Projects typically support business goals. For example, the achievement of a business goal may depend on ready availability of accurate information to management. The strategy that management defined to achieve this goal was to implement a data warehouse. This was the main reason for initiating the data warehouse project in step 2.

For this example, project goals must be defined that clearly specify WHAT information is needed to support the business goals. And of course, the business goals and project goals must both be known if the project is to achieve those goals. They must fully define WHAT results will achieve those goals.

Step 4: What Are the Business Problems or Opportunities?

The business problems or opportunities are generally well known; in many cases they are the reasons for establishment of the project. But it is important here to apply the complete goal analysis step 4 as discussed earlier. This identifies all relevant business issues: problems, threats, and opportunities for the business areas. It additionally identifies their strengths and weaknesses. These all provide input to the next step, to decide specific strategies to be followed by the project.

Step 5: What Strategies Address the Problems or Opportunities?

The understanding gained from step 4 above enables specific features or characteristics of the project to be defined. These are strategies to address identified issues, using relevant technologies and drawing on specific strengths (or addressing weaknesses) as required.

From this examination, the best strategies are selected to achieve the project goals and business goals. These project strategies clearly define WHAT the project has to DO to achieve the project and business goals (but not yet how). It is typically only in the technical design of the project that the detailed tactics for implementation are defined, that determine HOW the strategies will be implemented.

Step 6: What Are the Performance Measures to Achieve?

Now performance measures can be defined to ensure that the project strategies established in step 5 are correctly implemented. These criteria typically define measures that enable the functionality of implemented project strategies to be tested. They permit assessment of the ability to support achievement of related project or business goals.

Step 7: What Business Functions Are to be Supported?

From the steps above, a clear definition of business and project mission, as well as business and project goals, issues, strategies, and performance criteria will emerge. But during these steps, some changes may have occurred in the specification of the project that could affect other parts of the organization.

This step therefore provides an important cross-check. All areas and functions that are affected by the project are listed, so representatives from those areas can be identified in the next step.

Step 8: Who Is Responsible from Each Function?

A *Project Strategy–Function Matrix* is developed in this step. This lists relevant business strategies and all project strategies—each as a row, with all affected areas and functions as columns. Primary responsibility for each business or project strategy is shown as a solid bullet in the relevant column. An open bullet shows secondary responsibility of all other affected columns.

Step 9: Schedule Project Participation by Business Experts and IT Experts

The matrix developed in step 8 allows primary and secondary responsibility areas or functions to be identified for each strategy row. It also allows all strategies for an area or function column to be readily identified, by reading down that column. Managers, business experts, and IT experts, with detailed knowledge of each relevant business or project strategy can now be easily identified. Their knowledge will be needed to develop a strategic data model. This uses strategic data modeling, a methodology that is discussed in Chapters 3 and 4.

REFERENCES

Ackoff, R.L. (1981) "On the Use of Models in Corporate Planning," *Strategic Management Journal*, 2, 353–359.

Drucker, P.F. (1974) *Management: Tasks, Responsibilities, Practices*, New York: Harper & Row.

Finkelstein, C.B. (1992) *Information Engineering: Strategic Systems Development*, Sydney, Australia: Addison-Wesley; Chapters 9–12.

Porter, M. (1980) *Competitive Strategy: Techniques for Analyzing Industries and Competitors*, New York: Free Press.

Rowe A.J., Mason R.O., Dickel K.E. and Snyder N.H. (1990) *Strategic Management and Business Policy: A Methodological Approach*, 3rd edn, Reading, MA: Addison-Wesley.

CHAPTER 3

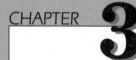

Data Modeling

A Window into the Enterprise

Just give me a street map and a destination address. I can find my own way . . . any time, any place, anywhere.

—Anonymous Traveller

This chapter discusses the principles of data modeling. A data model details the data that an organization needs to function effectively. A data model comprises data maps and data definitions in a data dictionary, which is called a *repository*. Data mapping is used to develop data maps; business normalization is used to identify metadata definitions to be stored in a repository. We will use data for knowledge management later in this chapter. We will apply the principles of data mapping that we learn here to develop a strategic data model in Chapter 4 from the strategic business plans in Chapter 2.

NOTE. *If you are experienced in data modeling, we recommend that you at least skim-read this chapter. You may find that some concepts are applied differently by the EEP methodology than what you are accustomed to. You may also decide to read the section titled* Structure Entities *in full. Structure entities allow you to take expert knowledge—held as tacit knowledge by some business experts—and make it explicit as expert knowledge for all to share. Structure entities are based on Fifth Business Normal Form (5BNF) as used by business-driven Information Engineering (IE) and by Enterprise Engineering (EE).*

So why do we need to learn data modeling and data mapping to build a Data Warehouse or an Enterprise Portal (EP)? Consider how we find our way in a strange city. We can hire a taxi. But if we need a car to get around, we would instead rent a car.

With a taxi we can rely on the driver's knowledge of the city; we do not need to know its layout. We place ourselves in the driver's hands. But we have no way of knowing whether the driver is taking the long route to our destination, at a higher cost.

With a rental car, we accept the fact that we must find our own way. We ask for a street directory. But if no directory is available we instead ask for directions to our destination. With verbal directions there is a high probability that we will get lost, while written directions may be more reliable . . . provided they are correct. Once again, to reach our destination we must depend on someone else.

We accept as normal that a city map or a street directory is available to help us find our way around a strange city. From the layout of the city, knowing where we are and where we want to go, we can find our way around any city. Without this capability, we have no alternative but to rely on others.

The Importance of Maps

A street directory has a list of street names and suburbs, which refer to relevant map pages in the directory and grid references on those pages.

With a street directory we can determine the best route to take to reach our destination. From a broad perspective, we use the city map in the inside front cover showing the layout of the city to decide where we are, and where we want to go. We can then identify the alternative routes to take.

As we cross each grid in the city map we turn to the more detailed map page within the directory, where we can see the detailed layout of that part of the city.

With a street directory, we can decide ourselves the most appropriate route to take: we do not depend on the accuracy of others. We can determine the most relevant route based on our requirements:

- If we want to get there quickly, we take the fastest route possible—such as a freeway if one is available. We find the nearest on-ramp, decide which off-ramp to take and where to go from there.
- If we want a more leisurely scenic route, we may travel using a different direction.

The route we choose depends on our requirements, traffic conditions, and also the mode of transport available—which involves technology.

Information for Decision Making

Unfortunately, most organizations do not have the corporate equivalent of a city map and street directory. When they need information for decision making they must ask someone else. They must also depend on others for the accuracy of that information.

In designing and building systems to provide information, we depend on many people. Generally the end users of the system—typically experts in that part of the business—are most qualified to decide what business processes and data are needed to provide the required information. Computer experts build required databases and systems based on the defined requirements of the business experts.

Data modeling has evolved as a methodology to document corporate data—using a schematic data map and a data dictionary (collectively called a data model), conceptually corresponding to the city map and list of streets in a street directory.

But data may exist as different versions in various parts of the enterprise to support business processes that use that data. If one data version is changed, all versions of that same data must be changed if information derived from the data is to be consistent. A data model enables these different data versions to be integrated as one shared data version—implemented as shared databases.

A street directory is unique to a city and is available for use when needed. Each organization is unique—and its data model is unique and must be developed. Broad industry data models ("templates" or "universal models") may be available, but if they are used each organization has to tailor the template to develop its own data model. This chapter shows components of a data model, then discusses how data maps are developed. We will see how they are used for Data Warehousing and EPs in Chapter 4.

Data modeling is used by business experts, and by computer experts. Business experts are analogous to the people who live in a city and know its layout through personal experience. They are the operational users and managers who know how the business operates. Operational users have vital knowledge of the organization; they know what data is needed for different business processes. Similarly, senior and middle managers know the information they need for decision making based on defined strategic plans. This information is generally derived from operational data and stored in a Data Warehouse.

Computer experts must participate: they are analogous to the surveyors or builders of the city. They are responsible for formally documenting and maintaining the data maps defined by the business experts. They work in a design partnership with these business experts, providing methodology guidance and technical support when needed. They later build the data warehouses, databases, and information systems based on the data models, to be used by the business experts.

The Data Modeling Phase

Data Modeling is a major component of business-driven *Information Engineering* (IE) and its later development, *Enterprise Engineering* (EE) [Finkelstein 1989, 1992]. It is used extensively by the Engineering Enterprise Portals (EEP) methodology. The following paragraphs show where Data Modeling exists in the EEP Systems Development Life Cycle (SDLC).

Business-driven Enterprise Engineering supports all SDLC phases in Figure 3-1. Phases above the line are *Technology-Independent* and focus on the business. These are Strategic Business Planning, Data Modeling, and Function Modeling.

The Strategic Directions set by management provide input to Strategic Business Planning, as discussed in Chapter 2 and shown in Figure 3-1. These plans indicate Information Requirements of management and provide input to Data Modeling. The data models show the data relevant to the organization. How data and information are used depend on defined business processes. Plans and data models define Information Usage and provide input to Function Modeling—which comprises Activity Modeling and Process Modeling.

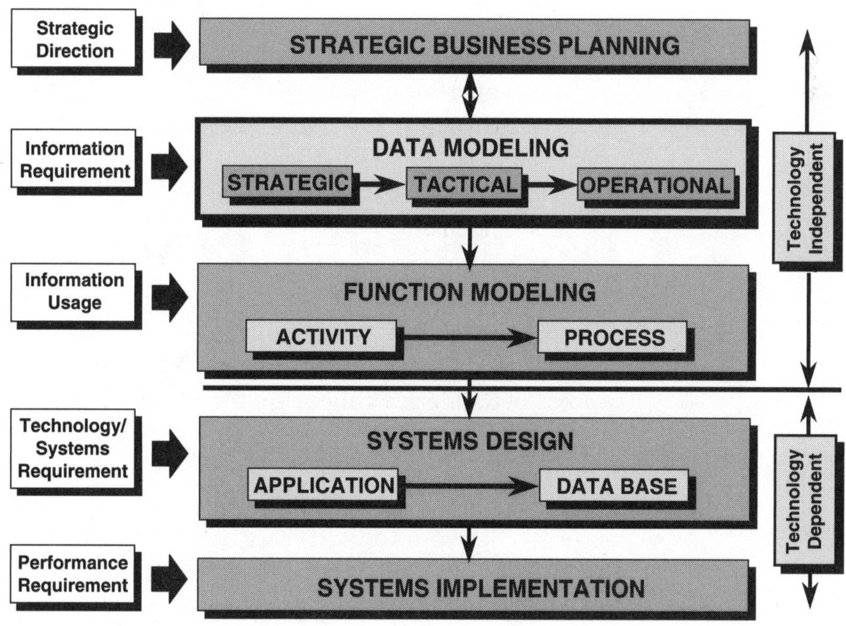

Figure 3-1 Data Modeling in the EEP Systems Development Life Cycle.

The phases above the line in Figure 3-1 therefore define business requirements and are Technology-Independent, while phases below the line are *Technology-Dependent*. These are Systems Design and Systems Implementation.

The Technology and Systems Requirements of the business provide input to Systems Design. Client/Server, Object-Oriented and Internet technologies are used in this phase for Application Design and Database Design of data warehouses—and of systems and databases to be deployed on corporate intranets or the Internet as Enterprise Portals. Identified Performance Requirements then provide input required by the Systems Implementation phase.

Looking at the Data Modeling phase of Figure 3-1 in more detail, we can see that Strategic Business Planning identifies Information Requirements of management and so provides input to this phase. The Strategic Plans from Chapter 2 provide input to Strategic Modeling, to develop a Strategic Data Model. The analysis of this Strategic Model produces project plans; we will discuss the analysis and content of these project plans in Chapter 4.

The Strategic Model and Tactical Business Plans all provide input to Tactical Modeling to develop Tactical Data Models. These Tactical Models, with Operational Business Plans, then provide input to Operational Modeling to develop Operational Data Models.

DEFENSE NOTE *As discussed in Chapter 2, Defense Departments use this terminology differently. Strategic data models are at the highest level, then operational data models. Tactical data models are at the most detailed logical data modeling level in Defense.*

Data Modeling Concepts

A knowledge of data modeling is vital for success in data warehousing. It is one of the key techniques of the EEP methodology. We can define the process of data modeling as follows:

> Data Modeling is a process used to identify, communicate, and record details about data and the relationships that exist between data, with its own terminology and conventions.

The above definition of data modeling does not assume any prerequisite knowledge of computers. Instead it requires knowledge of the business.

Data modeling uses terminology and conventions so that it can be used as a common communication medium between business experts and systems experts.

Reference material for the data modeling and the data mapping concepts covered in this chapter can be found in books and articles by Peter Chen [1976], Edgar (Ted) Codd [1970, 1979 and 1988], Chris Date [1986], Clive Finkelstein [1989 and 1992], Terry Halpin [1995] and others. Self-study courses by Clive Finkelstein on *Data Modeling Concepts, Business Normalization Concepts* and *Data Modeling Case Study Workshop*—to qualify as a Certified Business Data Modeler (CBDM)—can be found in [Finkelstein 1999].

A business is comprised of organizational units, business functions, or business processes. These are subsets of the business that we will refer to collectively as *Model Views*. We will use a terminology of data entities, data attributes, and data associations (or just entities, attributes, and associations) to represent, in a data model, the data and information of a Model View that represents part of the business. These terms are defined in detail below.

A *Data Model* includes a schematic representation of entities and associations (called a *Data Map*—analogous to the maps in a street directory) and details of entities and attributes (called an *Entity List*—which is analogous to a list of street names and other details in the street directory).

A Simple Data Map

A schematic data map shows each *Entity* as a rectangular box. The name of the entity is written within the entity box, in capitals and in the singular for a single occurrence of the entity as shown in Figure 3-2 with EMPLOYEE, SKILL and JOB. There may be many employees, skills, and jobs. However, we will use each entity box to show the data that we need to know about *each* employee (so representing *all* employees), and similarly for skills and jobs.

Attributes may optionally be listed within the entity box, as shown in the SKILL entity. These are written in lower case to distinguish them from the entity name. They also are written in the singular, to represent a single occurrence of each attribute.

A connecting line called an *Association* joins two entities that are related in some way. Symbols drawn on each end of an association line describe the relationship that exists between the two entities. We will discuss these symbols in more detail shortly.

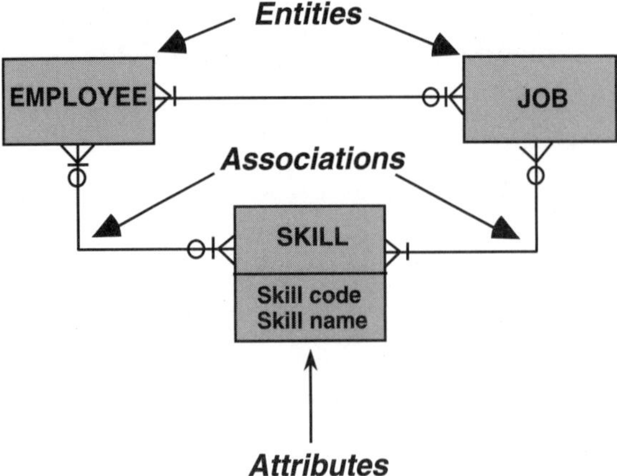

Figure 3-2
A Simple Data Map of Entities, Attributes and Associations.

A data map thus comprises entity boxes (optionally containing attributes) joined by association lines. It shows data entities of interest and indicates by the associations how those entities are interrelated. Related groups of entities are included in model views for those parts of the organization that are interested in the entities.

This data map notation can be drawn by hand or it can be drawn by Computer-Aided Software Engineering (CASE) modeling tools. CASE tools enable data maps to be drawn in different formats. They allow any changes to be easily made so that all data maps can be maintained up to date. We will use CASE tools extensively in later chapters.

Definition of a Data Entity

We will now examine the *data entity* further. It is defined as follows:

> A Data Entity is something of interest that we may need to refer to later. It is a logical representation of data to be stored in a database in a computer, or in a register file or some other storage format if not yet on computer.

We will use the logical term *data entity* (or just *entity*) rather than the more physical term *file* or *record*. When data modeling we are not yet concerned with the physical representation of an entity: merely that it does logically exist and will be stored for later reference. It is only during the Systems Design phase that we decide how the entity will be physically stored. This depends on the technology that is available, and on system and performance requirements when implemented.

An entity is always written in the singular to represent a single occurrence of the data that it represents. It is also written in capitals to distinguish it from attributes (which are in lower case). Examples of entities and the data they represent are:

EMPLOYEE	Data we need to store about each employee.
JOB	Data we need to store about each job.
SKILL	Data we need to store about each skill.

Definition of a Data Attribute

Examining a *data attribute* in greater detail, we see that:

> Data Attributes are contained in data entities. Attributes provide details that describe the entity in which they reside.

We will use the logical term *data attribute* (or merely *attribute*) rather than the physical terms *data item, data element*, or *data field*. During later steps in operational data modeling we will define the logical data type of the attribute (text, money, number, etc.). However, we will not decide the physical data type and representation of the attribute until physical Database Design is carried out (in the Systems Design phase of Figure 3-1) when we know more about the business requirements and the performance requirements for implementation.

An attribute name is always singular, to refer to *one* occurrence of the data that it represents. It is also written in lower case to distinguish it from entities (which are written in upper case).

An attribute should be qualified to avoid any ambiguity, typically by the name of the entity in which it resides. Thus *employee name, employee address*, and *employee phone number* are clearly different to *customer name, customer address*, and *customer phone number*. If we used only *name, address*, and *phone number* it would not be obvious when we were referring to customers, instead of employees. Prefixing the entity name avoids this ambiguity.

Definition of Data Associations

Data associations are vital to data mapping, as they help indicate relevant business rules. We define a *data association* as follows:

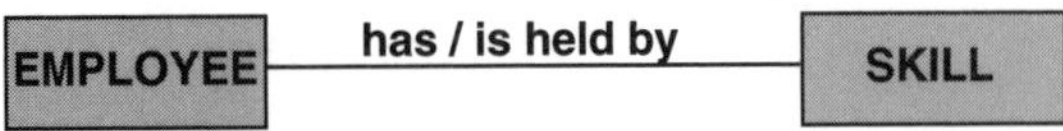

Figure 3-3 An association between two entities may optionally be named.

An Association is shown by a line joining two entity boxes, to represent a relationship that exists between the relevant entities. It models business rules for those entities.

We will use the term *association* to refer to the logical connection between the related entities, rather than use the more physical term *relationship* (which refers to the physical connection between tables in a database, as discussed in Part 2).

During Database Design in the Systems Design phase we decide how associations are to be physically implemented. This depends on the database technology that will be used, and also the system and performance requirements when implemented.

A name may optionally be written on an association line to define the meaning of the connection between related entities. The association in Figure 3-3 between EMPLOYEE and SKILL is not yet fully defined. However, reading from left to right, the data map shows that *employee has skill*. Reading from right to left it shows that *skill is held by employee*.

Figure 3-3 shows only one association line between a pair of entities. If more than one association is drawn between two entities it generally indicates that more detailed entities exist. These entities should be added to the data map to show more clearly the business rules they represent.

Associations use symbols at each end for schematic representation of business rules. These symbols show association degree and nature.

Association Degree

Symbols are added to each end of an association line to indicate the *cardinality*, or *degree*, of the association as shown in Figure 3-4. In this book we will use the term *degree* (rather than *cardinality*) when we refer to associations.

In Figure 3-4, a "crow's foot" (also called a "chicken foot") represents *one or many* occurrences of the entity that it touches. The absence of a crow's foot indicates *one* occurrence of the entity. This convention for *one* (i.e. no crow's foot) will be used for data mapping in this book.

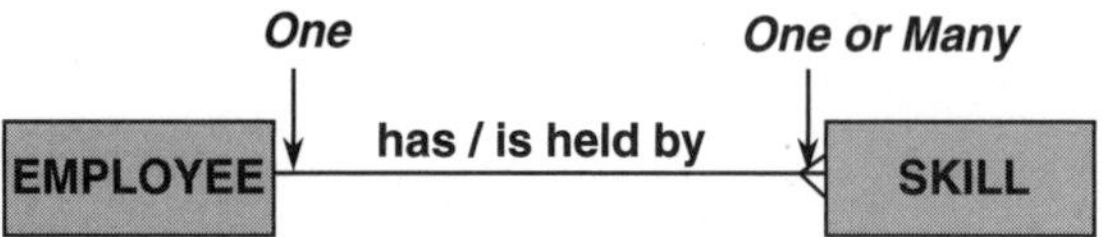
One
One or Many
EMPLOYEE
has / is held by
SKILL
An employee has one or many skills.
A skill is held by one employee.

Figure 3-4
Association *Degree* or *Cardinality* represents *one*, or *many*, occurrences.

When reading the meaning of the association, the first entity referenced always is expressed in the singular. The second entity is plural if the association degree is *one or many*; it is singular if the degree is *one*. We see that the association has now taken on greater meaning. Reading the example from left to right and applying these rules, we read that *an employee has one or many skills*. From right to left it means *a skill is held by one employee*. We can now represent business rules and meaning schematically.

We now see a critical benefit of data mapping, as the interpretation *a skill is held by one employee* provides immediate feedback. We instinctively think "why only one?" The statement raises an obvious question: *can a skill be held by one or many employees?* If true, it suggests that the association should be changed to *one or many* at EMPLOYEE.

Other meanings may also apply, such as *teaches/is taught by*, or *learns/is learned by*. Rather than draw these as additional association lines between the two entities, we will later see that more detailed review of these meanings will help us to identify different types of employees using subtype entities of INSTRUCTOR and STUDENT.

Other Data Modeling methods use different conventions to represent degree. For example, the IDEF1X notation (used extensively by the U.S. Department of Defense) uses a bullet to represent one or many, as with –•, while other methods use a different notation for *one*, with a vertical bar across the line.

However, in this book we will use the convention of a *crow's foot* on the association line to represent an association degree of *one or many*. We will use the *absence of a crow's foot* on the line to represent an association degree of *one* (and no more than one).

Association Nature

Other symbols are added to each end of an association line to show *association nature*. In this book we will use the abbreviation: *nature*.

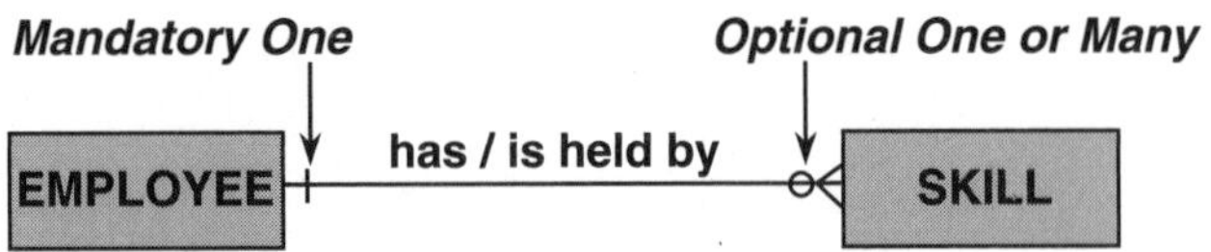
Mandatory One
Optional One or Many
EMPLOYEE
has / is held by
SKILL
An employee may have one or many skills.
A skill must be held by one employee.

Figure 3-5 Association *Nature* can show *may* (optional) or *must* (mandatory).

In Figure 3-5, a "bar" across an association line means *mandatory*, and is expressed as *must*. A "zero" on a line means *optional*, and is expressed as *may*. These both represent the association *nature*.

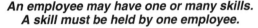

Association nature enables us to provide additional detail in the business rules expressed by the above example. Reading from left to right and showing in *bold* the application of the notation for nature, we can see that *an employee may have one or many skills*. Reading from right to left means *a skill must be held by one employee.*

Based on feedback from this interpretation, we may decide to clarify the meaning as shown next in italic: *an employee may have zero, one or many skills* and *a skill must be held by one (and only one) employee.*

We again naturally ask "why" with the latter statement. As expressed, the business rule is clear: *a skill must be held by one (and only one) employee*. But does that mean—if we have more than one employee with a skill—all but one employee with that skill must leave? That's a strange way to run a business! The feedback forces us to ask the question: *can a skill be held by one or many employees?* If true, the interpretation in Figure 3-5 is wrong. The degree at EMPLOYEE must be changed to *mandatory one or many*—to mean: *a skill must be held by at least one or many employees*. This is certainly more realistic.

We are beginning to glimpse some of the power of data mapping: it helps us clarify data meaning. In turn, this requires the participation of business experts. Knowledge of the business is therefore vital for success in data mapping and in data modeling.

Using Nature for More Complex Business Rules

We will now look at a third notation for nature: both a zero and a bar together—meaning *Optional becoming Mandatory*, or *will*. This enables

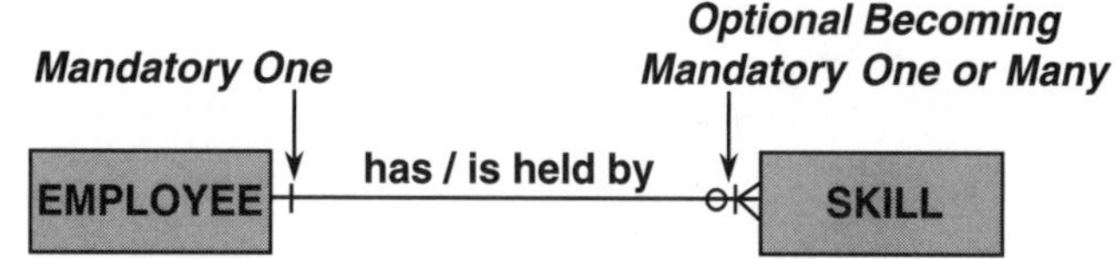
Optional Becoming
Mandatory One or Many
Mandatory One
has / is held by
EMPLOYEE
SKILL
An employee will (eventually) have one or many skills.
A skill must be held by only one employee.

Figure 3-6
A more complex association nature, showing *will* for time-dependence.

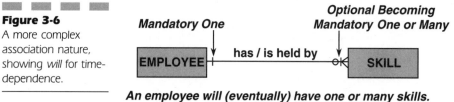

us to represent more complex business rules. For example, in Figure 3-6, starting from the EMPLOYEE entity, the data map expresses the rule: *an employee will (eventually) have one or many skills.* From the SKILL entity it shows the earlier interpretation: *a skill must be held by only one employee.*

This models the situation where an employee initially has no skills, but will acquire at least one or many skills eventually (i.e. over time). This skill acquisition may occur with formal training, or on-the-job experience gained over time. And of course quite independently, the data map could also show a degree of *mandatory one or many* at EMPLOYEE—as we discussed earlier—to represent the business rule that *a skill must be held by at least one or many employees.*

Situations like Figure 3-6 that require the use of *optional becoming mandatory* typically model business rules for complex business processes. Examining and modeling these processes in more detail may lead to the identification of other entities, attributes, and associations that should be added to include other business requirements in the data model.

Summary of Association Degree and Nature

We have now covered the following data mapping concepts:

- An entity box represents data stored for later reference, and is named in capitals and in the singular.
- Attributes describe the entity where they reside. They are written in lower case and singular, typically qualified by the entity name.
- An association is a line showing that the two entities joined by it are related. The association may optionally be named.

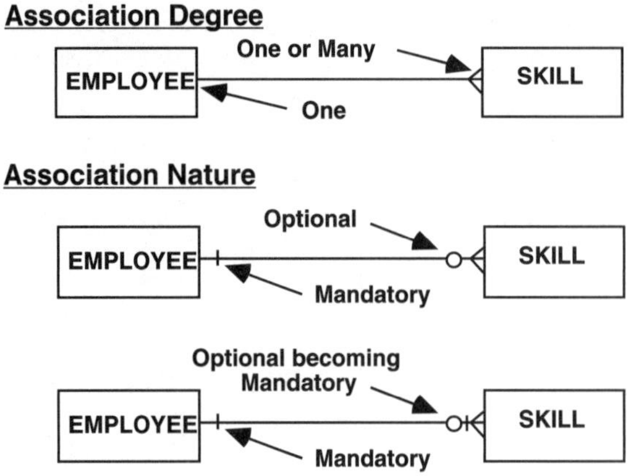

Figure 3-7 Summary of association degree and nature.

- Only one association line is used between each pair of entities. The use of more than one line to express different association meanings generally indicates the existence of more detailed subtype entities.

An association uses symbols at each end to show association cardinality or *degree*, and association *nature*, as illustrated in Figure 3-7.

- A *crow's foot* indicates an association degree of *one or many*.
- The *absence of a crow's foot* indicates a degree of *one*.
- A *bar* across the line indicates a nature of *mandatory*, or *must.*
- A *zero* across the line shows a nature of *optional*, or *may.*
- A *zero and bar* indicate a nature of *optional becoming mandatory*, or *will*.

Data Entity Types

We are now ready to discuss the different types of entities used in data maps. Six data entity types are used to show clearly the data and information of interest to different business areas within an organization. With alternative names shown in brackets, these entity types are:

- *Principal (supertype) entities*—contain common data that is to be shared throughout an organization.

- *Type entities*—used for Project Management and Data Warehousing or EP purposes and which indicate the existence of secondary (subtype) entities.
- *Secondary (subtype) entities*—contain data that is not shared throughout the organization or where privacy or security controls must be enforced.
- *Intersecting (associative) entities*—result from the decomposition of *many-to-many* associations and represent potential business activities, business processes, and operational systems.
- *Role entities*—define business interrelationships and business roles.
- *Structure entities*—capture business knowledge as expert rules.

These entity types illustrate business knowledge in schematic data maps so business requirements can be clearly identified.

Principal (Supertype) Entities

A *Principal* entity is of interest to many functional areas throughout an organization. As discussed earlier, these functional areas may be organizational units, business functions, or business processes and are collectively referred to as *Model Views*. Typically Principal entities contain common data shared by many model views.

A Principal entity is also called a "supertype" entity. This similarly represents common data shared throughout the organization, but we will use the term "Principal" entity in this book.

A Principal entity must be uniquely identified by at least one key attribute, called a "primary key." Primary keys originate in Principal entities.

The example in Figure 3-8 shows the Principal entity EMPLOYEE in the model view HR (i.e. managed by the *Human Resources Department*) but shared throughout the enterprise. It contains attributes in an Entity List, documented according to the following conventions:

- An entity list contains the name of the entity in capitals.
- Attributes that reside in the entity list follow within brackets and are separated by commas. These are *employee number, employee name*, and *employee address.*

Data Map

EMPLOYEE

Entity List		***View***
EMPLOYEE	***(employee number#, employee name, employee address)***	**HR**

Figure 3-8
A Principal (supertype) entity data map and entity list for the HR model view.

- Notice that *employee number* is underlined and has a suffix "#"—which is pronounced "key." This convention is used to show that the attribute *employee number key* is a primary key.

Figure 3-9 shows that a principal entity, when later physically implemented in a database, typically becomes a database table. We will use XYZ Corporation—introduced in Chapter 2—as a continuing example, and so examine the XYZ EMPLOYEE table.

The attributes of the entity become columns of the database table, as shown in Figure 3-9 for the EMPLOYEE database table. Each occurrence of the entity is implemented as a row in the table. Two employees are shown in the EMPLOYEE database table—employee numbers 1234 and 4567 for the fictitious employee names: "John Smith" and "Jack Brown" respectively.

Because *employee number#* is underlined in the entity list (to show that it is a primary key) each employee number in the table must be unique. This uniqueness is clear in the above example. Of course, we are not limited to using numbers for primary keys. We could alternatively use *employee code#* or *employee id#*—or any other term for an underlined primary key that uniquely identifies each employee.

Type Entities

A *Type* entity indicates that other entities may also exist for each Principal entity (Figure 3-10).

Database Table: EMPLOYEE

Employee Number	*Employee Name*	*Employee Address*
1234	***John Smith***	***1 First St, Anywhere***
4567	***Jack Brown***	***2 Second St, Any City***

Figure 3-9
An entity is later physically implemented as a database table.

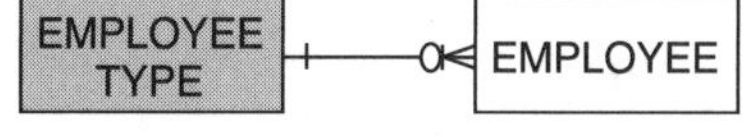

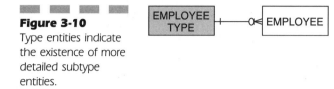

Figure 3-10 Type entities indicate the existence of more detailed subtype entities.

Type entities are used during data mapping for project management purposes. For example, when initially mapping the example above, only EMPLOYEE was identified at first. But closer examination indicated that:

- The Human Resources Department of XYZ manages EMPLOYEE details of employees' numbers, names, and addresses, and all other areas of the business also share this data.
- The Sales Department and Management Services Department of XYZ stated, however, that there were specific details they needed to know about Sales Persons and Managers.
- This indicated the potential existence of other entities to represent two subtypes of XYZ employees: SALES PERSON and MANAGER.
- The entity EMPLOYEE TYPE was added to record the existence of these other entities. It is called a "Type" entity.

The entity EMPLOYEE TYPE indicates that detailed entities exist for the principal entity EMPLOYEE. These are SALES PERSON and MANAGER, called "subtype" or "secondary" entities. We will examine SALES PERSON and MANAGER in more detail shortly.

EMPLOYEE TYPE may later be implemented as a database table called "Employee Type" in a Data Warehouse or EP, to hold derived information that is aggregated from detailed operational data. For example, XYZ managers may want to know the *total number of employees of each type.* This is derived by counting the total occurrences of Sales Persons and of Managers.

Figure 3-11 shows the Entity List for EMPLOYEE TYPE, with attributes of <u>*employee type number#*</u> and *employee type name*. The key attribute *employee type number#* is added to the end of EMPLOYEE as a foreign key. Because it is also a key attribute, it has the "#" suffix—but it is *not* underlined. This convention distinguishes a foreign key from a primary key (which *is* underlined). As before, we are not limited to using numbers only for employee type. We could instead use *employee type code#* or *employee type id#* or other terms to identify each employee type.

Figure 3-11 Data Map and Entity List for a Type entity—with a common, joining key.

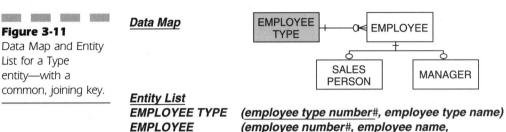

Data Map

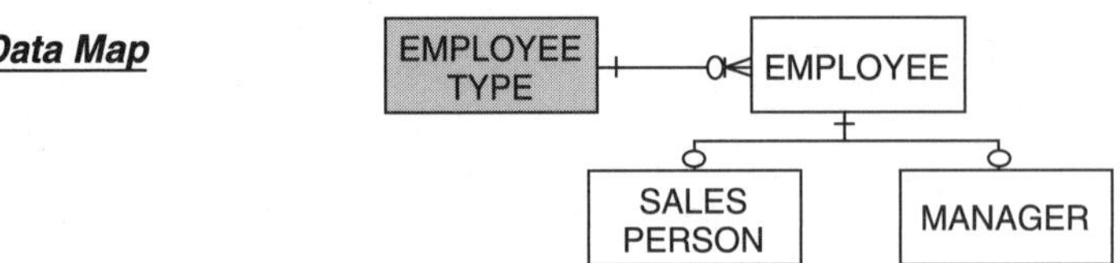

Entity List

EMPLOYEE TYPE ***(employee type number#, employee type name)***
EMPLOYEE ***(employee number#, employee name, employee address, employee type number#)***

We can see that *employee type number#* is a common key attribute in EMPLOYEE TYPE and in EMPLOYEE. It indicates an association exists between these entities that is *mandatory one* (at EMPLOYEE TYPE) to *optional becoming mandatory many* (at EMPLOYEE). This is characteristic of the association between a Type entity and its related Principal entity, interpreted as *an employee type will have one or many employees of that type.*

When implemented in the XYZ database as an Employee Type table, we see that the *Employee Type Number* column may contain values such as those in Figure 3-12.

This concept has been used in business for many years. Sometimes codes or numbers become part of the vocabulary or jargon of an organization. For example, type codes may be used as follows:

- Sales Persons may be called "code 1" persons.
- Similarly Managers may be called "code 2" persons.

The concept has also been used in Systems Development, likewise for many years, where data fields in a record are used to indicate the relevant record format. For example:

- The Sales Person record may be a "code 1" record format.
- The Manager record may be a "code 2" record format.

Figure 3-12 Typical data values for a Type entity.

Employee Type Number	Employee Type Name
0	EMPLOYEE
1	SALES PERSON
2	MANAGER

This has typically been indicated by a special data field in the record called a "record type code," containing "1" for Sales Person records and "2" for Manager records. Other attributes can exist in a Type entity, such as required for a Data Warehouse or EP. For instance, the earlier example: "total number of employees of each type" is represented by the attribute name (also the column name, when implemented) of *total employees this type*.

Secondary (Subtype) Entities

While Principal entities are shared throughout an organization, some data is of interest only to specific functional areas (i.e. model views). These are called "Secondary" entities. They are also called "subtype" entities, but we will use the term "Secondary" in this book.

Secondary entities contain data not shared throughout the organization, or where privacy or security controls must typically be exercised. They appear only in those model views that have an interest in, or privacy or security authorization over, access to the data represented by those secondary entities. In the example in Figure 3-13, the secondary entities are shaded. They are specific employee types.

- We saw that EMPLOYEE is a Principal (supertype) entity.
- SALES PERSON and MANAGER are Secondary (subtype) entities. They were identified from the Type entity EMPLOYEE TYPE.

Secondary entities participate in a categorizing hierarchical association as shown: with a *mandatory one* association (at the Principal entity) and an *optional one* association (at the Secondary entity).

The Entity List for the Secondary entities in Figure 3-14 shows that the SALES PERSON and MANAGER entities are not accessible by other model views—for privacy or security reasons.

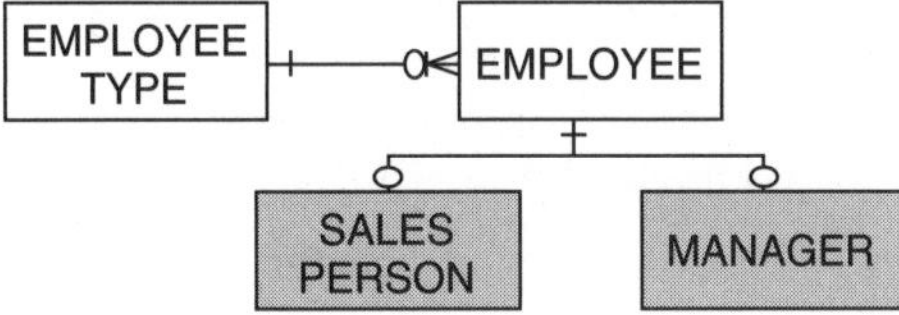

Figure 3-13 An example of Secondary (subtype) entities for a Principal entity.

Figure 3-14 Entity List for Secondary (subtype) entities in specific Model Views.

Entity List (Partial)		View
EMPLOYEE	(*employee number#*, employee name, employee address)	HR
SALES PERSON	(*employee number#*, sales person quota, sales person sales, sales person commission)	SALES
MANAGER	(*employee number#*, manager title, manager reporting level)	MGT

SALES PERSON contains the attributes *sales person quota, sales person sales*, and *sales person commission* which are of interest only to the Sales Department (SALES) model view. This Department exercises privacy and security control over these attributes: they represent sensitive data that are not relevant to other parts of XYZ. MANAGER contains the attributes *manager title* and *manager reporting level* which are of interest only to the XYZ Management Services (MGT) model view.

Notice that SALES PERSON and MANAGER have the same primary key *employee number#* as for EMPLOYEE. It is this common primary key that establishes the categorizing hierarchical *mandatory one* to *optional one* association between EMPLOYEE and each secondary entity.

"Exclusive" Type Entities

We previously discussed the association in the Data Map, namely:

- mandatory one (at EMPLOYEE TYPE) to optional becoming mandatory many (at EMPLOYEE).

This was illustrated in Figure 3-13. We discussed that there *will eventually be one or many* employees for each Employee Type. However *mandatory one* at EMPLOYEE TYPE also indicates that each Employee exclusively can be of *one (and only one)* Employee Type. It is therefore called an *Exclusive* Type entity. Expressed more clearly, the Exclusive Type entity Data Map in Figure 3-13 indicates that:

- an employee who is an XYZ Sales Person cannot later be promoted to a Manager, and
- an employee who is an XYZ Manager cannot later be promoted to a Sales Person.

If the data map correctly models the "Promotion" business rules of the organization, this interpretation suggests that XYZ does not promote from within. Instead, it implies that new managers or sales persons are appointed from outside, by recruitment. If it is correctly modeled, this would *not* be a good employer to work for if you were looking for advancement through promotion!

"Inclusive" Type Entities

Contrast the example in Figure 3-13 now with the example in Figure 3-15—with a modified (highlighted) association—namely:

- mandatory one or many (at EMPLOYEE TYPE) to optional becoming mandatory many (at EMPLOYEE).

The earlier *mandatory one* (i.e. "Exclusive") at EMPLOYEE TYPE is now a *mandatory one or many* in the data map in Figure 3-15. This shows an *Inclusive* Type entity. It indicates that each XYZ Employee can be of *one or many* Employee Types (*but at least one*). The data map now indicates an alternative interpretation, namely that:

- an XYZ Sales Person can later be promoted to a Manager,
- an XYZ Manager can later be promoted to a Sales Person, and
- an XYZ employee can also be both a Sales Person and a Manager at the same time.

If the data map correctly models the "Promotion" business rules of the organization, this now suggests an interpretation that XYZ will promote from within. It allows XYZ Managers also to be Sales Persons. Alternatively it enables XYZ Sales Managers to carry a sales quota: as a personal sales quota; or as an aggregate sales quota of all the Sales Persons who report to that Sales Manager.

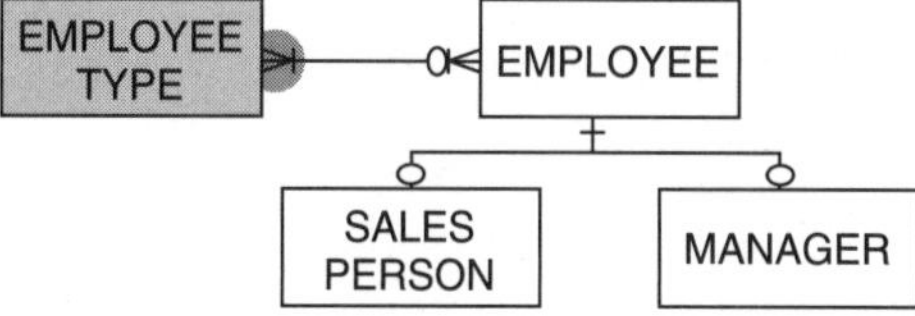

Figure 3-15
An Inclusive Type entity, with *mandatory many* at the Type entity.

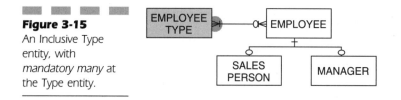

This models a more flexible business rule. We now see more of the power of data mapping—it enables alternative business rules to be evaluated. These flexible rules will be defined by examining the *many-to-many* association between EMPLOYEE TYPE and EMPLOYEE, when we discuss *Role Entities* shortly.

Intersecting (Associative) Entities

Consider now the data map example in Figure 3-16 that illustrates the business rule:

> An employee must have at least one job, but can have many jobs. A job will eventually be filled by at least one or many employees.

This data map illustrates a *many-to-many* association. In its present form it is very difficult to determine which jobs an employee has held (over time, or at the same time), or which employees fill (or have filled) a job.

To resolve these questions, a *many-to-many* association must be decomposed. This requires the addition of an intermediate entity to the data map, called an "intersecting" entity. It is also called an "associative" entity, but we will use the term "intersecting" in this book. The *many-to-many* association between EMPLOYEE and JOB is decomposed in Figure 3-17.

- A new entity is drawn between the two entities. This is called an "Intersecting" entity and is shaded in Figure 3-17.
- The name of this entity typically is based on the two original entity names. The Intersecting entity in Figure 3-17 is thus called EMPLOYEE JOB.
- The *many-to-many* association is decomposed into two *one-to-many* associations.

Figure 3-16
The business meaning of *many-to-many* associations is hard to determine.

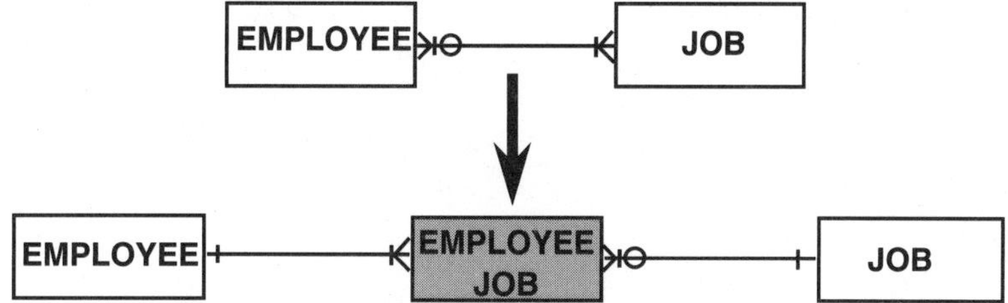

Figure 3-17 Many-to-many associations are resolved by an intersecting entity.

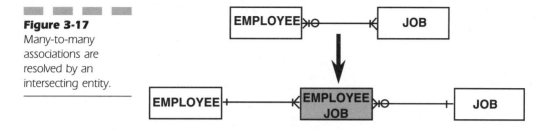

Intersecting entities, formed by decomposing *many-to-many* associations, are extremely important in data mapping—they indicate activities, processes, or systems, as follows:

> An Intersecting entity typically indicates existence of a business activity, a business process, or an operational system.

A business *activity* comprises one or more related business processes. Figure 3-17 therefore indicates the potential existence of:

- a business activity: Employee Job Allocation Activity (say), or
- a business process: Employee Job Appointment Process (say), or
- an operational system: Employee Job Assignment System (say).

This is a powerful characteristic of intersecting (associative) entities in data mapping. The activity, process, or system name that is identified depends on the business needs and terminology. The steps involved in decomposing a *many-to-many* association follow, and are illustrated in Figure 3-18. For each *many* end of the association:

- an association degree of *one* touches an original entity, and is of *mandatory* nature.
- an association degree of *many* touches the Intersecting entity.

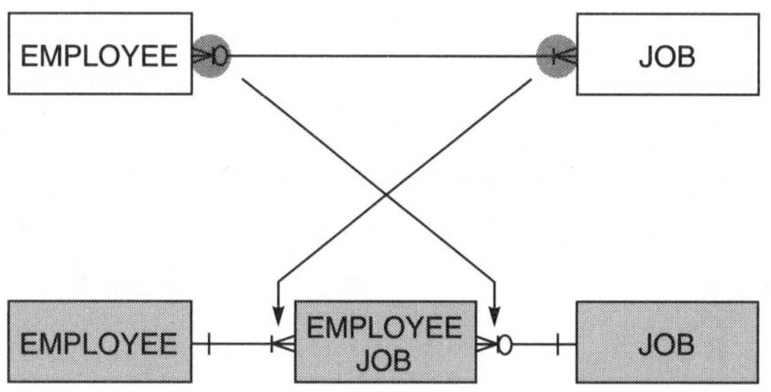

Figure 3-18 Steps involved in decomposing a *many-to-many* association.

EMPLOYEE JOB ***(employee number#, job number#,*** ***employee job start date, employee job salary)***

Figure 3-19 The primary key of an intersecting entity comprises the primary keys of the entities it joins.

The association nature at the *many* end of the association is moved across to touch the Intersecting entity as in Figure 3-18. The implied business rule is then reviewed for validity—as *optional, mandatory*, or *optional becoming mandatory* – depending on the business rules that apply to the Intersecting entity after decomposition.

The interpretation of the business rule for association nature often becomes clearer by considering it from the perspective of the business activity, business process, or system identified by that entity.

The primary key of an Intersecting entity is typically made up of the primary keys of the entities that it joins.

Figure 3-19 shows EMPLOYEE JOB with an underlined combined primary key: *employee number#, job number#*. This is called a *compound primary key*. The XYZ *Employee Job* database table is shown in Figure 3-20.

From this, we can now determine, for a given XYZ employee number, all of the jobs held by that person. For example:

- Employee 123 started job 65 on 12 Dec 1993 on a $30,000 salary.
- Employee 123 started job 89 on 04 Jan 1996 on a $35,000 salary.

Similarly, for a given XYZ job number we can find all employees who have occupied that job. For example:

- Employee 456 first held Job 65 from 25 Mar 1990, on $45,000.
- Employee 123 then held Job 65 from 12 Dec 1993, on $30,000.

Figure 3-20 Sample data for the Employee Job database table.

Database Table: Employee Job

Emp No	Job No	Start Date	Salary
123	65	12 Dec 1993	30,000
123	89	04 Jan 1996	35,000
456	65	25 Mar 1990	45,000

Role Entities

Let us now refer back to the example in Figure 3-15 of an "Inclusive" Type entity, where an employee could be both a Sales Person and a Manager. This was represented by a *many-to-many* association between EMPLOYEE TYPE and EMPLOYEE.

We now know that this *many-to-many* association indicates the potential existence of an Intersecting entity. However, this example is, in fact, a special case of the *many-to-many* association rule that results in a Role entity, as shown in Figure 3-21.

The intersecting entity formed by decomposing the *many-to-many* association between EMPLOYEE TYPE and EMPLOYEE in Figure 3-21 is called EMPLOYEE ROLE. It is a *Role* entity—a special case of the *many-to-many* rule when used with an Inclusive Type entity:

> A many-to-many association between a Type entity and its Principal entity indicates the existence of a Role entity.

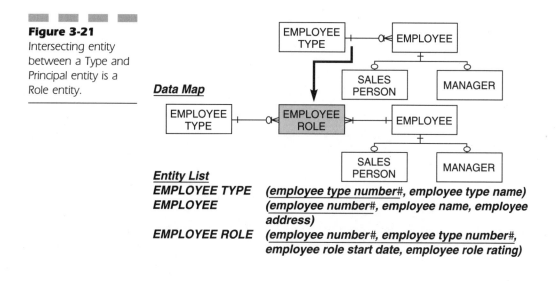

A Role entity specifies the different types (or "roles") that a Principal entity can take with an Inclusive Type entity. As for an Intersecting entity, a Role entity has a compound primary key: employee number#, employee type number#—from the primary keys of EMPLOYEE and EMPLOYEE TYPE. As a Role entity is a special case of an Intersecting entity, it indicates the existence of either:

- a potential XYZ Employee Role Management Activity (say), or

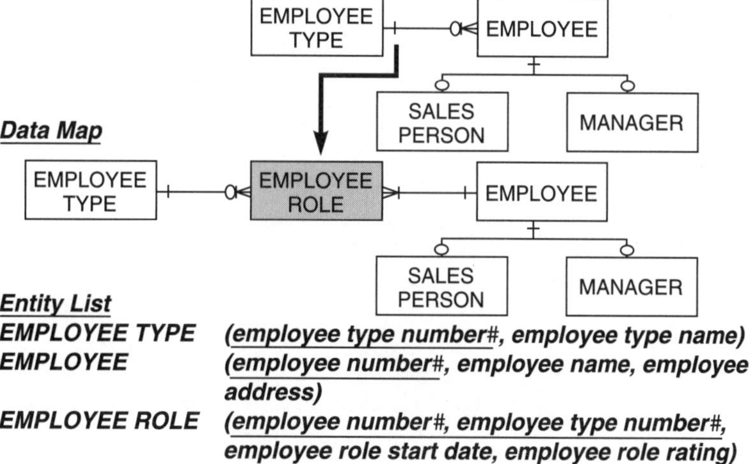

Figure 3-21 Intersecting entity between a Type and Principal entity is a Role entity.

- a potential XYZ Employee Role Management Process (say), or
- a potential XYZ Employee Role Management System (say).

The following example enables us to record the date each employee started in a role (as an XYZ Sales Person or Manager) as well as the performance rating of that employee in each role.

The XYZ *Employee Role* table in Figure 3-22 shows that employee 123 started as a Sales Person (i.e. Type 1—see Figure 3-12) on 12 Dec 1993 and had a performance rating of 3. Employee 123 became a Manager (i.e. Type 2) on 4 Jan 1996 and had a rating of 2. Similarly Employee 456 started as a Sales Person on 25 Mar 1990 on a rating of 2, and then became a Manager on 14 Apr 1992 on a rating of 4. Notice the last line, showing that employee 456 became a Sales Person *again*, on 20 May 1996, on a rating of 3. This raises a difficulty:

- As EMPLOYEE ROLE has a compound primary key of: *employee number#, employee type number#*, we can record details for each employee in each role.
- Employee 456 is a Sales Person, twice. This means we can record details of 456 as a Sales Person from 1996, but if we did that, we would then lose the history of 456 as a Sales Person from 1990.
- To correct this problem we therefore need to enable an employee to occupy a role many times.

This capability can be provided, by making *employee role start date#* also a primary key—adding to the attribute name a suffix "#" (i.e. "key"), and underlining it to signify that it is a primary key. Thus an employee's rating now depends on the *employee number#*, the *employee type number#*, and the *employee role start date#*.

Figure 3-22
Typical data for a Role entity, implemented as a Role table.

Database Table: Employee Role

Emp No	Type No	Start Date	Rating
123	1	12 Dec 1993	3
123	2	04 Jan 1996	2
456	1	25 Mar 1990	2
456	2	14 Apr 1992	4
456	1	20 May 1996	3

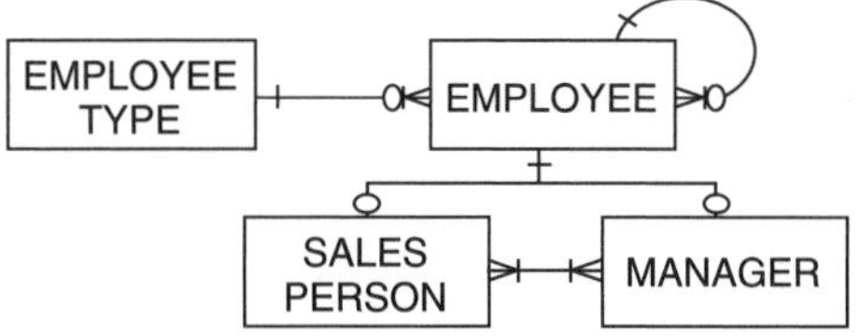

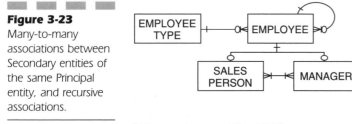

Figure 3-23 Many-to-many associations between Secondary entities of the same Principal entity, and recursive associations.

Structure Entities

Sometimes we need to show associations between Secondary entities under the same Principal entity. The example in Figure 3-23 shows a *many-to-many* association between SALES PERSON and MANAGER.

Of course, we now know that a *many-to-many* association indicates the potential existence of an Intersecting entity: SALES PERSON MANAGER in this example. But what if we had other Secondary entities, such as CLERK and SUPPORT PERSON—similarly related to other entities also with *many-to-many* associations?

We would then have to add a number of Secondary and Intersecting entities to the data map in Figure 3-23:

- *Secondary entities:* CLERK and SUPPORT PERSON
- *Intersecting entities:* SALES PERSON MANAGER; as well as CLERK SALES PERSON and CLERK MANAGER; and also SUPPORT PERSON SALES PERSON and SUPPORT PERSON MANAGER.

Considering that any number of Secondary entities can exist under a Principal entity, to any depth, this approach using Intersecting entities adds complexity to the data map. It does not represent business knowledge clearly, which should be our main objective.

And what about the other association above: between EMPLOYEE and itself. This is called a "recursive" (or "convoluted") association. How should we represent that association?

This dilemma can be modeled more simply, using a *Structure* entity, shown by EMPLOYEE STRUCTURE in Figure 3-24. The *many-to-many* association between SALES PERSON and MANAGER, and the recursive association at EMPLOYEE, have now been replaced by this new Structure entity. The name of this entity may use "structure" as a suffix (e.g. EMPLOYEE STRUCTURE), or instead may use RELATED EMPLOYEE (say) or EMPLOYEE RELATIONSHIP.

Figure 3-24 shows that Structure entities typically exhibit a characteristic *mandatory one to optional many* association between the

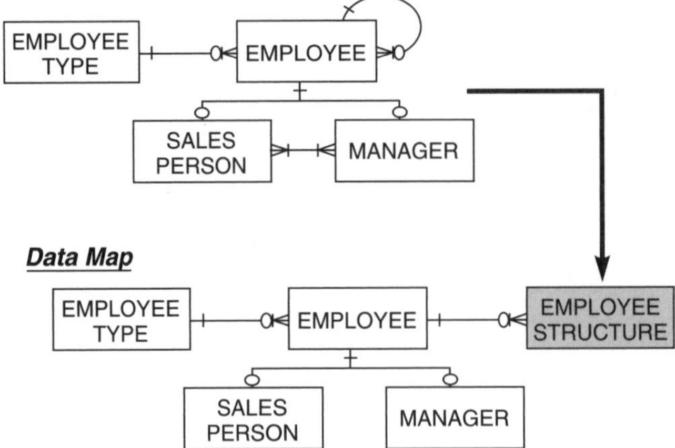

Figure 3-24 Complex interrelationships are represented by a Structure entity.

Principal entity and the Structure entity. Structure entities are said to be in Fifth Business Normal Form (5BNF) [Finkelstein 1989, 1992]. They enable us to record complex relationships that exist between:

- occurrences of Secondary entities, or
- occurrences of Secondary and Principal entity occurrences, or
- different occurrences of a Principal entity.

These complex interrelationships typically involve expert business knowledge. We will shortly see that a Structure entity can be used to represent expert rules for knowledge management purposes.

A Structure entity has several possible 5BNF Entity List formats [Finkelstein 1989, 1992]. The numbers in the discussion below are keyed to the Entity List Formats shown in Figure 3-25:

1. *Format 1* uses as a compound key the primary key of the Principal entity (*employee number#*)—but duplicated to identify related occurrences (as *related employee number#*). Format 1 is used when a Principal entity is of only one type and can never change. *Employee number#* is all that is needed for identification.
2. *Format 2* uses as a compound key the primary key of the Principal entity (*employee number#*), plus the primary key of the Type entity (*employee type number#*)—duplicated for related occurrences (*related employee number#* and *related employee type number#*). Format 2 applies when a Principal entity is of

Figure 3-25
Typical Entity List formats for Structure entities.

Data Map

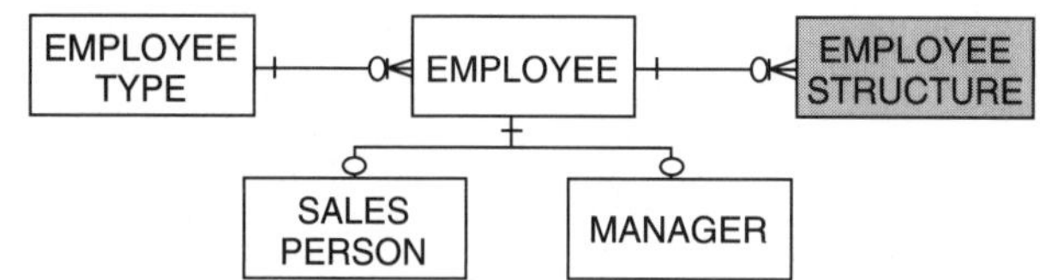

Entity List Formats

1. ***EMPLOYEE STRUCTURE*** ***(employee number#, rel employee number#)***

OR ...

2. ***EMPLOYEE STRUCTURE*** ***(employee number#, employee type number#, rel employee number#, rel employee type number#)***

OR ...

3. ***EMPLOYEE STRUCTURE*** ***(employee number#, employee type number#, rel employee number#, rel employee type number#, relationship reason)***

many types; *employee number#, employee type number#* both are needed for unique identification.

3. *Format 3* is similar to Format 2 and provides a reason why the two occurrences are related (as *relationship reason*). It may suggest an expert rule as discussed shortly. Alternatively, *relationship reason id#* could be used in Format 3 as a foreign key, to establish an association to a separate entity called REASON with the attributes:

   REASON (*relationship reason id#, reason description)*

Any number of "reasons" for knowledge management purposes can thus be defined for the relationship between entity occurrences.

The table in Figure 3-26 is based on Format 3 from Figure 3-25. Attribute names are column names in the Employee Structure table. So we can clearly explain the XYZ sample data in the table; however, we have used *employee type name* and *related employee type name* data values, instead of *employee type number* and *related employee type number*. In practice, these latter columns with numbers are normally implemented in a physical Structure table—rather than names.

Figure 3-26 shows the content of a typical Structure table. Manager 1358 manages XYZ employees 1362 and 1556 in a *Manager Reporting* relationship. Manager 1358 also manages XYZ employees 1460 and 1661 in a *Sales Reporting* relationship. The left to right relationship in the

Figure 3-26
A typical table for a Structure entity.

Employee Number	Employee Type	Employee Number	Employee Type	Relationship Reason
1358	Manager	1362	Manager	Manager reporting
		1460	Sales person	Sales reporting
		1556	Manager	Manager reporting
		1661	Sales person	Sales reporting
1362	Manager	262	Sales person	Sales reporting
		1132	Sales person	Sales reporting
		1441	Sales person	Sales reporting
1556	Manager	1333	Sales person	Sales reporting
		1512	Sales person	Sales reporting

table thus represents a "Manager Reporting" relationship, or a "Sales Reporting" relationship.

Manager 1362 in turn manages employees 262, 1132, and 1441 in a *Sales Reporting* relationship. Manager 1556 also manages employees 1333 and 1512 in a *Sales Reporting* relationship.

Looking further at the table and following the right to left relationship, we can also see that XYZ employee 1441 reports to Manager 1362, who in turn reports to Manager 1358. The right to left relationship thus represents the "Reports to" relationship.

Assume now that 1512 is the sales person responsible for Customer ABC. If 1512 is ill and so is absent from work, who is an alternative sales person to call on ABC? Employee 1333 cannot automatically be used. Figure 3-26 shows only that 1333 and 1512 both report to manager 1556. This fact does not indicate at all whether 1333 has any knowledge of Customer ABC.

However, an additional line has now been added in Figure 3-27—shown in bold italic. The last line now of the table shows that 1441 is related to 1512, as they both have common knowledge of Customer ABC. This indicates that 1441 can therefore visit Customer ABC, if 1512 is unavailable. This is an example of expert knowledge recorded by XYZ in the table. This is a powerful characteristic of Structure entities: they can be used to capture expert rules for knowledge management purposes.

The left to right "Manager Reporting" and "Sales Reporting" relationships, and the right to left "Reports to" relationships, are also examples of expert rules: these are reporting rules well known by all XYZ employees, but not known at all outside the organization. However, the fact that

Figure 3-27
The last line is an example of "expert" knowledge.

Employee Number	Employee Type	Employee Number	Employee Type	Relationship Reason
1358	Manager	1362	Manager	Manager reporting
		1460	Sales person	Sales reporting
		1556	Manager	Manager reporting
		1661	Sales person	Sales reporting
1362	Manager	262	Sales person	Sales reporting
		1132	Sales person	Sales reporting
		1441	Sales person	Sales reporting
1556	Manager	1333	Sales person	Sales reporting
		1512	Sales person	Sales reporting
1441	***Salesperson***	***1512***	***Sales person***	***ABC Knowledge***

1441 and 1512 both have common knowledge of Customer ABC was not well known. Previously, only the individuals concerned knew of their common knowledge.

Now that the XYZ expert rule is represented in the table, it is available to all who are authorized to access that table. Structure entities therefore can implement expert rules for knowledge management so that the knowledge is readily accessible. Structure entities also allow changes in knowledge to be made easily by changing the relevant data values.

We will now consider a Structure entity example documenting the roles taken by organizations in their dealings with each other—as Suppliers, Customers, and Competitors—in the Organization Role Structure entity represented by the table in Figure 3-28.

From the interrelationships documented in Figure 3-28 we can see that:

- Org No XYZ has Org Role Type of "Supplier" to:
  - Rel Org No KLM, with Rel Org Role Type of "Customer."
  - Rel Org No MNO, with Rel Org Role Type of "Customer."
  - Rel Org No PTC, also with Rel Org Role Type of "Customer."

This is well known to staff who work in the Sales Dept, but is not at all known by any staff who work outside Sales. Examining the table further, we see that:

Figure 3-28 Interrelationships between Suppliers, Customers, and Competitors.

ORGANIZATION ROLE STRUCTURE			
Org	**Org Role**	**Rel Org**	**Rel Org Role**
XYZ	Supplier	KLM	Customer
		MNO	Customer
		PTC	Customer
XYZ	Customer	Brink	Supplier
		PMM	Supplier
XYZ	Competitor	MPP	Competitor
		PXM	Competitor
		Brink	Competitor

- Org No XYZ also has Org Role Type of "Customer" to:
  - Rel Org No Brink, with Rel Org Role Type of "Supplier."
  - Rel Org No PMM, also with Rel Org Role Type of "Supplier."

This information is known by the staff who work in the Purchasing Dept, but it is not known by staff who work outside Purchasing. The final part of the table then shows:

- Org No XYZ additionally has Org Role Type of "Competitor" to:
  - Rel Org No MPP, with Rel Org Role Type of "Competitor."
  - Rel Org No PXM, with Rel Org Role Type of "Competitor."
  - Rel Org No Brink, with Rel Org Role Type of "Competitor."

Once again, this information is known by the staff who work in the Marketing Dept, but it is not known by any staff who work outside Marketing. But now we see in Figure 3-29 that:

- Brink is both a Supplier and a Competitor. This was not known before. With this new knowledge, XYZ would most likely add a clause to its Supplier Purchase Agreement to prevent Brink from withholding supply from XYZ for competitive advantage.

Figure 3-29 More than one interrelationship can exist with another organization.

ORGANIZATION ROLE STRUCTURE			
Org	**Org Role**	**Rel Org**	**Rel Org Role**
XYZ	Supplier	KLM	Customer
		MNO	Customer
		PTC	Customer
XYZ	Customer	Brink	Supplier
		PMM	Supplier
XYZ	Competitor	MPP	Competitor
		PXM	Competitor
		Brink	Competitor

What does this mean?

Figure 3-30
Typical content of an Organization Structure entity

ORGANIZATION STRUCTURE			
Org	**Org Type**	**Rel Org**	**Rel Org Type**
XYZ	Unit	Finance	Department
		Marketing	Department
		Sales	Department
ABC	Parent	KLM	Subsidiary
		MNO	Subsidiary
		PTC	Subsidiary
		Brink	Subsidiary
PXM	Parent	MPP	Subsidiary
		PMM	Subsidiary
MNO	Shareholder	PXM	Parent

This is an example of expert knowledge that was not previously known by XYZ. Now that it has been discovered, this knowledge enables more effective Supplier Management.

We will consider another example, based on an Organization Structure entity. This shows business relationships between organizations, such as "Unit" (for Business Unit), Parent, and Shareholder in the table in Figure 3-30, which tells us that:

- *Org No* XYZ has *Org Role Type* of "Unit," specifying that it has an internal structure of:
  - *Rel Org No* "Finance," with *Rel Org Role Type* "Department."
  - *Rel Org No* "Marketing," with *Rel Org Role Type* "Department."
  - *Rel Org No* "Sales," with *Rel Org Role Type* "Department."

This is well known to all staff who work for XYZ, but is not known outside XYZ. We also see from the table that XYZ Corporate Dept has added other relationships that are of interest to it: those between Parent and Subsidiary organizations, and between Shareholder and Parent:

- *Org No* ABC has *Org Role Type* of "Parent" to:
  - *Rel Org No* KLM, with *Rel Org Role Type* of "Subsidiary."
  - *Rel Org No* MNO, with *Rel Org Role Type* of "Subsidiary."
  - *Rel Org No* PTC, with *Rel Org Role Type* of "Subsidiary."
  - *Rel Org No* Brink, with *Rel Org Role Type* of "Subsidiary."
- *Org No* PXM has *Org Role Type* of "Parent" to:
  - *Rel Org No* MPP, with *Rel Org Role Type* of "Subsidiary."
  - *Rel Org No* PMM, with *Rel Org Role Type* of "Subsidiary."
- *Org No* MNO has *Org Role Type* of "Shareholder" to:
  - Rel Org No PXM, with Rel Org Role Type of "Parent."

Organizations typically report annually a list of their largest shareholders, and so shareholder relationships like these are in the public domain. But when we consider Organization Structure and Organization Role Structure together, some interesting expert knowledge emerges—as shown in Figure 3-31.

In Organization Structure at the top of Figure 3-31, we see that KLM, MNO, PTC, and Brink are all sister organizations with the same parent, ABC. But from the Organization Role Structure we can see that KLM, MNO, and PTC are customers of XYZ. However, Brink, a sister company, is a Competitor. What if they share with Brink (our competitor) information about XYZ that they learn as our customers? Brink could then use this for competitive advantage.

Now we have knowledge of this close relationship, it would be wise to include a restraint clause in their Sales Agreements with XYZ—to prevent this sharing with Competitor Brink. Otherwise this would be a competitive threat to XYZ. This knowledge is often called "Market Intelligence" in real life. Experienced staff may have tacitly known of this relationship between their customers and a competitor. But these Structure entities now make this knowledge explicit. The tables in Figure 3-31 bring related knowledge together so that it is clearly apparent to all. It can be acted on for marketing, purchasing, sales, and other management purposes.

Figure 3-31 Expert knowledge in two Structure entities.

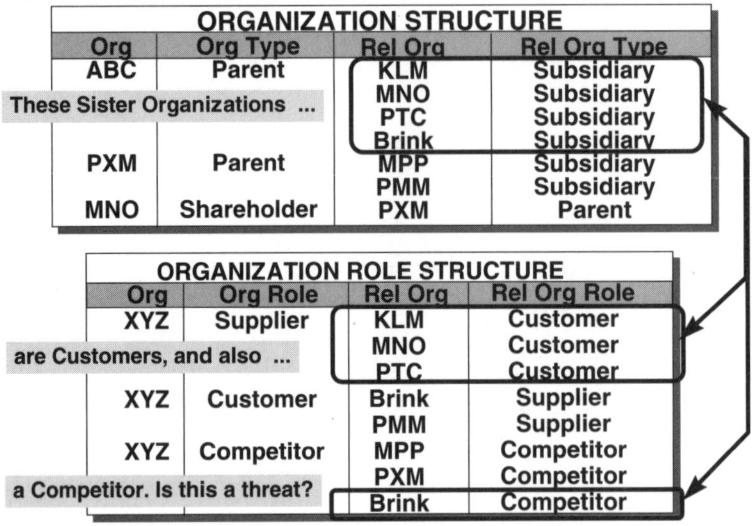

ORGANIZATION STRUCTURE

Org	Org Type	Rel Org	Rel Org Type
ABC	Parent	KLM	Subsidiary
		MNO	Subsidiary
		PTC	Subsidiary
		Brink	Subsidiary
PXM	Parent	MPP	Subsidiary
		PMM	Subsidiary
MNO	Shareholder	PXM	Parent

These Sister Organizations ...

ORGANIZATION ROLE STRUCTURE

Org	Org Role	Rel Org	Rel Org Role
XYZ	Supplier	KLM	Customer
		MNO	Customer
		PTC	Customer
XYZ	Customer	Brink	Supplier
		PMM	Supplier
XYZ	Competitor	MPP	Competitor
		PXM	Competitor
		Brink	Competitor

are Customers, and also ...

a Competitor. Is this a threat?

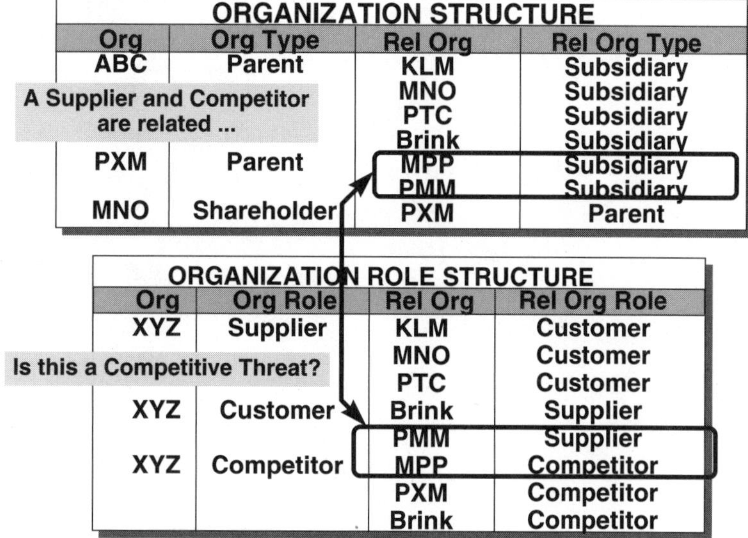

Figure 3-32 Market intelligence derived from two Structure entities.

Again referring to Organization Structure now as the top table in Figure 3-32, we also see that:

- PXM (a Competitor—see bottom table) is the parent of MPP and PMM, who are therefore subsidiaries of PXM.
- The first subsidiary is MPP, which is another Competitor. But the second subsidiary is PMM, which is a Supplier.

What if PXM (its Parent), asks PMM (a Supplier) to withhold supply from XYZ for the competitive benefit of MPP (a Competitor subsidiary of PXM)? This would be a competitive threat to XYZ. It may be possible to avoid it by a competitive restraint clause in the Supplier Purchase Agreement for PMM. We now see that Structure entities can provide an enormous amount of useful expert knowledge. It is important to be aware of this, to manage customers and suppliers, and to compete effectively.

Finally, referring to Figure 3-33, we also see that:

- MNO, a Customer of XYZ . . . is also a shareholder of PXM.

But PXM is a Competitor of XYZ. This is a competitive threat. MNO could potentially use knowledge it learns about XYZ as its customer, and can share that knowledge with PXM (an XYZ Competitor). This is a competitive threat to XYZ. It may require a restraint clause in the

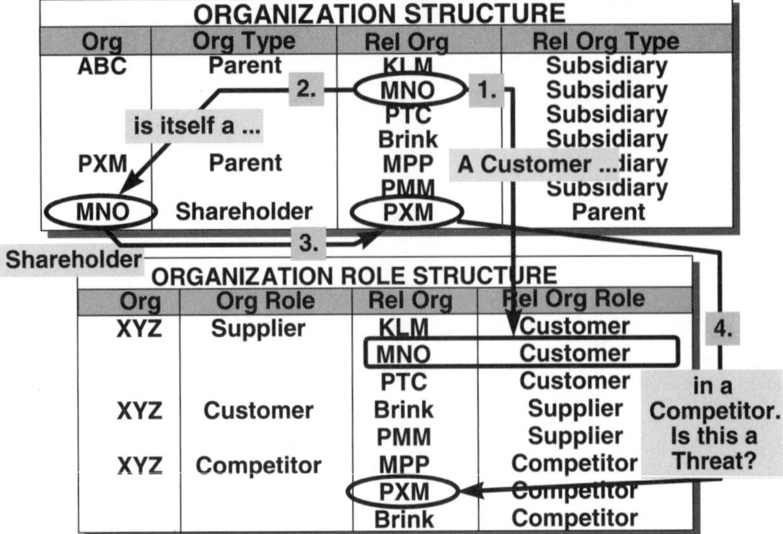

Figure 3-33 Further Market intelligence from two Structure entities.

MNO Sales Agreement to prevent this happening. Of course, legal restraints discussed in this and the earlier examples offer no guarantee that these competitive threats will not arise. Experienced staff normally hold this knowledge. But these examples show how this knowledge is now more accessible in Structure entities for explicit and proactive knowledge management.

Summary of Entity Types

We have now covered the main entity types that are used by the EEP methodology. Other entity types are also used by EEP, but are outside the scope of this book. These include *Rule* entities, *Rule Structure* entities, and *Condition* entities. Figure 3-34 summarizes the main entity types:

- EMPLOYEE and JOB are Principal (supertype) entities—with attributes shared by all. These typically become databases in a Data Warehouse or Enterprise Portal.
- EMPLOYEE TYPE is a Type entity—used for project management purposes. Type entities often contain aggregate or derived data for Data Warehouse or EP access.

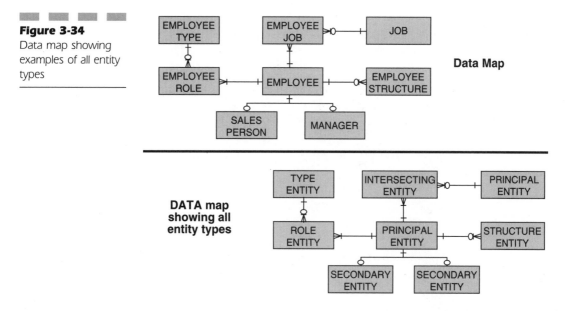

Figure 3-34
Data map showing examples of all entity types

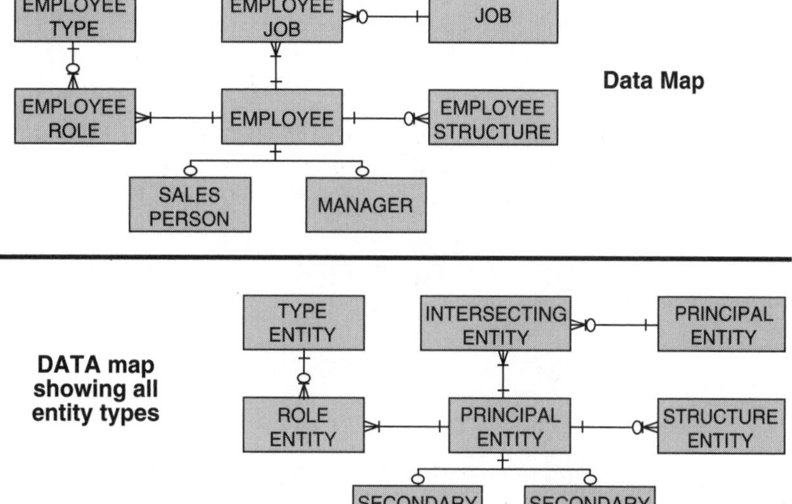

- SALES PERSON and MANAGER are Secondary (subtype) entities—which contain attributes that are not to be shared or over which security or privacy control must be exercised.
- EMPLOYEE ROLE is a Role entity—showing the roles valid for a Principal entity. It implements the *many-to-many* association of an Inclusive Type entity.
- EMPLOYEE JOB is an Intersecting (associative) entity—identifying potential business activities, business processes or systems. Intersecting entities typically indicate potential data sources for extraction and transformation of summary information in Data Warehouse or EP databases, as discussed in Part 2.
- EMPLOYEE STRUCTURE is a Structure entity—which shows interrelationships between entity occurrences. This indicates expert knowledge, which can represent explicit rules for knowledge management.

We have now covered the basic principles of data mapping. We will see that we can use these concepts to represent business strategies schematically, to develop a "picture" or "window" into the enterprise. We will later use this capability in Chapter 4 to develop a schematic strategic data model from strategic business plans for data warehouse or EP development.

Associations Represent Strategies

We will now use our acquired data mapping skills to represent strategies schematically. We will identify alternative strategies by modifying the data maps that we define. This will help us later in Chapter 4, when we develop a strategic model for the XYZ data warehouse.

Associations represent business strategies schematically in a data map. The XYZ *Employee Skills Strategy* is shown as a data map in the example in Figure 3-35.

The association degree and nature from the data map are initially used, and are refined to express the relevant business interpretation. The statements suggested by the data map are shown in brackets and in italic. These bracketed statements in Figure 3-35 are not normally included. They are shown in brackets here only for our clarification.

As expressed in Figure 3-35, this strategy indicates that a new skill cannot be introduced *unless there is at least one employee with that skill*. This is rather restrictive: it indicates that an employee already must have the new skill before that new skill can be introduced. This may only be achieved by hiring a new employee who already has the new skill.

In other words, the organization represented by this data map does not train its existing employees in new skills; it will only hire new employees who already have the desired new skill. This would not be a good organization to work for if you are ambitious and want to learn new skills on the job.

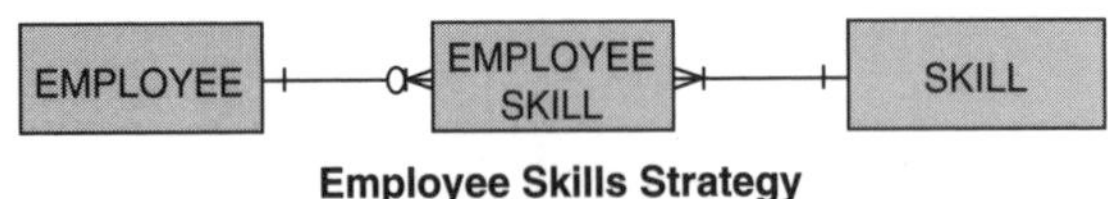

Figure 3-35 A data map representing the Employee Skills strategy.

- We hire employees who presently have none of our skills, but we will train them *(shown by optional becoming mandatory, one, or many at EMPLOYEE SKILL).*
- Each employee must have demonstrated an ability to be trained, however (*shown by mandatory one at EMPLOYEE).*
- We must have at least one employee, but we need many (*shown by mandatory many at EMPLOYEE SKILL)* for each skill (*shown by mandatory one at SKILL).*

How would this data map change to represent an ability to learn new skills on the job? It requires an association degree or nature to be modified, as shown in Figure 3-36 for an alternative strategy.

An Alternative Strategy

We see now that the association nature of *mandatory* at EMPLOYEE SKILL has changed to *optional becoming mandatory* at EMPLOYEE SKILL (shaded in the data map in Figure 3-36). The *Refined Employee Skills Strategy* shows the business interpretation of this simple change, with the variations highlighted in bold italic.

As the association from EMPLOYEE to EMPLOYEE SKILL in Figure 3-36 has been unchanged, the first paragraph is unaffected. But the association from SKILL to EMPLOYEE SKILL has been changed by the modified optional association nature (shown shaded) at EMPLOYEE SKILL. The second paragraph shows a new strategy expressing the intent of this change: in bold italic.

The third paragraph expresses a further refinement in bold italic—to hire from outside only for those skills that are uneconomical to develop from within. These new employees must then be able to train the present employees.

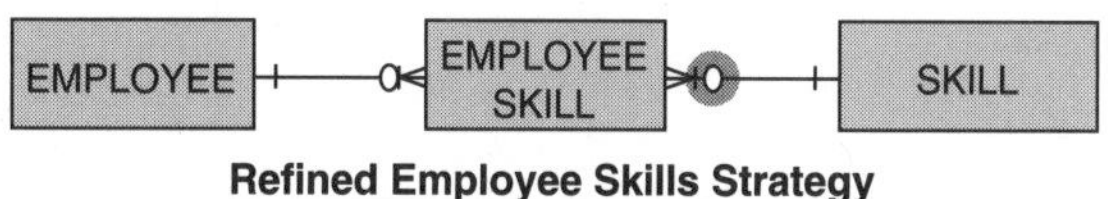

Figure 3-36 The data map is modified for an alternative Employee Skills strategy.

- We hire employees who presently have none of our skills, but we will train them. Each employee must have demonstrated an ability to be trained.
- ***For new skills we need to develop, we will train our present employees where possible so that eventually we will have at least one employee, but we need many*** for each skill.
- ***We will only hire new employees from outside for any new skills that are not economical for us to mount training programs for our present employees. Where feasible, these new employees will train our present employees.***

We now see a further power of Data Modeling: it enables business rules and strategies to be shown schematically in a data map. By questioning, it leads to the identification of alternative strategies.

A data map can also be used for "what if" strategy setting, discussed next for the examples in Figures 3.37 and 3.38.

Strategy Review Using Associations

The examples in Figure 3-37 show strategy interpretation for Employees in Jobs, when the association degree or nature has been varied at EMPLOYEE JOB.

Each numbered association example in Figure 3-37 is highlighted in bold using the same numbers in the discussion below. The interpretation of each strategy is summarized in brackets and italic.

1. *Optional becoming Mandatory One*: "An employee will be appointed to only one job, and can never have another job." *(Each employee has only one, lifetime job.)*
2. *Optional becoming Mandatory Many*: "An employee will be appointed to a job, and can be appointed to many jobs over time." (*Each employee will be guaranteed one or many jobs.*)
3. *Mandatory Many*: "An employee must initially be appointed to a job, and can be appointed to many jobs over time." *(Each employee must have at least one job.)*
4. *Optional Many*: "An employee may never be appointed to a job, or may be appointed to many jobs over time." *(Some employees*

Figure 3-37
Alternative strategies identified by modifying associations.

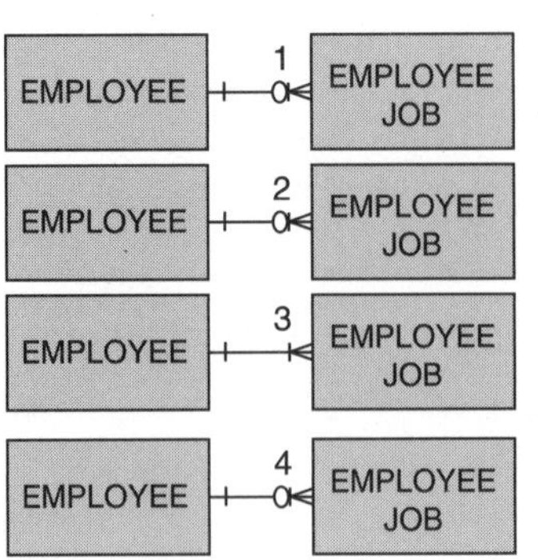

"An employee will be appointed to only one job, and can never have another job."

"An employee will be appointed to a job, and can be appointed to many jobs over time."

"An employee must initially be appointed to a job, and can be appointed to many jobs over time."

"An employee may never be appointed to a job, or may be appointed to many jobs over time."

may not have any job to do, but they are still considered employees.)

Figure 3-38 illustrates further strategy interpretations for Jobs filled by Employees, again when the association degree or nature is varied at EMPLOYEE JOB.

Each association discussion is again highlighted in bold below, with the example number from Figure 3-38. The strategy interpretation is summarized in brackets and italic.

5. *Optional becoming Mandatory One*: "A job will be filled by only one employee, and can never have any other employee." *(One job, one employee.)*
6. *Optional becoming Mandatory Many:* "A job will eventually be filled by one employee, and can be filled by many employees over time." *(Jobs will be reassigned.)*
7. *Mandatory Many:* "A job must initially be filled by at least one employee, and over time can be filled by many employees." *(No job can be vacant.)*
8. *Optional Many:* "A job may never be filled, or over time may be filled by many employees." *(Some jobs may never be filled.)*

We have now covered the main concepts of data modeling. We have not dealt with the related subject of Business Normalization, which is a major component of business-driven Enterprise Engineering. This subject is introduced in [Finkelstein 1989, 1992]. It is covered in detail in the self-study courses in [Finkelstein 1999].

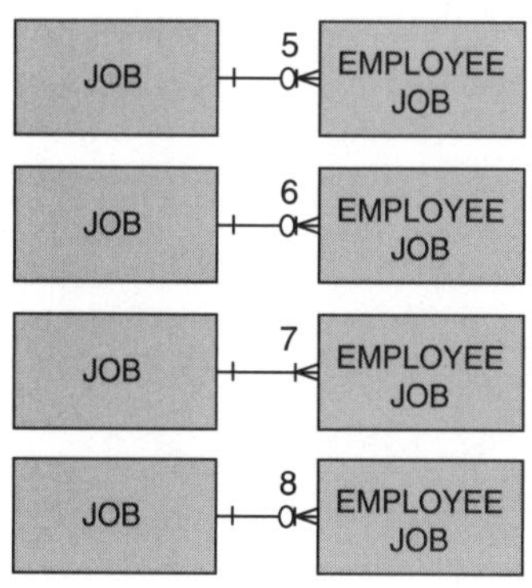

"A job will be filled by only one employee, and can never have any other employee."

"A job will be filled by one employee, and can be filled by many employees over time."

"A job must initially be filled by at least one employee, and over time can be filled by many employees."

"A job may never be filled, or over time may be filled by many employees."

Figure 3-38 Further alternative strategies identified by modifying associations.

However, we will now use our knowledge of data modeling and mapping to develop strategic data models from strategic business plans. This is the focus of the next chapter.

REFERENCES

Chen, P. (1976) "The Entity-Relationship Model: Towards a Unified View of Data," *ACM Trans. on Database Systems*, 9–36.

Codd, E.F. (1970) "A Relational Model for Large Shared Data Banks," *CACM*, 13(6): 377–387.

Codd, E.F. (1979) "Extending the Database Relational Model to Capture More Meaning," *ACM Trans. on Database Systems*, 4(4): 397–434.

Codd, E.F. (1988) Domains, Keys and Referential Integrity in Relational Databases, *InfoDB*, San Jose, CA: Colin White Consulting.

Date, C. (1986) *An Introduction to Database Systems - Volume 1*, 4th edn, Reading, MA: Addison-Wesley.

Finkelstein, C. (1989) *An Introduction to Information Engineering*, Sydney, Australia: Addison-Wesley. [ISBN: 0-201-41654-9]

Finkelstein, C. (1992) *Information Engineering: Strategic Systems Development*, Sydney, Australia: Addison-Wesley. [ISBN: 0-201-50988-1]

Finkelstein, C. (1999) *Certified Business Data Modeler Self-Study Course Series*, Perth, Australia: Information Engineering Services Pty Ltd (IES). The CBDM Course Series is available in PowerPoint or in intranet-delivered versions from the IES Online Store. Go to the IES Web site at http://www.ies.aust.com/~ieinfo/ or the Visible Australia web site at http://www.visible.com.au/ and click on the Online Store link from either Web site.

Halpin, T. (1995) *Conceptual Schema & Relational Database Design*, Sydney, Australia: Prentice-Hall. [ISBN: 0-13-355702-2]

CHAPTER 4

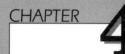

Strategic Modeling

A Map for the Future

I know the information that I need. Just show me how I can get to it, and let me look at other relevant information at the same time.

—Anonymous Manager

Now that we have covered the concepts of data modeling in Chapter 3, we understand more clearly how we can satisfy the management request above. We know that a data map is a visual way of looking at the data and information of an organization. It also shows related data and information associated with relevant areas of interest.

This chapter discusses the principles of strategic data modeling. It uses data mapping to develop a strategic map from strategic business plans, defined as discussed in Chapter 2. We will apply these principles using the strategic plans defined for XYZ Corporation in that chapter to develop a strategic model and project plans for data warehouses and Enterprise Portals.

XYZ Strategic Plan

We will use the Strategic Plan in Chapter 2 as a catalyst to identify information needed by management to achieve the goals, objectives, strategies, and key performance indicators detailed in those plans.

To show the development of a Strategic Model, we will use an Integrated Computer-Aided Software Engineering (I-CASE) software tool, Visible Advantage. Visible Advantage is available in three editions: the Enterprise Architecture (EA) edition; the Data Warehousing (DW) edition; and the Educational (ED) student edition. The EA and DW editions are both available as a single-user (Standalone) version and a multi-user (Collaborative Server) version [see Visible Advantage]. The main screens of these two editions are shown in Figures 4-1 and 4-2. The ED student edition is a limited-capacity Standalone version, but having the functionality of the EA edition. Any of these Visible Advantage editions can be downloaded for free evaluation as discussed in the References at the end of this chapter. The ED student edition of Visible Advantage is also included as part of the [CBDM] course series [Finkelstein 1999].

The Enterprise Architecture edition of Visible Advantage supports all of the SDLC phases in Figure 3-1, namely:

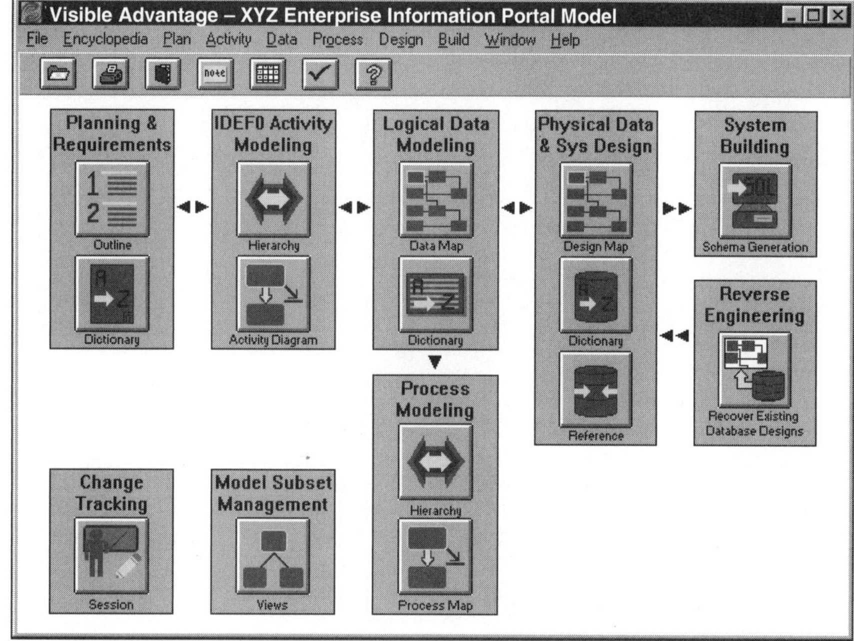

Figure 4-1 The main screen of Visible Advantage Enterprise Architecture (EA) edition.

- Strategic Planning (see the Planning & Requirements buttons) of Figure 4-1
- Data Modeling (see the Logical Data Modeling buttons)
- Function Modeling (see the IDEF0 Activity Modeling and Process Modeling buttons)
- Systems Design (see the Physical Data & Sys Design buttons)
- Implementation (see the System Building buttons)

The EA edition supports Forward Engineering, Reverse Engineering, and Business Reengineering all in the one tool, as shown by the arrowheads in Figure 4-1.

Figure 4-2 shows that the Data Warehousing edition does not include the Activity Modeling or Process Modeling components of the Enterprise Architecture edition. Both editions, however, can easily use the same project encyclopedia (repository). For example, any activity models or process models defined in the EA edition cannot be seen or used by the DW edition, but they still remain in the encyclopedia.

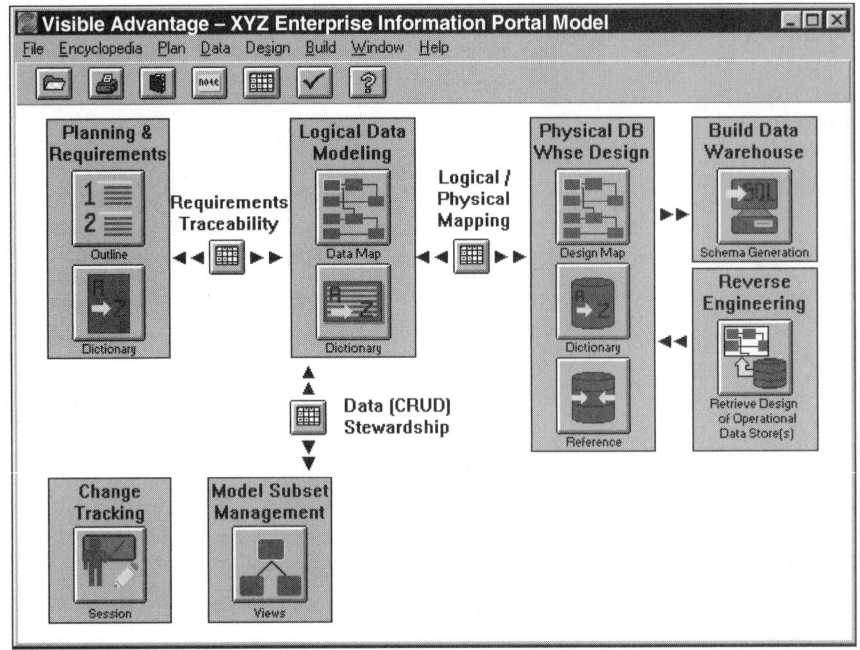

Figure 4-2 The main screen of Visible Advantage Data Warehousing (DW) edition.

The Need for Feedback to Management

Strategic Plans, to be effective, must be implemented at all management levels throughout an organization. Figure 4-3 shows that feedback is needed for management review and refinement. It shows that business-planning methods help staff develop detailed plans at lower levels. Business-driven data modeling helps them to identify their information needs, based on those plans.

Figure 4-3 provides immediate feedback that can suggest refinements to the plans. Identified information will be included in a Data Warehouse or EP, derived from data in operational databases. This will be discussed in later chapters.

The XYZ Mission, Policies, Issues, Strengths, Weaknesses, Goals, Objectives, Strategies, and Key Performance Indicators (KPIs)—all defined as the XYZ Strategic Plan in Chapter 2—were entered into the Planning Dictionary of Visible Advantage. The Planning Report in Figure 4-4 documents these statements and will be used as a catalyst for strategic modeling in the following pages.

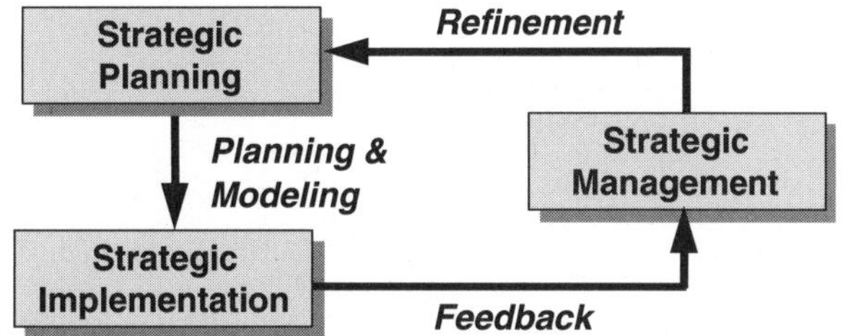

Figure 4-3 Strategic Planning Feedback from Implementation.

The feedback from Strategic Business Planning in Figure 4-4 leads to the refinement of plans and identification of information needs to be satisfied by a Data Warehouse. It results in databases and systems to deliver management information at all levels of XYZ, to help managers carry out their responsibilities and achieve their defined plans.

The XYZ Planning Statements in Figure 4-4 were entered into Visible Advantage as shown in Figure 4-5. This shows the hierarchical nature of those statements. The Statement–View Matrix in that figure shows how these statements guide managers of XYZ Departments.

Figure 4-6 shows that the Mission, Asset Growth Policy, and Profitability Policy are shared by all Departments. Figure 4-7 shows that the Sales and Marketing Departments need to work together to achieve the Market Share and Market Analysis Strategies and KPIs.

We will mainly use the Mission statement to help us develop an initial strategic data model for XYZ. The statements will be used as a catalyst in a facilitated modeling session with the same managers of XYZ as in the Strategic Planning session in Chapter 2.

Facilitated Modeling Session for the Strategic Data Model

The XYZ Mission in Chapter 2 identified major areas of XYZ, by underlining nouns, as follows:

> Develop, deliver and support <u>products</u> *and* <u>services</u> *which satisfy the* <u>needs</u> *of* <u>customers</u> *in* <u>markets</u> *where we can achieve a return on* <u>investment</u> *of at least 20 percent pa within two years of market entry.*

Participants in a Facilitated Strategic Modeling session were therefore drawn from relevant business areas. Invited to this session were the

Figure 4-4 XYZ Major Strategic Planning Statements.

Thu Jun 10 12:43:09 1999 Page 1

XYZ Enterprise Portal Model **Planning Statement Report**
All Statements in XYZ Corporate

Statement: **A. XYZ Mission**
Category: Mission
Text: Develop, deliver, and support products and services which satisfy the needs of customers in markets where we can achieve a return on investment of at least 20 percent pa within two years of market entry.

Statement: **B1. Asset Growth Policy**
Category: Policy
Text: Monitor performance of all aspects of our business so that each activity has a favorable effect, directly or indirectly, on our mission ROI.

Statement: **B2. Asset Growth Issues**
Category: Issue
Text:
- Many investments in declining markets
- High market entry cost into marginal markets
- High debt levels for assets in sunset markets

Statement: **B3. Asset Disposal Strategy**
Category: Strategy
Text: Identify assets that cannot provide a return within two years consistent with the mission ROI, and dispose of them at the best possible price.

Statement: **B4. Asset Disposal Objective**
Category: Objective
Text: Following Board approval, dispose of all non-performing assets within 12 months.

Statement: **C1. Profitability Policy**
Category: Policy
Text: Monitor financial performance of all activities to ensure that profit and cash flow projections are achieved according to, or ahead of, plan.

Statement: **C2. Profitability Issues**
Category: Issue
Text:
- Delayed financial reporting
- High interest costs
- Poor cash flow management

Statement: **C3. Profitability Strengths**
Category: Strength
Text:
- Profitable
- Cash-rich

Statement: **C4. Profitability Weaknesses**
Category: Weakness
Text:
- Poor financial reporting
- Poor budget control

Figure 4-4
(Cont'd) XYZ Major Strategic Planning Statements.

Statement: **C5. Financial Reporting Strategy**
Category: Strategy
Text: Implement flexible financial reporting systems able to be introduced at any organizational level, and which can provide profit and loss statements for any defined reporting frequency, with associated balance sheet statements.

Statement: **C6. Financial Reporting Objective**
Category: Objective
Text: Implement financial reporting systems within 6 months that provide profit and loss, balance sheet, and cash flow reporting within 1 day of the close of any defined financial period.

Statement: **C7. Budget Control Strategy**
Category: Strategy
Text: Establish and maintain strong budgetary controls for all expenditure, linked directly to revenue achievement. All financial statements must clearly show actual revenue and expenditure against budget, and indicate percentage change from the previous reporting level.

Statement: **C8. Budget Control Objective**
Category: Objective
Text: Implement budget control systems directly linked to financial reports based on the budget control strategy within 6 months.

Statement: **D1. Market Share Policy**
Category: Policy
Text: Achieve the targeted annual market share for the chosen market segments of XYZ.

Statement: **D2. Market Share Issues**
Category: Issue
Text:
- No market share info. (unavailable or inaccurate)
- Market definition (growth rates and size N/A)
- Corporate image (poor)
- Product Range Definition (limited)
- Pricing Policy (high and inflexible)

Statement: **D3. Market Share Strengths**
Category: Strength
Text:
- Large, cash-rich organization
- Experienced, capable staff

Statement: **D4. Market Share Weaknesses**
Category: Weakness
Text:
- Poor financial control and management
- Arrogant, reactive corporate culture
- Poor customer service and products
- Limited experience in a competitive environment

Figure 4-4 (Cont'd) XYZ Major Strategic Planning Statements.

Statement: **D5. Market Share Strategy**
Category: Strategy
Text: Achieve the targeted annual market share based on the Unit Market Share KPI for the chosen market segments of XYZ.

Statement: **D6. Unit Market Share KPI**
Category: Key Performance Indicator
Text: The Unit Market Share KPI monitors Market Growth in Total Units and Unit Sales Growth targets by quarter. These targets are managed by varying total and proportional funding for advertising and product cost reduction technologies, to achieve decreases in sales price with consistent gross margins. The Unit Market Share KPI Spreadsheet defines each of these targets.

Statement: **E1. Market Analysis Policy**
Category: Policy
Text: Analyze existing and emerging markets on a regular basis, to assess market growth, potential market size, and potential market competition.

Statement: **E2. Market Survey Strategy**
Category: Strategy
Text: Ensure regular surveys are undertaken to determine market size and our market share, and to understand the needs and the expectation characteristics of our chosen and potential market segments.

Statement: **E3. Product Range Strategy**
Category: Strategy
Text: Establish and maintain a product range definition that recognizes the strength of our products and technology, and the capabilities for bundling products into innovative packages.

Statement: **E4. Pricing Strategy**
Category: Strategy
Text: Establish and maintain a pricing policy which will sustain long-term achievement of market share targets by market segment, consistent with achieving profitability targets.

Marketing Manager, Sales Manager, the CFO (Finance Manager), Product Development Manager, and R&D Manager, who were all earlier involved in the Strategic Planning session.

From Chapter 3, we now know that the underlined nouns in the Mission statement also indicate major data entities. Discussing the Mission with the managers, the Marketing Manager tells us that:

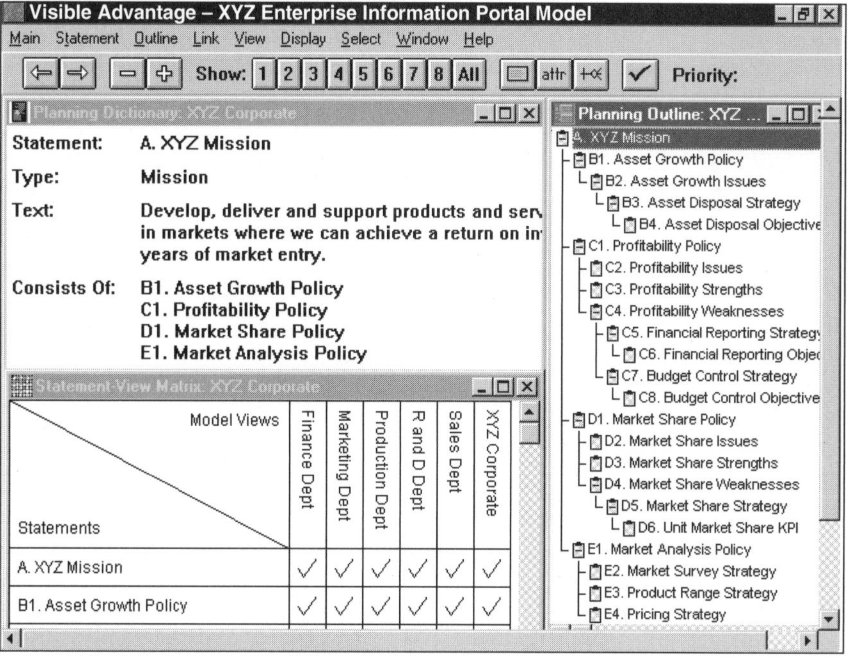

Figure 4-5 The Planning Dictionary and Statement–View Planning Matrix.

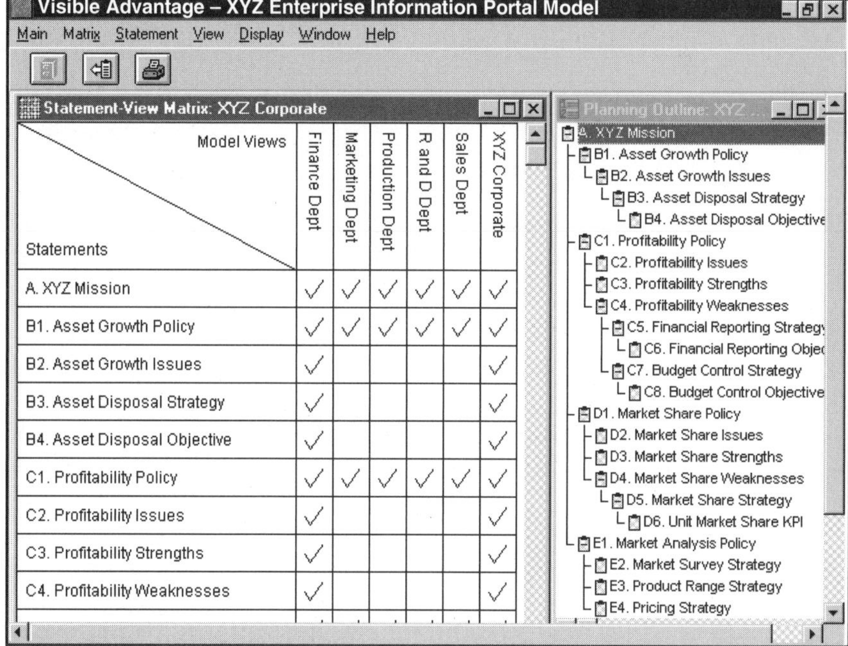

Figure 4-6 All Departments are responsible for the Mission and major policies.

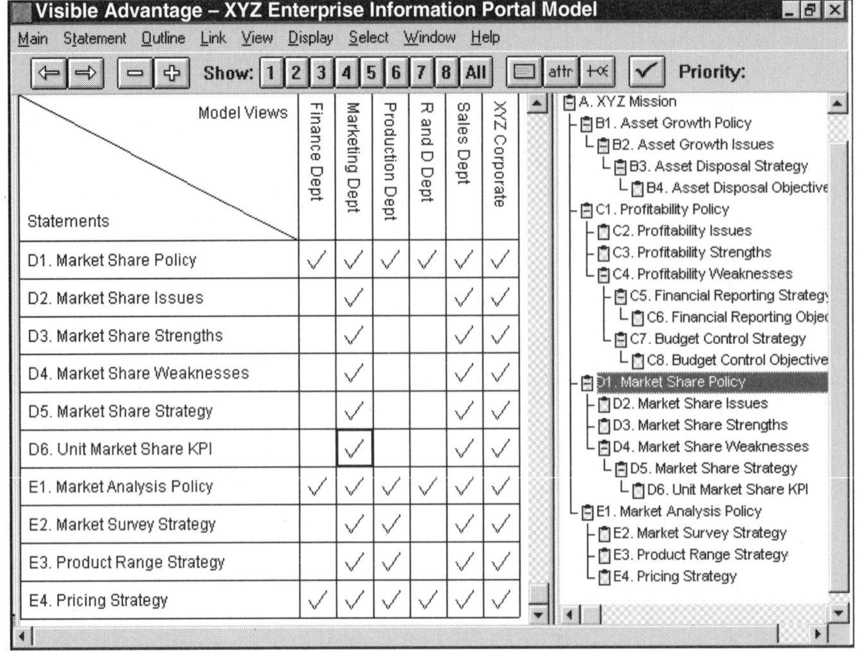

Figure 4-7 The Market Share statements involve both Sales and Marketing Departments.

> Our markets have many needs that we address, but there must be at least one need that we are in business to satisfy for a market to be relevant to us.

From this statement, it is clear that XYZ is interested in markets and needs. This is shown schematically in a data map as follows:

A MARKET has *many* needs, but at least one need addressed by XYZ. The association at NEED is therefore shown as *mandatory many*. The Marketing Manager further states that "*a need may be held by many markets*"; the association at MARKET is thus *optional many*.

Next, as we saw in Chapter 3, the *many-to-many* association between MARKET and NEED is replaced by an *intersecting* entity to identify specific needs for each market.

The line between MARKET and MARKET NEED shows an association of *mandatory one to mandatory many*. This represents the Marketing Manager's business rule that a market *must* have a need for *at least one (or many)* of the products and services that are provided by XYZ, to be a market of interest to XYZ. But the association between NEED and MARKET NEED is *mandatory one to optional many*. This indicates that zero, one, or many markets *may* have a particular need.

Identification of Activities and Processes in a Data Model

We saw in Chapter 3 that an intersecting entity represents business activities or processes. We can now see that MARKET NEED is a high-level representation of the business activity: *Market Needs Analysis Activity*. These entities are entered into the Data Modeling phase of Visible Advantage, as shown in Figure 4-8.

Figure 4-8 shows each entity and its attributes, displaying <u>*market id#*</u> and <u>*need id#*</u> as primary keys of MARKET and of NEED, each with a # suffix

Figure 4-8
Partial Strategic Data Map for Marketing.

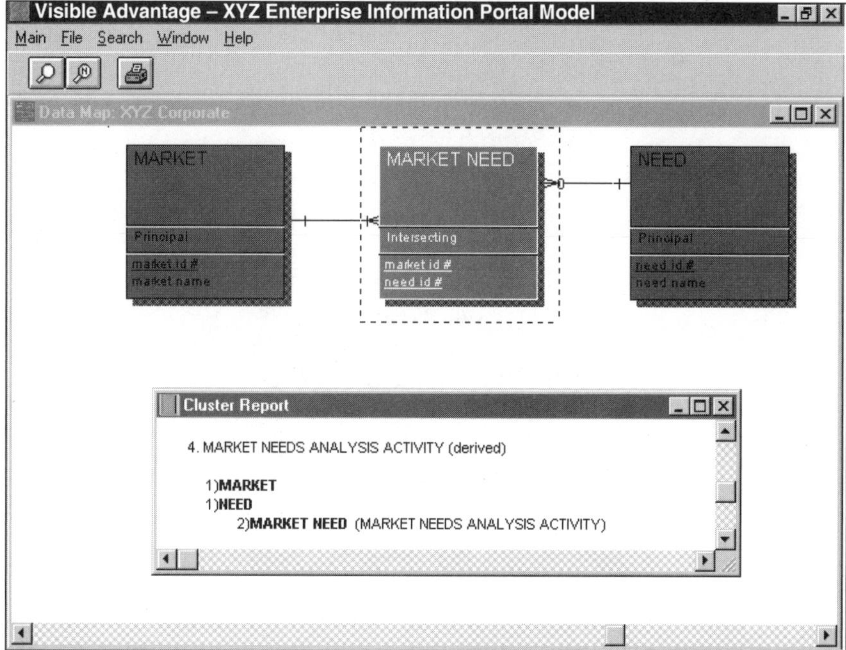

and underlined. The intersecting entity MARKET NEED shows these two key attributes also—as a compound primary key. The non-key attributes of *market name* and *need name* have also been defined. Figure 4-8 is a typical strategic model with only limited attribute details defined: mainly primary keys and foreign keys. But we will omit displaying attributes in later figures of this chapter, as we focus mainly on entities and associations in strategic modeling.

Derivation of Project Plans from a Data Model

Notice that there is an extra window in Figure 4-8, showing a Cluster Report. This illustrates that automatic analysis is carried out by Visible Advantage to derive project plans for activities, processes, or systems represented in a data model. It shows an automatically derived project plan for the *Market Needs Analysis Activity* of MARKET NEED.

Using Engineering Enterprise Portals (EEP), this analysis has identified potential source data that could be extracted from an existing *Market Needs Analysis System*, relevant to markets and needs. Data from this system may perhaps be aggregated and stored as totals in the Market and the Need databases of a Data Warehouse.

MARKET NEED is displayed on the last line in bold. It is called a *Cluster End-Point.* The name of the activity (in brackets following it) was explicitly defined when the intersecting entity was entered. It has "2)" preceding it. This indicates that Visible Advantage has determined that MARKET NEED source data is in phase 2 of an EEP project for Market Needs Analysis. MARKET and NEED above it are also in bold, each with "1)" preceding it. This indicates that they will be implemented in phase 1 of the project; they are both Principal entities and so will be typically implemented as databases using EEP.

We can now see that the Cluster Report in Figure 4-8 is a simple project plan derived from this data model. It can be viewed in Outline format as shown in the figure, with each higher project phase number indented one position to the right as a conceptual Gantt Chart. This derivation was achieved automatically by Visible Advantage through applying the rules of entity dependency. The principles of entity dependency analysis are described in Chapter 3 of [Finkelstein 1992].

Further Expansion of the Strategic Data Model

We will now continue the Facilitated Strategic Modeling session. The Sales Manager and Marketing Manager both take up the discussion:

> "A customer must be allocated to at least one market so that we can sell effectively. Some customers participate in many markets," says the Sales Manager. The Marketing Manager further adds: "We should be aware that a new market initially has no customers, as we first develop that market."

We now see that customers are in many markets, which have many customers. We show this schematically in the data map as follows:

A CUSTOMER can belong to many markets of XYZ, but at least one. The association at MARKET is thus *mandatory many*. A MARKET may have many customers; the association at CUSTOMER is *optional many*. The many-to-many association of CUSTOMER and MARKET is therefore replaced by an intersecting entity, to identify customers in each market—as shown next.

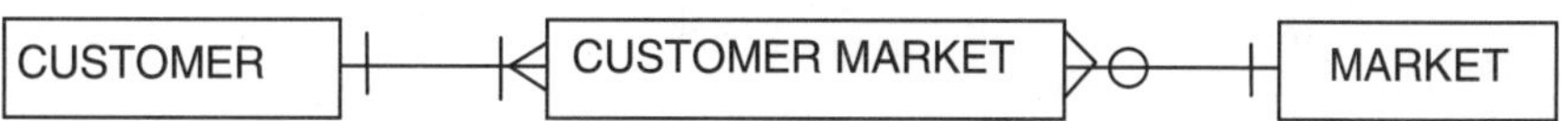

The line between CUSTOMER and CUSTOMER MARKET shows an association of *mandatory one to mandatory many*. This represents the business rule that a customer *must* belong to *at least one (or many)* markets of interest to XYZ. But the association between MARKET and CUSTOMER MARKET is *mandatory one to optional many*. This indicates that a market *may* have zero, one, or many customers.

Once again, this intersecting entity is a high-level schematic of a business activity or business process. CUSTOMER MARKET therefore represents the Customer Marketing Activity—which is of interest to both the Sales Manager and Marketing Manager. These entities are added to the Strategic Data Model in Figure 4-9.

This shows the Customer Marketing Activity in the Cluster Report window. Visible Advantage shows most of these entities in bold. This convention is used to indicate that Customer Marketing Activity directly depends on the entities above it in bold, representing the Customer and

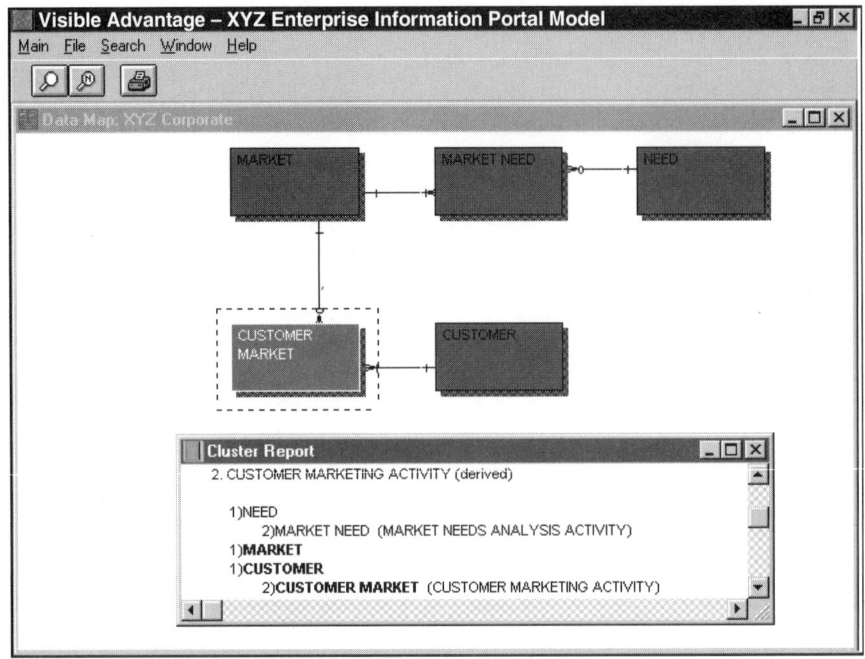

Figure 4-9
The *Customer Marketing Activity,* in the XYZ Strategic Data Model.

Market databases. It shows that CUSTOMER MARKET is in phase 2, dependent on CUSTOMER and MARKET, both of which are in phase 1. It has now identified potential source data for the Customer and Market databases in the Data Warehouse that could be extracted from an existing XYZ Customer Marketing System.

Notice, however, that the Market Needs Analysis Activity from Figure 4-8 is also included in the Cluster Report window of Figure 4-9. But here, NEED and MARKET NEED are now not shown in bold. This "not bold" convention is used by Visible Advantage to indicate that the Market Needs Analysis Activity is a prerequisite activity for the Customer Marketing Activity. Why is this so?

We now see that Visible Advantage has automatically applied the earlier business rule that a market must have at least one need. The data model therefore shows that—to be effective in customer marketing—the market needs of customers in those markets must first be known. This is a reasonable assumption. Visible Advantage has automatically used the earlier business rule to identify other potential source data for Customer and Market databases in the warehouse. It further indicates that Market Needs Analysis Activity is a common, shared activity that can be used whenever there is a reference to a market in any activity.

We can now see from Figure 4-9 that the principle of entity dependency, applied automatically by an I-CASE tool such as Visible Advantage, is a powerful technique. It not only identifies potential databases in a warehouse, but it also indicates potential systems that can provide source data for extraction—to populate those databases in the warehouse or EP. This is discussed in more detail in Part 2 of the book.

Our focus here has been the development of a strategic data model for a data warehouse or EP. However, entity dependency also has many other uses:

- It is used to derive project plans from data models to build new systems, for Forward Engineering projects.
- It is used to identify shared, cross-functional business processes for reengineering, required in Business Re-Engineering projects. This is discussed in Chapter 12.
- It is used to derive project plans from data models that have been extracted from database designs of existing systems, for Systems Reengineering projects. This is discussed in Chapter 13.
- It is used to identify shared, reusable business objects (such as Customer or Market) to be implemented using object-oriented development tools.

We will now continue our Facilitated Strategic Modeling session with the XYZ managers. The Product Development Manager and R&D Manager both take up the discussion:

> "In R&D we develop products that are designed to satisfy the needs of our customers, from Market Needs Analysis carried out by Marketing. A product must address at least one of those needs to be worthwhile investing R&D effort," says the R&D Manager. And the Product Development Manager adds: "This ensures that every product is relevant to at least one market—a market that has needs addressed by that product."

We can see from this statement that there is a *many-to-many* association between PRODUCT and NEED, resulting in the PRODUCT NEED intersecting entity—for the *Product Needs Analysis Activity*. Furthermore, the association from PRODUCT to PRODUCT NEED is *mandatory one to mandatory many*. These two entities are added to Figure 4-10.

Similarly, there is a *many-to-many* association between PRODUCT and MARKET, resulting in the PRODUCT MARKET intersecting entity and the *Product Marketing Activity*. A PRODUCT to PRODUCT MARKET association is

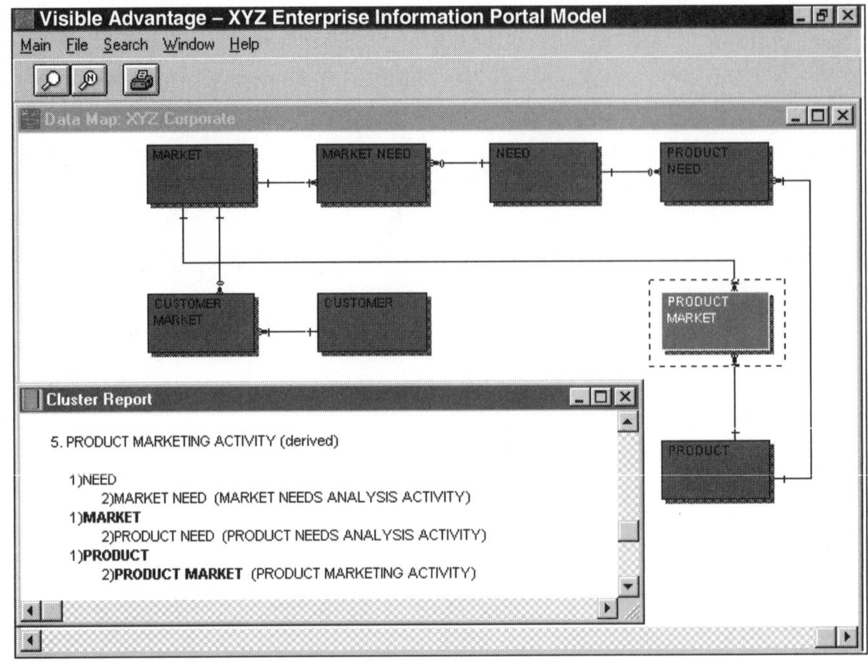

Figure 4-10 Adding Product Marketing, Product Development, and R&D perspectives.

mandatory one to mandatory many. This intersecting entity is also added to the strategic model in Figure 4-10.

We can now see the result of these additional entities in the Cluster Report window of Figure 4-10. It indicates that the *Product Marketing Activity* (and any Product Marketing Systems) potentially may provide source data for the Product and Market databases—because they are all shown in bold. But it also shows the *Market Needs Analysis Activity* and *Product Needs Analysis Activity* as prerequisite activities—as they are *not bold*. Systems associated with these also may provide relevant source data for the Product and Market databases.

Looking further at the data map in Figure 4-10, the Sales Manager then makes the following observation:

> You know, it is our job in Sales to make sure that our customers purchase many products, and of course we sell products to many customers. Isn't there a many-to-many association between Customer and Product for our Customer Product Sales Activity?

That is exactly right! We add an intersecting entity in Figure 4-11 to the strategic data model, with a *mandatory one to optional becoming*

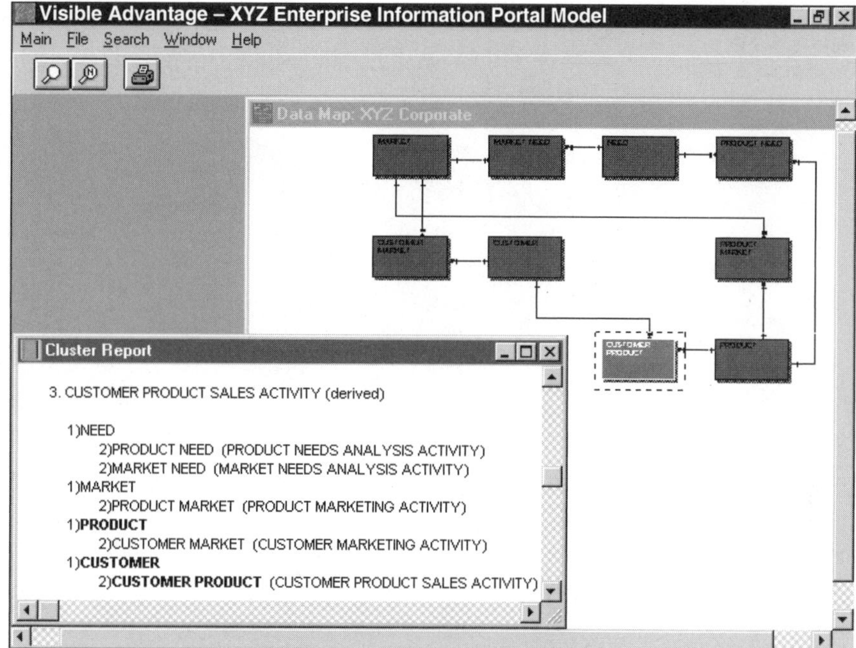

Figure 4-11 The *Customer Product Sales Activity* added to the Strategic Model

mandatory many association between CUSTOMER and CUSTOMER PRODUCT. There is also a *mandatory one to optional many* association between PRODUCT and CUSTOMER PRODUCT.

The Cluster Report now shows that this activity provides source data to (and uses data from) the Customer and Product databases in the Data Warehouse. Other source data can potentially be extracted from prerequisite Customer Marketing, Product Marketing, Market Needs Analysis, and Product Needs Analysis Activities and systems.

We now see another valuable intersecting entity—between NEED, CUSTOMER, MARKET, and PRODUCT—as CUSTOMER MARKET PRODUCT—for the *Customer Market Product Sales Activity*. This is shown in Figure 4-12. The CFO from the Finance Dept then contributes to the discussion:

> This activity is the financial reason for our existence. Without sales of products to customers in markets, we cannot issue orders and invoices for payment. These are charged against revenue and expenditure financial accounts and are reported in our Profit and Loss (Nett Income) Statement.

The CFO continues to comment on the Customer Market Sales Activity:

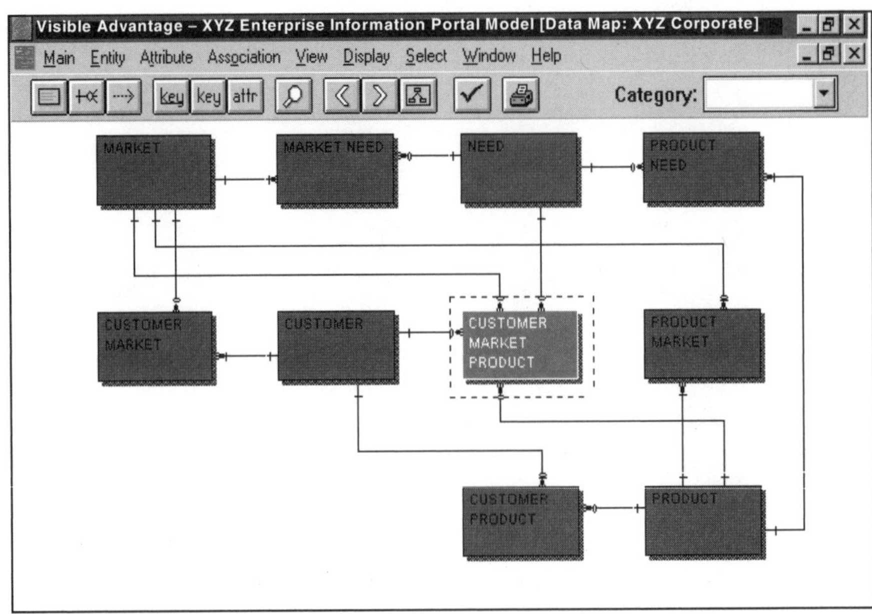

Figure 4-12 The *Customer Market Product Sales Activity* is central to the warehouse.

> Our investments in markets where we sell products are shown in our Balance Sheet Statement, also. These Financial Statements are issued based on our monthly, quarterly, and annual reporting periods.

To which the Marketing Manager and Sales Manager both add:

> And don't forget that we budget our expenditure for these periods from projected sales, and we later check these projected budgets against the actual financial results that are achieved for each period.

We now have some more entities to add to Figure 4-13. FINANCIAL ACCOUNT has a *mandatory one to optional many* association between FINANCIAL ACCOUNT and CUSTOMER MARKET PRODUCT. And FINANCIAL STATEMENT has a *mandatory one to mandatory many* association to FINANCIAL ACCOUNT. BUDGET has a *mandatory one to optional many* association to FINANCIAL STATEMENT. Finally, PERIOD (representing time) is associated with many entities, with *mandatory one to optional many* associations as illustrated in Figure 4-13.

We can see that CUSTOMER MARKET PRODUCT is central to this strategic map. In fact, we could continue the facilitated strategic modeling session and use all of the Planning Statements in Figure 4-4. At a more detailed tactical and operational modeling level we would eventually identify

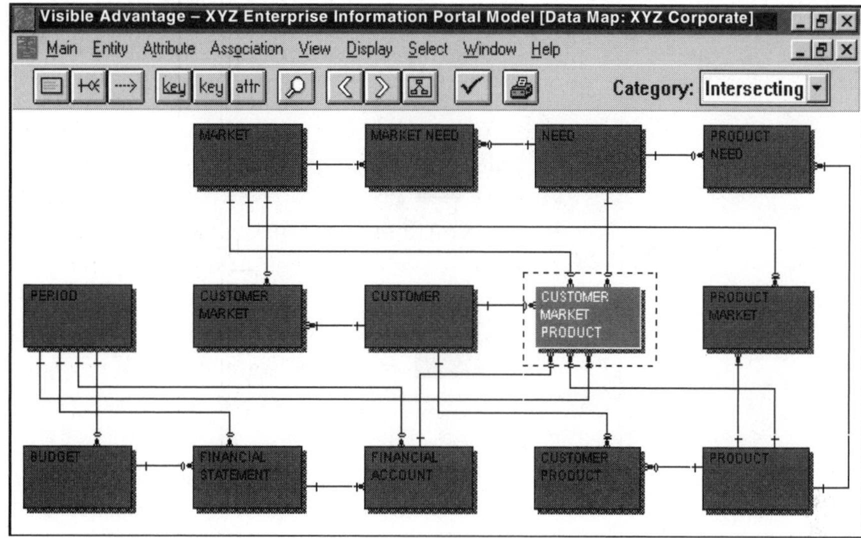

Figure 4-13 The XYZ Strategic Data Model, now including Financial entities.

entities used by the Order Entry, Sales Invoicing, Budgeting, and Financial Reporting systems that are typical of XYZ Corporation and most organizations.

We have so far only used the Mission statement from Figure 4-4 in this facilitated strategic modeling session. We have identified 14 entities in the initial strategic data model. A typical facilitated strategic modeling session runs over two days, using a whiteboard to develop the strategic data map rather than actively entering it into Visible Advantage as we have done in this chapter. In this two-day session, typically 90–120 entities are drawn on whiteboards [Finkelstein 1989, 1992]. These entities are then entered separately—away from the managers—into an I-CASE tool such as Visible Advantage for entity dependency strategic analysis such as discussed above.

For this chapter, we have deliberately focused our attention on the Mission statement. This statement is usually covered in the first hour of the two-day facilitated session. But this example has discovered enough entities to illustrate the main EEP principles involved in strategic modeling. We can now identify some of the core dimensions in the strategic model for access in the Data Warehouse or Enterprise Portal.

Identification of Core Dimensions for the XYZ Data Warehouse

Figure 4-14 shows the strategic map from Figure 4-13, but restricted to display only the Principal entities that are directly associated with CUSTOMER MARKET PRODUCT. It further includes BUDGET and FINANCIAL STATEMENT because of their business significance.

Figure 4-15 shows *Customer Market Product Sales Activity* as a Cluster Report on the screen. NEED, MARKET, CUSTOMER, PRODUCT, and PERIOD are all in phase 1. These are all major dimensions for access, using multidimensional EIS, DSS, and OLAP Data Warehousing products.

We can see that BUDGET is in phase 2. FINANCIAL STATEMENT and FINANCIAL ACCOUNT are in phases 3 and 4. And the cluster end-point, CUSTOMER MARKET PRODUCT, is in phase 5. By entity dependency analysis, Figure 4-15 also identifies systems from the following activities as potential data sources:

- Market Needs Analysis Activity
- Customer Marketing Activity
- Product Needs Analysis Activity
- Product Marketing Activity

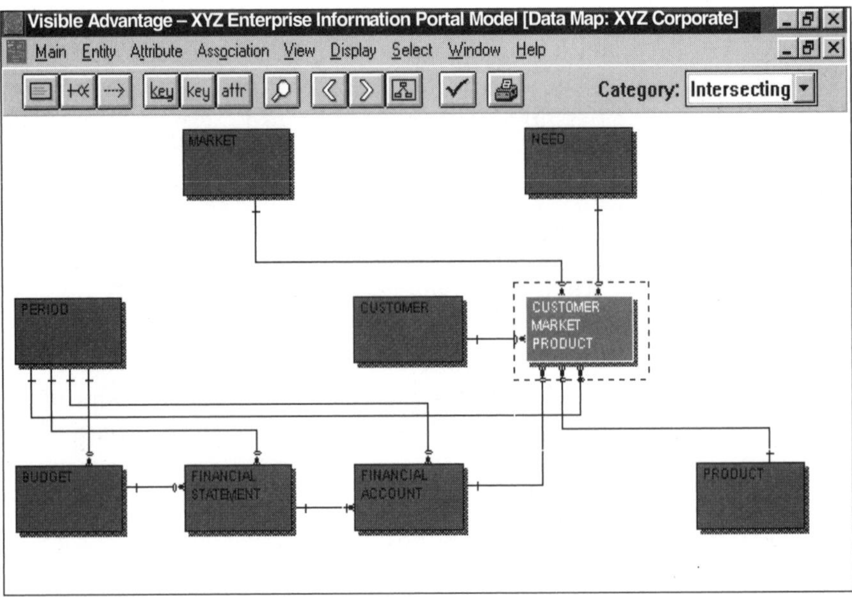

Figure 4-14 The Core Dimensions are indicated by Principal entities.

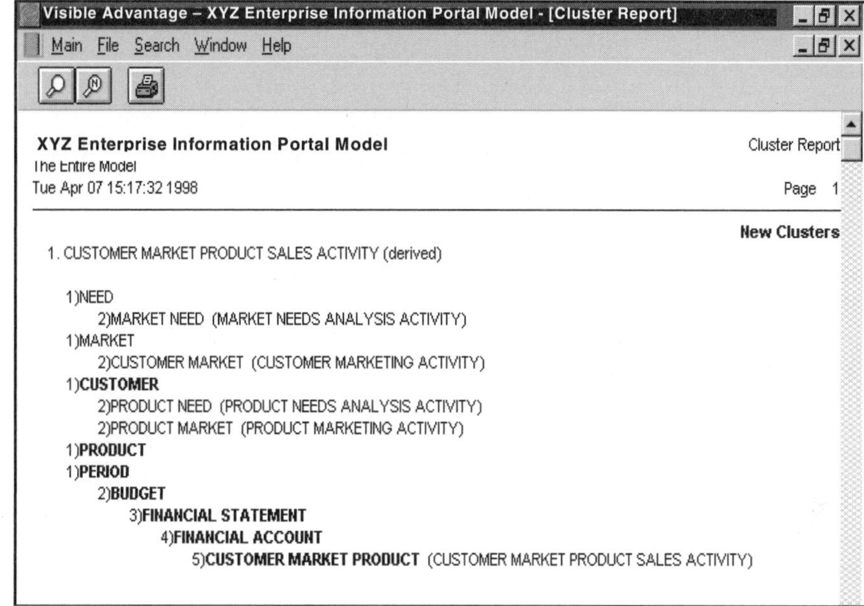
Visible Advantage – XYZ Enterprise Information Portal Model - [Cluster Report]

Main File Search Window Help

XYZ Enterprise Information Portal Model — Cluster Report
The Entire Model
Tue Apr 07 15:17:32 1998 — Page 1

New Clusters

1. CUSTOMER MARKET PRODUCT SALES ACTIVITY (derived)

1)NEED
2)MARKET NEED (MARKET NEEDS ANALYSIS ACTIVITY)
1)MARKET
2)CUSTOMER MARKET (CUSTOMER MARKETING ACTIVITY)
1)**CUSTOMER**
2)PRODUCT NEED (PRODUCT NEEDS ANALYSIS ACTIVITY)
2)PRODUCT MARKET (PRODUCT MARKETING ACTIVITY)
1)**PRODUCT**
1)**PERIOD**
2)**BUDGET**
3)**FINANCIAL STATEMENT**
4)**FINANCIAL ACCOUNT**
5)**CUSTOMER MARKET PRODUCT** (CUSTOMER MARKET PRODUCT SALES ACTIVITY)

Figure 4-15 The *Customer Market Product Sales Activity* cluster.

The complete Cluster Report for the XYZ Strategic Model in Figure 4-13 has now been included as Figure 4-16. We will use this next, to help us identify attributes for specific information that is needed by Finance, Marketing, and Sales managers from the Data Warehouse. We will also use it in the concluding section of this chapter to develop Project Maps—to implement the Data Warehouse by progressive delivery of Data Marts.

Identification of Information Needs for the Data Warehouse

In Chapter 2 we discussed the Market Share Strategy and Unit Market Share KPI that were defined. These statements were entered into the Planning Dictionary of Visible Advantage in Figure 4-4. They are repeated in Figure 4-17.

We will use the statements in Figure 4-17 as catalysts to identify information needed by the Marketing Manager and Sales Manager.

The *Market Share Strategy* measures market share based on total number of units sold annually in a market. It refers to the *Unit*

Figure 4-16
The Complete Cluster Report for the XYZ Strategic Model.

XYZ Enterprise Portal Model **Cluster Report**
The Entire Model
Thu Jun 10 15:17:32 1999 Page 1

1. CUSTOMER MARKET PRODUCT SALES ACTIVITY (derived)
    1)NEED
        2)MARKET NEED (MARKET NEEDS ANALYSIS ACTIVITY)
    1)MARKET
        2)CUSTOMER MARKET (CUSTOMER MARKETING ACTIVITY)
    1)**CUSTOMER**
        2)PRODUCT NEED (PRODUCT NEEDS ANALYSIS ACTIVITY)
        2)PRODUCT MARKET (PRODUCT MARKETING ACTIVITY)
    1)**PRODUCT**
    1)**PERIOD**
        2)**BUDGET**
        3)**FINANCIAL STATEMENT**
            4)**FINANCIAL ACCOUNT**
                5)**CUSTOMER MARKET PRODUCT**
                    (CUSTOMER MARKET PRODUCT SALES ACTIVITY)

2. CUSTOMER MARKETING ACTIVITY (derived)
    1)NEED
        2)MARKET NEED (MARKET NEEDS ANALYSIS ACTIVITY)
    1)**MARKET**
    1)**CUSTOMER**
        2)**CUSTOMER MARKET** (CUSTOMER MARKETING ACTIVITY)

3. CUSTOMER PRODUCT SALES ACTIVITY (derived)
    1)NEED
        2)PRODUCT NEED (PRODUCT NEEDS ANALYSIS ACTIVITY)
        2)MARKET NEED (MARKET NEEDS ANALYSIS ACTIVITY)
    1)MARKET
        2)PRODUCT MARKET (PRODUCT MARKETING ACTIVITY)
    1)**PRODUCT**
        2)CUSTOMER MARKET (CUSTOMER MARKETING ACTIVITY)
    1)**CUSTOMER**
        2)**CUSTOMER PRODUCT** (CUSTOMER PRODUCT SALES ACTIVITY)

4. MARKET NEEDS ANALYSIS ACTIVITY (derived)
    1)**MARKET**
    1)**NEED**
        2)**MARKET NEED** (MARKET NEEDS ANALYSIS ACTIVITY)

5. PRODUCT MARKETING ACTIVITY (derived)
    1)NEED
        2)MARKET NEED (MARKET NEEDS ANALYSIS ACTIVITY)
    1)**MARKET**
        2)PRODUCT NEED (PRODUCT NEEDS ANALYSIS ACTIVITY)
    1)**PRODUCT**
        2)**PRODUCT MARKET** (PRODUCT MARKETING ACTIVITY)

6. PRODUCT NEEDS ANALYSIS ACTIVITY (derived)
    1)NEED
        2)MARKET NEED (MARKET NEEDS ANALYSIS ACTIVITY)
    1)MARKET
        2)PRODUCT MARKET (PRODUCT MARKETING ACTIVITY)
    1)**PRODUCT**
        2)**PRODUCT NEED** (PRODUCT NEEDS ANALYSIS ACTIVITY)

Figure 4-17
Key Performance Indicators relating to Market Share.

Statement: **D5. Market Share Strategy**
Category: Strategy
Text: Achieve the targeted annual market share based on the Unit Market Share KPI for the chosen market segments of XYZ.
Statement: **D6. Unit Market Share KPI**
Category: Key Performance Indicator
Text: The Unit Market Share KPI monitors Market Growth in Total Units and Unit Sales Growth targets by quarter. These targets are managed by varying total and proportional funding for advertising and product cost reduction technologies, to achieve decreases in sales price with consistent gross margins. The Unit Market Share KPI Spreadsheet defines each of these targets (see Figure 2-11).

Market Share KPI, documented in the spreadsheet in Figure 2-11. We asked the Marketing Manager what information was needed to assess changes in market share and market growth:

> Well, I need to evaluate the impact of technology investments that we make each period for products in markets, so that we can reduce the sales price while still realizing our standard margin. I must know the advertising for each product in each period and the total amount spent by product each period.

From this statement, we can see a number of attributes that need to be added to the PRODUCT MARKET entity, as well as a primary key of *period id#* to track these amounts over time. These are:

PRODUCT MARKET (product id#, market id#, period id#, product market cost reduction funded amount, product market advertising amount, product market total funded amount)

We also need to decide how we should represent the time period. A useful approach is to use a primary key of period id#, recording for each period the period start date, the period duration and unit of time used, and the period end date—as follows:

PERIOD (period id#, period name, period start date, period duration, period unit, period end date)

Figure 4-18
Attributes added to Entities, for the *Unit Market Share KPI*.

MARKET	(market id#, period id#, market name, market total unit size this period, market growth rate from last period, market total units for xyz, market share for xyz, market share growth rate from last period, market target units sold in period, market actual units sold in period)
PERIOD	(period id#, period name, period start date, period duration, period unit, period end date)
PRODUCT MARKET	(product id#, market id#, *period id#*, product market cost reduction funded amount, product market advertising amount, product market total funded amount)

We will defer a more detailed discussion of this representation of time until Chapter 5, when we consider performance monitoring. Returning to the Marketing Manager, we ask about other information that is needed for the *Unit Market Share KPI* Spreadsheet in Figure 2-11.

> I need to know the total size of each market in units for each period, from which the spreadsheet will calculate the market growth rate from the last period. And with the total units that we do sell in each market, it calculates our market share and the market share growth rate from the last period.
>
> Also, so I can make forward projections I need to know the target units that we plan to sell over the next few periods for each market—and of course the actual units that we do sell.

This results in a number of attributes being added to the MARKET entity in Figure 4-18. This figure also summarizes the attributes we added above to the PERIOD and PRODUCT MARKET entities.

These attributes were added to the relevant entities in a Model View in Visible Advantage for the Marketing Department. This model view includes the *Product Marketing Activity* from Figure 4-10, and is shown in Figures 4-19 and 4-20.

We can clearly see the attributes that have been added to MARKET and to PRODUCT MARKET in Figure 4-19, both in the Data Map window on the right and for the MARKET entity also in the Data Dictionary window on the left.

In Figure 4-20 we see the entire data map for Marketing, but this time without the attribute detail. *Mandatory one to optional many* associations between PERIOD and MARKET, and also PERIOD and PRODUCT MARKET were defined when period id# was added as a primary key to each entity.

Notice that PRODUCT, PERIOD, and NEED are all positioned to the left, vertically aligned in Phase 1. Then MARKET and PRODUCT NEED are positioned to their right, in Phase 2. PRODUCT MARKET and MARKET NEED are

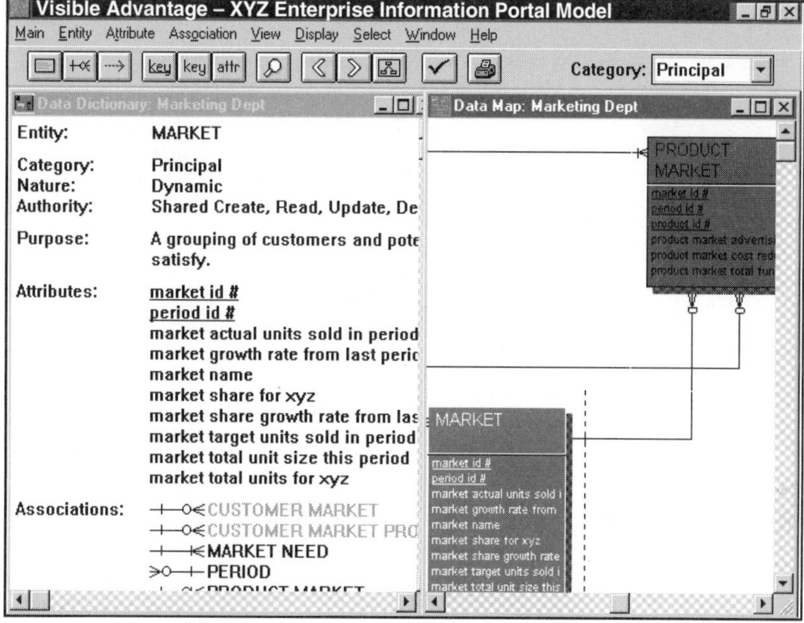

Figure 4-19 Attributes for the *Unit Market Share KPI* in the Strategic Model.

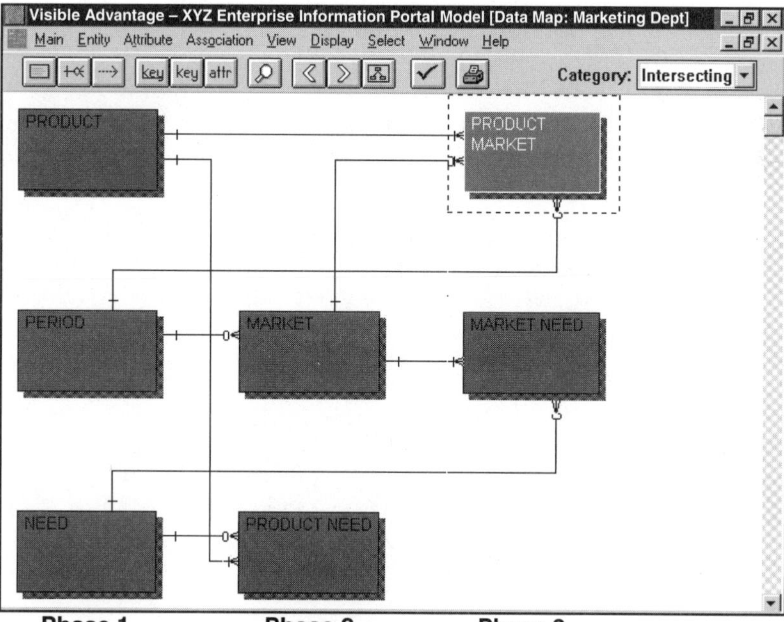

Figure 4-20 Product Marketing data map displayed in Pert Chart format.

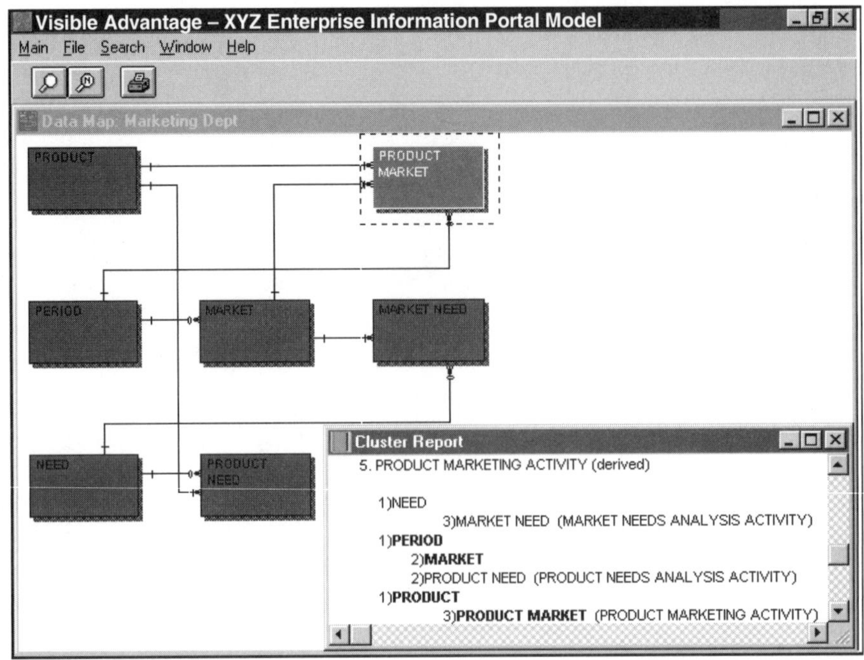

Figure 4-21 The Product Marketing data map, also showing the Cluster Report.

then positioned at the far right, in Phase 3. This reflects the *Product Marketing Activity* cluster—with PERIOD added—which is shown again in Figure 4-21.

We clearly see in Figures 4-20 and 4-21 that the data map has been drawn by Visible Advantage in a Pert Chart format. This is automatically diagrammed for visual examination of entities in a project plan format, so that attributes for information to be provided by the Data Warehouse, or EP can be readily identified.

We will now complete this chapter by discussing the development of Data Mart, Data Warehouse, and EP Project Maps. We will conclude by examining several Project Maps from real-life projects.

Development of Data Mart, Data Warehouse, and EP Project Maps

The Cluster Report in Figure 4-16 shows each activity in the strategic model, with each entity indented by phase as we discussed earlier—like a conceptual Gantt Chart. Some of these activity clusters represent potential Data Marts, as separately implementable Data Mart subprojects for the Data Warehouse.

We will use the Cluster Report to decide whether there is a logical order for progressive delivery of Data Marts. To help us think of systems that provide source data for Data Marts, we will replace the suffix of "activity" by "data mart" in the following discussion.

We saw earlier that some clusters appear as prerequisite activities in other clusters. We will now see that they also help us to develop Data Mart Project Maps. These schematically show steps involved in the progressive implementation of the Data Warehouse.

We will start with the *Market Needs Analysis Activity* cluster from Figure 4-16, as follows.

4. MARKET NEEDS ANALYSIS ACTIVITY (derived)
1)**MARKET**
1)NEED
2)MARKET NEED (MARKET NEEDS ANALYSIS ACTIVITY)

This cluster includes the Market and Need databases in Phase 1 and so represents a *Market Needs Data Mart*. We see that the cluster has only bold entities within it. As it has no prerequisite activities with entities that are not bold, it is not dependent on any other clusters. It is therefore drawn as a box, with the name of the Data Mart within it.

Market Needs

When we examine the Cluster Report in Figure 4-16 further, we see that the *Market Needs Analysis Activity* appears in all other clusters. The *Market Needs Data Mart* is therefore a prerequisite for the Data Marts populated by source data from systems for the other activities. It becomes the Stage 1 Data Mart project for the warehouse.

Now let us look at the cluster for the *Customer Marketing Activity*.

2. CUSTOMER MARKETING ACTIVITY (derived)
1)NEED
2)MARKET NEED (MARKET NEEDS ANALYSIS ACTIVITY)
1)**MARKET**
1)CUSTOMER
2)CUSTOMER MARKET (CUSTOMER MARKETING ACTIVITY)

Because *Market Needs Analysis* is a Stage 1 Data Mart and the *Customer Marketing Activity* is dependent on it, Customer Marketing becomes a Stage 2 Data Mart as follows:

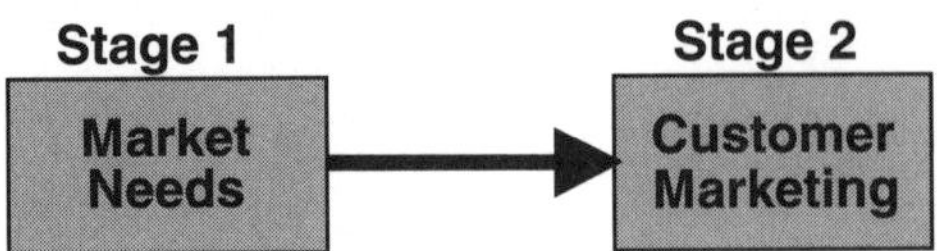

The arrow joining these two Data Mart project boxes shows the sequence of implementation: from Stage 1 to Stage 2. We now continue our examination of Figure 4-16.

The *Market Needs Data Mart* is a prerequisite also for the *Product Marketing Activity* and the *Product Needs Analysis Activity*. These become Stage 2 Data Mart projects also. But, when we look at these two clusters we see that each is a prerequisite of the other.

5. PRODUCT MARKETING ACTIVITY (derived)
   1)NEED
      2)MARKET NEED (MARKET NEEDS ANALYSIS ACTIVITY)
   1)**MARKET**
      2)PRODUCT NEED (PRODUCT NEEDS ANALYSIS ACTIVITY)
   1)**PRODUCT**
      2)**PRODUCT MARKET** (PRODUCT MARKETING ACTIVITY)

6. PRODUCT NEEDS ANALYSIS ACTIVITY (derived)
   1)NEED
      2)MARKET NEED (MARKET NEEDS ANALYSIS ACTIVITY)
   1)MARKET
      2)PRODUCT MARKET (PRODUCT MARKETING ACTIVITY)
   1)**PRODUCT**
      2)**PRODUCT NEED** (PRODUCT NEEDS ANALYSIS ACTIVITY)

From this, we realize that they are interdependent; one cannot be implemented without the other. We represent this by using a double-headed arrow as highlighted by the surrounding box. We add this to Stage 2 of the evolving Data Mart Project Map below.

We can now see that there are two alternatives for implementing the Stage 2 Data Marts. The *Customer Marketing Data Mart* can be implemented first. Or instead, the *Product Marketing Data Mart*—which includes the *Product Needs Data Mart* – can both be implemented. Either alternative can be implemented before the other. Or both can be implemented in parallel if development resources are made available, once the *Market Needs Data Mart* has been built.

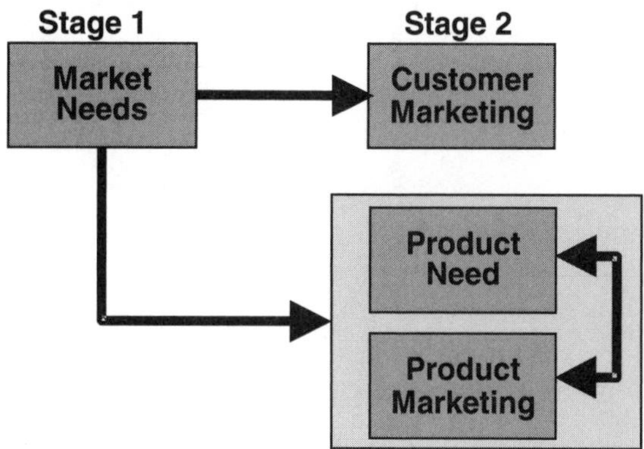

Now let us consider a Data Mart that is populated from source data extracted from the *Customer Product Sales Activity*. Systems for this activity—to provide source data for a *Customer Product Data Mart*—are at the tactical and operational levels of XYZ. They are associated with Order Entry, Inventory, Shipping, and Sales Analysis.

3. CUSTOMER PRODUCT SALES ACTIVITY (derived)
 1)NEED
  2)PRODUCT NEED (PRODUCT NEEDS ANALYSIS ACTIVITY)
  2)MARKET NEED (MARKET NEEDS ANALYSIS ACTIVITY)
 1)MARKET
  2)PRODUCT MARKET (PRODUCT MARKETING ACTIVITY)
 1)**PRODUCT**
  2)CUSTOMER MARKET (CUSTOMER MARKETING ACTIVITY)
 1)**CUSTOMER**
  2)**CUSTOMER PRODUCT** (CUSTOMER PRODUCT SALES ACTIVITY)

We can see that each activity we have discussed earlier in this section is a prerequisite to this activity. Therefore the *Customer Product Data Mart* is a Stage 3 project. It is added to the Data Mart Project Map as follows. We can now see that there is a clear order emerging for progressive implementation of these Data Marts.

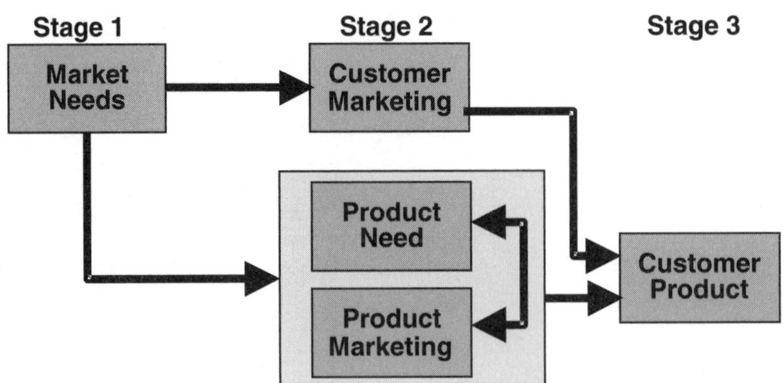

Now we will examine the last cluster, the *Customer Market Product Sales Activity*. This also will become a Stage 3 Data Mart project.

1. CUSTOMER MARKET PRODUCT SALES ACTIVITY (derived)
    1)NEED
        2)MARKET NEED (MARKET NEEDS ANALYSIS ACTIVITY)
    1)MARKET
        2)CUSTOMER MARKET (CUSTOMER MARKETING ACTIVITY)
    1)**CUSTOMER**
        2)PRODUCT NEED (PRODUCT NEEDS ANALYSIS ACTIVITY)
        2)PRODUCT MARKET (PRODUCT MARKETING ACTIVITY)
    1)PRODUCT
    1)**PERIOD**
        2)BUDGET
            3)FINANCIAL STATEMENT
                4)FINANCIAL ACCOUNT
                    5)CUSTOMER MARKET PRODUCT
                        (CUSTOMER MARKET PRODUCT SALES ACTIVITY)

As this activity does not include the *Customer Product Sales Activity*, the *Customer Market Product Data Mart* can be implemented in parallel with the *Customer Product Data Mart* if development resources are made available. It is added as a Stage 3 Data Mart project. The final Project Map is documented as Figure 4-22. It shows the implementation sequence for delivery of Data Marts that are immediately usable, while also progressively implementing the Data Warehouse or Enterprise Portal.

As discussed at the beginning of this section, We used the Cluster Report to help us identify source data from systems associated with activities in that report. We added "Data Mart" to the end of the cluster

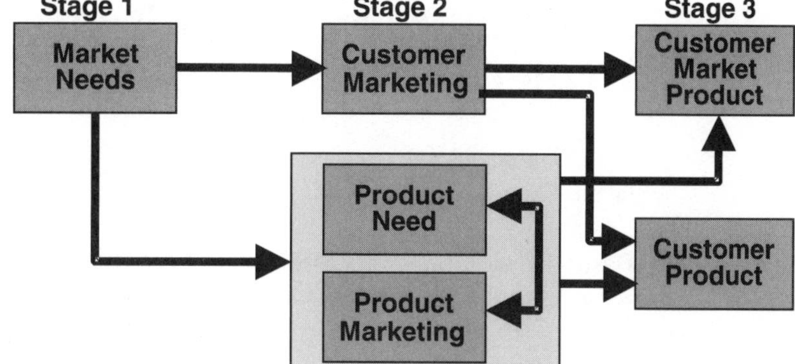

Figure 4-22
The Final Project Map for implementation of the Data Warehouse.

names to help us think about these source data systems, for progressive delivery of Data Marts and the Data Warehouse. In Figure 4-14, we looked at some core dimensions for multidimensional access to the Data Warehouse. These are now illustrated again in Figure 4-23, with the *Customer Market Product Data Mart* as the central focus.

The extraction and transformation of source data to populate these Data Marts and the Data Warehouse is the focus of Part 2 of the book. We will conclude this chapter by reviewing the Project Maps developed for some real-life projects.

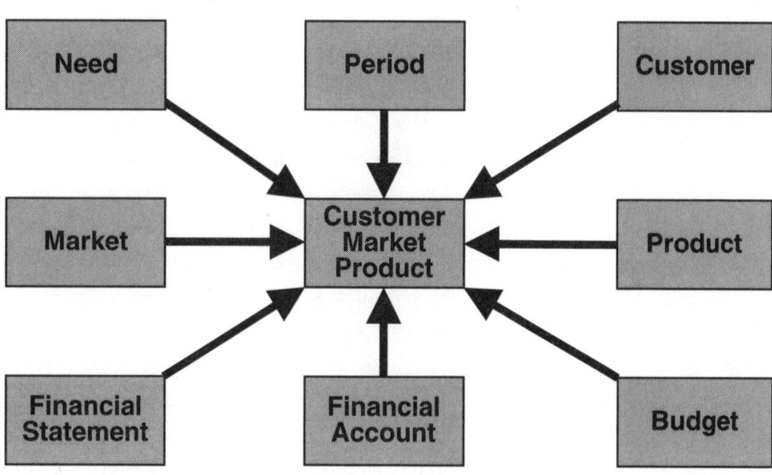

Figure 4-23
The Core Dimensions for the *Customer Market Product Data Mart.*

Project Maps from Real-Life Projects

We will discuss two projects. The first project is in the Public Sector: a large Federal Government Department. The second project is in the Private Sector: a Regional Bank. Both of these were large projects for Data Warehouses. The Bank project also addressed redevelopment of some of the operational systems that provide data to the warehouse. These systems focused on the competitive opportunities presented by global electronic banking using the Internet.

Public Sector Project Example

The Government Department delivers a number of services nationally to persons who make up the population of the country—who are referred to as their "customers." They focus strongly on identifying the needs of each customer, so that they can provide the most relevant services to address the needs of each person.

The Data Warehouse project started with a Facilitated Strategic Modeling session conducted by Clive Finkelstein over two days, attended by very senior managers in the Department and using as a catalyst their Strategic Plans defined for 1995–2005. The strategic model was developed on whiteboards and then entered into Visible Advantage for analysis and development of a Strategic Information Systems Plan (SISP) for the Data Warehouse. This took a total of three weeks. Project Maps for progressive delivery of Data Marts to implement the Data Warehouse are summarized in the following figures.

The services offered to customers depend on the roles that a person can take. A person role may be as an active customer, a past customer, or as a potential customer. The Department is also interested in the dependents of persons who are customers. All of these persons, their dependents and person roles are managed by PERSON STRUCTURE as a *Related Persons Knowledge Base*.

The cluster identified as the *Person Role Management Activity* is a prerequisite of the *Customer Needs Management Activity*, as shown in Figure 4-24. This shows a *Person Role Management Activity* project box in Stage 1, with a project box for *Customer Needs Analysis Activity* in

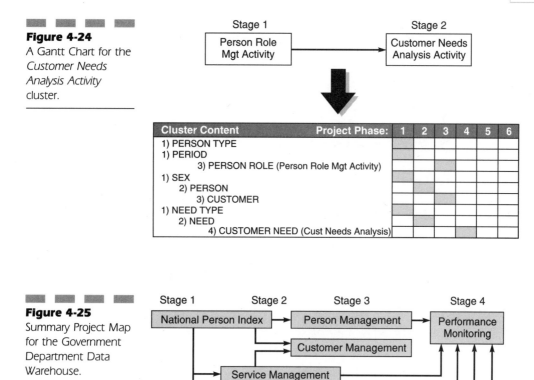

Figure 4-24
A Gantt Chart for the *Customer Needs Analysis Activity* cluster.

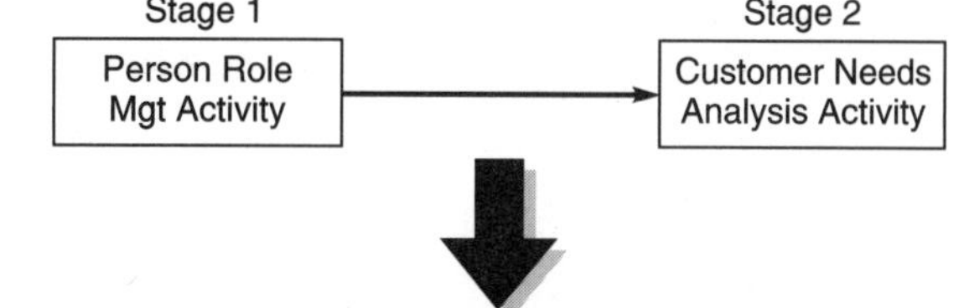

Cluster Content	Project Phase: 1	2	3	4	5	6
1) PERSON TYPE	■					
1) PERIOD	■					
3) PERSON ROLE (Person Role Mgt Activity)			■			
1) SEX	■					
2) PERSON		■				
3) CUSTOMER			■			
1) NEED TYPE	■					
2) NEED		■				
4) CUSTOMER NEED (Cust Needs Analysis)				■		

Figure 4-25
Summary Project Map for the Government Department Data Warehouse.

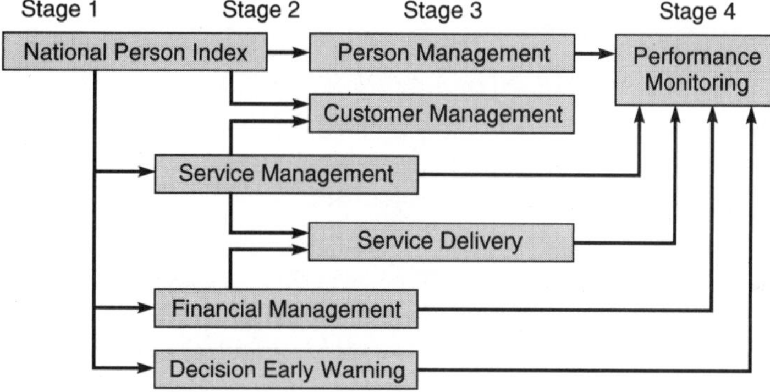

Stage 2. The sub-phases for entities within the cluster are shown in Figure 4-24 as a Gantt Chart for project management.

Figure 4-25 shows a Summary Project Map for the Data Warehouse in this Government Department. The *Person Role Management Activity* and the *Related Persons Knowledge Base* represent the *National Person Index Data Mart*. As this is a fundamental starting point for the Data Warehouse, it appears in Stage 1.

Data Marts for *Service Management, Financial Management*, and *Decision Early Warning* are in Stage 2. Stage 3 Data Marts are *Person Management, Customer Management*, and *Service Delivery*. Finally, *Performance Monitoring* is a Stage 4 Data Mart.

Each of these Data Marts draws on source data from many systems and databases at the operational level of the Department. More detailed activities for these systems are shown in Figure 4-26, within each larger shaded Data Mart.

Private Sector Project Example

The Private Sector example was a project for an innovative Regional Bank. This Bank has been operating since 1994 with Banking Systems implemented using Distributed Client/Server technologies. A project was initiated in 1997 to redevelop systems for Global Electronic Banking, with a Data Warehouse later for management information. This was a large Forward Engineering project that identified at the same time, the information needed by management.

The project team comprised Banking experts as well as IT experts. The strategic model was developed over two days by Clive Finkelstein in a Facilitated Strategic Modeling session. It was entered into Visible Advantage for analysis, then formally presented to other Banking experts in another day, for review.

Here the power of a data model to communicate business meaning became apparent. In a group modeling session a banker came up to the whiteboard to discuss a section of the data model. He suggested a competitive opportunity for the bank to expand its markets using the Internet for global electronic banking. He used the data model to illustrate. He was correct, but Clive pointed out other opportunities he had overlooked. Both were deep in conversation for 15 minutes before Clive realized what was happening . . .

Now let us tell you about the Bank. The banker had been speaking Korean; he knew no English for it was a South Korean Bank! Clive was using English; he did not know Korean! The only communication medium was the data model—but with it, each understood precisely what the other person was saying!

So we now see that there is hope that business managers and IT people (who also speak different languages) will eventually understand each other, by using a data model to communicate in business terms—yet also appreciate the IT implications!

From this initial four-week SISP project, the bank then developed detailed tactical and operational data models of priority areas of interest over the following four months. The IT project members then developed

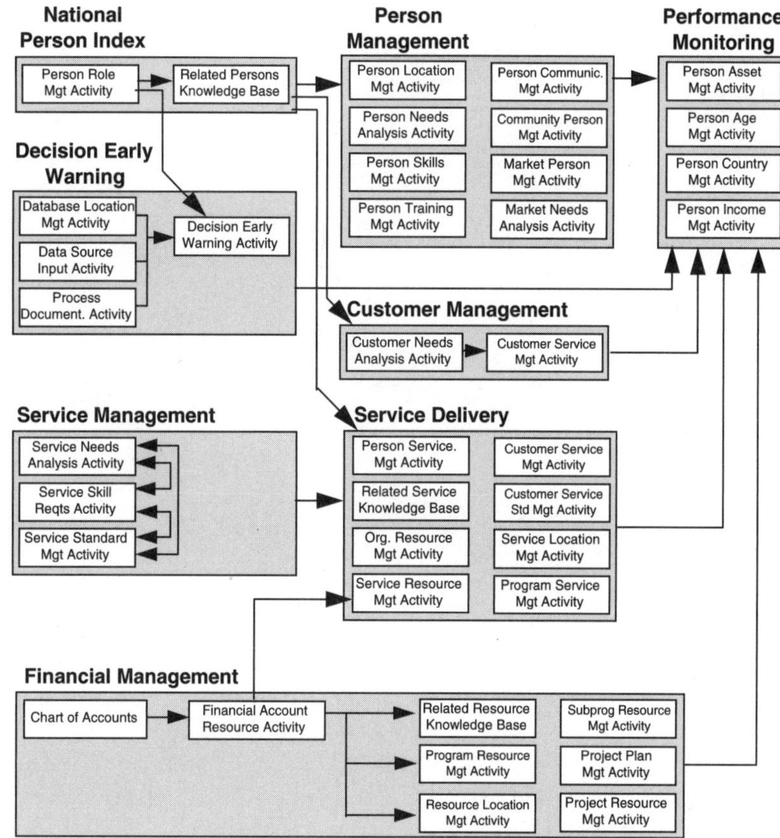

Figure 4-26 Activities and Systems that provide Source Data to these Government Department Data Marts.

object-oriented process models from the data models using Enterprise Engineering and Visible Advantage. They built systems rapidly in Java to enable the Bank to take advantage of the widest future deployment capability. By using business objects built this way, they achieved high object and code reuse and a rapid change capability.

Following this analysis and review, the Strategic Information Systems Plan (SISP) Report was documented. The total elapsed time for Strategic Modeling was three weeks, with a further week for translation of the SISP Report to Korean. Following this four-week strategic modeling project, the SISP Report and Summary Project Map were presented to senior managers of the Bank, as shown in Figure 4-27. This SISP Report can be read online or downloaded from the IES Web Site as discussed shortly.

Figure 4-28 shows the *Customer Management* Project Map. This was identified as the highest priority area for management. The *Customer*

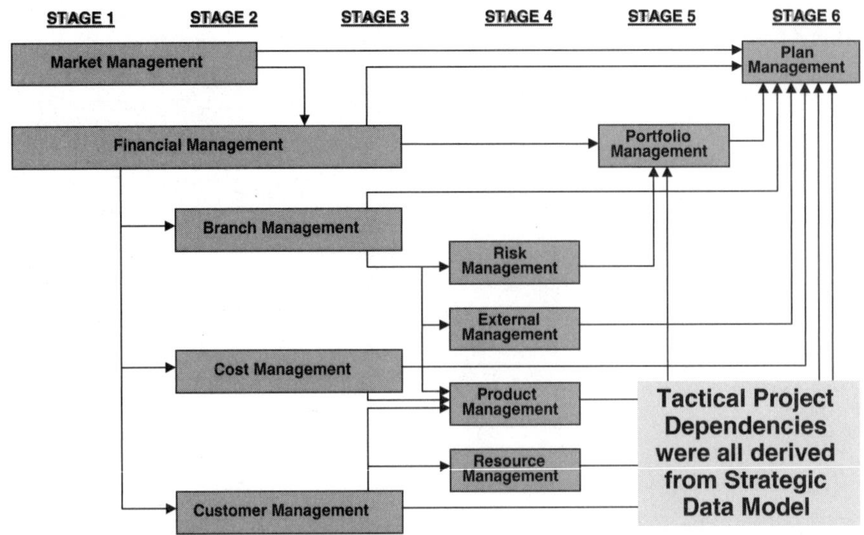

Figure 4-27 Summary Project Map for a Regional Bank.

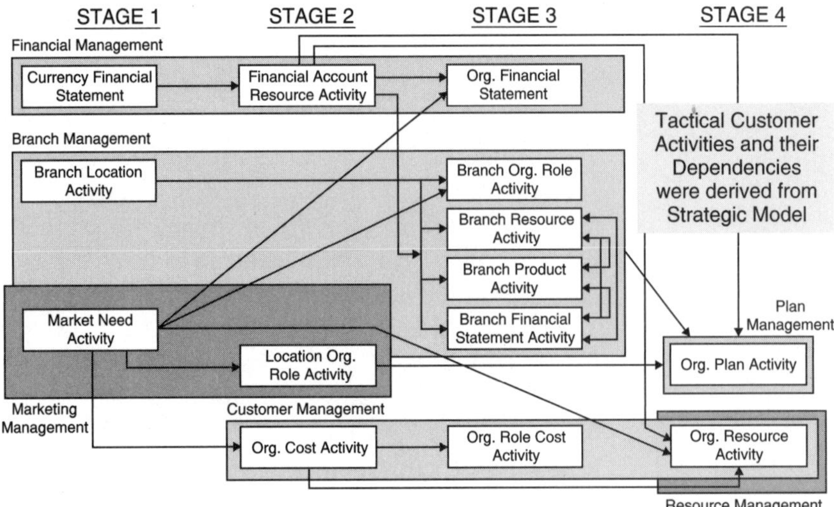

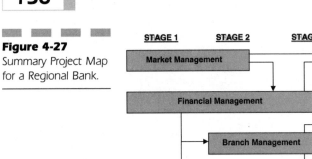

Figure 4-28 The *Customer Management* Project Map, showing prerequisite activities.

Management and *Customer Risk Management* activities then became the initial focus for detailed Tactical and Operational Modeling.

The senior management review examined the Summary Project Map in Figure 4-27 and detailed Customer Management Project Map in Figure 4-28, to identify priority activities. These activities became the focus of the tactical and operational data modeling projects, followed by process modeling and Java implementation, based on the Systems Development Life Cycle in Figure 3-1.

This Bank Project is documented on the Internet. It is available to be read online via the World Wide Web [see IES Web Site]. Alternatively it can be downloaded as Word documents for offline reference.

Two documents are provided. The first is a News Article describing the project. The second document is the Strategic Information Systems Plan (SISP) Report, in English. It includes a cover page for each Appendix, describing the content of each appendix and how it is used. The Appendix contents are of course *Bank Confidential* and so have not been placed on the Internet.

We are now ready to discuss the concepts of Decision Early Warning. This is covered in the next chapter. That chapter also provides a framework that we will later use in Part 2 of the book to manage Data Warehouse and Enterprise Portal projects, based on the analysis and documentation that we have produced in this Part 1.

REFERENCES

Finkelstein, C. (1989) *An Introduction to Information Engineering*, Sydney, Australia: Addison-Wesley. [ISBN: 0-201-41654-9]

Finkelstein C. (1992) *Information Engineering: Strategic Systems Development*, Sydney, Australia: Addison-Wesley. [ISBN: 0-201-50988-1]

Finkelstein C. (1999) *Certified Business Data Modeler Self-Study Course Series*, Perth, Australia: Information Engineering Services Pty Ltd.

[CBDM] This Course Series includes the Data Modeling Concepts course, the Business Normalization Concepts course and the Data Modeling Case Study Workshop. The Educational student edition of the Visible Advantage I-CASE tool is included (see below). The Course Series is available in PowerPoint or in intranet-delivered versions for purchase from the Online Stores of the Visible Web site at http://www.visible.com.au/ or the IES Web site (below).

[IES Web Site] This Web site is located at http://www.ies.aust.com/~ieinfo/. It includes descriptions of many projects, accessible from the Resources link on any page. This links to a Project Planner page. For example, the Regional Bank project discussed in this chapter was for Kwangju Bank in South Korea. The News Article and SISP Report for this project can be read online or downloaded from the Project Planner page. Details about the CASE tools used on the project and detail project phase descriptions for Information Engineering and Enterprise Engineering projects are also available from this page. The IES Web site includes many papers and articles relating to Data Warehousing, Methodologies, Business Re-Engineering, XML, Internet/intranet technologies and other topics—all accessible from the Resources link on any page.

[Visible Advantage Data Warehouse Edition] A free, full function Data Warehouse (DW) edition of Visible Advantage can be downloaded for evaluation from the Visible or IES Web sites as discussed below for the Visible Advantage Enterprise edition.

[Visible Advantage Educational Edition] A full function Educational (ED) student edition of Visible Advantage for unlimited use—with a capacity limited to 50 entities—can be purchased from the Visible Web site at http://www.visible.com.au/ or the IES Web site at http://www.ies.aust.com/~ieinfo/. Click on the Online Store link from either web site. This student edition has adequate capacity for the Forward Engineering examples of Part 1 and for the Reverse Engineering examples included in Part 2 of this book.

[Visible Advantage Enterprise Edition] A free, full function Enterprise Architecture (EA) edition of Visible Advantage—with a capacity for large enterprise data models exceeding 2,000 entities—can be downloaded for evaluation from the Visible Web site at http://www.visible.com.au/ or the IES Web site at http://www.ies.aust.com/~ieinfo/. Click on the Online Store link. It can be used to install the EA edition or the Data Warehousing (DW) edition, but is limited to only 21 days' free use. Either edition can be purchased from the Online Store for unlimited enterprise use at the end of the 21-day, free-use period if required.

CHAPTER 5

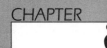

Engineering Enterprise Portals

Implementing Decision Early Warning

Just tell me of any problems before I have a crisis on my hands and give me all of the information I need, early enough, to make a correct decision.

—Anonymous Manager

This is not an unreasonable request by management, but it certainly has been difficult to satisfy! Knowledge management tools, such as Executive Information System (EIS), Decision Support System (DSS), Online Analytical Processing (OLAP), and *Decision Early Warning* (DEW) tools, are generally aimed at providing management with better information, more rapidly, in order to facilitate better decision making. This chapter illustrates the implementation of DEW for knowledge management using a data warehouse or an Enterprise Portal. By using DEW as our example, we are concentrating on what is perhaps the least used form of knowledge management and yet at the same time the most common form of business need. Other examples are discussed in Part 3.

Unfortunately many business decisions focus on "putting out the fires." Like a few sparks that can explode into a major fire if not extinguished early, many decisions are left until it is too late. A problem that would have been easy to resolve instead escalates into a major crisis by the time it is recognized. A DEW system identifies trends towards unacceptable performance, providing early warning to management, enabling them to make decisions that avoid the fires in the first place. With this knowledge of DEW, you can guide your organization through many types of organizational knowledge management activities.

EEP Framework Motivation

In this chapter we discuss DEW principles and present a framework for Engineering Enterprise Portals—an EEP Framework—that is also applicable for implementing other organizational knowledge tools. You can use the EEP Framework as a template, regardless of whether you are planning your initial or your one hundredth Enterprise Portal effort. Using the EEP Framework applies a methodology that provides a repeatable organizational knowledge management implementation process on which to base future implementation efforts.

From a practitioner perspective, an EEP Framework assists organizations with implementation. It is particularly useful as a template to link organizational strategic decision making with information technology-based support. An EEP Framework is a basis for repeatable implementation, a starting point for organizations yet to implement Enterprise Portals, and a means of comparing implementation expectations from one project against the results of others. The framework provides a necessary prerequisite for determining measurable improvement in organizational implementation capabilities.

Decision Early Warning Principles

While real-life applications have provided anecdotal data on the use of DEW as a focus for initial Enterprise Portal efforts, until now there has been little guidance on how DEW capabilities are actually implemented. Clive Finkelstein [1989, 1992] introduced some Decision Early Warning (DEW) concepts. Other concepts have been widely implemented to support organizational "question and compare" analytical activities [Koberg and Bagnall 1991]. DEW performance trend analysis is based on three decision-making principles: the development of performance measures; decision early warning periods and tracking mechanisms; and DEW performance trend analysis. Each is described below.

Performance Measure Development

To decide whether an organization is on track in pursuit of its goals and objectives, planning statements should be expressed in a way that leads to common understanding. They can take the form of quantitative goals and objectives, key performance indicators (KPIs), or critical success factors (CSFs). In this book, we will use the term *Performance Measure* to refer to all of these.

If they are to be measured, then it follows that these statements must be measurable. We saw in Chapter 2 that performance measures have three key characteristics: (1) they must clearly define *what* the measure is; (2) they must clearly define the *level* to be achieved; (3) they must clearly define *when* that level must be realized. This addresses the first principle of DEW.

In the absence of clear strategic business plans for an organization, using methodologies such as in Chapter 2, the information that management needs is difficult to determine. As Demming has warned:

Figure 5-1
Key Performance Indicators relating to Market Share.

Statement: **D5. Market Share Strategy**
Category: Strategy
Text: Achieve the targeted annual market share based on the Unit Market Share KPI for the chosen market segments of XYZ.

Statement: **D6. Unit Market Share KPI**
Category: Key Performance Indicator
Text: The Unit Market Share KPI monitors Market Growth in Total Units and Unit Sales Growth targets by quarter. These targets are managed by varying total and proportional funding for advertising and product cost reduction technologies, to achieve decreases in sales price with consistent gross margins. The Unit Market Share KPI Spreadsheet defines each of these targets (see Figure 2-11).

> ... the most important figures that one needs for management are unknown or unknowable but successful management must nevertheless take account of them [Demming 1986 p. 121].

This need not be so. We refer to discussion of the *Market Share Strategy*, based on the *Unit Market Share KPI* in Chapter 4. This appeared in Figure 4-17; repeated here as Figure 5-1. This performance measure is expressed as in Figure 5-1.

We saw in Chapter 4 that these statements resulted in attributes that were added to MARKET and PRODUCT MARKET (see Figure 4-18). Attributes were added so that the Marketing Manager and the Sales Manager could monitor achievement of market share by markets and products—by using the spreadsheet in Figure 2-11.

NOTE: *May we suggest that you now take a moment to review Figure 2-11 in Chapter 2. You will then better appreciate the discussion in the following paragraphs.*

Performance monitoring using this spreadsheet is largely reactive; it evaluates current performance against past results. It does not help managers make effective decisions for the future. An attempt was made to be proactive, by recording projected future sales targets for later comparison against actual results. If the target sales were achieved in each of the defined future quarters, the market share could then be calculated. Because this is forward-looking, it is more proactive. But we will see that it is still passive, as there is no clear way of fine-tuning progress towards targets.

One controlling mechanism offered by the spreadsheet is to vary expenditure on technology to reduce the cost price for products, so that the sales price can be decreased while maintaining a standard margin for consistent profitability. But technology investment can be a very coarse control; it may be difficult to relate broad investments back to precise cost reductions on specific products.

Another controlling mechanism used in the spreadsheet is advertising expenditure. But again, it can be very difficult to relate a particular sales campaign and expenditure back to precise sales volume increases in a specific product. We have all heard the common complaint of Sales Managers—expressed memorably by one, who said:

> Only 50 percent of what I spend on advertising is effective. But I have a problem. I don't know which half is the effective half!

The spreadsheet is certainly better than having no monitoring. But it is imprecise. It is difficult to determine cause and effect. There may also be many other factors that affect sales results and profitability that the spreadsheet does not even address. We will shortly see that Decision Early Warning performance monitoring provides additional controls that will enable a manager to fine-tune achievement of intermediate performance results, while moving towards a larger performance target.

This discussion of the development of performance measures is the first of the three DEW principles. We will now consider the second principle—presentation and tracking of periodic results using well-articulated graphs.

DEW Periods and Tracking Mechanisms

A standard DEW performance monitoring representation shows the performance measure as a range on the Y-axis and the reporting period on the X-axis. The actual performance is recorded within the range of upper and lower acceptable performance measures.

Once several periods of actual performance data have been recorded, it becomes possible to forecast a trend line using appropriate methods. Trend lines provide the "early warning" of performance that is moving towards unacceptable limits, and provide management with enough time to make a correction. This is proactive, a concern we had above with the passive spreadsheet used for performance monitoring of unit sales and market share.

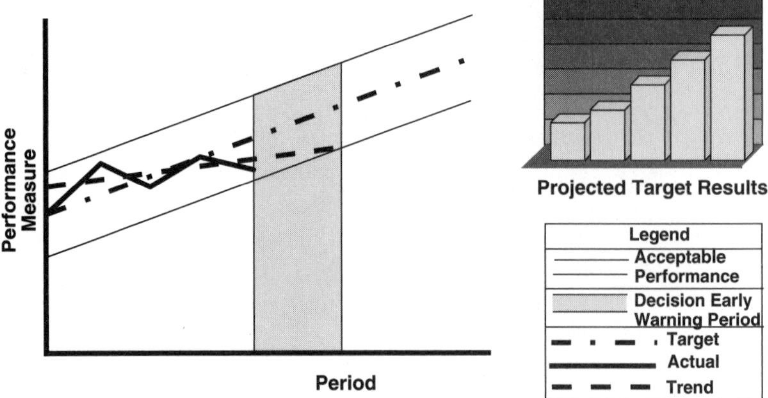

Figure 5-2 Decision Early Warning Concepts Illustrated.

Adapted from: C. Finkelstein, *Information Engineering: Strategic System Development,* Addison-Wesley, Reading, MA (1992).

The concepts of Decision Early Warning presentation and tracking mechanisms are illustrated in Figure 5-2.

DEW Performance Trend Analysis

Performance trend analysis is the third decision-making principle. As each actual performance result is recorded, it is checked to ensure it lies within the upper and lower boundaries of acceptable performance in Figure 5-2. If it falls outside these boundaries a manager is immediately notified by an *Exception Report*. The manager can take prompt action as this out-of-boundary result could indicate a crisis situation. It represents a "fire" to be put out.

As measurements are recorded, a trend may develop which indicates some future period when the trend line will cross into unacceptable performance. The period between the latest actual result and the time when a performance boundary will first be crossed is called the *Decision Early Warning Period*—shown as a shaded band along the X-axis in Figure 5-2. This period controls when a manager should be given early warning of an apparent trend. The early warning duration depends on the specific performance measure.

For example, to change a performance trend a manager may need to allocate further resources. These resources can be people, equipment, money, etc. In the *Unit Market Share KPI* example in Figure 5-1, the resource used was funding for technology investments and advertising. Other resources may also be allocated.

There may be a delay before those resources can be acquired: this is the *Resource Lead Time*. A further delay, called the *Resource Lag Time*, may occur before these resources can take effect, once acquired and allocated to address the problem. Finally a *Resource Safety Factor* may be required. The sum of these enables the Decision Early Warning Period to be calculated.

When it is seen that the trend will cross into unacceptable performance within the early warning period, the manager responsible for that performance measure should immediately be notified so that an early decision can be made to correct the trend.

Most performance measures are represented by a Decision Early Warning graph. At first glance, it would appear that each graph must be derived by a unique DEW system designed specifically for that measure. We will later see in this chapter that instead, a single generic DEW system can be developed for a data warehouse or an Enterprise Portal that provides DEW graphs for many different performance measures. We will see that—instead of a large organization-wide Enterprise Portal containing each and every periodic performance measure, indexed by time period and by other dimensions—a simpler approach can be used to achieve the same result.

DEW concepts directly complement Enterprise Portal capabilities by using direct output from existing systems. For example, an operational system can produce output values that represent actual performance results for a period. Once processed and delivered to managers, who are the intended users, these results are often unavailable also to other managers or users. An Enterprise Portal allows this processing to provide early warning for decisions that may also need to be made by others.

Decision Early Warning and Enterprise Portals

A wider interest in performance results becomes apparent from strategic business planning goal analysis. We discussed planning statements and relevant performance measures in Chapter 2. These were captured and entered into a CASE tool in Chapter 4, with standard data definitions, details describing data periodicity, and specific data quality attributes. Publication of these data details in a repository, such as Visible

Advantage in Chapter 4, makes these facts available to authorized managers or staff on an organization-wide basis.

The value of an Enterprise Portal is great, but consider the increased value added by cross-indexing formerly non-integrated data. Some of this is structured data in legacy files or relational databases. But as we discussed in Chapter 1, most organizations find that over 90 percent of their knowledge resource exists in text documents, in graphics or images, or in audio or video formats. While data warehouses focus on structured data, Enterprise Portals also include this greater unstructured data component.

In fact, the true value of Enterprise Portal comes from identifying factual relationships that were not previously available because the data was not integrated. These relationships can provide breakthroughs of business insight. They provide some of the motivation behind data mining and related topics.

Let us continue the example begun in the previous section. Somewhere in XYZ is a legacy system, such as the *Product Marketing System*, that produces the outputs: "pricing by market" and "pricing by product" on a periodic basis. Other legacy systems, such as the *Market Survey System* and *Market Analysis System*, produce "actual market share" and "actual market size," also periodically. Outputs from these legacy systems can be used to populate the Enterprise Portal.

For example, the operational *Customer Product Sales Analysis System* may add sales results to the Enterprise Portal on a daily basis while the *Product Marketing System, Market Survey System*, and the *Market Analysis System* results are added monthly. When metadata describing this data is published in the Enterprise Portal repository, and the actual results are periodically added to the EP, managers and their staff are able to access, integrate, and compare product and market data outputs.

If the organization determines a regular requirement for access to this type of integrated information, it can encode period-based conversion rules that are processed when the data is retrieved. This enforces organization-wide data and integration standards, increasing the accessibility of the organizational data assets.

Defining Decision Early Warning Metadata

In order to develop a DEW system, it is necessary to identify specific information that will be the focus of Enterprise Portal use analysis. To

Figure 5-3
Decision Early Warning Data Model.

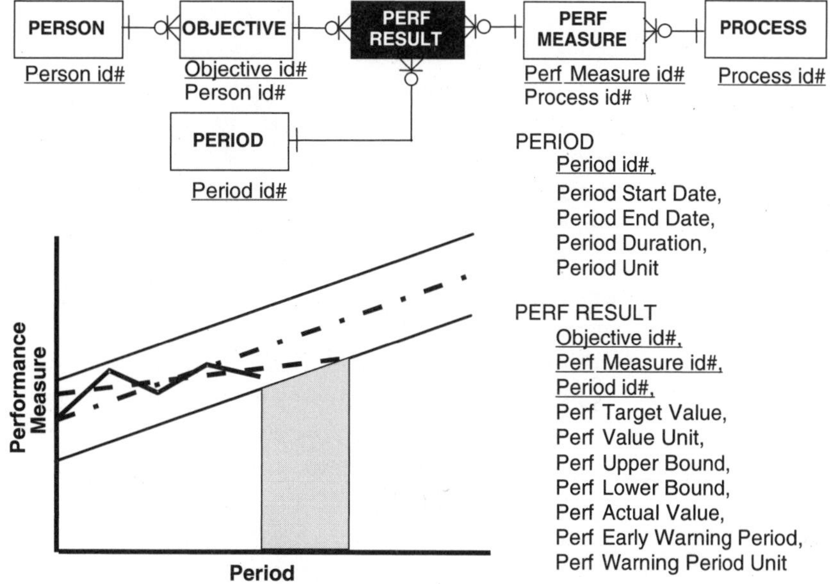

facilitate data integration, these requirements are generally specified using data models, such as in Figure 5-3. This is metadata that documents the facts and business rules that must be represented to satisfy user information needs.

In this example, an actual performance result (PERF RESULT) is specified in the data model of Figure 5-3. This data model shows that a PERSON (such as a manager) will be responsible for *one or many* objectives. An OBJECTIVE will have *one or many* performance measures (PERF MEASURE); while a PERF MEASURE can support many objectives. This *many-to-many* association between OBJECTIVE and PERF MEASURE is resolved by PERF RESULT, which records the actual result of the performance measure within a specific period. A PERF MEASURE is associated with a PROCESS that is carried out to derive the PERF RESULT. This PROCESS can be manual or automated, and is used to derive many performance results.

Figure 5-3 is a generic data map for any performance measure. It shows that each PERF RESULT is dependent on an OBJECTIVE (*objective id#*), a PERF MEASURE (*perf measure id#*) and a PERIOD (*period id#*). *Perf upper bound* and *perf lower bound* monitor performance within upper and lower boundaries, while *perf target value* and *perf value unit* indicate the target result to be achieved for a period. Execution of the related PROCESS (*process id#*) for the PERF MEASURE calculates the *perf actual value*. The trend line for *perf actual value*, calculated over several periods, can then be evaluated against the *perf early warning period*, expressed in *perf warning period unit*.

We discussed in Chapter 4 that we would defer until this chapter any discussion of the entity PERIOD, used for recording time. PERIOD uses the primary key *period id#*. This is a system-generated key that is automatically used to uniquely identify each time period. PERIOD is defined with non-key attributes of *period start date* and *period end date*. The *period duration* is calculated as their difference, expressed in units of *period unit*. However, PERIOD can be used more powerfully than this. For example, rather than calculate period duration—given any two values, the third value can be derived. This introduces an automatic event triggering capability that demonstrates a key benefit of using PERIOD to record time.

Given a *period start date* and *period duration*, the *period end date* can be calculated. This event triggers execution of the relevant PROCESS, which calculates the *perf actual value* for that period. This value is compared with the upper and lower bounds, as discussed above for exception reporting. The trend line is recalculated and compared to the *perf early warning period*. The next period automatically begins and runs for the defined period duration. The end of that period then triggers the following cycle . . . and so on.

Using Decision Early Warning Graphs

Figure 5-3 is a generic data model for any performance measure, but it also enables us to provide automatic performance monitoring within defined boundaries. For example, as a doctor places sensors on the skin of a patient and monitors heart performance with an ECG, so performance measures are "sensors" that allow managers to monitor corporate performance within defined boundaries. And as these sensors can be left in place by doctors for continuous monitoring of a patient in intensive care, so also these performance sensors can continuously monitor corporate performance in critical areas.

A pilot of an airliner submits a flight plan for travel between two cities. This flight plan is also fed into the automatic pilot, which can fly the plane unaided. It only notifies the pilot on an exception basis, or when an unacceptable performance trend is detected. An exception report can be given immediately the plane starts flying through a storm. But typically, early warning by radar is given several minutes before the storm is reached—so that the pilot can take over control from the automatic pilot and decide on an alternative course.

A manager can use a DEW graph to avoid corporate "storms." The manager defines upper and lower boundaries, and target values, for a performance measure over several future periods. For example, spreadsheet target sales (in Figure 2-11) can define unit sales targets for future periods of a *Unit Market Share KPI DEW* graph, similar to Figure 5-2. Upper and lower boundaries that may be acceptable for unit sales can also be defined for each future period. The *period duration* in Figure 5-3 specifies the frequency of performance monitoring, while *perf early warning period* controls early notification based on trend line analysis. This duration is expressed in units based on the *period unit*.

There are many types of periods relevant for performance monitoring. For example, a duration that is expressed in units of years, quarters, months, or weeks may be appropriate for financial or sales performance monitoring based on Accounting Periods. A duration expressed also in days, hours, or minutes may apply to Reporting Periods. And Performance Periods may require still closer monitoring in seconds, milliseconds—or even less, when real-time process control performance is measured.

Once started for a period, the DEW graph automatically monitors performance. It immediately reports to the manager on an exception basis if actual performance falls outside the defined boundaries. It notifies the manager automatically, if a trend line will cross into unacceptable performance within the *perf early warning period*.

It functions as an automatic pilot for the organization, monitoring performance unaided. A manager is only notified if an unacceptable performance trend is detected and a decision needs to be made. These corporate performance sensors can be left in place for those critical areas in an organization that show a need for close and frequent observation while they are in "intensive care."

A trend towards unacceptable future performance may require a change in the allocation of resources. Or it may trigger an assessment of other performance measures, based on more detailed controls at a lower organizational level. There may be other factors at those levels that could have resulted in the poor performance. Or there may be short-term actions that can be taken to correct this performance.

For example, a focused advertising campaign, together with customer purchase incentives and changes in sales commission, may be used to achieve a rapid increase in unit sales for specific products to correct an unacceptable sales performance trend. The manager is given sufficient warning to identify possible causes of the trend, and so can better determine the most effective correction action. This leads to proactive management action, using allocated resources to fine-tune progress over time towards larger defined targets or goals.

Metadata for Generic Decision Early Warning

We have now extended the DEW data map further in Figure 5-4 to provide a complete Generic Decision Early Warning data map. This also includes in the data model specific entities that record metadata. In this form, it can be used to define any current or future performance measures for DEW performance monitoring, with only a minimal amount of programming as discussed below.

In Figure 5-4, DATABASE contains the name of every database in the data warehouse or Enterprise Portal. A database has many tables within it; TABLE is used to contain the name of every table in each separate database. A table has many columns; COLUMN contains the name of each column of interest within a table. These columns typically represent derived data attributes that are performance measures.

A column has many rows; ROW represents each data value for the column. There can be millions of rows, representing millions of data values. These values are the source data used by the PROCESS to calculate the *perf actual value* for the PERF RESULT in each period, based on the

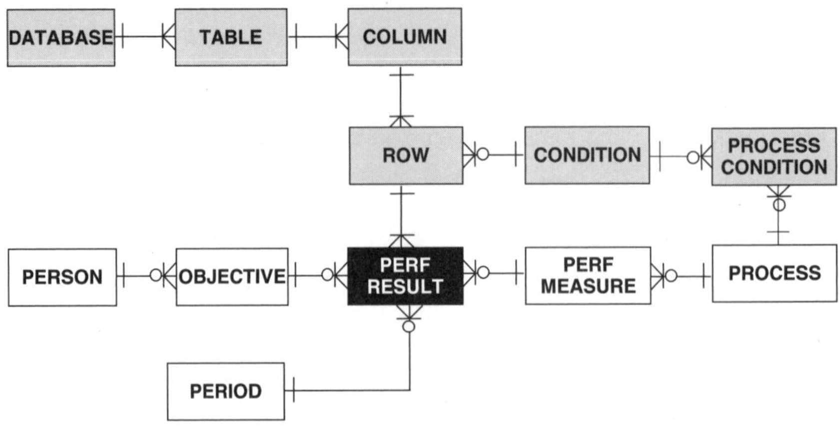

Figure 5-4 Complete Generic Decision Early Warning Data Map.

defined derivation formula for the derived attribute that represents the specific PERF MEASURE.

Not all data values may be relevant for the PERF MEASURE. Those that apply are defined by conditions that filter out relevant values. CONDITION contains the business rules or logic so relevant rows can be selected. For example, it can contain SQL WHERE clauses of a SELECT query to extract relevant data values. The data values that satisfy the relevant condition become the source data to be used as input to the specific PROCESS for the PERF MEASURE.

Figure 5-4 thus provides a capability for any performance measure to be added easily for automatic performance monitoring, with only a minimal amount of programming required. For a new PERF MEASURE to be added, the relevant DATABASE and TABLE in that database is selected first. The COLUMN in the table that represents the performance measure is then selected.

The PROCESS that is used to calculate data values in ROWS for the column is next defined; this typically is derived from data in other columns in the same or different tables. The PROCESS may have to be programmed if the column has not been previously used as a performance measure. Any programming language that can be automatically invoked can be used. The relevant PROCESS contains the name and location of the program or object-oriented (O-O) method written for the process, as well as other information needed to automatically invoke that executable process.

The CONDITION that is to be used to filter relevant data values from ROWS of the column is defined; this is written in a format acceptable to the process. For example, if the process is a query in SQL, the condition is written as a WHERE clause to be automatically executed as part of an embedded SQL SELECT statement.

Once the new performance measure has been defined to the DEW system as described above, it can now be used for automatic performance monitoring. For each future period the values of PERF RESULT are defined, as shown in Figure 5-3. These values may increase or decrease over different periods as shown in that figure. The *period start date, period duration*, and *period unit* are defined to control initiation and duration of each period. The *period end date* is calculated to terminate each period and start the next period.

On termination of a period, the PROCESS for the PERF MEASURE is also triggered. The program or O-O method for that PROCESS is then automatically invoked. This uses the related CONDITION to determine the ROWS that are to be used as source data for the process. The result of this, processing is a value that becomes the *perf actual value* in PERF RESULT for the specific period.

This actual value is compared against the upper and lower bounds as described earlier. The manager (identified by PERSON) is automatically notified on an exception basis if the result is outside bounds. The actual value is also used for trend calculations—as also described, the trend line is examined for that period. The manager is automatically notified on an early warning basis if the trend line will cross into unacceptable performance within the defined early warning period. The result is automatic performance monitoring—like an automatic pilot—notifying the responsible manager only if a decision is required, and providing information so that a correct decision can be made, early.

It is appropriate now for us to discuss how such a DEW system for automatic performance monitoring can be implemented. This is the subject of the next section.

Engineering Enterprise Portals Framework

DEFINITIONS

framework n.

1. A structure for supporting or enclosing something else, especially a skeletal support used as the basis for something being constructed.
2. An external work platform; a scaffold.
3. A fundamental structure, as for a written work or a system of ideas.

Synonym(s): No synonyms found for framework.

Definition of Framework: (*Source: American Heritage English Dictionary* © 1993 Houghton Mifflin Company).

Frameworks provide guides for assembling physical structures and for conceptual idea organization. Project frameworks help define the boundaries and characteristics of complex or information-intensive projects. Frameworks permit project teams to associate facts and to facilitate project knowledge development. The *EEP Framework* can be used to provide project templates for building and using data warehouses and Enterprise Portals. We will use these framework templates throughout the book. We will introduce the EEP Framework by using it to illustrate implementation of a DEW system.

By creating a project-specific EEP Framework, we can place project activities conceptually in context. Figure 5-5 presents an EEP Framework composed of 16 activities and three project phases: (I) Enterprise Portal Design; (II) Enterprise Portal Development; and (III) Enterprise Portal Deployment. You will notice that these three project phases correspond also to the Parts of this book.

Each activity produces a specific output. Acceptance of the output delivery signals completion of the activity. For example, the first activity in Figure 5-5, "identify user information requirements," results in the output labeled *verified metadata-based specifications*. Each output is designed to ensure that individual activities accomplish specific objectives.

While framework phases and activities are generally implemented sequentially as in any systems development activity, the actual ordering can be project-specific and thus somewhat flexible. There is room for iterative refinement of outputs within and between activities (following Boehm's [1986] familiar spiral model). But we all know that if you work in an environment orderly enough to permit a measured well-considered approach to this process, you can consider yourself lucky! The typical manager, faced with the problem of implementing the first organizational EP, is likely to face confusion.

Nevertheless, the framework in Figure 5-5 can be used as a starting point from which project-specific implementations can be developed. Each phase and activity is described briefly below. We will use the DEW system discussed in this chapter to introduce us to the framework. We will cover aspects of the EEP Framework in more detail in Part 2.

Phase I: Enterprise Portal Design

The first phase is devoted to a series of targeted, focused analyses. These are designed to understand and specify, precisely, the user requirements for information that are currently not met, and could be met by implementing an EP-based solution. We discussed in Chapters 2–4 the strategic business planning, data modeling, and strategic modeling methods that are used during Enterprise Portal Design. Ten activities make up this Phase I. Each is described below.

Figure 5-5
The EEP Framework.

No.	Name	Output
Phase I: Enterprise Portal Design		
1	Identify user information requirements	Verified metadata-based specifications
2	Assess need in light of potential EP solutions	Determination that EP represents a potential solution
3	Requirements verification and detailed legacy system reverse engineering	Metadata-based system requirements and data sources
4	Detailed initial solution design	Detailed description of the solution specification
5	ROI projection assessment	Data and operating parameters defining project ROI
6	Project planning and metrics collection	Project plan
7	Project kickoff	Project charter
8	EP requirements refinement and verification	Verification of the business requirements that the EP is developed to satisfy
9	EP logical design refinement and verification	Verification of a logical design satisfing the requirements verified by activity 8
10	EP physical design	Verification of a physical design satisfying the requirements verified by activity 8
Phase II: Enterprise Portal Development		
11	EP implementation (repeat until complete)	Characterized by implementation cycles
11.1	Previous cycle assessment and cycle planning	Focused plan for next implementation cycle
11.2	Planning of physical EP implementation	Desired EP data structure
11.3	Physical population of EP	Desired EP data
11.4	Test physical implementation	Validated EP data implementation
11.5	Integrate with appropriate EP data structures	Integrated EP data
11.6	Cycle metrics collection	Accessible models and associated information
Phase III: Enterprise Portal Deployment		
12	EP data publication	Users begin to access data
13	EP data use	Verification of data quality
14	EP data use assessment	Assessment of implementation success
15	EP data refinement planning	Future EP framework utilization planning
16	Framework and methodology refinement	Continually improving framework and methodology

Activity 1: Identify User Information Requirements

As with most technology-based solution methods, the framework first focuses on requirements. Strategic, tactical, and operational business plans, discussed in Chapter 2, document the information needed by managers to implement and realize their plans. These statements are used to define data models and metadata for information of interest to management.

Other statements that are descriptions of perceived data quality deficiencies must be translated into metadata specifications. Statements from users such as *we can't track our sales accurately* must be refined into data modeling specifications. In order to increase the precision and accuracy of the requirements specifications, users are taught to express their own requirements using data models. We saw briefly in Chapters 3 and 4 how data modeling is carried out with business users. Other examples will be covered later in the book.

Users work with business analysts to develop data models that describe their requirements. The business analysts read the diagrams in English (or other language) statements back to the users, to verify how accurately the data model expresses their business needs and also corrects the perceived data deficiencies. In this manner the team produces verified, metadata-based specifications. The above complaint may be translated into a metadata-based statement: *Organizationally we need to track product line unit sales results on a periodic basis.*

Activity 2: Assess Need in Light of Potential Enterprise Portal Solutions

Once the requirements have been specified and defined as metadata, they can be examined to assess their suitability for an Enterprise Portal solution. Many metadata specifications are associated with specific outputs from an existing system. Ideally, there is a direct correlation between the outputs of various legacy systems and metadata specifications. If not, transformation into a suitable format must occur and be documented.

The key is to identify the business processes that will benefit from an investment in making historical results (including recent results) more accessible. We saw how this identification can be made, by using strategic modeling as discussed in Chapter 4.

Good candidates for Enterprise Portal solutions are requirements specifications of legacy system outputs for information that does not exist elsewhere in the organization. Thus, the output of activity 2 is an assessment of metadata where an Enterprise Portal is a likely solution. Later chapters address this in considerable detail.

Activity 3: Requirements Verification and Detailed Legacy System Reverse Engineering

Once the decision has been made to attempt an EP-based solution, the project team uses the strategic model and project maps from Chapter 4 for more detailed tactical and operational data modeling. Both user and business analyst problem understanding will have matured as a result of the previous activities. Requirements verification then is an important opportunity to refine the initial solution and ensure that the new understanding still warrants an Enterprise Portal solution.

The refined metadata becomes the focus of a reverse engineering exercise [Aiken 1996]. Project maps and project plans, developed as described in Chapter 4, are also used as the basis for reverse engineering each relevant legacy system as a source of input to the EP. In many of these systems an automated solution may be specified. The quality of the metadata will determine the certainty whereby a solution can be specified, as well as the effectiveness of automation. The output of activity 3 is verified, metadata-based system requirements and identification of legacy data sources that provide the information required. Examples of this activity are provided later, in Part 2.

Activity 4: Detailed Initial Solution Design

Using the sources of information identified during activity 3, a detailed design is developed. For example, the generic decision early warning data model in Figure 5-4 enables entity and attribute metadata specifications to be documented as shown in Figure 5-6. We will use this DEW system example to show how the framework templates are used for implementation.

Almost any CASE tool can be used to generate database schemata from the metadata in Figure 5-6, to install the corresponding database tables of a generic DEW system. Again, almost any development tool or programming language can be used to build this system, once the DEW tables have been generated and installed.

As part of the solution methodology, the DEW system will eventually be tested with data values in various performance measure columns as source data input for each process, to validate that the system provides the required decision early warning capabilities.

Figure 5-6
Entity and Attribute Metadata for the Generic DEW Data Model.

PERIOD
period id#
period start date
period end date
period duration
period unit

PERF RESULT
objective id#
perf measure id#
period id#
perf target value
perf value unit
perf upper bound
perf lower bound
perf actual value
perf early warning period
perf warning period unit

DATABASE
database id#
database name

TABLE
table id#
table name
database id#

COLUMN
column id#
column name
database id#
table id#
process id#

PERSON
person id#
person name

OBJECTIVE
objective id#
objective name
objective description
person id#

PERF MEASURE
perf measure id#
perf measure name
process id#

PROCESS
process id#
process name

CONDITION
condition id#
condition name

PROCESS CONDITION
process id#
condition id#
process condition invocation
process condition program

ROW
row id#
row data value
column id#
table id#
database id#

Of course, this testing cannot be carried out until many of the following activities are completed. At that time, actual data values will be loaded into these DEW tables; that data will then be used to produce the designed DEW graphs as illustrated in Figure 5-2. Alternative scenarios will also be executed to reconfirm user and business analyst perspectives, in order to assess the effectiveness of the designed solution.

Activity 5: ROI Projection Assessment

Data and operating parameters defining project ROI should now be calculated. Some of the questions that should be asked follow, to assess the time and development cost of a DEW system.

- How many system items must be reverse engineered?
- How difficult is the process? For example, how well are the system items documented and understood?
- How much will it cost to reverse engineer each of them?
- What will it cost to buy or build relevant data analysis systems?
- What does the project cost when combining the individual totals?
- What kind of risk is inherent in our predictions?
- Does the ROI indicate that the value of the information provided will be worth this investment?

Our work is simplified here, using the solution methodology to implement the DEW system. In fact, we do not need to reverse engineer any databases to build this system—the metadata is largely defined in Figure 5-6. A DEW system can be used not only to access legacy systems, but also with newly installed systems [Aiken et al 1999]. For example, the process invoked on completion of a period can be a legacy system (a program, or a job comprising a series of programs) whose execution produces the actual value for PERF RESULT in that period as discussed in relation to Figure 5-4.

Put another way, a DEW system can be implemented on a microcomputer, where on completion of each period a command is sent to a mainframe. The mainframe initiates the relevant system, which completes its processing. The result is returned to the microcomputer for assessment against performance bounds and for trend analysis.

Here, the mainframe is being used as a performance monitoring peripheral by the DEW system microcomputer. Trend analysis of historical data—that normally would reside in, and be processed within, the Enterprise Portal—has now been reduced only to the actual value for the performance measure in each historical period. This volume of historical *result* data is typically orders of magnitude less than the historical *source* data. It can typically be stored quite economically within the DEW system microcomputer.

In this example, DEW system implementation is low cost—but it has a high-value ROI potential by providing easy and automatic performance monitoring using existing legacy systems. Such a system has the capability of not only paying for itself, but also generating a profit within a short time period. Part 2 provides guidance for more complex reverse engineering projects.

Activity 6: Project Planning and Metrics Collection

Assuming the ROI projections are favorable, the last preliminary activity is project planning. The detailed design exercise and ROI projection are sources of the project metrics and the projected work levels. Project maps and project plans, developed initially as discussed in Chapter 4 and refined when analysis has progressed into the design phase, are based on substantiated and verified details. The project plan is accompanied by a set of metrics characterizing the work accomplished to date.

Activity 7: Project Kickoff

If the previous activities in the Enterprise Portal Design phase have been completed successfully and satisfy ROI criteria, then Enterprise Portal implementation can begin. Activity 7 therefore becomes the project kick-off.

Activity 8: Enterprise Portal Requirements Refinement and Verification

The first step after assembling the project team is to verify that all have a shared understanding of the metadata-based requirements and design model developed by previous EEP activities. This is typically accomplished using joint modeling sessions. During these sessions business analysts, business experts, end users, and other Enterprise Portal implementation team members perform formal inspection of the requirements using high-resolution, large screen projectors and CASE tool support to verify the entities, attributes, associations, and definitions used to specify the EP requirements. During this activity the requirements are generally specified in terms of "what" data the Enterprise Portal will deliver to the users. In most instances this activity will result in clarification of certain aspects of the situation.

Activity 9: Enterprise Portal Logical Design Refinement and Verification

Once the newly constituted project team has formally verified the requirements, it must then determine the degree of fit between the initial logical Enterprise Portal design and the newly understood requirements models. Attention is then turned to determining "how" the data will be accessed and delivered to the Enterprise Portal users. Generally the support environment described above is also useful for these design activities which are now focused on how the data should be structured in order to deliver on the requirements specified previously. This step is usually much simpler than general system design activities because there are two assumptions that tend to focus Enterprise Portal design: (1) Enterprise Portal solutions are delivered via Internet technologies and (2) Enterprise Portal solutions are delivered using proved data warehousing hardware and software technologies.

Activity 10: Enterprise Portal Physical Design

Once the logical design has been verified and the implementation team has achieved a shared understanding with the business users and project sponsors, the physical design of the Enterprise Portal data structures can begin. This involves development of mapping, transformation, and migration rules for the requisite data items into a structure that is logically normalized to facilitate comprehensive understanding—but usually physically de-normalized to facilitate data delivery performance.

Phase II: Enterprise Portal Development

EP Development is also evolutionary in nature. Cycles implement plans, requirements, and designs developed during the Enterprise Portal Design phase, using project maps and project plans as described in Chapter 4. Cycles are repeated until the results are achieved or (in limited instances) the project is determined infeasible. Cycles are comprised of the activities in Figure 5-7.

EP Development is the focus of Part 2 of this book. We therefore will defer further discussion of these activities until Chapters 6–9. In Chapter 10 we will see examples of the application of these activities in real-life projects.

Phase III : Enterprise Portal Deployment

You will recall from our earlier discussions that the primary value in Enterprise Portal comes when a user is able to create new information

Figure 5-7
Enterprise Portal cycles for progressive implementation.

Activity 11.1:	Previous cycle assessment and cycle planning. Output: *focused plan for next implementation cycle.*
Activity 11.2:	Planning of physical EP implementation. Output: *desired* EP *data structure.*
Activity 11.3:	Physical population of EP. Output: *desired* EP *data.*
Activity 11.4:	Test physical implementation. Output: *validated* EP *data implementation.*
Activity 11.5:	Integrate with appropriate EP data structures. Output: *integrated* EP *data.*
Activity 11.6:	Cycle metrics collection. Output: *accessible models and associated information.*

out of previously non-integrated or disorganized information. We can now see that this is not the initial thrust of use. Instead, the initial focus is on ensuring the system provides the desired ROI. The subsequent focus is on providing the information prescribed in the system metadata, identified and verified during the Enterprise Portal *Design* phase and implemented in the Enterprise Portal *Development* phase. We will now discuss the activities carried out during the Enterprise Portal *Deployment* phase.

Activity 12: Enterprise Portal Data Publication

First, the data warehouse or Enterprise Portal data is published or released to the user community. In some instances, this exercise is trivial, in others very difficult. This activity is a major focus for both data warehouses and Enterprise Portals. We therefore consider a number of deployment alternatives in Part 3.

Activity 13: Enterprise Portal Data Use

At this point the users begin to access the Enterprise Portal. This is the first point where the effectiveness and quality of the Enterprise Portal solution can be assessed in a live environment. Changes or refinements may need to be made as a result of this feedback.

Activity 14: Enterprise Portal Data Use Assessment

EP data use is assessed periodically to gauge the implementation success. Success can be claimed when users recognize the Enterprise Portal as the authoritative source of the data that they need.

Activity 15: Enterprise Portal Data Refinement Planning

Future cycle planning is based on user reaction, discovery of new access, reference or analysis patterns, performance considerations, etc. The framework is typically re-entered in Phase I for this data refinement planning.

After the analysis is complete, the team summarizes and evaluates the metric data gathered periodically during analysis. This evaluation is used to establish and refine organizational productivity data used in planning future data warehouse and Enterprise Portal activity, and in strategically assessing enterprise integration efforts. Examples of summary information metrics collected include:

- the number of data entities analyzed;
- the number of duplicate data entities eliminated;
- the number of shared data entities identified;
- the expected financial benefit (and rationale);
- information describing the overall analysis throughput;
- assessment of the key specialist participation;
- reactions of systems management to the analysis.

The outputs of activity 15 become another set of measurements in the collection of metrics data for enterprise data integration analysis.

Activity 16: Framework and Implementation Refinement

One of the most important analysis closure items is collecting and recording implementation metrics, any refined procedures, tool and model usage data, and operational concepts. The outputs from activity 16 focus on assessing and improving the framework template steps from previous activities, and also improving subsequent implementation. Results and changes are archived to permit subsequent analysis. The nature of EEP analyses and all enterprise integration activities are such that benefits increase in value as they are integrated with each other.

The net worth of the analysis outputs cannot be evaluated immediately. This is because the overall contribution of these outputs towards data administration goals and enterprise integration activities often are apparent only in the context of longer-term reengineering activities. EEP analysis should be periodically reviewed in full hindsight to learn from successes as well as unexpected occurrences or failures. The activity results are improved procedures, data on tool and model usage, and activity template implementation assessment.

Framework Application Example: Where Next?

While use on a number of real-life applications has provided anecdotal data regarding DEW as a focus of Enterprise Portal efforts, practitioners lack guidance from these experiences when desiring to implement their own Enterprise Portals. The EEP Framework and DEW system outlined in this chapter enable organizations to plan, guide the implementation, develop practical expectations for, and assess implementation of initial Enterprise Portal efforts. It also enables organizations to refocus in-progress Enterprise Portal efforts that have become unfocused or have otherwise lost momentum.

DEW graphs are designed to ensure that organizations can navigate in changing performance environments. Adherence to the DEW principles can enable organizations to build flexible solutions guiding the archival and use of operational data. Flexibly archived data permits rapid response to strategic-level environmental changes requiring corresponding performance monitoring system modifications.

DEW systems are well suited for implementation and integration of operational, tactical, and strategic-level data. Data analyzed using DEW concepts can continue to play a valuable role as organizational data assets. It is particularly effective when used to provide organizations with a means of formally linking strategic decision making with information technology support.

The research community will similarly benefit from a framework that provides researchers with a process baseline for Enterprise Portal implementation. The EEP Framework provides a basis for repeatable implementation of Enterprise Portals, a starting point for organizations yet to implement Enterprise Portal, and for others a means of comparing implementation expectations against actual results. The framework is a necessary prerequisite for determining measurable improvement.

We have now reached the end of Part 1. In Part 2 we will use the framework to focus on aspects of Enterprise Portal Development.

REFERENCES

Aiken, P. (1996) *Data Reverse Engineering: Slaying the Legacy Dragon*, McGraw-Hill. [ISBN 0-07-000748-9] 394 pages.

Aiken, P.H, Ngwenyama, O.K. and Broome, L. (1999) "Reverse Engineering New Systems," *IEEE Software*, March/April, 16(2):36–43.

Boehm, B.W. (1986) "A Spiral Model of Software Development and Enhancement," *ACM SIGSOFT Software Engineering Notes* (August), 11(4):14–24.

Demming, E.F. (1986) *Out of the Crisis*, Center for Advanced Engineering Study, Massachusetts Institute of Technology, Cambridge, MA.

ISO (1996) ISO 11179:195–1996, *Information Technology – Specification and Standardization of Data Elements.*

Finkelstein, C. (1989) *An Introduction to Information Engineering*, Sydney, Australia: Addison-Wesley.

Finkelstein, C. (1992) *Information Engineering: Strategic Systems Development*, Sydney, Australia: Addison-Wesley.

Koberg, D. and Bagnall, J. (1991) *The Universal Traveler: A Soft-Systems Guide to Creativity, Problem-Solving & the Process of Reaching Goals*, Crisp Publications. [ISBN: 1560520450]

PART 2

Enterprise Portal Development

CHAPTER 6

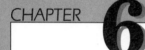

Metadata Analysis Dimensions

Knowledge is the small part of ignorance that we arrange and classify
—Ambrose Bierce

Enterprise Portals evolve from Date Warehouses and Data Marts. In Part 1 we focused on identifying the information to be delivered by Data Warehouses and Enterprise Portals. We developed data models and metadata that can be used for Data Warehouse Design as well as Enterprise Portal Design. In Part 2 we will set the scene for Enterprise Portal Development. However, so that we can introduce all of the necessary concepts first, we will first focus in Part 2 on Data Warehouse Development. We will particularly address metadata derived from operational databases and legacy systems by reverse engineering. But we will defer discussion of the final development and deployment of Enterprise Portals until later.

In Part 3, we will learn about XML (in Chapter 11), and see how XML utilizes metadata. We will then learn how XML can be used for business reengineering (Chapter 12) and also for systems reengineering (Chapter 13). The identified metadata from Part 2 will be used to address data quality issues, as we load data into the Data Warehouse (Chapter 14). Finally, in Chapter 15 we will bring all of these concepts together with a discussion of products that enable us to deploy Data Warehouses as Enterprise Portals.

In this chapter we will describe why it is necessary to first develop and analyze metadata in order to accurately engineer a Data Warehouse or an Enterprise Portal. Ignoring metadata analysis is a primary reason for implementation failure. Understanding the various dimensions of metadata analysis will enable you to understand the different types of analysis that can be performed on it. Generally, different Enterprise Portals can require different forms of metadata analysis, so key to the process is understanding the possibilities and selecting appropriate analysis forms.

Just as all systems have an architecture [Zachman 1987] whether they choose to treat it as an organizational asset or not [Spewak 1993], all systems also have an associated metadata engineering practice. For most organizations the term "system metadata" is a familiar phrase. However, many do not manage their metadata using currently available, modern, data engineering techniques. Typically, organizational interest in system metadata engineering has stopped when basic system documentation has been produced. While useful, this is the most primitive type of system metadata engineering.

To improve metadata engineering, organizations must focus on system metadata as an organizational asset, on system metadata engineering as an organizational strength, and on management of metadata assets as an ongoing activity.

The rest of this chapter is organized as follows. We differentiate between system metadata and traditional forms of system information according to metadata breadth; integration; uses/users; and deployment. System metadata integration and analysis are defined as a critical success factor in Engineering Enterprise Portals. The chapter closes by describing system metadata engineering and its value.

Enterprise Portal as Organizational Knowledge Management

EEP is a form of organizational knowledge management that satisfies organizational data requirements with Enterprise Portal-based solutions. This type of knowledge management depends on having access to massive amounts of organizational data in order to combine specific facts in ways that were either impossible or infeasible outside of the Enterprise Portal environment. The EP solution makes the integration of and access to previously unintegrated facts either possible or feasible or both.

Engineering your Enterprise Portal efficiently depends on structuring and implementing organizational knowledge management. You must first understand what organizational data is required to implement your organizational strategy successfully before you can arrange and classify it. For some organizations this task is relatively easy—for others it has been difficult. The task is inherently focused on organizational metadata.

You must develop physical metadata structures that are capable of managing data to help you meet your strategic information needs—this metadata-based approach will ensure that you rapidly develop flexible and adaptable structures that can be immediately useful. Formally specifying your warehouse or Enterprise Portal requirements in a manner that provides your organization with the required strategic, tactical, and operational data will help you develop your Enterprise Portal more quickly and more accurately than unstructured approaches.

What Is Metadata?

We discussed metadata briefly in Chapter 1. The term "metadata" enjoys widespread use but has no apparent formal definition within the research community. It is typically described as "data about data" in a manner that is consistent with ISO description 11179 as *the information and documentation which makes data sets understandable and sharable for users* [ISO 1996]. The prefix *meta-* is derived from definition 4 in Figure 6-1.

Metadata means transcending, being more comprehensive, and existing at a higher state of development than data. If we continue to define data—after Appleton [Appleton 1984]—as a specific combination of a fact and a meaning, then metadata would describe the fact/meaning combinations. Combined, the facts and meanings represent the formally managed organizational knowledge.

For example, data might be used to describe an individual customer. One or more sets of data (or data sets) might comprise the collection of data describing organizational customers. The metadata would be the collection of facts and meanings describing the data contained in the data set(s).

Figure 6-2 shows metadata from an example healthcare management system, describing the organizational concept of BED. Metadata describing the entity BED is composed of:

Figure 6-1
Definition of the prefix *meta-* (Emphasis added. *Source: American Heritage English Dictionary* © 1993 Houghton Mifflin).

meta- or met- pref.

1. a. Later in time: metestrus.
   b. At a later stage of development: metanephros.
2. Situated behind: metacarpus.
3. a. Change; transformation: metachromatism.
   b. Alternation: metagenesis.
4. **a. Beyond; transcending; more comprehensive: metalinguistics.**
   b. At a higher state of development: metazoan.
5. Having undergone metamorphosis: metasomatic.
6. a. Derivative or related chemical substance: metaprotein.
   b. Of or relating to one of three possible isomers of a benzene ring with two attached chemical groups, in which the carbon atoms with

Figure 6-2
A sample data entity and associated metadata.

Entity:	*BED*
Data Asset Type:	Principal Data Entity
Purpose:	This is a substructure within the Room substructure of the Facility Location. It contains information about beds within rooms.
Source:	Maintenance Manual for File and Table Data (Software Version 3.0, Release 3.1)
Attributes:	Bed.Description Bed.Status Bed.Sex.To.Be.Assigned Bed.Reserve.Reason
Associations:	>0-+ Room
Status:	*Validated*

- a purpose statement describing why the organization is maintaining information about bed as a business concept;
- sources of information about it;
- a partial list of the attributes or characteristics of the entity; and
- associations with other related data items; this one is read as "One room contains zero or many beds."

Generally organizations prefer to standardize data and processing. An example is the processing of all customer data with a single set of processes, instead of developing and maintaining many different processes to deal with each different customer type. Organizations can gain similar economies by managing metadata with standard routines. Unfortunately, most organizations don't maintain their metadata formally, much less process it using automated techniques. The need to integrate unintegrated data sets has been a primary motivation for many EEP efforts. System confusion resulting from organizational restructuring and mergers provides additional motivation.

Metadata continues to be a growing business interest and the subject of much systems research. The IEEE in conjunction with the National Oceanic and Aeronautic Administration has sponsored conferences devoted to the subject (whose proceedings have been posted on the Web—see [Griffioen 1996] and [Shklar 1997]) and metadata has been a popular research topic in Europe. (See for example [Lyytinen 1996; Lyytinen 1992; Edwards 1995].) A number of different types of metadata have been identified [Hsu 1994], [Weibel 1997], [Aiken 1999]. When engineering an Enterprise Portal, your initial focus will be on system metadata.

How Does System Metadata Differ from Traditional System Information?

Building on the definition of metadata, *system metadata* is data about a system that transcends, is more comprehensive, and must exist at a higher level of development than traditional system information. While a range of system metadata can be maintained, it usually encompasses at least the organizational structure of the system data. This permits automated processing of the system metadata queries and more easily incorporates other uses of automation.

Consider an example where system information was maintained as a word processing document by one of the organization's technical managers. A file on someone's PC isn't as valuable as an electronically published version that is accessible via an intranet file server. This form of system information management is better than situations that we have observed where key system information is maintained in the heads of the developers. The existence of system information is often unknown in these situations. Figure 6-3 is an email exchange with a colleague attempting to secure some system metadata.

Jeff was attempting to obtain system information documenting how to interpret parts of the organizational log file segments. The log file segments were the primary means of transporting organizational data

Figure 6-3
Email exchanged with Jeff regarding existence and location of some system metadata.

>Hi Peter - John Jeffress and I are looking for data element documentation for the AS/400 files. Do you know of any?
>Thanks,
>jeff
Hi Jeff,
I have a bunch of it but don't know which systems are on the AS/400. Which systems are you specifically looking into? I've posted a copy of one of the data dictionaries on my web pages at:
http://www.isy.vcu.edu/~paiken/home/DPS.ZIP
I'd suggest starting there and seeing if it has what you are looking for. If not, Bruce seems to know lots about the data documentation. Bruce's email is:
Bruce@a.large.retail.organization.com
Will you let me know what you find?
thank you
peter

Figure 6-4
The first few lines of the document named LOGSEG.DOC.

```
Introduction:
=============
IF YOU HAVE ANY CHANGES, CORRECTIONS, AND/OR
RECOMMENDATIONS FOR THE INFO BELOW, PLEASE CONTACT
JANE DOE VIA EMAIL OR AT # 6753.

YOUR INPUT IS SOLICITED.

Following file is designed to document:
   ...
```

between the retail store locations and the central office processing operations. The email exchange led us to a document labeled LOGSEG.DOC. The first few lines of this file are reproduced as Figure 6-4.

Notice how the general tone of the document introduction attempts to pull system information from developers. It requests them to report and describe changes to the log file segment information. The segment concerning customer information is stored in log file segment 2 or SEG02. The content of this segment is described in yet another document DPSLOGEXTSE.LIB shown as Figure 6-5.

Lack of a centralized repository has forced this organization to identify which managers they must turn to in order to obtain the system

Figure 6-5
Log file segment 2 documenting customer system metadata as reported in electronic document DPSLOGEXTSE.LIB.

```
(*************** segment 02 *****************)

seg02_type = packed record
      cust_lname        :  pac12;
      cust_fname        :  pac8;
      cust_m_init       :  pac1;
      cust_area_code    :  pac3;
      cust_exchange     :  pac3;
      cust_branch       :  pac4;
      cust_address      :  pac26;
      cust_city         :  pac16;
      cust_state        :  pac2;
      cust_zip          :  pac9;
      apt_po_box        :  pac8;
      company_name      :  pac26;
      tax_exempt_nbr    :  pac12;
      filler            :  pac2;
      end;
```

information. This situation resulted in a spiral—knowing that the metadata resources do not exist, the developers do not demand access to them. Organizational use/knowledge of system metadata was poor and developers use of it, low.

System metadata management involves management of system information that exceeds traditional system information in terms of system metadata: breadth; integration; uses/users; and deployment. Each is described in separate sections below.

System Metadata Breadth

System metadata engineering is more encompassing than traditional forms of system information. There are a number of system metadata types. Consider just one dimension:

- *Component* metadata describes various parts comprising the system (system components can include code, files, screens, interfaces, printouts, inputs, outputs, etc.);
- *Process* metadata describes system components structured into processes to support its mission;
- *User* metadata describes the consumers of system outputs in terms of their interaction with system components and users; and
- *Data* metadata describes system data as it is produced and consumed by system components, users, processes, etc.

Other combinations and metadata types are possible. Some of these have relatively narrow domain values. For example, data use is typically restricted to: *create*, *read*, *update*, *delete*, or *archive*.

Traditional system information describing files and panels might exist as a physical list of the attributes comprising the physical file in Figure 6-5 and another list (not integrated or otherwise connected) indicating attributes appearing on each display panel. A system metadata-engineering product would be given access to the set of facts documenting attribute appearances on display screens. System metadata would integrate the two lists, permitting a user to see all uses of a given attribute while browsing or querying system metadata. Another system metadata product might support interactive linking of system components, structured into system requirements. Technically accurate and complete metadata facilitates system understanding and metadata sharing among system users as well as metamodel-based sharing between systems.

System Metadata Integration

System metadata integration should be high; most useful individual metadata are related formally using organizationally standard meanings. System metadata integration is illustrated in Figure 6-6 which presents six possible system metadata relationships. It illustrates the existence of relationships between the previously described component, data, user, and process system metadata types.

The six individual relations in Figure 6-6 illustrate the existence of relationships between each metadata type.

R1 process and zero, one, or many users and each user is related to zero, one, or many processes;

R2 datum and zero, one, or many users and each user is related to zero, one, or many data;

R3 process and zero, one, or many data and each datum is related to zero, one, or many processes;

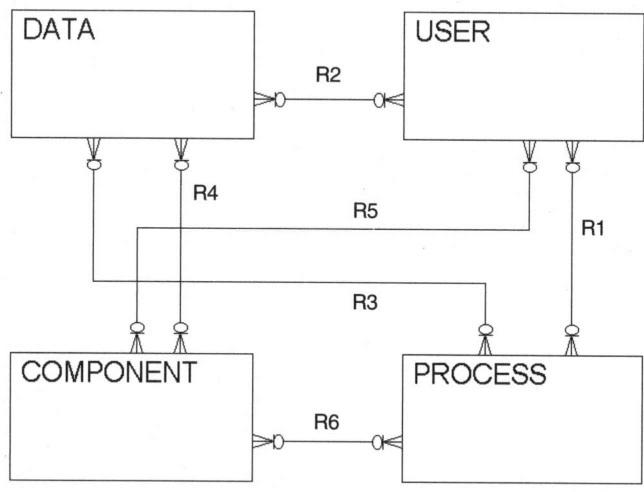

Figure 6-6 Illustration of the system metadata integration.

R4 datum and zero, one, or many components and each component is related to zero, one, or many data;

R5 components and zero, one, or many users and each user is related to zero, one, or many components; and

R6 process and zero, one, or many components and each component is related to zero, one, or many processes.

Metadata is most effectively managed using metamodels. Figure 6-6 illustrates the system metadata represented as a system metamodel. Metamodels are used to maintain and integrate metadata types. A system metamodel is a collection of metadata describing a system as an interrelated collection of system parts. The metamodel's focus is on describing the system architecture. As you might expect, system metamodels transcend non-metadata system descriptions. They are more comprehensive and exist at a higher state of development.

System metamodels are structurally stable, able to be queried programmatically, and are represented using relatively standard format. System metadata integration also permits programmatic control over the physical data using logical data manipulation such as SQL, graphical browsers, object manipulation techniques, etc. Increased metamodel scope and comprehensiveness results in increased metadata usefulness.

Figure 6-7 illustrates several other possible system metadata relationships describing data relationships between three system components: printouts; screens; and file elements. Integrated system metadata might report that screen element SE(Y) is the only panel attribute in the entire system where file element FE(X) is updatable by users or still further that screen element SE(Y), via FE(X), is used to create printout elements PE(L, M, N).

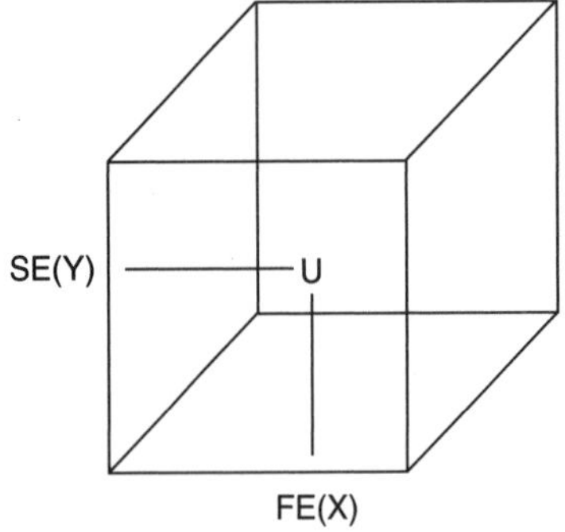

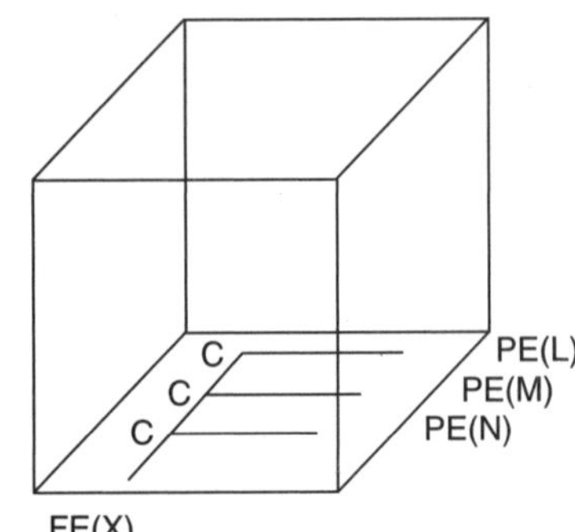

Figure 6-7 Sample representations of system metadata maintainable conceptually as a multidimensional metadata cube.

Figure 6-8
An example showing how metadata output can be used to report the destination and code-based origin of screen element (255).

Printout Element		Use	Screen Element		Code Element
PE(43)					
PE(44)		create			
PE(45)		read			
PE(46)	is used for	*update* by	SE(255)	Produced by	CE(1232)
PE(47)		delete	SE(434)		
PE(48)			SE(756)		
PE(49)			SE(1056)		
PE(50)					

Another example of integrated system metadata is shown in Figure 6-8. It illustrates integrated system metadata which might be queried to answer specific questions such as what screen elements can update printout element (PE) number 46? The example shows how the metadata reports that PE-46 can be updated by four screen elements. A metadata query might ask: "What code element produces screen element (255) and as what printout element does it appear?"

Metadata describing given system data can be considered as a multidimensional data source. This form of integrated system metadata engineering permits system developers and users to determine that information input-based system component NEW.ADDRESS is used to update file-based system seg02-based design object CUST_ADDRESS. Additional system metadata would also contain information such as the source of the input and the file(s) where CUST_ADDRESS is stored.

Another example of system metadata use would be the ability to quickly obtain the information that the three properties CUST_AREA_CODE; CUST_EXCHANGE; and CUST_BRANCH comprised a three-part compound key and that this key forms at least part of the key for 16 master files.

System Metadata Deployment

Contrast the previous description of a rather traditional approach to system metadata deployment with the integrated functionality illustrated by Figure 6-9.

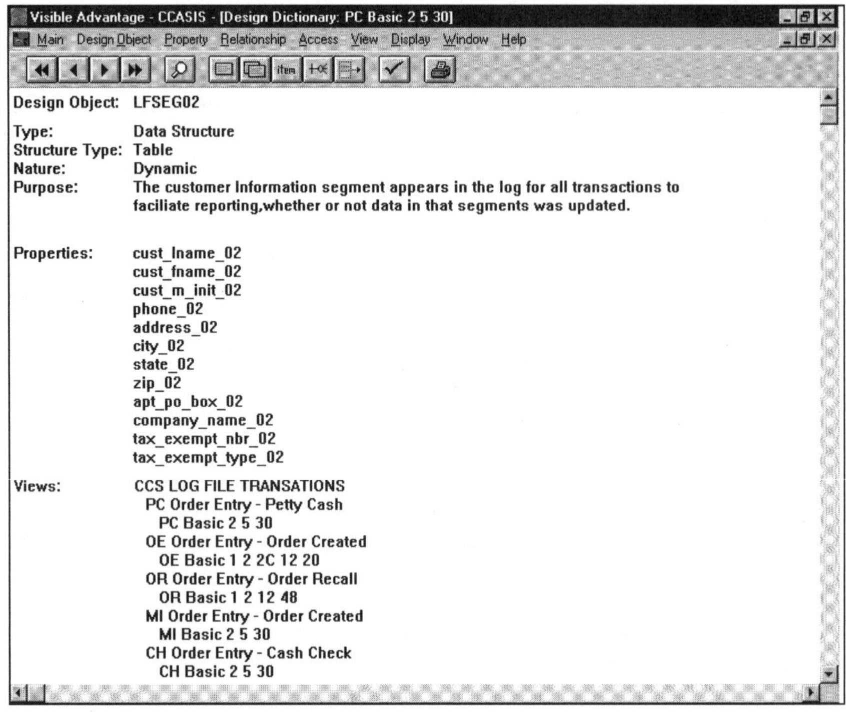

Figure 6-9 Hyperlinked CASE tool-based system metadata engineering. (*Source*: Screen snapshot from Visible Advantage)

Some advantages of this form of metadata engineering over previous approaches include:

- double clicking on the design object accesses the organizationally standard design object definition,
- double clicking on each of the design object properties also provides an organizational standard definition,
- additional navigational techniques will lead to any subsequent uses of each property in other design objects (such as foreign keys, etc.) as well as the data object's use in various system components, and
- all of the metadata items described above are managed using relational database technologies and are accessible via standard SQL queries.

High volume metadata typically requires implementation using commercial tool kits including online browsing capabilities; a central repository; interactive graphical analysis tools; and distribution via server or LAN/intranets. In order to permit storage and use of metadata in its most flexible and adaptable format, metamodels are typically implemented using relational database management technologies and as a result, metadata can be maintained as an electronic living document/project data repository. From data engineering, we also understand how:

- different combinations of facts can satisfy diverse user needs (for example, contrast operational data uses with warehouse data uses);
- to effectively share the commonly understood metadata within organizations and with business partners;
- systems tend to evolve at a rate that is faster than traditional documentation;
- these conditions dictate that metadata must be managed as a "living document" with easy access to shared, reconfigurable metadata.

This changes the focus on the contents from "getting it right" at data entry time to a different metadata engineering mindset involving iterative evolution of a continually improving solution.

An additional benefit of this approach is that the integrated metadata is maintained in its most flexible and adaptable format. Normalized metadata further ensures its utility during subsequent project activities, providing system developers, implementers, and users with programmatic analysis and interactive query access to comprehensive system descriptions. Maintained at a high level of granularity, metadata is variously combined to respond to user needs. Many different query types can be run against the normalized metadata, permitting metadata use outside data engineering contexts and in response to unforeseen uses.

System Metadata Uses/Users

Metadata users desire metadata access at workstations when working individually and with high-resolution projection capabilities when working with groups. They want to manipulate and analyze the metadata, to aid when performing their respective analysis and implementation tasks. System metadata should be developed to be used interactively, supporting real-time fact capture, organization, structuring, and presentation functions. It supports system development and maintenance activities [Aiken 1991] and as such it is available to business as well as technical users.

System information is developed to support development staff as they create or maintain system components. System metadata are sometimes produced as by-products of other activities. Key to effective metadata engineering is to satisfy differing user information needs with a core set of metadata. Metadata engineering can personalize and make more effective the communication about system issues between diverse metadata users who use it as a means of achieving shared understanding. System metadata users encompass a broader range of system personnel including system contractors; developers; architects; managers; and end users. Metadata users interactively query the system metamodel when exploring and analyzing system components and considering changes and implementing system components. The metadata engineering provides integrated understanding of the system so that future analyses can include factual information. Organizational development staff members become more valuable and valued as their familiarity with the metadata development and its use increases. This will result in higher technical competencies and increased productivity. In addition, it increases the relative worth of metadata users and the organization as a whole. Figure 6-10 differentiates among various system metadata users and their use of system metadata.

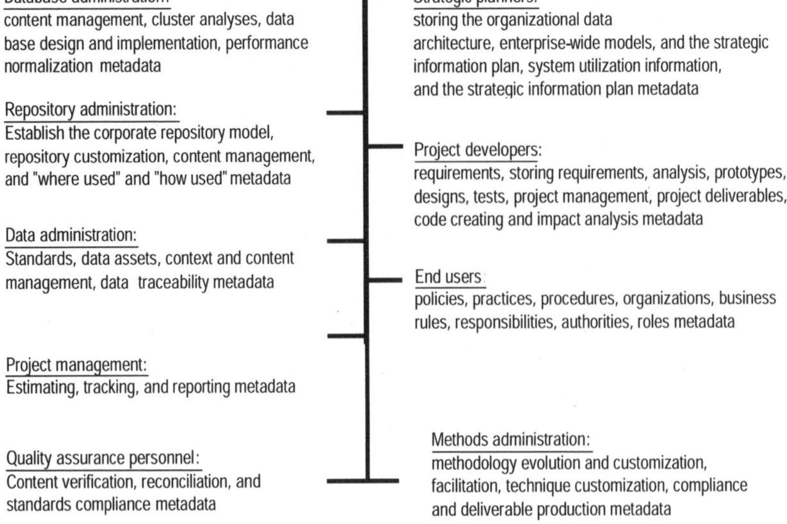
Database administration:
content management, cluster analyses, data base design and implementation, performance normalization metadata
Repository administration:
Establish the corporate repository model, repository customization, content management, and "where used" and "how used" metadata
Data administration:
Standards, data assets, context and content management, data traceability metadata
Project management:
Estimating, tracking, and reporting metadata
Quality assurance personnel:
Content verification, reconciliation, and standards compliance metadata
Strategic planners:
storing the organizational data architecture, enterprise-wide models, and the strategic information plan, system utilization information, and the strategic information plan metadata
Project developers:
requirements, storing requirements, analysis, prototypes, designs, tests, project management, project deliverables, code creating and impact analysis metadata
End users
policies, practices, procedures, organizations, business rules, responsibilities, authorities, roles metadata
Methods administration:
methodology evolution and customization, facilitation, technique customization, compliance and deliverable production metadata

Figure 6-10 System metadata uses/users (adapted from [Selkow 1990]).

Metadata use also range along a continuum from:

- relatively structured (use of metadata by new hires and interns to become more familiar with the system), to
- moderately structured (routine use by technical systems personnel to plan fix/enhancements), to
- unstructured (experienced developers and data analysts when considering strategic uses of organizational data assets).

The metadata uses correlate, ranging from relatively structured (programming-based system maintenance and enhancement) to unstructured (how to make the system Y2K analyses most efficient and effective).

System Metadata Engineering

Recall our modern definition of engineering from Chapter 1 as "elements of the arts and sciences used to make the mechanical properties of matter more useful as systems." Systems metadata engineering can be defined as the development and implementation of complex data products used to formally manage system facts that are useful to several types of system metadata users as they develop, manage, and evolve systems—in this case, data warehouses or Enterprise Portals.

System metadata engineering is the means of formally supporting the extraction of the metadata into a data management system and using the resulting repository capabilities to inform subsequent activities. System metadata engineering is the structured technique that is used to define, create, and maintain system metadata using system metamodels.

System metadata engineering is not a new technique but instead a formalization of the system fact management practices. Organizational implementation of formalized metadata engineering increases with organizational knowledge/abilities and situation dictates.

Organizations invest in system metadata to manage and maintain their systems more effectively. Metadata engineering results in system metadata specifications that satisfy metadata user requirements, typically providing access to requested metadata in a fashion supporting the rapid cognitive momentum required of these analysts [Woods 1984].

Metadata engineering benefits from the same sort of techniques that data engineers use when organizing and structuring business information to understand and meet the requirements of a given business function. The same enterprise integration principles that are used to manage data can be applied to system metadata. Metadata engineering can also benefit from leverage achieved by understanding a relatively large amount of information by modeling and managing a relatively small amount of metadata.

Developing and maintaining system metadata engineering practices represents a significant organizational accomplishment. As organizations become more proficient at system metadata engineering, the utility and ease of developing and maintaining the system metamodels will increase.

In this chapter we have described system metadata engineering as key to successful data warehouse and Enterprise Portal development. Figure 6-11 illustrates that the EEP methodology includes two dimensions of system metadata development. Do all situations call for application of a complete EEP cycle and management of the entire range of system metadata types? The answer is no.

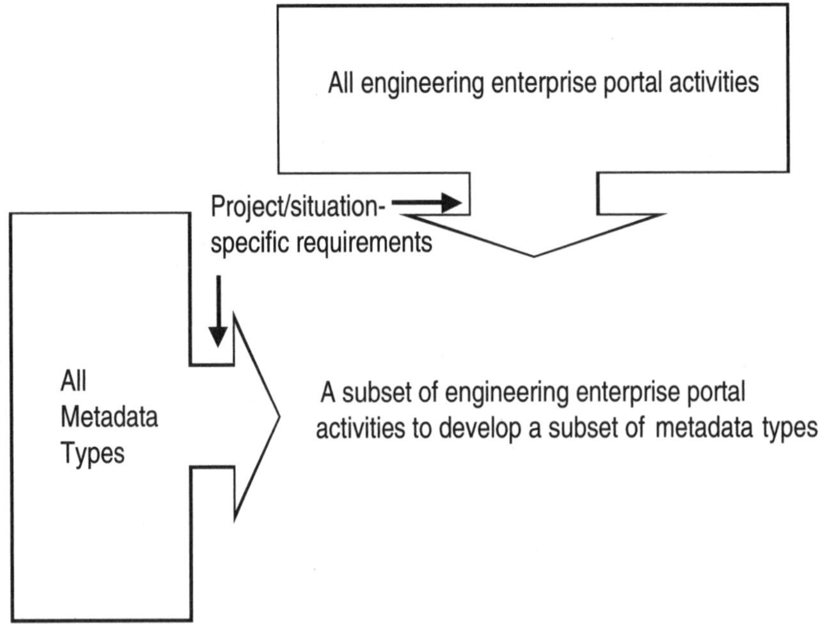

Figure 6-11 Not all metadata types and metadata engineering activities are required for engineering enterprise portals—the question is which ones are required for your project?

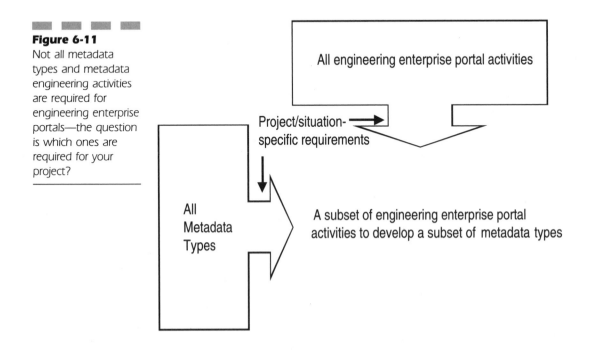

However, unless you understand the range of EEP activities and system metadata types, it is not possible to focus your efforts on those metadata engineering activities and metadata types required to help you develop an Enterprise Portal. Because different situations dictate different system metadata type usage and EEP activities, the key to effective and efficient EEP is determining what specific combination of EEP activities and system metadata types are required to engineer your Enterprise Portal.

Chapter 7 describes EEP activities in the context of the EEP activity cycle. Understanding cycle activities will help you determine which are required for your organizational Enterprise Portal effort. Chapter 8 is a detailed description of a range of system metadata types so that you can determine which subset is relevant for your Enterprise Portal effort.

REFERENCES

Aiken, P.H. (1991) "Hypermedia-based Requirements Engineering," in *Advanced Technology for Command and Control Systems Engineering*, S. J. Andriole, Reston, VA: AFCEA International.

Aiken, P.H., Ngwenyama, O.K. and Broome, L. (1999) "Reverse Engineering New Systems for Smooth Implementation," *IEEE Software,* March/April, 16(2):36–43.

Appleton, D. (1984) "Business Rules: The Missing Link," *Datamation* (October) 16(30): 145–150.

Boar, B., "Understanding Data Warehousing Strategically." White paper commissioned by NCR's Communication Industry Line of Business — posted on the WWW at: http://warehouse.chime-net.org/manage/stplan/bboar1.htm

Edwards, H. (1995) *The RECAST Method for Reverse Engineering,* Cambridge, MA: The Government Centre for Information Systems, Blackwell Publishers.

Griffioen, J., Yavatkar, R., *et al.* (1996) *Proceedings of the First IEEE Metadata Conference*, First IEEE Metadata Conference, NOAA Auditorium, NOAA Complex Silver Spring Metro Center 1301 East-West Highway, Silver Spring, Maryland, IEEE Publications Office, http://www.computer.org/conferen/meta96/meta_home.html

ISO (1996) ISO 11179:195 *Information Technology—Specification and Standardization of Data Elements*, Washington, DC: International Standards Organization.

Lyytinen, K. and Tahvanainen, V. (1992) *Studies in Computer and Communications Systems Volume 3: Next Generation CASE Tools*, Amsterdam: IOS Press.

Lyytinen, K. (1996) *The MetaPHOR Project - Metamodeling: Principles, Hypertext, Objects and Repositories.*

Selkow, W. (1990) "Strategic Information Planning: A New Framework," *Enterprise Systems Journal*.

Shklar, L., Au, E., *et al.*, (1997) *Proceedings of the Second IEEE Metadata Conference*, Second IEEE Metadata Conference, NOAA Auditorium, NOAA Complex Silver Spring Metro Center 1301 East-West Highway, Silver Spring, Maryland, IEEE Publications Office, http://www.computer.org/conferen/proceed/meta97/ http://www.llnl.gov/liv_comp/metadata/md99/md99.html

Spewak. S.H. (1993) *Enterprise Architecture Planning*, Boston, MA: QED Publishing.

Woods, D.D. (1984) "Visual Momentum: A Concept to Improve the Cognitive Coupling of Person and Computer," *International Journal of Man-Machine Studies*, 21: 229–244.

Zachman, J. (1987) "A Framework for Information Systems Architecture," *IBM Systems Journal*, 26(3): 276–292.

CHAPTER 7

Metadata Engineering Activities

All that is valuable in human society depends upon the opportunity for development accorded the individual.
—Albert Einstein

After describing the symbiotic relationship between system metadata engineering activities and reverse engineering, Chapter 7 describes the Enterprise Information Portal engineering activities and activity combinations that make up an EEP development activity cycle. We close the chapter by describing the conceptual to metadata conversion required to express organizational strategies as metadata and the physical to metadata conversion required to express legacy system information as metadata.

Enterprise Portal Engineering and Reverse Engineering

Your legacy systems are likely to be the source of major portions of the information maintained by your Enterprise Portal. In instances where your legacy system metadata isn't as useful as it could be, you may perform targeted reverse engineering analyses on your legacy systems in order to recover the system metadata. It is rare that data warehouses or Enterprise Portals exist without associated legacy systems.

All systems can be described as consisting of subsets of basic system components such as: hardware, software, people, procedures, and data. These components, in turn, are composed of elements. Thus, systems are composed of one or more components and each component is composed of one or more elements.

Legacy systems are often complex, developed using unarchitected metadata, a correspondingly large number of relationships between components, and little programmatic support. Legacy systems often contain thousands of elements that are related, with a correspondingly large number of relationships. With thousands of system elements relating to thousands of other elements, the process of mapping all of the elements to all other elements can appear quite daunting. Manually documenting and maintaining these relationships can require considerable resources. This system metadata can be difficult to maintain manually.

In this context, reverse engineering is concerned with effectively and efficiently making sense of and organizing legacy system metadata in coordination with EEP activities. Reverse engineering is the application of structured techniques to reconstitute the assets of a legacy system in situations where the system metadata doesn't exist; has deteriorated; or has become confused. Reverse engineering has broad technological application—such as evaluating CASE tools, developing client/server system architectures, year 2000 analysis, and enhancing system maintenance [Aiken 1996]. However, we will describe how reverse engineering and Enterprise Portal engineering are symbiotically linked.

Typically, system metadata is programmatically unavailable or disorganized before a reverse engineering analysis. Most of the EEP activities are complementary activities to reverse engineering. Reverse engineering is accomplished by identifying interrelated system data components and creating representations of them in another form or at a higher level of abstraction. Programmatically unavailable or disorganized system metadata is derived, extracted, understood, and used by subsequent EEP activities. The reverse engineering outputs are metamodels describing the system implementation, design, or requirements. Reverse engineering produces outputs for EEP. System metadata engineering is concerned with managing this repository of system metadata. The repository is in reality itself a data warehouse or Enterprise Portal for system metadata.

Enterprise Portal Development Phase Activities

Chapter 5 discussed the EEP Framework. Phase II addresses Enterprise Portal Development. Within Phase II, there are two subphases. These address Metadata Engineering (ME) and Metadata Implementation (MI). We will focus initially on Metadata Engineering.

Metadata Engineering activities are developed for capturing, organizing, structuring, and presenting system metadata in anticipation of their use during subsequent EEP activities. It is possible to develop a data warehouse or EP as a comprehensive set of activities, beginning at one point and proceeding through the entire Enterprise Portal Development activity cycle. While favored by some consulting practices, this approach is usually unnecessary. Enterprise Portal Development activities are driven by specific EP-based information requirements. Figure 7-1 illustrates the Enterprise Portal metadata engineering activity cycle.

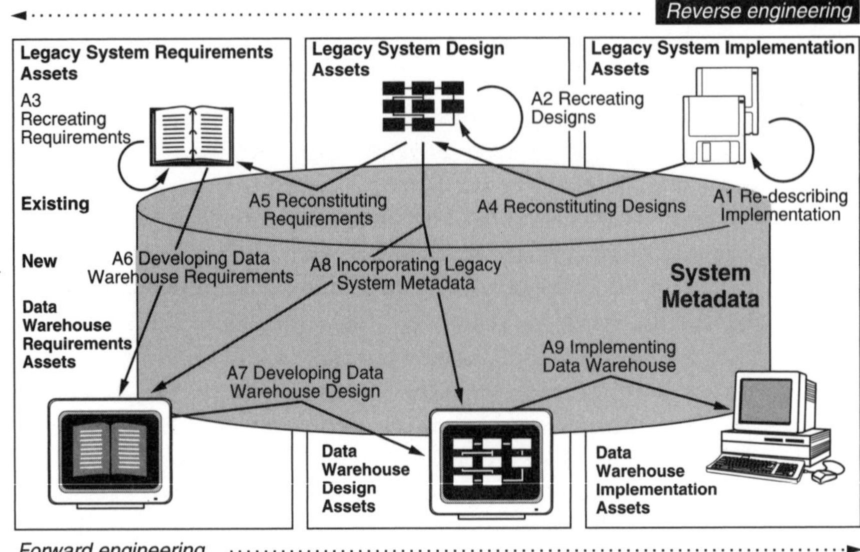

Figure 7-1 Enterprise Portal Metadata engineering activities illustrating their range and general flow (adapted from [Chikofsky 1990] and [Aiken 1998]).

System metadata is at the heart of metadata engineering (ME). In contrast to the standard, waterfall-based system development model, ME activities are not executed in strict-sequential fashion. While they generally flow as shown in the figure, you should always plan on an iterative refinement-based approach, such as the spiral model championed by Boehm [Boehm 1998] which incorporates system development practices such as multi-phase JAD sessions, iterative refinement, prototyping, etc.

The duration of each individual activity varies but generally increases with the activity number. Reuse of metadata and integration with existing components can significantly speed up ME activities and the iterative nature of the cycle makes precise measurements difficult. That is, A1 is generally the shortest duration and A6 generally takes longer than A5, etc. There are three classes of metadata engineering activities:

- *ME activities A1–A3* capture, organize, structure, and present re-created legacy system metadata without the benefit of derived or pre-existing legacy system metadata. For example, A2 manages the data of a design re-creation without any knowledge of the implementation metadata.
- *ME activities A4–A5* manage reconstituted legacy system metadata based on formal understanding of the system. For example, A4 involves understanding the system design by

examining its implementation metadata. This is a considerably different task than A2, which re-creates the design information without accessing the system implementation.

- *ME activities A6–A9* utilize the legacy system requirements, design, and implementation metadata developed as a result of A1–A5 to engineer a data warehouse or Enterprise Portal solution that meets organizational requirements.

Subphase I of Enterprise Portal Development is Metadata Engineering (ME). ME activities A1–A5 are designed to receive and manage the outputs of different reverse engineering analyses. ME activities A1–A8 represent various different types of metadata analyses that can contribute to Enterprise Portal development. Activities A1–A8 are fundamental and should be considered as part of a thorough reverse engineering exercise. Most Enterprise Portal development difficulties can be traced to informally structured ME or a failure to perform ME (A1–A8). *They all consist of the various pre-implementation analyses that should each be considered during Enterprise Portal Development*. Failure to consider or accurately assess the value of these analyses has been a primary reason for past data warehouse and EP project failures.

Phase II of Enterprise Portal Development is Metadata Implementation (MI) and consists solely of activity A9. Some organizations have had a tendency to jump many (or all) of ME activities A1–A8 and begin their Enterprise Portal development with activity A9.

Data warehouse and Enterprise Portal development is performed by building, refining, and using metamodel-based products that result from previous ME and MI activities. If you don't have access to the requisite metadata then you must perform a specific activity in order to produce it. In each of the subsections that follow, we will describe Enterprise Portal development activities in terms of a metamodel implementation along with several examples. When complete, users will have integrated access to all life-cycle metadata as well as other, integrated life-cycle products.

Reconstituting Original System Metadata (ME Activities A1–A3)

ME activities A1–A3 manage system metadata that describes legacy systems without making any improvements to the metadata. Instead, the focus is on providing improved access to system implementation, design, and requirements metadata.

ME Activity A1 creates a system for managing the redescribed legacy system metadata as the basis for subsequent ME activities. Implementation metadata that is produced includes lists of system components such as screens, files, and printouts. A1 examples include creating a system for managing the metadata that is used to manage descriptions of implemented screens, files, or printouts as comprised of their respective elements according to system—component—element hierarchies. Users can query the metadata and determine for each component, what are their respective elements? Taken as a whole this system metadata describes how the system functions and is constructed. As a result of A1, users can access legacy system implementation metadata and determine how the legacy system data functions and is constructed.

ME Activity A2 creates a system for managing the re-created design metadata of legacy systems as the basis for subsequent ME activities. A2 manages the metamodel components produced describing the logical system design metadata. Users access design metadata to determine how the legacy system components and/or elements consume, transform, and produce the organizational resources to meet customer information requirements. For example, electronically maintaining the schema of a legacy database is often easily accomplished using integrated database management environments.

ME Activity A3 creates a system for managing the re-created requirements legacy system metadata as the basis for subsequent ME activities. Once formally organized, these specifications provide an excellent basis for performing enterprise integration. Useful metamodel components managed by A3 include model-based integrated text and graphical system requirements, such as the original legacy system specifications and business rules.

Unless the implementation, design, or requirements legacy metadata already exists, you must perform A1–A3 if you are going to use this metadata to develop your data warehouse or Enterprise Portal. These standalone activities (A1–A3) must be implemented in situations where the legacy system metadata once existed but now the system requirements, design, and implementation system metadata must be re-created without the aid of other system metadata.

Improving Existing System Metadata (ME Activities A4–A5)

Under some circumstances, it is possible to reconstitute system design or requirements, utilizing the existing implementation and (in the case of re-creating requirements) the existing design assets as the basis for deriving relevant system metadata. Why would you want to re-create system designs and requirements for data warehouses or Enterprise Portals?

It is necessary during the system design phase to know the following.

- When it is important to understand the system as a series of interrelated data structure components.
- When it is important to understand why certain data design decisions were made (for example, the use of particular indexing schemes).
- When failure to fully understand the data design can lead to confusion between organizational business rules and technology-based constraints.

During the system requirements phase, the following factors must be considered.

- When nothing in system design addresses the organizational requirements, then these must be extracted, formalized, and understood in order to provide a solid basis for Enterprise Portal development.
- System requirements must be specified in order to provide formally the linkages between Enterprise Portal capabilities and organizational strategies.
- Mapping also permits programmatic control over the physical data using manipulation. Organization of metadata permits programmatic management of a system's logical and physical data structures.
- Metadata-based system implementations can be integrated with other similarly implemented metamodels providing the basis for enterprise integration.

While the re-creation-based ME activities (A1–A3) have value, combining and integrating individual system metadata products can make them more effective, compounding results and resulting in more valuable system metadata. ME activities A4–A5 improve system metadata value by reconstituting the system design and requirements metadata in cases where it doesn't exist; has deteriorated or become confused; or is otherwise unavailable.

ME Activity A4 creates a system for managing the reconstituted system design assets that are based on the existing implementation assets. This imposes the requirement that the implementation metadata must be integrated with the design metadata, when, for example, re-creating a legacy system database design. (When appropriate, A1 can be implemented to facilitate A4.) Users accessing metadata resulting from A1–A4 will be able to understand the system design metadata and trace design elements to their corresponding implementation metadata.

ME Activity A5 creates a system for managing the reconstituted system information requirements assets that are based on the existing legacy system design metadata. Metamodel components produced include integrated text and graphical-based system specifications and user requirements. For example, when re-creating existing system specifications and business rules using the system design metadata as the basis for more input is the result of A5, users are able to count on full integration of metadata from requirements to design to implementation. (Note: this requires the system requirements metadata to be integrated and managed with the system design and implementation metadata – A4 often precedes A5.)

ME activities A4–A5 also seek to improve the utility of system metadata, usually through system metadata integration and extension. An example would be the management of existing system metadata describing file layouts for customer data. This can be accomplished by integrating a list of all possible sources of customer data. This would include existing customer metadata, organizationally standardized descriptions, and associated screen elements.

Developing the Data Warehouse or Enterprise Portal (ME Activities A6–A9)

ME Activities A6–A9 specify metadata-based requirements, design, and implementation solutions that result in strategy-based data warehouse or Enterprise Portal implementation. This is accomplished by building on legacy system metadata gathered from earlier ME activities.

ME Activity A6 develops metadata-based Enterprise Portal requirements. The Enterprise Portal requirements can be expressed as data models specifying requirements capable of meeting user specifications. They are based on the metadata-based specification of the legacy system requirements understood as a result of previous ME activities. This establishes a mapping between legacy system metadata and Enterprise Portal components. It ensures that model-based requirements for the new data warehouse or Enterprise Portal are integrated with the requirements for the existing legacy systems. These requirements can also be based on reconstituted system requirements produced by A3 or A5.

ME Activity A7 develops the metadata-based Enterprise Portal design using the metadata-based requirements produced by A6. Metamodel components produced by A7 include model-based data design specifications for the new Enterprise Portal. The metadata-based design serves as a bridge integrating the newly specified EP requirements with the yet-to-be-created data warehouse or Enterprise Portal. For example, each individual requirement is typically associated with one or many Enterprise Portal design components.

ME Activity A8 incorporates integrated legacy system data design metadata into the Enterprise Portal requirements and design development. The use of existing system metadata provides a stable basis to specify the transformations required to use the legacy system metadata as the basis of the requirements and design for the new Enterprise Portal. Metadata components produced include formal linkages indicating sources, transformations, and destinations of data drawn from existing legacy systems (and if required, external sources). For example, prescribing that the customer data elements will be taken from specific log file segments. The knowledge of the log file segments came from reconstituted data design assets produced by either A2 or A4.

As we discussed earlier, A9 is what we referred to in the introduction as subphase II—Metadata Implementation (MI).

MI Activity 9 implements the data warehouse or Enterprise Portal, using the new warehouse or Enterprise Portal design produced by A7 and based on the existing legacy system metadata from A8.

Understanding these nine Enterprise Portal Development activities permits organizations a wide range of ME and MI activity combinations (ACs). Some ACs are shown in Figure 7-2. These range from managing redocumentation of existing legacy systems (AC-1); to enhancing system design metadata (AC-5); to performing data warehouse or Enterprise Portal development as part of an integrated system reengineering effort (AC-33) [Hodgson 1998].

Activity Combination	Implement activity	Preceded by activity	Preceded by activity	Preceded by activity	Preceded by activity	Preceded by activity	Preceded by activity	Preceded by activity
AC-1	1							
AC-2	2							
AC-3	3							
AC-4	4							
AC-5	4	1						
AC-6	5							
AC-7	5	2						
AC-8	5	4						
AC-9	5	2	4					
AC-10	5	4	1					
AC-11	5	2	4	1				
AC-12	6							
AC-13	6	2						
AC-14	6	4						
AC-15	6	4	1					
AC-16	7							
AC-17	7	3						
AC-18	7	5	4					
AC-19	7	5	4	1				
AC-20	8							
AC-21	8	7						
AC-22	8	7	3					
AC-23	8	7	5	4				
AC-24	8	7	5	4	1			
AC-25	9							
AC-26	9	6						
AC-27	9	6	2					
AC-28	9	6	4					
AC-29	9	6	4	1				
AC-30	9	8	7					
AC-31	9	8	7	3				
AC-32	9	8	7	5	4			
AC-33	9	8	7	5	4	1		
AC-34	9	8	7	6	5	6	5	4
AC-35	9	8	6					

Figure 7-2
Possible transformation activities indicating potential Enterprise Portal development options.

Some ACs are made up of activities not based on ME understandings reached by the previous ME activities. These include AC-1, AC-4, AC-6, AC-12, AC-16, AC-20, and AC-25. AC-12, for example, indicates the implementation choice to develop a warehouse or Enterprise Portal without formally understanding any aspects of the existing legacy systems.

In contrast, the remaining activity combinations indicate the choice to implement an Enterprise Portal using improved system metadata produced by the remaining activity combinations. For example, AC-26 through AC-29 specify activities available when the legacy system requirements closely match Enterprise Portal requirements. Such a situation might occur as a result of the utility of that system's data receiving higher recognition. A result could be a system extension exercise where its data management technology is altered to include providing access to archival data. AC-28 specifies engineering the Enterprise Portal by reconstructing your legacy system designs (A4), developing Enterprise Portal requirements from existing legacy system requirements (A6), and implementing the Enterprise Portal without first developing a system design (A9).

A comprehensive choice is AC-33 where the Enterprise Portal is implemented by reconstituting the data assets describing the existing legacy systems (A1). This system metadata is used to reconstitute the existing data design metadata (A4), which was in turn used to reconstitute system requirements metadata (A5). Once these are understood, the existing legacy system requirements metadata are specified (A6). From these the data warehouse or Enterprise Portal is redesigned (A7), legacy data is incorporated (A8), and the Enterprise Portal is implemented (A9).

The above discussion has proceeded as if the ME activities are executed sequentially. However, the iterative refinement nature of these activities also permits active repository metadata evolution and refinement as structural bugs are worked out of the system and more is learned about the nature of EEP.

Figure 7-2 also illustrates another possible course of EEP activities. It is AC-34 in Figure 7-3, which shows the repetition of A5/A6.

Figure 7-4 illustrates still another possible course of EEP activities. This is AC-35 in Figure 7-2, which represents the organizational decision to skip some prerequisite steps. Figure 7-4 shows the relevant metadata engineering activities.

Metadata Engineering Activity Cycle

The Metadata Engineering analysis cycle can be summarized in seven steps applied repeatedly:

1. Analyze a class of system objects to derive information for structuring queries.

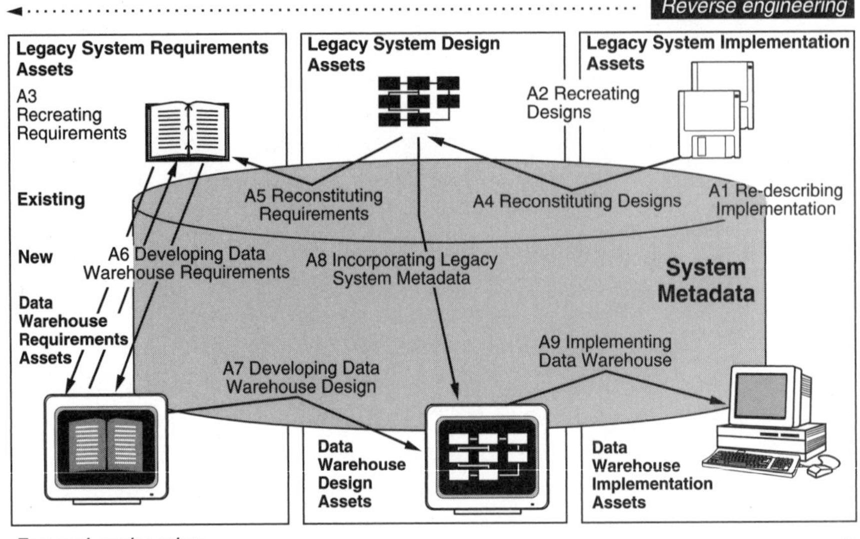

Figure 7-3
A variation on ME activity execution.

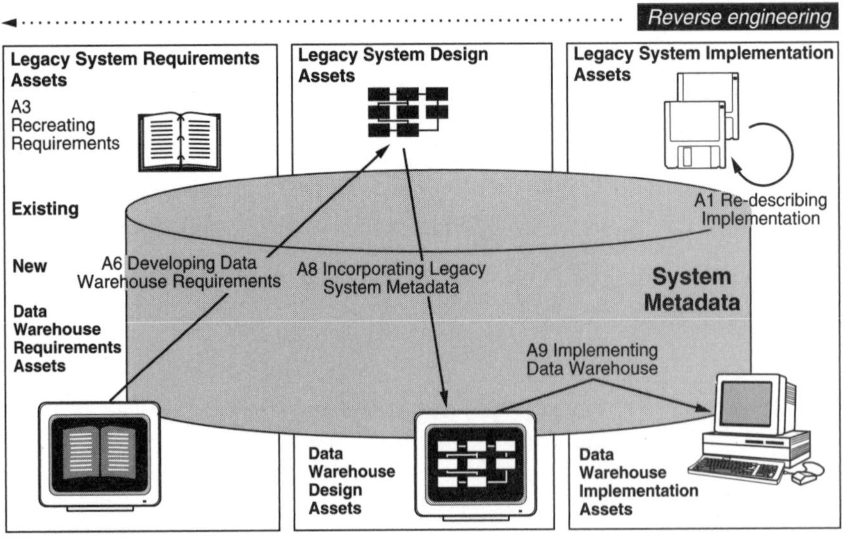

Figure 7-4
Another variation on ME activity execution.

2. Identify the most effective means of getting the system to report on itself.
3. Obtain the metadata.
4. Examine the extracted metadata for complexity analysis and validation.
5. Import the validated metadata into a repository.
6. Integrate the new metadata with the existing metadata.
7. Provide the enhanced metadata to the requesting user, verifying the metadata and its correctness.

The last step usually results in additional requests for metadata and the cycle begins again. To develop the metadata, this general model—extracting specific metadata characterizing aspects of the system, restructuring it, and integrating it with the existing repository contents—is repeated with many analysis variations. The variations consisted primarily of changing the source of the analysis inputs to include different system objects, the system documentation, or the metadata itself.

Some examples of metadata engineering extractions are discussed in this section. The extractions were imported into office suite-based spreadsheets for analysis. Statistical analysis provided information about relationships, their complexity, and their occurrence frequency, and was used to confirm the extracted metadata's correctness. A series of subsequent metadata manipulations transformed it into its repository-based format. After new metadata is imported into a repository, its relationships with existing metadata are derived.

A6–A8 each require the integration of organizational strategies into the Enterprise Portal design, and require that some legacy system metadata is also incorporated into the Enterprise Portal Design metadata produced during strategic modeling, and tactical and operational data modeling (as described in Part 1). Legacy system data is typically the main source of Enterprise Portal metadata and is integrated with the Enterprise Portal Design metadata. Two aspects of the metadata development process were described as A6–A9 previously. The Enterprise Portal development challenge is expressed in Figure 7-5 and its motivations include:

- System metadata-based management of legacy system data, legacy system metadata, and Enterprise Portal metadata.

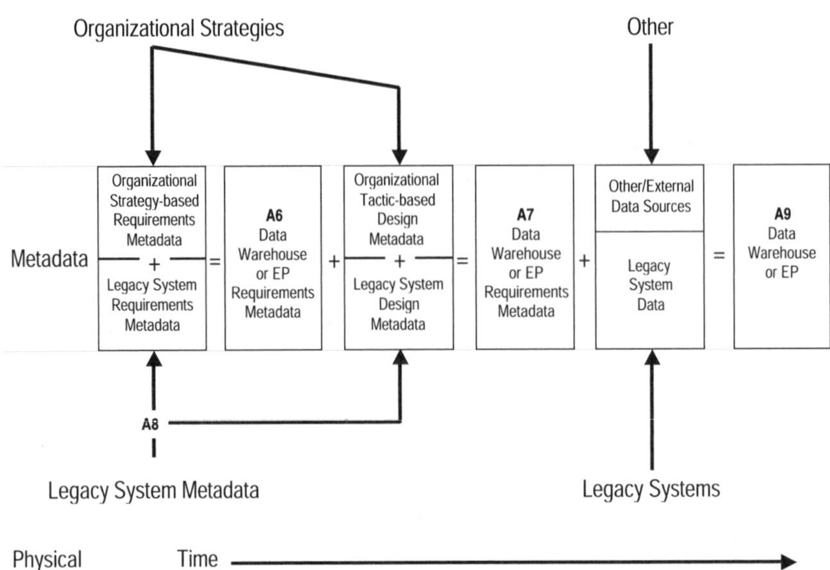

Figure 7-5 Integration of conceptual and physical metadata as ME Activities A6–A8.

- System metadata integration occurs in the form of mapping relations between the legacy system components and their data warehouse or Enterprise Portal counterparts
- System maintenance methods that synchronize the states of identical variables that exist as different system components in both legacy systems and the data warehouse or Enterprise Portal.
- More efficient data warehouse or Enterprise Portal maintenance methods.
- Greater shared understanding and use of organizational data.
- Permits direct mapping of strategic organization requirements onto data warehouse or Enterprise Portal capabilities.
- Ensures complete implementation of strategic organizational information requirements into warehouse or Enterprise Portal requirements, design, and implementation.
- CASE-based maintenance of organizational information strategy.
- Implement a Zachman Framework-based information architecture.

Only after you understand how your situation dictates the ME activities that need to be accomplished and what system metadata types will be required should you begin to link your organizational strategies to specific system metadata-based requirements and begin metadata implementation.

Some organizations are beginning to understand the value of system metadata. Customer feedback is prompting architecture of new systems so that their metadata is programmatically maintained and "queryable." Metadata produced by EEP generally increases in value as different metadata types are integrated and as the complexity of the data it describes and/or the system(s) that access it. Integration also permits homogeneous access technology and programmatic control over the physical data using organizationally standardized logical manipulation forms such as SQL, graphical browsers, object technologies, etc.

The next subsection of Chapter 7 addresses the question: How do I link my organizational strategies into the process? The top left part of Figure 7-6 illustrates this conceptual to metadata conversion. The next question is: how do I specify the metadata? The window in the bottom right of Figure 7-6 illustrates this physical text to metadata conversion process.

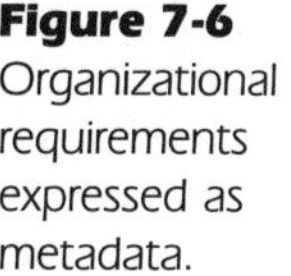

Figure 7-6 Organizational requirements expressed as metadata.

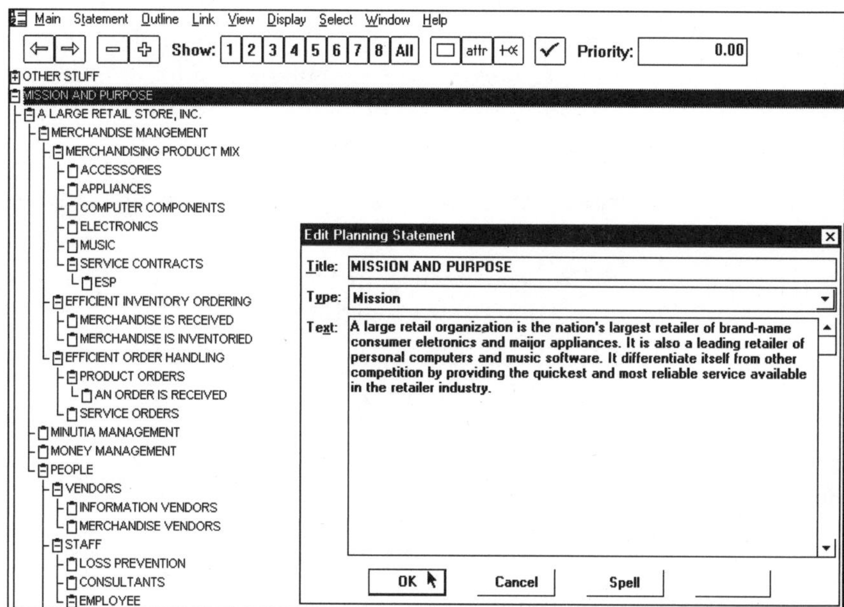

Expressing Organizational Strategy as System Metadata (Conceptual to Metadata Conversion)

In order to achieve this desired integration, the organizational strategy must be specified in a metadata format. Figure 7-6 illustrates a small part of organizational strategy that is maintained as system metadata. This example shows an organizational mission and purpose, defined using the Goal Analysis method discussed in Chapter 2. This statement would typically be captured during strategic modeling as discussed in Chapter 4.

As illustrated, each strategy system metadata element has a title, text, and a statement type using Visible Advantage. This CASE tool permits assignment of many statement-based metadata types. Strategy elements: mission, strengths, weaknesses, opportunities, threats, goals, strategies, critical success factors, objectives, policies, tactics, tasks, and other statement types are included. We will use these to develop our strategy-based system metadata example. Visible Advantage is user-extensible and allows other strategy elements to be easily added if required. The example follows the form specified by the metamodel shown as Figure 7-7.

The STRATEGY ROLE entity is used to specify the roles that are to be arranged among the various STRATEGY entities. Using this metadata structure, each STRATEGY entity can be related using the STRATEGY ROLE entity to other STRATEGY entities in a hierarchical fashion. Organizations can specify the hierarchy that they use to maintain their strategies. For example, deciding to implement strategy metadata structure as shown in Figure 7-8 implies four strategy rules as part of the Enterprise Portal requirements structure.

SR-1 One mission is supported by one or many strategies, tactics, and critical success factors.

SR-2 Each strategy or tactic is based on one or more opportunities/threats or strengths/weaknesses.

SR-3 Each strategy or tactic begets one or more policies—combined with an associated goal/objective pair.

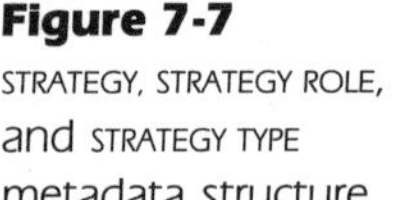

Figure 7-7
STRATEGY, STRATEGY ROLE, and STRATEGY TYPE metadata structure.

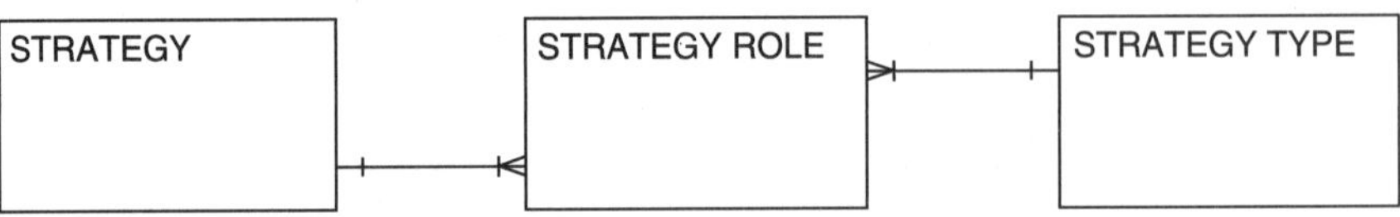

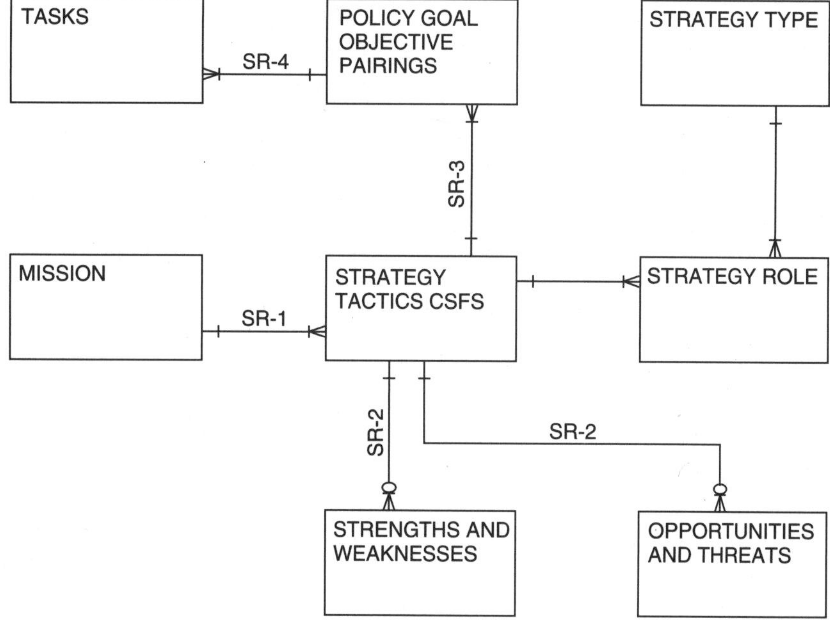

Figure 7-8 Example strategy metadata specification.

SR-4 Each policy begets one or more specific tasks.

Conceptually the organizational strategy was integrated with the existing system metadata as shown in Figure 7-9. It illustrates how the strategies were related to ten other metadata types.

Of course, the organization can choose to implement the template presented as Figure 2-3 of Chapter 2. Another example template on which organizational strategy can be implemented is shown in Figure 7-10.

Once the original structure is specified formally (according to Figure 7-8 or any other workable structure), the statements can be combined into views and formally related to other strategic objects as shown in Figure 7-11, or to specific metamodel decompositions as shown in Figure 7-12.

The key to development of useful (or better still, valuable) strategy-based system metadata is to develop, implement, and stabilize a structure before refining it. Use it to specify existing organizational strategies as metadata. This use will highlight potential conflicts and suggest refinements. Once formalized, the structure will keep the strategy development focused toward management at the right levels of abstraction.

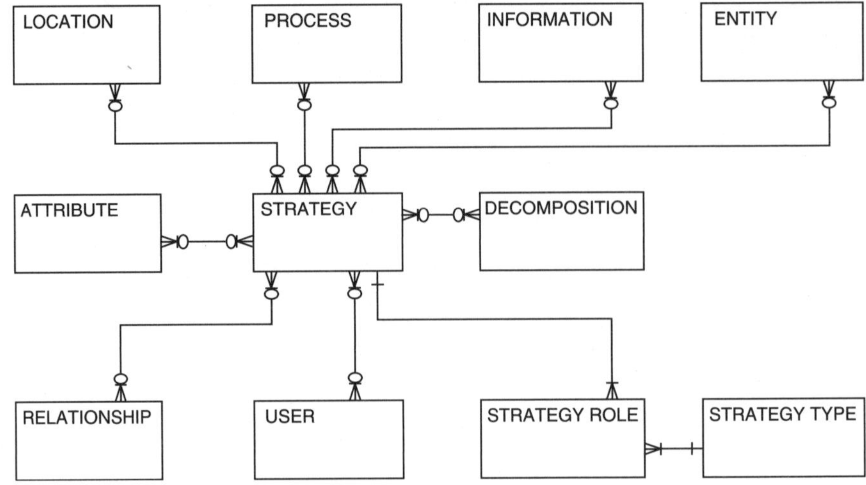

Figure 7-9 System metadata specification variation.

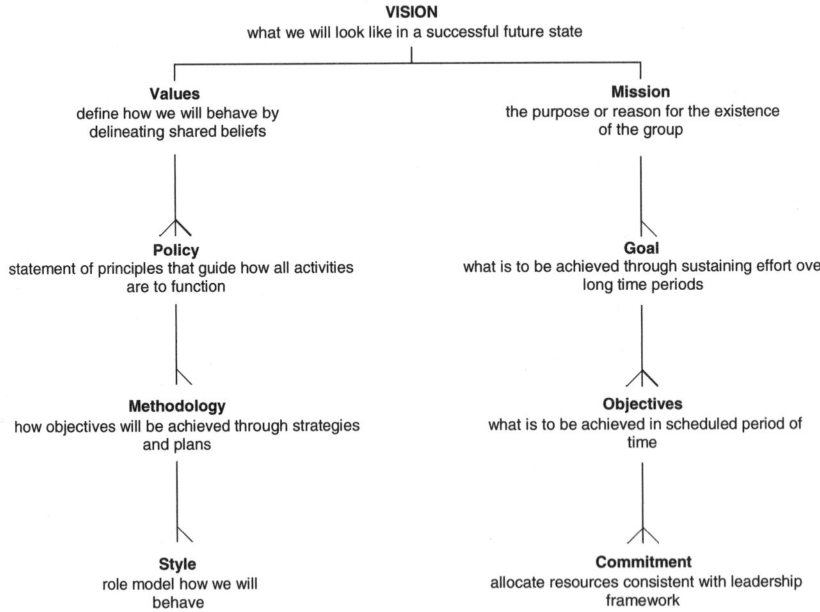

Figure 7-10 Another variation of metadata-based specification of strategy.

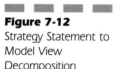

Figure 7-11 Strategy Statement to Data Object Mapping.

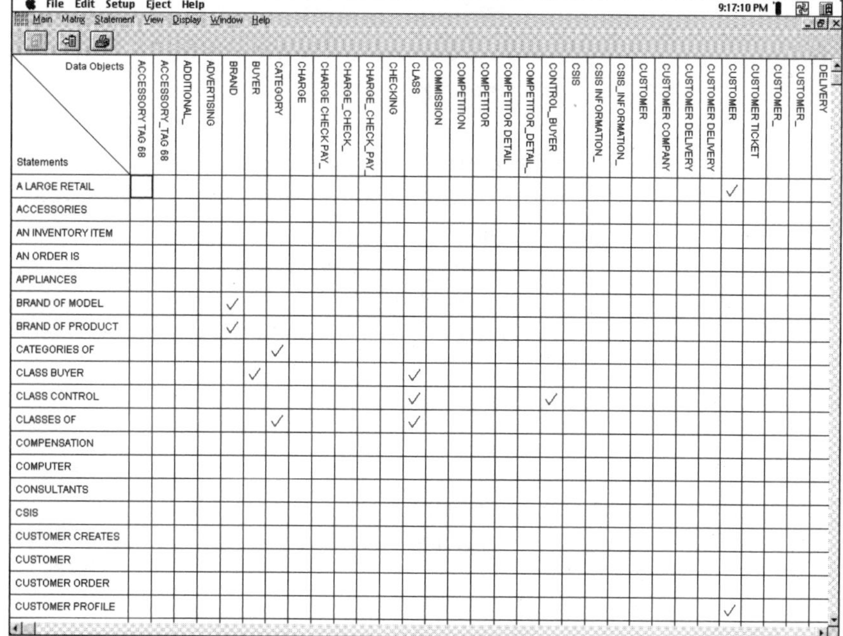

Statements \ Data Objects	ACCESSORY TAG 68	ACCESSORY_TAG 68	ADDITIONAL_	ADVERTISING	BRAND	BUYER	CATEGORY	CHARGE	CHARGE CHECK PAY_	CHARGE_CHECK_	CHARGE_CHECK_PAY_	CHECKING	CLASS	COMMISSION	COMPETITION	COMPETITOR	COMPETITOR DETAIL	COMPETITOR_DETAIL_	CONTROL_BUYER	CSIS	CSIS INFORMATION_	CSIS_INFORMATION_	CUSTOMER	CUSTOMER COMPANY	CUSTOMER DELIVERY	CUSTOMER DELIVERY	CUSTOMER	CUSTOMER TICKET	CUSTOMER_	CUSTOMER_	DELIVERY
A LARGE RETAIL																											✓				
ACCESSORIES																															
AN INVENTORY ITEM																															
AN ORDER IS																															
APPLIANCES																															
BRAND OF MODEL					✓																										
BRAND OF PRODUCT					✓																										
CATEGORIES OF							✓																								
CLASS BUYER						✓							✓																		
CLASS CONTROL													✓						✓												
CLASSES OF							✓						✓																		
COMPENSATION																															
COMPUTER																															
CONSULTANTS																															
CSIS																															
CUSTOMER CREATES																															
CUSTOMER																															
CUSTOMER ORDER																															
CUSTOMER PROFILE																											✓				

Figure 7-12 Strategy Statement to Model View Decomposition Mapping.

File Edit Setup Eject Help
9:17:38 PM
Main Matrix Statement View Display Window Help

Statements \ Model Views	Catch All (Contains	Catch all for CUSTOMER	chapter 08	Circuit City	CSIS PRODUCT	CSIS Tables supporting	CUSTOMER	CUSTOMER (FROM CSIS)	CUSTOMER (LFSs)	CUSTOMER LFS EXCLUDE	CUSTOMER ORDER	CUSTOMER ORDER	CUSTOMER PAYMENT	FINANCE PAYMENT	INVENTORY	LFSs supporting	Miscellaneous Cash	Mission	Objectives	OR BASIC	OR OPTIONAL	Order Entry - Order Created	ORDER ENTRY - ORDER	Order Entry - Order Recall	Out of Stock	PRICE	PRICING/PROMOTION	Product	Product (Derived from CSIS	Product (from Sales	RECEIPT
A LARGE RETAIL				✓																											
ACCESSORIES																															
AN INVENTORY ITEM IS																															
AN ORDER IS																															
APPLIANCES																															
BRAND OF MODEL				✓																								✓		✓	
BRAND OF PRODUCT				✓																								✓		✓	
CATEGORIES OF				✓																								✓		✓	
CLASS BUYER				✓																								✓		✓	
CLASS CONTROL				✓																								✓		✓	
CLASSES OF				✓																								✓		✓	
COMPENSATION																															
COMPUTER																															
CONSULTANTS																															
CSIS																															
CUSTOMER CREATES																															
CUSTOMER DATAMART																															
CUSTOMER ORDER		✓		✓			✓	✓	✓			✓																			

Expressing Legacy System Attributes as System Metadata (Physical to Metadata Conversion)

Some metadata subset is often maintainable using CASE tools—especially if a CASE tool was used to develop the system. However, since organizational CASE tool use has fallen by almost a third in recent annual measurements—from an apparent peak of 62 percent of organizations surveyed in 1993 to 54 percent in 1994 and still further to 42 percent in 1995 [Touche 1995 and 1996]—it is clear system managers cannot count on CASE tool-based metadata support.

What follows is a description of the implementation of an employment-related model view containing seven entities with a relational database management system (RDBMS) as part of metadata engineering activity A4. The sequence of Figures 7-13–7-17 illustrates how to maintain system metadata describing system entities, attributes, and relationships as

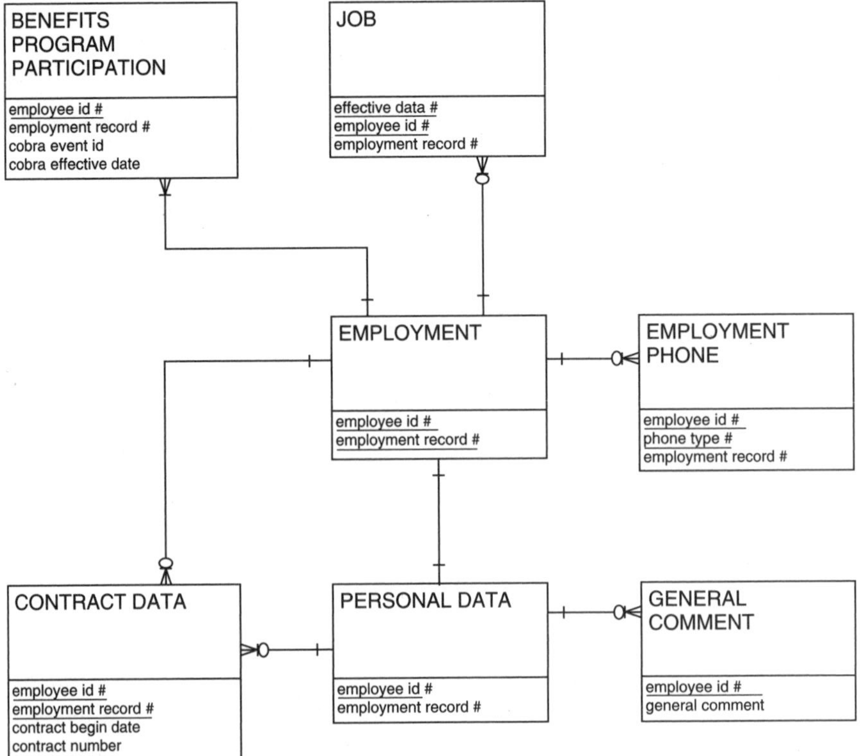

Figure 7-13 Employee model view decomposition contents represented by metadata contained in subsequent figures.

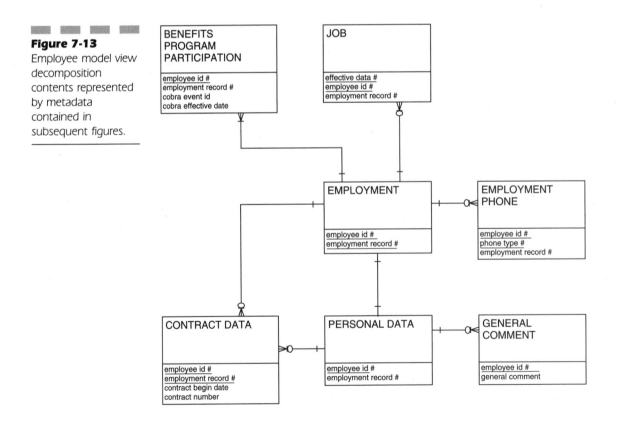

Figure 7-14 Metadata describing the entities in model decomposition (employment).

PK Entity ID	Entity Name	Entity Purpose
E1	PERSONAL DATA	PERSONAL DATA is one of the core records in the database. Use it to record personal and demographic data about an employee or applicant including name, address, birth date, and ethnic group.
E2	EMPLOYMENT	EMPLOYMENT is one of the core records in the database. Use it to record an employee's employment-related data that doesn't tend to change, such as hire date, termination date, and company service date.
E3	JOB	JOB is one of the core records in the database. Use it to record an employee's job history data such as actions taken, department, job code, location, and salary history. You can create one or many JOB records for an employee.
E4	EMPLOYMENT PHONE	Use EMPLOYMENT PHONE to record phone numbers that relate to an employees work environment. The field 'phone_type' identifies the type of phone number entered.
E5	BENEFITS PROGRAM PARTICIPATION	BENEFITS PROGRAM PARTICIPATION is a record that defines the benefit program for which an employee is enrolled. It is used while processing Payroll and Benefits Administration.
E6	CONTRACT DATA	Use CONTRACT DATA to store details of employment contracts associated with JOBs.
E7	GENERAL COMMENT	Use GENERAL COMMENT to enter any general comments that you wish to retain relating to an employee's job or employment.

a series of tables. Other metadata components are implemented in a similar fashion. The model specifies facts to be maintained for employees as discovered by reverse engineering analysis. The reverse engineering revealed the design—specified as system entities, attributes, and relationships—as standard data model components shown in Figure 7-13.

Figure 7-14 describes the seven entities maintained as part of the employment model view decomposition.

Figure 7-15 is a table of the attributes comprising each entity in the decomposition. The table key is a combination of ENTITY ID and ATTRIBUTE ID. Rows in this table represent the fact that an entity has the associated

Figure 7-15 Model decomposition metadata describing each entity as comprised of a key attribute structure.

PK Entity ID	Attribute ID	Attribute Name	Relationship Information
E1	A1	employee id	PK
E1	A2	personal data	NK
E2	A1	employee id	PK
E2	A3	employment record	FK
E3	A1	employee id	PK
E3	A4	effective date	PK
E3	A3	employment record	FK
E4	A1	employee id	PK
E4	A3	employment record	FK
E4	A5	phone type	FK
E5	A1	employee id	PK
E5	A3	employment record	FK
E5	A6	cobra effective date	NK
E5	A7	cobra event id	NK
E6	A1	employee id	PK
E6	A3	employment record	FK
E6	A8	contract begin date	NK
E6	A9	contract number	NK
E7	A1	employee id	PK
E7	A10	general comment	NK

attribute as part of its composition. The relationship information column indicates whether the attribute is a primary key (PK), a foreign key (FK), or a non-key attribute (NK).

The next figure describes the relationships existing in the employment decomposition. The first relationship listed in Figure 7-16 indicates that entity (E3) job is related to entity (E2) employment. The relationship between the two entities can be stated as: "one employment instance

Figure 7-16 Data describing the relationships between the entities in employment model view decomposition.

Rel. id	Left id	Right id	Left entity relationship	Right entity relationship	MD
R1	E3	E2	optional many	mandatory one	1
R2	E4	E2	optional many	mandatory one	1
R3	E5	E2	mandatory many	mandatory one	1
R4	E7	E1	optional one or many	mandatory one	1
R5	E6	E1	optional many	mandatory one	1
R6	E6	E2	optional many	mandatory one	1
R7	E2	E1	mandatory one	mandatory one	1

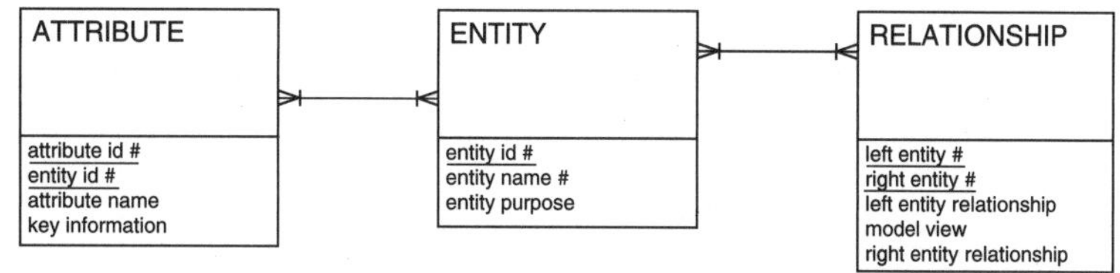

Figure 7-17 Three metamodel entities comprising a metamodel component that can store data models as metadata—a component of the data structure metadata.

may have many job records associated with it". A row corresponds to each entity-to-entity association.

Using these three tables, individual data models can be stored as metadata: "ATTRIBUTE"—usable as a component of many entities; "ENTITY"—comprised of attributes and key structures; and "RELATIONSHIP"—documenting associations existing among entities. The three describe a design implementation permitting many-to-many relationships to exist between entities/relationships and entities/attributes. Figure 7-17 illustrates a logical metamodel representing the relationship, entity, and attribute contents of employment.

REFERENCES

Aiken, P.H. (1996) *Data Reverse Engineering: Slaying the Legacy Dragon*, New York: McGraw-Hill.

Aiken, P.H. (1999) "Reverse Engineering of Data," *IBM Systems Journal,* 37(2): 246–269.

Boehm, B., Egyed, A. *et al*. "Using the WinWin Spiral Model: A Case Study," *IEEE Computer*, 31(7 July): 33–45.

Chikofsky, E. and J.C. III (1990) "Reverse Engineering and Design Recovery: A Taxonomy," *IEEE Software* 7(1): 13–17.

Hodgson, L. and Aiken, P.H. (1998) "Synergistic Dependence Between Analysis Techniques," *Information Systems Management.*

Touche, D. (1995, 1996) *Leading Trends in Information Services – The Annual Deloit and Touche CIO Surveys*, Deloit and Touche.

CHAPTER 8

Metadata Types

Acquire new knowledge whilst thinking over the old, and you may become a teacher of others.

—Confucius

Now that you understand the metadata engineering activities that produce specific system metadata products, we will describe the system metadata types, and how they are interrelated. Then you will be able to identify and obtain the metadata relevant to your EEP efforts from the entire range of possible system metadata.

System Metadata Types

The primary focus of Metadata Engineering (ME) activities is to identify and produce validated system requirements, design, and implementation-based metadata in preparation for Metadata Implementation (MI). The system metadata produced by ME activities A1–A8 is precise information required to understand those aspects of the legacy system metadata important to your EEP effort—information that was unavailable or disorganized prior to the effort. The system metadata is formalized in a system metamodel consisting of entities grouped according to various criteria as groups of related facts of interest. Data collections describing each class of facts are represented using metamodel entities. Each model entity is related to other entities through formally defined relationship structures.

For clarity, the primary entities in the system metamodel are organized and presented in three subsections (technically they are called model view decompositions) as shown in Figure 8-1. Each decomposition represents some non-exclusive subset of the entities and relationships contained in the entire metamodel. Each decomposition can be further decomposed. Data engineers and users focus their analyses on decompositions instead of attempting to comprehend the entire metamodel at once.

Of the three decompositions in Figure 8-1, two are required and the *Contextual Extensions Decomposition* is optional. The two required decompositions are often developed in parallel. They correspond to metadata capture (*Reverse Engineering Analysis Decomposition*) and metadata use (*Conceptual Structure Decomposition*). Implemented and organized in seven second-level decompositions, the system metadata

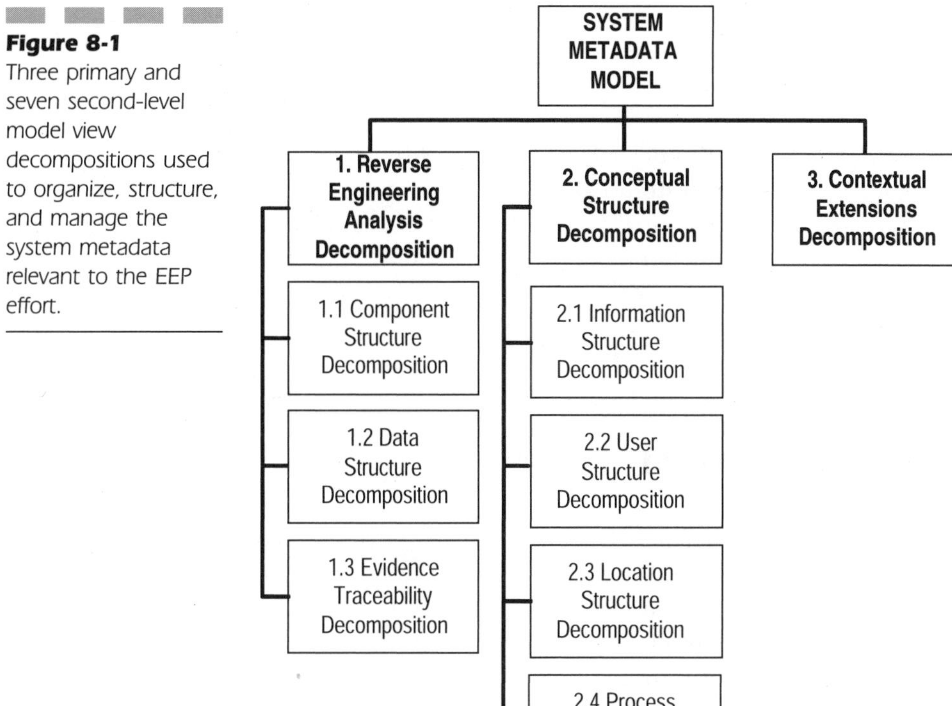

Figure 8-1 Three primary and seven second-level model view decompositions used to organize, structure, and manage the system metadata relevant to the EEP effort.

structure facilitates metadata capture and use. Figure 8-2 presents a metamodel of all of the entities in the two required decompositions.

This model is shown unnormalized with intersecting and type entities excluded to fit the presentation constraints. The entities comprising the *reverse engineering analysis decomposition* are enclosed in the light gray line (to the left of the diagram) while those in the *conceptual structure decomposition* are enclosed by the darker gray line (to the right of the diagram). Two structurally prominent associations (between ELEMENT–ATTRIBUTE and between PROCESS–DECOMPOSITION) formally relate the system metadata in these two decompositions. The two decompositions are comprised of 11 principal entities. Distribution of the 11 principal entities about the reverse engineering analysis and conceptual structure decompositions is shown as Figure 8-3. For example, the EVIDENCE entity appears only in the evidence traceability decomposition while the PROCESS entity appears in all of the conceptual structure second-level decompositions (2.1–2.4).

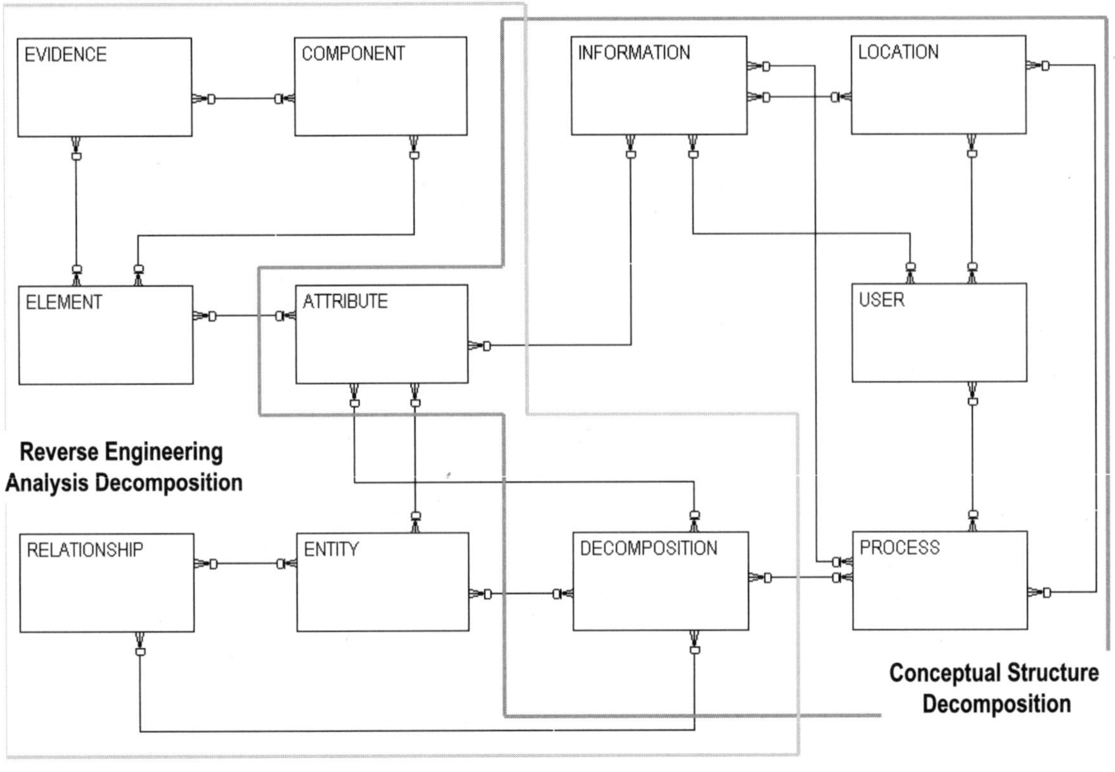

Figure 8-2
An unnormalized representation of entities and relationships comprising the required reverse engineering analysis and conceptual structure decompositions.

Figure 8-3
Decomposition/entity matrix—specifying the distribution of the 11 principal entities about the seven decompositions.

DECOMPOSITION:	ENTITIES:	Attribute	Entity	Model Decomposition	Relationship	System Component	Component Element	Evidence	Location	Information	User	Process
1. Reverse Engineering Analysis	1.1 Component Structure	X				X	X					
(Metadata Capture)	1.2 Data Structure	X	X	X	X							
	1.3 Evidence Traceability					X	X	X				
2. Conceptual Structure	2.1 Information Structure	X							X	X	X	X
(Metadata Use)	2.2 User Structure	X							X	X	X	X
	2.3 Location Structure	X							X	X	X	X
	2.4 Process Structure	X		X					X	X	X	X
3. Contextual Extensions												

Figure 8-4
Sixteen REQs implemented to maintain system metadata.

- Each COMPONENT contains zero, one, or many elements and each ELEMENT is a part of zero, one, or many components.
- Each ELEMENT is composed of zero, one, or many attributes and each ATTRIBUTE is a part of zero, one, or many elements.
- Each ATTRIBUTE is found in zero, one, or many entities and each ENTITY contains many attributes.
- Each ENTITY is related to one or many related entities.
- Each RELATIONSHIP is contained in one or many DECOMPOSITIONS and each DECOMPOSITION contains one or many RELATIONSHIPS.
- Each ENTITY can appear in one, or many DECOMPOSITIONS and each decomposition can contain zero, one, or many entities.
- Each EVIDENCE can support zero, one, or many components and each COMPONENT can be supported zero, one, or many evidences.
- Each EVIDENCE can support zero, one, or many facts represented as elements and each ELEMENT can be associated with zero, one, or many evidences.
- Each INFORMATION can be composed of zero, one, or many attributes and each ATTRIBUTE can be provided as part of zero, one, or many informations.
- Each INFORMATION can be consumed by zero, one, or many users and each USER can be provided to one or many informations.
- Each INFORMATION can be received by zero, one, or many locations and each LOCATION can be provided one or many informations.
- Each INFORMATION can be supplied to one or many processes and each PROCESS can require one or many informations.
- Each USER can reside at one or many locations and each LOCATION can have one or many users.
- Each USER can participate in one or many processes and each PROCESS can have one or many users.
- Each LOCATION performs one or many processes and each PROCESS is performed at one or many locations.
- Each PROCESS can be associated with one or many decompositions and each DECOMPOSITION can be associated with one or many processes.

The 11 entities are formally related, specifying a series of 16 system metadata requirements for implementing Enterprise Portal system metadata (we will refer to each as a "REQ"). They are listed in Figure 8-4. Some subsets of these specify the metamodel management capabilities for your data warehousing or Enterprise Portal effort.

The rest of this chapter describes how each second-level decomposition implements a related subset of the REQs, defining the entities at the same time. Each subsection that follows describes the decomposition contents, the relations, the REQs satisfied by the implementation, and physical metadata model specifications required to implement the decomposition. We will begin with the reverse engineering analysis decomposition. The next three subsections describe the composition and structure of the three decompositions that make up the reverse engineering analysis decomposition. If you understand the second-level decompositions individually, you will understand the entire meta-model.

Reverse Engineering Analysis Decomposition

This section describes the composition of the reverse engineering analysis decomposition. The metamodel representing the reverse engineering analysis decomposition is shown in Figure 8-5. This model decomposition consists of seven entities and relationships implementing nine REQs.

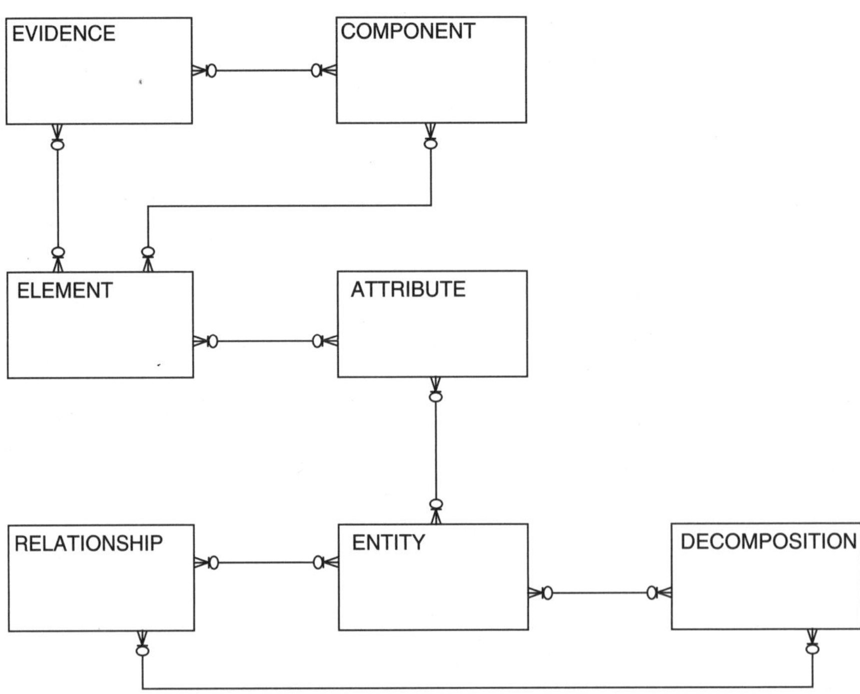

Figure 8-5 Entities and relationships comprising the reverse engineering analysis decomposition.

Figure 8-1 illustrated that the reverse engineering analysis decomposition is comprised of three second-level decompositions. These decompositions describe facts about the system's data structure, its component structure, and evidence traceability. This decomposition supports the capture of reverse engineering analysis outputs. Collectively, they prescribe the collection of system metadata entities specifying the facts used to represent much of the information produced by reverse engineering analyses.

Component Structure Decomposition

The component structure decomposition metadata describes the system as components formed of combinations of elements. Figure 8-6 illustrates seven data entities representing general classes of system components as: screens, interfaces, inputs, outputs, and printout elements.

Each component is comprised of system elements. For example, each system screen is composed of one or more screen elements. Each element can be linked via many-to-many relationships to the other six component classes. The associations are specified as many-to-many because each SCREEN ELEMENT can appear as many printout elements and each PRINTOUT ELEMENT can appear on many screens, etc. Comprehensive system metadata would permit, given any specific element, all associated elements to be determined.

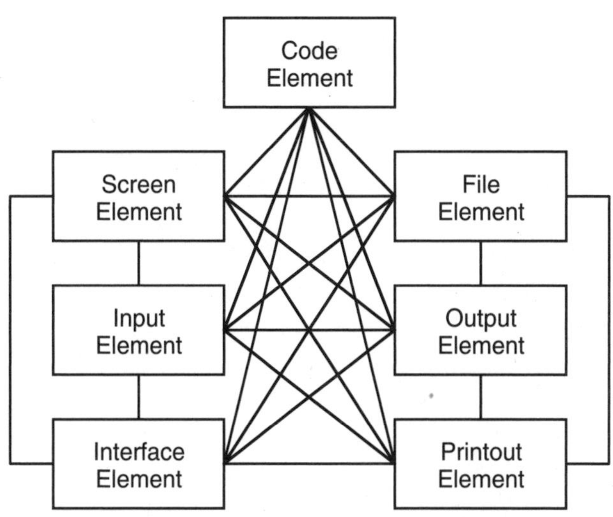

Figure 8-6 Seven classes of components illustrated using a simplified representation of many-to-many relationships existing between elements of each of system component.

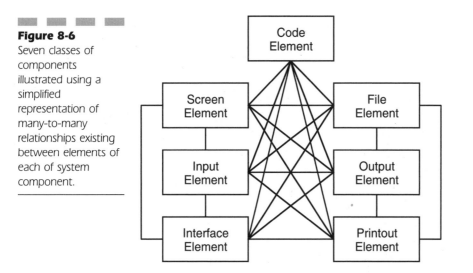

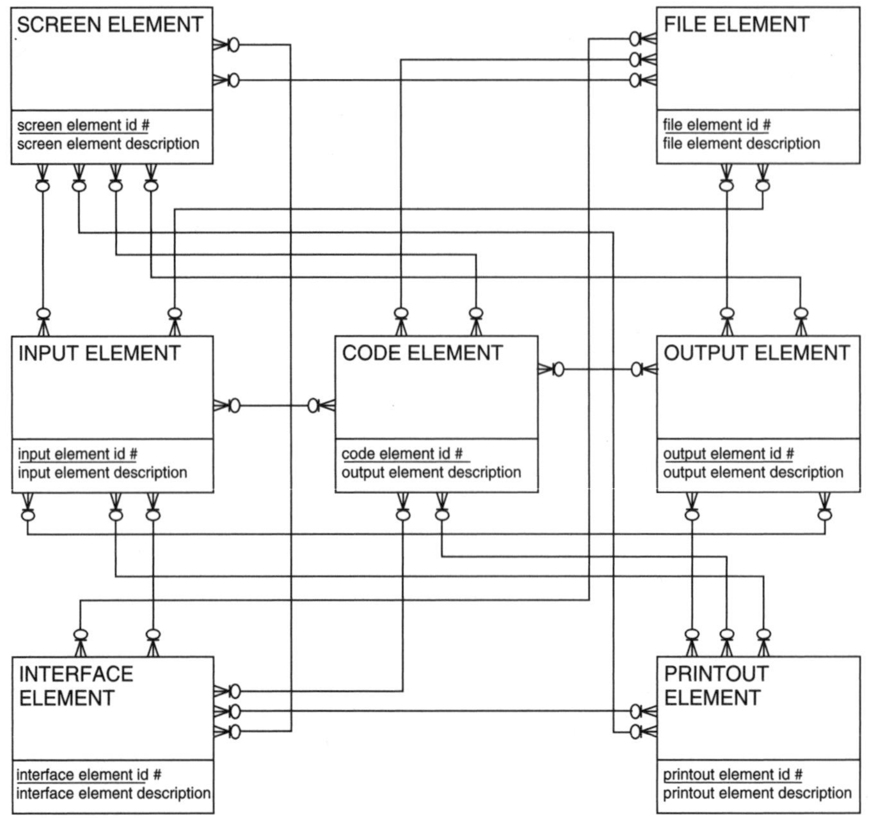

Figure 8-7 Representational system metadata specifications illustrating physical requirement for many-to-many relationships between elements.

By itself this metadata exceeds the comprehensiveness of system information documenting most legacy systems. These relationships form the basis for more complex system metadata, describing—for example—which screen elements are transformed into which printout elements. Without this basic system metadata, the more complex metadata cannot be developed.

Figure 8-7 shows a more formalized physical implementation of the requirements specified in Figure 8-6. The specific relationship notation is read as zero, one, or many to zero, one, or many. Given any specific component, all associated components can be determined.

NOTE. *Beginning with Figure 8-7, we will represent the system metadata specifications with standard information engineering techniques using entities, attributes, and relationships as described in Chapter 3. Many of the illustrations are made using* CASE *tool generated data model-*

ing techniques. We used Visible Advantage™ because of its support for this type of data reengineering. The methodology implemented is described in [Finkelstein 1992].

To understand the detail required to implement the specifications in Figure 8-7, consider the representation of relationships between ELEMENTS, SCREEN and PRINTOUT. Each SCREEN ELEMENT can appear on zero, one, or many screens and each SCREEN can contain zero, one, or many screen elements. This relationship is shown unnormalized in Figure 8-8.

To link elements of different components together, Figure 8-9 illustrates the conceptual system metadata requirement that each individual SCREEN ELEMENT can be linked to multiple printout elements and that each PRINTOUT ELEMENT can be linked to multiple screen elements.

Using this conceptual structure, specific screen elements can be related to printout elements with an implied intersecting entity resolving the many-to-many relationship between screen and printout elements. Figure 8-10 illustrates the physical implementation of this system

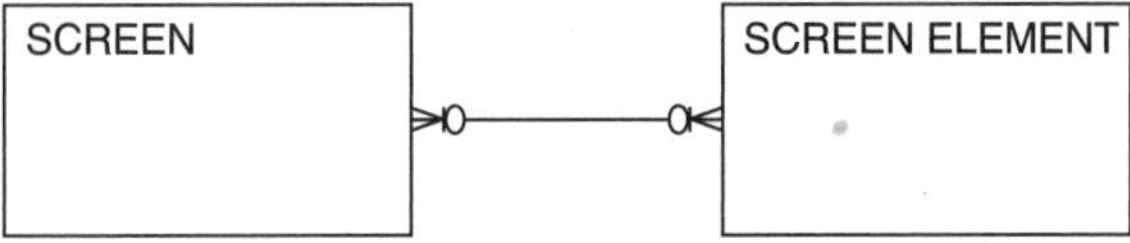

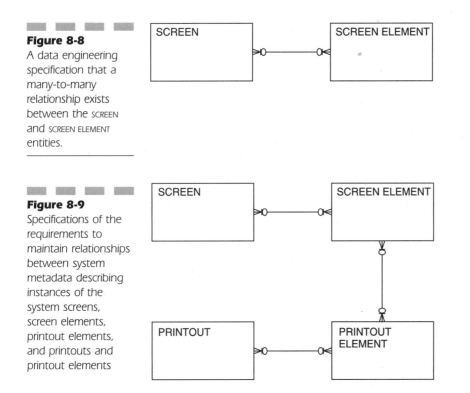

Figure 8-8
A data engineering specification that a many-to-many relationship exists between the SCREEN and SCREEN ELEMENT entities.

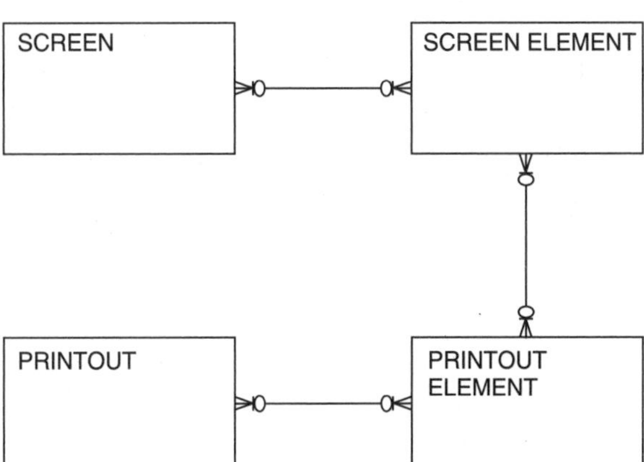

Figure 8-9
Specifications of the requirements to maintain relationships between system metadata describing instances of the system screens, screen elements, printout elements, and printouts and printout elements

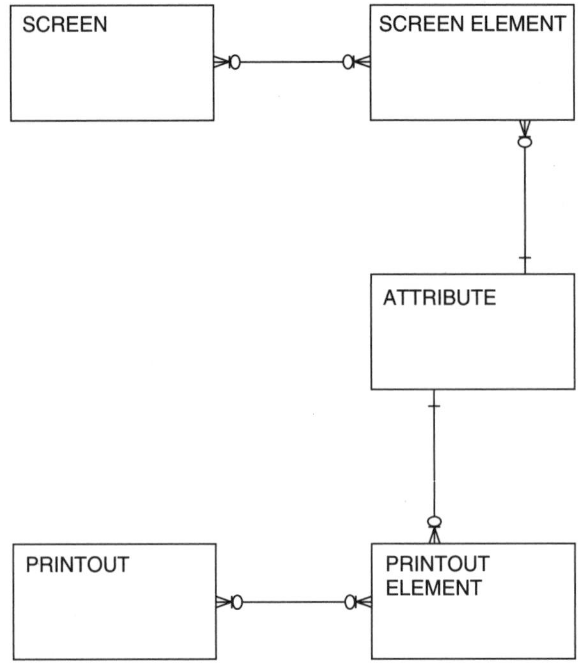

Figure 8-10 Use of the ATTRIBUTE principal entity to physically implement the many-to-many relationship between instances of SCREEN ELEMENT and PRINTOUT ELEMENT entities.

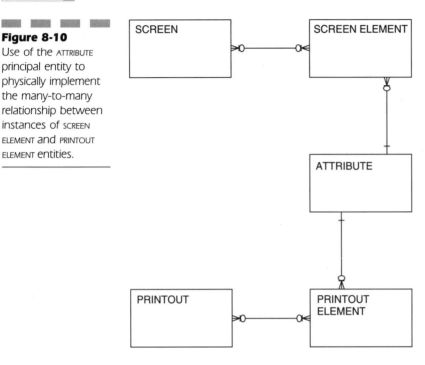

metadata structure with the principal entity: ATTRIBUTE. It is used to specify each relationship instance occurring between screen and printout elements as both relate to a single attribute.

The system metadata requirements illustrated in Figure 8-10 specifying management of the many-to-many relationship between screen and printout elements can be generalized to the creation of maintaining many-to-many relationships between all system elements described in Figure 8-6.

The model can be further generalized to a structure representing the relationship between all components and their respective elements. The component structure decomposition is populated by three principal entities—ATTRIBUTE, COMPONENT, and ELEMENT—and associated relationships describing the system structure from various component perspectives. The decomposition describes a metamodel structure for representing the relationship between each component and all related elements. The metadata structure specified in Figure 8-11 implements REQ-01 through REQ-03, which specifies that:

REQ-01 Each COMPONENT contains zero, one, or many ELEMENTS and each ELEMENT is a part of zero, one, or many COMPONENTS.

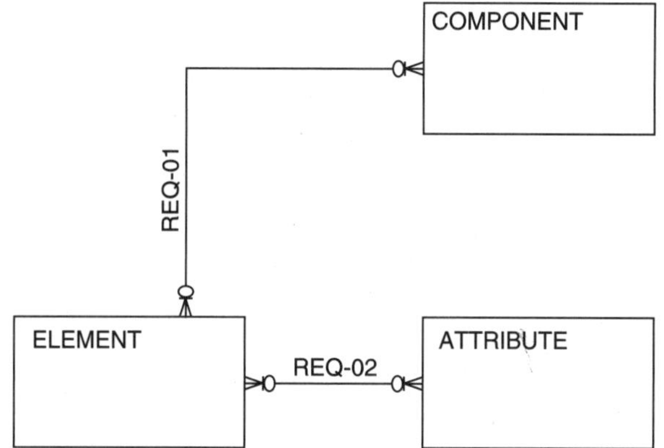

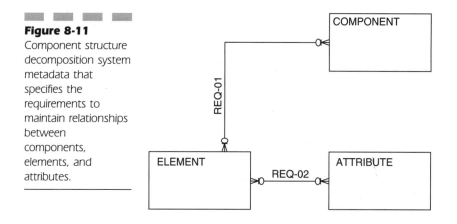

Figure 8-11 Component structure decomposition system metadata that specifies the requirements to maintain relationships between components, elements, and attributes.

This structure implements an "is a part of" relationship: screen elements are parts of screens; printout elements are parts of printouts; file elements are parts of files, etc. REQ-02 implements the same relationship structure for elements and attributes.

REQ-02 Each ELEMENT is composed of zero, one, or many ATTRIBUTES and each ATTRIBUTE is a part of zero, one, or many ELEMENTS.

A detailed physical implementation of this system metadata is shown in Figure 8-12.

By maintaining component types, the ATTRIBUTE entity can be used to maintain information linking elements of different types such as screens and printouts. For example, the many-to-many relationship between entities and attributes is resolved using the intersecting entity "X ENTITY ATTRIBUTE." Similar structures are implemented throughout the metamodel resolving each many-to-many relationship with an entity of the form "x ... ... ". These represent a data engineering solution to the requirements articulated in Figure 8-4. This more detailed metamodel includes two intersecting and three type entities not shown on Figure 8-2.

This presentation is optimized to illustrate the metamodel structure. Definitional material is minimized for this presentation to allow concentration on understanding the metamodel structure. The system metadata entities are defined with generic primary key definitions. They are implemented using the form <entity name id #>. All other information dependent on the entire key is referred to as a single group attribute of the form <entity name description>. So the name for the attribute entity is <attribute id> and all other attributes fully dependent on the

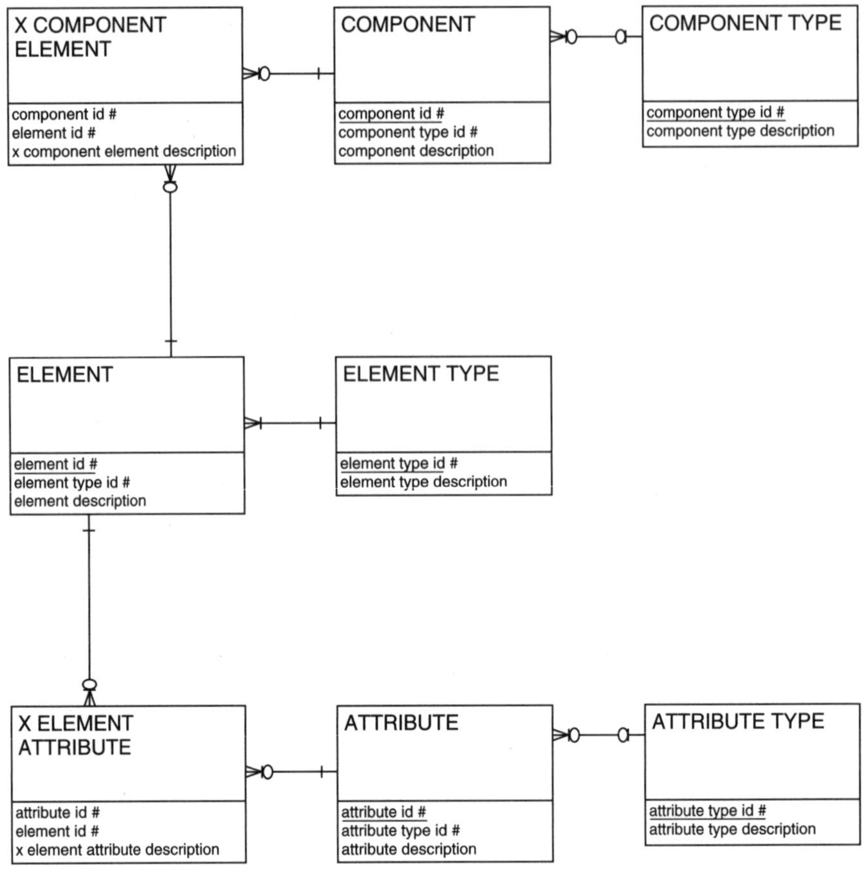

Figure 8-12 Physical implementation of the component structure decomposition—for use in maintaining facts that relate components, elements, and attributes.

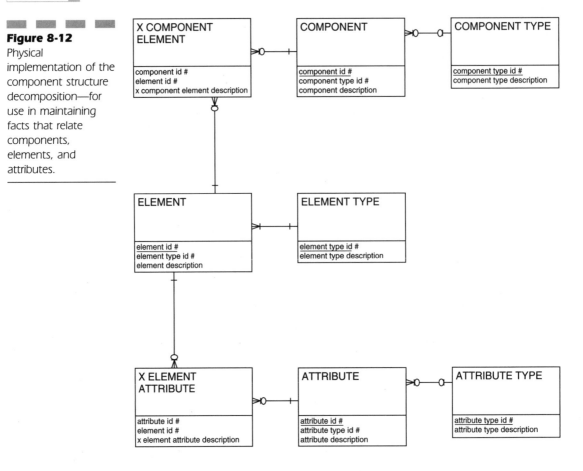

entire key for the attribute entity are contained as a group attribute <attribute description>.

The addition of a COMPONENT TYPE attribute permits a general meta-model structure to represent ELEMENT "screen element" using a type "SCREEN" and "SCREEN ELEMENTS" are part of COMPONENT TYPE "SCREEN". Maintaining COMPONENT TYPE, ATTRIBUTE TYPE, and ELEMENT TYPE data permits facts to be maintained which define screens as collections of screen elements, menus as collections of menu items, and files as collections of file elements, etc.

NOTE. *This structure is generally specified and could be further refined using a role entity to redefine the structure permitting many-to-many relationships between the ELEMENT and COMPONENT TYPE and between the COMPONENT and COMPONENT TYPES.*

Data Structure Decomposition

In addition to the composition of the system, a second set of basic representation requirements to provide for data system metadata management includes lists of:

- *Entities* conceptual system component entities are the conceptual things that a system tracks. They are facts about persons, places, or things about which the legacy system maintains information. Each entity can be comprised of many attributes and key structures. (As in data engineering, the entities could be also considered objects and implemented using object-based technologies.)
- *Attributes* The most common of metadata items, attributes are facts grouped as they uniquely describe entities. Each attribute can be a part of many entities.
- *Relationships* Narrative descriptions of possible correlations existing between entities as implemented by attributes acting as key. Relationships describe the ordinality and cardinality of the relationships between entities.

With this system metadata, a user, given an attribute, has the ability to determine: From what entity did it originate? Given an entity, what attributes formed the key structure(s)? Which were the non-key attributes? What other entities is it related to?

These facts are typically maintainable using CASE tools if they were used to develop the system. In this form the system metadata may be programmatically available. Figure 8-13 is a subset of Figure 8-2 illustrating the data structure decomposition. It implements REQs 03–06.

The first, REQ-03, describes the requirement that entities are comprised of attributes.

REQ-03 Each ATTRIBUTE is found in zero, one, or many ENTITIES and each ENTITY contains many ATTRIBUTES.

The second (REQ-04) indicates attributes are sharable among one or many entities.

REQ-04 Each ENTITY is related to one or many related ENTITIES.

REQs 05–06 describe the DECOMPOSITION entity as composed of a series of non-exclusive - smaller well-defined subsets of the entities and relationships—used to facilitate user understanding. The fifth REQ specifies a

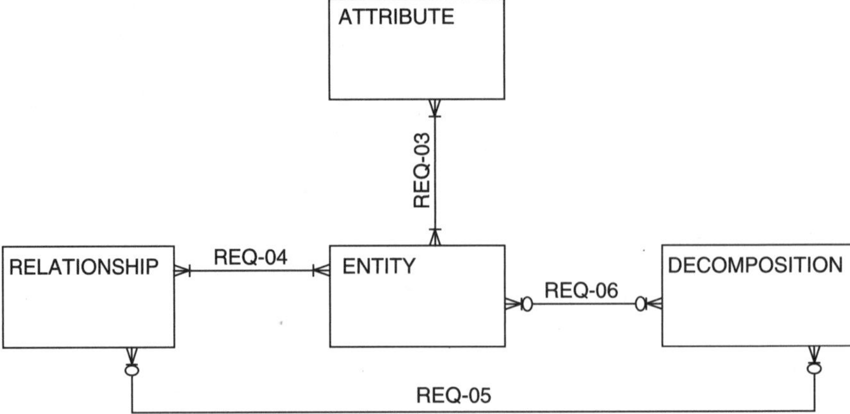

Figure 8-13 Data Structure Decomposition.

key metamodel relationship—providing for the integration of elements, entities, and decompositions. REQ-05 describes the requirement to represent the entity-to-entity relationships as they occur within each respective decomposition. It is implemented as the relationship entity with attributes similar to those specified in the other intersecting entities.

REQ-05 Each RELATIONSHIP is contained in one or many DECOMPOSITIONS and each DECOMPOSITION contains one or many RELATIONSHIPS.

REQ-06 specifies the mandatory membership of entities in one or more decompositions.

REQ-06 Each ENTITY can appear in one or many DECOMPOSITIONS and each DECOMPOSITION can contain zero, one, or many ENTITIES.

Thus, each ENTITY and ATTRIBUTE can appear in multiple decompositions of the entire model and each DECOMPOSITION can contain multiple entities and attributes. A detailed physical implementation of this system metadata is shown as Figure 8-14.

Within each system, a data engineering goal is to link each ELEMENT to one specific attribute integrating data with components such as files, screens, printouts—with decreasing numbers of unassociated elements serving as a measure of success. Organization-wide benefits can begin to accrue immediately when elements are formally related to specific attributes.

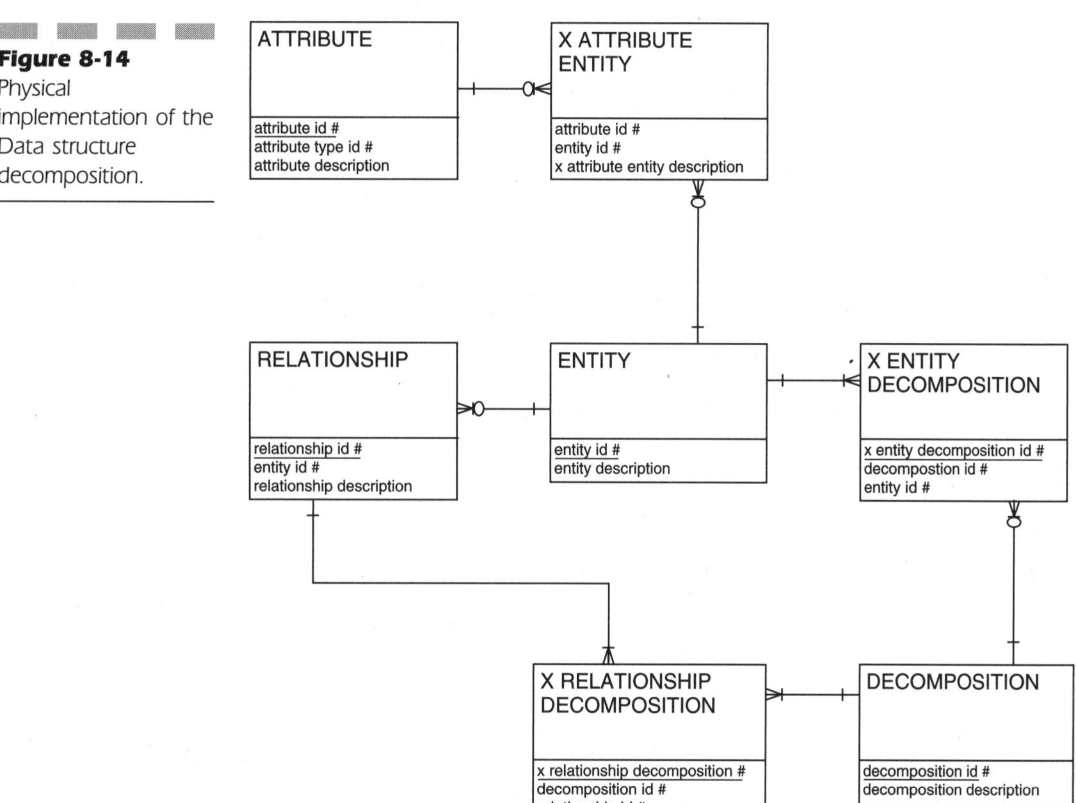

Figure 8-14 Physical implementation of the Data structure decomposition.

Evidence Traceability Decomposition

The evidence structure decomposition in Figure 8-15 is populated by three principal entities (COMPONENT, ELEMENT, and EVIDENCE).

The decomposition describes the specific evidence used to obtain the facts represented by the associated system metadata. The data source documenting the model component is maintained in the EVIDENCE entity. It represents system metadata requirements to maintain links between evidence and the facts in the metamodel. It implements two more REQs, completing the specification of this decomposition. They are:

REQ-07 Each EVIDENCE can support zero, one, or many COMPONENTS and each COMPONENT can be supported by zero, one, or many EVIDENCES.

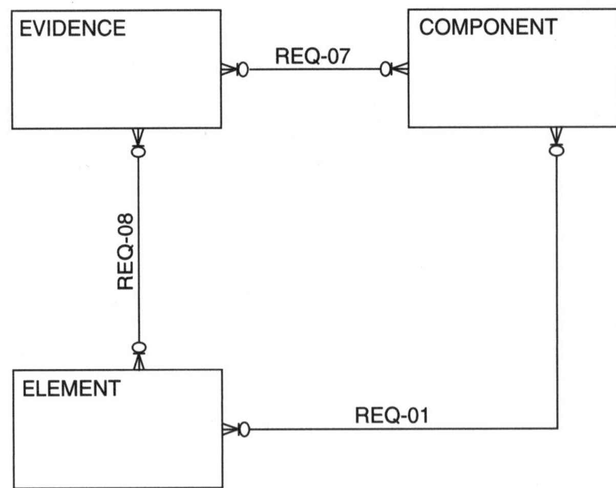

Figure 8-15
Evidence traceability decomposition.

REQ-08 Each EVIDENCE can support zero, one, or many facts represented as ELEMENTS and each ELEMENT can be associated with zero, one, or many EVIDENCES.

These entities (also shown unnormalized) permit each COMPONENT and ELEMENT to be linked to one or many evidences and to link each COMPONENT and ELEMENT to one or many EVIDENCE sources.

A detailed physical implementation of this system metadata is shown as Figure 8-16. It adds three intersecting entities to those presented in Figure 8-15.

To establish model traceability in reverse engineering contexts, and to provide the most complete set of documentation, the information source documenting system metadata facts is maintained in the EVIDENCE and corresponding EVIDENCE TYPE entities. Evidence traceability serves two purposes. The first purpose is to document the evidence used to establish the facts maintained by the metamodel. Second, once documented, the system metadata-based evidence becomes the primary source of future system documentation. The evidence traceability decomposition's system metadata documents the metamodel's validity. Data recording the source of the fact links system evidence with facts maintained in the metamodel. Each EVIDENCE is linked to one EVIDENCE TYPE and each EVIDENCE TYPE is associated with one or many evidences. Evidence types are maintained to increase the robustness of the evidence which can be represented and managed using the metamodel. Representative evidence types are shown as Figure 8-17.

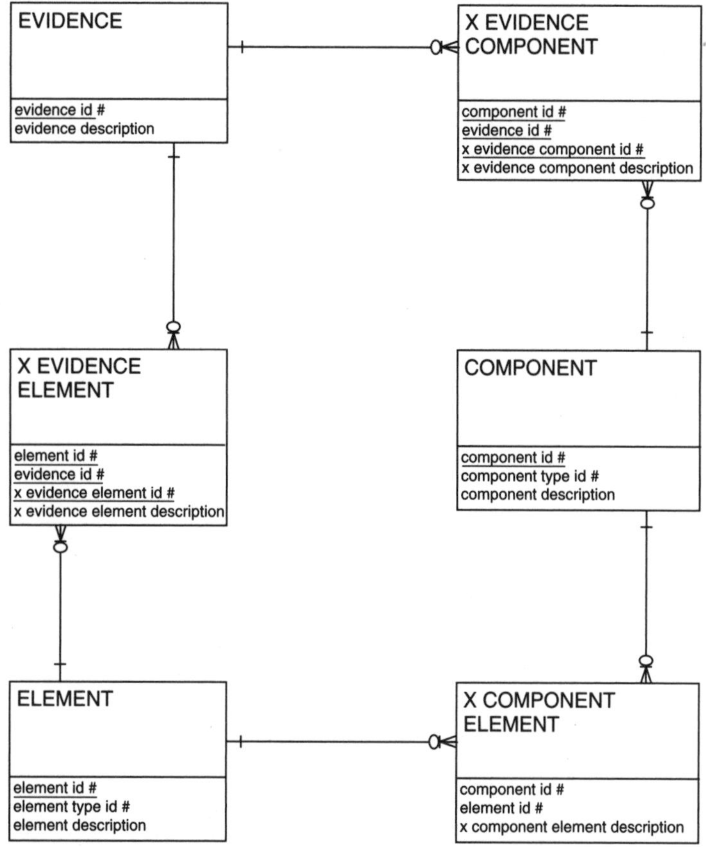

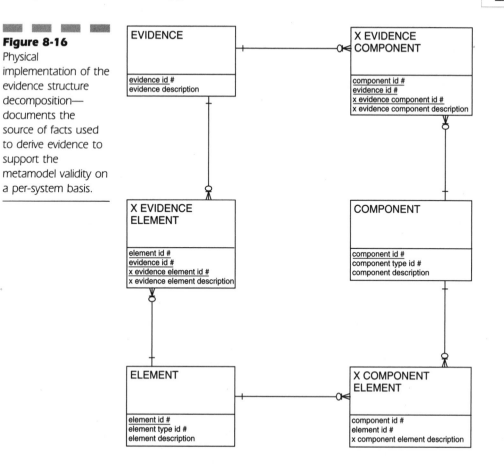

Figure 8-16 Physical implementation of the evidence structure decomposition—documents the source of facts used to derive evidence to support the metamodel validity on a per-system basis.

Figure 8-17 Evidence types.

Evidence Type	Examples
Domain specialists	Domain knowledge from the specialists, business rules
Processes	Functional descriptions, process models, code, user manuals
External data	Screen, report, interface specifications, interfaces to other systems
Conceptual data	Models, interface documentation
Internal data	Program variables, data element lists, tables, file layout structures
Policies	Directives, guidelines, planning statements
System	Program source, object code, job procedures, libraries, directories, test cases, schemas, copy libraries, make files, link maps, I/Os and other documentation, data

This achieves common data use throughout the metamodel and permits the implementation of consistent system metadata among the Enterprise Portal implementation and legacy systems. This mapping also permits programmatic control over the physical data using automated forms of manipulation. When fully normalized, system metadata is maintained in the reverse engineering analysis and the structural extensions decompositions.

When populated, the system metamodel described will maintain information as specific as:

- ATTRIBUTE X of SCREEN Y is a display of ENTITY Z (it is likely that attributes are displayed on multiple screens within the system);
- ENTITY W is generated by a code LOCATION X of JOB-STREAM Y that is maintained at LOCATION Z; and
- PRINTOUT W is related to ATTRIBUTE X of ENTITY Y and therefore it is by definition equivalent to input ELEMENT Z.

Conceptual Structure Decomposition

The conceptual structure decomposition specifies the requirements to store system metadata describing components from integrated location, user, information, and process perspectives. These perspectives should be seen as directly complementary with the Zachman Framework for Enterprise Architecture specification. The Zachman Framework was introduced in Chapter 1 and is illustrated in Figure 8-18 showing all six columns [Zachman 1987]. Many organizations use this framework articulation as the basis for their enterprise integration activities.

Mapping between the system metadata entities and the framework columns is as follows:

- The data column corresponds to the *what* perspective and maps to data maintained by the system metadata entity INFORMATION.
- The function column corresponds to the *how* perspective and maps to data maintained by the system metadata entity PROCESS.
- The network column corresponds to the *where* perspective and maps to data maintained by the system metadata entity LOCATION.

A FRAMEWORK FOR ENTERPRISE ARCHITECTURE ™

	DATA *What*	FUNCTION *How*	NETWORK *Where*	PEOPLE *Who*	TIME *When*	MOTIVATION *Why*	
OBJECTIVES/ SCOPE (CONTEXTUAL) *Planner*	List of Things Important to the Business Entity = Class of Business Thing	List of Processes the Business Performs Function = Class of Business Process	List of Locations in Which the Business Operates Node = Major Business Location	List of Organizations Important to the Business People = Class of Agent	List of Events Significant to the Business Time = Major Business Event	List of Business Goals/Strat. Ends/Means = Major Bus. Goal/ Critical Success Factor	OBJECTIVES/ SCOPE (CONTEXTUAL) *Planner*
ENTERPRISE MODEL (CONCEPTUAL) *Owner*	e.g. Semantic Model Ent. = Business Entity Reln. = Business Relationship	e.g. Business Process Model Proc. = Business Process I/O = Business Resources	e.g. Logistics Network Node = Business Location Link = Business Linkage	e.g. Work Flow Model People = Organization Unit Work = Work Product	e.g. Master Schedule Time = Business Event Cycle = Business Cycle	e.g. Business Plan End = Business Objective Means = Business Strategy	ENTERPRISE MODEL (CONCEPTUAL) *Owner*
SYSTEM MODEL (LOGICAL) *Designer*	e.g. Logical Data Model Ent. = Data Entity Reln. = Data Relationship	e.g. Application Architecture Proc. = Application Function I/O = User Views	e.g. Distributed System Architecture Node = I/S Function (Processor, Storage, etc.) Link = Line Characteristics	e.g. Human Interface Architecture People = Role Work = Deliverable	e.g. Processing Structure Time = System Event Cycle = Processing Cycle	e.g. Business Rule Model End = Structural Assertion Means = Action Assertion	SYSTEM MODEL (LOGICAL) *Designer*
TECHNOLOGY MODEL (PHYSICAL) *Builder*	e.g. Physical Data Model Ent. = Table/Segment, etc. Reln. = Key/Pointer, etc.	e.g. System Design Proc. = Computer Function I/O = Data Elements/Sets	e.g.Technology Architecture Node = Hardware/System Software Link = Line Specifications	e.g. Presentation Architecture People = User Work = Screen Format	e.g. Control Structure Time = Execute Cycle = Component Cycle	e.g. Rule Design End = Condition Means = Action	TECHNOLOGY CONSTRAINED MODEL (PHYSICAL) *Builder*
DETAILED REPRESEN-TATIONS (OUT-OF-CONTEXT) *Sub-Contractor*	e.g. Data Definition Ent. = Field Reln. = Address	e.g. Program Proc. = Language Stmt I/O = Control Block	e.g. Network Architecture Node = Addresses Link = Protocols	e.g. Security Architecture People = Identity Work = Job	e.g. Timing Definition Time = Interrupt Cycle = Machine Cycle	e.g. Rule Specification End = Sub-condition Means = Step	DETAILED REPRESEN-TATIONS (OUT-OF CONTEXT) *Sub-Contractor*
FUNCTIONING ENTERPRISE	e.g. DATA	e.g. FUNCTION	e.g. NETWORK	e.g. ORGANIZATION	e.g. SCHEDULE	e.g. STRATEGY	FUNCTIONING ENTERPRISE

John A. Zachman, Zachman International

Figure 8-18
The Zachman Framework for Enterprise Architecture.

- The people column corresponds to the *who* perspective and maps to data maintained by the system metadata entity USER.
- The time column (corresponding to the *when* perspective) is implemented structurally by time/date function-based indexing determined by the smallest addressable unit of time that can be reported (e.g., minutes, hours, days, weeks, months, etc.).
- The motivation column corresponds to the *why* perspective and it contains explicit referential links, specifically connecting Enterprise Portal information with the organizational strategy from the *planner, owner, designer, builder, sub-contractor*, and details vertically integrated perspectives (described in this chapter).

The conceptual structure decomposition specifies the requirements to store data describing the components from integrated location, user, information, and process perspectives. It specifies four new system metadata principal entities and describes nine additional REQs. The conceptual structure decomposition entities are shown as a simplified (unnormalized) version in Figure 8-19.

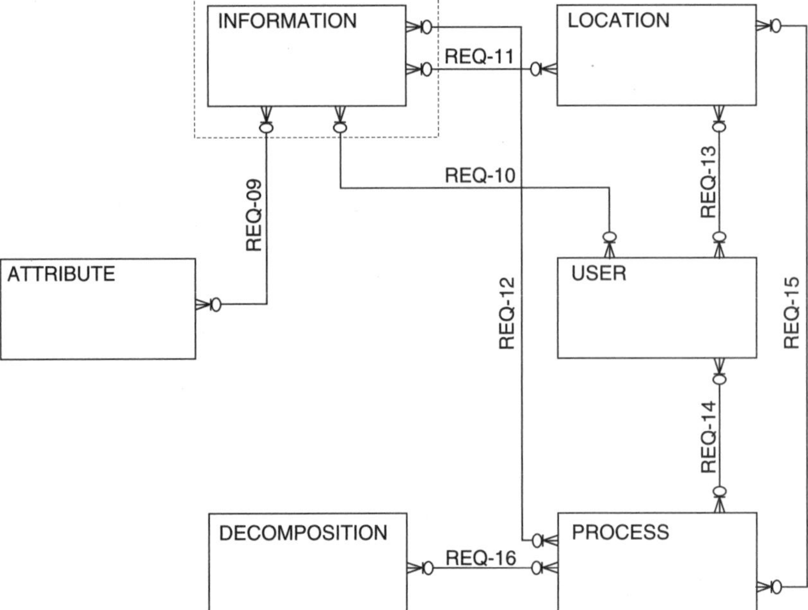

Figure 8-19 Unnormalized conceptual structure decomposition.

The conceptual structural decomposition implements the four remaining system metadata principal entities and integrates the previously introduced system metadata entities ATTRIBUTE and DECOMPOSITION. With the addition of this non-technical system metadata, the system metadata is robust enough to store the metadata facts required to engineer the Enterprise Portal. With the addition of the conceptual structural system metadata entities, the system metamodel can store information useful to component EEP analyses and specification. The four conceptual structure decompositions are described below.

Information Structure Decomposition

The information structure, user structure, and location structure decompositions (shown as Figure 8-20) are populated by the same five primary entities (ATTRIBUTE, USER, LOCATION, PROCESS, and INFORMATION).

The new entities are defined in Figure 8-21.

Following Appleton [Appleton 1984], the INFORMATION entity is used to identify specific attributes provided as INFORMATION in response to a specific request. Each INFORMATION can be composed of multiple ATTRIBUTES and each ATTRIBUTE can be provided as part of one or many INFORMATIONS.

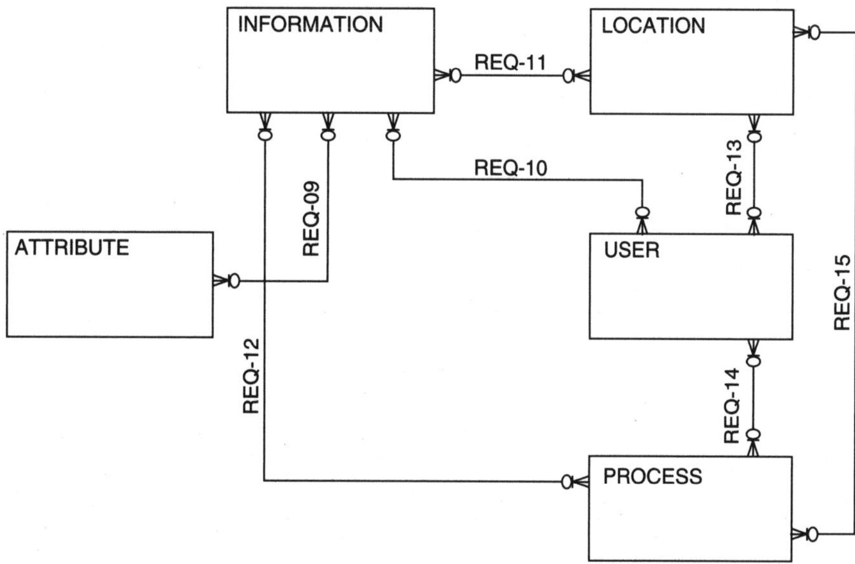

Figure 8-20 Information structure, user structure, and location structure decompositions are identically represented.

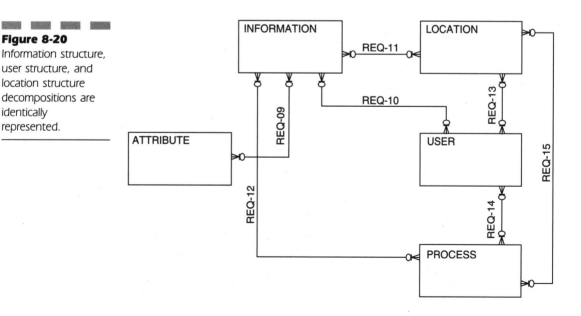

Figure 8-21
Metamodel entity definitions for the information structure decomposition.

Entity	Definition
INFORMATION	One or many attributes provided in response to a USER request
USER	A person who makes a specific request for INFORMATION
PROCESS	Organizational business process initiated in response to pre-defined external events are performed at one or many LOCATIONS by one or many users
LOCATION	Are defined as places where a specific INFORMATION is accessed or provided to specific USERS

The INFORMATION entity is used to identify specific attributes provided as INFORMATION in response to a specific request. This illustrates REQ-09.

REQ-09 Each INFORMATION can be composed of zero, one, or many ATTRIBUTES and each ATTRIBUTE can be provided as part of zero, one, or many INFORMATIONS.

The next three REQs concern representation of data at various locations; for various users; and produced or consumed by various processes.

REQ-10 Each INFORMATION can be consumed by zero, one, or many USERS and each USER can be provided to one or many INFORMATIONS.

REQ-11 Each INFORMATION can be received by zero, one, or many LOCATIONS and each LOCATION can be provided one or many INFORMATIONS.

REQ-12 Each INFORMATION can be supplied to one or many PROCESSES and each PROCESS can require one or many INFORMATIONS.

A detailed physical implementation of this system metadata is shown as Figure 8-22.

One or many USERS receive the information and each USER can request multiple types of INFORMATION. Each USER can reside at one or many LOCATIONS and each LOCATION can have many USERS. Each individual INFORMATION can be related to one or many PROCESSES and each PROCESS can require one or many INFORMATIONS. In addition, each INFORMATION is required by one or many LOCATIONS and each LOCATION requires one or many INFORMATIONS. Further, each LOCATION may perform many PROCESSES and each PROCESS may be performed at many LOCATIONS. Each PROCESS can be associated with one or many DECOMPOSITIONS and each DECOMPOSITION can be associated with one or many PROCESSES.

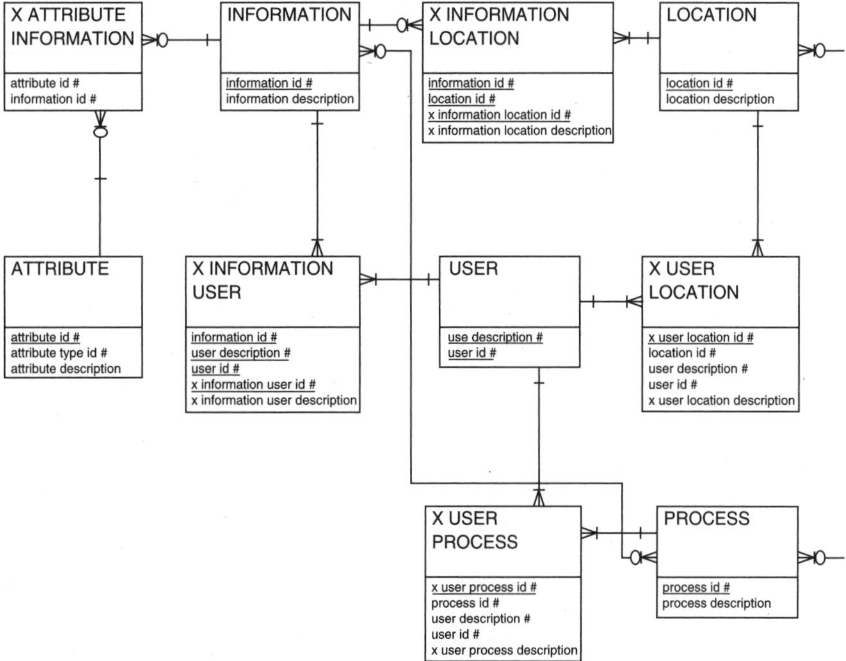

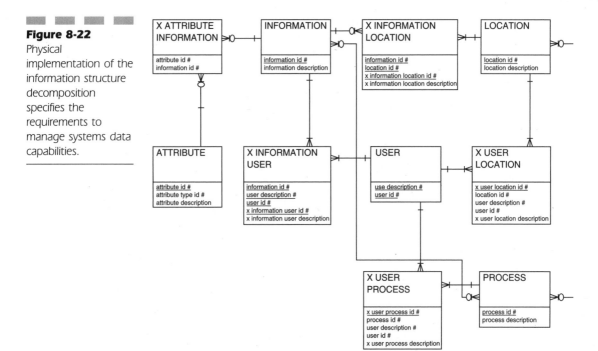

Figure 8-22 Physical implementation of the information structure decomposition specifies the requirements to manage systems data capabilities.

Once the information is accurately represented in the metamodel (after completion of Activities A1–A5), Enterprise Portal engineers can normalize the "as-is" (existing) data as represented by the ENTITY and ATTRIBUTE entities. These requirements provide the basis for the new Enterprise Portal data model and physical Enterprise Portal design and maintain links to other system metadata entities. Other aspects of the EP design, such as the development of user views, can be implemented using information stored in the intersecting entities between INFORMATION and USER.

User Structure Decomposition

The user structure decomposition is depicted identically to Figure 8-20 because it is populated by the same four principal entities (LOCATION, USER, PROCESS, and INFORMATION) but the focus of this decomposition is specifying how the system user characteristics can be managed programmatically. Users can be categorized by information and process affiliations. This implements many-to-many relationships among users, processes, and information. Users initiate processes to obtain information at specific locations. This decomposition implements two more REQS specifying user structure decomposition requirements:

REQ-13 Each USER can reside at one or many LOCATIONS and each LOCATION can have one or many USERS.

REQ-14 Each USER can participate in one or many PROCESSES and each PROCESS can have one or many USERS.

Location Structure Decomposition

As with the user structure decomposition, the focus of this decomposition is on the organizational location metadata and one additional REQ.

REQ-15 Each LOCATION performs one or many PROCESSES and each PROCESS is performed at one or many LOCATIONS.

Process Structure Decomposition

With the addition of the decomposition entity, the process structure decomposition in Figure 8-23 is identical to the information, process, user, and location decompositions. It implements the last REQ.

REQ-16 Each process can be associated with one or many DECOMPOSITIONS and each model decomposition can be associated with one or many PROCESSES.

The physical implementation is similar to that of the information structure decomposition. It is shown in Figure 8-24.

Contextual Extensions Decomposition

The contextual extensions decomposition is used to manage project-specific facts and builds onto the common metadata structure comprised of the other two decompositions. These extensions may require the addition of specific entities, attributes, or relationships to the system

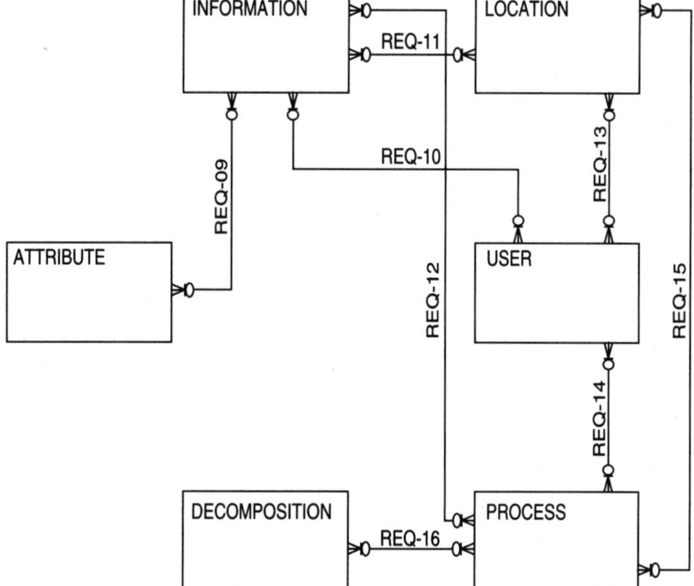

Figure 8-23 Process Structure Decomposition.

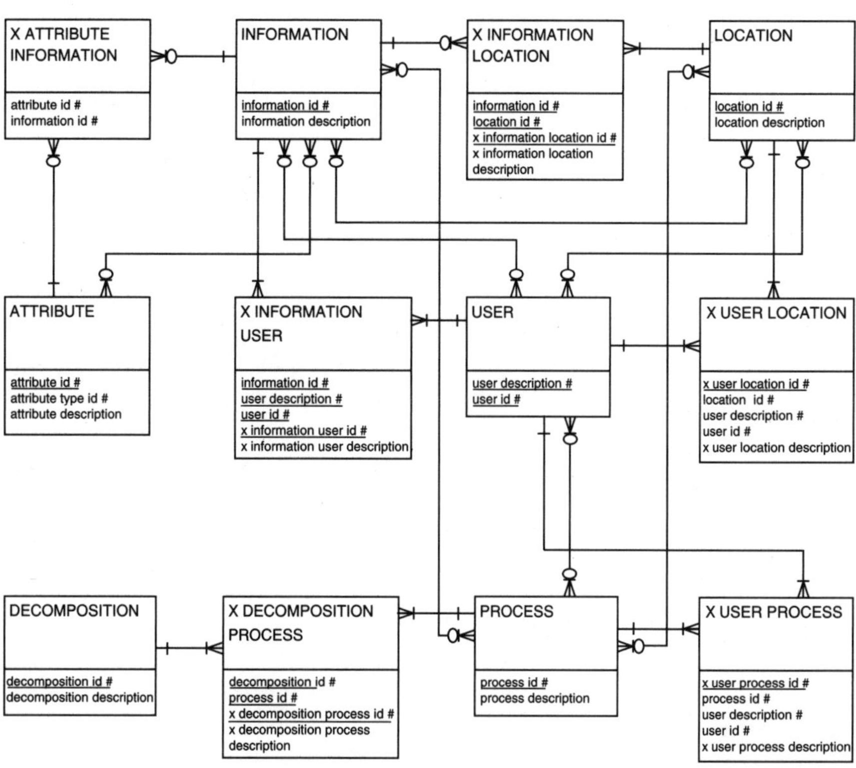

Figure 8-24 Process structure decomposition describes the requirements of programmatic management of process-based metadata.

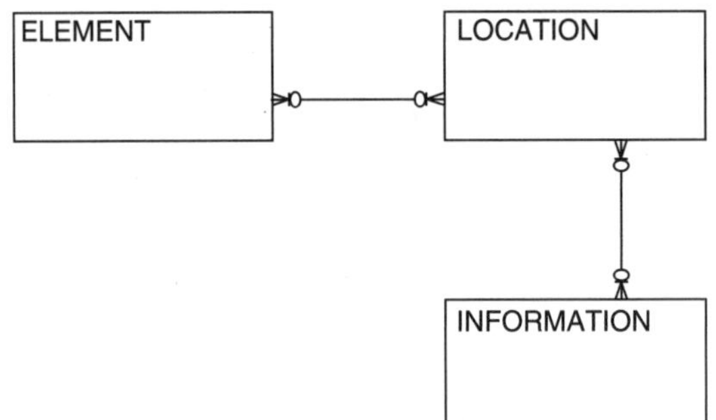

Figure 8-25
Sample relation extension useful when describing unintegrated, distributed data.

metamodel. For example, when working with distributed, unintegrated data, the *as-is* analysis may be aided by linking each INFORMATION directly with many elements and indicating that each ELEMENT can be associated with multiple locations as shown in Figure 8-25, which implements two potential REQs.

REQ-X Each INFORMATION can be associated with one or many LOCATIONS and each LOCATION can be associated with one or many INFORMATIONS.

REQ-Y Each LOCATION can be associated with one or many ELEMENTS and each ELEMENT can be associated with one or many LOCATIONS.

Its physical implementation is shown as Figure 8-26.

To provide another example of specific system metadata data extensions, consider the situation where the legacy environment is determined to be distributed in nature. Other specific system metadata attributes that can be captured might include those listed in Figure 8-27 (derived from [Inmon 1993]).

Contextual extensions may be implemented with the addition of specific attributes, entities, or relationships to the metamodel. Consider the situation where the legacy environment has been determined to be used to manage facts describing a distributed data implementation. Figure

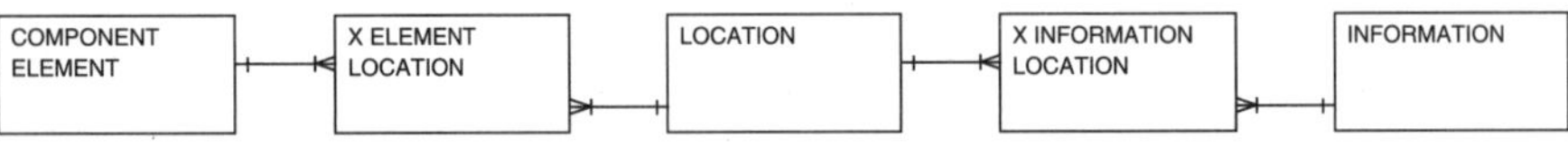

Figure 8-26
Sample relation extension useful when describing distributed data requirements.

Figure 8-27
A sample set of contextual extensions.

Type	Usage
Data usage type	operational or decision support.
Data residency	functional, subject, geographic, etc.
Data archival type	continuous, event-discrete, periodic-discrete.
Data granularity type	defining the smallest unit of addressable data as an attribute, an entity, or some other unit of measure.
Data access frequency	measured by accesses per measurement period.
Data access probability	probability that an individual ATTRIBUTE will be accessed during a processing period.
Data update probability	the probability that an ATTRIBUTE will be updated during a processing period.
Data integration requirements	the number and possible classes of integration points.
Data subject types	the number and possible subject area breakdowns.
Data location types	the number and availability of possible node locations.
Data stewardship	the business unit charged with maintaining the attribute.
Data attribute system	the component responsible for maintaining the attribute.component of record

8-28 shows how attributes can be extended from the three shown in Figure 8-14 to eleven under conditions when the attributes such as archival type and usage type are also maintained.

See also [Blaha 1995] for additional examples of idiosyncratic data implementations that can benefit from possible application of this technique and [Hainaut 1995], [Premerlani 1993] and [Edwards 1995] for other examples of context-specific system metadata.

Now you know that it is possible to accomplish data engineering as a comprehensive system examination, beginning at one point and proceeding through the entire system, but usually this approach is unnecessary. Different analyses require different system metadata and system metadata types. Once implemented, incremental builds can be used to extend system metadata maintained—making it a tool and not just a means of implementation by-product so it can continue to evolve in support of business needs. For possible future use, types include: a simple system migration; an architecture distribution; a system rehosting; or an

Figure 8-28 Attributes added to various entities describing project-specific data.

ATTRIBUTE
attribute archival type #
attribute id #
attribute usage type #
entity id #
attribute access frequency
attribute access probility
attribute name
attribute residency
attribute stewardship
attribute system of record
key information

internal data reorganization. Specific system metadata capture is driven by data engineering project goals, such as Y2K analyses. In some cases, certain analysis types provide incentives to capture certain additional system metadata supporting project-specific data engineering objectives.

REFERENCES

Appleton D. (1984) "Business Rules: The Missing Link," *Datamation* (October), **16**(30): 145–150.

Blaha, M. and Permerlani, W. (1995) "Observed Idiosyncracies of Relational Data Warehouse Designs," *Proceedings of the Second Working Conference on Reverse Engineering*, Toronto, Ontario, Canada, IEEE Computer Society Press.

Edwards, H. and Munro, M. (1995) "RECAST: Reverse engineering from COBOL to SSADM Specification," *Proceedings of the International Conference on Software Engineering*, Baltimore, MD, IEEE Computer Society Press.

Finkelstein, C. (1992) *Information Engineering: Strategic Systems Development*, Sydney, Australia: Addison-Wesley.

Hainaut, J. Englebert, V. *et al*. "Requirements for Information System Reverse Engineering Support," *Proceedings of the Second Working Conference on Reverse Engineering*, Toronto, Ontario, Canada, IEEE Computer Society Press.

Inmon, B. (1993) *Data Architecture: The Information Paradigm*, QED Technical Publishing Group.

Premerlani, W. J. and Blaha, M. (1993) "An approach for reverse engineering of relational data warehouses," *Proceedings of the IEEE*

Working Conference on Reverse Engineering, Baltimore, MD, IEEE Computer Society Press.

Zachman, J. (1987) A framework for information systems architecture, *IBM Systems Journal*, **26**(3): 276–292.

CHAPTER 9

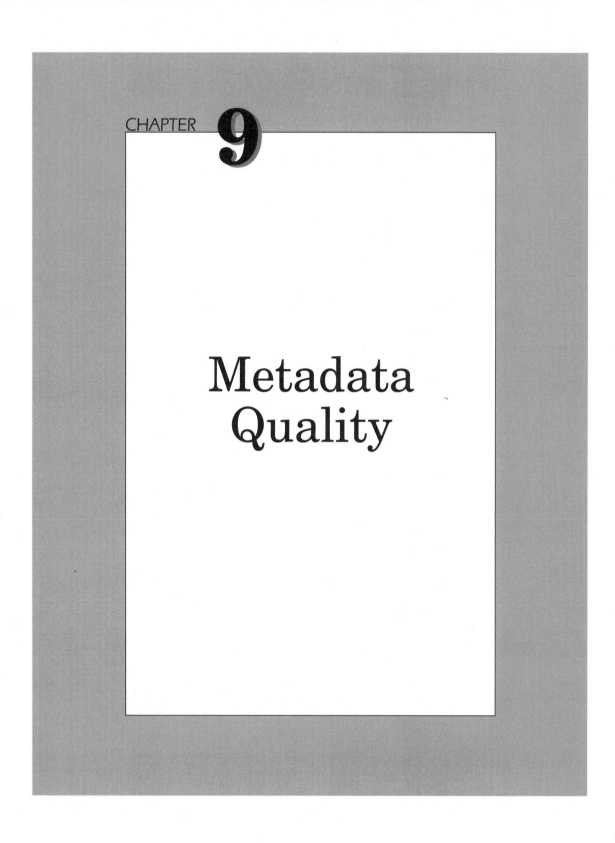

Metadata Quality

We are never so ridiculous by the qualities we have, as by those we affect to have.

—François de La Rochefoucauld

Metadata Implementation (MI) results from quality systems Metadata Engineering (ME) concepts. Organizational knowledge management and quality systems metadata engineering is required to implement your data warehouse or Enterprise Portal. The practice of quality systems ME will help you to populate these data structures with quality data resulting in higher usability for your warehouse or Enterprise Portal data.

Of course, you know that it is easier to build quality into a system than to attempt to "bolt it on" after its development and you have discovered its flaws. How often have you witnessed, much less participated in, true quality programs as part of systems development or observed their effective implementation? Not as often as you would like, we'll wager.

This chapter describes quality's key role as an integral part of EEP and quality metadata as a foundation on which Enterprise Portals must be built. We describe Enterprise Portal quality as a function of four quality dimensions. Each quality dimension is further specified as a number of Enterprise Portal quality attributes. The role of quality methods in EEP is also described in the context of a generalized eight-phase data life cycle. Enterprise Portal quality engineering depends on identifying the quality measures applicable to each of these four categories of data products and applying them in the appropriate phase. Understanding each quality dimension, its attributes, and the applicable data life-cycle methods will allow you to better focus phase-specific quality methods and, in particular, quality metadata engineering efforts. (Note: this chapter was co-authored by Youngohc Yoon).

What is Perfect Enterprise Portal Data?

Organizations are discovering that imperfect data is hidden in most information systems. The fact that most Enterprise Portals are new development projects has led to higher expectations and greater subsequent disappointments. Imperfect data negatively affects business operations and costs millions of dollars [GAO 1976]. Well-documented cases have questioned the credibility of entire classes of private sector and governmental data (see [Leipins 1989] and [Laudon 1986]). With the size of operational data warehouses and Enterprise Portals now measured in terabytes and Enterprise Portal investments costing millions, the importance of engineering quality into your warehouse or Enterprise Portal becomes obvious [Foley 1996]. As your organization relies more on Enterprise Portal and data integration for its business operations, so does its dependence on the quality of EP data and thus on the quality engineered into your Enterprise Portal. The data quality-related goal of EEP is to deliver as close to perfect data as possible.

The adjective *perfect* is defined by the 1993 *American Heritage English Dictionary* as "lacking nothing essential to the whole; complete of its nature or kind." When data supplied by a data warehouse or Enterprise Portal is accurate and lacking nothing essential, it can be described as perfect data. Data lacking anything required to respond to the customer's request is considered imperfect. Imperfect data is caused by either practice-oriented or structure-oriented causes.

Practice-oriented causes stem from a failure to rigorously apply EEP quality-engineering methods when capturing and manipulating data. Such causes typically include edit masking/range checking of input data, CRC-checking of data that has been transmitted, and other validation techniques. An array of EEP quality-engineering methods—such as those reported in surveys by [English 1996] and [Broussard 1994]—have been developed to resolve practice-oriented data quality problems.

Structure-oriented causes of imperfect data occur because of data and metadata that has been arranged imperfectly. For example: when the data is in the system but we just can't access it; when a correct data value is provided as the wrong response to a query; or when data is not provided because it is unavailable or inaccessible to the customer. Structure-oriented causes occur when developers focus within system boundaries instead of adopting an organization-wide perspective that integrates the development activities using a technology architecture.

Historically, attempts to define Enterprise Portal quality engineering have focused narrowly on presenting and correcting practice-oriented data problems, directing attention to surface problems and failing to address structural data quality issues. Failure to develop systems (including data warehouses and Enterprise Portals) as architecturally coordinated components results in fragmented data whose quality definitions apply at best within system boundaries. In these situations, practice-oriented perspectives lose their effectiveness beyond system boundaries. As a consequence, data interchange among associated legacy systems—with external partners and your Enterprise Portal—is more difficult.

In the next section, we will describe how four Enterprise Portal quality dimensions are required in order to address structure-oriented and practice-oriented causes of data imperfection.

Enterprise Portal Quality Dimensions and Attributes

The quality of Enterprise Portal data is perfect if it meets four dimensions of customer requirements shown in Figure 9-1.

The four dimensions are: data value quality, data representation quality, data model quality, and organizational Enterprise Portal data architecture quality. The dimensions correspond to the conceptual, logical, physical, and representation rows in the Zachman Framework. Figure 9-2 illustrates how these four dimensions of Enterprise Portal quality engineering correspond to the various Zachman Framework live view perspectives.

The quality of the Enterprise Portal architecture is determined by its capability to provide data for an entire organization as a single unit. The data model quality is based on its utility to multiple functional areas. Data value quality efforts can be focused because of a single logical storage location. Finally the quality of data representation is characterized by the various customer perspectives. Since the quality of these four deliverables combines to determine the Enterprise Portal quality,

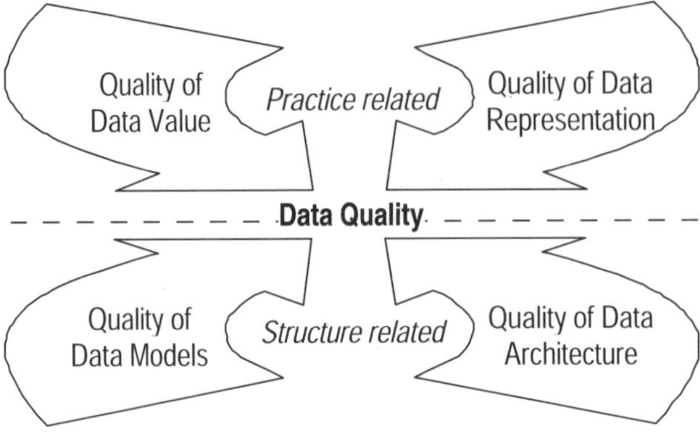

Figure 9-1 Refined dimensions of perfect Enterprise Portal data.

Figure 9-2
Four Enterprise Portal quality-engineering dimensions.

PERSPECTIVE	QUALITY DIMENSION
A single organizational perspective	Data Warehouse Architecture
Multiple functional area perspectives	Data Warehouse Models
A single logical location	Data Warehouse Values
Single customer perspectives	Data Warehouse
	Data Representation

perfecting the quality of these data quality attributes is the focus of the Enterprise Portal quality-engineering efforts.

Each dimension is comprised of multiple Enterprise Portal quality-engineering dimension attributes (we'll just call them attributes for short). When data supplied is accurate and meets all relevant attributes, it can be described as perfect data. Data lacking in any attribute that is required to respond to the customer's request is considered imperfect. The structure of the data quality metadata is summarized in Figure 9-3.

Unlike the framework, the data quality metadata is formally structured in a hierarchical fashion. One data architecture should be related to one or more data models that should determine one or more data values that should be represented by one or more data representations.

The next section presents our definitions of the data warehouse and Enterprise Portal quality dimension and associated attributes.

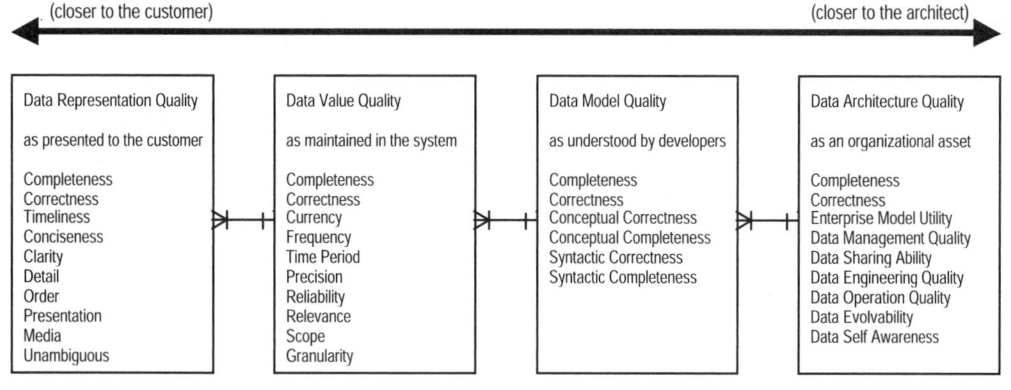

Figure 9-3
A comprehensive definition of Enterprise Portal quality metadata showing each dimension as composed of individual EP quality attributes.

Figure 9-4
Data value quality dimension attributes.

Value Attribute	Description
Completeness	Attributes of all entities requiring values have values stored.
Correctness	Data values maintained are free from fault, recording defects, or damage.
Currency	Data values maintained are the most up to date and match customer expectations.
Frequency	Data values are updated as often as the customer requires.
Time Period	Data values maintained cover the time period required by the customers.
Precision	Data values are maintained with the amount of precision required by the user. Precision refers to the measurement of detail used in specifying the data value.
Reliability	Data values stored can be depended on by the customer under stated conditions.
Relevance	Data values stored are directly responsive to the specific customer requirements.
Scope	Data values maintained match the breadth and depth of the customer request parameters.
Granularity	Data values stored hold the level of detail expected and accessible by the customer.

Data Value Quality

The quality aspect of data values has been long recognized as an important dimension of Enterprise Portal quality, and data warehouse or Enterprise Portal quality research has initially focused on perfecting the value dimension. Based on prior studies by Redman and Levitin and others (see [Redman 1992] and [Levitin 1995]), the quality attributes of data values are defined in Figure 9-4. For Enterprise Portal data to be of perfect value, all relevant attributes must also be perfect. For example, some organizational requirements emphasize data currency while others focus on the data precision to be maintained.

Data Representation Quality

Too often Enterprise Portal quality efforts end with the creation and maintenance of data values. However, work by Tuftee and others indicated that correct data values can, as in the Challenger disaster, be

Figure 9-5
Data representation quality dimension attributes.

Representation Attribute	Description
Completeness	Data presented to the customer lacks nothing with respect to the customer's information requirements.
Correctness	Data presented to the customer is free from retrieval fault, meaning that data is displayed unaltered from what was maintained, provided that the data stored is correct.
Timeliness	Data should be promptly presented to the customer at the time when it is needed.
Conciseness	Data presented to the customers should match the customers' breadth and depth requirements without missing any important data.
Clarity	Data is presented in a form that is easiest for the customer to understand given the circumstances of the request.
Detail	Data is presented in the level of detail most appropriate for the customer's need.
Order	Data is presented in a sequence fitting the customer's need and cognitive style.
Presentation	Data is presented in a format facilitating customer comprehension.
Media	Data is presented using media most effective for customer comprehension.
Unambiguity	Data presented to the customer requires no interpretation to comprehend the correct value.

imperfectly represented to customers [Tufte 1990]. This resulted in a second Enterprise Portal quality dimension—data representation quality (see also [Redman 1992] and [Fox 1994]). The attributes which determine the quality of data as represented to the customer are defined in Figure 9-5.

Data Model Quality

The data model quality dimension refers to the quality of Enterprise Portal metadata. A quality data model is essential to communicating with customers about data structure specifications. Reingruber and Gregory [1994] (see also [Fox 1994] and [Levitin 1993]) formally extended the definition of Enterprise Portal quality to include the quality of the data model. The attributes which determine the quality of data models are based on the work of [Fox 1994] (and others) and include those shown in Figure 9-6.

Figure 9-6
Data model quality dimension attributes.

Model Quality Attribute	Description
Completeness/Correctness	The model is composed of components representing all of the real-world system components. The model components—entities, attributes, and definitions—are arranged in a fashion representing the existing system.
Conceptual Completeness	The model is comprehensive enough to be used for a reference—containing complete metadata.
Conceptual Correctness	Both model component definitions and the relationships between the entities are free from fault. The model reflects the intentions of the modelers, and they did not make a mistake developing the model.
Syntactic Completeness	This quality attribute addresses the issue "Did the modelers include all of the information they desired in the model?" Is this model populated with sufficient data to be useful?
Syntactic Correctness	The model is developed and maintained according to generally accepted data modeling principles. That is, the modelers consistently and correctly applied the modeling technique to represent the entities, attributes, and their relationships.

Data Architecture Quality

Although some have recognized the importance of data architecture (see for example [Spewack 1993]), the possible, significant effect of organizational data architecture is not widely understood. Developers and vendors have typically taken task orientations when developing EPs. From the organizational perspective, absence of data definitions shared across functional areas makes data interchange among systems difficult and the need to coordinate it with an organizational data architecture obvious. This is especially true in situations when data usage crosses system boundaries, as it does at least twice when engineering enterprise portals: first as the system metadata goes from at least one legacy system to an EEP implementation; and second as the data from the legacy system is moved to the Enterprise Portal. The requirement that customers interact with multiple systems indicates a need for an organizational data architecture to coordinate cross-functional system developments is apparent

Figure 9-7
Data architecture quality dimension attributes.

Architecture Quality Attribute	Definition
Architectural Completeness	The architecture is comprehensive enough to be used by any functional areas of an organization which desire to utilize it.
Architectural Correctness	The information describing the architecture is correctly represented with the appropriate methodology. That is: "Can the organization use it to maintain uniform data definitions throughout the organization?"
Management Utility	This attribute concerns the organizational application of the data architecture in strategic planning and systems development. It is an indication of the data architecture's utility in managing the organization. Data architectures too often wind up as shelf-ware.
Data Management Quality	Data organization and all maintenance and enhancement facilities are data-driven. Models are developed and managed from an organization-wide perspective, guided by the organizational data architecture. Data is managed with distributed control from a centralized resource.
Data Sharing Ability	The data architecture is the framework serving as the basis for negotiating and implementing intra-organizational data exchange agreements. This organization-wide use is achieved through anticipating, defining, and managing data sharing requirements within the organization and among its business partners through the use of organization-wide standard metadata definitions.
Functional Enterprise Portal Quality	Data engineered in support of functional area requirements where data elements of functional systems are derived from organization metadata requirements and implemented in the organizational systems supporting information representation.
Data Operation Quality	EP quality engineering is instantiated as functional areas actively practice organizational functions and consistently apply EP quality engineering methods to data elements.
Evolvability	The organizational data architecture is maintained in a flexible fashion facilitating evolution to meet future requirements. This mostly concerns the physical implementation of the architecture. Maintaining it in a CASE tool with easy access to a repository is probably the most flexible and best alternative.
Organizational Self-Awareness	Self-awareness concerns whether entire organizations are aware of the utility and capabilities of the data architecture, and they will investigate its use and determine the types of value that it provides to them as they attempt to perform their function. Their feedback will help the data architects to further refine the architecture to make it more useful organizationally.

when numerous structural data problems exist. The attributes determining the quality of data architectures are shown in Figure 9-7.

The Enterprise Portal Data Life Cycle

The differences between practice and structure are also easily understood in the context of the Enterprise Portal data life cycle. Data quality efforts were originally focused on distinctions between data acquisition and data use cycles [Levitin and Redman 1993]. Data is stored between cycles as shown in Figure 9-8.

The life-cycle events of an individual datum include [Yoon and Aiken 1999]:

- use/input—as a control parameter, customer input, input from a screen, a record from a file;
- processing—by various system elements; or
- display/output—on screens, written to files, printed on reports

All of these facts were captured as system metadata and interrelated, comprising the standard CRUD matrix of the early 1980s [IBM 1981]. A refined and extended model of the Enterprise Portal data life cycle is presented in Figure 9-9.

Eight boxes represent eight phases: metadata creation, metadata structuring, metadata refinement, data creation, data utilization, data assessment, data refinement, and data manipulation. Next, we will present the Enterprise Portal data life-cycle phases as they occur in an Enterprise Portal context.

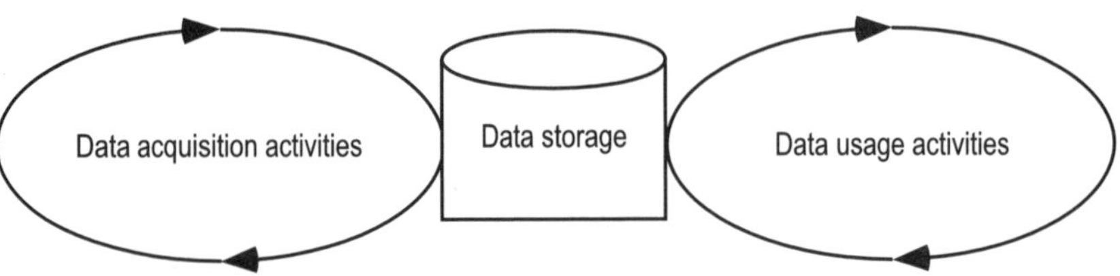

Figure 9-8 Levitan and Redman's Data Acquisition and Usage Cycles [Levitin and Redman 1993].

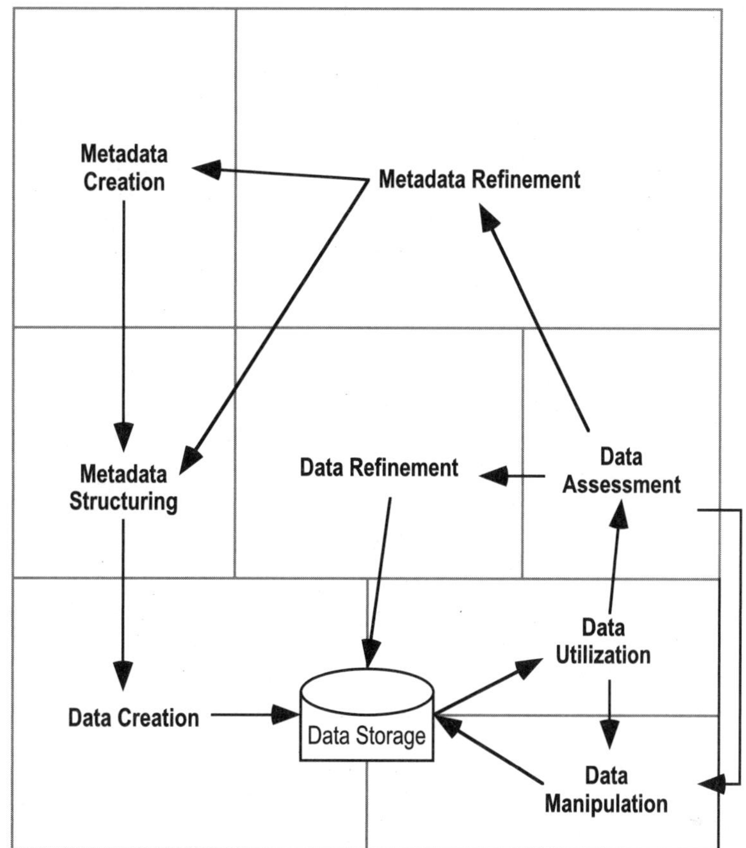

Figure 9-9 Eight-phase Enterprise Portal data life-cycle model.

Data Creation

Data creation occurs when data values are captured from some external source and stored in systems. Data sources can range from a point of sale terminal, to EDI, to floppy disk exchange, to the Internet or intranet. Data creation has been the most popular focus of Enterprise Portal quality-engineering efforts but for most Enterprise Portal efforts, the source of data warehouse or Enterprise Portal data is some organizational legacy system. Data value quality efforts are aimed at perfecting data values as they are captured and stored in your Enterprise Portal.

Data Utilization

Data utilization occurs as the Enterprise Portal data is provided as information in response to a request from a customer or a process. The focus of Enterprise Portal quality-engineering efforts for this phase is an appropriate data representation: taking data from a storage location and presenting it to a customer or a process. The data provided may or may not be assessed as described in the next phase.

Data Assessment

Often in response to complaints of imperfect data, Enterprise Portal data produced by a system is assessed formally or informally to determine its suitability for current or future use. If warehouse data is judged inadequate, the assessment should also determine if the problem is practice-orientated or structure-orientated or both. Practice-orientated problems are corrected through Enterprise Portal data refinement, while structure-orientated problems are amended through Enterprise Portal metadata refinement, creation, and structuring. Structural changes must be applied at an architectural level.

Data Refinement

If the cause of imperfect data is determined to be practice-orientated, the data values are corrected using data refinement procedures. Data refinement refers to the process of altering data within the existing structure of data. This has been a popular focus of data value quality engineering efforts (see for example [Morey 1982], [Laudon 1986], and [Ballou 1989]).

Data Manipulation

Often data is accessed to be altered, deleted, or otherwise manipulated. Data manipulation is the process of altering data forms or data values. Any change is potentially troublesome, and the Enterprise Portal quality-engineering considerations are similar to those described in the section describing data refinement. Data manipulation can also occur with or without data assessment.

Metadata Refinement

As the Enterprise Portal data structure evolves, some metadata will be determined to be incapable of meeting organizational information requirements and must be refined. Metadata refinement implements an iterative approach to refining the original requirements, correcting factual errors and evolving the Enterprise Portal structure to more correctly meet organizational requirements. This usually occurs in response to data assessment activities.

Metadata Creation

Each metadatum is created once. In situations where organizational data collection efforts are starting from scratch, Enterprise Portal architecture components can be developed with an understanding of organizational information needs based on the analysis of its mission, goals, objectives, and KPIs as discussed in Chapter 2. It is more likely that the organization has inherited its legacy data. In these situations, this metadata describes existing systems. These become the inputs to the development of the data architecture. This phase focuses on developing the framework for the Enterprise Portal architecture.

Metadata Structuring

For the remainder of its life, metadata is evolved. The term "structuring" indicates the iterative refinement process that occurs as the organizational Enterprise Portal metadata structure refinements are implemented.

Enterprise Portal Data Life Cycle Products

The eight data life-cycle phases in Figure 9-9 consume and produce with the inputs and outputs as shown in bold in Figure 9-10. These can be organized into four categories: (1) an organizational Enterprise Portal

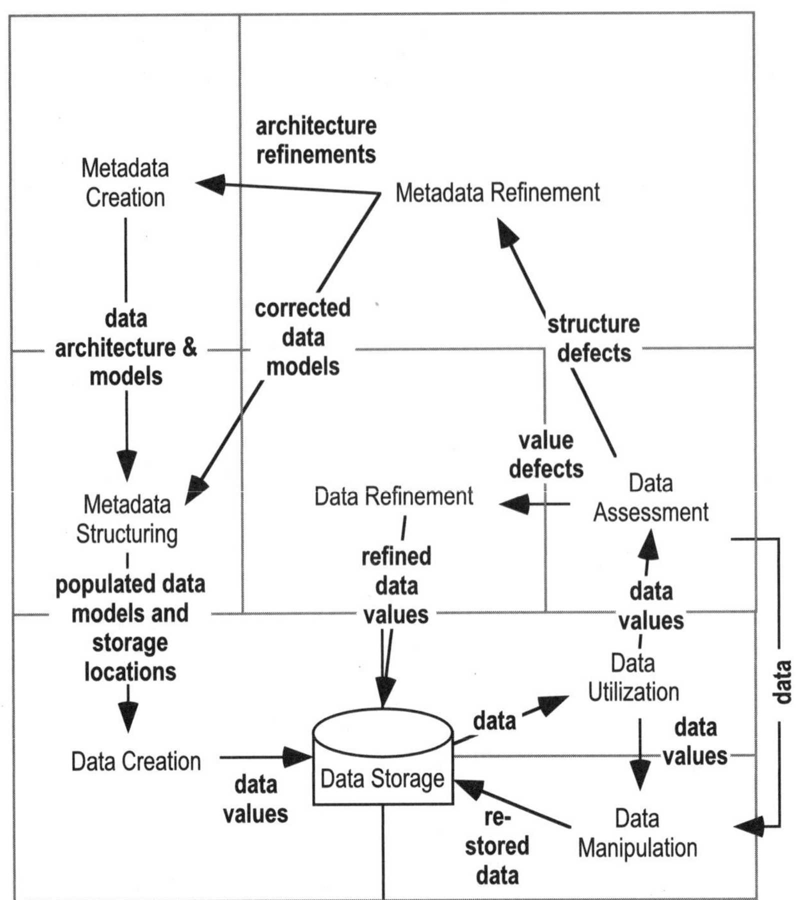

Figure 9-10 Data life-cycle model with the addition of input and output shown in bold.

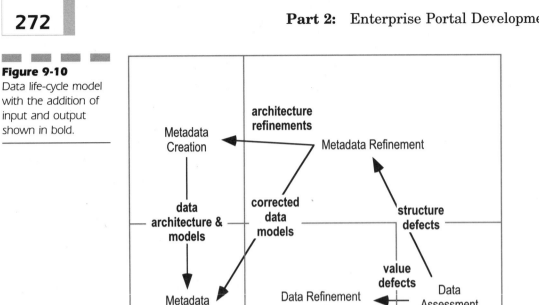

architecture; (2) a series of related Enterprise Portal models; (3) specific Enterprise Portal data values; and (4) Enterprise Portal representations.

As shown in Figure 9-11, each quality dimension focuses primarily on different phases in the data life-cycle model.

This dimension of Enterprise Portal quality-engineering efforts is most important at the data capture, data manipulation, and data restoring phases of the data life-cycle.

Because customers deal with data as represented—not as abstract data entities and/or values—the Enterprise Portal quality-engineering efforts have been extended to the data utilization phase to ensure the customers receive quality representation of the stored data values. For this dimension, Enterprise Portal quality-engineering efforts are focused

		Metadata			Data				
Dimension	Focus/Phase:	Refinement	Creation	Structuring	Creation	Manipulation	Refinement	Utilization	Assessment
Data Architecture Quality	Data architecture quality is the focus of metadata creation and refinement efforts.	↵	↵						↵
Data Model Quality	Data model quality is the focus of metadata refinement and structuring efforts.	↵		↵					↵
Data Value Quality	Data value quality is the focus of the data creation, manipulation, and refinements phases.				↵	↵	↵		↵
Data Representation Quality	Data representation quality is the focus of data utilization phase.							↵	↵

Figure 9-11
Metamodel quality dimensions related to data model life-cycle phases.

on representing the data value component to the customer during the data utilization phase.

- Data architecture quality is the focus of metadata creation and refinement efforts.
- Data model quality is the focus of metadata structuring efforts.
- Data value quality is the focus of the data creation, manipulation, and refinements phases.
- Data architecture and model quality are the focus of metadata refinement efforts.
- Data representation quality is the focus of data utilization and assessment phase.

Use Figures 9-11 and 9-12 to narrow the focus of your Enterprise Portal quality-engineering efforts. The perspective pertinent to each quality dimension is the basis for identifying a set of quality attributes for the dimension.

Development of the comprehensive Enterprise Portal quality metadata model will enable organizations to focus more effectively on the dimensions that enhance Enterprise Portal quality, pre-empting damage

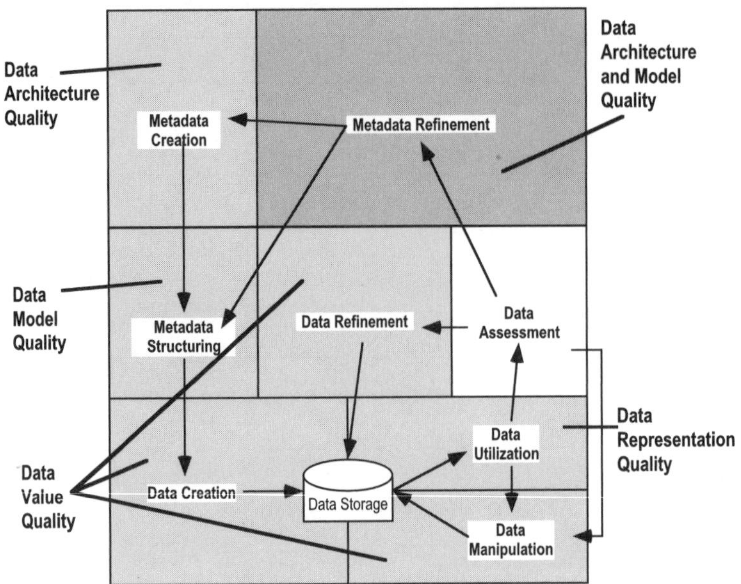

Figure 9-12 Matching Enterprise Portal quality dimensions with the primary focus of data life-cycle phases (the responding phases of the data life-cycle model)

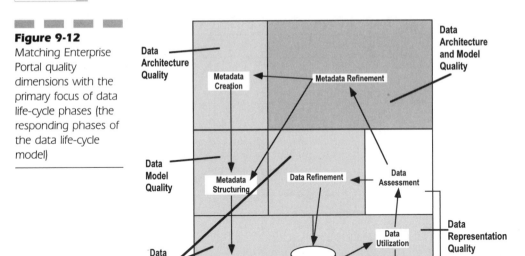

caused by imperfect data. However, Enterprise Portal quality-engineering efforts will be more effective if organization-wide quality guidance exists with respect to these four dimensions. Although our analyses revealed the existence of transformation points, further studies are required to identify the condition required for transformation points and the nature of each transformation. Using this information, Enterprise Portal quality-engineering methods most effective to each transformation point could be applied to improve the EP quality. Key to Enterprise Portal quality engineering is determining which of the EP quality-engineering attributes are required to perfectly respond to customer requests. Enterprise Portal quality-engineering efforts will be more cost-effective if organization-wide quality guidance with respect to the four dimensions exists.

REFERENCES

Ballou, D. and Tayi, G. (1989) "Methodology for allocating resources for data warehouse quality enhancement," *Communications of the ACM* (March) 32(3): 319–329.

Broussard, S. *et al.* (1994) *Data Warehouse Quality-Engineering Handbook Defense Logistics Agency*, Alexandria, VA.

English, L. P. (1996) "Help for data warehouse quality Problems—A number of automated tools can ease data cleansing and help improve data warehouse quality," *InformationWeek*, Issue: 600 (October 7).

Foley, J. (1996) "Databases—Towering Terabytes—Fast growing data warehouses are reaching terabyte size and creating a new elite among corporations," *Information Week*, Issue: 599 (September 30).

Fox, C., Levitin, A. and Redman, T. (1994) "The Notion of Data and Its Quality Dimensions," *Information Processing and Management*, 30 (1): 9–19.

General Accounting Office (1976) "Improvements Still needed in Federal Energy Data Collection, Analysis and Reporting," OSP-76-21; B-178205, Washington, D.C. (June 15).

International Business Machines Corporation (1981) *Business Systems Planning: Information Systems Planning Guide*, 3rd edn (July) GE20-0527-3 1981.

Knight, B. (1992) "The Data Pollution," *Computerworld* (September 28).

Laudon, K. (1986) "EP quality and due process in large interorganizational record systems," *Communications of the ACM* (January), 29(19): 4–11.

Liepins, G. (1989) "Sound data are a sound investment," *Quality Process* (September): 61–64.

Levitin, A. and Redman, T. (1993) "Models of Data (Life) Cycle with Applications to Quality," *Information and Software Technology* (April) 35(3): 216–223.

Morey, R. (1982) "Estimating and Improving the Quality of Information in a MIS," *Communications of the ACM* (May), 25(5): 337–342.

Porter, M.E. and Millar, V.E. (1995) "How Information gives you Competitive Advantage," *Harvard Business Review* (July–August): 149–160.

Redman, T. (1992) *Data Warehouse Quality Management and Technology*, Bantam Books.

Reingruber, M. and Gregory, W. (1994) *The Data Modeling Handbook: A best practice approach to building quality data models*, John Wiley & Sons, Inc.

Spewak, S.H. (1993) *Enterprise Architecture Planning*, Boston: QED Publishing.

Tsichritzis, D. and Fochovsky, F. (1982) *Data Models*, Engelwood Cliffs, NJ: Prentice-Hall.

Tufte, E. (1990) "Chartjunk and the Challenger" insert materials accompanying the text Envisioning Information Graphics Press, P. O. Box 430, Cheshire, CT 06410.

Yoon, Y., Aiken, P. and Guimaraes, P. "Managing Organizational Data Resources," *Quality Dimensions Information Resources Management Journal*.

Yoon, Y. and Aiken, P. (1999) "Defining Data Quality System Metadata: Toward a Life Cycle Approach to Data Quality Engineering," *Information Resources Management Journal* (in press).

Zachman, J. (1987) "Business Systems Planning and Business Information Control Study: A Comparison," *IBM Systems Journal*, 21(1): 31–53.

Additional Reading

Aiken, P. (1996) *Data Reverse Engineering*, McGraw-Hill.

Aiken, P. (1997) *Reengineering to Design Quality into Data*. Under review by the Communications of the ACM.

Aiken, P., Muntz, A. and Richards, R. (1994) "DoD Legacy Systems: Reverse Engineering Data Requirements," *Communications of the ACM* (May) 37(5): 26–41.

Appleton, D. (1984) "Business Rules: The Missing Link," *Datamation* 30(6): 145–150.

Wand, Y. and Wang, R. Y. (1996), "Anchoring Data Warehouse Quality Dimensions in Ontological Foundations," *Communications of the ACM* (November) 39(11): 86–95.

Wang, R. Y. and Strong, D. M. (1996) "Beyond Accuracy: What data warehouse quality Means to Data Consumers," *Journal of Management Information Systems* (Spring) 12(4): 5–34.

Wang, R. Y. and Strong, D. M. (1996) "Beyond Accuracy: What Data Warehouse Quality Means to Data Consumers," *Journal of Management Information Systems* (Spring).

Wang, R. Y. (1993) "Towards Total Data Warehouse Quality Management," chapter in *Information Technology In Action* (R. Y. Wang, editor) Englewood Cliffs, New Jersey, Prentice-Hall, pp. 179–197.

Wang, R. Y., Reedy, M. P., and Kon, H. B. (1995) "Toward quality data: An attribute-based approach," *Decision Support Systems* 13: 349–372.

Wang, R. Y., Storey, V. C., and Firth, C. P. (1995) "A Framwork for Analysis of Data Warehouse Quality Research," *IEEE Transactions on Knowledge and Data Engineering* (August) 7(4): 623–640.

Wilson, L. (1992) "Devil in your Data," *InformationWeek* (August), 48–54.

Wybo, M. D. and Goodhue, D. L. (1995) "Using interdependence as a predictor of data standards: Theoretical and measurement issues," *Information & Management* 29 (1995): 317–329.

CHAPTER 10

Metadata Project Example

If you give users a printed report, they have an answer for the moment. When you provide them an effective query tool and access to an Enterprise Portal, they have insight for the future.

—Marie Freeman

This chapter presents a relatively small-scale metadata engineering (ME) and metadata implementation (MI) example, illustrating the application of the concepts presented in Part 2. The example—a sales information project—is based on the experience of one of our clients, but it has been fictionalized as an XYZ Corporation project to avoid disclosing confidential client information. At project inception, the sponsoring Marketing Department was using unintegrated sales analysis and reporting systems that supported two unintegrated business units.

The sales analysts were presently spending 80 percent of their time on the mechanics of obtaining source sales data for analysis. Only 20 percent of their time was spent on actual analysis of the results. One project goal was to reverse this ratio, so that sales analysts would not spend more than 20 percent of their time on the mechanics of obtaining data. Other project goals were also set; these are detailed later in the chapter in the project specifications—specific data quality attributes included uniformity, currency, and consistency. The project was called the Sales Enterprise Portal (SEP) project. This chapter focuses on preparing the business case for the project. Later chapters will discuss the detailed implementation steps for the project.

Sales Enterprise Portal (SEP) Project Characteristics

You remember that we discussed some of the problems experienced by XYZ Corporation in Chapter 2. The example in that chapter focused on Market Analysis, defining *Market Share* and *Product Pricing* strategies, and *Unit Market Share KPI*. Management now need to address the problems discussed in that chapter. They have since been greatly magnified by the acquisition of two companies, which have different sales analysis systems. These subsidiary companies now operate as different business units. The Sales Enterprise Portal project has been established to integrate these systems and resolve their differences.

The Sales Enterprise Portal project effort was considered an incremental effort in a much larger reengineering strategy. That is, XYZ

Corporation had already seen the value of data as an organizational asset. They wanted to implement the SEP as one of several strategic investments designed to capitalize on their valuable organizational data. Other aspects of their reengineering strategy will be discussed in Chapters 12 and 13.

Over the past decade XYZ Corporation had acquired a number of companies, each with their own way of tracking and reporting sales data. None of the existing systems provided any archival capabilities or the ability to perform longitudinal analyses of the sales data. The SEP project was planned to support the organizational sales analysts' efforts by providing a single point of information for all organizational sales analysis.

The first sales analysis system (S1) processes sales data for one business unit. This is a partially implemented Commercial Off The Shelf (COTS) system that is run on an Amdahl mainframe. It was installed in the mid-1980s. Its data structure was physically implemented as VSAM files containing hundreds of attributes. At run time the physical files are redefined by application software to appear as distinct virtual database tables.

The second system (S2) processes sales data for another business unit. S2 uses different hardware—a Unisys mainframe. S2 was developed inhouse in the early 1970s using a homegrown, network-style Unisys database, with associated utility and other software programs.

The project objective is to integrate these two sales analysis systems into a Sales Enterprise Portal within a larger Enterprise Portal project. Figure 10-1 provides descriptive statistics, characterizing the data structures of S1 and S2.

While Figure 10-1 includes details of the number of relationships, entities, and attributes for each system, these are estimates only to indicate their relative complexity. There are no data models at present available for either system.

					APPROXIMATE NUMBER OF DATA				
			1999		*Records*				
System	**Platform**	**OS**	**Age**	**Structure**	**Physical**	**Logical**	**Relationships**	**Entities**	**Attributes**
S1	Amdahl	MVS	14	VSAM/virtual database tables	7 Million	2 Million	500	350	6500
S2	Unisys	OS 1100	27	DMS (network database)	5 Million	1 Million	1600	90	1500

Figure 10-1
Data characteristics of S1 and S2 Systems.

TABLE 10.1

Capital Budget Request Statement

The research group currently provides account-based point of sales analysis to the organization through the use of mainframe programs, databases, and spreadsheets. However, owing to processing constraints, the analysts are limited to the number of years of information they can view (2 years) and data granularity (they cannot easily access store-level data). In addition, sales across countries cannot be easily compared and many key issues hamper the organization from effectively analyzing sales. The purpose of this capital budget request is to gain approval to fund the Sales Enterprise Portal (SEP) project. This project will address the data access and availability limitations currently faced by the research group. The SEP will provide the following benefits:

- *Easy and quick access to multiple years of worldwide sales information. The sales analysis system will include data from the U.S., Canada, France, Germany, U.K., Italy, Spain, Australia, and Mexico.*
- *Allows for cross-country comparison of sales data in order to monitor quotas and inventory.*
- *Allows for more efficient allocation of resources, particularly manufacturing and media dollars.*
- *Allows for better sales and inventory management at the individual country level.*
- *Faster response times and more timely access to store-level data.*
- *Exception reporting.*
- *Time savings as analysts will be able to redirect time currently spent consolidating information instead to analyzing sales trends and identifying opportunities to expand sales.*

The SEP project will enable the organization to address questions which are very difficult to answer today, such as the identification of:

- *Global product performance across key countries*
- *Global brand analysis across key countries*
- *Quota projections for key products*
- *Advertising response for categories across key countries*
- *Analysis across companies for the requested categories*
- *Early TV reads in spot markets*

Benefits:

- *The research organization will be able to view worldwide data easily and quickly. The data will be clean, consistent and easy to access. This will provide the organization with access to various levels of data for timely and relevant analysis of toys.*
- *The group will have access to decision support tools that will enable analysts to immediately perform analyses based on the needs of the moment. Information will no longer be "program" driven, as access to it will be available to the end user as soon as he or she requests the information through the provided analytical tools.*
- *End users will obtain faster response to information requests, as the SEP can easily store and summarize large volumes of data.*
- *Exception reporting will be facilitated so less time will be spent on analyzing and compiling huge amounts of information.*
- *Delivery of analysis tools will virtually eliminate programming of information delivery applications, thus saving development money in the long term.*
- *These new tools will require minimal resources for global application rollout and support.*

- *Research analysts will be able to redirect the time currently spent consolidating information instead to analyzing sales trends and identifying opportunities to expand sales. Time will be redirected from data consolidation to providing:*
  - *More market analysis (TV and Test Markets)*
  - *International POS analysis for additional brands. Currently, only international sales are analyzed.*
  - *More depth to analysis for additional toys*
  - *Analysis across countries*

Sales Enterprise Portal Project Specifications

The first task for the IT Manager was to prepare the necessary documentation for approval of the project. A systems analyst (being groomed for greater responsibilities) was assigned to the project as Project Leader. The IT Manager handed her the *Capital Budget Request Statement* prepared by the Project Sponsor, the Marketing Manager. This is documented as Table 10.1. He asked the Project Leader to meet with the Marketing Manager and prepare any other documentation required by management.

On meeting with the Marketing Manager, the Project Leader learned that management had asked for further detail. They requested a statement describing the project vision, mission, and objectives. This had also been prepared by the Marketing Manager; provided as Table 10.2.

Based on the vision, mission, and objectives for the project, management then asked for further details before they would give approval for the project to begin. They requested a project plan and project scope. The Marketing Manager allocated this task to the Project Leader. They had asked for the project scope to include: the problems and/or opportunities to be addressed; the staff to be supported; the sales analysis data to be provided; and the processes, analysis areas, and data sources that would be involved. Management had asked for a statement of the project risk. And of course, they also needed an estimate of the project cost and completion time.

These project details took some time to prepare. They have been documented by the Project Leader in Table 10.3. The project cost and time estimates were then developed as discussed later in this chapter.

One problem leading to the initiation of this project concerned major differences between the current sales analysis systems, S1 and S2. Differences existed between the systems in: terminology; calendars;

TABLE 10.2

Project Vision, Mission, and Objectives

Summary of Project Vision, Mission, and Business Objectives

Project Vision

To develop and implement a business process utilizing worldwide corporate and competitive consumer sales and marketplace data for children's products and other corporate-related industries that allows global communication, information discovery and sharing, direct information flow on a timely basis, and that identifies opportunities to improve company performance and reduce risk.

Project Mission

Enhance the effectiveness and efficiency of worldwide research and strategic analysis by implementing a business process that enables users to quickly produce accurate reports, communicate timely and actionable analysis leading to clear global strategies and insightful analysis of strengths, weaknesses, opportunities, and threats. Through data discovery, the business system can also provide global sales and inventory management, and enable us to identify strategic opportunities.

Business Objectives

A. *Develop encompassing standardized definitions to address variances in global data sources and needs of users.*
   1. *Develop standardized terminology, addressing variances in global data sources*
      a) *Use of standardized data names*
      b) *Variances in calendars, classification, pricing, and comparison toys*
      c) *Current and new data sources from direct marketing, Internet, and advertising agency sources*
   2. *Design the process and system to allow smooth incorporation of data sources used by current and future customers*
      a) *Departments: Marketing, Field Sales, Advertising, etc.*
      b) *Affiliates: Canada, Europe, Japan, etc.*

B. *Streamline and enhance the data validation process and improve data integrity.*
   1. *Process should allow comprehensive electronic data inflow for*
      a) *The organization*
      b) *Affiliate*
      c) *Competitive source data*
   2. *Ensure data integrity through expanded validation and workflow methods using a redesigned validation process*

C. *Enhance customer service by providing more effective, efficient, and flexible analytical tools for research analysts and customers.*
   1. *Increase productivity through better time efficiency (20/80) and expand technical tools/capabilities with improved validation and integrity, employ new analytical tools*
   2. *Address unique needs of users with flexible global reporting formats*
      a) *Incorporate roll-up and drill-down capabilities*
      b) *Production needs for standard publications, ad-hoc reports, special projects, and new reporting formats*
      c) *Design multiple view capability, e.g., cross-country, category, brand, and retail store level*
   3. *Enhance training and feedback methods to elicit changing needs of customers by addressing needs of customer through identification of customer work processes and global issues*

TABLE 10.3

Sales Enterprise Portal Project Plan, Scope, Users, Sales Analysis, and Project Risks

The Project Plan
Elements of the project plan include reverse engineering to identify and document the existing system, deriving the fundamental system metadata, populating the architecture, and using it to make informed future system decisions. Deriving the core SEP metadata will initiate development of a corporate repository. This in turn will: lead to reduced time required to diagnose and correct system maintenance problems; protect the organization against risk due to loss of technical expertise; and increase the accuracy of system enhancement estimates.

Project Scope
What is the Problem or Opportunity?
Currently, the staff in Sales Research are spending excessive time gathering and consolidating information, leaving inadequate time for complete analysis of worldwide data. The completed SEP should greatly reduce the time needed to access data—and with improved validation processes in place, allow more time for in-depth analysis on products worldwide. At the present time, limited access to worldwide data sources and limited capabilities of information systems prevent analysts from quickly producing reports on a worldwide basis. The SEP aims to improve the situation in both of these areas.

Who does the Project Support?
The SEP is designed to support the needs of the analysts in Sales Research. It includes the development of an SEP that will have 100 users. Approximately 30 seats will be allocated to analysts and support staff in the Sales Research and IS departments; the remaining 70 seats will be allocated for use by the affiliates worldwide, distributed two to three per affiliate.

What Sales Analysis is Included in the Project?
According to the capital budget request, the SEP should provide tools to analysts and other users to view data at store level, across countries, across companies, *and over* multiple years. *In addition, the users will be able to independently create views from applications, reducing the dependence on programmers to obtain the needed views. However, to achieve success, the validation process will need to be redesigned to improve data integrity for both current and future systems. The SEP team will concentrate efforts in the following areas:*

Process Redesign
- *Improved data validation*
- *Standardization (data definitions, terminology, and classification)*
- *Innovative information delivery to customers*

Viewing Capabilities
- *Multiple company*
- *Multiple year*
- *Multiple country*
- *Store level*
- *Data discovery (hidden trends)*

Data Sources to be Included
- *POS*
- *Shipping*
- *Competitive (Retail Panel)*
- *Advertising,* Forecasting,* Allocation,* Carryover.**
  [* *Inclusion depends on availability of electronic data.*]

(Cont'd)

TABLE 10.3

(Cont'd)

What are the Risks?

With the current hiring freeze and reduced staff in Sales Research, the demand placed on current analysts will increase. Initially, the SEP project will demand more time and resources from the department as the analysts will help to determine the requirements for process redesign and system development and training. The IS department will also experience increased workload because they will need to support not only the systems in place, but also the new SEP application.

The project will also require an improvement in the work processes, primarily in the validation procedures. To reduce the time required for gathering and consolidating information on current and future systems, current staff will need to invest time redesigning and testing new procedures to improve data integrity. This will also affect delivery times of reports. This effort will involve all members of the Sales Research and Marketing IS staff.

retailer groupings; product identification and naming; analysis methods; advertising information; product comparison features; maintenance procedures; reports and more. In fact, as the Marketing Manager sponsor sadly commented: *the only commonality about S1 and S2 is that they are totally different!"*

Management asked for a statement summarizing how these differences would be resolved by the integrated sales analysis system. A summary of the organizational requirements to be addressed by S3, the new integrated system, was prepared and is documented in Table 10.4.

Sales Enterprise Portal Architecture

In addition to the hardware and software systems needed for physical access to the data, an analytical toolkit was planned to be used to insulate the sales analysts from having to access the SEP metadata directly. This is illustrated in Figure 10-2.

The analytical toolkit in Figure 10-2 provides the desired point-and-click, drill-down data access capabilities that are needed to achieve the sales analyst productivity increases promised in the project specifications. The final details that the Marketing Manager needs for the business case are the project cost and time estimates. These are the focus of the remainder of the chapter.

TABLE 10.4

Organizational Requirements for Common Sales Analysis

1. Common Terminology
- *Report Headings*
- *Data Definitions*
- *Rollup Definitions*
- *Toy Flags*
- *Retailer Flags*
- *Titles for Published Documents*

2. Common Calendar
- *Flexible Month Ending definitions*
- *Consistent with NPD Calendar*
- *Flexible Year Ending definitions*

3. Common Groupings of Retailers
- *Change Corporation/Accounts to RETAILERS*
- *Utilize same Retailers in Retailer Groups*
  - *Top Reconciled Retailers, etc.*
- *Create Retailer flags for dynamic processing needs*
  - *Discounters, Year End Retailers, Country, Worldwide, etc.*
- *Create ability to have customized grouping of Retailers*

4. Common Toy Master and Flags
- *Utilize Global Toy Master*
- *Incorporate Company reporting structure and Worldwide reporting structure*
- *Create numerous flags for flexible reporting needs*
- *Create numerous pricing fields*
  - *retail, average invoice, A-price, FOB, list*

5. Common Rollup Toy Numbers and Flags
- *Create flags to override member toy information*
- *Create price fields to override member toy information*
- *Provide rollup toy name*

6. Common Advertising Information
- *Create common flags*
- *Create common definitions*
- *Create common methods to view advertising information*

7. Incorporate "Actual vs Planned" Features
- *Store the "planned" information*
- *Show comparison of "actual vs planned"*

8. Incorporate Comparison Product Features
- *Utilize abilities to compare same toy year to year*
- *Add ability to select comparison toy for year to year comparisons*
- *Create comparison at the toy, rollup toy, and higher levels*

9. Incorporate Ability to Access Store Level POS by Market
- *One product, rollup product, and higher levels*
- *Various reports*
  - *Top Sellers in a Market*
  - *Spot TV Advertising Analysis*

(Cont'd)

TABLE 10.4 (Cont'd)

10. Common Maintenance Procedures

- *Data Cleaning*
- *Data Consolidation*
- *Retailer Maintenance*
- *Toy Maintenance*
- *Calendar Maintenance*
- *Categorization Maintenance*

11. Common Reports

- *By Toy*
- *By Retailer*
- *By a flexible dimension of time*
  - *week, month, quarter, annual, multiple years*
- *Seasonality Tracking by Week*
- *Year End Reconciliation*
- *Monthly Forecasts*
- *Worldwide reports with multiple views*
- *Country-specific reports with multiple views*
- *Maintenance reports*
- *Data "Early Warning" reports*

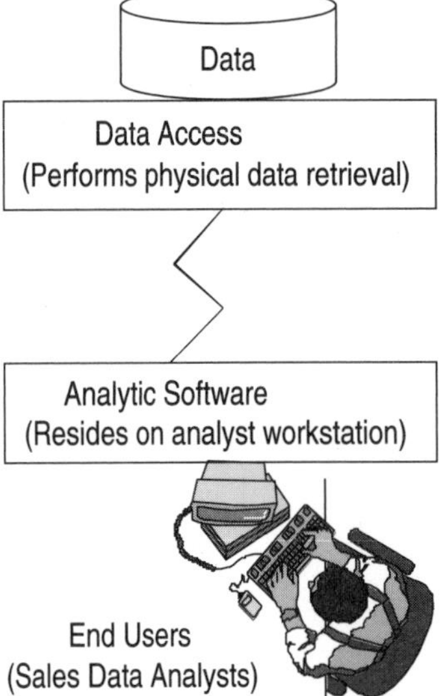

Figure 10-2 Sales Enterprise Portal architectural layers.

Data Reverse Engineering Plan

Data reverse engineering goals focus on correctly integrating and migrating data structures and data from S1 and S2 into S3 for use in the Sales Enterprise Portal (SEP). This data structure integration involves three operating systems, three hardware platforms, and three computing eras. As can be assumed, no pertinent S1 or S2 documentation existed. At best, available documentation is incomplete. But much of this has never been updated for years, although many systems changes have been made. The documentation that does exist is therefore out of date, and so is likely to be quite incorrect. It is a typical reverse engineering project.

The data reverse engineering challenge is to manage, understand, integrate, and convert thousands of data items for hundreds of thousands of records into data usable by the SEP. A metamodel is needed to provide structure for, and to facilitate, the data structure evolution. Two project characteristics motivate the use of metamodels for integrating metadata describing these three systems.

First, the documentation for S1 and S2 is insufficient to develop an understanding of their implemented data structures. Neither system was documented using traditional data models. For S1, the documentation comprises descriptions of thousands of possible run-time database tables. These descriptions are maintained manually, using tables. In addition, hundreds of undocumented modifications have been made to the system. It was customized to fit the evolving needs of the original sponsoring organization.

S2 is maintained by a single systems analyst who is (happily) the original system developer. The analyst can manipulate Unisys system utilities to obtain information and system descriptions that are needed for capital budget requests. However, no formal system documentation exists.

The data reverse engineering approach is illustrated in Figure 10-3, accomplished by the summarized steps below and discussed in more detail in the following sections:

1. Data reverse engineer S1 and S2;
2. Integrate S1 and S2 with S3;
3. Migrate the data from S1 and S2, populating the desired data structures and making it available to SEP system users;
4. Plan, develop, and implement an organizational SEP to maintain archival data (S4); and
5. Plan the conversion for the next release of the desired system (S3 v7), which will implement the data as a three-tier distributed data model.

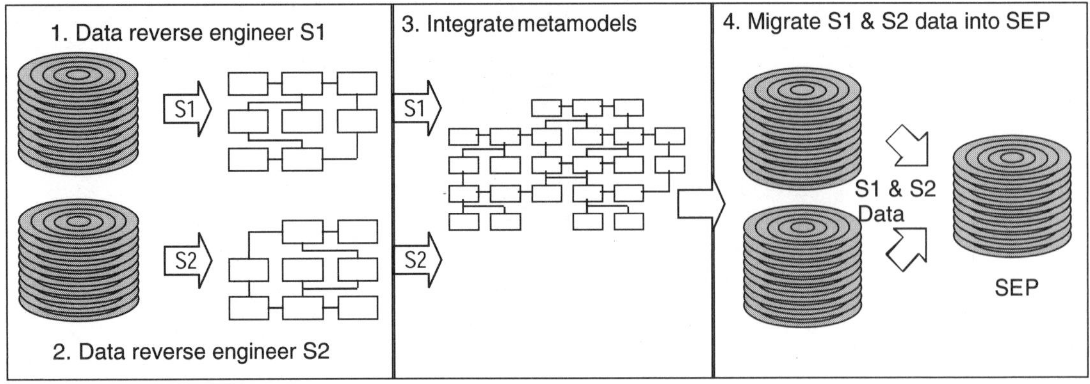

Figure 10-3
Data reverse engineering challenge.

Data Reverse Engineer S1 and S2

To obtain the metamodel representations and understand the data structures that are processed, it is necessary to reverse engineer S1 and S2. The approach to be used involves the application of formal data reverse engineering techniques to implement and populate the metamodel with metadata. This understanding will be documented using the metamodel format, discussed earlier in Part 2. Logical or conceptual data models have been the primary targets of many data reverse engineering activities. Examples are documented in [Andersson 1994], [Davis 1995], [Edwards and Munro 1995], [Aiken and Girling 1997], and [Aiken 1999]. A more complete description of this aspect of data reverse engineering analysis can be found in [Aiken 1998].

Integrate S1 and S2

Once the metadata for S1 and S2 has been reverse engineered in the previous step, it is integrated to determine data mappings needed to transform the data for use with the SEP. The data engineering challenge depicted in Figure 10-4 is to decide how to transform the existing entity

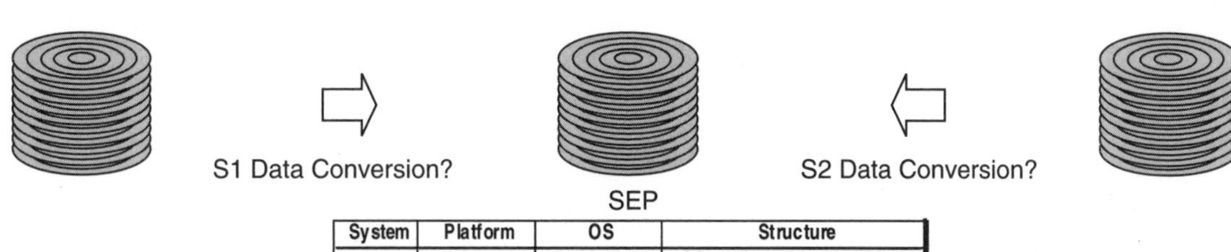

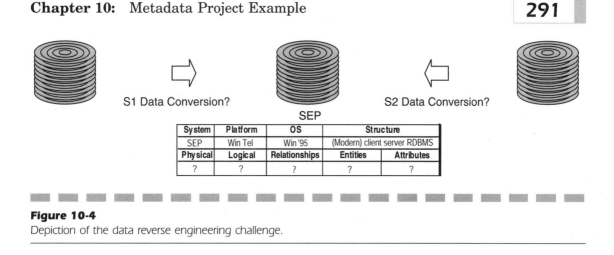

System	Platform	OS	Structure	
SEP	Win Tel	Win '95	(Modern) client server RDBMS	
Physical	**Logical**	**Relationships**	**Entities**	**Attributes**
?	?	?	?	?

Figure 10-4
Depiction of the data reverse engineering challenge.

and attribute structures—linked by hundreds of relationships (existing as separate systems)—into the desired single cohesive SEP system, S3.

First the metamodel is developed to accomplish conceptual data migration so that the physical data migration can be planned. Data engineers, in conjunction with system users, use the various decompositions to narrow and structure their focus. Metamodel reporting tools enable the engineers to map and report their progress.

The metamodel can be used to map facts and plan migration. For example, Figure 10-5 illustrates how the metamodel is used to map facts describing how entity DE(DE-A) is created by code element: CE(X), and is stored as file element: FE(Y). It provides comprehensive data regarding the sources and uses of all data items.

The mapped file element FE(Y) in Figure 10-5 is an instance of a physical data attribute in S1 or S2 that is identified as matching in S3. While the majority of these will be one to one, provisions in the metadata tool also permit one or many inputs from either S1 or S2 to be combined in S3, as well as attributes in S1 and S2 to be subdivided further in S3. In many cases these can be incorporated into the existing metadata as entities or attributes.

Migrate Data from S1 and S2

This step migrates the data from S1 and S2, populating the S3 data structures, thereby making that data available to the SEP users. Another example of metamodel use is shown in Figure 10-6. This

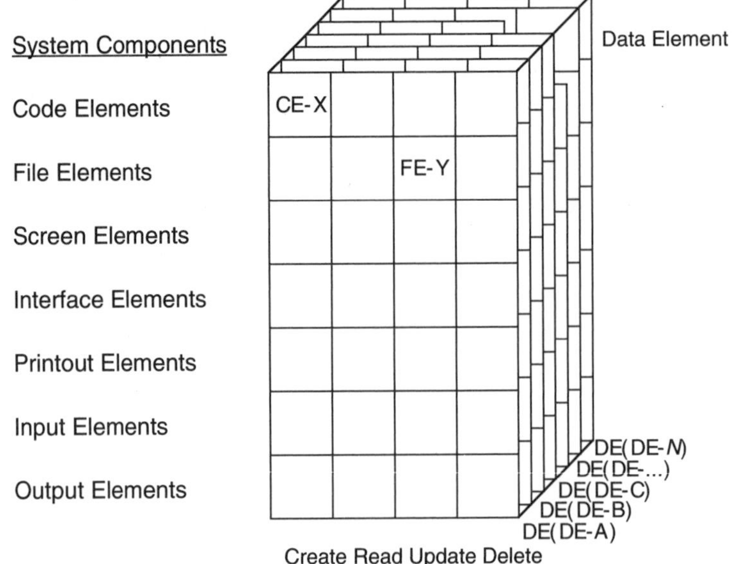

Figure 10-5 Metamodel integration supporting physical data migration.

answers the question, *What code element is responsible for handling the screen-based update of the variable that prints as printout element PE (46)?*

The metamodel is first queried by asking for the screen elements that can update PE(46). The result for this example is: SE(255), SE(434), SE(756), and SE(1056). The metamodel is queried again using these screen elements. The result indicates that code element CE(1232) produces the update to SE(255).

Figure 6-8 has been reproduced as Figure 10-6. This illustrates another metamodel use, which exceeds typical CASE tool capabilities in maintaining relationships between the system components: printout elements; screen elements; and file elements. This comprehensive, highly

Figure 10-6 An example showing how metadata is accessed by developers. Other potential choices are shown italicized.

Printout Element		Use		Screen Element		Code Element
PE(43)						
PE(44)		*create*				
PE(45)		*read*				
PE(46)	is used for	update	by	SE(255)	produced by	CE(1232)
PE(47)		*delete*		*SE(434)*		
PE(48)				*SE(756)*		
PE(49)				*SE(1056)*		
PE(50)						

developed data also exceeds what is normally available from typical system documentation.

Figure 10-5 shows how the metamodel can also be used to respond to the question: *Where did the value that is currently stored in FE(X) originate (where file element (X) = 'CUSTOMER.ADDRESS')?* For example, the metamodel shows that SE(Y) (screen element = "NEW.ADDRESS") is the only source of updates for FE(X). The metamodel can also be used to determine that FE(X) is used to create printout elements PE(L), PE(M), PE(N).

Another key use of metadata types is in the analysis of panels and/or screens. The design for S3 contains 1194 menu items. More than 39 processes and 890 individual workflow steps are defined by S3. The types of processes that users must perform can also be determined from the metamodel. A hierarchical layer structure of screen elements and screens was also created by the developers of S3, providing structures that combine panels into related process groupings.

Consider the value that this metadata can bring to a Year-2000 (Y2K) analysis. Using the metadata, DE(X) is determined to link back to FE(Y) in S1. Moving forward into S3, DE(X) is implemented in S3 as FE(Q). Conversion program (R) contains the code used to migrate the data—formerly maintained as S1(FE(X))—now to S3(FE(P)). In this fashion, the process of migrating data from S1 and S2 is: (1) organized according to existing data structures; (2) greatly facilitated using utility program generation; and (3) verified using actual output results.

A further programmatic use of the metadata is in support of database design. For example, development of user decompositions implements data stored in the intersecting entity between INFORMATION and USER, thus resolving instances of user and information needs. System security is also implemented using the same data extensions, as the basis for planning access levels and privileges. This enhances support of automated generation of system utilities, and the maintenance of system state changes.

Develop and Implement the SEP

From the preceding analysis, a plan can be prepared to develop and implement a Sales Enterprise Portal that maintains archival data for sales analysis purposes. Later in this chapter we will re-evaluate the benefits of metadata and the resources required to produce it, and—

where required—to obtain additional metadata guided by the previous results.

The Project Budget

The previous steps enable the development of a project budget. Analysis of this budget in Figure 10-7 indicates the SEP technologies that will be utilized by this investment. The Project Leader issues a Request for Information (RFI), comprising the project documentation prepared in Tables 10.1–10.4.

From the vendor RFI responses, two potential vendors were found to have suitable solutions. They had also worked closely with each other on past XYZ projects. They proposed hardware and software products and consulting support, which were discounted to a best-possible price. The project cost was estimated to be approximately $800K. With training, $700K was required for purchase of vendor system components and consulting.

Specialized hardware and integrated software form integrated warehousing packages on a multitude of platforms. With the current state of toolsets, only very specialized circumstances would dictate a home-grown solution. And purchase of a hardware/software combination is incomplete without setup assistance. As the tools mature and incorporate advanced interface technologies, the need for specialized setup assistance will diminish.

NOTE. *The setup activities involve metadata specification and exchange, as described earlier in this and other chapters of Part 2.*

For the near future, it is likely that investments in consulting support for initial setup, and for mapping legacy data into the SEP will be fruitful. The more that an organization prepares, using the methods outlined in this book, the more precise will be the communication between vendors, developers, clients, and management.

Of the project budget in Figure 10-7, $500K is for the integrated hardware/software combination—installed and set up by a single vendor who will provide necessary consulting support. The agreement covers the hardware acquisition/installation, software purchase, installation, and setup. A total of 15 days of consulting support was negotiated at a rate

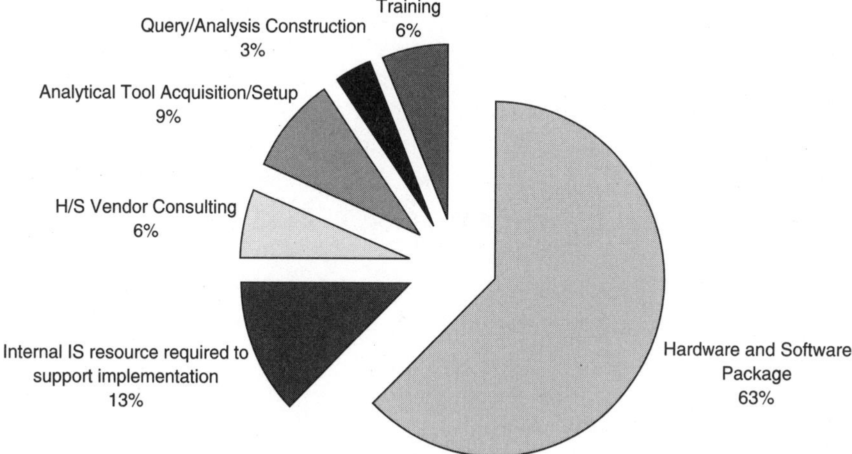

Figure 10-7 Project Budget for SEP implementation.

of $2,500/day for a two-person team. Their goal was to rapidly implement the hardware/software combination required to provide access to data requested by users.

The next largest budget component is an investment valued at $100/hour for 6 months, accounting for one-third of the non-hardware/software budget. Management plan to use this effort as an opportunity to develop organizational SEP expertise. The effort was placed in the hands of the Project Leader—supported also by Rising Star (RS), an individual within the IT organization who has demonstrated the requisite leadership, technical, and managerial abilities. The Project Leader and RS will coordinate the SEP reverse engineering, the installation by the two vendors of their components, and thousands of minor tasks required to implement the SEP. A large part of their focus is to closely coordinate the efforts of the two primary vendors. The vendors supply complementary packages that attractively reduce the coordination and communication requirements that are required, and cover key implementation aspects. Part of their charge from the IT Manager is to learn enough from the interaction with the two vendors to be able to accomplish the next SEP effort with less vendor reliance.

The second vendor negotiated a $100K agreement covering three implementation components: acquisition and installation of the analytic toolkit; its setup; and implementation of initial queries. A total of 25 days of consulting support was negotiated at a rate of $1,500/day for a two-person team, and 30 days at $680/day for a two-person team. The remaining $37,500 is the analytical software cost.

The second component required another setup step. It required the SEP data to be mapped to design concepts that are understood by the users. Necessary communication between vendors used to be the only point where metadata specifications were previously exchanged, as physical warehouse data is mapped to interface components accessed by users. The degree of metadata completeness and its quality influence the percentage of time that is devoted to metadata analysis, versus the non-value-added activity of metadata documentation. The goal of this group is to link the physical database attributes with the design-level descriptions in the analytical tool, correctly translating interface requests into physical data.

The lower of the two consulting fees covers specific, focused query development designed to provide end users with a basic query ability covering eight percent of their standard queries. It was hoped that the Project Manager and nominated staff would be able to implement similar enhancements after the end of the consulting. This final step develops an organization-specific toolkit providing the desired drill down and other popular data access and analysis functions. Representing just three percent of the total project costs, and eight percent of non-hardware/software costs, development of this capability to manipulate the system in this fashion was a stated management goal.

The remaining $50K was allocated for user training. The project was planned to take eight months.

Metadata Capture Plan

An additional project goal is to transfer much of the consultants' Enterprise Portal development knowledge to the organization. To accomplish this, XYZ included plans to capture and analyze the metadata. Table 10.5 is a User/Use CRUD matrix, which illustrates anticipated metadata uses according to the degree of structure and the user type. This will guide enterprise portal knowledge transfer during the project.

Figure 10-8 illustrates the XYZ Corporation Metadata Engineering plan for development of the Sales Enterprise Portal, illustrating the integration of metadata management requirements with the project activities and schedule. For the SEP, the metadata will be created largely by the vendors' consultants (who will begin to reuse it as soon as it is produced). It will be read by XYZ development staff as they verify and begin

TABLE 10.5

Metadata user/uses (in the form of an annotated CRUD Matrix)

DEGREE OF STRUCTURED METADATA USAGE

User type *CRUD values* **General metadata use**	**low (analysis)**	**moderate (design)**	**high (programming)**
Contractor *CREATE/read* Formalizing system knowledge into metadata	Describe, define, and validate the structure of Sales Enterprise Portal components and between the Sales Enterprise Portal and its interfaces	Extract and articulate system design information and describe it as metadata, processing table contents	Develop metadata precisely describing SEP implementation details (i.e. CRUD matrices detailing VSAM file/program interaction)
Development Staff *READ/create/update* Understand, validate, and evolve metadata in support of daily activities	(Extract and transform metadata in the same fashion as described above)	(Extract and transform metadata in the same fashion as described above)	(Extract and transform metadata in the same fashion as described above)
Data Architects *UPDATE/create/read* Enforce metadata development standards that range from structural to syntactical	Initial metadata development, oversight, and coordination focus on architectural derivation accomplished in partnership with end users and developers	Develop architectural component definitions, structural decompositions, and interaction diagrams	Describe data inputs, repository operations, transaction processing, and maintenance and development staff interaction
System End Users *READ/(indirect) update* Use as system "maps," diagnostic tools, as a means of communicating with other metadata uses	Introducing users to the system. *Can the system be used to accomplish …?*	Business practice realignment analysis focused on addressing gaps between system features and existing work practices. *Does the system maintain facts describing … ?*	User navigational support. *How does the system...?*
System Management *READ/(indirect) update* Use common dialog ensuring shared understanding of system facts	Evaluating proposed system changes, modifications, and enhancements. *Analyzing the build versus buy decision?*	Provide data for statistical analysis to guide metadata integration. *How to design fixes that strengthen rather than weaken system infrastructure?*	How to implement fixes in a timely and effective fashion. *Where does Sales Enterprise Portal calculate...?*

Figure 10-8
SEP Reengineering Project Plan

	Evidence	System Component	Component Element	Attribute	Entity	Relationship	Model Decomposition	Process	User	Location	Information
PHASE I — Project Definition											
Create a data administration team	CR	CR	CR								
Reverse engineering System X physical data design	CR			CR	CR	CR	CR				
Refine the current System X physical database design							RU				
Improve its overall performance				U	U	U	U				
Reconcile data from different sources				RU	RU	RU					
Establish guidelines			RU				RU	RU			
Create Repository	CR	CR	CR	CR	CR	CR	CR	CR	CR	CR	CR
Recreate a Business (logical) Model	CR	CR	CR	CR	CR	CR	CR	CR	CR	CR	CR
PHASE II — System X Data Reengineering											
Reverse engineering System X tables	RU	RU	RU	RU	RU	RU	RU				
Organize the data into Business Subject areas		R	R	R	R	R	C	CR	CR	CR	CR
Verify that all entity/tables names				RU	RU	RU	RU				
Identify keys, review usage, eliminate duplicates				RU	RU	RU	RU				
Establish table relationships based on known business rules				RU	RU	RU	RU				
Improve performance using optimization techniques				RU	RU	RU	RU				
Roll out the changes using CASE-generated data definition langu	RU	RU	RU	RU	RU	RU	RU	RU	RU	C	C
Establish a procedure for recording database-related issues	R	R	R	R	R	R	R	R	R	R	R
PHASE III — Create Conceptual Data Models											
Complete data model and business model for DB2 version											
Document the model				RU	RU	RU	RU				
Populate the Repository				RU	RU	RU	RU				
Complete data model and business model for MVS version											
Document the model				RU	RU	RU	RU				
Populate the Repository				RU	RU	RU	RU				
Reconcile differences between the MVS and DB2 versions				RU	RU	RU	RU				
PHASE IV — Create Improved System X logical view											
Creation of a 3NF logical data model of the current data structure				CR	CR	CR	CR				CR
Transform the physical model of Phase III into a logical model				CR	CR	CR	CR				CR
Description business requirements currently satisfied				RU	RU	RU	RU	RU	RU		RU

to use the metadata in support of their daily activities. The development staff will also contribute to its creation; they have a high level of knowledge and system expertise of S1 and S2. The metadata will also be used (read/update) by XYZ data architecture staff as they refine existing S1 and S2 metadata, adding derived (usually integrative) S3 metadata. An example includes relationships indicating use of a specific physical data attribute as a component of a system screen, in support of a specific process by a particular user.

Analysis of the integrated S3 Metadata User/Uses Project Plan in Figure 10-8 leads to corresponding Metadata Engineering goals in Table 10.6. These goals provide targets that can be used to stop, assess, and delimit reverse engineering efforts. The ME goals are different according to whether the metadata is *In Development* or *In Use*.

TABLE 10.6

Metadata Engineering Goal Summary

RELATIVE METADATA ENGINEERING GOALS

User Type	During Metadata Development	During Metadata Use
Consultant	Shift the source of system knowledge to development staff	Incorporate metadata into daily activities, increasing knowledge of system and productivity
Development Staff	Specify their system knowledge as metadata	Incorporate metadata into daily activities, increasing knowledge of system and productivity
System Architects	Responsible for overall metadata engineering and articulation of all components, details, and interrelations in the most comprehensive manner. Hold combined metadata refinement/ verification sessions with metadata users to structure, plan, and specify metadata. Sessions can range from architecture to implementation focus, included to group like-analysis work	Update metadata as the system evolves and is implemented as a series of controlled releases. Ensure metadata users understand the role and value of metadata and the fundamental ways that the repository/metadata combination can change the existing way of doing business. If possible, automate updates of metadata changes, and implement OLAP-based metadata access/analysis
System End User	Specify business knowledge relevant to metadata development—focus on matching system design with work-group-based system requirements	Metadata availability is used as a living document, with navigational aids and training materials, and develop specific system measures
System Management	Management needs to use accurate metadata-based SEP measures	Report productivity, plan enhancements/diagnose failures, and implement changes

Observations

Few CASE tools are capable of maintaining all of the required metadata associations. Many organizations have developed their own metadata model management support using, for example, combinations of spreadsheet, word processing, and database technologies. We used Visible Advantage in this and earlier chapters. This I-CASE tool is fully extensible, enabling it to record all relationships between all metadata types. It would be a logical choice if used in the Design and Development phases, as all metadata would already reside in the Visible Advantage encyclopedia (repository). Alternatively, standard office-suite software tools can be used although the process of mapping each element to all other elements is quite daunting if performed manually. It is difficult to maintain and requires substantial people resources. But if automated using this

CASE technology, Metadata Engineering activities are not resource-expensive. Server storage of a few hundred megabytes, relatively small equipment and staff resources—using I-CASE technology or standard office-suite software products—is all that is needed to implement Metadata Engineering.

Most of the Metadata Engineering will be accomplished using Visible Advantage. To reverse engineer the S1and S3 legacy files and databases, XYZ will utilize a combination of manual and automated approaches. Each system will be reverse engineered into separate encyclopedias (repositories) to maintain the metadata described in the previous sections. Where appropriate, these are merged together using Visible Advantage into a third encyclopedia for the integrated system, S3. Additional facilities for project management and spreadsheet analysis will be based on use of project management, word processing, spreadsheet, database, and presentation software capabilities of the standard office-suite software tools used by XYZ Corporation.

Useful metadata is an asset that most systems do not have. Formalizing informal system information management practices using Metadata Engineering requires development of a structure on which other activities can build. We will see in Chapters 12 and 13 how to integrate both reverse and forward engineering. This contributes general insights and project-specific results, broadening the perceived utility of Metadata Engineering when managing and maintaining systems.

From a project-specific perspective, the ability to carry out Metadata Engineering using office-suite-based metadata management tools is important. XYZ will benefit from using easily accessible metadata that accurately describes System (X) details in ways that transcend traditional documentation capabilities. The metadata will reside in the Repository, which will institutionalize this knowledge as a living document that can evolve with the system as it is modified to meet changing business demands.

Metadata Engineering can personalize and make more effective the communication about system issues between metadata users, as a means of achieving shared understanding. Metadata Engineering provides integrated understanding of systems so that future analyses can include factual information. Development staff will acquire further skills as they become familiar with the metadata development and use, with greater technical competency and pay-based rewards. Further, ME increases the relative worth of metadata users.

One general insight is an assessment of the effectiveness and efficiencies of integrated metadata management systems, indicating we have crossed a threshold of economic viability. Leveraging of data reverse engineering strategies, combined with technical advances in commercial tool suite integration, now permits organizations to rapidly develop Metadata Engineering environments. The relative ease and effectiveness whereby a lot of information is managed using a small amount of metadata can be easily demonstrated. Storing normalized metadata permits different metadata types to be integrated, bringing economies of scale to metadata management.

The discovery of core metadata holds one end of the transformation equation constant. If core metadata is defined, the community can shift focus from *what to store* to *how best to store it*. This can further extend increased: user, breadth, integration, currency, and CASE tool dimensions—with intriguing usage implications. The leverage obtained by maintaining metadata engineering products in a normalized format can assist users regarding the system: understanding; decision making; reimplementation; and the reimplemented support. This increases the perceived utility of Metadata Engineering beyond developers to include business systems analysts and end users—who are ready to adopt tools that simplify their understanding of the system.

There are several other insights. Metadata rapidly becomes a valuable organizational data asset. Reasonable investments in specific targeted reverse engineering can provide metadata that greatly facilitates system management and maintenance activities. A further insight is that metadata should be as accessible as possible, encouraging end users as well as implementation personnel to incorporate it as a regular part of their situation analysis and resolution activities. While each metadata type has an independent value, when integrated the metadata value compounds; users incorporate metadata into their task activities, in turn generating further metadata requirements. The organization benefits from this metadata feedback cycle. We will see powerful examples of the use and application of metadata in Part 3; it is an essential component for the development and deployment of Enterprise Portals.

If managers and other users, as well as system maintenance and development staff, cannot access the metadata, they are forced to develop and implement unique solutions to each business requirement. As we will see in Chapter 13, this leads to data and process redundancy, with high staff costs and poor organizational responsiveness. This leaves no room for process improvement or shared data development. Metadata engineering provides the data and measures for developing repeatable practices. As organizations become more proficient at metadata engineering, the utility and ease of developing and maintaining metadata will increase

In summary, technology now permits creation and maintenance of metadata that can become a valuable organizational asset. There are indications that new systems are likely to incorporate metadata engineering support as system developers adopt architecture-based development approaches. These suggest more widespread use of metadata engineering in system management and maintenance.

We have now completed Part 2 for development of Enterprise Portals. Part 3 describes the deployment of Enterprise Portals. We first discuss Extensible Markup Language (XML) concepts in Chapter 11. We examine the use of XML for Business Reengineering in Chapter 12. We then revisit the XYZ Sales Enterprise Portal project and other Enterprise Portal opportunities in Chapter 13, which examines integrated Business Reengineering and Systems Reengineering. Chapter 14 introduces methods to build a corporate quality culture for the integrated enterprise. Chapter 15 concludes by introducing emerging technologies that are becoming available for the further deployment of Enterprise Portals.

REFERENCES

Aiken, P. (1996) *Data Reverse Engineering: Slaying the Legacy Dragon*, McGraw-Hill, Chapters 18 and 19.

Aiken, P. and Girling, W. (1997) "Data Reengineering Fits the Bill," *InformationWEEK*, May 26, pp. 8A–12A.

Aiken, P. (1999) See Web site—http://fast.to/peteraiken for more details.

Aiken, P.H. (1998) "Reverse Engineering of Data," *IBM Systems Journal*, 37(2): 246–269.

Andersson, M. (1994) "Extracting an Entity Relationship Schema from a Relational Model," *Proceedings of the 4th Reengineering Forum*, September 19–21, 1994, Victoria BC, Canada. Volume 2, pp. 57-1 to 57-10.

Davis, K. (1995) "August-H: A Tool for Step-by-Step Data Model Reverse Engineering," *Proceedings of the Second Working Conference on Reverse Engineering*, IEEE Computer Society Press, Toronto, Ontario, Canada, July 14–16, pp. 146–154.

Edwards, H. and Munro, M. (1995) "Deriving a Logical Data Model for a System Using the RECAST Method," *Proceedings of the Second Working Conference on Reverse Engineering*, IEEE Computer Society Press, Toronto, Ontario, Canada, July 14–16, pp. 126–135.

PART 3

Enterprise Portal Deployment

CHAPTER 11

The Internet and XML

The Future of Metadata

> It is critical that you understand the meaning of the data that goes into the warehouse. ... You also need to know if your data is a complete record of the organization's activity. Maybe the data you really need is not recorded in your database at all.
>
> —IBM Software Solutions

Part 1 covered Enterprise Portal Design, while Part 2 addressed data warehouse development, for later evolution to Enterprise Portals. In Part 3 we focus on this evolution of data warehouses and their deployment as Enterprise Portals. We will examine technologies that offer new ways of delivering information from the data warehouse. This chapter addresses the Internet and intranets, and a vital technology for deploying data warehouses and Enterprise Portals: Extensible Markup Language (XML). Our brief introduction to XML in Chapter 1 will now be expanded to cover XML more completely in this chapter.

In earlier chapters we discussed that the only thing stable today . . . is change itself. Organizations must structure themselves to respond rapidly to change. They must change to a market-driven and customer-driven focus—rather than be organization-driven or product-driven as in the past. New business process opportunities can emerge from this customer-oriented focus, with new processes crossing previous functional boundaries. These cross-functional processes can lead to dramatic breakthroughs with reengineered business processes. The Enterprise Engineering Portals (EEP) methodology uses XML for Business Reengineering in Chapter 12, and for integrated Business and Systems Reengineering in Chapter 13.

Transformations of the 1990s

We begin this chapter by considering three major transformations, or shifts, that have occurred in the computer industry throughout the 1990s. Their impact extends far beyond that industry. They are also transforming business and society. They are moving us rapidly from the Industrial Age to the Information Age.

The First Shift: The Internet

The First Shift has already occurred: the impact that the World Wide Web is having on business today. With the introduction of Web browsers in the early 1990s, the Internet—already over 20 years old at that time—moved into the mainstream as organizations rushed to establish their own Web sites.

First-generation Web sites—using Hypertext Markup Language (HTML)—were used as billboards to the world. They provided static advertising and marketing information for the benefit of customers and suppliers. They implemented online information that was also available in print advertisements, or as documentation in book or manual formats. While effective with those static media, when transferred to a Web site they offered no benefit—only glitzy eye candy. These static Web sites also suffered from another disadvantage. While they were easy to visit, they were also easy to leave with the click of a mouse—when potential customers could not find what they needed.

Second-generation Web sites added interactivity and more content to provide further assistance. But alone, animated images or sounds and movie clips do not provide real benefit to visitors. They are still essentially "static" in their ability to bring real, bottom-line benefit to the business. They need to be integrated into the main purpose of the Web site—as demonstration aids, sales aids, or information aids, for example. When they provide this purpose-focused capability, they move their Web sites to the third generation.

Electronic Commerce sites that are extensively being established today are part of these third-generation Web sites. They have potential to generate major revenue and profit for the business. But many of these electronic storefronts are like the Lemonade stands of our childhood—the first tentative ventures into a New World of business. More is needed before the full potential of Electronic Commerce can be realized, as this and later chapters will explain.

The Second Shift: Java

The mid-1990s saw the start of the Second Shift: the emergence of Java as a programming language able to be executed anywhere regardless of hardware platform or operating system. Java was first developed by a team led by James Gosling at Sun Microsystems in 1991. It was planned as a portable language that could be executed from embedded devices such as TV set-top boxes. But its potential to become a major programming language that could transcend the hardware platform and operating system dependencies of other languages was also recognized. This saw the introduction by Sun in early 1995 of Java as a portable programming language. It was seen as the "Holy Grail of Computing": a hardware- and operating-systems-independent language.

Java presented a potential threat to Microsoft, as it could offer an alternative operating environment to Windows and threaten its desktop monopoly. Microsoft therefore embraced Java, but it added extensions to use Windows-specific capabilities—so limiting the portability of the language. This was the subject of a suit brought by Sun against Microsoft in 1997, decided against Microsoft in late 1998. The legal judgment required that Microsoft remove its Windows-specific Java extensions within 90 days of the ruling.

Java today is being adopted widely as a major object-oriented language across the industry. Java virtual machines are now available for all major operating system and hardware environments. Java compilers are also available for most operating systems: desktop, server, and mainframe. The shift to Java is gathering steam, but it will be many years before its full promise of "write once, run anywhere" can be fully realized.

The Third Shift: Extensible Markup Language (XML)

The Third Shift is the emergence of the Extensible Markup Language (XML) in the late 1990s. This shift is just starting. It promises to be as significant as the first two. It has the ability to bring real, bottom-line benefits to business—in cost reduction, in greater efficiency, in greater competition, and in greater revenue.

XML is one of the most significant developments of the computer industry since the World Wide Web and Java moved to their present positions of importance. For the next 2–5 years this will be one of the most important aspects of the Internet, and of systems development in general. It has the potential to move metadata and data administration also into the mainstream of systems development. XML will present major business opportunities, when used with the Internet, as a delivery channel for information from Data Warehouses and Enterprise Portals.

XML will be the successor to HTML for the Internet, intranets, and for secure extranets between customers, suppliers, and business partners. XML incorporates metadata in any document, to define the content and structure of that document and any associated (or linked) resources. It has the potential to transform the integration of structured data (such as in legacy files or relational databases) with unstructured data (such as in text documents, reports and emails, graphics and images, audio and video resources, and Web pages). XML will be a significant technology for the deployment of Data Warehouses and Enterprise Portals.

XML uses the Extensible Style Language (XSL) and the Extensible Linking Language (XLL) to achieve this integration. We will see that XML, XSL, and XLL allow the easy integration of dissimilar systems for multiple worldwide customers and suppliers in any industry. It permits the ready integration of those systems, regardless of whether they are legacy systems and databases, Electronic Data Interchange (EDI) systems, or Electronic Commerce. It represents the future direction of metadata and the important role that data administration will take in systems development in the years ahead.

There are steps that you can take now, to prepare today for the coming shift to XML.

Preparing for an XML World

XML assumes that your metadata has already been defined. This is necessary not only for the new systems that you want to develop, but also for the legacy systems and databases that you need to integrate with those new systems. XML will enable this integration to be carried out dynamically.

The knowledge of data modeling and strategic modeling that you gained in Part 1 from Chapters 3 and 4 will help you to define the metadata required by XML using these Forward Engineering methods of EEP. This will also enable you to eliminate redundant data versions and redundant processes, to develop integrated databases for the Internet and intranets. This is not just the responsibility of data administrators. It requires business knowledge also, gained by your knowledge of strategic business planning from Chapter 2.

The knowledge of the metadata types, metadata activities, and metadata capture techniques that you learned in Part 2 using the Reverse Engineering methods of EEP will also help you to extract the metadata from existing legacy systems and databases, or from relational or object databases. XML will enable you to combine reverse-engineered metadata from Part 2 with the forward-engineered metadata from Part 1, for the seamless structured and unstructured data integration that characterizes truly effective Enterprise Portals.

Interest in XML, metadata, and data administration will grow strongly. The XML specifications are now essentially complete [XML], while the XSL and XLL specifications were still evolving at the time of writing. These specifications are defined by the World Wide Web Consortium and are all available from their Web site [W3C].

Some browser support for XML was first included in Microsoft Internet Explorer 4.0. The Channel Definition Format (CDF) capability of Internet Explorer 4.0 was based on the use of XML. More complete support for XML is provided in Microsoft Internet Explorer 5.0 and Netscape Communicator 5.0. We will also see wide XML support added to DBMS products, to CASE tools, to Data Warehouse tools and also to Client/Server development tools. We will see a new generation of Knowledge Management tools evolve rapidly to take advantage of the structured/unstructured data integration opportunities offered by XML.

Several books provide good treatment of XML. An initial introduction to XML (and also Cascading Style Sheets) is provided by *XML: A Primer* [St Laurent 1998]. XML used for Web site development, with HTML, XSL, and XLL, is addressed in *XML: Extensible Markup Language* [Harold 1998]. *XML Complete* [Holzner 1998] covers the use of XML with Java. These can be used as detailed references in conjunction with the remainder of this chapter. *Web Farming for the Data Warehouse* [Hackathorn 1998] uses the Internet, intranets and XML for access to external data sources for warehouse deployment. This is addressed in more detail in Chapter 15, together with a discussion of XML-related products.

We will now examine XML concepts. In one chapter, of necessity this can only be an overview. More detail is available from the references above and at the end of the chapter. We will start with the initial purpose of XML, which was to provide a more effective capability for defining document content than that offered by HTML.

Some Problems Using HTML

Tim Berners-Lee at CERN, the originator of the World Wide Web (WWW) in 1990, developed Hypertext Markup Language (HTML) as a subset of the Standard Generalized Markup Language (SGML). A standard for the semantic tagging of documents, SGML evolved out of work done by IBM in the 1970s. It is used in Defense and other industries that deal with large amounts of structured data. SGML is powerful, but it is also very complex and expensive.

HTML was defined as a subset of SGML—specifically intended as an open architecture language for the definition of WWW text files transmitted using Hypertext Transport Protocol (HTTP) across the Internet. HTML defines the layout of a Web page to a Web browser running as an open architecture client. Microsoft Internet Explorer and Netscape Communicator share over 90 percent of the Web browser market; both are now available free.

An HTML page contains text as the content of a Web page, as well as tags that define headings, images, links, lists, tables, and forms to display on that page. These HTML tags also contain attributes that define further details associated with a tag. An example of such attributes is the location of an image to be displayed on the page, its width, depth, and border characteristics, and alternate text to be displayed while the image is being transmitted to the Web browser.

Because of this focus on layout, HTML is recognized as having some significant problems:

1. *No effective way to identify content of page* HTML tags describe the layout of the page. Web browsers use the tags for presentation purposes, but the actual text content has no specific meaning associated with it. To a browser, text is only a series of words to be presented on a Web page for display purposes.
2. *Problems locating content with search engines* Because of a lack of meaning associated with the text in a Web page, there is no automatic way that search engines can determine meaning—except by indexing relevant words, or by relying on manual definition of keywords.
3. *Problems accessing databases* We discussed earlier that Web pages are static. But when a Web form provides access to online databases, that data needs to be displayed dynamically on the Web page. Called "Dynamic HTML" (DHTML), this capability enables dynamic content from a database to be incorporated "on the fly" into an appropriate area on the Web page.
4. *Complexity of dynamic programming* DHTML requires complex programming to incorporate dynamic content into a Web page. This may be written as CGI, Perl, ActiveX, JavaScript, or Java logic, executed in the client, the Web server, the database server, or all three.

5. *Problems interfacing with back-end systems* This is a common problem that has been with us since the beginning of the Information Age. Systems written in one programming language for a specific hardware platform, operating system, and DBMS may not be able to be migrated to a different environment without significant change or a complete rewrite. Even though it is an open architecture, HTML also is affected by our inability to move these legacy systems to new environments.

Recognizing these limitations of HTML, the W3C SGML working group (now called the XML working group) was established in mid-1996. The purpose of this group was to define a way to provide the power of SGML, while also retaining the simplicity of HTML. The XML specifications were born out of this activity [XML].

XML retains much of the power and extensibility of SGML, while also being simple to use and inexpensive to implement. It allows tags to be defined for special purposes, with metadata definitions embedded internally in a Web document—or stored separately as a Document Type Definition (DTD) script. A DTD is analogous to the Data Definition Language script (DDL) used to define a database, but it has a different syntax.

As we discussed earlier, data modeling and metadata are key enablers in the use and application of XML. The Internet and intranets allow us to communicate easily with other computers. Java allows us to write program logic once, to be executed in many different environments. But these technologies are useless if we cannot easily communicate with and use existing legacy systems and databases.

In Chapter 1 we used an analogy based on the telephone. We can now make a phone call, instantly, anywhere in the world. The telephone networks of every country are interconnected. When we dial a phone number, a telephone assigned to that number will ring in Russia, or China, or Outer Mongolia, or elsewhere. It will be answered, but we may not understand the language used by the person at the other end.

So it is also with legacy systems. We need more than the simple communication between computers afforded by the Internet. True, we could rewrite the computer programs at each end in Java, C, C++, or some other common language. But that alone would not enable effective and automatic communication between those programs. Each program must know the metadata used by the other program and its databases so that they can communicate with each other.

Considerable work has been carried out to address this problem. Much effort has gone into definition and implementation of Electronic Data Interchange (EDI) standards. EDI has now been widely used for business-to-business commerce for many years. It works well, but it is complex and expensive. As a result, it is cost-justifiable generally only for larger corporations.

XML now also provides this capability. It allows the metadata used by each program and database to be published as the language to be used for this intercommunication. But distinct from EDI, XML is simple to use and inexpensive to implement. Because of this simplicity, as discussed in Chapter 1 we like to think of XML as:

XML is EDI for the Rest of Us

XML will become a major part of the application development mainstream. It provides a bridge between structured databases and unstructured text, delivered via XML then converted to HTML during a transition period for display in Web browsers. Web sites will evolve over time to use XML, XSL, and XLL natively to provide the capability and functionality presently offered by HTML, but with far greater power and flexibility. XML components are listed in Table 11.1.

The rest of this chapter provides an introduction to XML and DTDs, with only brief coverage of XSL, XLL, DOM, and RDF. Further information in each of these areas can be obtained from the book and Web site references provided at the end of the chapter.

TABLE 11.1

Components of XML

Acronym	Name	Description
XML	Extensible Markup Language	Defines document content using metadata tags and namespaces
DTD	Document Type Definition	Defines XML document structure (analogous to DDL schema)
XSL	Extensible Style Language	XSL or Cascading Style Sheets (CSS) separate layout from data
XLL	Extensible Linking Language	XLL implements multidirectional links (single or multiple)
DOM	Document Object Model	Implements a standard API for processing XML in any language
RDF	Resource Description Framework	W3 Interoperability Project for data content interchange

A Simple XML Example

We will start our introduction to XML with a customer example in Figure 11-1. This illustrates some basic XML concepts. It shows customer data (in italics), such as entered from an online Web form or accessed from a customer database. It shows the inclusion of metadata "tags" (surrounded by < and >)—such as `<customer_name>`.

The tag: *<customer_name>* is a start tag; the text following it is the actual content of the customer name: *XYZ Corporation*. It is terminated by an end tag: the same tag-name, but now preceded by "/"—such as *</customer_name>*. Other fields define *<customer_address>*, *<street>*, *<city>*, *<state>*, and *<postcode>*. Each of these tags is also terminated by an end tag, such as *</street>*, *</city>*, *</state>*, and *</postcode>*. The example concludes with *</customer_address>* and *</CUSTOMER>* end tags.

From this simple example of XML metadata, we can see how the meaning of the text between start and end tags is clearly defined. We can also see that search engines can use these definitions for more accuracy in identifying information to satisfy a specific query.

Even more effective applications become possible. For example, an organization can define the unique metadata used by its suppliers' legacy inventory systems. This will enable that organization to place orders via the Internet directly with those suppliers' systems, for automatic fulfillment of product orders. XML is enabling technology to integrate unstructured text and structured databases for next-generation E-Commerce and EDI applications. We will see examples of this and other XML applications in Chapters 12 and 15. The project example we discussed in Chapter 10 will be developed further with XML in Chapters 12 and 13.

The following pages now examine the XML syntax in more detail.

Figure 11-1
A simple XML example.

```
<CUSTOMER>
   <customer_name>XYZ Corporation</customer_name>
   <customer_address>
      <street>123 First Street</street>
      <city>Any Town</city>
      <state>WA</state>
      <postcode>12345</postcode>
   </customer_address>
</CUSTOMER>
```

XML Naming Conventions

An XML document must be "well formed." To be well formed, a document must obey the following rules:

- A tag name must start with a letter or underscore, with no spaces. Thus *person_id* is correct, but not *person id* or *1st name.*
- XML names are case sensitive. For example, *PERSON, Person*, and *person* are all different names.
- Each tag must have surrounding < and > indicators, as in the start tag `<tag_name>`.
- Each start tag must also have an end tag, as in `</tag_name>`.
- If a tag is empty, it must still have an end tag or empty tag such as `<CUSTOMER></CUSTOMER>` or `<country/>` (i.e. Empty).
- Attribute values are preceded by an = sign and are surrounded by double or single quotes, such as `version="1.0" standalone="YES"`.
- The characters <, >, &, ", or ' cannot be used in XML except when replaced by their "escaped" versions. Thus the character string `<` represents "<" at all times until it is to be displayed. Similarly `>` is ">," `&` is "&," `"e;` is ", and `'` is '. These character sequences are called "predefined entity references."

A well-formed document example follows in Figure 11-2.

Notice that double quote characters in Figure 11-2 surround the attribute values of `PERSON`, declared on the first line with the values: `person_id="p1100" sex=".M"`.

The XML Document Prolog

Every XML document starts with an XML declaration as part of its prolog. This declaration must be the first statement on the first line of the document. It is defined as a processing instruction (surrounded by <? ... ?> tags) such as:

```
<?xml version="1.0" standalone="yes"
encoding="Unicode"?>
```

Figure 11-2 Example of a Well-Formed XML Document.

```
<PERSON person_id="p1100" sex="M">  (Attributes in Element)
   <person_name>                                   (Children of
      <given_name>Clive</given_name>              "person_name"
      <surname>Finkelstein</surname>                  Element)
   </person_name>
   <email>cfink@ies.aust.com</email>
   <company>
      Information Engineering Services Pty Ltd
   </company>
   <country>Australia</country>
   <phone>+61-8-9309-6163</phone>
   <fax>+61-8-9309-6165</fax>
</PERSON>
```

The <?xml specifies that the document uses XML syntax. An XML parser or application can analyze the content of the document prior to it being processed. The tag "XML," "xml," or any upper and lower-case combination of this sequence of letters is reserved and cannot be used in any tag name.

The version number is specified for compatibility with future XML versions. The standalone specification indicates whether a Document Type Definition is included in-line ("standalone=yes") or out-of-line in an external file ("standalone=no"). We will discuss this shortly in relation to *DOCTYPE Declarations*.

The "encoding" statement specifies the language-encoding format used by the XML document. XML has been defined so it can be used with any language, such as English, European, and Middle Eastern languages, as well as double byte Asian languages—Japanese, Chinese, or Korean.

DOCTYPE Declarations

A Document Type declaration ("DOCTYPE") immediately follows the <?XML ... ?> statement. Every XML document contains a root name, which includes all other XML tag names. The DOCTYPE statement identifies the specific root name used by the document. It also identifies the location of the Document Type Definition (DTD) file that is to be used with the document.

A DOCTYPE declaration has the following formats, with examples:

```
<!DOCTYPE root_element_name [ ... ]>
                  OR
<!DOCTYPE root_element_name SYSTEM "DTD_URL">
```

```
1. <!DOCTYPE CUSTOMER [ ... ]>
2. <!DOCTYPE CUSTOMER SYSTEM "customer.dtd">
3. <!DOCTYPE supplier PUBLIC
   "http://www.ind-xml.com/supplier.dtd">
```

The first example specifies that the DOCTYPE is declared internally in the same document. We will see an example of this format shortly.

The second example declares that an external DTD is used as a private file ("`SYSTEM`"). It is the DTD file that is located at the relative Uniform Resource Locator (URL) "`customer.dtd`" within the same Web site directory.

The third example specifies that the DTD is `PUBLIC`. It is the DTD file at the absolute URL "`http://www.ind-xml.com/supplier.dtd`".

URL and URI

These DOCTYPE examples use relative or absolute URLs to identify the location of an external DTD file. But files and other resources can be moved to different URL locations. With HTML Web pages, every link that refers to a moved resource must be updated to refer to its new URL. HTML links can be from Web sites anywhere in the world. These can all refer to the same URL. Relocating a resource to a different URL can therefore require considerable maintenance work.

To overcome this problem, in time XML and XLL will enable resources to be located instead by a Uniform Resource Identifier (URI). Distinct from a URL, a URI can never change. XLL, with XLinks and XPointers, defines a URI. The URI always points to that resource. We cover these in *Extensible Linking Language*, later in this chapter.

XML Comments

Comments can be used in an XML document to describe the purpose, intent, and use of different statements. Comments can also document and separate logical sections of a document.

Comments in XML are defined similarly to HTML comments, surrounded by `<!-- ... -->` tags. For example:

```
<!-- This is a comment and is not processed -->
```

Comments can contain any data except the literal string "-->" but may not be placed inside an XML tag. In the next two examples, the first comment is wrong; the second comment is correct:

```
<customer_name <!-- Defines customer name --> >
  (incorrect-comment is inside tag)
<!-- Defines customer name --> <customer_name>
  (correct-comment is outside tag)
```

However, comments can be used to surround and hide tags, such as:

```
<-- The following tag is used only for retail customers
<retail-code>2</retail-code>
and is ignored for wholesale customers -->
```

An XML parser or XML application cannot process the `<retail-code>` tag until the surrounding comment is removed, or until the tag is moved outside the comment. While it remains within the comment, for XML processing purposes the tag does not exist.

Processing Instructions

Processing instructions (PIs) declare applications that will be used to process part (or all) of an XML document. Like comments, they are not part of the XML document. An XML processor must pass a PI unchanged to the relevant XML application. A PI has the format:

```
<?PI_target_name PI_data?>
```

The *PI_target_name* identifies the application. The *PI_data* following the *PI_target_name* is optional; it is specified by and used by the PI application. We saw a PI example in *XML Document Prolog*. A document to be processed by an XML parser or processor was declared by the PI statement:

```
<?xml version="1.0" standalone="yes" encoding="Unicode"?>
```

XML applications should process only the targets they recognize. PI names that begin with "XML", in any combination of upper or lower case, are reserved for use in XML standards. PIs are used for document-specific application processing.

PIs can also utilize NOTATION declarations and NOTATION attributes. We will discuss these briefly later.

CDATA Sections

A document may contain markup characters such as <, >, &, “, or ‘ that should be ignored by an XML parser or processor. An example is a source code listing within an XML document. To prevent characters in the listing from being recognized incorrectly as XML markup characters, a CDATA section can be used. For example:

```
<![CDATA[
*x = &a;
c = (i <= 5);
]]>
```

The CDATA section begins with the string: “`<![CDATA[`” and ends with the string “`]]>`.” All other character data between these strings is passed directly to the relevant application. Clearly, the only character string that cannot occur in a CDATA section is “`]]>`.”

We will see later that an XML Attribute containing character data is declared with “`CDATA`.” This is not to be confused with the use of a CDATA section, which is intended only to isolate markup characters so they can be passed unprocessed to an XML application.

XML Elements, Attributes, and Entities

XML defines metadata tags using elements, attributes, and entities. In the following sections we will first learn how XML uses these to declare metadata tags. We will then discuss how this use differs from data modeling. The chapter concludes by describing how CASE tools can be used to define data modeling entities, attributes, and associations, for automatic generation of XML declarations.

Declaring XML Elements

The tags that we have seen are all examples of XML “elements.” An element is a named metadata tag that is declared in a DOCTYPE statement. As we have seen, a DOCTYPE can be defined externally in a DTD file, located using a relative or absolute URL. Alternatively, a DOCTYPE can be defined internally. It is included in-line, immediately following the

Figure 11-3 DOCTYPE declaration for the Customer example in Figure 11-1.

```
<?XML version="1.0" standalone="YES"?>
<!DOCTYPE CUSTOMER
[
<!ELEMENT CUSTOMER ANY>
<!ELEMENT customer_name (#PCDATA)>
<!ELEMENT customer_address EMPTY>
<!ELEMENT street (#PCDATA)>
<!ELEMENT city (#PCDATA)>
<!ELEMENT state (#PCDATA)>
<!ELEMENT postcode (#PCDATA)>
]>
```

XML processing declaration. Figure 11-3 shows an internal declaration of the DOCTYPE statement that is used with the customer example in Figure 11-1.

The DOCTYPE statement in Figure 11-3 defines the XML root name as <CUSTOMER>. Square left and right brackets ([...]) follow, surrounding all element declarations. The DOCTYPE root name <CUSTOMER> is declared as an ELEMENT, specified to be ANY (case-sensitive). This indicates that any element, as well as parsed character data (shown as italics in Figure 11-1) can appear in a <CUSTOMER> element.

Each element must be uniquely named within an XML document. As a DOCTYPE declaration can be defined using more than one DTD, the concept of namespaces has been included in XML. This allows an alias to be assigned to a DTD. The namespace alias can then be used to qualify named elements that would otherwise violate this rule, so ensuring uniqueness. This is discussed later in the chapter.

The declaration of an XML Element in Figure 11-3 has the format:

```
<!ELEMENT element-name content_type>
```

As with all XML tags, the *element-name* starts with a letter or underscore, can have no spaces and all names are case sensitive. Thus *Customer, customer*, and *CUSTOMER* are different XML element-names. Because of this and to avoid confusion, it is recommended that an element-name be declared using a case-sensitive name that always refers to that same element. Once declared, that *element-name* is used as the *tag-name*; the terms *element-name* and *tag-name* are therefore synonymous.

The *content_type* of an Element can have values of ANY, EMPTY, (#PCDATA), or a (Child List) as discussed next.

We discussed an example of ANY in relation to the root name element <CUSTOMER> in Figure 11-3. This indicates that any element, as well as parsed character data, can appear within it.

By default, tags are *non-empty* and are followed by data (see italics in Figure 11-1). An element is declared EMPTY if it normally has no data. For example, the element <customer-address> in Figure 11-1 contains <street>, <city>, <state>, and <postcode> elements within it. These are called child elements. As the parent element, the data for <customer-address> is provided by its child elements. The <customer-address> element is therefore declared in Figure 11-3 to be EMPTY.

Figure 11-3 declares the <customer_name> element is (#PCDATA). This specifies that the element contains "Parsed Character Data." In Figure 11-1, we now know that *XYZ Corporation* is character data that is parsed by an XML parser, or processed by an XML application.

Similarly, the <street>, <city>, <state>, and <postcode> elements in Figure 11-3 are also declared to be (#PCDATA). Note that <postcode> in Figure 11-1 contains the numeric characters: "12345," not the numeric value. For example, consider the following element declaration and corresponding tag:

```
<!ELEMENT customer_balance (#PCDATA)>
........
<customer_balance>$15,500.00</customer_balance>
```

Before the <customer_balance> data of $15,500.00 can be processed by an XML application, it must first be converted from the numeric characters "$15,500.00" to the numeric currency value of $15,500.00.

When we consider address data in an application, there are many variations. For example, in addition to the street number and name, some customers may have a floor or level number, and/or an apartment, suite, or flat number. We could define each of these as separate elements within <CUSTOMER>. But this data could be considered as part of the normal content for the <street> element. Some customers may need two or more <street> elements. For others, <postcode> may not be available and so could be omitted.

To this point there is nothing in the declaration of CUSTOMER to control whether any or all of the declared elements must exist. We can provide extra control by specifying a *content model* (also called a *child list*).

Figure 11-4 Constraints added to the CUSTOMER DOCTYPE Declaration.

```
<?XML version="1.0" standalone="YES"?>
<!DOCTYPE CUSTOMER
[
<!ELEMENT CUSTOMER ANY>
<!ELEMENT customer_name (#PCDATA)>
<!ELEMENT customer_address (street, city, state, postcode)>
<!ELEMENT street (#PCDATA)>
<!ELEMENT city (#PCDATA)>
<!ELEMENT state (#PCDATA)>
<!ELEMENT postcode (#PCDATA)>
]>
```

We indicate in Figure 11-4 that `<customer_address>` has a *(child list)*. This child list is a content model, which specifies that `<customer_address>` has child elements of *(street, city, state, postcode)*. This comma-delimited format indicates that each customer address has only one *<street>*, *<city>*, *<state>*, and *<postcode>* element. Each element must appear in the specified sequence.

When a child list is defined using commas, each element is mandatory and must exist in that sequence. Alternatively, if any elements validly may not exist, they can be separated by " | " to indicate optionality, such as:

```
<!ELEMENT customer_address (street | city | state |
postcode)>
```

If we also add a *<contacts>* element, with child elements of *<phone>*, *<fax>*, *<mobile>* (cell phone), and *<email>* elements, we find even more variations. We therefore need to be able to specify the number of occurrences of child elements that are valid.

Figure 11-5 adds validity constraints to child elements by including a suffix character attached to the child name. A suffix of "?" specifies that zero or one occurrence of the child element may exist within the parent element. A suffix of "*" specifies that zero or more occurrences may exist, while a suffix of "+" specifies that at least one or more occurrences of the relevant child element must exist within the parent element. No suffix indicates that the element must exist only once.

Examining Figure 11-5 further, we see that *<customer_address>* must have at least one *<street>* element, but it can have more *street* occurrences (street+). There must be only one

Figure 11-5 Further constraints added to the CUSTOMER DOCTYPE declaration for customer _address and contacts.

```
<?XML version="1.0" standalone="YES" ?>
<!DOCTYPE CUSTOMER
[
<!ELEMENT CUSTOMER ANY>
<!ELEMENT customer_name (#PCDATA)>
<!ELEMENT customer_address (street+, city, state, postcode?)>
<!-- ? = zero or one; * = zero or more; + = one or more -->
<!ELEMENT street (#PCDATA)>
<!ELEMENT city (#PCDATA)>
<!ELEMENT state (#PCDATA)>
<!ELEMENT postcode (#PCDATA)>
<!ELEMENT contacts (phone+, fax*, mobile?, email?)>
<!ELEMENT phone (#PCDATA)>
<!ELEMENT fax (#PCDATA)>
<!ELEMENT mobile (#PCDATA)>
<!ELEMENT email (#PCDATA)>
]>
```

`<city>` and one `<state>` element (no suffix). But the `<postcode>` element is optional; there may be none, or one occurrence (`postcode?`). The comma delimiters specify that the elements must appear in the declared sequence.

We may want to show that a valid `customer_address` can have several addresses within it. We can place these child elements all within brackets, with the relevant group suffix character following the right bracket. We also use surrounding brackets to group other elements.

```
<!ELEMENT customer_address
    (street+ | (city, state) | postcode)+>
```

The above fragment indicates by outer brackets with a suffix "+" that there must be at least one or more groups of addresses. Within an address group, there must be one or more `street` elements (`street+`) OR a `city` element followed by a `state` element OR a `postcode` element). Of course, all elements can also exist in the above example.

In Figure 11-5 we also saw new element declarations of `<contacts>`: `<phone>`; `<fax>`; `<mobile>`; and `<email>`. We see that `<contacts>` has a content model with child elements of `(phone+, fax*, mobile?, email?)>`.

Based on the suffix attached to each of the `<contacts>` child names, Figure 11-5 specifies that there must be at least one or more `<phone>` occurrences (`phone+`) and zero or more `<fax>` occurrences (fax*). There can be zero or one <mobile> occurrence (mobile?), and also zero or one <email> occurrence (email?).

We can use a content model that includes PCDATA. For example, we can alternatively specify <phone> and <fax> by the fragment:

```
<!ELEMENT phone (#PCDATA | (country-code, area-code,
phone-number))*>
<!ELEMENT fax (#PCDATA| (country-code, area-code, phone-
number))*>
  <!ELEMENT country-code (#PCDATA)>
  <!ELEMENT area-code (#PCDATA)>
  <!ELEMENT phone-number (#PCDATA)>
```

There can be zero or more <phone> and <fax>—by the suffix "*" after the outer brackets. These can contain parsed character data, or they may optionally have a child element group in the sequence of (<country-code>, <area-code>, and <phone-number>). All content models that include PCDATA must have this format: PCDATA must come first, vertical bars must separate all elements or element groups, and the entire outer group must be optional.

These constraints enable an XML parser or XML application to confirm the validity of the document, by checking the number of child element occurrences within each parent element. They validate these occurrences against those specified by the child list constraints associated with the parent element in an internal DOCTYPE declaration, or a DOCTYPE in an external DTD.

Declaring XML Attributes

An element may contain one or more attributes to provide additional details about that element. Figure 11-2 earlier included an example of attributes for the PERSON element. This specified a PERSON occurrence, with a unique identification attribute called *person_id* and another attribute called *sex*, repeated now in Figure 11-6.

Figure 11-6 The PERSON Element, with Attributes.

```
<PERSON person_id=''p1100'' sex=''M''>
```

This example shows that attributes and their values are enclosed within the < and > characters of the start tag for an element, immediately following the element name.

Each attribute of an element is declared in `DOCTYPE ATTLIST`, using the format in Figure 11-7. The `ATTLIST` format specifies the *`element_name`* and then defines an *`attribute_name`* as a unique XML name within all of the element's attributes. It observes all of the rules detailed earlier in *XML Naming Conventions*.

The *`type`* specification in Figure 11-7 is defined from an enumerated list of valid values: `(CDATA | ID | IDREF | IDREFS | ENTITY | ENTITIES | NMTOKEN | NMTOKENS | NOTATION)`.

`CDATA` represents "Character Data," as a character data type that is non-markup text. This is somewhat analogous to a Data Definition Language (DDL) SQL data type of `VARCHAR`, as used by DBMS products.

***NOTE** that XML does not support the other DDL data types such as* numeric *or* decimal *(with a defined length and precision), or* money, currency, *or* CHAR *(with a defined length), or* float, bit, Boolean, *or other data types. XML is used and read as text. An XML application must convert and validate these other data types. In the topics following* When to Use Elements, Attributes, *or* Entities *we will later discuss how these other data types can be supported.*

We will continue with the other *`type`* declarations for Figure 11-7. `ID` represents an identifying attribute such as a primary key, with a unique name within the element. There can only be one attribute in an element that is specified with a *`type`* of `ID`.

Where an element must have a compound primary key for uniqueness (see Chapter 3), a single unique primary key is defined. In data modeling this is called a "surrogate key." The compound primary keys are instead defined as foreign keys with a *`type`* of `IDREF` or `IDREFS`. These are discussed shortly.

Furthermore, the value of each ID attribute must be unique for all occurrences of the relevant element. This follows the uniqueness rule of primary keys that we discussed in Chapter 3: a primary key cannot have

Figure 11-7
The ATTLIST Format.

```
<!ATTLIST element_name attribute_name type "default value">
Where type = (CDATA | ID | IDREF | IDREFS | ENTITY | ENTITIES
      | NMTOKEN | NMTOKENS | NOTATION)
```

duplicates. The earlier PERSON example has a unique value of "p1100" for the attribute named *person_id*, repeated as Figure 11-6.

An attribute can be defined as a foreign key, with a type of IDREF. Or several attributes can all be specified as foreign keys, each with a type of IDREFS. This offers more flexibility. It is used to specify many foreign keys. The referenced IDREF attribute name must also exist elsewhere, in an element where it is also declared as an ID or IDREF attribute. As we discussed earlier, IDREF or IDREFS can be used to specify compound primary keys, where a single primary (surrogate) key is specified with a type of ID.

In Figure 11-7 the type declarations ENTITY and ENTITIES define an attribute name, or attribute names, with associated substitution text. These declare entity references. The defined entity name can be used as a shorthand notation, analogous to a macro; it is replaced by the substitution text wherever it is used as an attribute value for the declared element. Entities can be used within the main body of the XML document, or in a DTD. We will cover *Entity Declarations* shortly.

Note that the use of ENTITY and ENTITIES by XML is different to the use of these terms in data modeling and normalization. We will consider these differences further in the topic *When to Use Elements, Attributes, or Entities.*

NMTOKEN and NMTOKENS types specify that the value of an attribute must be a valid XML name (NMTOKEN) or valid multiple XML names (NMTOKENS). A program can use an attribute of this *type* to manipulate XML data. For example, it can be used to associate a Java class with an element. A Java API can then be used to pass the data to a method for that class.

A NOTATION type typically is used to specify an application to process an unparsed value of an attribute. A NOTATION attribute is associated with a NOTATION declaration in a DTD. This declares the specific application program name to be invoked. We saw earlier that applications can be declared in a Processing Instruction (PI). This declares the *PI_target_name* as the application, with associated PI_data.

We will now discuss the "default value" specification in Figure 11-7. This is used to define a list of valid values for an attribute, or it can declare an attribute as being *#REQUIRED, #IMPLIED*, or *#FIXED*.

For example, attributes of PERSON in Figure 11-6 are specified by an ATTLIST declaration in Figure 11-8. We can see that *person_id* is an ID attribute. Every PERSON occurrence must have a unique

Figure 11-8
A list of valid attribute values.

```
<!ELEMENT PERSON EMPTY>
   <!ATTLIST PERSON person_id ID #REQUIRED>
   <!ATTLIST PERSON sex (M | F) #IMPLIED>
   <!ATTLIST PERSON status (employee | trainee) "employee">
   <!ATTLIST PERSON company CDATA #FIXED "XYZ">
```

person_id value. Further, this ID attribute is mandatory (#REQUIRED).

The attribute sex in Figure 11-8 has valid values of "M" (Male) or "F" (Female). Any other values are invalid. This attribute example is #IMPLIED. It is not mandatory for a value to be supplied. The sex attribute can be omitted if it is not known.

A default value can be provided if an attribute is able to be omitted. In the example, status can only have valid values of "employee" or "trainee." If not specified, status defaults to "employee".

Finally, an attribute can be declared as #FIXED. This allows a default value to be supplied for an attribute, which cannot be changed. Figure 11-8 shows that company is character data (CDATA). It has a default value (#FIXED). This attribute is not provided in a document. It is automatically supplied as the value "XYZ".

Another example of element and attribute declarations is provided in Figure 11-9. This defines a PHOTO element in XML, so it can be used by HTML to display an image on a Web page. The src attribute specifies the location of the photo image source file. It contains character data (CDATA) and is mandatory (#REQUIRED). The width, depth, border, and alt specify the image dimensions and border thickness, as well as alternate text that is displayed while the image file is being transmitted. These are all character data (CDATA) and are optional (#IMPLIED).

Figure 11-9
Attribute declarations for the PHOTO element.

```
<!ELEMENT PHOTO EMPTY>
   <!ATTLIST PHOTO src CDATA #REQUIRED>
   <!ATTLIST PHOTO width CDATA #IMPLIED>
   <!ATTLIST PHOTO depth CDATA #IMPLIED>
   <!ATTLIST PHOTO border CDATA #IMPLIED>
   <!ATTLIST PHOTO alt CDATA #IMPLIED>
```

Valid XML Documents

An XML document must not only be well formed as discussed earlier, it must also be valid. An XML document is valid if the document tags and their data content agree with the ELEMENT and ATTLIST declarations in the Document Type Definition (DTD). We discussed that a DTD is analogous to a DDL schema for a DBMS, but with different syntax. A DOCTYPE declaration for the earlier PERSON examples, together with the defined document tags and data content, is shown in Figure 11-10.

From Figure 11-10, we see that a PERSON document has two attributes: a *person_id* which must be unique (ID #REQUIRED) and sex. This is an optional attribute (#IMPLIED), but if provided it can only have the values (M | F).

A PERSON must have at least one or more *names* (name+). A *name* has zero or more *given_name* (given_name*) and at

Figure 11-10
A valid internal DTD, with defined XML tags and data content.

```
<?xml version="1.0" standalone="yes"?>
<!DOCTYPE PERSON
[
<!ELEMENT PERSON
   (name+, email*, company?, country?, phone*, fax?, mobile*)>
   <!ATTLIST PERSON person_id ID #REQUIRED>
   <!ATTLIST PERSON sex (M | F) #IMPLIED>
<!ELEMENT name (given_name*, surname+)>
<!ELEMENT given_name (#PCDATA)>
<!ELEMENT surname (#PCDATA)>
<!ELEMENT email (#PCDATA)>
<!ELEMENT company (#PCDATA)>
<!ELEMENT country (#PCDATA)>
<!ELEMENT phone (#PCDATA)>
<!ELEMENT fax (#PCDATA)>
]>
<PERSON person_id="p1100" sex="M">
   <person_name>
      <given_name>Clive</given_name>
      <surname>Finkelstein</surname>
   </person_name>
   <email>cfink@ies.aust.com</email>
   <company>Information Engineering Services Pty Ltd </company>
   <country>Australia</country>
   <phone>+61-8-9309-6163</phone>
   <phone>(08) 9309-6163</phone>
   <fax>+61-8-9309-6165</fax>
   <mobile>+61-411-472-375</mobile>
   <mobile>0411-472-375</mobile>
</PERSON>
```

least one or more *surnames* (surname+). The document shows examples of these tags with the relevant data content.

A PERSON can have zero or more *email* addresses (email*), zero or one *company*, *country*, or fax number (company?, country?, fax?), and zero or more *phone* or *mobile* numbers (phone*, mobile*). We can see in Figure 11-10 that two phone numbers and two mobile numbers are provided as part of the PERSON document content. The data tags and content agree with the DOCTYPE declaration. The PERSON root name and its contents therefore comprise a valid XML document.

Entity Declarations

XML uses the term ENTITY to declare a substitution name for insertion of predefined values. This is quite different from the use of the term "entity" in data modeling. We discuss this later in the chapter, in the topic *When to Use Elements, Attributes, or Entities*.

There are two types of entity declarations. The first is a *General Entity* declaration. This can be used inside the main body of an XML document or in a DTD section, where it is called an *internal entity reference*. It can be used externally to a document, when it is called an *external entity reference*. A general entity reference is distinguished by a prefix "&."

We saw internal general entity references earlier, in *XML Naming Conventions*. XML supplies five predefined entities—< (which is replaced by <), > (by >), & (by &), " (by ") and ' (by '). The replacement text replaces an internal entity reference only when it is displayed, or is about to be processed by an application. For example, the internal entity reference "&IES;" can be declared with text "Information Engineering Services Pty Ltd." This text automatically replaces "&IES;" wherever it occurs, but only when that entity is displayed or passed to an application. Internal entities can contain references to other internal entities, but they cannot be recursive.

Distinct from an internal entity reference, the replacement text for an external entity reference immediately replaces that entity wherever it occurs. An XML parser or processor processes the replaced text as if it was an original part of the document.

An entity name must be a unique XML name. It is declared together with the replacement text. This text is substituted for the entity

Figure 11-11 General entity declaration and usage examples.

```
Format:
   <!ENTITY entity_name "replacement text">                    (Internal)
   <!ENTITY entity_name SYSTEM URL">                           (External)
Declaration Examples:
   <!ENTITY IES "Information Engineering Services Pty Ltd">
                                                               (Internal)
   <!ENTITY copy99 "© Copyright 1999">                         (Internal)
   <!ENTITY ref1 SYSTEM http://www.ref.com/ref1.xml">          (External)
Usage Examples:
   "&IES;" is replaced later by Information Engineering
      Services Pty Ltd"
   "&copy99;" is replaced later by * Copyright 1999"
   "&ref1;" is replaced immediately by the content of document
      ref1.xml"
```

wherever it occurs. Figure 11-11 shows the internal and external format and examples for a general entity.

The format and two examples of an internal entity are illustrated in Figure 11-11. The first declares "`&IES;`" as an internal entity reference for *Information Engineering Services Pty Ltd.* The second declares "`©99;`" as a shorthand for the text © *Copyright 1999. Whenever* "`&IES;`" or "`©99;`" are found internally within a document they are replaced by that text, but only when the document is about to be processed or displayed.

The third example in Figure 11-11 declares an external entity "`&ref1;`" as a shorthand reference for the document "`ref1.xml`." This is located externally at "`http://www.ref-xml.com/ref1.xml`." (This is a fictitious URL.) Because it is an external entity reference, it is immediately replaced by the content of the document "`ref1.xml`."

An entity can be a convenient shorthand way of including a much larger amount of text, as shown in Figure 11-11. It also provides an XML document with a single point for declaration of text that can change. If volatile text appears in many places of an XML document, a general entity can be used in each place. The replacement text is defined once only when the entity is declared. Whenever that text is later changed, the updated text automatically replaces every occurrence of that entity.

We discussed that there are two types of entities. The second type is a *Parameter Entity* declaration, which can only be declared inside a DTD. A parameter entity reference is distinguished by a prefix "`%`".

Figure 11-12 now shows the declaration format and examples of a parameter entity, which uses a prefix "`%`"—distinguished from general

Figure 11-12
Parameter entity declaration and usage examples.

```
Format:
   <!ENTITY % entity_name "replacement text">        (Internal)
   <!ENTITY % entity_name SYSTEM URL">                (External)
Declaration Format:
   <!ENTITY % person SYSTEM person.dtd">              (External)
   <!ENTITY % idr 'ID #REQUIRED >                     (Internal)
Usage Examples:
   <!DOCTYPE PERSON SYSTEM %person;>                  (External)
   ........
   <!ATTLIST PERSON person_id %idr;>                  (Internal)
```

entities that use a prefix of "&." A parameter entity is declared in a DTD, which can be internal or external. If declared in an internal DTD, it is used within that same document similar to a general entity. If declared in an external DTD, it references a URL where the DTD exists.

In the first example of Figure 11-12, the `%` character—followed by a space—declares that `person` is an external Parameter Entity. It specifies that content for "`%person;`" (no spaces) is located in the DTD file "`person.dtd.`" The content of this DTD file immediately replaces "`%person;`" as if it was an original part of the document.

The second example declares "`%idr;`" as an internal Parameter Entity that is to be immediately replaced by the text '`ID #REQUIRED.`' The example shows an `ATTLIST` declaration for `person_id` (as an attribute of `PERSON`) with "`%idr;`" as an internal Parameter Entity. This is replaced immediately by "`ID #REQUIRED`," as if it had been written:

```
<!ATTLIST PERSON person_id ID #REQUIRED>
```

Any amount of replacement text can be declared for general entities and for parameter entities. This text is surrounded by quotes. As we have seen, entities can be declared to insert fragments or complete paragraphs of standard "boiler-plate" text in a document. That insertion is immediate for parameter entities or external general entities. Insertion is deferred for internal general entities; the entity is replaced by the text only when it is about to be displayed, printed or passed to an application for processing.

Namespaces

XML requires that each element name is unique within a document, and also that each attribute name is unique within an element. These names can be declared in an internal DOCTYPE for the document, or can be specified in a DOCTYPE declared externally in a DTD whose location is referenced by the document DOCTYPE. Once defined, the element and attribute names constitute a "markup vocabulary".

A problem exists if different XML processors or applications all use the same names for different purposes. A single document may also include tags for more than one application. Because of these different markup vocabularies, there are potential problems of recognition and name collision. Software modules must be able to recognize the tags and attributes that they are designed to process, even in the face of naming collisions.

The role of XML namespaces is to provide a mechanism that overcomes these problems. Names can be qualified by a namespace prefix so that they are universally unique. XML Namespaces are now documented as a W3C "recommendation," the first step for acceptance as a standard [Namespaces]. This recommendation specifies that:

> An XML namespace is a collection of names, identified by a URI reference, which are used in XML documents as element types and attribute names. XML namespaces differ from the "namespaces" conventionally used in computing disciplines in that the XML version has internal structure and is not, mathematically speaking, a set.
>
> Names from XML namespaces may appear as qualified names, which contain a single colon separating the name into a namespace prefix and a local part. The prefix, which is mapped to a URI reference, selects a namespace. The combination of the universally managed URI namespaces and the document's own namespace produces identifiers that are universally unique. [Namespaces]

An example of a qualified name as an element type of `price` for use in EDI applications is illustrated in Figure 11-13. (This is not a formal EDI specification, and the referenced URI is fictitious.)

Figure 11-13 is an example of a local namespace with a limited scope. It declares an XML namespace (`xmlns:`) prefix of "`edi`," located at the URI '`http://ecommerce.org/schema`'. As it is declared within the element `retail_price`, its scope applies until the end tag `</retail_price>` is reached. The example prefixes "`edi:`" to the `price` element and to the `status` attribute of the `tax` element. These are both children within the `retail_price` parent element.

A namespace declaration applies to the element where it is specified and to all elements within the content of that element, unless overridden by another namespace declaration. With the `edi:` prefix in Figure 11-13, the `price` element and `status` attribute each now

Figure 11-13 Namespace definition and use for elements.

```
<retail_price xmlns:edi='http://ecommerce.org/schema'>
  <!-  The namespace for the 'price' element, and the
    'status' attribute of the 'tax' element, is located at
    'http://ecommerce.org/schema' -->
  <edi:price unit='Euro'>2.50</edi:price>
  <tax edi:status="Exempt">Meat</tax >
</retail_price>
```

has a unique name within the scope of the `retail_price` parent element.

More detail about namespaces can be obtained from the W3C recommendation and associated references, available from the [Namespaces] Web site.

Extensible Style Language (XSL)

The XSL specification is based on the Document Style Semantics and Specification Language (DSSSL) and Cascading Style Sheets (CSS). It is simpler than DSSSL and more powerful than CSS. While not yet a recommendation at the time of writing, it has progressed through a number of drafts. It will soon become an integral part of XML. We will briefly introduce XSL in this section. Further detail can be found in [Harold 1998]. The latest XSL specifications are available from the [XSL] Web site.

An XSL style sheet is itself an XML document. It has elements that are rules defining how the data contents of specific tags are to be displayed on screen or printed. An XSL processor uses a specified XSL style sheet to process an XML document. The output that is generated is an HTML file that can then be stored in a Web server, ready to be transmitted to a Web client and viewed with a Web browser.

A single XSL style sheet can be used by many XML documents. An organization may choose to define a corporate XSL style sheet that is to be used by all departments. If required, a department can override certain corporate styles by defining its own styles first. A parameter entity is then used to include the corporate style sheet automatically. XML always processes the first occurrence of a declaration that it encounters, ignoring later occurrences of that same declaration. Because they are processed first, only the departmental styles that have been specified therefore override those same relevant corporate styles.

Figure 11-14
XSL Style Sheet format.

```
<xsl>
   <rule>
      <target-element type="tagname"/>
      action
   </rule>
   <rule>
      <target-element type="tagname"/>
      action
   </rule>
</xsl>
```

The root element of an XSL style sheet is called `<xsl>`. Each `<xsl>` element contains one or more `<rule>` elements. Each rule specifies a *target* and an *action*. The *target* is an expression that defines which XML elements the *rule* applies to. The *action* specifies the list of *flow objects* that are to be generated when the rule is applied. A *flow object* is typically HTML markup and/or text that will become part of the output. Figure 11-14 shows the format of an XSL style sheet.

An XSL processor uses the style sheet to process tags in an XML document. Each time a `<tagname>` is found in the document that matches a `<target-element>` for a *rule* in the style sheet, the processor carries out the specified action for that rule. The action usually specifies HTML tags that will surround the data content of the located XML `<tagname>`.

HTML compresses white space (such as carriage returns, new lines or space characters) all as a single space character. This can be overridden by surrounding preformatted text with `<PRE>` ... `</PRE>` tags. A new line can be forced in an HTML file with a `<BR>` tag. A new paragraph can be forced with a `<P>` tag.

The HTML tags `<DIV>` ... `</DIV>` and `<SPAN>` ... `</SPAN>` can be used to apply formatting to regions of text. The <SPAN> tag is used to apply specified formatting in-line, as part of a sentence for example. The `<DIV>` tag is used to separate a block of text from other text, as if it was surrounded by `<P>` ... `</P>` tags for a new paragraph.

In contrast, XML preserves white space. To continue to maintain this white space after an XML document is converted to HTML, the tags can be included as part of the action for an XSL rule. Figure 11-15 illustrates the use of a `<DIV>` tag for all tags in an XML document, setting the style for the entire document to a font size of 12 point and using the font family of Arial.

Figure 11-15 Converting from XML to HTML, with a global font size and font family.

```
<xsl>
  <rule>
  <root/>
    <HTML/>
    <BODY>
      <children/>
    </BODY>
    </HTML>
  </rule>
  <rule>
    <target-element/>
    <DIV style="font-size: 12pt; font-family: Arial;">
      <children/>
    </DIV>
  </rule>
  <rule>
    <target-element type="person_name"/>
    <H2>
      <children/>
    </H2>
  </rule>
</xsl>
```

The first `<rule>` in Figure 11-15 specifies an empty `<root/>` tag. The action therefore applies to all tags and their content in the document. It declares `<HTML>` ... `</HTML>` and `<BODY>` ... `</BODY>` tags to surround `<children/>`, so applying these tags around the whole document. This converts the XML document to an HTML file.

The second `<rule>` provides a global style for every *`<target-element>`* in the document. This uses a font-size of 12 pt and a font-family of Arial. <DIV> also places the `<children/>` data content each on a new line, for each XML tag in the document.

The third `<rule>` specifies the *`<target-element type="person_name,"`* such as in Figure 11-10. It specifies that all *`<person_name>`* elements will be surrounded by `<H2>` ... `</H2>` tags. The output HTML file will display each person's name (all data content between *`<person_name>`* ... *`</person_name>`* tags) in the HTML Heading 2 format for the relevant browser.

XSL also allows elements to be targeted by attribute. This is very flexible as it can target all elements that have a certain attribute, or that have a certain attribute with a specific value, or an element whose ancestors have an attribute with a specific value, and more. Figure 11-16 documents the format, with a typical example.

Figure 11-16 locates all `PERSON` elements. Of these elements, it selects the *`person_id`* attribute with the value of "`p1100`" and

Figure 11-16
An XSL rule based on an Attribute Value.

```
Format:
<attribute name="attribute-name" value="attribute-value"/>
Example:
<rule>
   <element name="PERSON"
      <attribute name="person_id" value="p1100"/>
      <target-element type="person_name"/>
      <SPAN style="font-weight: bold">
         <children/>
      </SPAN>
   </element>
</rule>
```

locates the target element of `<person_name>`. <SPAN> includes all of the target-element and its children, which are made **bold** by the style specification `font-weight: bold`.

This example located a specific occurrence of an element based on the value of the attribute, `<person_id>`. *If instead* `<person_id>` was declared as an element of type `ID`, it could be explicitly referenced by an XSL `ID` attribute, such as:

```
<id attribute="attribute-name"/>
```

Formatting rules can also be specified to apply to elements based on their position in the parent element. This is specified by adding "`only`" and "`position`" attributes to the element or target-element tags.

The value "`of-type`" *used with* "`only`" specifies that the target be the only element of its type that is a child of its parent. The value "`of-any`" specifies that the target be the only element of any type of its parent.

The "`position`" attribute has four valid values: "`first-of-type`," "`last-of-type`," "`first-of-any`," and "`last-of-any`." The first rule locates the target that is the first child of a specified type of its parent. The second rule locates the last child of the specified type of its parent. The third and fourth rules locate the first child (or the last child) of any type of the parent.

In addition, content can be added as part of an XSL action following a rule. Additional text can be included that is not present in the XML document. For example, the internal general entity "`&M;`" (defined as "AUD") adds this prefix to prices in Figure 11-17, denominating prices in Australian dollars as AUD$15,500.00 (say).

If required, prices can instead be denominated in US dollars just by changing the declaration of the entity "`&M;`" instead to "USD".

Figure 11-17 Adding content to <price> in an XSL action.

```
<rule>
   <target-element type="price"/>
      &M; <children/>
</rule>
```

To this point, we have used <children/> to include children of the specified element in the output. We can be more specific with *Select*.

Selected Elements

When a target is matched, an action that includes a <children/> tag outputs all children of the element that matched the target, perhaps also applying other rules recursively to the children. These children are output in the order in which they appear in the XML document. The <select-elements> tag allows some children to be included in the output, while others are excluded. The order that included children are output can also override their order in the XML document.

The <target-element> tag applies patterns to the input; the <select-elements> tag applies patterns to the output to organize, reorder, and select the exact elements to appear in the rendered output. Figure 11-18 shows how we use <select-elements> to present the PERSON details of Figure 11-10 in a specific order.

Figure 11-18 has now changed the order of the tags in Figure 11-10 to display a person's *name* first at the start of a new paragraph <P>, followed by *company*, then *phone*, *fax*, and *email*.
 places

Figure 11-18 Presenting XSL output in a specific order.

```
<rule>
   <target-element type="PERSON"/>
   <select-elements>
      <P>
      <target-element type="name"/> <BR/>
      <target-element type="company"/> <BR/>
      <target-element type="phone"/> <BR/>
      <target-element type="fax"/> <BR/>
      <target-element type="email"/>
      </P>
   </select-elements>
</rule>
```

each of these on a new line. Note that neither `country` nor `mobile` is a specified `<target-element>` in the list of `<select-elements>`. They are therefore omitted from the output.

XSL Macros

In some cases, you may want to apply the same action on multiple elements. For example, you may have specific elements for managers, other elements for salespersons and still different elements for clerks. But you may want each of these separate job titles all to be formatted in the same way. XSL *macros* can be defined to apply the same group of complex rules to different objects.

The XSL `<define-macro>` tag uses an attribute name that becomes the name of the macro. The macro specifies relevant replacement text together with one or more `<contents/>` tags that specify where the contents of the relevant element are to be placed. Macros are declared in an XSL style sheet outside of a rule.

XSL Named Styles and Embedded Scripts

Named styles can be used similar to macros, to apply style properties. For example, the `<define-style>` tag allows a series of Cascading Style Sheet (CSS) style values to be used with a defined style name. Styles can also be included in XML tags; but this tends to defeat the intent of XML and XSL, which is to separate content from layout.

XSL style sheets can also contain *embedded scripts* that are written in JavaScript. These scripts can be executed by XSL as it processes an XML document, or they may be passed to the output HTML file so they can be executed by a Web browser.

This overview of XSL has provided a small insight into its power. As we have seen, it can be used to provide great flexibility for processing and formatting an XML document as an HTML file. And it can be expanded further with JavaScript. Using the power of XML with the syntax of XSL, very powerful rules can be defined to format the data content of an XML document. The XSL concepts are covered well in [Harold 1998]. The complete XSL specifications are available from the [XSL] Web site.

We have examined XSL syntax and examples, but in practice we expect that XSL will be generated using other tools. For example, we anticipate that developers of word processing software packages will offer an XSL generation option. This could convert existing or new style templates automatically into XSL style sheets. HTML editing packages should also allow style templates to be defined and generated as XSL style sheets using a similar approach.

Once generated, the look and feel of an XML document—converted to an HTML Web file under control of an XSL style sheet—can be changed merely by making appropriate style changes using the word processor or HTML editor. The changed XSL code will convert the generated HTML file then to the new style.

Document Object Model (DOM)

We have seen that an XML parser or processor is used to analyze an XML document. If it is well formed, and agrees with its DTD (and so is valid), the document is then passed to another application for processing. XSL is an application that is used to process and convert an XML document, formatting its output as an HTML file. Enterprise and other applications may need to carry out other processing against an XML document or an HTML file. A way is needed to access the content of XML or HTML files using a programming language.

Recognizing this need, the W3C has produced specifications for the Document Object Model (DOM). This is now a recommendation of the W3C; the DOM specifications are now available from the [DOM] URL.

DOM Specifies XML Program Interface

XML can be used to define the metadata vocabulary used by many disciplines. The structure of an XML document is clearly defined by its metadata, as well as the meaning of its data content. DOM defines a standard programming interface that can be used by a wide variety of environments and applications. DOM is a language-independent specification using the Object Management Group (OMG) Interface Definition Language (IDL), defined in the CORBA 2.2 specification. Any language can therefore use the DOM. In addition to the OMG IDL, language bindings are provided for Java and for ECMAScript—an industry-standard scripting language based on JavaScript and Jscript.

The DOM is an object model based on object-oriented design. The DOM recommendation specifies that *documents are modeled using objects, and the model encompasses not only the structure of the document, but also the behavior of a document and the objects of which it is composed. ... As an object model, the DOM identifies:*

- *the interfaces and objects used to represent and manipulate a document*
- *the semantics of these interfaces and objects—including both behavior and attributes*
- *the relationships and collaborations among these interfaces and objects.*

DOM Core and DOM HTML

The DOM has two parts: *DOM Core* and *DOM HTML*. The DOM Core represents the functionality used by XML documents. It also serves as the basis for DOM HTML. It documents functions to *create, set, get, replace*, and *remove* any objects of an XML document that can be written using XML, XSL, or XLL syntax. Using the DOM, a complete XML document—or any object within it—can be created, read, updated, or deleted as if it was part of a file or database.

It is important to note that DOM is not a binary specification. DOM programs written in the same language will be source code compatible across platforms, but DOM does not define any form of binary interoperability. It is not a set of data structures; it is an object model that specifies interfaces for managing XML and HTML documents.

The DOM is not a competitor to the Component Object Model (COM). It can be implemented using language-independent systems like COM or CORBA, or it can be implemented with language-specific bindings like Java or ECMAScript bindings as discussed earlier.

Extensible Linking Language (XLL)

The main reason for the rapid growth of the WWW and browsers in the early 1990s was largely due to HTML links. The ability to point and click on a link in a document, and be taken immediately to another document anywhere in the world, is now a familiar concept.

We discussed earlier that links based on a Uniform Resource Locator (URL) are vulnerable to change. If the targeted resource is moved, all URL links pointing to the target must be explicitly updated to point each URL to the target in its new location. In contrast, a Uniform Resource Identifier (URI) need never be changed.

If a link must point not to the start of a target HTML document, but instead to a point within that document, an anchor point must be used. The HTML anchor point must be inserted within the target document, at the relevant point. This target anchor point is then included as a suffix to the link, separated from the URL by a "#."

In HTML a link is specified with the <A> tag. In XML, almost any tag can be a link; elements that include links are called *linking elements*. The Extensible Linking Language (XLL) specifies how linking elements and URIs are defined and used. XLL is implemented using *XLinks* and *XPointers*. A linking element can specify a *Simple Link* or *Extended Links*.

Simple XLinks

A simple linking element is specified by `xlink:form="simple"`. Each linking element contains an `href` attribute; its value is the URI of the target (linked) resource. Three linking examples follow in Figure 11-19. These are examples of *simple* XLinks, similar to standard HTML links.

The first example in Figure 11-19 uses a `<store_link>` element and relative URL to link to the HTML page "`store.html`" when the active underlined text: Enter our Online Store is clicked. The start tag is terminated by the end tag `</store_link>`.

Figure 11-19 Example of "simple" Xlinks defined by XLL.

```
<store_link xlink:form="simple" href="store.html">
     Enter our Online Store</store_link>
<home_page xlink:form="simple" href="http://
www.visible.com.au/">
     Visible Systems Australia Pty Ltd Home Page</
home_page>
<image xlink:form="simple" src="visible-logo.gif"
     href="storeohtml"=/>
```

The next example uses a *<home_page>* element to specify an absolute URL for the active underlined Visible Systems Australia Pty Ltd Home Page text. This link is terminated by *</home_page>*.

The final example is an image link using the relative URL for the GIF file "*visible-logo.gif*." This last example is simplified by declaring the *xlink:form* attribute FIXED in a DTD, as shown in Figure 11-20.

Link elements may contain three optional attributes that specify how the link is to be used and how the target resource will be displayed in relation to the current page. These are *show*, *actuate*, and *behavior*.

The *show* attribute has three values: *replace*, *new*, and *embed*. With *show="replace"*, the target document is displayed in the same window as presently used by the current page. This is analogous to the default behavior of standard HTML links. In contrast, *show= "new"* displays the target document in a new window—analogous to the behavior of an HTML link set to *_blank*. Or with *show="embed"*, the target document is inserted into the current document—similar to an HTML server *include* statement.

The *actuate* attribute has two values: *user* and *auto*. A specification of *actuate="user"* indicates that the link is to be traversed only when the user clicks on it. This is the default action. The alternative specification of *actuate="auto"* indicates that the link is to be followed automatically whenever another targeted resource of that same link element is traversed.

The *behavior* attribute passes included data to an application specified to read that data. The specific data and how it is used is determined by the application. For example, the sound file "welcome.au" could play when the relevant link is traversed.

Figure 11-20 Example of a FIXED xlink:form attribute.

```
<!ELEMENT image EMPTY>
<!ATTLIST image
    xlink:form  CDATA  #FIXED "simple"
    src         CDATA  #REQUIRED
    href        CDATA  #REQUIRED
    alt         CDATA  #IMPLIED
    height      CDATA  #IMPLIED
    width       CDATA  #IMPLIED>

<image src "visible-logo.gif" href="store.html"/>
```

Figure 11-21 Using the `show`, `actuate`, and `behavior` XLink attributes.

```
<!ENTITY % link
     "xlink:form CDATA  #FIXED   'simple'
     href           CDATA  #REQUIRED
     show           CDATA  (new | replace | embed) 'replace'
     actuate        CDATA  (user | auto) 'user'
     behavior       CDATA  #IMPLIED"

<!ELEMENT home_page (#PCDATA)>
<!ATTLIST home_page %link;>

<home_page href="http://www.ies.aust.com/~ieinfo/"
     show="new" behavior="sound: welcome.au">
```

Like all attributes, `show`, `actuate`, and `behavior` must be declared in an `ATTLIST` for the link element. Figure 11-21 illustrates this, using the parameter entity "`%link;`" for convenience.

The parameter entity "`%link;`" is a single declaration that specifies all of the XLink attributes. The *<home_page>* `ELEMENT` then uses "`%link;`" to declare its `ATTLIST`. This inserts the `ATTLIST` XLink declarations into the *<home_page>* `ELEMENT`.

The *<home_page>* tag can now be used in an XML document to link to the IES Web site as shown in Figure 11-21. The IES home page is displayed in a *new* window and the sound "*welcome.au*" is played. The default *show*="*replace*" has been overridden, while the second default attribute *actuate*="*user*" has been used as declared.

So far we have discussed *simple* links. These are very similar to the standard links used by HTML. They are in-line links that are unidirectional; they are traversed from one link to the target. XLL is more powerful than HTML. It also supports *extended* links. These can define multidirectional links—with many links to many targets, as well as out-of-line links that reference a link file.

Extended XLinks

Distinct from HTML, an *extended* link can point to more than one target. It is declared by the attribute *xlink:form*="*extended*". The targets are defined in locator elements as children of the linking element, rather than use an *href* attribute in the linking element. The *show*,

Figure 11-22 Using child elements to implement XLL extended links.

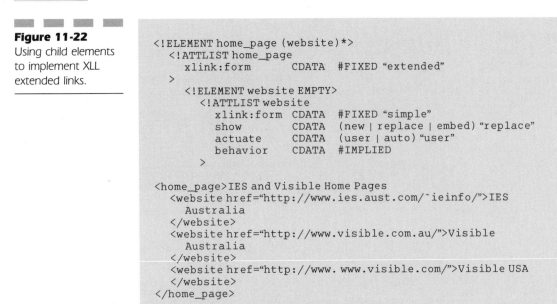

```
<!ELEMENT home_page (website)*>
   <!ATTLIST home_page
      xlink:form       CDATA  #FIXED "extended"
   >
      <!ELEMENT website EMPTY>
         <!ATTLIST website
            xlink:form  CDATA  #FIXED "simple"
            show        CDATA  (new | replace | embed) "replace"
            actuate     CDATA  (user | auto) "user"
            behavior    CDATA  #IMPLIED
         >

<home_page>IES and Visible Home Pages
   <website href="http://www.ies.aust.com/˜ieinfo/">IES
      Australia
   </website>
   <website href="http://www.visible.com.au/">Visible
      Australia
   </website>
   <website href="http://www. www.visible.com/">Visible USA
   </website>
</home_page>
```

`actuate`, and `behavior` attributes can be specified with each locator element.

Figure 11-22 specifies an extended `<home_page>` parent element with multiple `<website>` child links within the parent. Each child link now specifies the `href` attribute for its relevant text link. Defaults are used for `show` and `actuate`, but optional `behavior` attributes have not been included.

Implementing Uniform Resource Identifiers (URIs)

All of the links defined in this section, both simple and extended, are *inline* links based on URLs. XLL also supports *out-of-line* links. The links between documents are not present in the documents themselves, but are stored in separate XLL documents or files. Thus they become URIs. They never change in the linking documents, which always specify the same XLL document or file. This is analogous to indirect addressing. Any required changes are made only in the XLL document; the linking documents are unaffected.

This capability will lead to innovative new applications, as links can be maintained quite separate from the content of the document. For example, an XML document can have its links defined out-of-line in an XLL document or file. An HTML page can then be generated, using XML to specify the structure and content of data in a database. As the data changes dynamically in the generated HTML, the links embedded in that data can also change dynamically using XLL. Additional logic can also be provided using XSL `<rules>` or with embedded JavaScript. The application potentials are endless.

XPointers

To this point we have used *XLinks* to point to a specific resource, which may be an HTML page. XPointers are used to point to precise locations within a resource: a section, part, chapter, clause, or specific text in an unstructured textual document. Or it may point to a specific record in a legacy file, or a specific row and column of a certain table in a database. They are more powerful than HTML anchors.

HTML requires that anchors be physically inserted at the relevant position in the target document. In contrast, XPointers are specified without requiring any changes to the target document. Unlike HTML anchors, XPointers can point to ranges or spans rather than a specific point. For example, an XPointer can select a particular part of a document so that it can be copied or loaded into a program.

Absolute XPointers: An XPointer location can be specified as `id`, `root`, `html`, or `origin`. An `id` location selects the document element that has an ID-type attribute with the specified value. A `root` location selects the root element of a document and has no arguments; it selects the entire document. An `html` location selects a named anchor in an HTML document, for compatibility with HTML. The `origin` pointer is used in conjunction with one or more relative location terms—discussed next.

Relative XPointers: The `id`, `root`, `html`, and `origin` specify absolute locations: they can find an element in a document regardless of other contents of the document. But sometimes you may need to locate the first or the last element of a given type. Or instead, the next or preceding element, or the first (or last, next, or previous) child (or parent) of a specified type. These are all relative locations. They utilize the following location terms:

- `child:` searches the immediate children of the specified source element.
- `descendent:` searches all descendents of the source, not just the immediate children.
- `ancestor:` searches all ancestors of the source, starting from the nearest.
- `preceding:` searches all elements that occur before the source element in the document.
- `following:` searches all elements that occur after the source element in the document.
- `psibling:` selects the element that precedes the source element in the same parent element.
- `fsibling:` selects the element that follows the source element in the same parent element.

These relative XPointers provide a powerful location capability within unstructured text documents, as well as within structured legacy files or databases. They can specify ID values or particular values of elements and/or attributes.

Finally a selection can be made by `string`. This can be used to point into non-XML data, or into XML data that contains large amounts of text. A specific character, or range of characters, can be selected.

Figure 11-23 provides several examples that illustrate the use of XPointers. Each URL can be used as the `href` attribute value in a simple or extended XLink.

The first URL example in Figure 11-23 specifies the HTML document `articles.htm` in the IES Web site, at the anchor point "`#TEN`." When activated, this link positions the browser to display a list of

Figure 11-23 Examples of XPointers specified in Xlink URLs.

```
http://www.ies.aust.com/~ieinfo/articles.htm#html(TEN)
http://www.ies.aust.com/~ieinfo/ten.xml|id(ten03)
http://www.ies.aust.com/~ieinfo/ten.xml|root(),following(2)
http://www.ies.aust.com/~ieinfo/ten.xml|root(),string(2,
"IES,"1, 3)
```

published free quarterly newsletters, called: *The Enterprise Newsletter (TEN)*.

The second URL example locates an element in the document `ten.xml`, which has an `id` value of `ten03`. The "|" character (instead of the anchor point character "#") selects only the specified element.

The third URL example selects the second element (2) following the root element of `ten.xml`.

Finally, the fourth example uses a `string` to select the second occurrence of the string "`IES`." The two digits after the string specify the first character, and the number of characters, that are to be selected. This selects the entire string "`IES`".

Resource Description Framework (RDF)

Metadata that is used by various industries, communities, or bodies can be used with XML, XSL, and XLL to define markup vocabularies. The W3C is developing a standard framework that can be used to define these vocabularies. This is called the *Resource Description Framework* (RDF). It is a model for metadata applications that can support XML applications. RDF is an attempt by the W3C to build standards for XML applications so that they can interoperate more easily. The current status of RDF is available from the [RDF] Web site.

General Markup Vocabularies

We earlier referred to *Channel Definition Format* (CDF), supported by Microsoft in Internet Explorer 4.0. This is based on XML. Other examples are Netscape's *Meta Content Framework* (MCF), the *Open Software Description* (OSD) defined by Marimba and Microsoft, and the *Web Interface Definition Language* (WIDL) by webMethods. These vocabularies use unique language for communication.

Channel Definition Format (CDF): Microsoft has submitted CDF to the W3C as a standard, but it may remain a Microsoft-only standard. CDF provides a standard set of tags for defining push channels. These automate the flow of data from a Web server, pushed to a browser. CDF comprises a DTD that points the browser to relevant content, with descriptive content information and a schedule for downloads.

Meta Content Framework (MCF): Netscape extended original work done by Apple to navigate in 3D through a Web site. They converted it to XML as the Meta Content Framework. The current MCF model uses XML to create information nodes describing Web sites and pages. These nodes can include other nodes and can link across multiple files, creating a web of metadata that reflects the web of HTML underneath.

Open Software Description (OSD): The OSD was developed to deliver software and software updates over the Internet, not just Web pages. OSD can automatically download and install programs and packages in Java and in platform-specific code. Marimba is interested in using OSD for Java; Microsoft will use it to deliver Windows software. The OSD specifies information that is used to install the same software on multiple platforms, even if the code to be downloaded will change depending on the platform. OSD files specify program dependencies, allowing Java programs to download packages and Windows programs to download required DLLs. It expands the current OBJECT and APPLET HTML tags. OSD is designed to work with CDF as well; channels can be used with OSD files to update software automatically and regularly.

Web Interface Definition Language (WIDL): WIDL provides information about available Web services to client machines, allowing them to automate web-based processes. Programs use WIDL without needing a browser. For example, a shipping clerk who needs to track thousands of packages can use WIDL to connect lists of tracking numbers to the relevant FedEx, DHL, or UPS Web sites. We will see other applications that use WIDL in Chapter 12.

WIDL makes it easy to connect clients to back-end systems through Web interfaces. It is a tool to connect and automate systems, converting applications using sophisticated interfaces to access data and databases. Parts of WIDL may become obsolete as XML is more widely used, when programs are able to parse XML data easily without the need for a separate interface. WebMethods has promised WIDL interface capabilities for C, C++, Java and Visual Basic. We could expect them also to update WIDL to reflect advances in XML.

Special Purpose Markup Vocabularies

There is considerable effort in some industries to define a standard vocabulary, using XML for their metadata. Markup languages have been defined for: *Mathematics Markup Language* (MathML); *Chemical Markup Language* (CML); *Open Financial Exchange* (OFX); *Internet Content Exchange* (ICE); *Speech Markup Language* (SpeechML); *JavaBean Markup Language* (JBL); *Synchronized Multimedia Integration Language* (SMIL); and *Wireless Markup Language* (WML).

The [W3C] and [RDF] Web sites are two good starting points for more information. They will point you to specific Web sites that provide additional details about the above markup languages.

XML Resolves Many HTML Problems

Early in this chapter we discussed a number of problems associated with the use of HTML. XML resolves many of these problems, as discussed next.

1. *XML defines content of page* We now know that XML offers a powerful way to define tags describing the content of a document. This document can be unstructured text, or it can be graphics, images, audio or video files, or it can be structured data in legacy files, relational or object databases.
2. *Search engines can locate XML content* Search engines can precisely locate required content based on defined XML tags. This content has more meaning than earlier search methods that rely only on word indexes or manually defined keywords.
3. *XML can integrate dissimilar data sources* XML can be used to define the structure of legacy files, relational and object databases, as well as unstructured text, graphics, images, audio, or video. This makes it easier to integrate data content sourced from dissimilar systems and databases.
4. *Easier dynamic programming* XML and DOM simplify programming to incorporate dynamic content from different data

sources. DOM offers a language-independent interface for processing XML documents.

5. *Easier interfacing with back-end systems:* XML and DOM have been designed to interface with back-end systems. Markup languages such as WIDL also provide this capability.

When to Use Elements, Attributes, or Entities

The terminology used by XML differs in context from the terminology we used for data modeling in Parts 1 and 2. In data modeling, an entity contains attributes. With XML, an element can represent both data modeling entities and attributes. For example, XML can declare data modeling attributes as elements. These are then declared hierarchically as the children of a parent element that represents the data modeling entity.

To illustrate further, Figure 11-24 shows a typical data map and data dictionary as used by Visible Advantage, the CASE tool we used in Parts

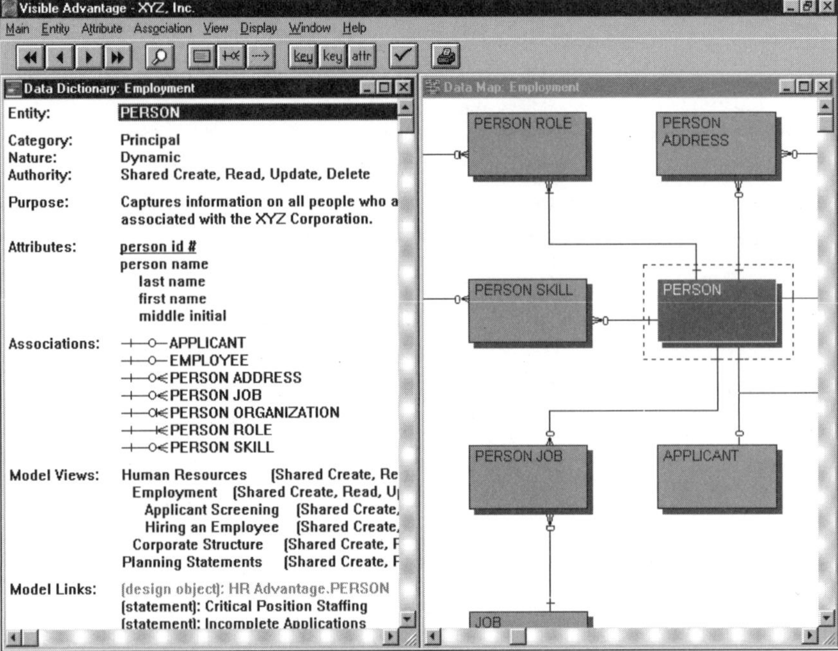

Figure 11-24 CASE Tool details for the Element PERSON.

1 and 2 for Data Warehouse and Enterprise Portal design and development. In Figure 11-24 a Data Map window is displayed for the *Employment* area within XYZ. A Data Dictionary window is synchronized with it and tiled to its left.

When an entity is selected in the Data Map window of Figure 11-24, the metadata details of that entity are automatically displayed in the Data Dictionary window. We can see that the selected PERSON entity contains a number of attributes. In data modeling entity list notation (see Chapter 3), this is documented as:

```
PERSON(person id#, person name (last name, first name,
middle initial))
```

Note that *person name* is a group attribute, containing each attribute that follows in brackets. Expressing this entity in XML, PERSON and its attributes can be declared as elements, hierarchically nested as shown in Figure 11-25. The *Employment* model view in the figure is declared as the root name of the document, and is also called Employment.

NOTE. *PERSON is an XML element, but it is called an "entity" in data modeling terminology (see Chapter 3). The metadata details describing the element PERSON in Figure 11-24 can be declared as XML attributes.*

Figure 11-25 An Internal DTD for Figure 11-24, with XML tags and data content.

```
<?xml version="1.0" standalone="yes"?>
<!DOCTYPE Employment
[
<!ELEMENT Employment ANY>
   <!ELEMENT PERSON (person_id, person_name)>
      <!ELEMENT person_id (#PCDATA)>
      <!ELEMENT person_name
         (last_name, first_name, middle_initial)>
            <!ELEMENT last_name (#PCDATA)>
            <!ELEMENT first_name (#PCDATA)>
            <!ELEMENT middle_initial (#PCDATA)>
]>
<Employment>
   <PERSON>
      <person_id>771144</person_id>
      <person_name>
         <last_name>Finkelstein</last_name>
         <first_name>Clive</first_name>
         <middle_initial>B</middle_initial>
      </person_name>
   </PERSON>
</Employment>
```

Figure 11-25 contains the data modeling entity PERSON, declared as XML element PERSON. As XML names are case-sensitive, the element name is in upper case—following the data modeling notation convention for entities in capitals as discussed in Chapter 3.

The *Employment* document in Figure 11-25 can also declare the other data modeling entities displayed in Figure 11-24. For example, SKILL and PERSON SKILL entities could be declared as the XML elements SKILL and PERSON_SKILL.

The data modeling attributes *person id#* and *person name* in the entity list are declared as XML elements person_id and person_name. These element names have been declared in lower case, following the convention for data modeling attributes (see Chapter 3). The child list (person_id, person_name) within the PERSON element declares—with a comma-separator—that these are mandatory.

The group attribute (*person name*) in the entity list is declared in Figure 11-25 as the XML element person_name, with child elements of *(last_name, first_name, middle_initial)*. These child elements are all mandatory. XML tags and data content at the end of Figure 11-25 illustrate the hierarchical nature of these element declarations through nesting. The person_id element has a value of "771144" as an actual value for this primary key element.

Creating XML DTD Files

We can now see why knowledge of the metadata used by an organization is essential if XML is to be used effectively. The examples in this chapter focused on metadata for one data modeling entity: PERSON, and declared some of its data modeling attributes. In real life, we saw in Parts 1 and 2 that an enterprise has many hundreds (or thousands) of entities, and thousands of attributes. To manually declare each of these to XML is impractical; an automated approach is needed.

The earlier chapters of the book used various methods to identify this metadata. In Part 1 we used Forward Engineering methods: strategic business planning (Chapter 2); data modeling (Chapter 3); strategic modeling (Chapter 4); and Decision Early Warning (Chapter 5). In Part 2 we used Reverse Engineering methods to extract and capture metadata that exists in legacy databases and systems. We used a CASE tool, Visible Advantage, to capture this metadata in a repository. With this CASE tool, we can use the defined metadata to generate automatically the database tables, columns, and indexes needed to implement a Data Warehouse or Enterprise Portal.

Through our Forward Engineering and Reverse Engineering focus in Parts 1 and 2, the hard work has already been done. The metadata has been identified and captured. It can be used to generate the databases needed by the data warehouse or enterprise portal.

So why can't the metadata in the CASE tool repository also be used to generate the DTD files needed for XML?

We believe that an automatic XML DTD generation capability will be supported soon by some CASE tool vendors. It is not a difficult task as we will soon see. To misquote Neil Armstrong, *One small step for a CASE tool; one giant leap for business!* CASE vendors that provide this capability will be the winners in the new business and computing environment that is emerging with Internet, intranet and extranet technologies, with Java, and with XML.

Let us examine how this could be achieved. We will continue to use Visible Advantage as our CASE tool example; the concepts apply also to other CASE tools. The approach that we will use next is only one of several possible methods.

Using CASE Tools to Generate XML DTD Files

In Figure 11-24 the Data Dictionary window at left contains data modeling details, and also: all attributes of PERSON; associations to other entities related to PERSON; model views interested in PERSON; and design object and planning statement model links from PERSON. One or many occurrences of these exist for each entity as we discussed in Chapter 4. This is illustrated in Figure 11-26 by a box surrounding each group of multiple occurrences. We will discuss the labels attached to each box shortly.

The CASE tool uses these details as its metadata (*CASE metadata*), to manage details about enterprise entities, attributes, and associations (*enterprise metadata*) defined in its repository. *CASE metadata* can be used by XML applications when they process the enterprise data content identified by XML data tags declared from the *enterprise metadata*. This is the "giant leap" above.

Visible Advantage uses enterprise metadata definitions of entities and attributes in its repository to generate Data Definition Language (DDL)

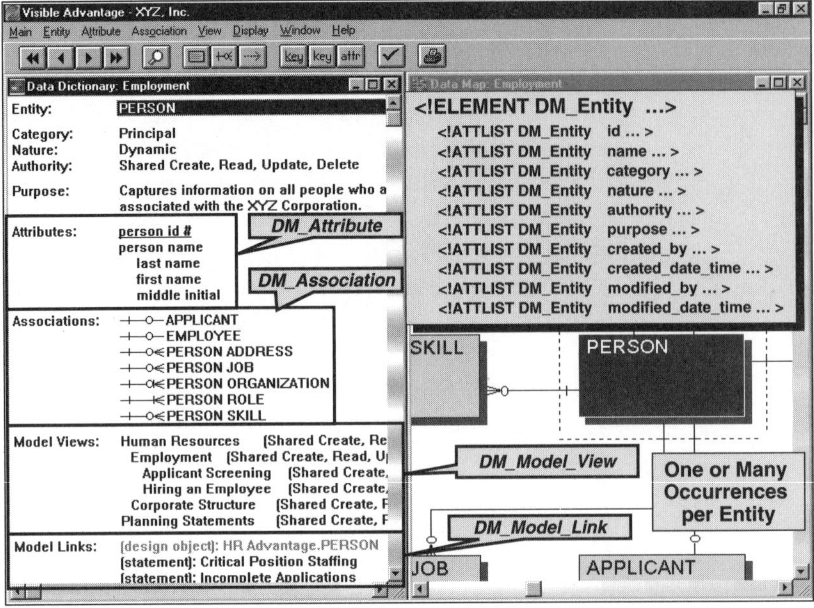

Figure 11-26 CASE Tool details for the Element PERSON. Boxes surround multiple occurrences of CASE metadata details.

schema scripts automatically for DBMS products. As the DDL syntax can differ between DBMS products, Visible Advantage uses a scripting language to generate the DDL `CREATE TABLE`, `CREATE INDEX` and other DDL statements for the target DBMS. These specify table and column definitions generated from data modeling entity and attribute metadata, to install these in a physical database.

The logical source of metadata definitions for XML is the enterprise metadata captured in CASE tools as discussed in Parts 1 and 2. We believe that XML element and attribute declarations in the future will be automatically generated by CASE tools, using CASE metadata and similar scripting capabilities that these tools already use to generate DDL schemata automatically for different DBMS products. This will be a key enabler of XML, from the wider use of enterprise metadata defined by data administrators.

Specifying Data Modeling Entities

The CASE metadata details in Figure 11-26 can be declared as attributes in an XML `ATTLIST` for the XML element: *`DM_Entity`* (say). We have used this element name with the prefix *DM_* (for data modeling) to distinguish it from other CASE metadata elements. CASE tools typically support many methodologies. They may need to use *OO_Entity* (or *OO_Class*) for elements generated from object-oriented CASE metadata, for example. The prefix identifies the methodology.

Do not confuse this use of methodology prefixes with the prefixes that are used for namespaces, as discussed earlier. Each CASE tool vendor will define its CASE metadata. Namespaces can then be used (as defined for XML) to prevent name collisions with the XML names used by different vendors for their specific CASE metadata.

A fragment of the `DM_Entity` XML `ELEMENT` and `ATTLIST` declarations defined from CASE metadata is displayed in Figure 11-26 and is defined in more detail in Figure 11-27.

Several incomplete XML attribute declarations in Figure 11-26 follow the `DM_Entity` element declaration. Figure 11-27 shows that the XML attributes `id`, `name`, `category`, `nature`, `authority`, `created_by`, and `created_date_time` are specified as "`REQUIRED;`" there must be one, and only one, occurrence of each of these XML attributes in a declared `DM_Entity`. The attributes `purpose`, `modified_by`, and `modified_date_time` are optional and so are specified as "`IMPLIED`."

```
<?XML version="1.0" standalone="YES"?>
  <!DOCTYPE Employment
  [
  <!ELEMENT Employment ANY>
    <!ELEMENT DM_Entity
      (DM_Attribute+, DM_Association+, DM_Model_View+, DM_Model_Link*)>
      <!ATTLIST DM_Entity  id                       ID     #REQUIRED>
      <!ATTLIST DM_Entity  name                     CDATA  #REQUIRED>
      <!ATTLIST DM_Entity  category  (Principal | Type | Intersecting |
                         Secondary | Structure | Role)    # REQUIRED>
      <!ATTLIST DM_Entity  nature (Dynamic | Static)     # REQUIRED>
      <!ATTLIST DM_Entity  authority(Create | Read | Update |
                                   Delete)  # REQUIRED>
      <!ATTLIST DM_Entity  purpose                  CDATA  #IMPLIED>
      <!ATTLIST DM_Entity  created_by               CDATA  # REQUIRED>
      <!ATTLIST DM_Entity  created_date_time        CDATA  # REQUIRED>
      <!ATTLIST DM_Entity  modified_by              CDATA  #IMPLIED>
      <!ATTLIST DM_Entity  modified_date_time       CDATA  #IMPLIED>
  ]
```

Figure 11-27
XML `ELEMENT` and `ATTLIST` CASE Metadata Declarations for `DM_Entity` in Model View Employment.

In Figure 11-26, the box surrounding the attributes for PERSON is labelled to indicate that each *Attribute* is defined by an XML element: *DM_Attribute* (say). Because many attributes exist for each entity, each is defined as a child element of *DM_Entity*. Similarly each *Association* is defined as a child element: *DM_Association* (say). Additionally, *Model View* and *Model Link* entries in Figure 11-26 are defined as child elements: *DM_Model_View* and *DM_Model_Link* (say).

Figure 11-27 shows that there must be at least one *DM_Attribute* child element (DM_Attribute+) for each *DM_Entity*. Each data modeling entity must at least have a primary key. The + suffix indicates that there can be more occurrences of *DM_Attribute*. These occurrences define other primary keys, foreign keys, or non-key attributes (see Chapter 3).

The + suffix for *DM_Association* (DM_Association+) specifies there must be one or more association occurrences in a *DM_Entity*. Good data modeling practice ensures that a data modeling entity does not exist as an isolated island of data; it is associated with at least one or more other entities. There must also be one or more *DM_Model_View* (DM_Model_View+) child elements, while there may be zero or more *DM_Model_Link* child elements (DM_Model_Link*) for each *DM_Entity*.

Figure 11-27 lists these as valid child element declarations of *DM_Entity* for each of these child elements. We will not refer to these further, except for *DM_Attribute* which will be used with *DM_Entity* to generate an XML DTD as shown in Figure 11-25.

The *Category, Nature*, and *Authority* details in Figure 11-26 can only have certain values. These values are specified when an entity is first entered or later changed in Visible Advantage. The valid values are shown in Figure 11-28 as a dialog box. Figure 11-27 therefore declares the *Category*, *Nature*, and *Authority* values in brackets. Valid category values are (*Principal | Type | Intersecting | Secondary | Structure | Role*). Valid *nature* values are (*Dynamic | Static*). Valid authority values are (*Create | Read | Update | Delete*). Only these values can be used; each of these XML attributes is #REQUIRED. Other XML attributes are declared as #REQUIRED or #IMPLIED as discussed earlier.

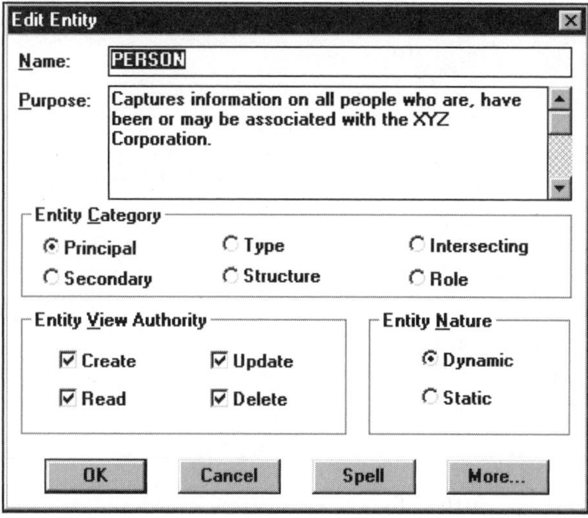

Figure 11-28 CASE metadata valid values for definition of a data modeling entity.

Specifying Data Modeling Attributes

CASE metadata is also captured for data modeling attributes and associations, as well as for planning statements, activities, processes, objects, methods, physical database designs, and more. Each of these is also declared as an XML element as shown in Figure 11-26. For our purposes, however, we only need to consider the `DM_Attribute` child element. For example, metadata from Figure 11-26 for the primary key attribute *person id#* is shown in Figure 11-29 as a dialog box.

The CASE metadata in Figure 11-29 is declared in Figure 11-30 as an XML `ATTLIST` for the XML element `DM_Attribute`. This shows that each dialog box detail of Figure 11-29 is declared as an XML attribute of the XML element `DM_Attribute`. Attributes in the declaration that are mandatory are shown as `#REQUIRED`. Those details that are optional (such as length and precision) are shown as `#IMPLIED` as they depend on the specified domain value. For example, domain values of `character`, `numeric`, and `decimal` require a `length` attribute. Domains of `numeric` and `decimal` may also optionally specify the `precision` as a number of decimal places.

`Alias` and `purpose` are optional attributes and are shown as `#IMPLIED`. But as for data modeling entities, good practice recommends that all data modeling attributes should have a defined purpose description.

Edit Primary Key Attribute
Entity: PERSON
Attribute: person id
Alias:
Purpose: Uniquely identifies an occurrence of person.
Domain: System Generated Id
Length: Precision: Edit Domain
System Controlled
Model View Authority
Read
Update
Spell OK
More... Cancel

Figure 11-29 CASE metadata for the *person id#* primary key attribute. These valid values are declared in Figure 11-30.

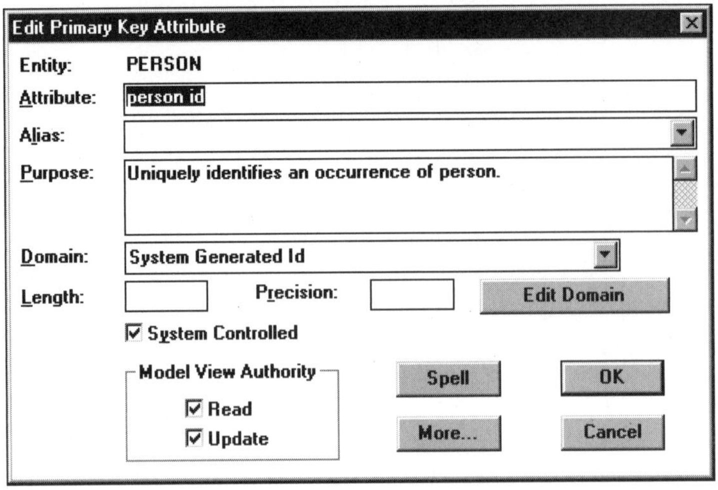

The XML *type* attribute in Figure 11-30 specifies valid values of *Primary-Key*, *Foreign-Key*, *Non-Key*, and *Group* for data modeling attributes. For attributes that are children of another *DM_Attribute* of *type="Group"* (such as *person_ name*), each child *DM_Attribute* specifies its parent in the XML *group* attribute (such as *group="person_name"*). An example of this is shown later in Figure 11-31.

Notice in particular the list of valid values for the *domain* attribute in Figure 11-30. This is #REQUIRED: it specifies the data type of the attribute defined in the enterprise metadata. Typical valid values are listed here. Visible Advantage can easily be extended to add other enterprise-defined data types to the list of valid domains. Examples are *State*, *SSN*, and *Skill Level*. Once added, any domain value can be easily selected as the data type for an attribute used in the enterprise.

We discussed earlier that data content in an XML document is expressed as character data (CDATA). We considered an XML data example showing a *customer_balance* of $15,500.00. The numeric characters used for this value must be converted by an XML application to the numeric value of $15,500.00 before it can be used for calculation purposes. The data type of each enterprise metadata attribute can be determined by the XML application from the XML *domain* attribute in the XML *DM_Attribute* element, as declared in Figure 11-30.

Figure 11-31 shows the *CASE Metadata* XML element tags and attribute data content that has been automatically generated from the

Figure 11-30 XML ELEMENT and ATTLIST Declarations for *DM_Attribute* based on CASE metadata valid values in Figure 11-29.

```
<!ELEMENT DM_Attribute
  <!ATTLIST DM_Attribute id         ID             #REQUIRED>
  <!ATTLIST DM_Attribute entity     CDATA          #REQUIRED>
  <!ATTLIST DM_Attribute attribute  CDATA          #REQUIRED>
  <!ATTLIST DM_Attribute type       (Primary-Key|Foreign-Key|
                                    Non-Key | Group) #REQUIRED>
  <!ATTLIST DM_Attribute group      CDATA          #IMPLIED >
  <!ATTLIST DM_Attribute alias      CDATA          #IMPLIED >
  <!ATTLIST DM_Attribute purpose    CDATA          #IMPLIED>
  <!ATTLIST DM_Attribute domain     (Character | Text | Flag |
                                    Money | Numeric | Decimal |
                                    Float | Integer |
                                    System_Generated_Id|Date|
                                    Date_Time|Time)#REQUIRED>
  <!ATTLIST DM_Attribute length     CDATA          #IMPLIED>
  <!ATTLIST DM_Attribute precision  CDATA          #IMPLIED>
  <!ATTLIST DM_Attribute authority  (Read | Update) #REQUIRED>
```

declarations of *DM_Entity* in Figure 11-27 and of *DM_Attribute* in Figure 11-30. The *CASE Metadata* content for PERSON from Figure 11-26 is now included in Figure 11-31 as the data content for the *DM_Entity* occurrence of PERSON. *CASE Metadata* content for the *person id#* primary key displayed in Figure 11-29—and other attributes earlier displayed in Figure 11-26—are shown in Figure 11-31 as XML attribute content for *DM_Attribute* elements of *person id*, *person name*, *last name*, *first name*, and *middle initial*.

The resulting XML *CASE Metadata* in Figure 11-31 can be automatically generated by CASE tools from *Enterprise Metadata*. This is analogous to generated CREATE TABLE declarations as the DDL for a target DBMS. When processed by an XML processor or XML database (see Chapter 15), the final *Enterprise Metadata* XML tags and content are as shown in Figure 11-32.

Similarly, other CASE metadata can be declared as XML elements for planning statements, activities, processes, objects, methods, database designs, and more. The generated enterprise metadata in Figure 11-32 can be used for import and export data interchange between different enterprise data sources. This enables XML to integrate dissimilar legacy files or relational databases. Examples of XML applications that integrate different data sources are discussed in Chapters 12 and 15.

The XML declarations in Figure 11-27 and Figure 11-30 document the CASE metadata used to manage data modeling entities and attributes in

```
<Employment>
   <DM_Entity  id="E1245"
      name="PERSON"
      category="Principal"
      nature="Dynamic"
      authority="Shared Create, Read, Update, Delete"
      purpose="Captures information on all people who are, have been or may be
      associated with the XYZ Corporation"
      created_by="CBF"
      created_date_time="Feb 12, 1999 10:15:00">
   <DM_Attribute id="A3152" entity="PERSON" attribute="person id" type="Primary-Key"
      purpose="Uniquely identifies an occurrence of person."
      domain="System Generated Id" authority="'Read, Update">
   <DM_Attribute id="A3153" entity="PERSON" attribute="person name" type="Group"
      purpose="To identify the person.">
   <DM_Attribute id="A3154" entity="PERSON" attribute="last name" type="Non-Key"
      group="person_name" purpose="A person's last name used to identify the person."
      edit rule="add now & modify later" domain="Character" length="30"
      authority="Read, Update">
   <DM_Attribute id="A3155" entity="PERSON" attribute="first name" type="Non-Key"
      group="person_name" purpose="The first name of a person."
      edit rule="add now & modify later" domain="Character" length="30"
      authority="Read, Update">
   <DM_Attribute id="A3156" entity="PERSON" attribute="middle initial"
      type="Non-Key" group="person_name" purpose="Middle initial of a person's
      name, used for identification of the person."
      edit rule="add now & modify later" domain="Character" length="30"
      authority="Read, Update">
</Employment>
```

Figure 11-31
Generated CASE Metadata XML tags and data content for *DM_Entity* and *DM_Attribute*.

the Visible Advantage CASE tool. The generated CASE metadata in Figure 11-31 is used to import and export enterprise metadata between this and other CASE tools that declare CASE metadata differently. Each vendor can publish its CASE metadata in a unique namespace. Once published, these CASE metadata declarations can be used to define a common CASE metadata vocabulary. An approach can be used to integrate CASE metadata in Figure 11-31 with other CASE metadata that is similar to the multiple supplier application described in Chapter 12. This will enable enterprise metadata to be easily imported and exported between different CASE tools in the future, using a common repository.

We will now use the XML concepts covered in this chapter for other purposes: using XML as a Business Reengineering technology in Chapter

Figure 11-32 Output from XML Processor or XML database of generated *Enterprise Metadata* tags from Figure 11-31, with relevant data content.

```
<?xml version="1.0" standalone="yes"?>
   <!DOCTYPE Employment
   [
   <!ELEMENT Employment ANY>
      <!ELEMENT PERSON (person_id, person_name)>
         <!ELEMENT person_id (#PCDATA)>
         <!ELEMENT person_name
            (last_name, first_name, middle_initial)>
               <!ELEMENT last_name (#PCDATA)>
               <!ELEMENT first_name (#PCDATA)>
               <!ELEMENT middle_initial (#PCDATA)>
   ]>
   <Employment>
      <PERSON>
         <person_id>771144</person_id>
         <person_name>
            <last_name>Finkelstein</last_name>
            <first_name>Clive</first_name>
            <middle_initial>B</middle_initial>
         </person_name>
      </PERSON>
   </Employment>
```

12, and for integrated Business and Systems Reengineering in Chapter 13. We consider enterprise quality initiatives in Chapter 14. We conclude the book by discussing other business and systems reengineering opportunities in Chapter 15 that are based on the use of XML, and the central role taken by Enterprise Portals in deploying these as XML applications.

REFERENCES

Document Object Model (DOM) Specifications—http://www.w3.org/TR/REC-DOM-Level-1/

Hackathorn, R. (1998) *Web Farming for the Data Warehouse*, Morgan Kaufman, ISBN: 1-55860-503-7. Includes use of XML for data sources from Internet (368 pages).

Harold, E. R. (1998) *XML: Extensible Markup Language*, IDG Books, ISBN: 0-7645-3199-9. Covers XML, XSL, and XLL with HTML (426 pages + CD-ROM).

Holzner, S. (1998) *XML Complete*, McGraw-Hill, ISBN: 0-07-913702-4. Covers XML with focus on Java (516 pages + CD-ROM).

XML Namespaces Specifications—http://www.w3.org/TR/REC-xml-names/

Resource Description Framework (RDF) Specifications—http://www.w3.org/Metadata/RDF/

St Laurent, S. (1998) *XML: A Primer*, MIS Press [IDG Books], ISBN: 1-55828-592-X. A good basic introduction to XML (348 pages).

Extensible Linking Language (XLL) Specifications—http://www.w3.org/XLL/

Extensible Markup Language (XML) Specifications—http://www.w3.org/XML/

Extensible Style Language (XSL) Specifications—http://www.w3.org/XSL/

W3C, WWW Consortium and associated specifications—http://www.w3.org/

XML Books. The IES web site at http://www.ies.aust.com/~ieinto/ and the Visible Australia web site at http://www.visible.com.au/ both list many HTML, XML, Data Warehousing, and Corporate Portal books. Each listed book has a direct link to Amazon.com so that you can review these books then purchase those that interest you.

XML Information Web Sites

- WWW Consortium—Specifications and Standards—http://www.w3.org/
- Microsoft XML Scenarios Web Site—http://microsoft.com/xml/scenario/intro.asp
- XML.com Web Site—http://www.xml.com/
- James Tauber's XMLINFO Web Site—http://www.xmlinfo.com/
- James Clark's XML Web Page—http://www.jclark.com/xml/
- Robin Cover's XML Resources—http://www.sil.org/sgml/xml.html
- Microsoft XML Site—http://www.microsoft.com/xml/
- Microsoft XML Workshop Web Site—http://www.microsoft.com/workshop/xml/toc.htm
- Web Farming Web Site—http://www.webfarming.com/

XML Development Tools: Validating Parsers

- Microsoft's MSXML Parser—http://www.microsoft.com/standards/xml/xmlparse.htm
- IBM's Alphaworks XML for Java Parser—http://www.alphaworks.ibm.com/formula/xml
- Data Channel's DXP Parser—http://www.datachannel.com/products/xdk/DXP/index.html
- Object Design's eXcelon XML database—http://www.objectdesign.com/
- TclXML Parser (based on TCL—instead of Java or C)—http://tcltk.anu.edu.au/XML/

XML Development Tools: XML Browsers

- Peter Murray Rust's Jumbo Browser—http://vsms.nottingham.ac.uk/vsms/jumbo
- Netscape's Mozilla Browser—http://www.mozilla.org/
- Microsoft Internet Explorer 5.0—http://www.microsoft.com/
- Netscape Communicator 5.0—http://www.netscape.com/

CHAPTER 12

Using XML as a Business Reengineering Technology

... Downsizing and restructuring only mean doing less with less. Reengineering, by contrast, means doing more with less. ... Nor is re-engineering the same as quality improvement, total quality management (TQM), or any other manifestation of the contemporary quality movement ... Quality programs ... aim to do what we already do, only to do it better ... Re-engineering seeks breakthroughs, not by enhancing existing processes, but by discarding them and replacing them with entirely new ones.

—Michael Hammer and James Champy

The Internet and corporate intranets present opportunities to reengineer business processes for direct access between customers and suppliers. Reengineering for this environment requires close integration of business plans, business processes, and business information, to ensure that systems are built that are closely aligned with strategic directions. A new generation of I-CASE tools is emerging that can automatically analyze data models based on the metadata, to identify cross-functional processes. These present reengineering opportunities that benefit from the open architecture environment of the Internet and intranets. The emergence of the Extensible Markup Language (XML) offers a metadata technology that presents significant opportunities for business reengineering. This chapter discusses reengineering opportunity analysis of metadata, as used by the Engineering Enterprise Portals (EEP) methodology. It uses Business Reengineering and XML in the metadata project example that we first discussed in Chapter 10.

The Problems Of Change

The Internet and its corporate counterpart, the intranet, are transforming the competitive landscape with a rapidity and in ways never thought possible [Finkelstein 1996]. Organizations are faced with unprecedented competition on a global basis. To compete effectively, they must change. Those that fail to see the need for change will not survive.

This change, in most cases, involves reengineering the business. This chapter shows how a focus on business reengineering, and development of information systems that directly support strategic business plans, allows managers to take control and turn tomorrow's chaotic environment to their competitive advantage by using the Internet and intranets.

To succeed in today's environment an organization must focus first on customers and markets, rather than on products and production. To compete effectively in today's market environment, flexibility is key: time to market has to go to virtual zero [Zachman 1992]. This suggests a strategy of *Assemble-to-Order:* of products, custom-built from standard components, and tailored to each customer's specific needs.

An assemble-to-order strategy applies not only to manufacturing and assembly, but to most service industries as well: such as custom-tailored banking or insurance products, or government services. It also applies to systems development. The solutions are well known. They involve the integration of business and IT: integration on the business side using strategic business planning and business reengineering; and integration for IT using client/server systems and object-oriented development.

The Internet and intranets also assist. The emergence of XML offers a powerful metadata technology to achieve integration of dissimilar systems. It presents significant reengineering opportunities.

We will first discuss well-known problems associated with manual and automated systems. We will then see how data models and metadata can help us identify reengineering opportunities for business processes. We will discuss how open architecture environments established by Internet and intranet technology, with XML, can be utilized to reengineer processes in ways that were difficult to achieve before.

Manual Processes and Systems

Consider a typical business that accepts orders for products or services from the Sales Dept, as placed by customers. These orders are processed first by the Order Entry Dept, and then by the Credit Dept. Each department needs details of the customer, such as name and address, and account balance, and details of the order. These are saved in customer files and order files, held and maintained by each department as shown in Figure 12-1. They represent source data that is used in the sales analysis system, S1, discussed in Chapter 10.

In satisfying these orders, items used from inventory must eventually be replaced. These are ordered by the Purchasing Dept from suppliers, and are then later paid by the Accounts Payable section of the Accounts Dept. Details of name and address, and the account balance due to the supplier, are also saved in supplier files and creditor files. These are held

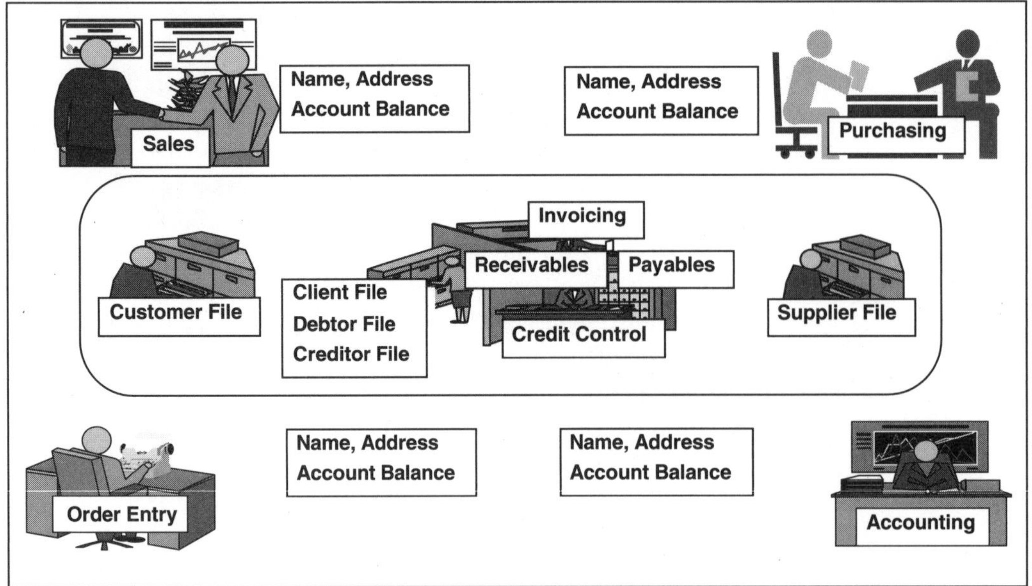

Figure 12-1
The same data often exists redundantly in an organization. Each redundant data version must be maintained current, and up to date. This invarably leads to the evolution of redundant processes.

redundantly and are maintained separately by each department as also shown in Figure 12-1.

To ensure these redundant data versions are kept current and up to date and that all versions consistently refer to the same information, any change to one data version must also be made to all other affected versions. For example, a customer notifies the Sales Dept of a change of address. That address change must be made not only in the Sales Dept customer file, but also in the customer file maintained by the Order Entry Dept. The same customer details are held and maintained redundantly by the Credit Dept in their client file and by the Invoicing Section of the Accounts Dept in their debtor file.

And if the customer also does business with the organization as a supplier, that change of address must be made to the supplier file maintained by the Purchasing Dept and to the creditor file maintained by Accounts Payable in the Accounts Dept. The address change must be made to *every* redundant data version, so that all information about the customer is correct and is consistent across the organization.

This is not a computer problem: it is an organization problem! But its resolution over the years has defined the manual processes and the organizational structures adopted by countless organizations. In our earlier example, processes are defined to capture the details of customers and make changes to those details when needed later, as in the change of customer address. Many of these processes are also redundant, but are necssary to maintain the data versions all up to date. Redundant data thus leads to redundant processes.

And of course, people have been allocated to carry out these redundant processes in each department. This staffing is unproductive and adds nothing to the bottom line: in fact, it reduces profitability. It introduces unnecessary delays in serving the customer, so reducing customer service—leading often to competitive disadvantage.

Automated Processes and Systems

In the 1980s office automation was introduced to solve the problem. But this focused on the symptom: the time that an Address Change Form took to reach each affected department. It did not address the true problem, the redundant data—it only sped up the paper! To resolve the problem common data (name and address in our example) should be stored once only, so all areas of the business that are authorized to access it can share the same data version. This is illustrated in Figure 12-2.

While name and address is common to many areas, there is also data needed only by certain areas. For example, an organization may have more than one role in its business dealings with XYZ Corporation. This is shown by Organization Role in Figure 12-2: one role may be as a customer; another role as a supplier.

As a further example, the Credit Dept must ensure that the value of the current order, when added to the outstanding debtor balance still to be paid (maintained by the Accounting Dept) does not exceed the customer's credit limit. And the Accounting Dept must be aware of the creditor balances that are due to be paid to organizations that we deal with as suppliers. While this data is specific to each of these areas, an organization's name and address is common—regardless of its role as a customer, or as a supplier—and so is shared by all, as shown in Figure 12-2.

It is in the identification of common data that the greatest impact can be made on the efficiency and responsiveness of organizations to change.

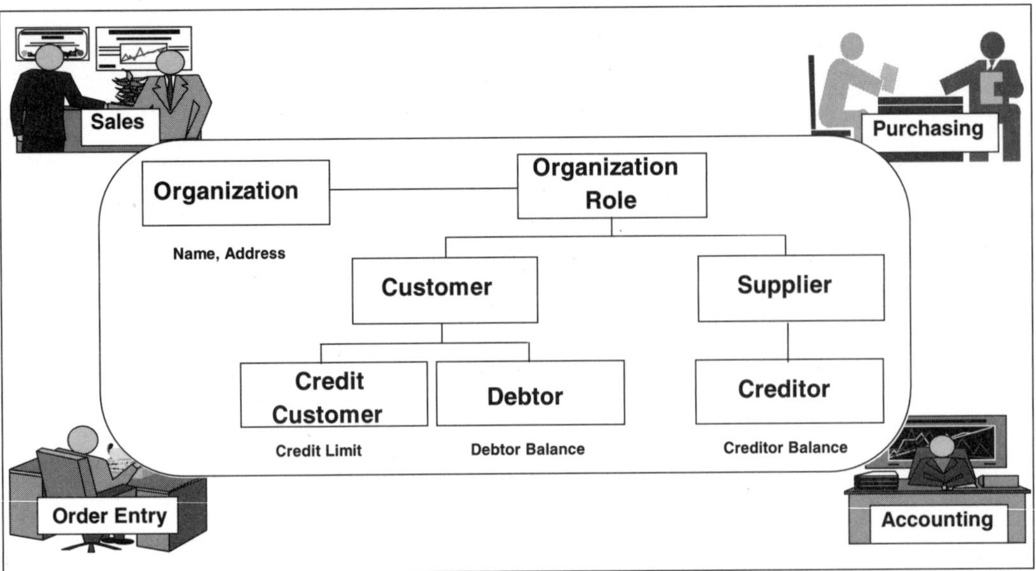

Figure 12-2
Common data can be shared as one data version, and made available to all authorized to use it. Specific data is then managed by each area that needs it.

Once applied, changes made to common data are available immediately to all areas that need the data to be current. And because common data is stored only once, redundant processes that maintain redundant data are no longer needed. Business processes that evolved over many years to ensure all areas had access to needed data (by each department maintaining its own data version) now share common data and are immediately aware of any changes.

The First Era of the Information Age

The way in which an organization structures itself today, when common data is readily available and can be easily shared, is quite different from the way it had to be organized when that data was difficult to obtain. New business processes emerge that often cross previous functional boundaries. This leads to *Business Reengineering* (BRE).

The strong inerest in Business Process Reengineering (BPR) addresses only a subset of the broader area of business reengineering.

Organizations that approach BPR without recognizing and first correcting the redundancy problems of organizational evolution discussed above, are inviting trouble. This is discussed further, shortly.

We are now seeing the emergence of the *New Corporation*, defined by [Tapscott and Caston 1992] as *the fundamental restructuring and transformation of enterprises, which in turn cascades across enterprises to create the extended enterprise and the recasting of relationships between suppliers, customers, affinity groups and competitors.* In their book [Tapscott and Caston 1993] they discuss that organizations today are now moving from the First Era of the Information Age to the Second Era.

They categorize the First Era by the traditional system islands built for established organization structures, using computers for the management and control of physical assets and facilities, for the management and support of human resources, and for financial management and control systems. Computers have automated the existing processes used by an organization, replicating redundant data and manual processes with redundant files or databases, and redundant computer processing. But these automated systems are far more resistant and difficult to change than the manual systems they replace.

Organizations have buried themselves in computer systems that have now set like concrete; the computer systems introduced to improve organizational responsiveness now inhibit the very business changes needed to survive!

One of the original roles of middle managers was to implement internal procedures and systems that reflected directions and controls set by senior management. Their other role was to extract specific information needed by senior management for decision making from underlying operational data at all levels of an organization. Organizations that downsized by only eliminating middle managers are now vulnerable. But those that downsized also by eliminating redundant data as well as redundant processes have enjoyed dramatic cost reductions—while also ensuring that accurate information is made available for management decision making.

It is true that with accurate, up to date information available electronically and instantly, many layers of management in the First Era are no longer needed. But if this accurate information is not available, organizations invite disaster if they do not first implement effective systems to provide that information before removing middle managers. Only when the earlier problems of redundant data and redundant processes are resolved can downsizing truly be effective. Then decision making can be faster, when access to acurate, up to date shared information is available corporate-wide.

The Second Era of the Information Age

Tapscott and Caston next described the Second Era of the Information Age as that which supports open, networked enterprises. These new corporations move beyond constraints of oranizational hierarchy. In this Second Era, reengineered processes and systems in the new corporation not only cross previous functional boundaries. They move beyond the organizational hierarchy—utilizing computer systems that can directly link suppliers and customers. For example, insurance companies link directly with agents who sell their products: insurance policies that are uniquely tailored to satisfy their customers' exact insurance needs. With the Internet today, we are now moving into the Second Era.

Similarly airlines link with travel agents and convention organizers. The services they offer are not only booked airline flights, but also accommodation, car rental, and business meetings or holidays tailored uniquely to each customer's needs. In addition: banks provide direct online account access for their customers; manufacturers link to terminals in the trucks of their suppliers for just-in-time delivery; and governments provide information kiosks for public access, so that people can obtain the specific inormation they need. These are all examples of business reengineering, in the spirit so memorably encapsulated in the title of a landmark paper: *Reengineering Work: Don't Automate, Obliterate* [Hammer 1990].

The important point to recognize with *Business Reengineering*, and its subset of *Business Process Reengineering*, is their vital link with the development of computer application systems. But systems development has seen dramatic change. Integrated CASE tools (I-CASE) and methodologies are available that automate most manual, error-prone tasks of traditional systems development. They result in the rapid development of high quality systems that can be changed easily, and fast, resolving many of the problems discussed earlier.

An understanding of computer technology was a prerequisite of the traditional systems development methods of the First Era, and it was hard for business managers to participate effectively. The new generation of I-CASE tools for the Second Era achieves dramatic success by harnessing the knowledge of business experts. Business managers and their staff—not computer analysts—have this knowledge. When business experts work in a design partnership with computer experts using the Engineering Enterprise Portals (EEP) methodology, redundant data and processes are readily identified.

Using the knowledge of business experts across different areas that share common data, integrated databases that eliminate redundant data and redundant processes are defined using business-driven I-CASE tools. Automatic analysis of common data by these tools identifies new business processes that cross functional boundaries, and where appropriate also cross enterprise boundaries as discussed later. These cross-functional processes are automatically identified by the software and suggest common, shared processes. These can be identified and implemented across an organization for improved efficiency and effectiveness. Reengineering opportunities thus emerge.

Databases and systems are designed which are of high business quality, implemented by computer experts using the most appropriate computer technology for the business: decentralized in a client/server environment, or instead centralized. Databases can be automatically generated for any SQL-dialect RDBMS, such as IBM DB2, Oracle, CA/Open-Ingres, Sybase, Microsoft SQL Server and other RDBMS products. These systems can be built using a wide variety of computer languages or development tools, as object-oriented systems that share common data and common logic. This enables systems to be built rapidly and changed easily. The I-CASE tools discussed earlier automatically derive object-oriented logic from integrated data identified by the business experts.

The result is a dramatic gain in systems development and maintenance productivity and quality. Systems can now be built rapidly to meet the changing business requirements imposed by the intense competitive environment of today. These systems become competitive weapons that achieve success, not just by eliminating redundant data and processes, and duplicated staffing—so leading to huge cost savings. They also provide management with accurate, up-to-date, consistent information that was difficult, if not impossible, to obtain with confidence before. In this way, IT achieves its true potential, as corporations move to the Second Era of the Information Age.

The rest of this chapter illustrates how this is achieved, using XML and the Internet and intranets for deployment.

Business Reengineering for the Second Era

As discussed above, we need to consider not only redundant data versions, but also the redundant processes that have evolved to keep redundant data versions up to date. Integrated data models not only eliminate redundant data versions, they also eliminate redundant processes. Data and processes represent *Business Information* and *Business Processes* which both must support *Business Plans* defined by management, as shown in Figure 12-3.

Business Reengineering from Business Plans

Business plans represent the ideal starting point for Business Reengineering, as they apply at all management levels. When defined explicitly by senior managers, we saw in Chapter 2 that they are strategic business plans. When defined by middle managers they are tactical business plans. At lower management levels they are operational business plans. We will use the generic term Business Plan to refer to all of these.

Business plans define the directions set by management for each business area or organizational unit. They indicate the mission of the area and its defined policies, critical success factors, its goals, objectives, KPIs, strategies, and tactics. They are catalysts for definition of business processes, business events, and business information as follows.

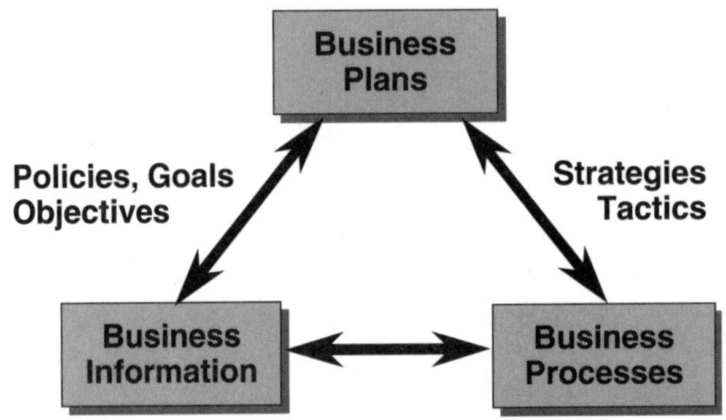

Figure 12-3 Business Reengineering improves all three areas essential to business effectiveness: Business Plans, Business Processes, and Business Information.

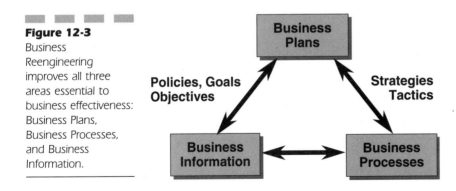

We saw in Chapter 2 that *Policies* are qualitative guidelines that define boundaries of responsibility. In a data model, policies are represented by related groups of data entities. The data entities defined within a business area thus together represent the policies that apply to the management and operation of that area. A policy also establishes boundaries for business processes that are carried out by one business area, and processes that relate to other business areas.

An example of a policy is:

Employment Policy: We only hire qualified employees.

Critical Success Factors (CSFs), *Key Performance Indicators* (KPIs), or *Key Result Areas* (KRAs) define a focus or emphasis that is intended to achieve a desired result. They lead to the definition of goals and objectives. *Goals* and *objectives* are quantitative targets for achievement. Goals are long-term; objectives are short-term as discussed in Chapter 2.

They indicate *WHAT* is to be achieved, and have quantitative characteristics of *measure*, *level*, and *time*. The *measure* is represented by data attribute(s) within entities. The *level* is the value to be achieved within an indicated *time* for the goal or objective. These attributes represent management information and are generally derived from detailed attributes by processes at the operational level. They provide information that managers need for decision making. An example of a measurable objective is:

Hiring Objective: To be eligible, an applicant must exceed a score of 70 percent on our Skills Assessment Test at the first attempt.

There are many alternative strategies that managers may use to obtain the information they need. Strategies may contain more detailed tactics. Strategies detail WHAT has to be done. Tactics define how the information is provided and how it is derived. Together they lead to the definition of business processes. Examples of a strategy and business process are:

Assessment Strategy: Interview each applicant and match to Position Criteria, then administer the relevant Skills Assessment Test.

Evaluation Process:

1. Review the completed Application Form to ensure all questions have been satisfactorily completed.
2. Check that required references have been provided.
3. Select and administer relevant Skills Assessment Test.
4. Note total time taken to complete all questions.

5. Mark responses and calculate overall score.
6. Write score and completion time on Application Form.

A strategy is initiated by a *Business Event*, which in turn invokes a business process. Without a business event, nothing happens: business plans, policies, goals, objectives, strategies, and processes are merely passive statements. A business event initiates a business activity or activities—i.e. business process(es). An example is:

Interview Event: Schedule an interview date with the applicant.

Documented planning statements of mission, critical success factors, policies, goals, objectives, KPIs, strategies, tactics, and business events are allocated to the business area(s) or organization unit(s) that are represented as model views. The model views involved in, or responsible for, those statements are displayed in a *Statement—Model View Matrix* or a *Statement—Organization Unit Matrix*, similar to Figures 4.5–4.7 for strategic modeling in Chapter 4. This enables the subset of planning statements for each area or unit to be clearly identified. Business plans that define future directions to be taken by an organization represent the most effective starting point for Business Reengineering. But in many organizations today the plans are obsolete, incomplete, or worse, non-existent. In these cases, another apex of the triangle in Figure 12-3 can be used as the starting point: either business processes, or business information.

Business Reengineering from Business Processes

Existing business processes, reviewed and documented by narrative description and/or Data Flow Diagrams (DFDs) show how each process is carried out today. Business areas or organization units that are involved in, or responsible for, a process are identified and documented in a *Process–Model View Matrix* or a *Process–Organization Unit Matrix*, similar to Figures 4.6 and 4.7 with only "Process" statement types displayed.

A business event is the essential link between a business plan and a business process. In the plan, an event is defined as a narrative statement. It can be a physical transaction that invokes a business process. Or it may represent a change of state. The strategy or tactic that is initiated by an event is documented in an *Event–Strategy Matrix*. This link must be clearly shown. The process invoked by each event should also be clearly indicated: documented in an *Event–Process Matrix.*

Without links to the plan, the business reason(s) why the process exists is not clear. It may be carried out only because "*we have always done it that way.*" If the process cannot be seen to support or implement part of the plan, or provide information needed for decision making, then it has no reason to remain. As the past fades into history, it too can be discarded as a relic of another time. To reengineer these processes without first determining whether they are relevant also for the future is an exercise in futility. Worse still, the danger is that management feel they have done the right thing ... when they may have only moved the deck-chairs on their own "Titanic."

If the process is essential, then the strategies implemented by the process must be clearly defined. Associated goals or objectives must be quantified for those strategies. Relevant policies that define boundaries of responsibility for the process and its planning statements must be clarified. Missing components of the plan are thus completed, with clear management direction for the process.

The third apex of Figure 12-3 is an alternative starting point for Business Reengineering. In fact, business information is a far more powerful catalyst for reengineering than business processes, as we will soon see.

Business Reengineering from Business Information

Data models developed for business areas or organization units should ideally be based on directions set by management for the future. These are defined in business plans. Where business plans are not available, or are out of date, or the reasons why business processes exist today are lost in the dark recesses of history, data models of business information provide clear insight into future needs.

Data models can be developed from any statement, whether it be a narrative description of a process, or a statement of a policy, goal, objective, or strategy as we saw in Chapter 4. The redundant data versions that have evolved over time (see Figure 12-1) are represented as data models consolidated into integrated data models. Data versions from different business areas are integrated so that all areas that need access to it can share any common data. Regardless of whichever area updates the common data, that updated data is then available to all other areas that are authorized to see it (Figure 12-2).

With this integration, redundant business processes—earlier needed so redundant data versions could be maintained up to date—are no longer required. Instead, new processes are needed. As common data is integrated across parts of the business, data that previously flowed to keep the redundant data versions up to date no longer flows. With integrated data models, implemented as integrated databases, data still flows to and from the outside world—but little data flows inside the organization. The original processes that assumed data existed redundantly may no longer work in an integrated environment. New, integrated, cross-functional processes are required.

But how can cross-functional processes be identified? Data Flow Diagrams provide little guidance in this situation. And *Affinity Analysis* provides little help either. This technique has been used by many CASE tools to group related entities into business areas or subject areas. But it is highly subjective. It depends on the knowledge that the data modeler has of the business; of data modeling; and the thresholds that are set. As a technique, it is not repeatable. It is potentially dangerous, as indicated next.

Where allowance is made for its subjectivity, affinity analysis can be still be useful. But when its results are accepted blindly, without question, the end result can be disaster. It lacks rigor and objectivity. It can lead to the grouping of more data in a subject area than is needed to deliver priority systems. This will require more resources to develop those systems; they will take longer and cost more. This is merely embarrassing, as in: "*the IT department has overrun its budget yet again.*"

But the real danger is that essential, related data may not be included in the subject area. This related data may indicate interdependent processes that are needed for the priority processes to function. The end result? When delivered, the systems may not support all business rules that are essential for correct functioning of the business process. The systems may be useless: developed at great cost, but unable to be used. This situation is not just embarrassing: it is disastrous! At best, it represents wasted development time and cost. At worst, it can affect an organization's ability to change rapidly, to survive in today's competitive climate.

Identifying Business Processes from Data Models

Related data that indicates existence of interdependent processes leads to the definition of cross-functional processes, derived from data models. These suggest reengineered business processes. Business processes can be identified from the analysis of data models, based on the concepts of *Entity Dependency* discussed in Chapter 4 in relation to Figures 4.9–4.11. It is an objective technique, described in [Finkelstein 1992]. Its importance for Data Administrators was acknowledged in [McClure 1993]. Entity dependency is rigorous and repeatable: it can be applied manually or can be fully automated. When used to analyze a specific data model, the same result is *always* obtained—whether the analysis is done by man or machine.

Entity Dependency Analysis

Entity dependency automatically identifies all data entities that a process is dependent upon, for referential integrity or data integrity reasons. It automatically identifies interdependent processes and indicates cross-functional processes. We will see that it uncovers and provides insight into business reengineering opportunities.

Consider the following example, based on the analysis of a data model developed for the business processes discussed earlier in this chapter: involved in Sales and Distribution. Figure 12-4 shows an integrated data model that consolidates the previously separate functions of Order Entry, Purchasing, Product Development, and Marketing. This data model was expanded to operational detail from the strategic model discussed in Chapter 4. It represents business processes in each of these business areas, stated as follows:

Order Processing:

A customer may have many orders. Each order must comprise at least one ordered product. A product may be requested by many orders.

Purchase Order Processing:

Every product has at least one supplier. A supplier will provide us with many products.

Product Development:

We only develop products that address at least one need that we are in business to satisfy.

Marketing:

We must know at least one or many needs of each of our customers.

We will use Figure 12-4 to illustrate an important EEP principle, used to identify process reengineering opportunities from a data model. We saw in Chapter 3 that this principle is stated as: *intersecting entities in a data model represent functions, processes, and/or systems.* This leads to identification of cross-functional processes that arise from integration of the Order Entry, Purchasing, Product Development, and Marketing functions—as we shall see.

Referring to Figure 12-4, ORDER PRODUCT is an intersecting (or "associative") entity formed by decomposing the many-to-many association between ORDER and PRODUCT. It represents the *Order Entry Process* used in the Order Entry business area. This provides source data for the sales analysis system, S1, discussed in Chapter 10. When implemented it will be the Order Entry System; but we will focus on identifying processes at

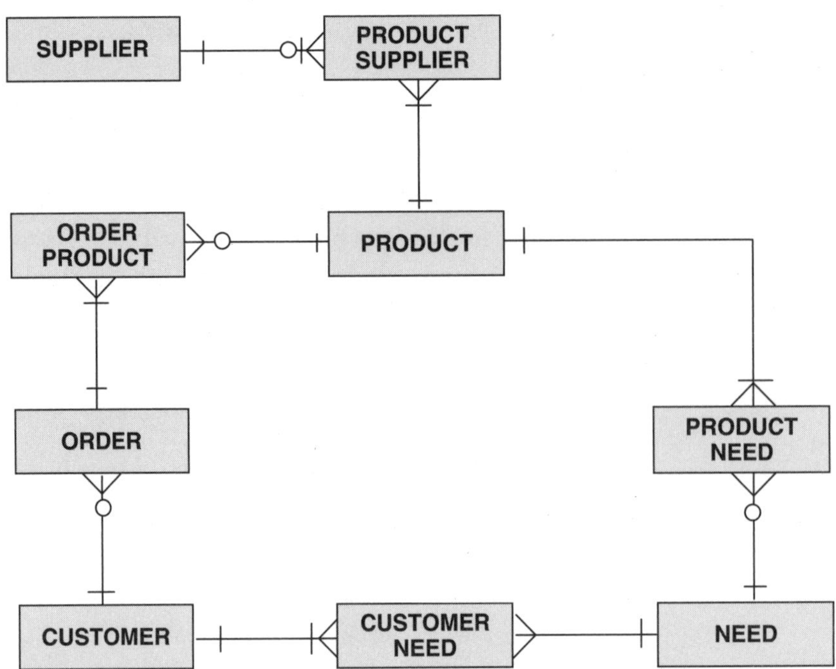

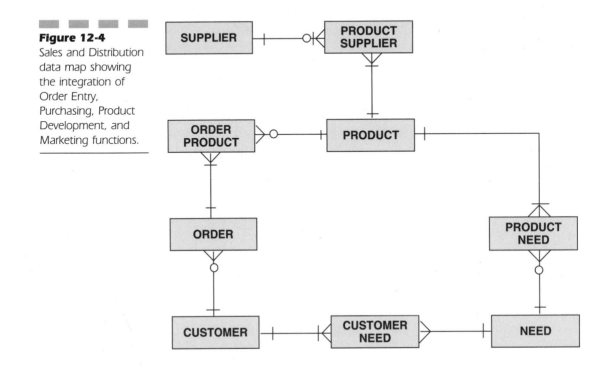

Figure 12-4 Sales and Distribution data map showing the integration of Order Entry, Purchasing, Product Development, and Marketing functions.

this stage. Similarly, PRODUCT SUPPLIER is an intersecting entity that represents the *Product Supply Process* used in Purchasing. PRODUCT NEED is the *Product Development Process* used in the Product Development area. Finally, CUSTOMER NEED is the *Customer Needs Analysis Process* used in Marketing.

The data model in Figure 12-4 is common to many organizations and industries. We will use it to illustrate reengineering opportunity analysis. For example, by inspection we can already see reengineering opportunities to integrate some functions based on our understanding of the business. But what of other business areas where mandatory rules have been defined that we are not aware of? How can we ensure that these mandatory rules are correctly applied in our area of interest? The complexity of even this simple data model requires automated entity dependency analysis [Finkelstein 1992].

Reengineering analysis of the data model in Figure 12-4 was carried out by Visible Advantage, which fully automates entity dependency analysis for Business Reengineering. The results are shown in Figure 12-5, showing part of the Cluster Report produced from the data model also displayed in Figure 12-5.

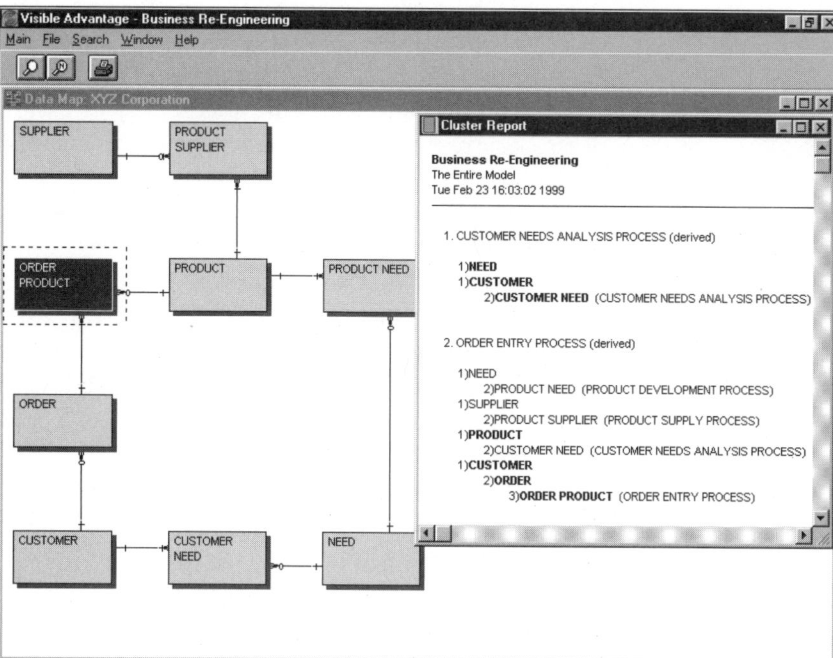

Figure 12-5
Entity dependency analysis of the data model in Figure 12-4.

Each potential function, process, or system represented by an intersecting entity (as discussed above) is called a *Cluster*. Each cluster is numbered and named, and contains all data and processes required for its correct operation. A cluster is thus self-contained: it requires no other mandatory reference to data or processes outside it. Common, interdependent, or instead mandatory, data and processes are automatically included within it to ensure its correct operation.

Figure 12-5 shows Cluster 2, representing the *Order Entry Process*. It has been automatically derived from the data model through entity dependency analysis. Each cluster addresses a business process and is a potential sub-project; common data and processes appear in all clusters that depend on the data or process. The intersecting entity that is the focus of a cluster appears on the last line.

An intersecting entity indicates a process; the name of that process is shown in brackets after the entity name. The intersecting entity on the last line of the cluster (ORDER PRODUCT in Figure 12-5) is called the "cluster end-point." It is directly dependent on all entities listed above it that are in **bold:** it is interdependent on those above it that are not in bold; these represent prerequisite processes of the cluster end-point process.

Interdependent entities represent common data and processes that are also shared by many other clusters. Thus we can see in Cluster 2 that the *Order Entry Process* (the cluster end-point) depends on the prerequisite processes: *Product Supply Process*, *Product Development Process*, and *Customer Needs Analysis Process*.

Figure 12-6 next shows in Clusters 3 and 4 that the first two of these processes are fully interdependent: a product supplier cannot be selected without knowing the needs addressed by the product (as each supplier names its products differently to other suppliers).

Notice that a right-bracketed number precedes each entity in Figures 12-5 and 12-6: this is the project phase number of the relevant entity in the process. Shown in outline form, with higher-numbered phases further indented to the right for each cluster, it represents a conceptual Gantt Chart—the Project Plan for implementation of the process. This Project Plan is automatically derived by Visible Advantage, also by using entity dependency analysis.

A cluster in outline form is used to display a data map automatically. For example, Visible Advantage aligns each entity vertically by phase, from left to right, so that the data map is automatically displayed in Pert Chart format as shown in Figure 12-7.

Alternatively, entities can be displayed horizontally by phase, from top to bottom, in Organization Chart format as illustrated in Figure 12-8. An

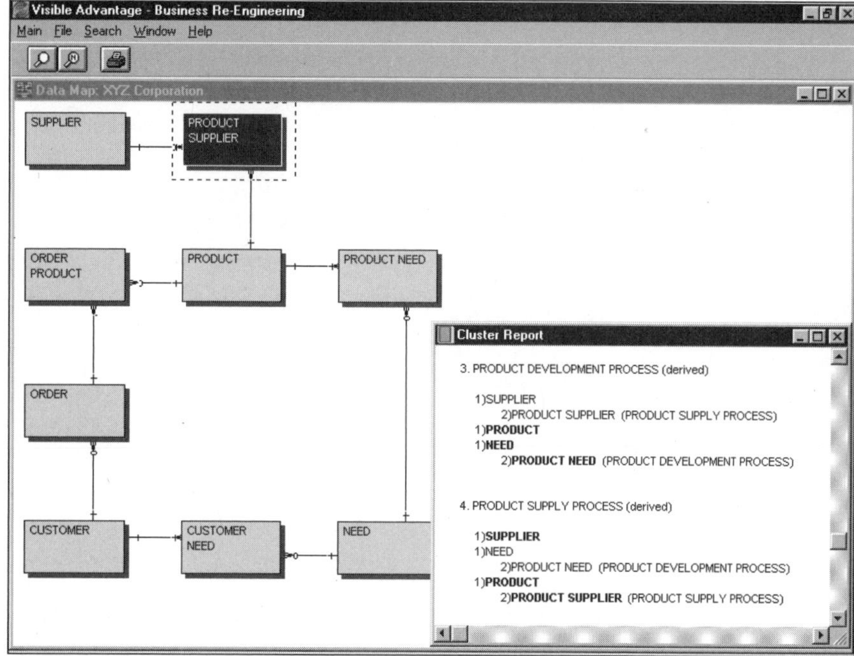

Figure 12-6 Further entity dependency analysis of Figure 12-4, showing that the *Product Development Process* and *Product Supply Process* are both interdependent.

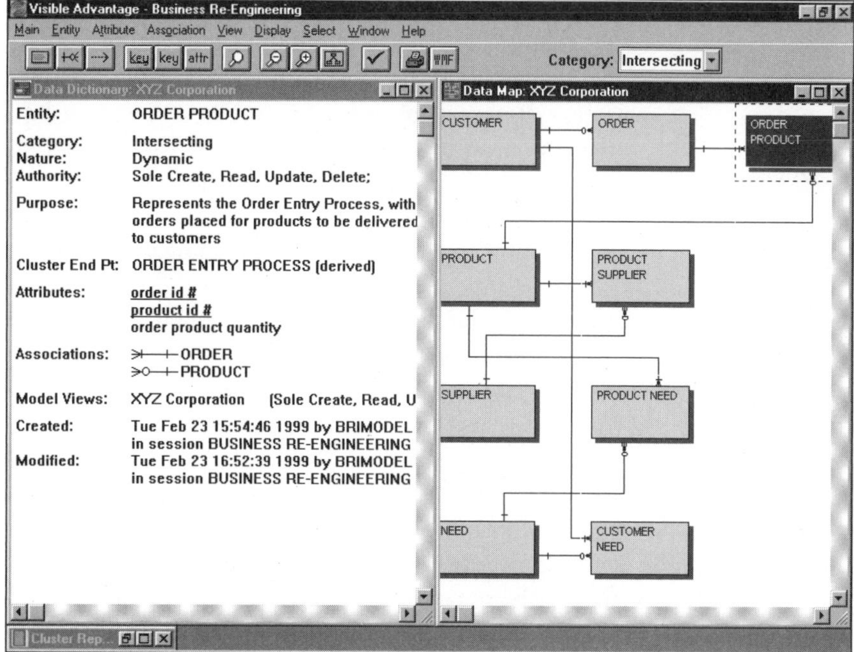

Figure 12-7 Pert Chart data map format, with entities vertically aligned by phase from left to right. Entities in higher numbered phases are positioned further to the right.

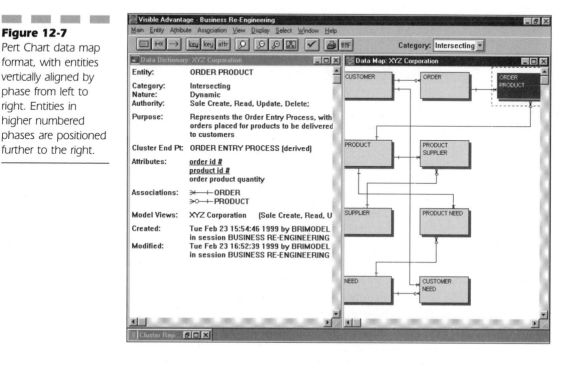

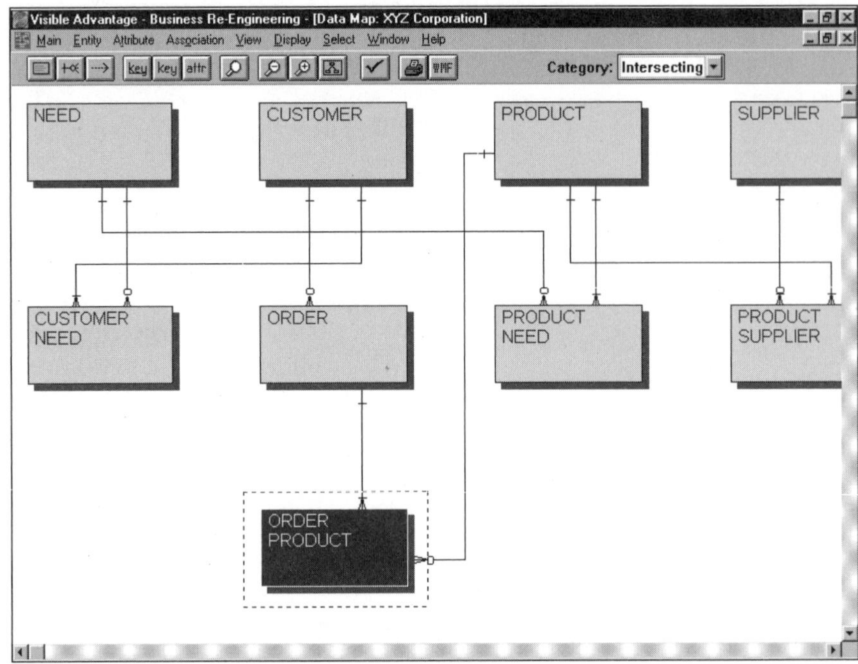

Figure 12-8 Organization Chart data map format, with entities horizontally aligned by phase from top to bottom. Higher numbered phases representing operational level entities are automatically displayed lower in the organization chart hierarchy.

entity name is displayed in an entity box; the attribute names may also optionally be displayed in the entity box. And because the data map is generated automatically, it can be displayed using different data modeling conventions: such as IE notation, or instead by using the IDEF1X data map notation.

This ability to automatically generate data maps in different formats is a characteristic of the latest generation I-CASE tools: data maps can be displayed from clusters. They do not have to be manually drawn; they can be automatically generated. When new entities are added, or associations changed, affected data maps are not changed manually: they are again automatically regenerated.

Similarly, process maps can be generated from data models. For example, data access processes (Create, Read, Update, Delete), that operate against entities as reusable object-oriented methods, can be automatically generated as object-oriented process maps by such I-CASE tools. So why have these processes all been included in Cluster 2 in Figure 12-5 for the *Order Entry Process*? I-CASE tools such as Visible Advantage provide direct assistance for Business Reengineering.

Identifying Cross-Functional Business Processes from Data Models

We saw in Figure 12-4 that a PRODUCT **must** have at least one SUPPLIER. Figure 12-5 thus includes the *Product Supply Process* to ensure that we are aware of alternative suppliers for each product. But where did the *Product Development Process* and *Customer Needs Analysis Process* come from?

The data map in Figure 12-4 shows the business rule that each PRODUCT **must** address at least one NEED relating to our core business. Similarly the data map follows the Marketing rule that each CUSTOMER **must** have at least one core business NEED. The *Product Supply Process*, *Product Development Process*, and *Customer Needs Analysis Process* have therefore all been automatically included as prerequisite, interdependent processes in Figure 12-5.

The sequence for execution of these processes is shown in Figure 12-9.

Figure 12-9 shows each cluster as a named box, for the process represented by that cluster. Each of these process boxes is therefore a sub-project for implementation. As we saw in Chapter 4, this diagram is called a *Project Map*—as it suggests the development sequence for each sub-project that implements each relevant process.

We can now see some of the power of entity dependency analysis: it automatically applies business rules across the entire enterprise. The I-CASE tool becomes a business expert: aware of all business facts. It determines whether other business areas should be aware of relevant business rules, data, and processes. It derives a Project Map for project management of each sub-project needed to implement those processes as computer systems. This is illustrated in Figure 12-9.

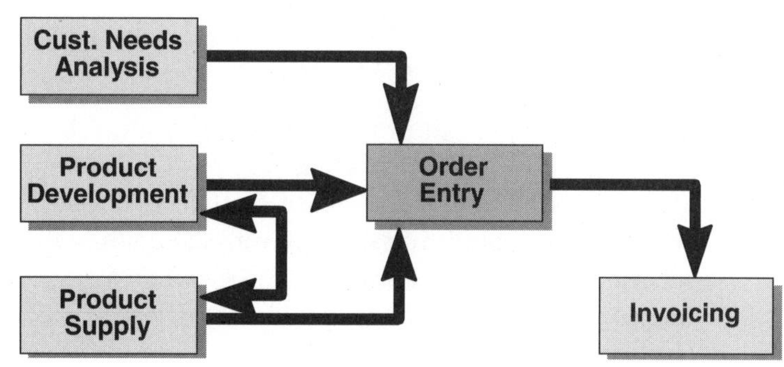

Figure 12-9
The Order Entry Process in this Project Map depends on prerequisite, interdependent processes to its left. They suggest reengineering opportunities for Order Entry.

So what do these prerequisite, interdependent processes suggest? How do they help us to identify reengineering opportunities? And how can we use the Internet?

Reengineering Opportunity Analysis

The Project Map in Figure 12-9 is used for reengineering opportunity analysis. It enables us to identify reengineering opportunities. It shows that the prerequisite processes for the Order Entry Process are cross-functional; these separate processes can be integrated.

To illustrate, consider the following scenario for the Order Entry Process—*before Business Reengineering:*

Customer: *Customer 165 here. I would like to order 36 units of Product X.*

Order Clerk: *Certainly ... Oh, I see we are out of Product X at the moment. I'll check with the Warehouse. I will call you back within the hour to let you know when we can expect more of Product X into stock.*

Customer: *No don't bother, I need to know now. Please cancel the order.*

Clearly, this example shows that the Order Clerk has no access to the Inventory Control System in the Warehouse. There is no way to determine when outstanding purchase orders for out-of-stock products will be delivered. It requires a phone call to the Warehouse staff to get that information. A call-back in an hour is no longer responsive for today's customers. The sale was therefore lost.

Now consider the same scenario—*after Business Reengineering:*

Customer: *Customer 165 here. I would like to order 36 units of Product X.*

Order Clerk: *Certainly ... Oh, I see we are out of Product X at the moment. One moment while I check with our suppliers. ... Yes, we can deliver 36 units of Product X to you on Wednesday.*

What has happened in this scenario? Product X was out of stock, so the *Product Supply Process* then automatically displayed all suppliers of Product X. The Purchasing function had been reengineered so the Order Clerk could link directly into each supplier's inventory system to check the availability and cost of Product X for each alternative source of supply. For the selected supplier, the Clerk placed a purchase order for immediate shipment and so could confirm the Wednesday delivery date with the customer.

But there are problems with this approach, due to incompatibilities between suppliers' Inventory Control Systems and the Order Entry System. There may also be incompatibilities between the Operating Systems, Data Base Management Systems, LANs, WANs, and EDI data formats used by these organizations. We will discuss these problems and their resolution using the Internet, shortly.

The reengineered *Product Supply Process* discussed above seems revolutionary, but other industries that also take orders online consider this inter-enterprise approach to Order Entry the norm.

Consider the travel industry. We phone a travel agent to book a flight to Los Angeles (say) because we have business there. We need to fly there on Wednesday evening, for business on Thursday and Friday. But we also decide to take the family and plan to stay for the weekend, returning Sunday evening. The travel agent uses an Airline Reservation terminal to book seats on suitable flights. These are ordered from an inventory of available seats offered by relevant suppliers: the airlines.

Let us now return to the customer on the phone—still talking to the Order Clerk, who says:

> **Order Clerk:** *By the way, do you know about Product Y? It allows you to use Product X in half the time. I can send you 36 units of Y as well for only 20 percent more than your original order. If you agree, we can deliver both to you on Wednesday.*
>
> **Customer:** *OK. Thanks for that suggestion, and Wednesday is fine. I look forward to receiving 36 units each of Products X and Y on that day.*

The *Product Development Process* displayed related products that met the same needs as Product X. This suggested that Product Y may be of interest. An order for Y, based on the current order for X, was automatically prepared and priced—and Y was in stock. This extension to the order only needed the customer's approval for its inclusion in the delivery.

What has happened here? We see that the *Product Development Process* has also been reengineered. Product X satisfies certain needs (see PRODUCT NEED in Figure 12-5). Other products may also satisfy those needs, as indicated by Product Y above.

Once again, this is commonplace in the travel industry. The travel agent knows the customer will be in Los Angeles over several nights and so asks whether any hotel accommodation is needed. If so, a booking is made at a suitable hotel using another supplier's system: Hotel Reservations.

The customer continues with the Order Clerk, who now says:

Order Clerk: *We find that customers using Product X also enjoy Product Z. Have you used this? It has the characteristics of . . . . . . and costs only . . . . . . Can I include 36 units of Product Z as well in our Wednesday delivery?*

Customer: *Yes. Thanks again. I confirm that my order is now for 36 units each of Products X, Y, and Z—all to be delivered on Wednesday.*

Finally, the *Customer Needs Analysis Process* knew that customers in the same market as Customer 165, who also used Products X and Y, had other needs that were addressed by Product Z. A further extension to include Z in the order was automatically prepared and priced. Z was also in stock and was able to be included in the delivery, if agreed.

This is analogous to the travel agent asking if a rental car and tour bookings were also needed: quite likely if a family is in Los Angeles and thus near the many LA tourist locations for a weekend.

Instead of waiting for stock availability from the Warehouse in the first scenario based on separate, non-integrated processes for each function, the reengineered scenario let the Clerk place a purchase order directly with a selected supplier so that the customer's order could be satisfied. And the Product Development and Customer Needs Analysis processes then suggested cross-selling opportunities based first on related products, and then on related needs in the customer's market.

Reengineered, cross-functional processes identified using entity dependency analysis can suggest reorganization opportunities. For example, interdependent processes may all be brought together in a new organizational unit. Or they may remain in their present organizational structure, but be integrated automatically by the computer only when needed—as in the reengineered scenario discussed above.

But what about the incompatibilities we discussed earlier with inter-enterprise access to suppliers' Inventory Systems? The Internet and XML offer us dramatic new ways to address these otherwise insurmountable incompatibilities.

The Status of Internet and Intranet Technologies

The Internet has emerged since 1994 as a movement that will see all businesses interconnected in the near future, with electronic commerce as the norm. Let us review the status of Internet and intranet technologies today.

A Status Update of Internet and Intranet Technologies

- Web browsers are now available for all platforms and operating systems, based on an open architecture interface using HyperText Markup Language (HTML). A key factor influencing future computing technologies will be this open architecture environment.
- The Web browser market will be largely shared between Microsoft and Netscape. The strategy adopted by Microsoft has seen it rapidly gain market share at the expense of Netscape: it has used its desktop ownership to embed its browser technology (Internet Explorer) as an integral component of Windows NT and Windows 98.
- The Internet is based on TCP/IP communications protocol and Domain Naming System (DNS). Microsoft, Novell, and other network vendors recognize that TCP/IP and DNS are the network standards for the Internet and intranets. This open architecture network environment benefits all end users.
- The battle to become THE Internet language—between Java (from Sun) and ActiveX (from Microsoft)—will likely be won by neither. Browsers will support *both* languages, and will automatically download from Web servers, as needed, code in either language (as "applets") for execution. Instead, the winners of this battle will again be the end users, who will benefit from the open architecture execution environment.
- XML will be the successor to HTML for the Internet, intranets, and for secure extranets between customers, suppliers and business partners. XML incorporates metadata in any document, to define the content and structure of that document and any associated (or linked) resources. It has the potential to transform the integration of structured data (such as in relational databases or legacy files) with unstructured data (such as in text, reports, email, graphics, images, audio, and video).
- Data Base Management System (DBMS) vendors (those that plan to survive) will support dynamic generation of HTML using XML, with transparent access to the Internet and intranets by applications using XML tools. They will accept HTML input direct

from Web forms, process the relevant queries using XML for integration of dissimilar databases and generate dynamic XML and HTML Web pages to present the requested output.

- Client/Server vendors (again those that plan to survive) will also provide dynamic generation of HTML for browsers that will be used as clients, with transparent access to the Internet and intranets for XML applications built with those tools. Client code, written in either ActiveX or Java, will both be supported and downloaded as needed for execution, and for generation of dynamic HTML output to display transaction results.
- Data Warehouse and Data Mining products will provide a similar capability: accepting XML input and generating HTML output if they are to be used effectively via the intranet and Internet. And also Screen Scraper tools that provide GUI interfaces for Legacy Systems will become Internet-aware: accepting 3270 data streams and dynamically translating them to, or from, HTML to display on the screen. XML will provide an integration capability for easy migration of Legacy Systems to the Internet and intranets.

Development Tool Directions

The list in the previous section indicates that most DBMS and Client/Server tools will interface directly and transparently with the Internet and intranet. Web browsers, Java, HTML, XML, the Internet, and intranets will all provide an open architecture interface for most operating system platforms. Previous incompatibilities between operating systems, DBMS and client/server products, LANs, WANs, and EDI disappear—replaced by open architecture HTML, XML, and Java.

The open architecture environment enjoyed by the audio industry—where any CD or tape will run on any player, which can be connected to any amplifier and speakers—has long been the holy grail of the IT industry. Finally, once the industry has made the transition over the next few years to the open architecture environment brought about by XML, Internet, and intranet technologies, we will be close to achieving that holy grail!

The client software will be the Web browser, operating as a "fat" client by automatically downloading Java or ActiveX code when needed. Client/

server tools will typically offer two options, each able to be executed by any terminal that can run browsers or XML-aware code:

1. Transaction processing using client input via Web forms, with dynamic XML and XSL Web pages presenting output results in a standard Web browser format, or
2. Transaction processing using client input via client/server screens, with designed application-specific output screens built by client/server development tools. This optional client environment will recognize XML and XSL, dynamically translating and presenting that output using designed application-specific screens.

These client/server development tools will provide transparent access to database servers using XML-access requests, whether accessing operational data, Data Warehouses, or Enterprise Portals. In turn, the database servers will process these requests—transparently using conventional languages, Java, or ActiveX to access new or legacy databases as relevant. These may be separate servers, or instead may be mainframes executing legacy systems.

Web servers will then operate as application servers, executing Java, ActiveX, or conventional code as part of the middle tier of three-tier client/server logic distribution, with database servers also executing Java, ActiveX, or conventional code as the third logic tier.

Influence of XML

We discussed in Chapter 11 that XML allows metadata used by each program and database to be published as the markup language to be used for intercommunication. XML is simple to use and inexpensive to implement. It will become a major part of the application development mainstream. It provides a bridge between structured databases and unstructured text, delivered via XML then converted to HTML during a transition period for display in Web browsers. Web sites will evolve over time to use XML, XSL, and XLL natively to provide the capabilities and functionality presently offered by HTML, but with far greater power and flexibility. XML is enabling technology to integrate unstructured text and structured databases for next-generation electronic commerce and EDI applications.

Development will be easier: many of the incompatibilities we previously had to deal with will be a thing of the past. Open architecture development using XML and the technologies of the Internet will also be part of the intranet: able to use any PC and any hardware, operating system, DBMS, network, client/server tool, Data Warehouse, or Enterprise Portal. This will be the direction that the IT industry will take for the foreseeable future.

Even more effective applications become possible. For example, once the metadata has been captured from the two sales analysis systems (S1 and S2) that we discussed in Chapter 10, XYZ can use XML to integrate these systems in S3. XML can also be used to define the unique metadata used by many suppliers' different inventory systems. This will enable XYZ to place orders via the Internet directly with those suppliers' systems, for automatic fulfillment of product orders to satisfy its customers' orders, as we saw in the reengineered Order Entry dialog with the customer earlier. This latter multiple supplier example is discussed next.

Business Reengineering and the Internet

We now see that the rush to implement systems based on Internet and intranet technologies will resolve the incompatibility problems we discussed earlier. XML will become the standard interface between the Order Entry system and the multiple suppliers' systems.

Suppliers are providing a capability for the world to order products via the Internet, using XML to make these order requests. These XML transactions are sent from the customer's browser to the suppliers' Web servers. XML metadata tags define the relevant field names and contents as discussed in Chapter 11. The input transaction is processed by the selected supplier's Inventory Control System and ordered products are shipped directly to the nominated customer delivery address.

Using XML for Multiple Suppliers

An example of an XML application that integrates multiple suppliers' inventory control systems is discussed next. A full description of this application can be viewed online from the XML section of the Microsoft Web site [XML Scenarios].

The Multiple Suppliers Microsoft scenario discusses an unnamed company that needs to order parts from multiple suppliers, to be used for the manufacture of products. Purchase orders are placed depending on the suppliers' current prices and available inventory. Each supplier's inventory control system uses different terminology to identify its parts, their availability and price. Because each system has different metadata, it is difficult to integrate those systems with the company's own inventory control system.

With XML and each supplier's URL, the latest quotes can be automatically obtained from the relevant supplier's parts catalog, or via a database query to the supplier's back-end inventory control system. The Microsoft [XML Scenarios] Web site provides an example of the XML quote format, reproduced here as Figure 12-10.

The application uses the Allaire ColdFusion Application Server. The server automatically makes hourly requests to each supplier for the latest quotes. Figure 12-10 illustrates the XML-structured data snippet that is received, with the product name, price, and available quantity. The supplier's name is then added to the quote and together with a date/time stamp, it is integrated with quotes from the other suppliers. The integrated quotes XML document from the Microsoft [XML Scenarios] Web site is repeated here as Figure 12-11.

Figure 12-11 shows the ColdFusion conversion of each supplier's quote and inventory data format into an XML document of all supplier quotes. The converted supplier metadata and the data from these dissimilar supplier back-end systems can now be integrated with the company's own inventory control system.

All supplier data from Figure 12-11 is presented in a Web browser as an HTML table, able to be sorted on columns. When the company's Purchasing Officer accepts a specific supplier's quote, the selected supplier's Purchase Order (PO) Form is then automatically displayed. When the PO Form has been completed, it is transmitted directly to the supplier for

Figure 12-10
Hourly supplier quote format, using XML and ColdFusion. *Source*: [XML Scenarios].

```
<QUOTE>
  <PRODUCT>M8 metric wing nut, steel, zinc</PRODUCT>
  <PRICE>$7</PRICE>
  <AVAILABLE>2000</AVAILABLE>
</QUOTE>
```

Figure 12-11 ColdFusion adds Supplier's Name and Date/Time around XML Quote snippet from Figure 12-10, to create an integrated XML Quote document. *Source:* [XML Scenarios].

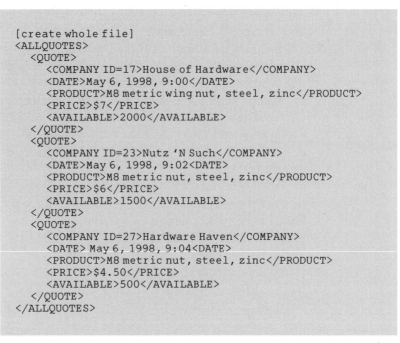

```
[create whole file]
<ALLQUOTES>
   <QUOTE>
      <COMPANY ID=17>House of Hardware</COMPANY>
      <DATE>May 6, 1998, 9:00</DATE>
      <PRODUCT>M8 metric wing nut, steel, zinc</PRODUCT>
      <PRICE>$7</PRICE>
      <AVAILABLE>2000</AVAILABLE>
   </QUOTE>
   <QUOTE>
      <COMPANY ID=23>Nutz 'N Such</COMPANY>
      <DATE>May 6, 1998, 9:02<DATE>
      <PRODUCT>M8 metric nut, steel, zinc</PRODUCT>
      <PRICE>$6</PRICE>
      <AVAILABLE>1500</AVAILABLE>
   </QUOTE>
   <QUOTE>
      <COMPANY ID=27>Hardware Haven</COMPANY>
      <DATE> May 6, 1998, 9:04<DATE>
      <PRODUCT>M8 metric nut, steel, zinc</PRODUCT>
      <PRICE>$4.50</PRICE>
      <AVAILABLE>500</AVAILABLE>
   </QUOTE>
</ALLQUOTES>
```

processing and delivery of the ordered parts. The supplier's PO details are then inserted via SQL into the company's PO-Tracking database.

The reengineered XYZ Order Entry System from the earlier Customer–Order Clerk dialog can apply a similar solution using XML. A computer-generated XML transaction can be sent to the Web site of each supplier of an out-of-stock product. Based on the product availability from each supplier, a Purchase Order is then issued for the selected supplier—who now can deliver directly to the customer as discussed earlier in the Customer–Order Clerk dialog in *Reengineering Opportunity Analysis*.

Other XML Scenarios

A number of other XML applications are also included in the Microsoft [XML Scenarios] Web site. Those available online as at March 1999 are listed below; the Multiple Suppliers application discussed above is listed as example 3.

1. Integrated Maintenance and Ordering using XML
2. Automating Customer Service with XML

3. Creating Multi-Supplier System with XML
4. Improving Online Shopping with XML
5. Personal Investment Management Using XML
6. Interactive Frequent-Flyer Web Site using XML
7. Consumer Product Ratings Online with XML
8. Purchasing and Supplier Data Integration with XML
9. Time and Attendance: Integrating Data with XML

Microsoft presents XML applications on the [XML Scenarios] Web site using a common format: a statement of the business problem; a discussion of the role of XML; an application description; a graphic illustrating the application; and an example of the XML solution. This illustrates some of the many applications being reengineered through the use of metadata and XML. We will discuss some of these applications further in Chapter 15.

New reengineering opportunities emerge from immediate access to customers and suppliers via the Internet. But this also means that *the chaos of redundant data that exists in most enterprises ... will now be visible to the world!*

If the redundant data problem is not resolved and reengineered processes implemented as discussed in this chapter, the chaos created by that data and process redundancy will now be apparent to customers from the front window of each organization's Web site. Not by what can be done, but rather by what an organization *cannot do* when compared with competitors. Customers will therefore leave with the click of a mouse and go to those competitors that can and will offer them the service they demand.

To reengineer only by improving processes using Business Process Reengineering (BPR) is like closing the barn door after the horse has bolted! Existing processes must be related back to business plans. Only those processes that support plans relevant to the future should be considered for reengineering. If a process is important and there are no plans today to guide the process, then plans must be defined that will provide the needed process guidance for the future. If this is not done, then BPR has the same long-term impact on an organization's competitiveness as rearranging the deckchairs had on the survival of the Titanic.

We saw earlier that business plans include policies, goals, objectives, KPIs, strategies, and tactics. Managers may need information for decision making that is not presently available in the enterprise. This information may be derived from data that does not exist today. Thus no processes will presently exist to provide that information, or maintain non-existent data up to date. By looking at processes only, BPR may never identify the need for this new information, data, and processes.

However, business plans provide a catalyst for definition of data and information in data models defined at each relevant management level. These data models are analyzed automatically by entity dependency to determine interdependent processes. In turn, these suggest cross-functional reengineered processes. Entity dependency analysis derives project plans automatically that are needed to implement the databases and systems required by those reengineered processes.

Only when all three apexes in Figure 12-3 are addressed can Business Reengineering fully consider the needs of the business for the future. These are the three steps to success in BRE. Only then can reengineered organizations be built that are effective, efficient, best-of-breed, and able to compete aggressively in the future.

Chapter 13 next discusses the integration of Business and Systems Reengineering. Chapter 14 describes how to establish a quality culture for a reengineered organization. Chapter 15 concludes by discussing how XML, Internet, and Intranet technologies all provide the assistance required for the business transformation that will be necessary to survive and prosper in the future—using these technologies to deliver information for knowledge management, decision support and integrated systems through the use of Enterprise Portals.

REFERENCES

Finkelstein, C. (1992) *Information Engineering: Strategic Systems Development*, Reading: MA Addison-Wesley. [ISBN 0-201-50988-1].

Finkelstein, C. (1996) *The Competitive Armageddon: Survival and Prosperity in the Connected World of the Internet.* Download from the "Papers" section of the IES Web Site located at—http://www.ies.aust.com/~ieinfo/

Hammer, M. (1990) "Reengineering Work: Don't Automate, Obliterate," *Harvard Business Review*, Cambridge, MA (Jul–Aug).

McClure, S. (1993) "Information Engineering for Client/Server Architectures," *Data Base Newsletter*, Boston, MA (Jul–Aug).

Tapscott D. and Caston, A. (1992) "Paradigm Shift: Interview with Tapscott and Caston," *Information Week* (Oct 5).

Tapscott, D. and Caston, A. (1993) *Paradigm Shift: The New Promise of Information Technology*, New York: McGraw-Hill.

Microsoft XML Scenarios Web site—http://microsoft.com/xml/scenario/intro.asp

Zachman, J. (1992) *Framework for Enterprise Architecture.* Download from the "Papers" section of the IES Web site at—http://www.ies.aust.com/~ieinfo/

CHAPTER 13

Enterprise Portals and Reengineering Technologies

Can you remember why reengineering was such a good idea in the first place?

—Oracle Corporation

In the Fall 1994 issue of the *CALS/Enterprise Integration Journal*, Oracle Corporation ran an advertisement. Over the caption "Can you remember why reengineering was such a good idea in the first place?" it showed a photograph of an individual sitting on a bench—alone. An overcoat is draped to one side and a paper cup sits on the other side. The individual's head rests face down on a pair of hands with intertwined fingers—a very worried posture. The implication is that the head-hanging individual is apparently attempting to determine where the reengineering project had gone wrong and how to get it back on track. Oracle is advertising its reengineering capabilities and has apparently decided the "fix-the-reengineering-projects-gone-astray" business is a good one to pursue. This chapter describes three important uses in reengineering contexts for the metadata engineering products produced in Part 2.

1. First, Enterprise Portals play a critical deployment role when reengineering legacy systems. The Engineering Enterprise Portals (EEP) methodology enables metadata to be used to accurately plan a systems reengineering project. During reengineering, EEP can be used as a framework to guide the process and assess progress towards reengineering goals. When implementing a reengineered solution, metadata can be used as a decision-making framework to assess integration priorities. In short, the use of EEP can be a critical success factor when reengineering legacy systems—without it, the systems reengineering effort will not be fact-based and will require many more resources to complete.
2. Second, Enterprise Portals can be valuable components as part of business reengineering solutions. Although business reengineering has both a mixed track record and perception by the business community, it has nevertheless achieved significance—as a management tool and in achieving quantum improvements in organizational performance. Solid understanding of the essential capabilities of Enterprise Portals can do much to leverage business reengineering efforts and avoid differences between desired organizational abilities and technical capabilities—the cause of many business reengineering failures.

3. Third, systems reengineering and business reengineering can play complementary roles when performed in an integrated fashion around Enterprise Portal-based solutions. Organizations should explore the potential benefits of an integrated approach incorporating aspects of both systems and business reengineering. When focused around Enterprise Portal solutions they can lead to optimal organizational investments in reengineering efforts.

Organizations risk failure when embarking on reengineering ventures without explicitly considering the potential role and integration value of enterprise portal technologies. After a brief explanation of the two reengineering types, this chapter discusses each of them in the following sections. Much of the material in this chapter is based on research reported in [Hodgson and Aiken 1997] and [Aiken and Hodgson 1998].

Two "Flavors" of Reengineering

When using the term reengineering, it is important to differentiate between business reeengineering and systems reengineering. The two terms mean different things to different consitituencies. We addressed business reengineering in some depth in Chapter 12. We will quickly review the basics here. Business reengineering has been defined by Hammer and Champy as:

> The fundamental rethinking and radical redesign of business processes to achieve dramatic improvements in critical, contemporary measures of performance, such as cost, quality, service, and speed
>
> [*Hammer and Champy 1993*]

At its core, business reengineering involves radical improvement of the processes used by organizations to accomplish their mission. Figure 13-1 illustrates the major steps involved in business reengineering: mobilization, diagnosis, redesign, and transition. Business reengineering became one of the top management tools of the 1990s because—when implemented correctly—it has a proven ability to achieve success in many business environments.

In contrast, the accepted definition of systems reengineering comes from Chikofski and Cross as:

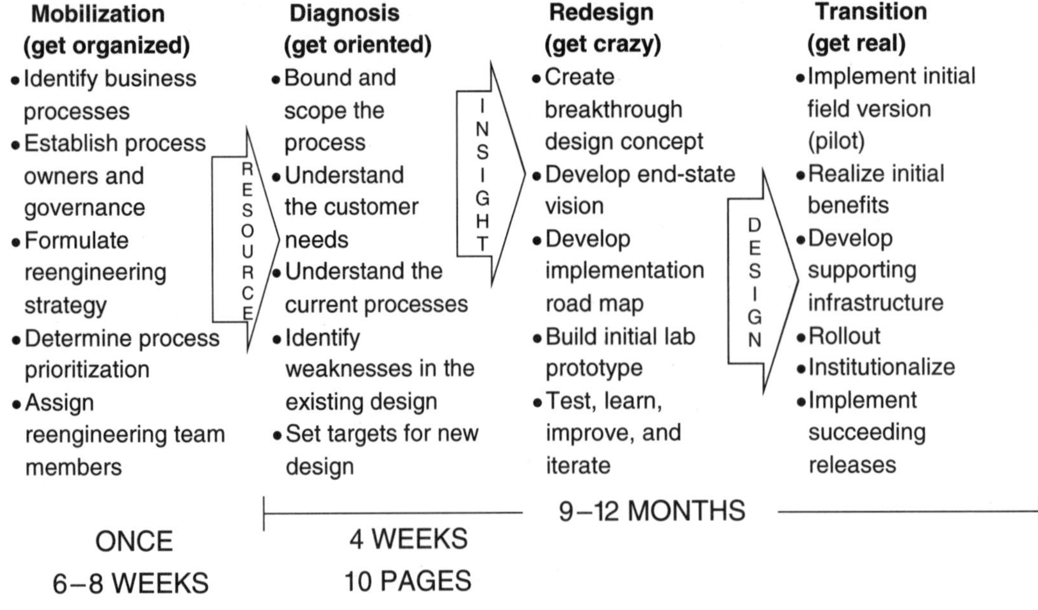

Figure 13-1
Hammer's Description of Business Reengineering.

> A structured technique aimed at recovering rigorous knowledge of the existing system to leverage enhancement efforts
>
> [*Chikofski and Cross 1990*]

Systems reengineering is the process of examining, documenting, and analyzing an existing legacy system in order to obtain details of value from it, before developing a new and improved version. Details of value that are obtained from a legacy system are generally metadata-based. They can include system-based descriptions of business processes, data models, and business rules, for example.

Systems reengineering is distinguished from other system enhancement methodologies by both reverse and forward engineering activities that are generally integrated sequentially. If the system is not first reverse engineered using a structured reverse engineering methodology, it cannot be reengineered.

Figure 13-2 illustrates that design recovery or requirements recovery must first take place before redesign or recoding, for an enhancement project to qualify as a system reengineering project. The metadata gained

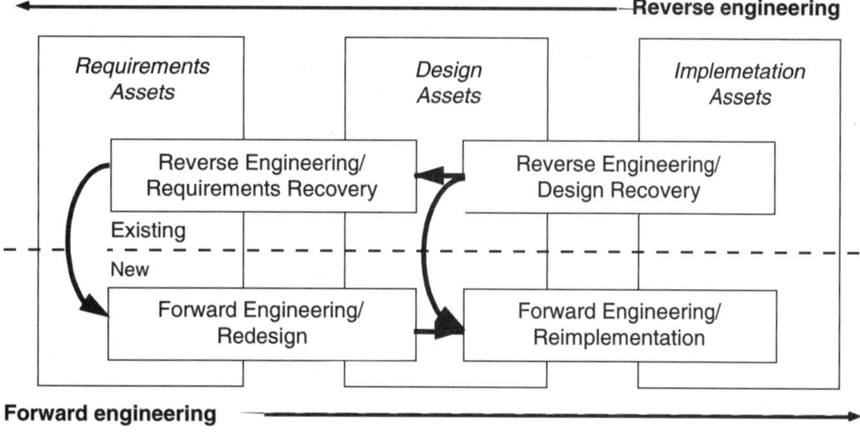

Figure 13-2 Reengineering is based on integrated reverse and forward engineering.

from these recovery techniques provides the basis for integrating the reverse and forward engineering steps.

Enterprise Portals for Legacy System Reengineering Deployment

Legacy Systems

A *legacy* is something handed down from an ancestor or a predecessor or from the past [American Heritage English Dictionary 1993]. *Legacy systems* are defined as standalone applications built using the technology of a prior era [Ulrich 1994]. They have been stereotypically and perhaps unfairly described as existing software systems whose plans and documentation are either poor or nonexistent [Connall and Burns 1993].

Legacy systems are often quite large and/or complex. Many legacy systems evolved in response to locally optimized user needs, instead of being developed to support an organization-wide enterprise integration or strategic planning effort. Performance problems have arisen as user requirements have evolved and the system developers have been unable to keep pace with the change requests [Software 1990]. As a result, legacy systems have attracted attention because of poor performance characteristics or disproportionate resource consumption. In addition, increased corporate volatility resulting from mergers, takeovers, and other corporate restructuring has transformed a number of well-planned and well-implemented organizational systems into chaos [Ulrich 1994]. These factors have combined and as a result, many organizations are burdened with costly legacy systems.

A primary cause for concern is that software does not age gracefully [Jones 1994]; the rate of change of software is between 5 and 7 percent each year, for as long as the software is operational and in use. Over time, the changes tend to degrade the program's original structure. Difficulty in understanding the system results in increased difficulty performing both maintenance and reengineering.

A common characteristic shared by most legacy systems is that they are very difficult to replace. A GSA publication [GSA 1993 p.6] reports two key factors:

1. It is generally not cost-effective to completely redesign the system from scratch. For example, it is not cost-effective if it would cost $1 million dollars to replace a legacy system with resulting savings of only $75,000 a year. Management may require a much higher payback before approving the replacement of such a system.
2. To make matters more difficult, replacement of legacy systems causes disruption in an organization. A need to replace a legacy system to integrate data and information often highlights a lack of integration in the organization itself. Managers may resist reorganizing if the changes impact their organization. In addition, users accustomed to the existing systems will often resist moving to different systems.

Legacy systems are typically complex; developed using unarchitected metadata with little programmatic support. They may contain thousands of elements that are interrelated. With thousands of system elements related to thousands of other elements, the process of mapping all of the elements to all other elements is daunting. Manually documenting and maintaining these relationships can require considerable resources. This system metadata can be very difficult to maintain manually.

Because systems consist of multiple components it is not possible to understand them from a single perspective. Common system definitions include components such as: hardware; software; people; procedures; and/or data. There exist corresponding reengineering technologies for each class of system components. The most popular types of systems

TECHNIQUE	
Focus	**Answers questions like**
Hardware focused	How does this hardware ... ?
Software focused	What does this software do ... ? How does this software perform ... ?
Program focused	What does this program do ... ? How does this program perform ... ?
Database focused	What information is stored in this database?
Data focused	What information does this organization require and produce?

Figure 13-3
Three primary types of reengineering techniques

reengineering technologies have been: software, database, and data reverse engineering. The focus of each is shown in Figure 13-3.

Systems reengineering can be distinguished from program reengineering by the analysis scope. If the scope of a project is a single program—or limited to a related family of programs—the project is considered to be program reengineering. An analysis scope that encompasses a complete system requires that the project be defined as a systems reengineering effort. If the project scope is also system-wide, then some form of data reverse engineering is also required. Data reverse engineering ensures that projects consider the system from the perspective of the source and the use of data by other system components. This understanding is gained by applying structured data reverse engineering to the system.

Program reengineering has been the focus of most automation efforts. Database reengineering has also been automated in some instances [Blaha and Permelani 1995]. We also saw in Chapters 10 and 12 that reengineering can often be semi-automated. However, the semantic understanding that must be extracted from legacy systems requirements requires some human-assisted processes.

Planning for Legacy Systems Reengineering

When planning for systems reengineering, EEP metadata can be used to plan the reengineering project. The framework described in Chapter 5 is used to guide the EEP methodology. During project planning the core metadata framework supports EEP project planning data. Where multiple systems are being merged, the legacy system metadata can be queried to determine the gross size and content of the system data for preliminary data integration priorities. Finally, metadata can be used for project milestone planning, to assess progress toward reengineering goals.

Enterprise Portals all share common, re-usable Web-based code and use browser-based information delivery. When considering a legacy system reengineering project, it is useful to remember two important points:

1. Thirty percent of application code is typically involved with user interface issues.
2. Everyone knows how to use the Web and Web browsers.

Organizations used to expend many resources to design standard user interfaces for an entire organization. The rise of the Web has eliminated all such arguments. In most instances, the economies of scale in using reusable code outweigh the cost of custom development. Organizations that focus on building a core competency for Web-based delivery of future application program developments immediately benefit by not having to study and code user interface routines. Instead, one component of the project cost equation is held fixed: organization-wide delivery of information in the future will use Internet technologies—whether delivered via the Internet, intranet, or extranet. Organizations will find it difficult to justify why an extra 30 percent (say) of a project cost should be spent to develop a unique user interface. By using a common, Web-based delivery standard based on cross-platform browser capabilities, organizations can eliminate much of the expense of user interface analysis. When developed as a core IT competency, this will dramatically reduce the time and cost spent in delivering information organization-wide. This use of browser interfaces will lead to virtual ubiquitous computing.

Similarly, the training budgets associated with system implementation will also decrease. Knowing and understanding basic Web-based interface navigation, information retrieval, and interaction techniques, will become a common skill, known even by children before entering high school. Past, present, and future organizational computing environments determine the basic set of information delivery primitives. Web-based navigation and information delivery techniques, using non-platform-specific browser technologies, will lead to significant decreases in the costs associated with new systems development. By using Java code (say), to develop systems that are portable across platforms and browsers, organizations will be able to maintain a single set of code for organization-wide delivery. Implementation of code reuse will increase proportionately.

We can approach legacy system reengineering projects with the understanding that information from these systems will be delivered via Enterprise Portals. These Enterprise Portals will deliver information organization-wide via intranet and Internet technologies, using browsers that everyone will know how to use, with a single set of common code for use on any platform. Carefully focused reverse engineering analysis of legacy system(s) metadata will identify core metadata required to deliver required information to system end users. In short, use of the EEP methodology will be a critical success factor when reengineering legacy systems—without it, the reengineering effort will not be fact-based and will require many more more resources to complete.

During Reengineering Analysis

During reengineering, the EEP framework in Chapter 5 guides the process and assesses progress towards reengineering goals. The framework specifies the focus of reverse engineering analyses: identifying and analyzing metadata that is required to provide solutions that satisfy user requirements. An integrated series of models are developed and used to coordinate and establish communication about the project among business users, technologists, and management. Models are used to achieve agreement on items such as the project scope, boundaries, and primary areas of focus. The EEP framework specifies a destination for each metadata component developed as part of the reverse engineering process. Reengineering progress can be assessed by the number of populated metadata entity classes and the quality of metadata facts stored in the metamodels.

Figure 13-4 summarizes two reengineering alternatives. The top of Figure 13-4 depicts how current legacy systems reengineering involves many-to-many transformation structures to map system functionality and data items from the existing legacy system to the reengineered system. In contrast, two key transformations are illustrated in the bottom part of Figure 13-4, associated with Enterprise Portal deployment.

The first maps legacy system metadata from the old system into an intermediate format. Because the core metadata is unchanged from system to system, this mapping format is reusable in any legacy system reengineering. Relevent metadata from the legacy system is mapped

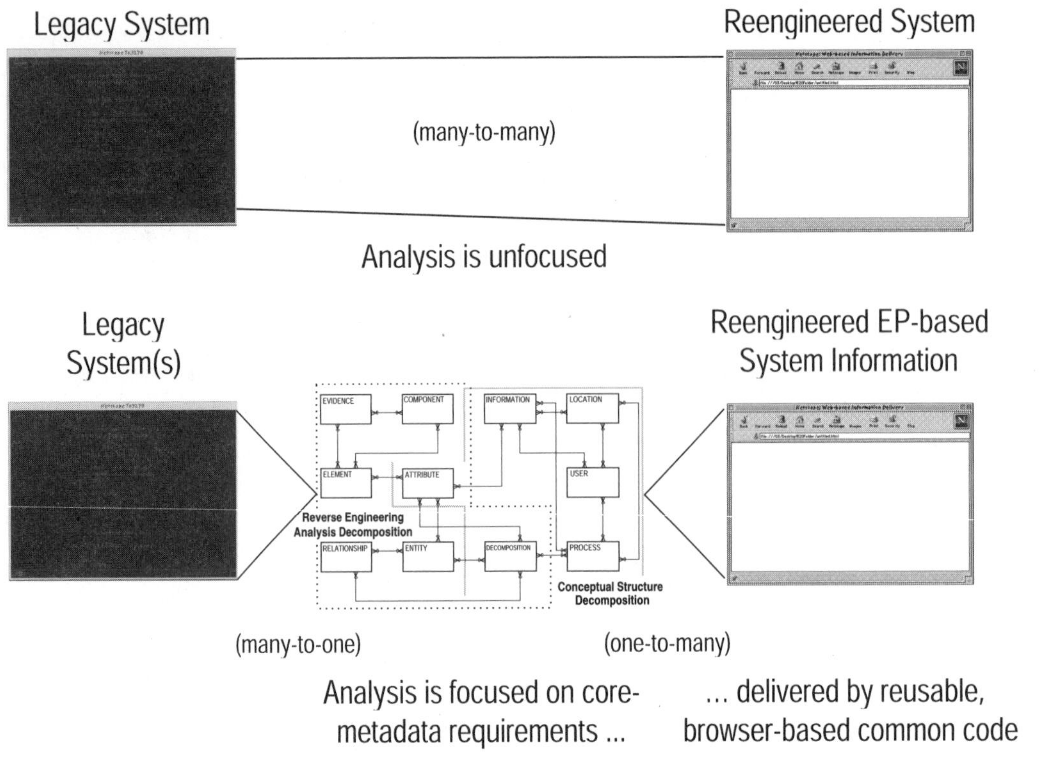

Figure 13-4
Enterprise Portal-based development holds the requirements dialog and information delivery mechanisms fixed.

onto the core metadata model, providing a definite place to map each metadata component.

The second key transformation maps the legacy metadata (already mapped to the core metadata) into generic components of the Enterprise Portal. Because portals focus on information delivery, this mapping can be quite simple: such as a database form or query combination. Obviously, templates can be used so that high reuse can be achieved with great efficiency. Holding fixed the two ends of the transformation equation considerably simplifies the analysis. Using the potential metadata as the focus, the reengineering becomes a series of definable steps required to transform a fact-based, "as-is" (current) model of an existing system into the precise "to-be" form of Web-based information delivery from the Enterprise Portal that is required by users.

Implementing Reengineered Solutions

When implementing a reengineered solution, the metadata can be used to establish integration priorities. By defining legacy system metadata first, if required its naming conventions can be absorbed into the newly deployed Enterprise Portal. Because all metadata is held in a common repository-based format, the metadata is also available for use during the forward engineering stage of the new Enterprise Portal. The Enterprise Portal repository facilitates development, providing a reference point for Enterprise Portal developers to access common metadata—such as data item names, domains, and associated processes. The metadata serves as the basis for system documentation. The metadata repository is also used to build a configuration management schema for subsequent system maintenance.

Naturally, one task most able to benefit from the metadata is data conversion. Much analysis work for this task is accomplished early in the reengineering cycle, when reengineering solution requirements are specified using legacy-systems-based metadata. When implementing the reengineered solution, the metadata can be used as a decision-making framework for setting integration priorities.

Enterprise Portals for Business Reengineering Solution Deployment

Enterprise Portals can also be valuable components of many business reengineering solutions. Information technology plays a key role in business reengineering. A solid understanding of the essential capabilities of enterprise portals can do much to avoid differences between organizational and technical capabilities: the cause of many past business reengineering failures.

Two frequent occurrences have caused many business reengineering efforts to fail. The first cause of failure is when there is little or no involvement from the IT Department. Where IT participation is weak—or worse, is non-existent—during reengineering planning and execution, there has been found to be a high potential for failure. Unfortunately many technologists concentrate their analysis on aspects of technical system implementation, as they have trouble interacting with end users because of a lack of business vocabulary. Another fault of technologists has been a focus on modeling at the expense of forward progress on the project—the dreaded *analysis paralysis* problem. Not involving IT staff in earlier reengineering phases can result in the typical statement:

> Yes, the new system that you desire can be developed—but it will take three years and cost $3 million!

Assuming that IT staff are available for the project team, they contribute to current analysis by producing selected, focused reverse engineering analyses on legacy system components that yield metadata useful to the business reengineering effort. These can address factual data required by the reengineering team. They can also introduce the concepts of EEP to the non-technical team members as a cost-effective means of delivering integrated enterprise information. By understanding the difference between the simplicity of Enterprise Portals and the complexity of individually developed solutions, they can focus more directly on output specification.

The second cause of business reengineering failure is that solutions specified by the reengineering team are often conceived and described as separate standalone systems. A statement such as: *This would be easier to implement if all of the information was available in one system, as a standalone information kiosk* assumes a non-integrated solution from the outset. When specifications such as these are delivered to technical developers, they may not consider that the users are making a bad choice when specifying new systems in this way. After all, the most glamorous job in the development community is in *new development*—it is no wonder that these requests are rarely questioned.

This thinking must be changed. IT staff must be involved throughout the entire reengineering project. Their main role is to describe the fact-based, data capabilities of the existing systems, as well as to help users understand the alternative information options that are available as output from an Enterprise Portal.

The message is clear—once your IT staff understand how to implement Enterprise Portals, involve them early during business reengineering projects and use them to keep the solutions focused on easy-to-implement Enterprise Portal technologies.

Integrated Systems and Business Reengineering

More important than performing business reengineering or systems reengineering in isolation is the potential synergy to be gained when they are implemented in complementary roles; when they are performed in an integrated fashion using Enterprise Portal-based solutions.

When focused on Enterprise Portal solutions, these projects can lead to optimal organizational investments in reengineering efforts. After all, what is the likelihood that some business processes will also have to be reengineered to take full advantage of the opportunities presented by systems reengineering efforts? Quantum improvements in information delivery from system reengineering projects usually have business structure implications, and result in new or different ways for an organization to accomplish its activities. The reverse is also true: when performing a business reengineering effort, the organization may determine the need for new technology support. Before embarking on separate business reengineering or systems reengineering projects, organizations should first explore the possibilities of an integrated approach incorporating aspects of both systems and business reengineering. This will be illustrated with two short examples.

A Business Reengineering Example

One business process selected for business reengineering in Chapter 12 was the *Product Supply Process*. A goal was to eliminate much of the overhead and non-value-added work associated with purchasing many small, low-cost items. In XYZ Corporation, the Purchasing Department had the responsibility for every purchase that was made, even those purchases of low cost, where they could add little value. For example, most purchases for office supplies are typically below $50. But the need to issue Purchase Orders only from the central Purchasing Department adds approximately $150 to the cost of every purchase made!

The XYZ business reengineering team instead developed a reengineered solution using Web browsers and Web forms, similar to the *Multiple Supplier* XML example discussed in Chapter 12. Their solution supported a browser-based workflow purchase order form, using corporate charge cards for payment.

However, their initial request for IT support failed. The business reengineering team requested acquisition and installation of the required database components to implement a browser-based purchasing solution. External consultants had helped the users develop the solution, but the IT Department of XYZ had not been involved. Imagine the surprise and disappointment of the consultants and users when IT staff said they could not implement their solution; the IT Department first had to decide which DBMS product they should standardize, organization-wide, to provide Web-based support! And of course, the database technology—used by the browser purchasing package requested by the users and consultants—was not even on the finalized list of databases under consideration!

The IT staff argued that they first should repeat the evaluation stage when they filtered out candidate database technologies. They also insisted that they had to play an active role in the database technology standardization effort. Little progress was made; the first business reengineering effort had run into a technological brick wall and eventually collapsed from inertia.

A Systems Reengineering Example

The systems reengineering example was based on a business unit that needed to install a new, integrated Human Resources and Payroll system. The solution was to be implemented using client/server technologies to replace legacy mainframe systems that were 20 years old. Some of the project team saw the project as a simple system replacement. That is, only technical questions regarding the implementation were of interest to the reengineering team. Their concern was the ability to process 125,000 payroll transactions on a regular basis.

This thinking reflected the conventional systems approach to reengineering, as automating existing functions. But viewed from a systems reengineering perspective, it was clear that the required workflow and technology changes required a much broader scope. For example, the reengineering project scope relabeled the "employment process" instead as the "task accomplishment process." This reflected the fundamental manner in which the new thinking of systems reengineering had altered the nature of accomplishing things–from one of merely hiring someone to actually completing a specific task! Technical training was included to familiarize users with the new reengineered systems and introduce them to new technologies where appropriate.

Integrated, Metadata-based Reengineering

The term "synergistic dependence" describes situations where the overall reengineering effort is dependent on synergies resulting from successful business reengineering/systems reeengineering (BR/SR) integration. The *American Heritage English Dictionary* defines the noun *synergy* as "the interaction of two or more agents or forces so that their combined effect is greater than the sum of their individual effects." The term *synergistic dependence* illustrates the interdependency between BR and SR efforts, as well as their mutual dependence on IT to successfully achieve greater-than-incremental change. Situations are defined as synergistically dependent if they require successful integration of both BR and SR in order to be economically feasible.

Business reengineering and systems reengineering are often implemented separately, in an uncoordinated fashion. Yet practitioners have found that BR can influence SR, and that SR can benefit from the application of BR concepts. This indicates that potential synergies can result when BR and SR are pursued in an integrated fashion. This chapter presents an integrated BR/SR approach that has been successfully applied in practice. Guidance provided in the chapter will enable you to use or develop your own version of this process and gain from the resulting synergies.

Because BR and SR are interdependent, it is clear to us that successful reengineering requires integrated business reengineering and system reengineering activities. The interdependencies can be managed through competent use of metadata-based management technologies. Figure 13-5 relates to a project [Hodgson and Aiken 1997] that employed different technological support for increased integration. Figure 13-6 shows that the key integration role is metadata-focused when performing systems and business reengineering.

There are four possible integrations between systems and business reengineering. These are shown in Figure 13-7. The simplest form is *administrative integration*, where each reengineering effort notifies its respective counterpart that it has completed a business or system re-engineering effort. If there are no exchange requirements between BR

Figure 13-5 How IT was used in a series of reengineering projects [Hodgson and Aiken 1997].

Data modeling / Procedural models / Mathematical models / Semantic network / Outline tools / Model exploration / Visualization software / Library services / Data bases / Multimedia / Hypertext and Hypermedia / Micro-observatory / Microcomputer laboratory / Survey Technology / Video and sound recording / Spreadsheets / Presentation Graphics / Data analysis tools / Statistical analysis / Environments for inquiry / Problem-solving programs / Control systems / Control of equipment / Computer-aided design / Construction of graphs and charts / Word processing / Outlining / Graphics / Spelling, grammar, etc. / Symbolic expressions / Desktop publishing / Presentation graphics / Electronic mail / Bulletin boards / Computer conferences / Synchronous comp. conf. / Audio and video teleconferences / Gopher / Authored hypertext environments / Collaborative data environments / Group decision support systems / Shared document preparation / Social spreadsheets / Drawing and painting programs / Music making and accompaniment / Interactive video and hypermedia / Animation software / Multimedia composition tools

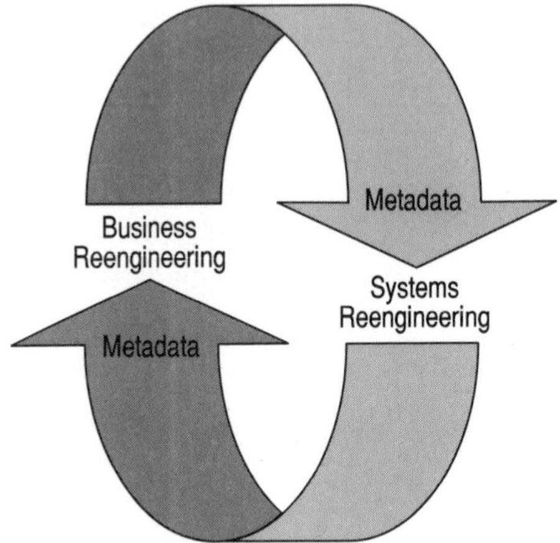

Figure 13-6 Metadata links Business Rengineering and Systems Reengineering efforts.

and SR, then they can be integrated administratively as shown in the first line of Figure 13-7.

For *sequential integration*, one reengineering approach is performed—then when complete, the requisite corollary reengineering is notified. If the outputs can be treated as distinct, then the two analysis techniques can be integrated sequentially as shown in the second line of Figure 13-7.

Reciprocal integration involves products being exchanged during the course of reengineering. This indicates that BR and SR interact at a level that requires minimally coordinated reciprocal integration as shown on the third line of Figure 13-7.

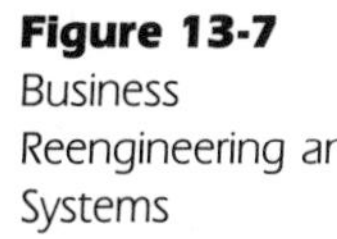

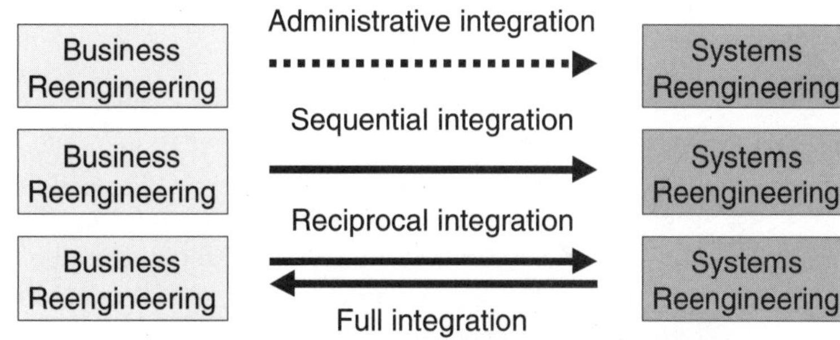

Figure 13-7 Business Reengineering and Systems Reengineering integration options (adapted from [Golden and Ramanujam 1985]).

Full integration has a different orientation, requiring simultaneous implementation of business and systems reengineering. Full integration (the last line of Figure 13-7) is an ideal state with optimal integration between BR and SR for balanced implementation of organizational strategy. Future environmental scenarios recognize industry restructuring that results in drastically different information needs and increasing value of the data needed to facilitate improvements in organizational dexterity. Only rarely is it possible to implement new business processes without corresponding technical changes. Similarly, most major systems reengineering efforts benefit from analysis of related business practices.

BR and SR can be integrated along two dimensions: process interdependencies and information sharing. Process interdependency analysis reveals several areas where the outputs of a BR process should be immediately used by an SR process and vice versa. In addition, the effort benefits from information accruing in a common repository. This permits use of standard project information and increases information sharing effectiveness. Several similarities exist. Both BR and SR:

- involve attempts to make major improvements that leverage knowledge of existing conditions;
- employ iterative prototyping approaches that evolve solutions (as opposed to specifying solutions); and
- can be enhanced with effective IT application.

IT projects provide an opportunity to integrate these two techniques in a manner that improves overall reengineering effectiveness. Information technology enables teams to spend more time concentrating on the analysis process and less on its mechanics. It facilitates the team's development of more complex and in-depth analysis of the meta-information during reengineering, which can speed up the reengineering process.

The remainder of the chapter shows how: business and systems reengineering can be integrated in order to leverage reengineering investments; structured project information maintained in a reengineering repository can facilitate ongoing and future efforts; and by evolving slightly, the organizational IT function can make a major contribution to these reengineering efforts. We will discuss an integrated business and systems reengineering (IBSR) method comprised of six processes. These are presented using Gane and Sarson process decomposition. We will provide a summary of the meta-information maintained using the repository. Finally, we will briefly discuss how an IT organization can evolve to facilitate IBSR implementation.

Integrated Business and Systems Reengineering (IBSR)

The IBSR model was derived from the two models presented earlier, describing Business Reengineering in Figure 13-1 and Systems Reengineering in Figure 13-2. An overview of the IBSR model is shown as a process decomposition hierarchy in Figure 13-8. The example used in the following diagrams relates to a real-life project carried out for a large Government Department.

In the model explanations that follow Figure 13-8, **bold** type refers to process names, *italic* type indicates data flow names, underlined type is used for internal data store names, and ***bolditalic*** type refers to external entities.

IBSR Model Context Diagram

The IBSR context diagram in Figure 13-9 defines the scope of integrated BR/SR, indicating it receives two inputs as compound data flows from two entities that are external to the system. Information describing *business characteristics* is received from the ***business environment***, as also is *system evidence* about the performance of the ***legacy system***

Figure 13-8 IBSR Model Process Decomposition.

Integrated Business and Systems Reengineering

- 1.0 Preliminary BPR Tasks
  - 1.1 Identify Business Processes
  - 1.2 Establish Process and System Owners
  - 1.3 Formulate Reengineering Strategy
- 2.0 Preliminary SR Tasks
  - 2.1 Candidate System Screening
  - 2.2 Non-Technical Feasibility Assessment
  - 2.3 Technical Feasibility Assessment
  - 2.4 Integrated Evidence Assessment
- 3.0 Reengineering Project Definition
  - 3.1 Determine Process and System Priorities
  - 3.2 Assign Reengineering Team Members
  - 3.3 Reengineering Project Planning
- 4.0 Situation Diagnosis
  - 4.1 Bound and Scope Processes
  - 4.2 Reverse Engineer Existing System
    - 4.2.1 Target System Analysis
      - 4.2.1.1 Cycle Planning
      - 4.2.1.2 Evidence Acquisition
      - 4.2.1.3 Evidence Analysis
      - 4.2.1.4 Straw Model Development
      - 4.2.1.5 Model Refinement and Validation
      - 4.2.1.6 Model Storage and Organization
    - 4.2.2 System Packaging
    - 4.2.3 System Integration
    - 4.2.4 System Transfer
    - 4.2.5 Project Metric Evaluation
    - 4.2.6 Methodology Evaluation
  - 4.3 Understand Customer Needs
  - 4.4 Understand Current Process
  - 4.5 Understand Existing IT Use
  - 4.6 Identify Weakness In Existing Process
  - 4.7 Understand Potential IT Use
  - 4.8 Set New Design Targets
- 5.0 Iterative Redesign
  - 5.1 Create Breakthrough Design Concept
  - 5.2 Screen for Rapid Technology Application
  - 5.3 Develop End State Vision
  - 5.4 Implement Process Prototype
  - 5.5 Implement System Prototype
  - 5.6 Test Learn Improve and Iterate
- 6.0 System and Process Redeployment
  - 6.1 Field Prototype Organizationally
  - 6.2 Realize and Document Benefits
  - 6.3 Develop Supporting Infrastructure
  - 6.4 Reengineering Results Rollout
  - 6.5 Institutionalize Organizationally
  - 6.6 Implement Succeeding Releases
  - 6.7 Implement Reengineered System

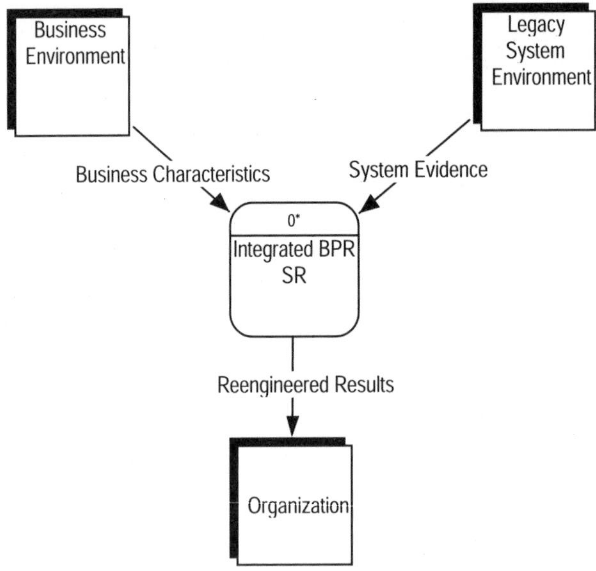

Figure 13-9 IBSR Model: Context Diagram.

environment. The process outputs, in the form of *reengineering results*, are evaluated by the ***organization*** for effectiveness and efficiencies.

Process 0: Integrated Business/Systems Reengineering

The first level of model decomposition breaks the **Integrated BR/SR** process into the six sub-processes shown in Figure 13-10. Each is explained briefly below and in more detail in the next sections.

1. The first process **preliminary BPR tasks** accepts *business characteristics* from the ***business environment***. It can also receive *system performance characteristics* from the *preliminary SR tasks* process. **Preliminary BPR tasks** produces two outputs, a general *reengineering strategy* and a *system to process mapping* indicating which legacy information systems are associated with each business process.
2. The **preliminary SR tasks** process prioritizes and focuses on determining which systems should be considered for

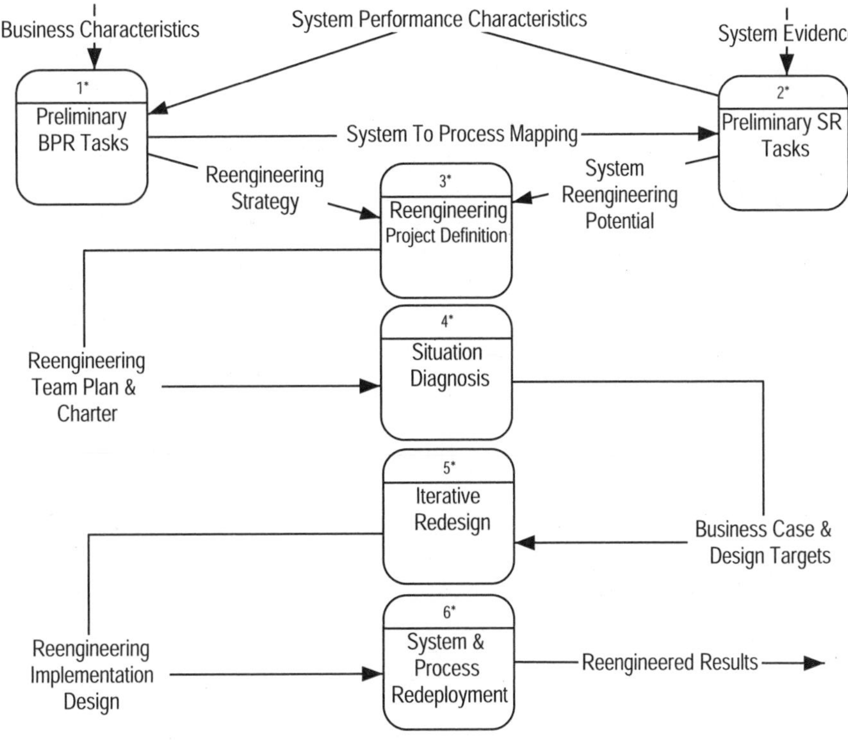

Figure 13-10 Process 0: Integrated BR/SR.

reengineering by identifying the *system reengineering potential* of possible efforts.

3. Process 3, **reengineering project definition**, incorporates both *reengineering strategy* and *system reengineering potential(s)* into the strategic process of defining a specific reengineering effort. The output of this process is a *reengineering team plan and charter* detailing: the process to be reengineered; the project scope; the associated systems to be reengineered; and the reengineering team members.
4. Reverse engineering is performed as an integrated portion of the **situation diagnosis** process. As a result of a combination of system reverse engineering and other diagnostic activities, the *business case and design targets* are developed as process outputs.
5. The **iterative design** process involves development and evaluation of successive solution refinement. When complete, the *reengineering implementation design* forms the basis for the **systems and process redeployment** efforts.

6. During the last process, **systems and process redeployment**, the reengineered processes and systems are institutionalized and fine-tuned to maximize organizational benefits. Periodically, the effort is evaluated to determine if it continues to meet the evolving reengineering design targets.

Virtually all of the information created as part of IBSR is stored in the reengineering repository. For clarity here, the repository is not shown but implied on the process diagrams with the exception of processes 4.2 (Figure 13-17) and 4.2.1 (Figure 13-18)—where development of repository inputs are the primary focus. Meta-information stored in the repository includes models used to store, manage, and communicate project information. The repository forms the basis for integrated reengineering project information. The repository enables IBSR efforts to access an evolving repository containing the latest version of the enterprise's official standardized, integrated reengineering information. Repository contents that are created during each process are cataloged after the IBSR model presentation.

Process 1: Preliminary BR Tasks

Figure 13-11 is a decomposition of the **preliminary BR tasks** process. Information comprising the *business characteristics* data flow consists of three sub-flows: *current business practices*, *customer feedback*, and *organizational structure data*. Information about the *current business*

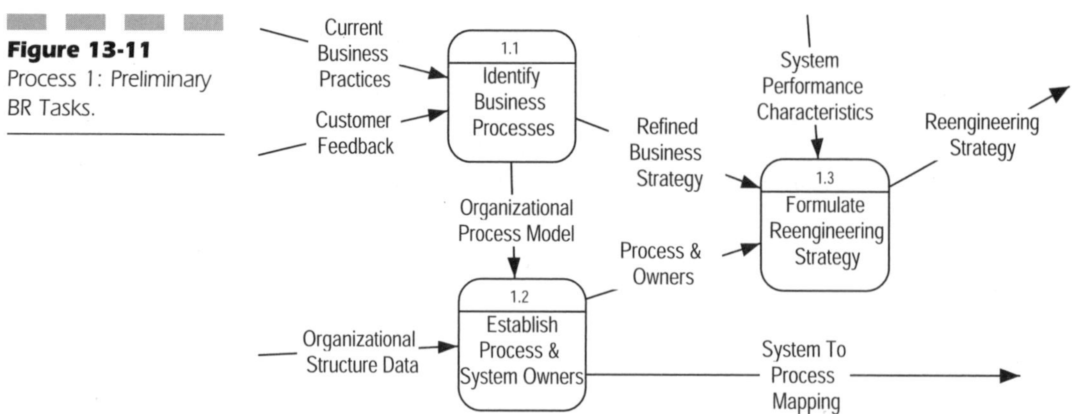

Figure 13-11 Process 1: Preliminary BR Tasks.

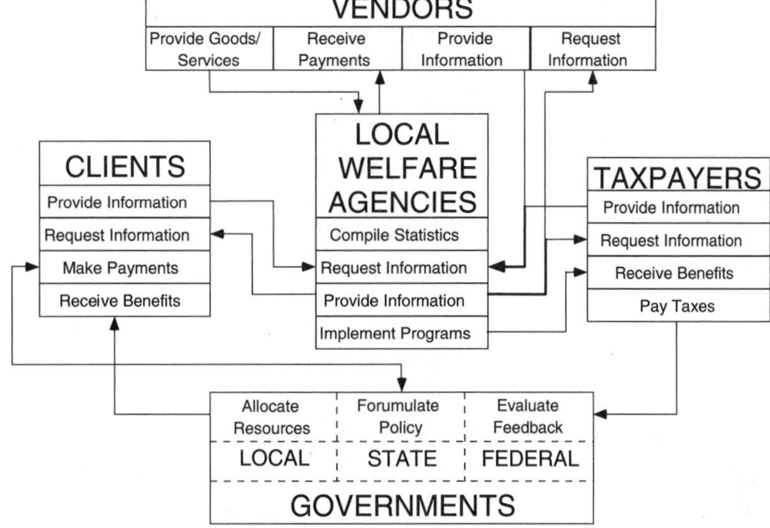

Figure 13-12 Sample Organizational Process Model for a Government Department.

practices is combined with *customer feedback* to perform a key reengineering activity—**identify business processes.**

This results in an *organizational process model* (see Figure 13-12 for an example), the first of many pieces of information stored in the repository. The model contains the first definition of the processes that the organization can reengineer. Development of the *organizational process model*, when combined with *customer feedback*, should also result in a *refined business strategy*.

The next process is **establish process and system owners**. An understanding of the technical organizational systems associated with each organizational processes and the responsible owners is developed. An example Process to System Mapping Matrix is shown as Figure 13-13. The *refined business strategy* is combined with *system performance characteristics*. The *process & owners* data flow results in the **formulation** of an **organizational reengineering strategy**.

Process 2: Preliminary SR Tasks

Figure 13-14 shows that the **preliminary SR tasks** are aimed at rapidly identifying those systems most likely to benefit from IBSR. **Candidate system screening** uses the *system to process mapping* and *system*

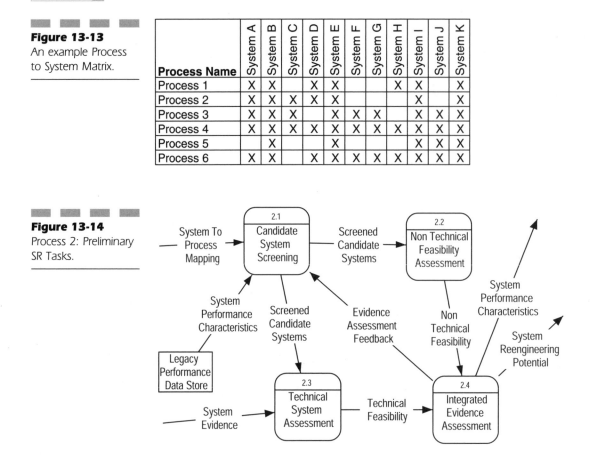

Figure 13-13 An example Process to System Matrix.

Process Name	System A	System B	System C	System D	System E	System F	System G	System H	System I	System J	System K
Process 1	X	X		X	X			X	X		X
Process 2	X	X	X	X	X				X		X
Process 3	X	X	X		X	X	X		X	X	X
Process 4	X	X	X	X	X	X	X	X	X	X	X
Process 5		X			X				X	X	X
Process 6	X	X		X	X	X	X	X	X	X	X

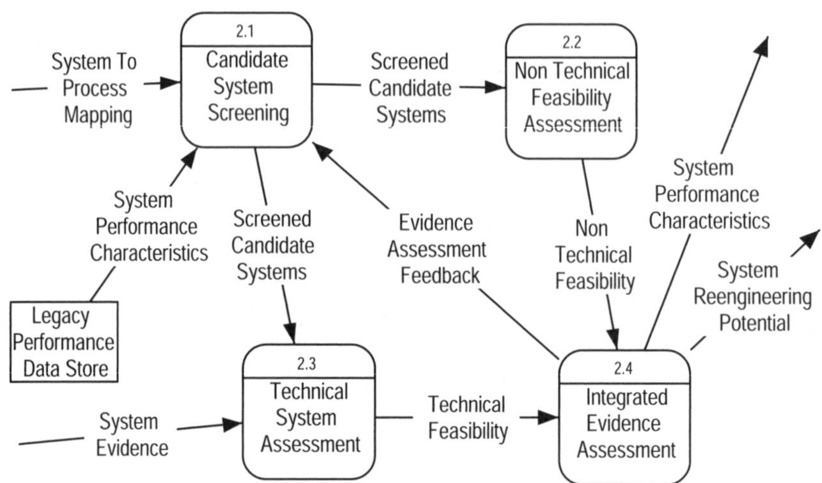

Figure 13-14 Process 2: Preliminary SR Tasks.

performance characteristics to filter the legacy systems for systems that: have disproportionate complaints; incur high maintenance costs; lack flexibility; or are problematic. The screening focuses detailed feasibility analysis on those systems where reengineering will be able to produce the desired synergies. The *screened candidate systems* are subject to both **technical** and **non-technical assessments** producing *technical* and *non-technical feasibilities*. The **integrated evidence** is **assessed** in light of the *reengineering strategy*.

When *system evidence* enters **technical system assessment**, some of the system evidence indicates how "problematic" each system is. "Problematic" systems can be symptomatic of dysfunctional or sub-optimal associated processes. This may trigger an associated BR effort. A data flow describing *system performance characteristics* can flow to **preliminary BR tasks** permitting either **preliminary BR tasks** or **pre-**

liminary SR tasks to initiate a reengineering effort. The other output from the **preliminary SR tasks** process is an assessment of the *system reengineering potential* synergies associated with specific business process/system reengineering combinations.

Process 3: Reengineering Project Definition

Figure 13-15 illustrates **reengineering project definition** where *reengineering strategy* and *system reengineering potential* are assessed in light of *organizational reengineering strategy* to **determine process and system priorities**. Trying to identify possible synergies, various process/system combinations are examined and ranked according to their reengineering potential. The resulting *reengineering priorities* serve to focus the search for *potential team members*.

Reengineering teams are typically comprised of both technical and non-technical members who have knowledge of organizational processes and have the associated systems technical abilities. When the *team composition* and the *reengineering priorities* have been determined, **reengineering project planning** can begin. This produces the *team charter*, the *team composition*, the *reengineering priorities*, and the *project plan*.

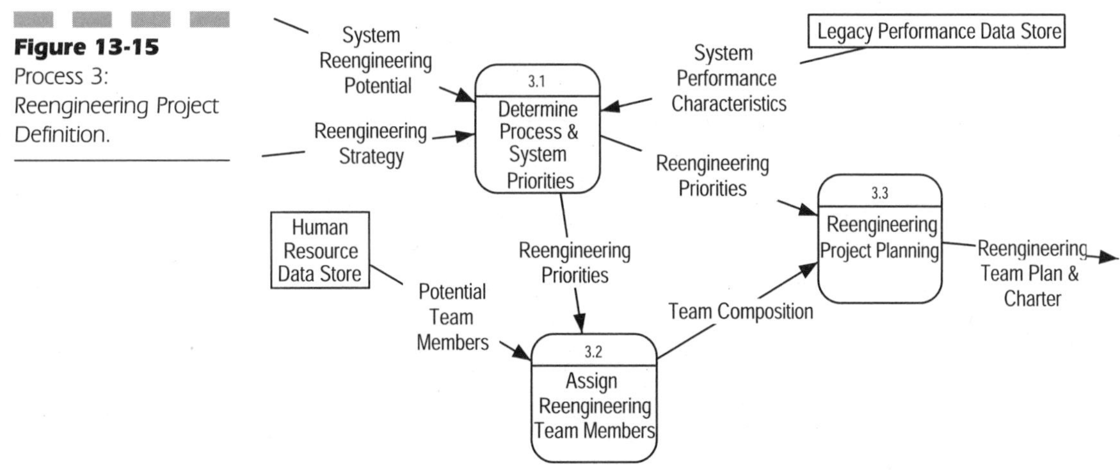

Figure 13-15 Process 3: Reengineering Project Definition.

Process 4: Situation Diagnosis

Figure 13-16 illustrates **situation diagnosis**. Once the *reengineering team, plan, and charter* have been developed, the team can begin to **bound and scope** the target **process**. The *organization process model* is re-verified to ensure the model (from **preliminary BR tasks**) still reflects the organizational processes—as the thinking surrounding the model may have evolved. Assuming they are synchronized, the target process is analyzed to determine the specific role it plays in organizational operation. From **bound and scope processes** flows a list of *systems to be reengineered* and *bound and scoped process* descriptions. The **reverse engineer existing system** process decomposes two levels further (described below) and produces *system reverse engineering information* that is stored in the repository for reuse by the **understand existing IT use** process.

The other output from IBSR Model Process Component (abbreviated below as IMPC) 4.1 are the *bound and scoped processes* data flows that serve as input along with feedback (from the repository) to the process **understand customer needs**. *Verified customer needs* are required to **understand** the **current process**. When the reengineering team is

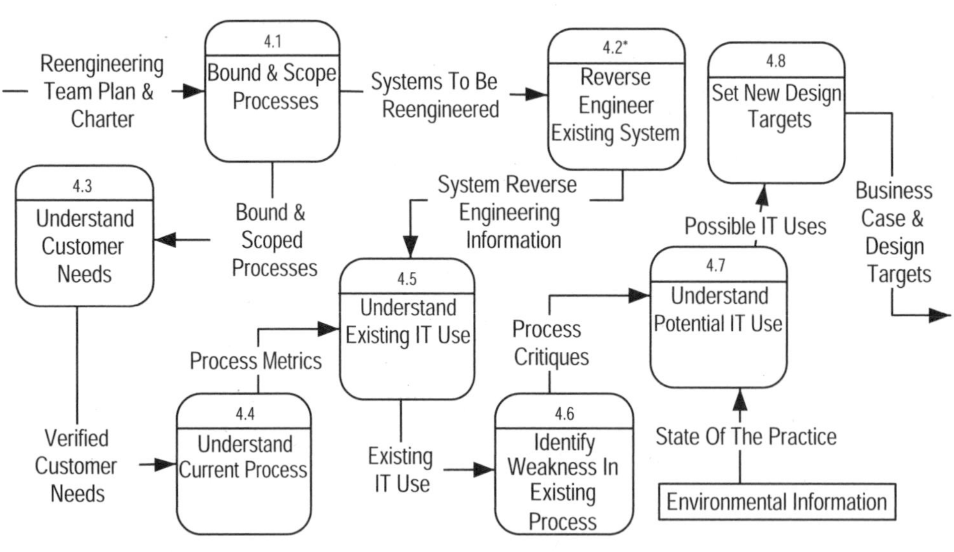

Figure 13-16
Process 4: Situation Diagnosis.

capable of describing a process using its own *process metrics*, it is described by: an overview of the process (what the process does, why is it carried out, and who uses it); and the process inputs and outputs, in a form comprehensible by anyone in the organization. Graphical process models can be used to identify value-adding work.

Once the process is understood it is used to **understand** the **existing IT use** in the process. Understanding why the current design does not perform better comes from understanding the underlying sources of problems and where the opportunities exist for extending the output of the process in order to add more value. The existing design understanding—in the form of *system reverse engineering information*—is incorporated into the process of developing requirements for the new process and setting the performance objectives.

Some *system reverse engineering information* should be accessible from the repository, to be used by the **understand existing IT use** process. The *existing IT use* is compared with the *process metrics* to **identify weaknesses in existing process**. This understanding is documented as *process critiques*. **Understand possible IT use** compares the *process critique* against the *state of the practice* information, inspiring *possible IT uses* in a reengineered process. The *possible IT uses* and the *process critiques* are used to **set new design targets** for the reengineered process.

Process 4.2: Reverse Engineer Existing System

IBSR model processes 4.2 and 4.2.1 are primarily concerned with developing repository inputs. Figure 13-17 **reverse engineer existing system** begins by accepting the list of *systems to be reengineered* and performing **target system analysis** until the system has been reverse engineered. (Process 4.2 is decomposed and described in the next section.) A system has been reverse engineered when *integrated target system models* have been stored in the repository. Once the reverse engineering is completed, **system asset packaging** occurs as *integrated target system models* are prepared for use in other processes (for example, IMPC 4.5 in Figure 13-16).

The system assets can be made more useful with a **system asset integration** process that integrates individual model components into larger, more comprehensive information collections. The resulting

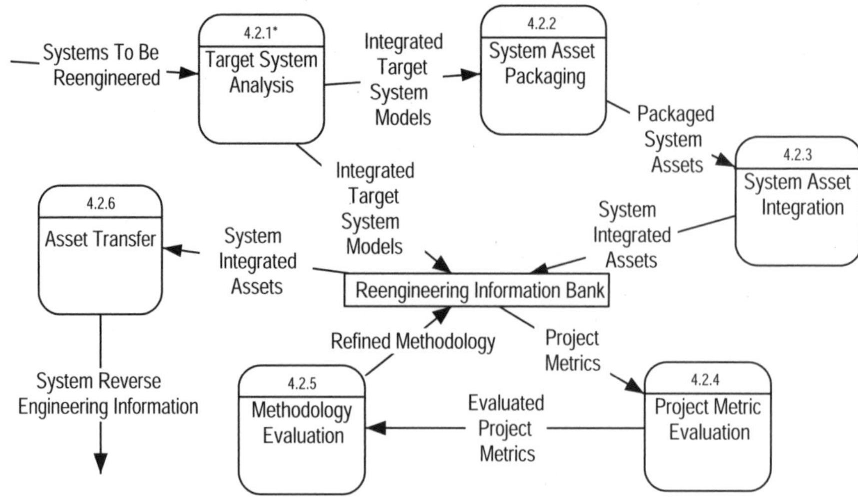

Figure 13-17 Process 4.2: Reverse Engineer Existing System.

integrated system assets are stored in the repository. Some of the *integrated assets* require additional processing (for example, development of associated user education materials) before they can be **transferred** for other uses as *system reverse engineering information*. Periodically, **project metric evaluation** is performed where the *evaluated project metrics* are tabulated, evaluated, and used as input to a **methodology evaluation** assessment. Improvements to the methodology are stored in the repository.

Process 4.2.1: Target System Analysis

Target system analysis (Figure 13-18) serves as the "main line" system reverse engineering activity. It is performed until the desired outputs, *integrated target system models*, are produced and stored in the repository. **Cycle planning** evaluates and incorporates previous cycle results, identifying the area of highest risk associated with lack of knowledge, specifying analysis targets, and a plan for the modeling cycle.

The output, a plan for obtaining desired results from the next cycle, focuses on specific *desired evidence lists*. The **evidence acquisition** process consists of looking for missing evidence, and collecting, cataloging, and structuring evidence. The outcome is *organized evidence* that is passed to **evidence analysis** where it is analyzed for appropriateness and model development potential.

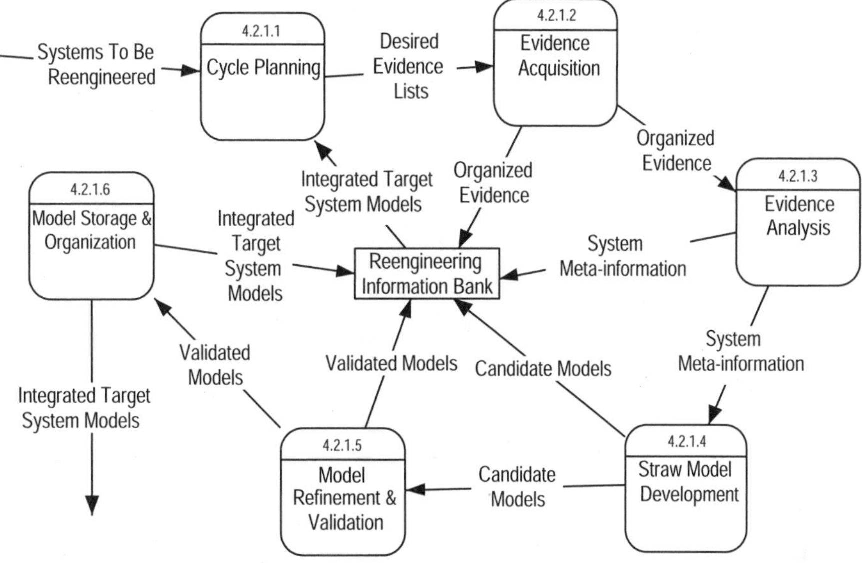

Figure 13-18 Process 4.2.1: Target System Analysis.

Useful *system meta-information* (or information about the structure of the information stored in the target system) is passed to **straw model development** where it is structured into *candidate models*. System users and technical personnel often participate in **model refinement and validation** activities geared toward refining the models by correcting deficiencies, error identification, new knowledge discovery, and normalization. The results are clearer, more comprehensive, more accurate, *validated models*. The last step in **target system analysis** is **model storage and organization** where the *validated models* are collected, cataloged, and structured for archival and configuration management purposes.

Process 5: Iterative Redesign

The next to the last IBSR process is **iterative redesign** in Figure 13-19. It evolves both a new process and supporting systems required to implement it. For this diagram, the IMPC 5.5 (on the left) is shown primarily as a process-oriented activity. Similarly, IMPC 5.2 and 5.4 (on the right) are primarily technology-based activities. IMPC 5.1, 5.3, and 5.6 are joint process/technology activities.

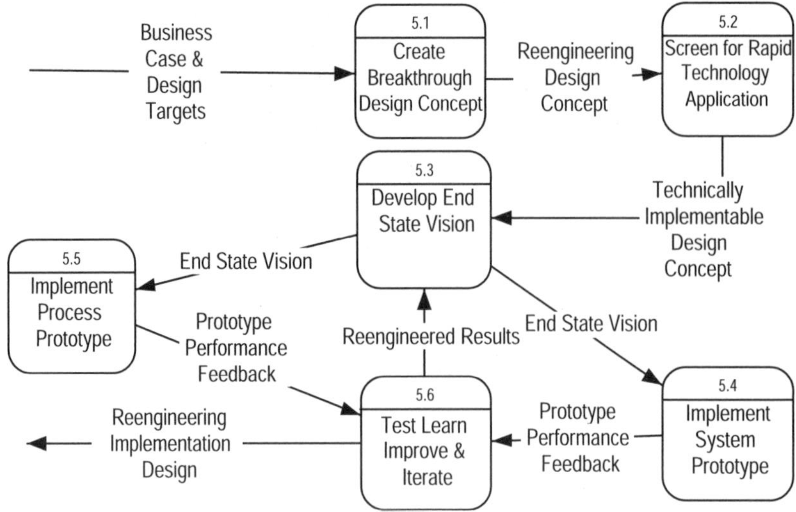

Figure 13-19
Process 5: Iterative Redesign.

Iterative redesign begins with the *business case and design targets* feeding a procedure called **create breakthrough design concept**. This is somewhat akin to the Far Side™ cartoon showing a blackboard full of calculations that converge on the phrase "and then a miracle occurs." Happily, in practice there are many techniques for developing breakthrough design concepts that are output as a new *reengineering design concept*.

For example, we discussed in Chapter 12 the entity dependency analysis technique—used for automated analysis of integrated data models to identify prerequisite independent and interdependent processes. These processes, within a target process represented by a data model cluster, often suggest breakthrough process redesign alternatives.

It will be no surprise to learn that the characteristics of reengineered processes include a list remarkably similar to modular program design in structured systems development: simplicity and integration; few interfaces and little non-value-adding overhead; multiple process versions; avoiding complexity and special cases; deferred, aggregated, and automated control; shared common information resources; coherence and consistency; and exploitation of non-linearity.

The redesigned concept is **screened for rapid technology application** to ensure that it can be quickly and efficiently implemented using existing or feasible improvements in organizational IT. The result, a *technically implementable design concept*, is passed to the **develop end state vision** process. The *end state vision* is passed to two parallel processes: **implement system prototype** and **implement process prototype**. Both produce *prototype performance feedback* from which lessons are **learned**, additional **testing** occurs and **iteration** continues until the reengineering team is satisfied it has evolved a *reengineering implementation design*.

Process 6: Systems Redeployment

The last process is **systems redeployment** in Figure 13-20. The first step is to take the *reengineering implementation design* out of the laboratory-like environment that it has been confined to until this point, and **field the prototype organizationally** for a trial period. The *prototype results* are used to **realize and document benefits**—demonstrating both proof of concept and tangible advantages from implementing the reengineered systems and processes.

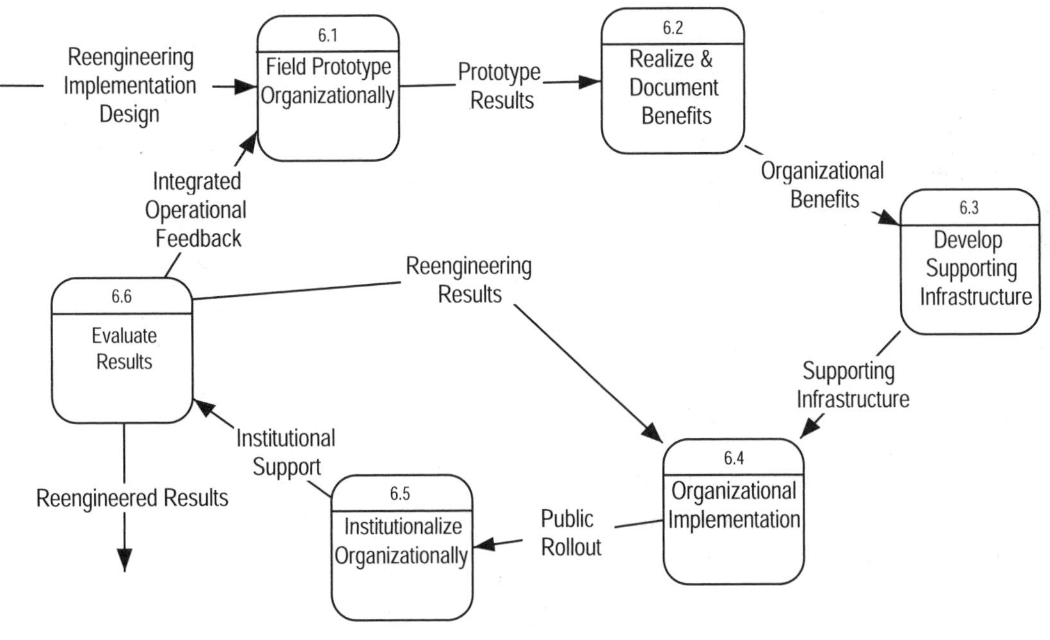

Figure 13-20
Process 6: Systems Redeployment.

The process of **realizing and documenting benefits** also serves to assess the *organizational benefits*. Once understood, these must be prepared for institutionalization by **developing** a **supporting infrastructure**. When the *supporting infrastructure* has sufficiently evolved, the team executes an **organizational implementation** and **institutionalized** reengineering results **organization-wide**. Since organizational resistance to change can be very strong, the process success depends on the reengineering team making it easier for the members of the organization to embrace the new system than to continue to use the old one. Iterative refinement continues as the organization **evaluates** the **results**. It sends the *reengineered results* back to the **organizational implementation** as well as forward to the next iteration.

Repository Metadata Development

The IBSR model presented is easier to develop, with benefits accruing to the reengineering effort, when the reengineering results are maintained as live documents in the repository. Future project planners can gain from prior experiences as well. Analysis of the repository meta-information gives an indication of the continuing need to develop and manage information and matrices—such as matrices linking functions to processes, data to processes, and processes to locations. Figure 13-21 illustrates the repository meta-information by including a number of data flows arranged by process output.

Successful reengineering often requires integrated BR and SR activities—IBSR can guide this process. Demonstrating that business and systems reengineering can be effectively integrated at the process level leads to the possibility that new reengineering economies of scale can be achieved. This in turn can lower individual project break-even points. Future BR and SR projects should be examined for synergistic dependencies. There are three areas critical to successful IBSR implementation: (1) appropriate use of IT; (2) management maturity; (3) IT evolution.

Appropriate use of IT permits integration of BR and SR in a manner such that IBSR can be used to successfully implement major organizational strategies. Most of this IT support currently exists as components that need to be integrated under a common analysis environment. More importantly, common information exchange techniques must be

Process 1: **Preliminary BR Tasks** Outputs
- a refined business strategy
- meta-information structure development and population of organizational customer feedback data
- the organizational process model
- a list of the organizational processes and associated process owners
- a formal system to process mapping indicating the systems associated with each process and the associated system owners
- the organizational reengineering strategy

Process 2: **Preliminary SR Tasks** Outputs
- lists of candidate systems for reengineering
- technical and non-technical feasibility assessments for each candidate system
- some initial system evidence
- an assessment of each candidate system's reengineering synergy potential

Process 3: **Project Definition** Outputs
- organizational reengineering priorities
- reengineering team charter
- reengineering team composition
- reengineering project plan

Process 4: **Situation Diagnosis**
- bound and scoped process descriptions
- process specific verified customer needs
- existing process users of IT
- systems associated with the target process
- system reverse engineering information
- critiques of the existing processes
- possible IT users in the new process design
- the reengineering effort business case and design targets

Process 4.2: **Reverse Engineering** Outputs
- integrated target system models
- integrated system assets
- project metrics
- methodology refinements

Process 4.2.1: **Target System Analysis** Outputs
- previous cycle results
- evaluations of previous cycle results
- evolving areas of highest risk
- analysis target specifications
- plans for the current modeling cycle
- system evidence
- system meta-information
- candidate and validated system models
- integrated target system models

Process 5: **Iterative Redesign** Outputs
- technically implementable reengineering design concept
- an end state vision
- system and process implementation data
- performance feedback
- reegineering results
- reengineering implementation design

Process 6: **Reimplementation** Outputs
- forms of institutional support
- organizational benefit
- supporting infrastructure
- organizational implementation
- institutional support
- reengineering results
- operational feedback
- prototype implementation results

Figure 13-21
Repository meta-information organized by process output.

developed so that this information is readily exchangeable between tool components. XML offers a lot of potential in this regard.

Before IBSR can be implemented, there are several organizational prerequisites. First, management should recognize the need for different information needs or for dramatically improved value from current data.

Integrated reengineering plans must function as strategic blueprints that link reengineering to: organizational strategy; reengineering priorities; system consolidation, information integration, system development, and post implementation engineering plans.

As its organizational role changes from producer to enabler, or from Implementation Agent to Strategic Partner, IT can play a leading role in reengineering. Some IT staff are motivated by fear; they feel that if they do not take a leading role in reengineering, they will risk losing their influence in the enterprise. They feel that if they do not participate actively, the IT function will bear the blame if the effort is a failure.

Consequently, the IT Department must shed some inappropriate practices before it can realize its potential in reengineering. IT methodologists must guard against a tendency to over-analyze, a fondness for existing systems, and constrained thinking due to over-reliance on earlier, inappropriate methodologies.

Traditional IT processes for system delivery are much too slow for today's pace of rapid business change. The functionally based reporting structure of most IT Departments can be counter-productive in an environment of rapid systems delivery. As a result, systems are too costly to build using the development practices of yesterday. This must be fixed. Enterprise Portals are not the only answer. But as the tools for Enterprise Portal development rapidly evolve in the coming years they will help resolve some of these IT problems.

REFERENCES

Aiken, P. and Hodgson, L. (1998) "Synergistic Dependence Between Analysis Techniques," *Information Systems Management* (Fall): 55–67.

Blaha, M. and Permerlani, W. (1998) "Observed Idiosyncracies of Relational Data Warehouse Designs," *Proceedings of the Second Working Conference on Reverse Engineering*, Toronto, Ontario, Canada, IEEE Computer Society Press.

Chikofski, E. and Cross, J. (1990) "Reverse Engineering and Design Recovery: A Taxonomy," *IEEE Software*, (January), 7(1): 13–17.

Hammer, M. and Champy, J. (1993) *Reengineering the Corporation: A Manifesto for Business Revolution*, Harper Business.

Hodgson, L. and Aiken, P. H. (1997) "Synergistic Dependencies: the Role of Information Technologies in Business Process Reengineering and

Systems Reengineering," *9th Software Technology Conference*, Salt Lake City, UT.

Additional Reading

Brynjolfsson, E. and Hitt, L. (1995) "The Productive Keep Producing," *InformationWEEK*, Sept. 18. (http://techweb.cmp.com/iw/545/graphics/iw500d.pdf).

Caldwell, B. (1994) "Missteps, Miscues: Business reengineering failures have cost corporations billions," *InformationWEEK* (June 20): 50–60.

Deloitte and Touche (1997) *1996 CIO Survey*, National Office, Ten Westport Road, Wilton CT, 203/761-3000 (1997) (http://www.dttus.com/dttus/publish/cio/key.htm).

Karr, R.N. Jr. (1993) *Data Management Issues Associated with Stovepipe Systems*, General Services Administration, Information Resources Management Service, Policy Analysis Division (October), KMP-94-1-I.

King, S. (1995) *How to Fail*, NAPM Insights (February) pp. 50–52.

Proceedings of the First Working Conference on Reverse Engineering, May 21–23, 1993—Baltimore, MD IEEE Computer Society Press 233 pages.

Proceedings of the Second Working Conference on Reverse Engineering, July 14-16, 1995—Toronto, Ontario, Canada IEEE Computer Society Press 335 pages.

Proceedings of the Third Working Conference on Reverse Engineering (WCRE '96), November 8–10, 1996—Monterey, CA IEEE Computer Society Press 312 pages.

Proceedings of the Fourth Working Conference on Reverse Engineering (WCRE '97), October 6-8, 1997—Amsterdam, The Netherlands IEEE Computer Society Press 248 pages.

Proceedings of the Fifth Working Conference on Reverse Engineering, (WCRE '98) October 12–14, 1998—Honolulu, Hawaii IEEE Computer Society Press 256 pages.

CHAPTER 14

Implementing Organizational Quality Initiatives

As databases become larger, the chances of errors goes up; our ability to deal with them goes down, because we haven't developed defense systems against anomalies and errors.
—Kamran Parsaye of IntelligenceWare, Inc.

One of the most useful ways of demonstrating the utility of the Enterprise Portal approach to your organization is to use it to resolve a data quality issue. This chapter illustrates how Enterprise Portal solutions can be used to address enterprise data quality problems. These situations offer a good place for organizations to begin practicing their Engineering Enterprise Portal (EEP) expertise because they are usually well bounded, very visible, and produce tangible, easily quantifiable results that will help organizations build the critical momentum required to achieve quantum improvements in their data quality. [Note: this chapter was co-authored by Wendy Wood.]

Data Quality Problem Characteristics

Unfortunately, organizations have been continually discovering that imperfect data often causes significant system-related problems and negatively affects operations. Addressing data quality problems costs organizations, consuming significant resources that could be applied otherwise. It also costs organizations two intangible costs: organizational trust and time. Quality problems should be found before damage is done ... like finding a virus before it can wipe out your hard drive. The cost of imperfect data, while perhaps difficult to measure directly, can be assessed using indirect indicators. Consider the following results reported over the years by [Knight 1992], [Wilson 1992], [Liepins 1989], [GAO 1976], [Laudon 1986], [Loebl 1990].

- Half of information executives in one survey reported losing valuable data with at least 20 indicating losses of $1 million;
- 70 percent of IS managers responding to an MIT survey reported their business processes had been interrupted at least once by imperfect data;
- imperfect databases costing organizations millions of dollars; and

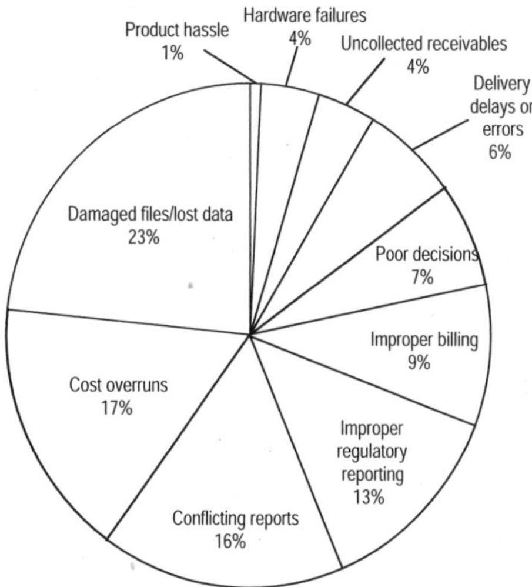

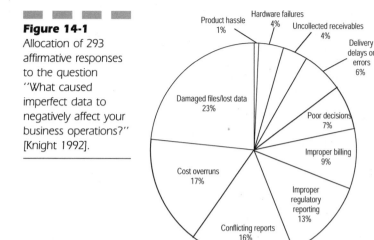

Figure 14-1
Allocation of 293 affirmative responses to the question "What caused imperfect data to negatively affect your business operations?" [Knight 1992].

- well-documented cases have questioned the credibility of entire classes of private sector/governmental data.

Sixty percent of IS managers at $20 million companies responded affirmatively to the question "Has corrupted, incorrect, or incomplete data ever negatively affected your business operations?" Various reported negative impacts of imperfect data are detailed in Figure 14-1.

The question then becomes "how does an organization approach the reengineering of data; correcting structural problems associated with task-oriented systems development and increasing the rigor of the organizational data quality methods?" Figure 14-2 presents the results of one investigation into how organizations have attempted to address data quality problems. It fails to show structure-oriented data quality method application [Wilson 1992].

Practice-Oriented Quality Problems

We illustrated in Chapter 9 that imperfect data can result from practice-oriented and structure-oriented reasons. Practice-oriented reasons stem from the failure to rigorously apply data quality methods (often when capturing and maintaining data). Examples of practice-oriented reasons are entry errors, incomplete data, and collection errors shown in Figure 14-3. Although these errors can be addressed by practice-oriented data

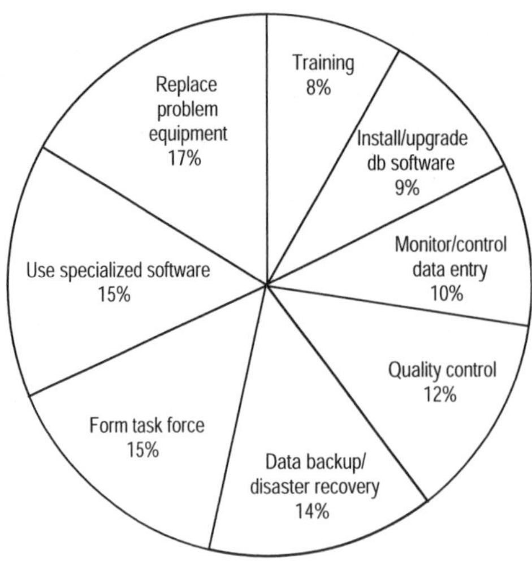

Figure 14-2 Allocation of responses, indicating steps that 258 organizations are taking to improve their data quality [Knight 1992].

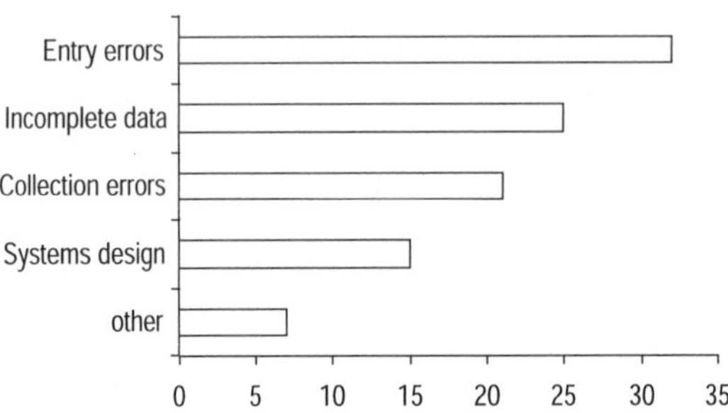

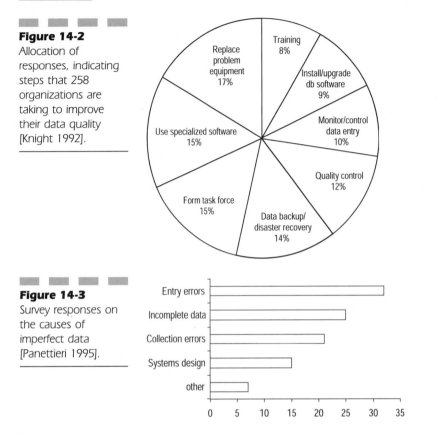

Figure 14-3 Survey responses on the causes of imperfect data [Panettieri 1995].

quality method application, methods are relatively few, they have been recently developed, and are not widely practiced.

Structure-Oriented Quality Problems

Structure-oriented problems are often caused by system developers focusing on task automation instead of adopting an organization-wide perspective and developing their systems to be a contributing component of the organizational information system infrastructure. Data definitions are similarly bound and not useful organization-wide, making data interchange more difficult for internal systems and external partners. Moreover, any data quality efforts are limited by task perspectives, decreasing their effectiveness beyond system boundaries. As data usage specifications are extended beyond the original task, requirements and designs are modified, resulting in brittle systems. This brittleness has made it difficult to implement data structure modifications and consistently apply data quality methods.

The question arises, if data quality problems are so pervasive and so dangerous, why haven't organizations taken a more proactive approach to data quality? The answers are relatively simple.

- *It is dangerous—they'll come after you!* Any data quality group effort started with the organization will immediately become the focal point of much activity. Unless adequately funded, data quality efforts are likely to be swamped as they do their job raising awareness of organizational data quality issues.
- *It is likely to be misunderstood.* As you attempt to begin to change the organizational data, the data quality effort will be the first one to be blamed as operational data problems appear and you may have to spend a lot of effort explaining why the problem predated your efforts to correct it.
- *You could make things worse.* It has been common for data quality efforts to make existing situations worse before improving them. An especially complex reconciliation is correcting keys; this is made particularly difficult when only business processes are available to fix them and the business process requires deactivating and reactivating. Another problem with using existing business processes is that notifications and workloads can increase dramatically.
- *Now you get to fix it.* Now that you have attention focused on these issues you must secure the resources required to address the problems discovered. As a side effect, these corrections have often resulted in quantum increases in certain business transactions that are certain to increase the popularity of the data quality efforts when they have been linked back to you.

It has been difficult to start these initiatives. They require support from upper management, in most cases requiring a metric-based justification. They require knowledgable people who can help the new initiative to understand the:

- business context of the data uses,
- rules used by the business that are applied to the data, and
- business processes that are based on these rules.

Obtaining all of these resources has been a challenge that few organizations have been able to reach. For the industry, data quality has been estimated to be a $4 billion problem annually. We will use an example in this chapter to illustrate a data quality project, based on a major telecommunication firm. As in the other examples, this organization has been fictionalized to prevent disclosure of sensitive company details. We will refer to the company as a business unit of XYZ Corporation, called: "XYZ Telecom."

Data Quality Project Example

In our example, XYZ Telecom had identified a major data quality problem associated with assignment of telephone numbers to customers—telephone number data. Opening up new sets of telephone numbers incurs a fixed cost involving tens of thousands of dollars owing to the costs of reprogramming the infrastructure, and the switching network, to accommodate the new prefixes. At a University where one of your authors was affiliated, the prefix was 828 (in order to spell out the university initials "VCU"). When the University had used all ten thousand telephone numbers within the 828 set, it became necessary to add another set. Based on the initial plan, the local telephone provider began issuing numbers prefixed with 827.

The University had probably not used all ten thousand numbers. Of those that it had used, many had been retired or were otherwise no longer in service. But the organization was unable to tell which numbers were in use, and which were not in use. Issuing a currently used number to a new subscriber would disrupt existing services to the University. It would also subject XYZ Telecom to penalties that could approach the cost of opening up a new prefix series. XYZ Telecom wanted to postpone incurring the cost of setting up the new prefix as long as possible, but in the absence of good data on number usage it seemed to have no other choice.

Obviously, the focus of this example was not confined just to the problem of managing the University telephone numbers, but was widespread across all aspects of the business. The total cost of adding a new set of numbers normally cost XYZ approximately $2.50 for each of the ten thousand new numbers that would then become available to assign to new customers. As in any capacity planning exercise, an organizational goal would be to postpone the expansion to the 827 numbers as long as possible. The application of data quality methods to the existing data enabled recovery of unused numbers at a cost of 50 cents each; this resulted in the recovery of almost 300,000 telephone numbers from 23 XYZ Telecom offices. We will discuss this data quality example in the rest of this chapter.

Data Quality Context Understanding

More and more, organizations are establishing data quality programs as cost centers. That is, the data quality initiative must continually prove that it is saving the organization more than it is costing it. This is a relatively good model to follow. As with any startup initiative, it is important to demonstrate tangible benefits early. It is important to tackle a well-bounded, very visible problem first that enables you to produce easily quantifiable results. Consequently, it is important to identify what are the major classes of organizational data quality problems and their relative impact on the organization. The three-pronged approach to data quality developed for XYZ Telecom can be described as follows and is illustrated more completely in Figure 14-4.

The key to the approach in Figure 14-4 is careful integration of three components, combined with Enterprise Portal deployment as we will see in Chapter 15. *Quality methods* include any number of techniques based on the idea of building quality into the capture and maintenance of data. These include continuous data improvement, data baselining, statistical data control, and application of the cost of quality models. *Technologies* that are useful to data quality improvement include logic and logic programming, reusability, relational and statistical programming languages, relational database, and client/server technologies. *Data analysis* requires selection and application of one or more of data analysis techniques, such as those listed in Figure 14-4. Different categories of analysis tools exist.

Process Analysis

Process analysis tools assist in identifying problems with processes such as manufacturing, shipping or order fulfillment. Process analysis tools highlight areas of poor performance and assist in identifying the causes of problems.

Figure 14-4 Analysis, quality, and technology-driven approach to addressing data quality problems with Enterprise Portal solutions.

Quality
Focus on the data itself

Apply quality improvements *continuously* and *systematically*
Empower the data domain expert

Data Analysis
Formatting data and metadata for accessibility and understanding

Technology
Take full advantage of new technologies, integrating them with the existing solution set mix

Enterprise Portal Delivery
Deliver the newly cleaned up data using EP technologies

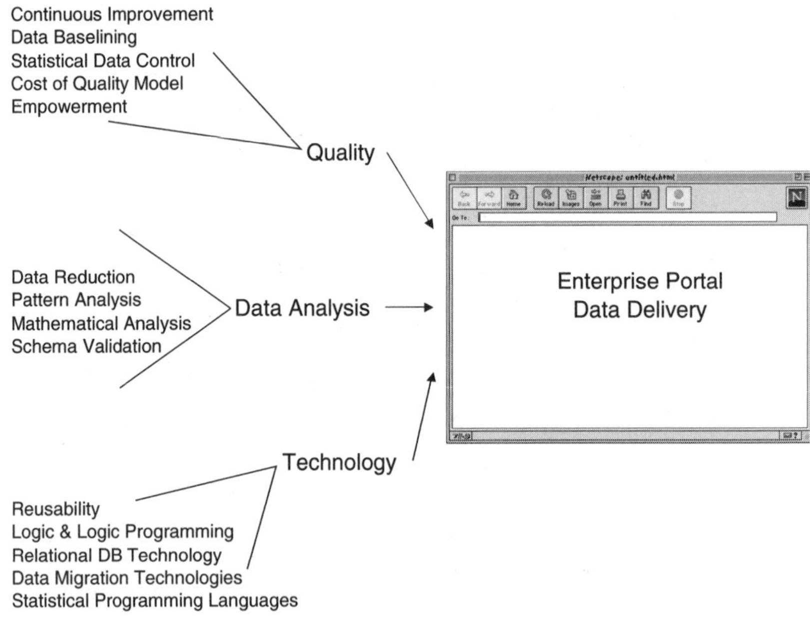

Aggregation Analysis

Aggregation analysis tools examine hierarchical or multidimensional aggregations of data in ways that are useful for summarizing information at different levels of detail for reporting budget, sales, or inventory data such that items of interest can usually be broken down into more detail.

Data Mining

Data mining tools search for previously unknown patterns in data in order to reveal useful facts about the data that would be hard to discover any other way using automatic or manual search techniques.

Query

General purpose query and reporting tools aim to put simple graphical interfaces onto the front end of databases in order to simplify the task of formulating queries and present results in graphical formats. Query tools are good for ad-hoc analysis, but do not provide the performance needed to tackle large process analysis and aggregation analysis problems.

General Purpose

General purpose tools such as databases, spreadsheets, and statistics packages and the ever popular Office suites can be configured to perform high-level preliminary analyses for a wide variety of problems. General purpose tools tend to be difficult to configure and slow when performing analysis on large data sets.

OLAP

Online analytical processing (OLAP) is a recent term coined by Dr. Codd. The term has been applied to a wide variety of analysis tools, data warehouse products and multidimensional databases.

Multidimensional databases

Multidimensional databases aggregate data into data structures well suited for rapid response to queries requesting summary data—for example, requesting total sales, broken down by country. Unfortunately, there are currently no standards defining access to the hypercube-based data structures used by multidimensional databases.

GIS

Geographic information systems (GIS) are used to analyze geographical information—displaying sales volumes on a map, along with census data.

The next section will describe one promising new technology—semi-automated data profiling and mapping—to illustrate the tools that will become more available to data quality analysts. Peter Phaal [1999] maintains a Web page with a listing of various data analysis tools. The brief definitions that are listed above Figure 14-4 were extracted from his listings.

The key to using data analysis tools is to understand the nature of the required analysis, select the correct tool or toolset, and correctly apply the analysis method(s). As depicted in Figure 14-5, this process begins with an examination of the raw data.

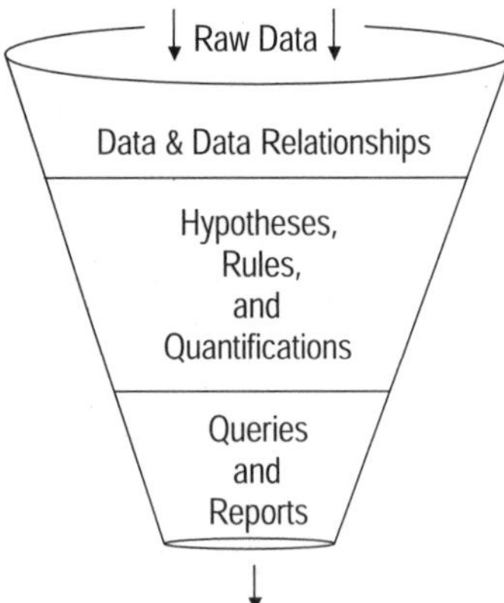

Figure 14-5 Data quality problem determination process.

This initial superficial examination of the raw data is carried out to discern gross understanding of the data and data relationships. As the understanding becomes clearer, hypotheses, rules, and other quantification about the data can be formulated. The analysis then shifts to verify these using a series of queries, reports, etc. A data quality problem cause is formulated as these are proven or disproved, as shown in Figure 14-6.

Building Quality into Data

The process of applying data quality consists of three closely related processes:

- *Data Analysis*—analyzing, then documenting the quality of the source data and testing the integrity of extracted data at each stage of the development process.
- *Data Monitoring*—auditing and monitoring data quality and integrity at each data hand-off in the data warehouse workflow.
- *Data Resolution*—analyzing, reconciling, and resolving data discrepancies between multiple sources.

When people speak about data quality, most often they refer to the *data reconciliation* component of data quality—also known as *data synchronization*, or *data resolution*. Data resolution is often required because

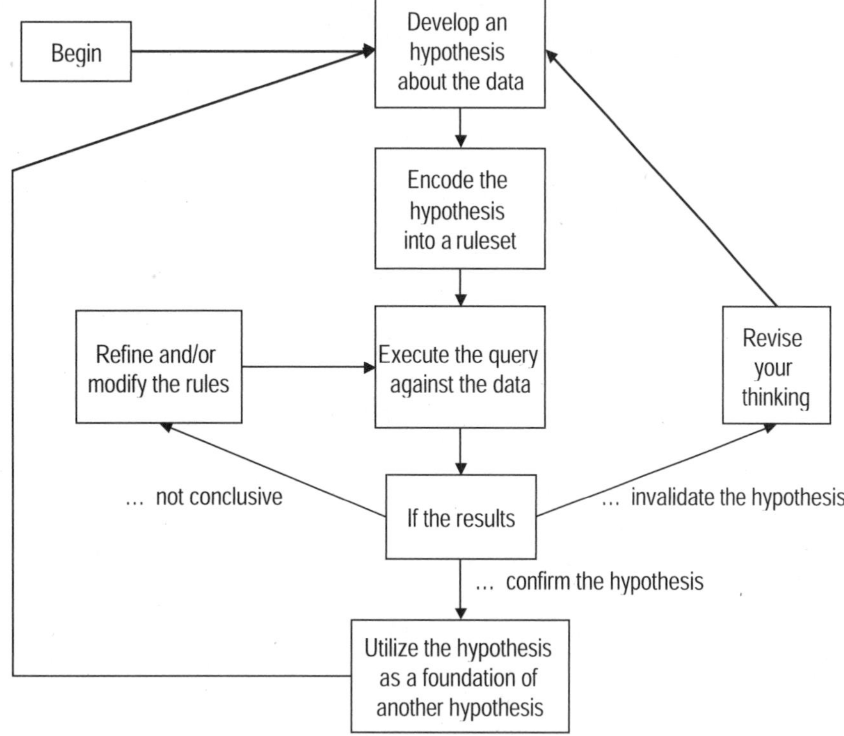

Figure 14-6 Iterative approach to data analysis.

source data from multiple systems cannot be merged correctly or the data may need additional information or transformation for use in Enterprise Portals.

Advanced Technologies—Data Profiling and Mapping

One of the most promising tools available to XYZ Telecom for the data quality project example enabled XYZ analysts to perform data profiling and mapping in a semi-automated fashion. The tool used was Migration Architect from Evoke Software. Full information about this product is available from the www.evokesoft.com Web site. While this tool can also be applied to many of the other data and metadata engineering tasks described in this book, we will confine our discussion to its application in the data quality environment—since its use here is probably the least understood. Other applications will then become obvious. Please note that the discussion focuses on just a portion of the tool functionality.

Of course, an alternative to using an automated tool is manual profiling. Manual profiling is a time-consuming, labor-intensive, error-prone operation that locates the documentation—if it exists—then attempts to understand it, and determine whether the structure of the data matches the stated documentation. It involves getting the user community mobilized to assist in the process, coordinating among the participating departments, and training participants in solution-development methodologies. With all of this effort often required, it is easy to see why the process of understanding legacy data typically consumes 50 percent of data quality effort initiatives. Put another way, $500,000 of a $1 million data quality project can be spent evaluating, validating, and cross-checking the data. Another 20 percent is then spent correcting the data problems that are found, with the remaining 30 percent in implementing the correction.

However, the semi-automated approach allows analysts to be vastly more productive—by examining and inferring the true data structures directly from the data. The toolkit-based approach ensures quick, accurate, verifiable results, dramatically reducing project risk and cost, and accelerating project completion. Figure 14-7 illustrates the XYZ Telecom use of the tool to access organizational data stored in different data stores.

The data analysts of XYZ Telecom accomplished much of the analysis above in an integrated environment. Data analysts are able to examine and understand the content and structure of the legacy data sources. Once understood, the data source transformation can be specified, the source of data pollution and abnormalities identified, and the individual data items corrected. Users then must verify all results through interactive sessions. In a data quality context, the environment is used to support hypothesis generation and validation through *Data Profiling* and *Data Mapping.*

Data Profiling

Data profiling is accomplished using three sequential steps, with each step building on the information produced in the previous steps. The goal of data profiling is to discover the true nature of the data structures using advanced inference analysis. The software applies a complex series

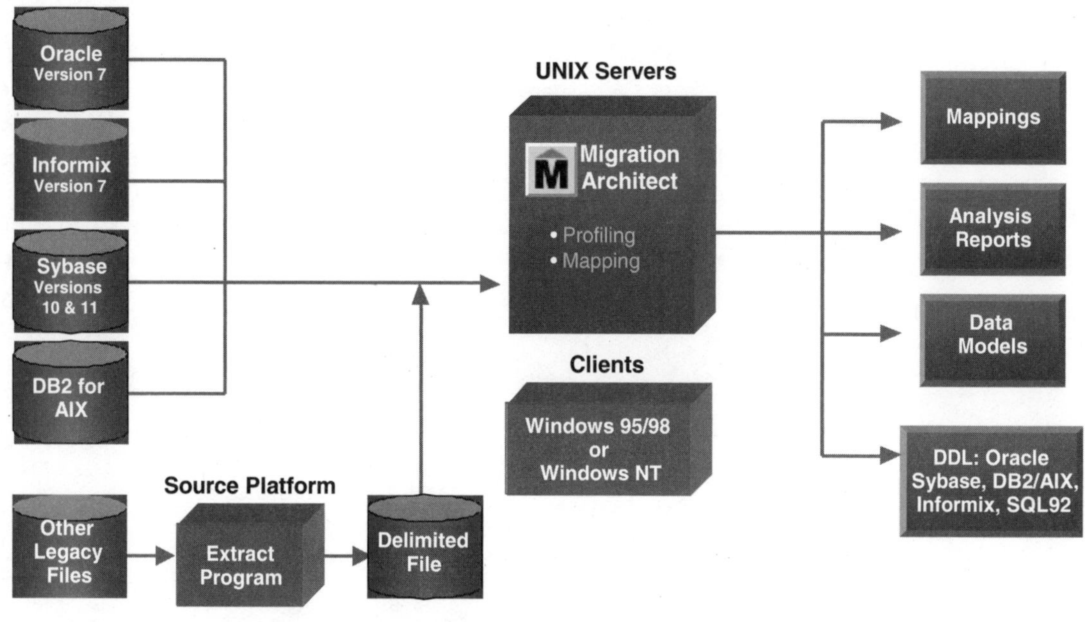

Figure 14-7
Use of the toolkit in a multi-use, multipurpose environment.

of algorithms to automatically discover and infer critical information about data from disparate data sources. This information is provided to analysts as they iteratively build their understanding of the actual data source.

The three steps correspond to three dimensions: down columns (*Column Profiling*); across rows (*Dependency Profiling*); across tables (*Redundancy Profiling*)—providing the analysts with a thorough understanding of data content, structure, quality, and integrity. Arranging the data profiling procedures in this fashion increases the effectiveness of determining structural associations within legacy data. Each step is described below in relation to the XYZ Telecom example.

Column Profiling

The data analysts examine each data column's data values using the toolkit software. It provides detailed information describing the characteristics of each column: the data type and size; range of values; and the

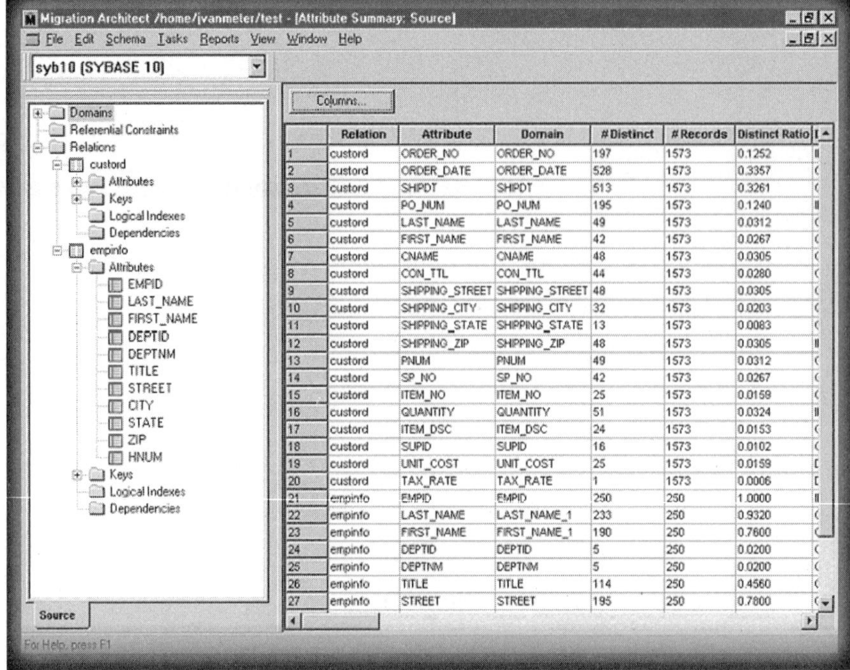

	Relation	Attribute	Domain	# Distinct	# Records	Distinct Ratio
1	custord	ORDER_NO	ORDER_NO	197	1573	0.1252
2	custord	ORDER_DATE	ORDER_DATE	528	1573	0.3357
3	custord	SHIPDT	SHIPDT	513	1573	0.3261
4	custord	PO_NUM	PO_NUM	195	1573	0.1240
5	custord	LAST_NAME	LAST_NAME	49	1573	0.0312
6	custord	FIRST_NAME	FIRST_NAME	42	1573	0.0267
7	custord	CNAME	CNAME	48	1573	0.0305
8	custord	CON_TTL	CON_TTL	44	1573	0.0280
9	custord	SHIPPING_STREET	SHIPPING_STREET	48	1573	0.0305
10	custord	SHIPPING_CITY	SHIPPING_CITY	32	1573	0.0203
11	custord	SHIPPING_STATE	SHIPPING_STATE	13	1573	0.0083
12	custord	SHIPPING_ZIP	SHIPPING_ZIP	48	1573	0.0305
13	custord	PNUM	PNUM	49	1573	0.0312
14	custord	SP_NO	SP_NO	42	1573	0.0267
15	custord	ITEM_NO	ITEM_NO	25	1573	0.0159
16	custord	QUANTITY	QUANTITY	51	1573	0.0324
17	custord	ITEM_DSC	ITEM_DSC	24	1573	0.0153
18	custord	SUPID	SUPID	16	1573	0.0102
19	custord	UNIT_COST	UNIT_COST	25	1573	0.0159
20	custord	TAX_RATE	TAX_RATE	1	1573	0.0006
21	empinfo	EMPID	EMPID	250	250	1.0000
22	empinfo	LAST_NAME	LAST_NAME_1	233	250	0.9320
23	empinfo	FIRST_NAME	FIRST_NAME_1	190	250	0.7600
24	empinfo	DEPTID	DEPTID	5	250	0.0200
25	empinfo	DEPTNM	DEPTNM	5	250	0.0200
26	empinfo	TITLE	TITLE	114	250	0.4560
27	empinfo	STREET	STREET	195	250	0.7800

Figure 14-8 Column Range Profiling. The # Distinct column, compared with the # Records column, can often indicate the presence of anomalies in the actual data values.

frequency of occurrences for each discrete value. The resulting understanding is of the "true" as opposed to the documented metadata values with automated attribute reporting. In this manner the data analysts can positively verify data conformity requirements and locate unused attributes, shown in Figures 14-8–14-10.

Figure 14-8 displays the data content of each attribute in the right-hand pane, for those relations (tables) selected in the explorer-like left-hand navigation pane. For example, we see for each attribute of the CUSTORD and EMPINFO tables the number of distinct values and the number of records that exist. Unexpected differences between the number of distinct values displayed and the corresponding number of records for an attribute can sometimes indicate the presence of possible data anomalies, such as invalid data values, or instead missing or corrupted values.

Figure 14-9 shows the result of actual data analysis for each listed attribute. The documented data type (specified in the relevant DBMS catalog) for each attribute is used to examine the actual data in that column across all records. Differences are noted in the relevant *Inferred Data Type* column and the *Data Type Flag* for each source

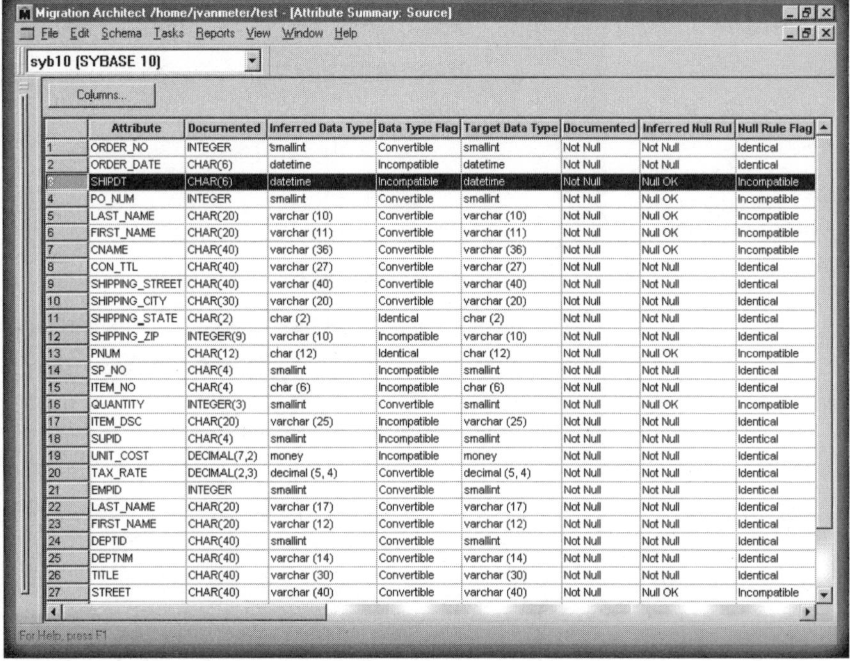

	Attribute	Documented	Inferred Data Type	Data Type Flag	Target Data Type	Documented	Inferred Null Rul	Null Rule Flag
1	ORDER_NO	INTEGER	smallint	Convertible	smallint	Not Null	Not Null	Identical
2	ORDER_DATE	CHAR(6)	datetime	Incompatible	datetime	Not Null	Not Null	Identical
3	SHIPDT	CHAR(6)	datetime	Incompatible	datetime	Not Null	Null OK	Incompatible
4	PO_NUM	INTEGER	smallint	Convertible	smallint	Not Null	Null OK	Incompatible
5	LAST_NAME	CHAR(20)	varchar (10)	Convertible	varchar (10)	Not Null	Null OK	Incompatible
6	FIRST_NAME	CHAR(20)	varchar (11)	Convertible	varchar (11)	Not Null	Null OK	Incompatible
7	CNAME	CHAR(40)	varchar (36)	Convertible	varchar (36)	Not Null	Null OK	Incompatible
8	CON_TTL	CHAR(40)	varchar (27)	Convertible	varchar (27)	Not Null	Not Null	Identical
9	SHIPPING_STREET	CHAR(40)	varchar (40)	Convertible	varchar (40)	Not Null	Not Null	Identical
10	SHIPPING_CITY	CHAR(30)	varchar (20)	Convertible	varchar (20)	Not Null	Not Null	Identical
11	SHIPPING_STATE	CHAR(2)	char (2)	Identical	char (2)	Not Null	Not Null	Identical
12	SHIPPING_ZIP	INTEGER(9)	varchar (10)	Incompatible	varchar (10)	Not Null	Not Null	Identical
13	PNUM	CHAR(12)	char (12)	Identical	char (12)	Not Null	Null OK	Incompatible
14	SP_NO	CHAR(4)	smallint	Incompatible	smallint	Not Null	Not Null	Identical
15	ITEM_NO	CHAR(4)	char (6)	Incompatible	char (6)	Not Null	Not Null	Identical
16	QUANTITY	INTEGER(3)	smallint	Convertible	smallint	Not Null	Null OK	Incompatible
17	ITEM_DSC	CHAR(20)	varchar (25)	Incompatible	varchar (25)	Not Null	Not Null	Identical
18	SUPID	CHAR(4)	smallint	Incompatible	smallint	Not Null	Not Null	Identical
19	UNIT_COST	DECIMAL(7,2)	money	Incompatible	money	Not Null	Not Null	Identical
20	TAX_RATE	DECIMAL(2,3)	decimal (5, 4)	Convertible	decimal (5, 4)	Not Null	Not Null	Identical
21	EMPID	INTEGER	smallint	Convertible	smallint	Not Null	Not Null	Identical
22	LAST_NAME	CHAR(20)	varchar (17)	Convertible	varchar (17)	Not Null	Not Null	Identical
23	FIRST_NAME	CHAR(20)	varchar (12)	Convertible	varchar (12)	Not Null	Not Null	Identical
24	DEPTID	CHAR(40)	smallint	Convertible	smallint	Not Null	Not Null	Identical
25	DEPTNM	CHAR(40)	varchar (14)	Convertible	varchar (14)	Not Null	Not Null	Identical
26	TITLE	CHAR(40)	varchar (30)	Convertible	varchar (30)	Not Null	Not Null	Identical
27	STREET	CHAR(40)	varchar (40)	Convertible	varchar (40)	Not Null	Null OK	Incompatible

Figure 14-9 Column Data Type Profiling. Notice differences between the *Documented* and *Inferred* Data Type and Null Rule columns, plus the *Data Type Flag* and *Null Rule Flag* columns.

data attribute, as well as its ability to be converted to the specified *Target Data Type* for that attribute. The *Documented Null Rule* and *Inferred Null Rule* columns indicate differences in the expected and actual *Null* values, with a summary in the *Null Rule Flag* column.

A summary of the analysis in Figures 14-8 and 14-9 is then displayed in Figure 14-10. Each attribute can be selected in turn, for examination in the top Attribute Summary Window. Figure 14-10 shows that HNUM is selected. The Domain Detail Window at the bottom then displays actual values that exist for that selected attribute, and the number of rows containing each value (frequency). These are apparently home phone numbers; each phone number value occurs 2 or 3 times of the 234 distinct values in 250 records.

Dependency Profiling

During dependency profiling, the XYZ analysts used the toolkit to investigate, hypothesize, and confirm attribute connections with other attributes within the same table, as shown in Figures 14-11 and 14-12 for the XYZ Telecom project. Information uncovered helps them to document

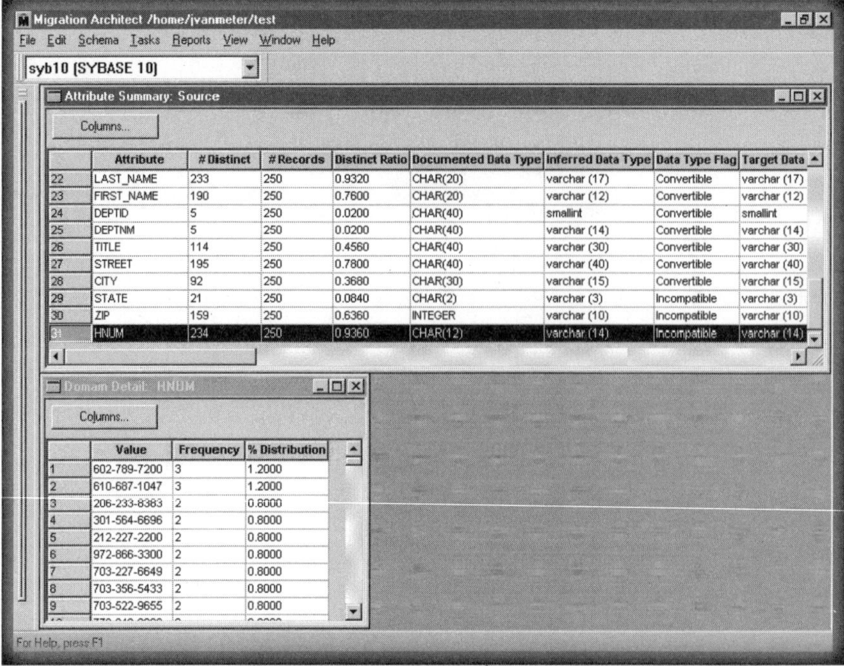

Figure 14-10 Column Profiling Summary. Notice the highlighted row in the top Attribute Summary Window, with the actual data values that exist for that attribute in the bottom Domain Detail Window.

"true" within-table commonalities, working and inactive dependencies, and principal keys—increasing still further their understanding of the XYZ legacy data. The profiling also exposes structural inconsistencies across rows because it reveals the actual source data structures and permits the description of the factual data schematic.

As shown in Figure 14-11, the toolkit analyzes the various columns selected by the data quality analyst. Based on its algorithmic inference capabilities, in an automated fashion it "discovers" relationships—proposing several functional dependencies within the table. Figure 14-12 shows how the analyst has confirmed several of the relationships and promoted the inferred relationships to formal relationships.

Redundancy Profiling

The XYZ analysts used redundancy profiling to inspect data properties across all data sources. These are placed side by side for comparison. Suspected repetitious or overlapping columns can be identified as well as potential homonym and synonym problems. Perhaps most valuably, the analysis can quickly locate integration points by finding columns

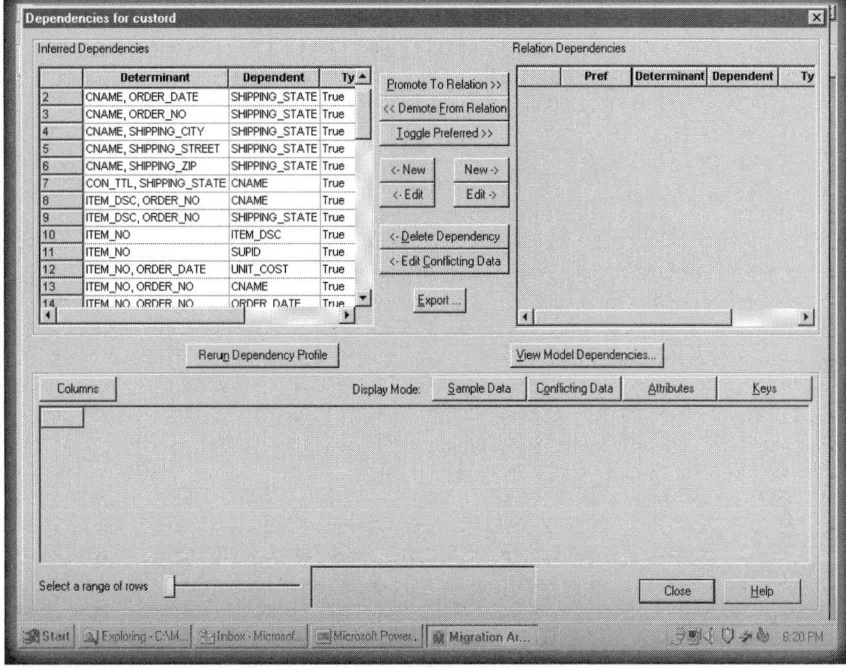

Figure 14-11 Dependency Profiling. Automated "discovery" of potential dependencies between columns.

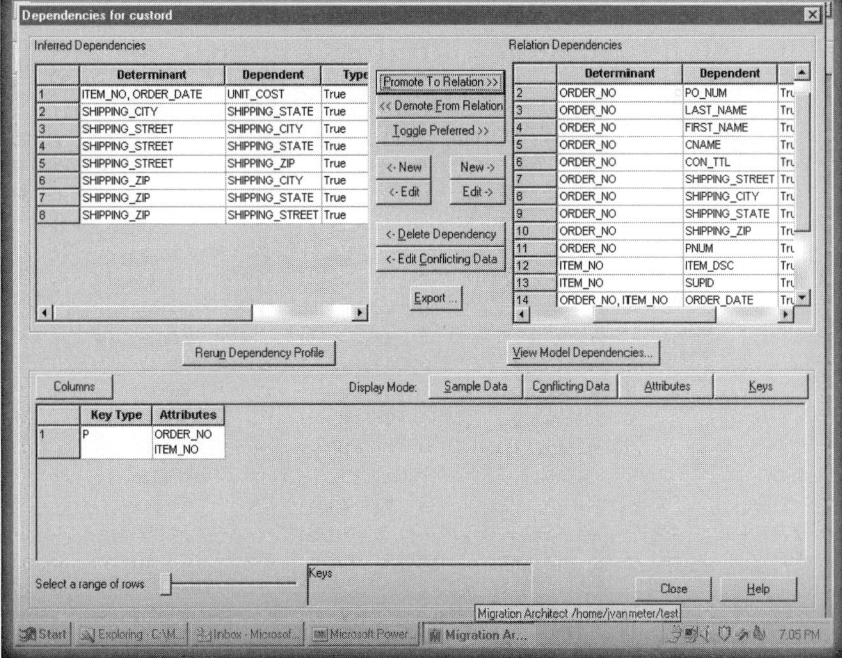

Figure 14-12 Dependency Profiling. Analyst acceptance of proposed dependencies between columns.

with common value sets. This can lead to decisions as to which columns are dependent on other colums and which are used to link data items across tables, as in Figure 14-13.

Figure 14-13 allows the user to merge domains. It presents the user with domains that are candidates for merging and information to assist their decision. For a given row, the first column represents the estimated percentage of overlap of domain values between the values associated with Domain 1 and the values associated with Domain 2. In other words, of the combined values for *Shipping_State* and *State*, 70 percent of them exist in both files. The amount of programming and documentation that would be required to determine and reflect this for all the domains across sets of files is considerable—however, the toolkit makes the information very accessible.

Figure 14-14 illustrates the Domain Comparison Detail showing frequencies for the same values across two different tables. The first two columns give values and frequency information for *custord.SUPID.* The next two columns give values and frequency information for *empinfo.EMPID*. From the sample shown it is clear that *custord* is a transaction file and *empinfo* is a reference file with a many-to-one relationship between the two files.

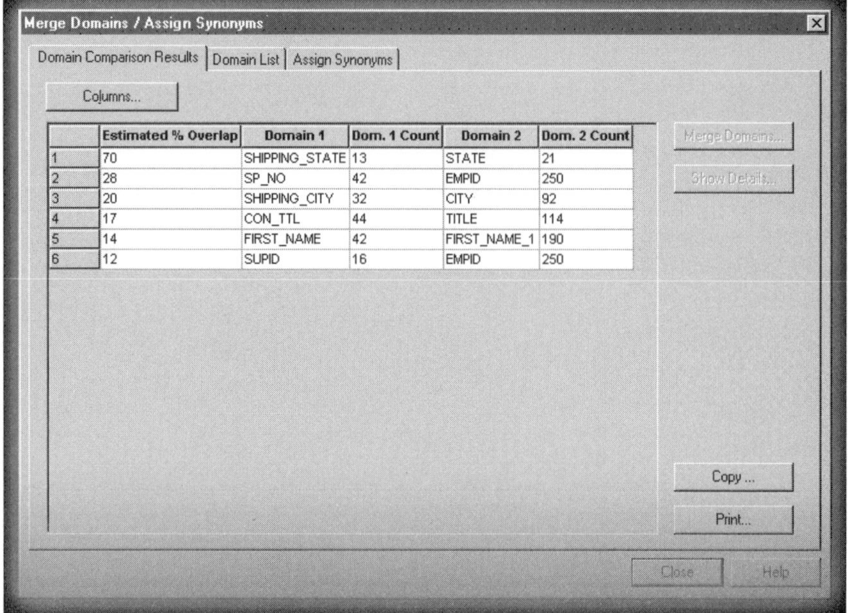

	Estimated % Overlap	Domain 1	Dom. 1 Count	Domain 2	Dom. 2 Count
1	70	SHIPPING_STATE	13	STATE	21
2	28	SP_NO	42	EMPID	250
3	20	SHIPPING_CITY	32	CITY	92
4	17	CON_TTL	44	TITLE	114
5	14	FIRST_NAME	42	FIRST_NAME_1	190
6	12	SUPID	16	EMPID	250

Figure 14-13 Redundancy Profiling. Notice domain counts for potential key joins.

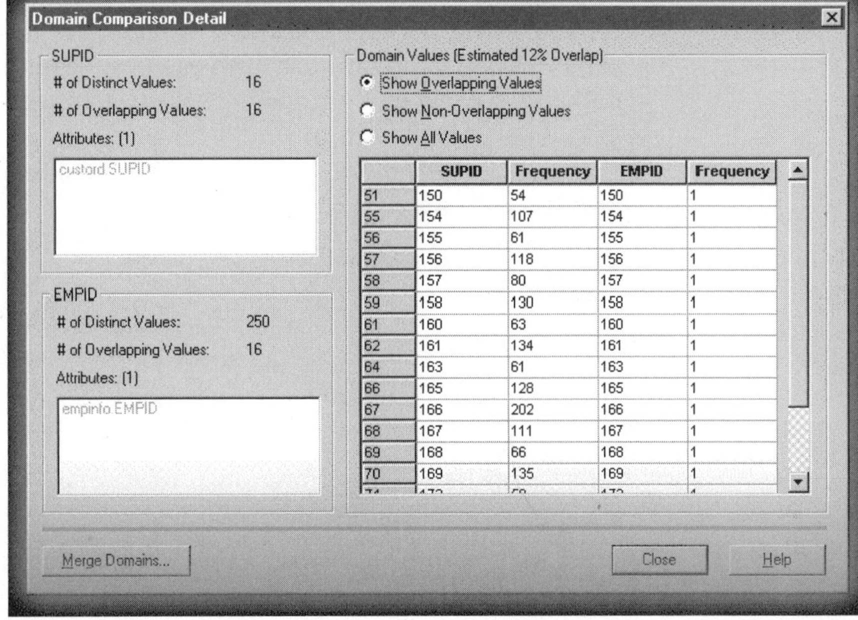

Figure 14-14 Redundancy Profiling. Notice the actual domain values for use in key joins.

Data Mapping

Building on the information composite produced from the Data Profiling series of steps, the toolkit incorporates another three-step sequence (Data Mapping). This modifies the data archetype, broadening the extent of analysis for: *normalization; model enhancement;* and *transformation mapping*.

Normalization

The Normalization process formulates a systematic relational model founded on data profiled from previous stages. This establishes whether the design findings are maintained by the data, reducing possible project delinquency in the execution period.

Model Enhancement

Using the model enhancement capabilities, users can adjust the normalized model to sustain application improvements by adding data structures to uphold new requirements, or by adding indexes and denormalizing the structures to enhance performance. This also adds flexibility to the model to tolerate analyst editing, and to ensure that adjustments and additions are adequately maintained. After the enhancement, the software presents the Data Definition Language (DDL) in a relevant DBMS dialect such as Oracle, Informix, Sybase, or DB2.

Transformation Mapping

Transformation Mapping features outline the route from data source to data objective, and plots a course for later data conversion cycles. The toolkit develops transformation charts that display the kinship between columns in the source files and tables in the updated model. This occurs after data model alterations are completed. Each level of automated profiling and mapping analysis requires information gathered from all the preceding levels to create a precise, usable system summary that is supported entirely by the data. This step reveals needed information for developers to design conversion routines that move data from the original database to the target database. It determines processing necessary for subsequent data movement, extraction, scrubbing, transformation, and loading. Using information developed from all five previous steps, the analyst can build transformation maps of attributes from source to target as shown in Figure 14-15.

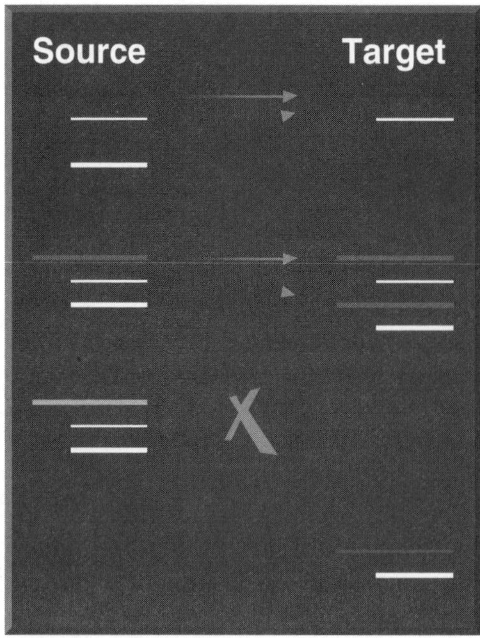

Figure 14-15 Transformation Mapping using Migration Architect [Evoke Software].

Results: Enterprise Portal Solutions to Data Quality Problems

Following this analysis of XYZ Telecom data using Migration Architect, the XYZ data quality group provided access to all of the information on the relative population of various XYZ data warehouse tables, for deployment by an Enterprise Portal in Chapter 15.

Figure 14-16 shows a tabular presentation of these results, while Figure 14-17 illustrates a graphical example. Presentation of these results brought an ovation for the data quality analysts from the Data Warehouse Board of Directors of XYZ Telecom. More importantly, the analysis identified more than 4.7 billion empty bytes in just three data warehouse tables—again reducing the need to upgrade company infrastructure capacity—and made a strong case for normalization of the data. (Note: an important foundation of data quality is to use meaningful data names, but note that these attribute names have been purposefully changed for confidentiality.)

In order to ensure adequate sampling, "population" counts were run on all the tables to be analyzed. These counts ended up having a value of their own as they pointed out that some tables were so unnormalized that significant amounts of space were being wasted. This is a concern to a data warehouse that deals in large volumes for the enterprise data that it already supports, and has much more waiting "in the wings" to be included in the warehouse. A decision was made to produce this analysis for all the tables in the data warehouse to support better space utilization. The results were displayed graphically in Figure 14-17.

Other reported accomplishments after one year of toolkit use by XYZ Telecom include:

- Use of the toolkit to preserve multi-million dollar discounts received from the US Postal Service for providing garbage-free inputs to their systems. That is, the mailings that originate from the organization are sorted according to USPS specifications and are error free.
- The toolkit has been used to provide the only accurate measurable views of how effectively certain processes work.
- An important accomplishment concerned matching the skills required to support the toolkit with the skills of one of the XYZ analysts. The knowledge of this analyst had great benefit for both the individual and the process.

ATTRIBUTENAME	populated row	total table rows	% populated	unpopulated rows	% unpopulated
TLAI	19411389	19411760	0.99998	371	0.00002
LPOD	19395288	19411760	0.99915	16472	0.00085
LPON	19395287	19411760	0.99915	16473	0.00085
CC_STAT	19356073	19411760	0.99713	55687	0.00287
ISD	19316716	19411760	0.9951	95044	0.0049
ICSD	18743765	19411760	0.96559	667995	0.03441
FCC	17428033	19411760	0.89781	1983727	0.10219
FSC	17428033	19411760	0.89781	1983727	0.10219
MCA	17122708	19411760	0.88208	2289052	0.11792
MCB	17122708	19411760	0.88208	2289052	0.11792
MCC	17122708	19411760	0.88208	2289052	0.11792
MCD	17122708	19411760	0.88208	2289052	0.11792
CTOT	15476866	19411760	0.79729	3934894	0.20271
RLS	13906921	19411760	0.71642	5504839	0.28358
CCLB	13899841	19411760	0.71605	5511919	0.28395
CAA	13746558	19411760	0.70816	5665202	0.29184
EUAC	12434941	19411760	0.64059	6976819	0.35941
CLS	11148418	19411760	0.57431	8263342	0.42569
SLINES	11060647	19411760	0.56979	8351113	0.43021
LSLC	10989398	19411760	0.56612	8422362	0.43388
EN_IND	3114450	19411760	0.16044	16297310	0.83956
CC2_STAT	1935771	19411760	0.09972	17475989	0.90028
ALC	1130691	19411760	0.05825	18281069	0.94175
RI	1130681	19411760	0.05825	18281079	0.94175
IBNG	1120435	19411760	0.05772	18291325	0.94228
BAI	895721	19411760	0.04614	18516039	0.95386
BCI	539893	19411760	0.02781	18871867	0.97219
TAI	482158	19411760	0.02484	18929602	0.97516
FSI	369127	19411760	0.01902	19042633	0.98098
DHE	363919	19411760	0.01875	19047841	0.98125
DHS	363919	19411760	0.01875	19047841	0.98125
SA_IND	349515	19411760	0.01801	19062245	0.98199
CC_STAT	135582	19411760	0.00698	19276178	0.99302
LNPA	109664	19411760	0.00565	19302096	0.99435
LNXX	109664	19411760	0.00565	19302096	0.99435
C3PS_CT	77594	19411760	0.004	19334166	0.996
DLINES	42657	19411760	0.0022	19369103	0.9978
LST_CT	34093	19411760	0.00176	19377667	0.99824

Figure 14-16

Tabular presentation of table population statistics. This identifies the percentage of data populated in each column.

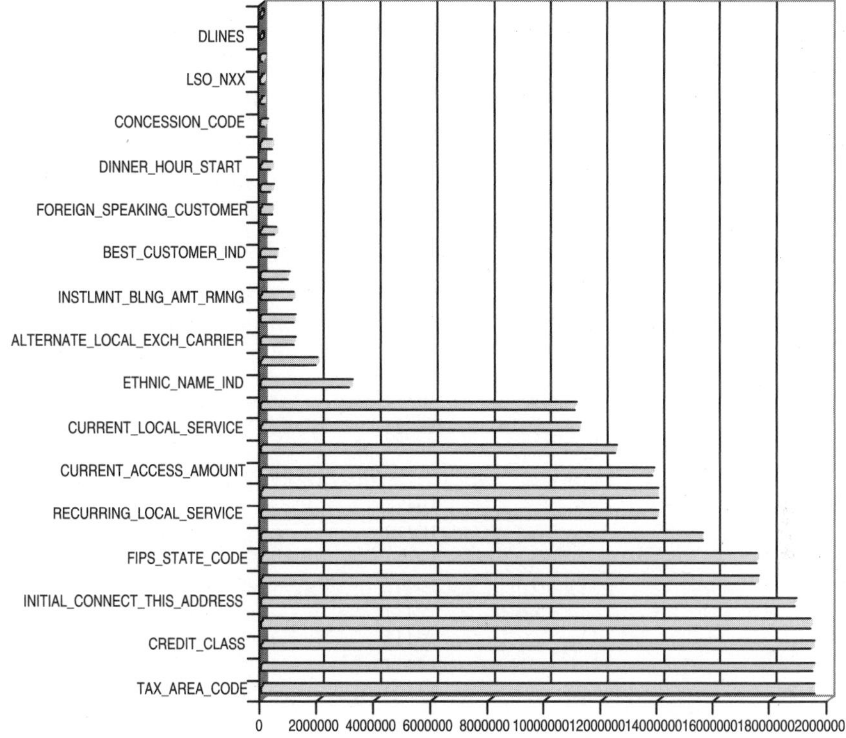

Figure 14-17 Graphical Presentation of Same Data. Lightly populated data columns are at top, heavily populated columns at bottom.

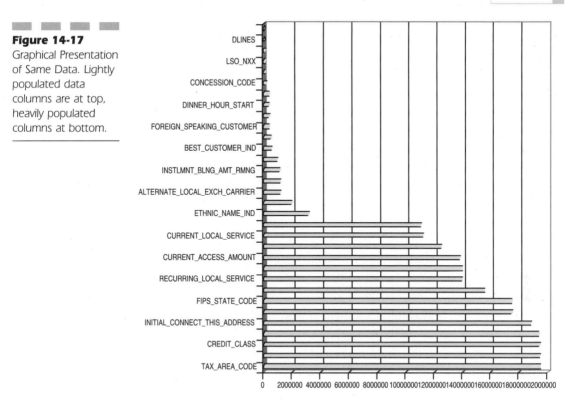

- Since installing the toolkit early in the year, hundreds of files have been processed by the domain profiling process. Many of the files have been taken through initial stages of normalization.

Before this project, data quality was assumed always to be perfect. These quality assumptions were often later found to be wrong. The analysts now have a tool they can use to assess actual data quality—by live analysis of relevant legacy data sources. Their decisions are now based on the *actual* data quality, rather than what the data quality *should be* in an ideal world. As the XYZ analysts now say: "there is no substitute for examining and analyzing the actual data itself."

XYZ management now understands that data quality exercises can in fact be a profitable venture for organizations. It can provide immediate, tangible benefits. Key is being able to articulate these benefits to management to gain approval to initiate data quality efforts and then rapidly deliver them. Now with high quality data, the resulting information can be used for deployment in Enterprise Portals in Chapter 15.

REFERENCES

Evoke Software Web site—http://www.evokesoft.com/

General Accounting Office (1976) Improvements Still needed in Federal Energy Data Collection, Analysis and Reporting, OSP7621; B178205, Washington, DC, June.

Knight, B. (1992) "The Data Pollution," *Computerworld*, September 28.

Laudon, K. (1986) "Data quality and due process in large interorganizational record systems," *Communications of the ACM* (January) 29(19): 411.

Liepins, G. (1989) "Sound data are a sound investment," *Quality Process*, September: 61–64.

Loebl, A. (1990) "Accuracy and Relevance and the Quality of Data," in (Liepins, G.E. and Uppuluri, V.R.R., eds) *Data Quality Control: Theory and Practices*, New York: Marcel Dekker, pp. 105–143.

Panettieri, J. (1995) "Security The good news," *Information Week*, Issue 555, 27 Nov., p. 32.

Phaal, P. (1999) maintains a Web page with a listing of various data analysis tools (Peter_Phaal@CQMInc.com) http://www.cqminc.com/analysis/analysis.htm

Wilson, L. (1992) "Devil in your data," *InformationWeek*, August 31, pp. 48–54.

Additional Reading

Aiken, P., Muntz, A. and Richards, R. (1994) "DoD Legacy Systems: Reverse Engineering Data Requirements," *Communications of the ACM* (May) 37(5): 2641.

Aiken, P., and Piper, P. (1995) "Estimating Data Reverse Engineering Projects," *Proceedings of the 5th annual Systems Reengineering Workshop* (Johns Hopkins University Applied Physics Laboratory Research Center Report RSI95001) February 79, 1995, Monterey CA, pp. 133–145.

Aiken, P. (1997) "Organizational Incentives for Data Reverse Engineering," scheduled to appear in the *IBM Systems Journal* 36(1).

Hossein Arsham "Statistical Data Analysis: Prove It with Data" http://ubmail.ubalt.edu/~harsham/stat-data/opre330.htm#rwisaq Home Page: http://ubmail.ubalt.edu/~harsham/index.html

Ballou, D. and Tayi, G. (1989) "Methodology fo allocating resources for Data Quality Enhancement," *Communications of the ACM* (March) 32(3): 319–329

Butler, S., Diskin, D., Howes, N. and Jordan, K. (1999) "Architectural Design of the Common Operating Environment for the Global Command and Control System," forthcoming in *IEEE Software*.

Constance, P. "DISA tries to save some of CIM as Pentagon kills off program," *Government Computer News* 12696.

Broussard, S. et al. (1994) *Data Quality Engineering Handbook*, Defense Logistics Agency, Alexandria, VA.

English, L. (1999) *Improving Data Warehouse and Business Information Quality*, New York, NY: John Wiley.

Fox, C., Levitin, A. and Redman, T. (1994) "The Notion of Data and Its Quality Dimensions," *Information Processing and Management*, 30(1): 919.

Enterprise Reengineering (1996) "Who's Talking Now: Cynthia Kendall on Reengineering the Defense Department," *Enterprise Reengineering* (March) 38.

Levitin, A. and Redman, T. (1993) "Models of Data (life) Cycle with applications to quality," *Information and Software Technology* (April) 35(3): 216–223.

Levitin, A. and Redman, T. (1995) "Quality Dimensions of Conceptual View," *Information Processing & Management* 31(1): 81–88.

Morey, R. (1982) "Estimating and Improving the quality of information in a MIS," *Communications of the ACM* (May) 25(5): 337–342.

Nguyen, B. (1993) *A Method for Implementing Data Administration: A Combat Command Model*, Office of the Deputy Assistant Secretary of Defense (Civilian Personnel) May.

O'Brien, J. (1993) *Management Information Systems: a managerial end user perspective*, Irwin.

O'Neill, E. and VizineGoetz, D. (1988) "Quality Control in Online Databases," *Annual Review of Information Science and Technology*, 23: 125–156.

Paige, Jr., E. (1995) "From the Cold War to the Global Information Age," *Defense Issues* 10(34) (Prepared remarks by Emmett Paige Jr., assistant secretary of defense for command, control, communications and intelligence, to the Catoctin Chapter of the Armed Forces Communications Electronics Association, Fort Ritchie, Md., Feb. 27, 1995).

Paige, Jr., E. (1996) "Six Emerging Trends in Information Management *Defense Issues* 11(16) (Address by Emmett Paige Jr., assistant secretary of defense for command, control, communications and intelligence, at the American Defense Preparedness Association's Information Management for the Warfighter Symposium, Vienna, Va., Feb. 29, 1996).

Redman, T. (1992) *Data Quality Managment and Technology*, Bantam Books.

Reingruber, M. and Gregory, W. (1994) *The Data Modeling Handbook: A best practice approach to building quality data models*, John Wiley & Sons, Inc.

Smith, M. (1994) *The DOD Enterprise Model: A White Paper*, Project Enterprise Office of the Director of Defense Information, January.

The Standish Group Report: Migrate Headaches, 1999.

Svanks, M. (1988) "Integrity analysis methods for automating data quality assurance," *Information and Software Technology* (December) 30(10): 595–605.

Tsichritzis, D. and Fochovsky, F. (1982) *Data Models*, Engelwood Cliffs, NJ: Prentice Hall.

Tufte, E. (1990) "Chartjunk and the Challenger," insert materials accompanying the text *Envisioning Information* Graphics Press, P. O. Box 430, Cheshire, CT 06410.

Yoon, Y. and Aiken, P. (1996) "An Evolving Concept of Data Quality," working paper in preparation for submission to the *Journal of Managment Information Systems* (May) 1996.

Evoke's Migration Architect: Advancing the Science of Data Migration, Kathleen Hendrick, Stephen D. Hendrick, IDC Bulletin #18318 - February 1999.

Acknowledgements

The author would like to acknowledge the excellent work done by Wendy Wood (Data Quality Manager, Paobell). Wendy provided much of the material for Chapter 14 and co-authored it with Peter Aiken.

CHAPTER 15

The Central Role of Enterprise Portals

The Web has opened up a whole new set of markets. A retailer can let its vendors look into its sales data. An HMO can open up a window for its insurers to look into their database. A bank can open up a window for its depositors to look at their account data. We're entering a transition zone in which data warehouses are changing from cost centers to profit centers.

—Michael Saylor, CEO—MicroStrategy

In Part 1 we covered Enterprise Portal Design. In Part 2 we addressed Enterprise Portal Development. We used the EEP methodology for Data Warehouses and Enterprise Portals. We introduced technologies for Enterprise Portal Deployment in Part 3 that offer great potential for the future.

We examined XML-related technologies in Chapter 11. We saw the potential in Chapter 12 of XML as a Business Rengineering technology. Chapter 13 described an integrated Business Reengineering and Systems Reengineering methodology that is used to build Enterprise Portals. Chapter 14 then focused on important aspects of quality.

This chapter discusses other XML applications for delivery by Enterprise Portals. It addresses "web farming" methods that are used with Internet and intranet technologies. It considers new deployment technologies and products to manage information from Data Warehouses and Enterprise Portals and disseminate it to interested users. It brings together methods and technologies used throughout the book. It concludes by describing the major role that Enterprise Portals will take in the enterprise of the future.

Typical XML Applications

Microsoft has published several innovative XML applications on its [XML Scenarios] Web site. We applaud their initiative in placing these application descriptions in the public domain. As at March 1999 their Web site included the following applications:

1. Integrated Maintenance and Ordering using XML
2. Automating Customer Service with XML
3. Creating Multi-Supplier System with XML
4. Improving Online Shopping with XML
5. Personal Investment Management Using XML
6. Interactive Frequent-Flyer Web Site using XML

7. Consumer Product Ratings Online with XML
8. Purchasing and Supplier Data Integration with XML
9. Time and Attendance: Integrating Data with XML

We discussed application 3 in Chapter 12. We will briefly examine some of the remaining applications in the following pages. We have included some of the information flow diagrams from the Microsoft [XML Scenarios] Web site. You can visit their Web site for further details. As we discuss these applications, see if you can identify a common trend emerging to indicate the direction businesses will take in the years ahead, as they grasp the opportunities for competitive advantage that are presented by XML, the Internet, and intranets and apply them to the evolution of Enterprise Portals.

Integrated Maintenance and Ordering

Airlines have a common business problem in maintaining their aircraft and other equipment. The high safety standards that they set for airline operations also point to similar high standards in their use of Information Technology. Yet the airline industry is no different from most other industries; their systems and databases have evolved over many years. Consequently they also struggle with non-integrated legacy systems and databases, and with the problems of redundant data and processes that we discussed in Chapter 12.

Most airlines therefore experience high maintenance costs due to non-integrated data and processes, together with a high manual workload. Many data resources exist as legacy files, relational databases, and supplier catalogs that have different formats, different metadata, and that may even operate on different platforms with dissimilar operating systems and DBMS products. They are non-integrated—one could almost say, disintegrated—systems.

Yet in this environment, in the event of aircraft or equipment malfunctions airline maintenance staff must identify the cause of a problem and its solution, and then access the airline's Inventory System for the necessary parts needed to correct the problem. When these parts are not in inventory, they must order new parts from suppliers. But this process is still manual for many airlines.

To reengineer the Maintenance and Ordering process, the Microsoft [XML Scenarios] Web site describes an XML application using Microsoft products and other third-party software tools. Refer to the Microsoft Web site for details of each of these products.

This application allows simultaneous access to all relevant data and to an automated ordering system from airline suppliers. XML is used to intelligently link various sources of reference data, suppliers' parts catalogs, and ordering processes. An XML database is used to integrate data from various documents and data sources. Purchase orders are sent to the selected supplier's Commerce system for parts ordering and execution, with the following benefits to the airline:

- Maintenance productivity is increased.
- Ordering is done on timely basis.
- Aircraft down times are reduced.

Figure 15-1 illustrates the information flow. Details about relevant parts may exist in supplier catalog formats, in Microsoft Word, or in Adobe Acrobat Portable Document Format (PDF) documents. These information sources are all converted to XML and stored in an XML database.

A browser is used to search the XML database for information about broken parts and the relevant corrective actions. All searches are made using XML metadata tags. The solution to a problem may require replacement parts, details of which are initially retrieved from the Inventory database using ODBC. If insufficient parts are in stock, an order is placed with the relevant supplier. A Purchase Order Form is sent from the browser to the supplier's Commerce Server to order the required parts. Figure 15-2 shows part of the XML used to implement this application.

The *Part Information* in Figure 15-2 describes each `<PART>`. XML tags identify the `<PARTLIST>`, with the part number `<PART-NUM>`, the `<PART-NAME>` and number of `<UNITS-PER-ASSEMBLY>`. The installation instructions `<INSTALL-INFO>` and `<SUPPLIER-NOTE>` provided by the supplier are included as documented notes, with additional `<AIRLINE-CAUTION>` notes that have been added by the airline.

The *Inventory Information* in Figure 15-2 indicates the current `<INVENTORY>` for the `<PART-NUM>` and `<PART-NAME>`. The `<LOCAL-INVENTORY>` indicates the `<AVAILABLE>` quantity and `<LOCATION>` of the specified part in the airline's warehouse. Each `<SUPPLIER>` of that part is identified by `<NAME>`. The `<COMMERCE-SERVER-URL>` of each supplier is provided as part of the XML data for that part.

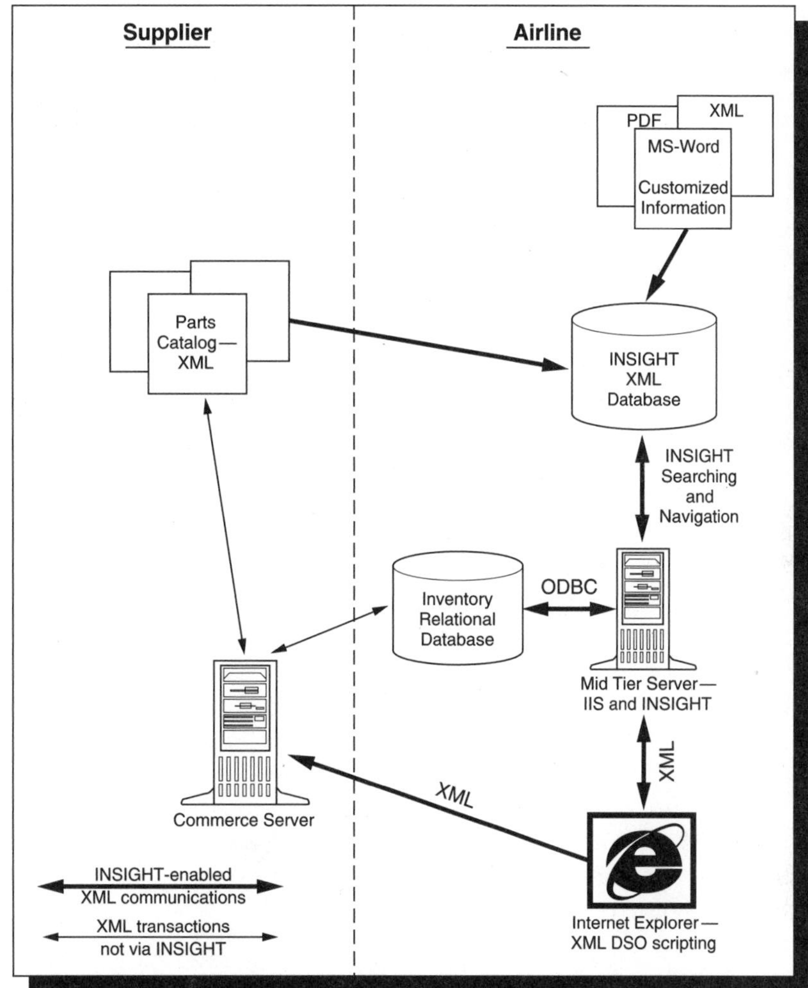

Figure 15-1 Integrated Maintenance and Ordering Information Flow. *Source*: [XML Scenarios] Web site.

If there is insufficient available quantity of a required part in the airline's Inventory Control System, an online browser Purchase Order Form can be completed by the airline maintenance technician, requesting parts from that supplier. This is sent directly to the supplier's Commerce Server to be processed by its Inventory Control System for automated replacement part ordering.

Significant benefits result from using XML for this application. XML achieves integration of unstructured data in Word or PDF documents with structured data from the airline's inventory database, and from supplier catalogs maintained by each separate supplier. An automated purchase order is sent directly to a selected supplier's Web site to replace

Figure 15-2 Maintenance and Inventory Details in XML. Source: [XML Scenarios] Web site.

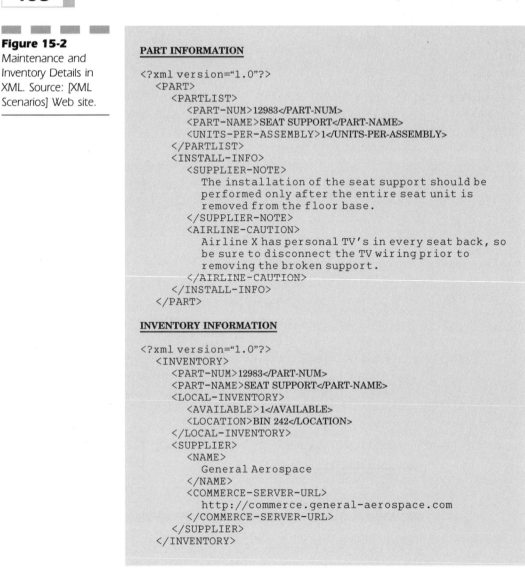

PART INFORMATION

```
<?xml version="1.0"?>
  <PART>
    <PARTLIST>
      <PART-NUM>12983</PART-NUM>
      <PART-NAME>SEAT SUPPORT</PART-NAME>
      <UNITS-PER-ASSEMBLY>1</UNITS-PER-ASSEMBLY>
    </PARTLIST>
    <INSTALL-INFO>
      <SUPPLIER-NOTE>
        The installation of the seat support should be
        performed only after the entire seat unit is
        removed from the floor base.
      </SUPPLIER-NOTE>
      <AIRLINE-CAUTION>
        Airline X has personal TV's in every seat back, so
        be sure to disconnect the TV wiring prior to
        removing the broken support.
      </AIRLINE-CAUTION>
    </INSTALL-INFO>
  </PART>
```

INVENTORY INFORMATION

```
<?xml version="1.0"?>
  <INVENTORY>
    <PART-NUM>12983</PART-NUM>
    <PART-NAME>SEAT SUPPORT</PART-NAME>
    <LOCAL-INVENTORY>
      <AVAILABLE>1</AVAILABLE>
      <LOCATION>BIN 242</LOCATION>
    </LOCAL-INVENTORY>
    <SUPPLIER>
      <NAME>
        General Aerospace
      </NAME>
      <COMMERCE-SERVER-URL>
        http://commerce.general-aerospace.com
      </COMMERCE-SERVER-URL>
    </SUPPLIER>
  </INVENTORY>
```

parts in the airline's inventory as required. The original business process has been reengineered and dramatically simplified.

Automating Customer Help Desk Service

With most Help Desk applications, it is very difficult to provide an automated capability so that customers can themselves locate the solution to a problem they are experiencing. Help Desk staff assist the customer in this task. They refer to a knowledge base of known problems and solutions. Once a new problem has been identified and its solution has been determined, documentation about the problem and solution should be added to the knowledge base as soon as possible, so that this information can be used by other customers and Help Desk staff.

Help Desk technical fixes and workarounds or solutions are typically stored as whole documents, making topic retrieval difficult. An approach is needed that can verify the integrity of source information about a problem and its solution, then update or share information across separate documents. An automated way of identifying solutions to problems is needed.

XML can provide considerable assistance to this application. XML metadata tags can be inserted in relevant text documents to allow the text to be searched readily for specific topics. XML can also be used to describe structured data in Product databases. XML allows Help Desk Problem and Solution documents to be authored on a collaborative basis. The following example on the Microsoft [XML Scenarios] Web site illustrates the use of XML to achieve this, showing the use of XLL to link directly into an SQL database for query purposes.

Figure 15-3 illustrates the information flow for this example. A customer fills out a Problem Form using a browser, entering the Customer ID, the product, and a description of the problem. An automated search parses the problem description, using XML metadata tags for searching XML documents, or full-text if the document is non-XML. The search is carried out against the XML knowledge base to locate the problem and the relevant solution. This is integrated with an SQL database that contains relevant information also about the customer. The solution in XML is converted to HTML and sent to the customer.

If no solution can be located, the problem is forwarded automatically to a Help Desk engineer using a template that includes the customer details from the SQL database together with relevant parts data and problem details previously retrieved from the XML knowledge base. The engineer determines an appropriate solution for the problem, then stores the solution in the knowledge base with XML tags automatically inserted from the XML Form. The solution is sent to the customer, and is also available for future customer requests relating to that problem.

Figure 15-4 shows the XML, SQL, and XLL logic used for this application. The first section shows *Customer Data Integrated with the Problem Description.* This integrates data from the Customer SQL table with a description of the problem. A `<sqllink>` XML tag has been defined to

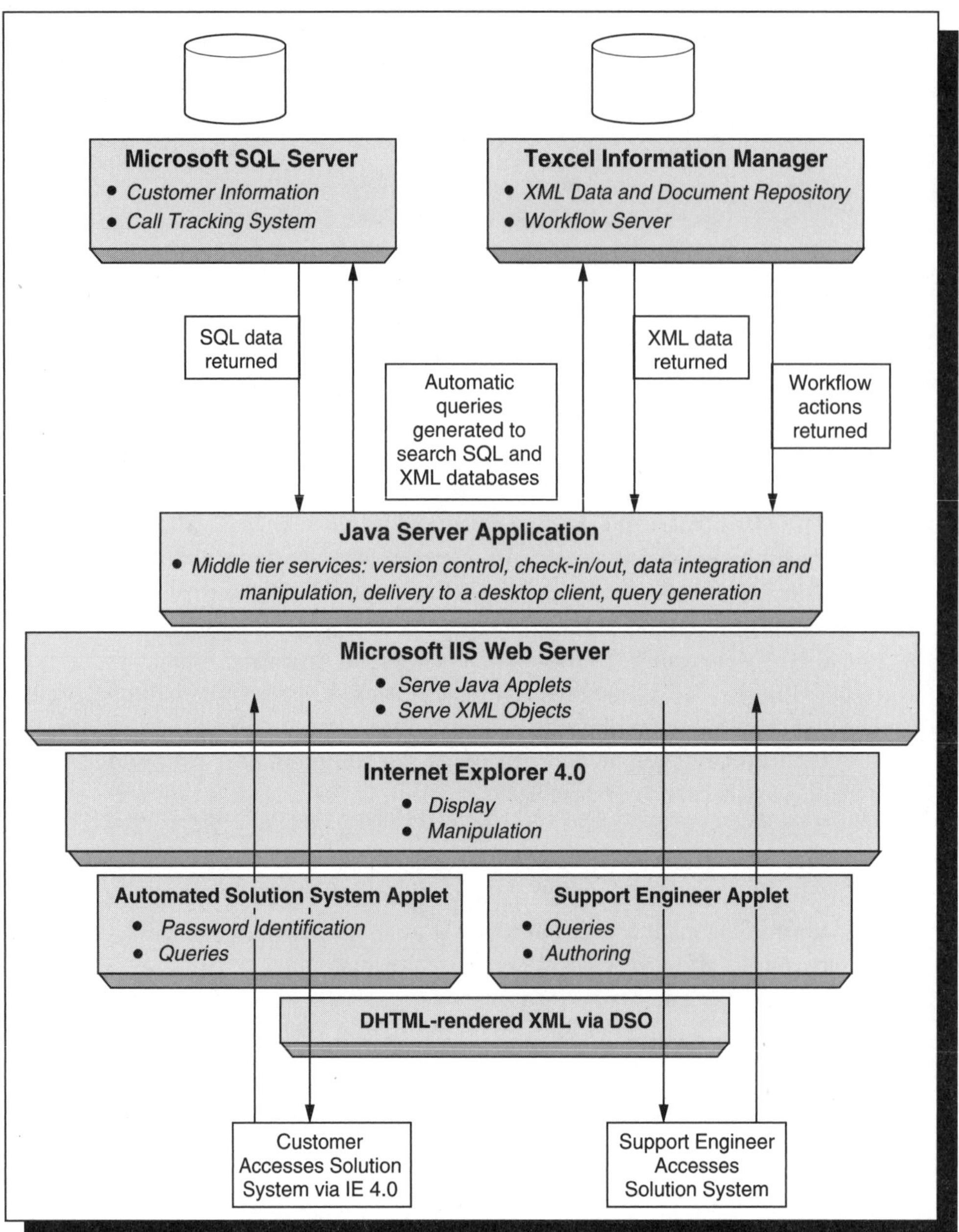

Figure 15-3
Automated Customer Service Help Desk Information Flow. *Source*: [XML Scenarios] Web site.

Customer Data Integrated with the Problem Description

```
<?xml version="1.0"?>
  <solution id="solution-1000">
    <!-- This is from the Microsoft SQL Database -->
    <sqllink xml:link="simple"
      href="http://sqlserver//getSQLinfo?SQL=
      'SELECT owner,date,product-type,product-name
      WHERE call-id = test.call.1'">
    <!---RESULTS:
      <solution-info>
        <owner>Derek Yoo</owner>
        <date>Sat Jan 31 22:30:50 1998</date>
      </solution-info>
      <product-grp>
        <product-type>SST</product-type>
        <product-name>Self Service Terminal 100A</product-name>
      </product-grp>
      <problem-grp>
        <problem-statement>
          Terminal 100A will not recover from a power failure. Screen remains blank
          after power is restored.
        </problem-statement>
      </problem-grp>
    -->
```

Solution Specification

```
    <solution-grp>
      <solution-statement>
        <!-- This part of the solution statement is authored by the Solution
        Engineer -->
        <para>
          The solution is to simply turn the main power switch for the terminal off
          and then on again.
        </para>
        <para>
          Please refer to <imlink xml:link="simple"
            href="http://imserver//getIMinfo="helpdb@
            Tech_Manual.xml#section1.child(2,para)">
            Paragraph 2, Section I of Tech_Manual.xml</imlink>.
      </solution-statement>
      <testing-steps>
        <step></step>
      </testing-steps>
      <additional-resources>
        <graphiclink xml:link="simple"
          href="file://localfileserver/graphics/image_of_part.gif">
        <weblink xml:link="simple"
          href="http://www.texcel.no/support">
      </additional-resources>
    </solution-grp>
  </solution>
```

Figure 15-4
Automated Customer Service Help Desk XML, SQL, and XLL Logic. *Source*: [XML Scenarios] Web site.

access a Microsoft SQL Server database. An XLL simple link points to "sqlserver" and specifies the "getSQLinfo" routine for processing the SQL SELECT statement that follows. The query results are integrated by this routine with the XML tags that are included within the <!-- RESULTS ... --> XML comment.

The <solution-info> includes the author name (<owner>) and <date> to be used if a new solution statement has to be written. This would be an assigned Help Desk person (or a default name) and the current date and time. The <product-grp> defines the <product-type> and <product-name>. The <problem-grp> and <problem-statement> then document the description of the problem as entered by the customer.

A solution to the problem is provided by the *Solution Specification*. In the <solution-grp>, we can see a <solution statement> made up of paragraphs (<para>). The second paragraph contains an XLL simple link to paragraph 2 of section 1 of the Technical Manual—an XML document in "Tech_Manual.xml." Any <testing-steps> follow; however, the <step> statements are empty in Figure 15-4. If any <additional-resources> are needed, they are included in the <graphiclink> and <weblink> tags. We can see that an XLL simple link points to a GIF image of the part and another link points to additional support resources.

The use of XML in this application has automated what was previously a labor-intensive process, ensuring that both structured and unstructured data sources can be drawn on intelligently to resolve the customer's problem.

Improving Online Shopping

Online shopping is growing rapidly, particularly in the sale of books online. Amazon.com sells books only via the Internet, and is the largest bookstore in the world. Following its success, there are now many online book stores. But comparison shopping from each of these stores has been difficult. A shopper wanting to purchase a specific book must visit each online store to find out the price and availability of the book. But each of these stores is different. Web shoppers must know each merchant that sells products of interest, how to conduct a search for the product in their store, then compile and compare the results from each store. Searches using HTML search engines often present a lot of irrelevant information.

What is needed to improve the shopping experience is an online shopping guide that searches for a product from multiple merchants and compares the results from those merchants.

An XML Shopping Guide application searches a number of online book stores for a specific book title or author. The HTML data returned from search queries by each store is converted to a standard structure for each product category, using XML tags and data extracted from the HTML response.

Figure 15-5 shows the information flow for the online shopping guide. A search for a specific book accesses an SQL database, which returns details of all merchants who sell that book. Each merchant's store is visited automatically for the latest information about the book. The HTML response that is received includes each merchant's book price, its availability, the book format (hardback, paperback, audio cassette), and the shipping cost.

The different formats and metadata used by each store are converted to a common XML format, shown in Figure 15-6. The results from all merchants are converted back to HTML and displayed in the shopper's browser. The list of books can be viewed, grouped, or sorted by clicking on the author, title, price, or availability column headings. The XML data is

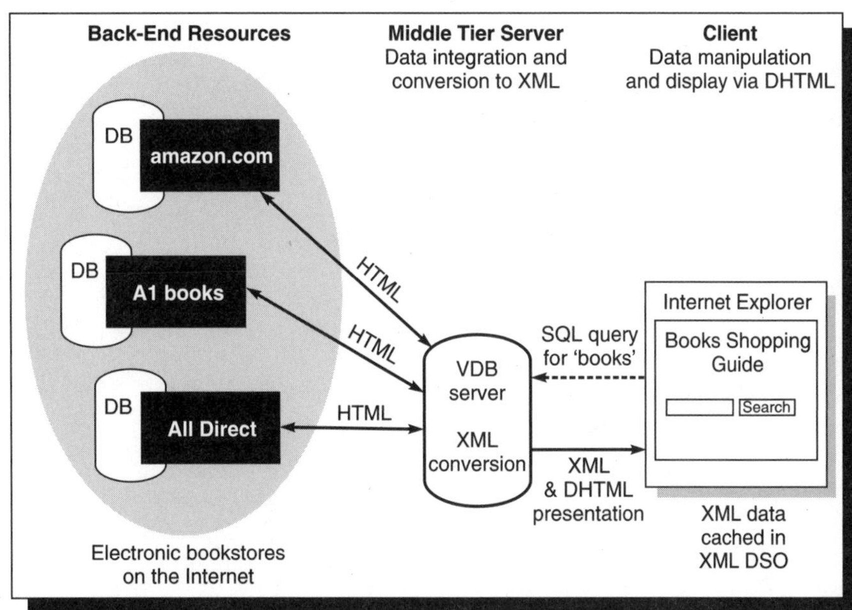

Figure 15-5 Improving Online Shopping Information Flow. *Source*: [XML Scenarios] Web site.

cached at the shopper's browser so that this data manipulation all represents local processing, with no remote access needed.

In Figure 15-6 we see an XML example of merchants who sell a specific book: *Eiger Dreams* by Jon Krakauer. The DOCTYPE specifies a root name of <Booklist> and the DTD file "book.dtd." A <Booklist> can contain many books. Figure 15-6 shows only one <Book>; its <Title> and <Author> are indicated. The information about this book from each merchant then follows as a series of deals. Each <Deal> includes the <Merchant>, the <Format> of the book, its <Price>, and its <Availability>.

The shopper can click on a "Details" button to get additional information from any store, such as a description of the book. When a purchase decision is made, the "Buy Now" button for the selected merchant is clicked. The shopper is then automatically sent from the Online

Figure 15-6
Improving Online Shopping XML Logic. *Source*: [XML Scenarios] Web site.

```
<?xml version="1.0"?>
  <!DOCTYPE Booklist SYSTEM "book.dtd">
    <Booklist>
      <Book>
        <Title>Eiger Dreams</Title>
        <Author>Krakauer, Jon</Author>
        <Deal>
          <Merchant>Amazon.com</Merchant>
          <Format>Paperback</Format>
          <Price>$10.36</Price>
          <Availability>Ships in 1 day</Availability>
        </Deal>
        <Deal>
          <Merchant>A1books</Merchant>
          <Format>paperback</Format>
          <Price>$10.00</Price>
          <Availability>2-3 days</Availability>
        </Deal>
        <Deal>
          <Merchant>A1books</Merchant>
          <Format>audio</Format>
          <Price>$17.50</Price>
          <Availability>2-3 days</Availability>
        </Deal>
        <Deal>
          <Merchant>All Direct</Merchant>
          <Format>paperback</Format>
          <Price>$9.71</Price>
          <Availability>2-3 days</Availability>
        </Deal>
      </Book>
    </Booklist>
```

Shopping Guide directly to that merchant's store to order the book online.

XML has been used here to satisfy a need created by the diversity of choices presented by the Internet. A useful service is provided to the shopper, who goes to just one place—the Online Shopping Guide—to purchase a required book to satisfy a need for low price or early delivery. The book merchants also benefit; they have had an opportunity to sell books to shoppers who may otherwise never have been able to find them. While only well-known online bookstores may have benefited before, now smaller stores have an opportunity to sell their books also. They can compete online equally with the larger bookstores, to the benefit of the shopper.

Personal Investment Management

With the move to online securities trading by individuals using the Internet, online brokers need to provide a personalized service for their clients. As well as maintaining details of each client's investment portfolio, data also needs to be combined from many sources: from Moodys, from Standard & Poors, from EDGARS for SEC filings, from financial analysts, and based on personal profiles.

The Microsoft [XML Scenarios] Web site describes a personal investment application for employees of a company. It shows how XML and third-party software tools can be used to create on-demand reports of employees' short-term and long-term investments for retirement and other purposes. A search engine locates XML content, structure, and metadata, searching for metadata tags and data within tags. XML and non-XML data can be accessed, tracked, and versioned, to provide financial advice based on various "what-if" scenarios.

The application extracts data about each employee from a Human Resources relational database, with each employee's investment portfolio stored in an object database. This HR and Portfolio data is transformed to XML data. "What if" requests are entered using an XML-based form and relevant financial data is obtained from external sources as illustrated in Figure 15-7. This is delivered to the employee's browser as XML, then displayed via dynamic HTML for analysis. The resulting XML data is shown in Figure 15-8.

In Figure 15-8, each `<portfolio>` is described by several attributes. These define the employee's name, with the `<risk>` and

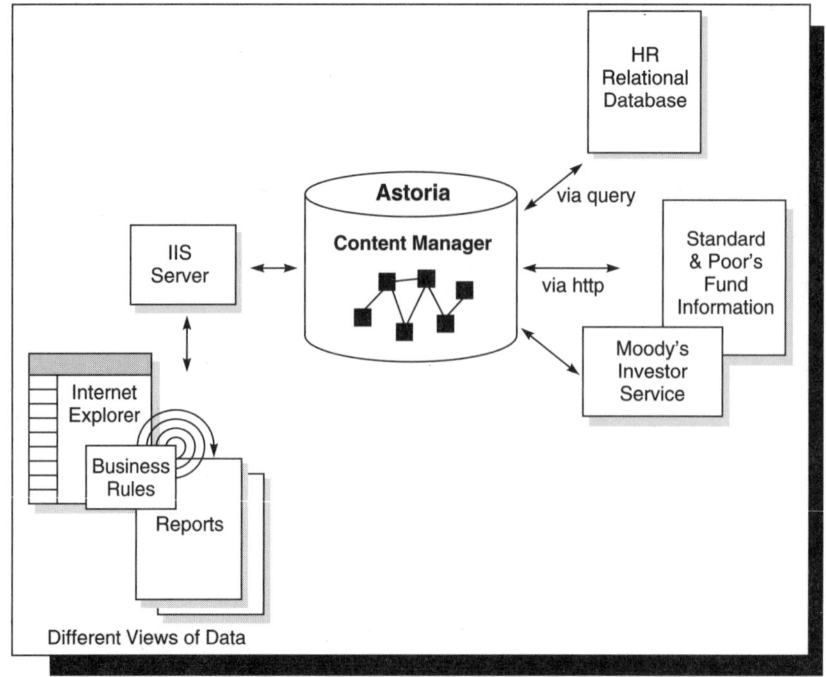

Figure 15-7 Personal Investment Management Information Flow. *Source*: [XML Scenarios] Web site.

<return> categories established for that portfolio. Information about the employee's <profile>, with attributes specifying the employee's name, employee number, and database source are also documented.

Several <analystreports> are defined in Figure 15-8. These include links to external sources for <Moodys>, and for Standard & Poors <SP>. These are followed by <investments>. The <shortterm> investments are for <moneymarket> and <bond> investments, while the <longterm> investments are for <retirement>—comprising <ira>, <beforetaxsavings>, and <collegefund> investments.

Time and Attendance System

Many organizations have older legacy systems, with data to be integrated with other data in relational databases for processing. This application illustrates how XML was used to implement a Time and Attendance Recording System for a company. Employees are able to

```
<portfolio name="Mary Weber" risk="balanced" return="medium"/>
  <profile name="Weber, Mary Ann" employee="82340" source="HRdatabase"/>
    <analystreports>
      <Moodys source="http://www.moodys.com/profiles/webermary"/>
        <description source="Astoria.Moody.Description.complete"/></Moodys>
      <SP source="http://www.ratings.com/funds/profile/weberma">
        <description source="Astoria.SP.Description.partial"/></SP>
    </analystreports>
    <investments>
      <shortterm>
        <moneymarket type="taxexempt" name="Phoenix"/>
        <bond type="taxable" name="BioTech"/>
      </shortterm>
      <longterm>
        <retirement>
          <ira contribution="maximum"/>
          <beforetaxsavings source="HRdatabase"/>
          <collegefund name="NY Aggressive Fund"/>
        </retirement>
      </longterm>
    </investments>
  </portfolio>
```

Figure 15-8
Personal Investment Management XML Logic. *Source*: [XML Scenarios] Web site.

submit their timecards via a corporate intranet for online manager approval. Data in the timecards is integrated with employee data from a Human Resources database and from a corporate-wide Directory Service database. It is then output as batch data files ready for processing by a legacy Payroll System as illustrated in Figure 15-9.

Each employee has a dynamically generated, personalized Web page that maintains details of the weekly schedule from the current date, the work status, vacation due, and weekly hours. For each date, the employee can specify the number of hours worked and the days on vacation. Only valid alternatives are presented to the employee for selection, based on details of the employee and position.

When these timecard details have been entered by the employee, the timecard is automatically sent to the employee's manager. All timecards for employees who report to that manager are queued for approval. The manager can drill down to obtain additional details about an employee, to approve or reject the timecard. An email message is then automatically sent to each employee, indicating the time of approval or the reason for rejection.

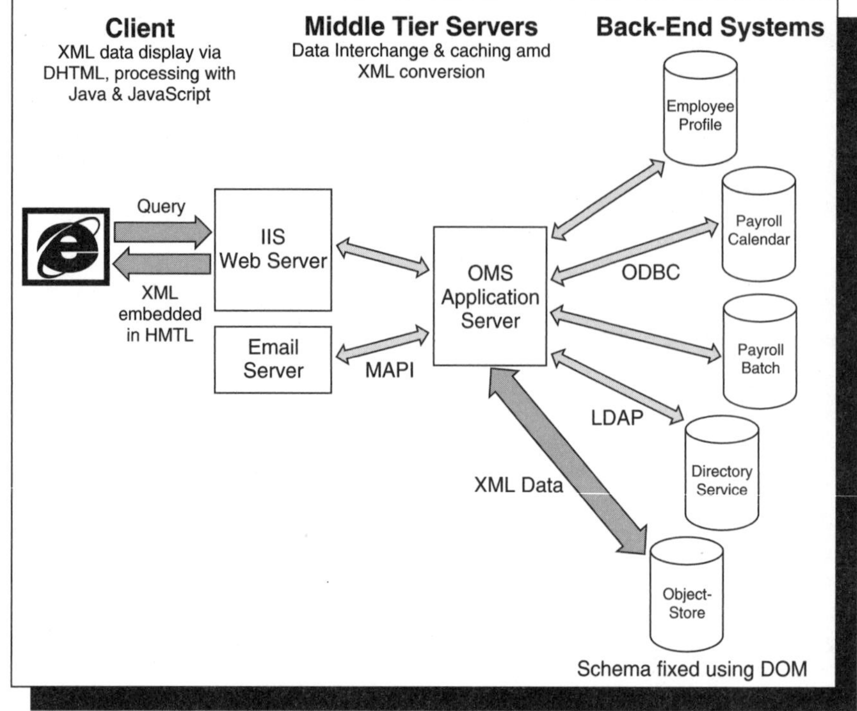

Figure 15-9 Time and Attendance System Information Flow. *Source*: [XML Scenarios] Web site.

This application used the Document Object Model (DOM). As we discussed in Chapter 11, DOM defines a language-independent interface for processing XML and HTML documents. DOM was used to build XML and HTML documents dynamically, accessing the legacy files and relational databases with interface code. A complete description of this application is available from the [XML Scenarios] Web site.

Figure 15-10 shows typical contents of a `<BATCH>` XML root document produced by this system. The employee is identified by the `<PAYEE>` tag, with attributes detailing the employee's *`serial`* number, *`fullname`*, *`manager`*, *`department`*, *`hired`*, *`termed`*, *`status`*, and *`email`* address that have been extracted from the Human Resources database. The `<PAYHRS>` tag includes `<PAYHR>` tags for the employee. These include `<PAYHR>` attributes of *`effective`* or *`exempt`*, *`manager`*, *`department`*, *`status`*, *`type`*, *`shift`*, *`days`*, and *`hours`* that are worked.

`<PAYBAL>` attributes are provided for *`group`*, *`hours`*, *`effective`*, *`starting`*, and *`ending`* dates and times. The `<PAYCARDS>` tag includes (in `<PAYCARD>`) the timecard details

`Batch.xml` **from Time and Attendance System**

```
<!DOCTYPE BATCH SYSTEM>
<BATCH>
  <PAYEE SERIAL="000000" FULLNAME="Sample,Patricia C." MANAGER="000000Z"
    DEPARTMENT="000000" HIRED="1989-08-01 00:00:00" TERMED="1997-09-29 00:00:00"
    STATUS="A" EMAIL="Patricia.Sample@somecompany.com" />
    <PAYHRS>
      <PAYHR EFFECTIVE="1998-03-15 00:00:00" MANAGER="000000" DEPARTMENT="000000"
        EXEMPT="N" STATUS="A" TYPE="RF" SHIFT="1" DAYS="5"
        HOURS="40.00" HIRED="1997-09-29 00:00:00" CURRENT="0" />
      <PAYHR EXEMPT="N" STATUS="A" TYPE="RF" SHIFT="2" DAYS="5" HOURS="40.00"
        EFFECTIVE="1998-04-01 00:00:00" MANAGER="000000" DEPARTMENT="000000"
        CURRENT="0" />
      <PAYHR EXEMPT="N" STATUS="A" TYPE="RF" SHIFT="1" DAYS="5" HOURS="40.00"
        EFFECTIVE="1998-04-15 00:00:00" MANAGER="000000" DEPARTMENT="000000"
        CURRENT="1" />
    </PAYHRS>
    <PAYBALS>
      <PAYBAL GROUP="003" HOURS="0.0" EFFECTIVE="1998-04-12 00:00:00" />
      <PAYBAL GROUP="006" HOURS="0.0" EFFECTIVE="1998-01-01 00:00:00"
        STARTING="1997-12-29 00:00:00" ENDING="1998-12-29 00:00:00" />
      <PAYBAL GROUP="007" HOURS="0.0" EFFECTIVE="1998-01-01 00:00:00"
        STARTING="1997-12-29 00:00:00" ENDING="1998-12-29 00:00:00" />
      <PAYBAL GROUP="008" HOURS="0.0"></PAYBAL>
    </PAYBALS>
    <PAYCARDS>
      <PAYCARD SERIAL="000000" PERIOD="1998-06-07 00:00:00"
        FULLNAME="Sample,Patricia C." EMAIL="Patricia.Sample@somecompany.com"
        MANAGER="000000" DEPARTMENT="000000" EXEMPT="N" STATUS="A" TYPE="RF"
        SHIFT="1" DAYS="5" HOURS="40.00" EFFECTIVE="1998-04-15 00:00:00" />
        <PAYCODES>
          <PAYCODE CODE="002" PERIOD="1998-06-07 00:00:00" MON="8.0" TUE="8.0"
            WED="8.0" THU="8.0" FRI="8.0" SAT="0.0" SUN="0.0" TOTAL="40.0"
            SUBMITTED="1998-06-17 10:13:06" SUBMITTER="000000" />
        </PAYCODES>
        <SUBMITTED DATE="1998-06-17 10:13:06" SERIAL="000000"
          FULLNAME="Sample,Patricia C." STATUS="SUBMITTED">
        </SUBMITTED>
      </PAYCARD>
    </PAYCARDS>
  </PAYEE>
</BATCH>
```

Figure 15-10
Time and Attendance System XML. *Source*: [XML Scenarios] Web site.

completed online by each employee reporting to the manager. Details from the timecard include attributes of *`serial`*, *`period`*, *`fullname`*, *`email`*, *`manager`*, *`department`*, *`exempt`*, *`status`*, *`type`*, *`shift`*, *`days`*, *`hours`*, and *`effective`* date and time.

The relevant <PAYCODES> for each employee have been extracted from the Payroll database. They include <PAYCODE> attributes of payroll *code* and the weekly *period* date. The hours worked each day for *mon*, *tue*, *wed*, *thu*, *fri*, *sat*, *sun*, and the *total* hours worked for the week have been extracted from the timecard. These are included as <PAYCODE> attributes, along with the date *submitted* and the *submitter* identification. Concluding the XML output file is a <SUBMITTED> tag, with attributes for submission *date*, the employee's *serial* number, *fullname*, and *status*.

Other XML Applications

In Chapter 12 and this chapter we have discussed six applications showing different examples of the use of XML. Full details about these are available from the Microsoft [XML Scenarios] Web site. Other applications on this Web site as at March 1999 were:

- Interactive Frequent-Flyer Web Site using XML
- Consumer Product Ratings Online with XML
- Purchasing and Supplier Data Integration with XML

These applications are described on the [XML Scenarios] Web site in terms of the business problem and the role taken by XML. An information flow diagram is provided, together with a discussion of the operation of the XML application. An extract of the XML specification used to implement the relevant application is then provided.

A Common Theme of XML Applications

With this review of the power and flexibility of XML and related technologies, using the Microsoft [XML Scenarios] examples as a catalyst, we can see a common theme emerging. This has not been difficult; you already saw the commonality of these examples long before now—didn't you!

You are completely correct! Every one of these applications—regardless of how they were processed before—is now an Internet or intranet application. The application has been Web-enabled. Its interface is a Web browser. The user interface has been simplified. It is now a common point-and-click browser interface, with online forms for data input.

Tables, reports, and other results are dynamically generated as XML and HTML output. These have replaced the many different interfaces used by legacy systems, relational databases, client/server products, and off-line reference documents. Instead of a multitude of input formats and user instructions, with significant operator training overheads, we see a simple, well-understood interface that can be used with any application.

> Using XML, each of these applications can now be deployed as an Enterprise Portal application.

An Enterprise Portal benefits an organization not only by using its corporate intranet for ready access to knowledge resources—both structured and unstructured—within the enterprise. Great benefit can be gained by using the Enterprise Portal also for access to knowledge resources outside the enterprise, via the Internet. This has been very difficult before; the task is now much simpler by using XML technologies.

Internet-Based Knowledge Resources

We have discussed how XML will enable intelligent searches to be carried out in the future based on metatags, as search engines and Web resources support XML more completely. XML also enables us to search and locate non-text information such as graphics, images, photos, audio, or video resources. These are largely omitted from today's Internet searches via search engines.

Harnessed using XML and related technologies, the Internet, intranet, and extranet represent a valuable knowledge resource that enterprises will use for competitive advantage. Little has been drawn from these sources for today's data warehouses. Yet they will provide valuable input for the Enterprise Portals of tomorrow. This leads us to the concept of *Web Farming.*

Web Farming

Web farming carries out intelligent Web searches using HTML, the Resource Description Framework (RDF), and XML to locate the

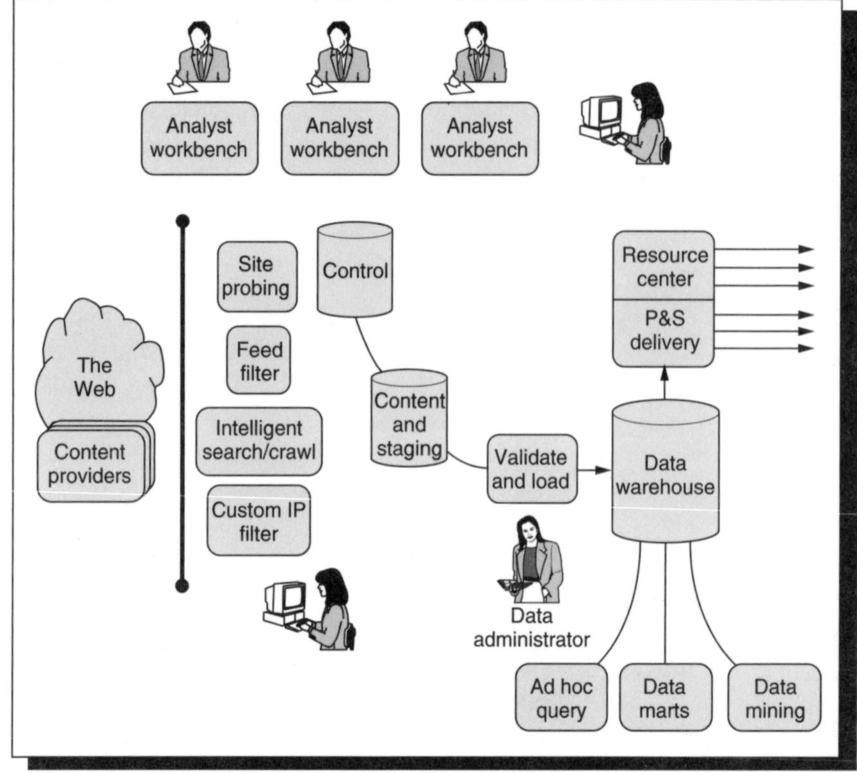

Figure 15-11 Web Farming, used to extract knowledge resources from the Internet. *Source*: [Hackathorn 1999].

information and content that is relevant to an organization. It has been defined by Richard Hackathorn as:

> Web farming is the systematic refining of information resources on the Web for business intelligence
> —[Hackathorn 1999]

Web farming refers to the cultivation and harvesting of data, information, and knowledge resources, obtained from the Internet, intranets, and extranets. Figure 15-11 shows that content is extracted from relevant sources identified by searches via XML, RDF, or HTML. It is then transformed, staged, validated, and loaded into a data warehouse for access via publish and subscribe (P&S) delivery as knowledge. Hackathorn uses a four-stage methodology, using farming as a metaphor as illustrated in Figure 15-12.

Stage 1: Getting Started documents the external factors critical to the enterprise. Some factors will have been identified from strategic business

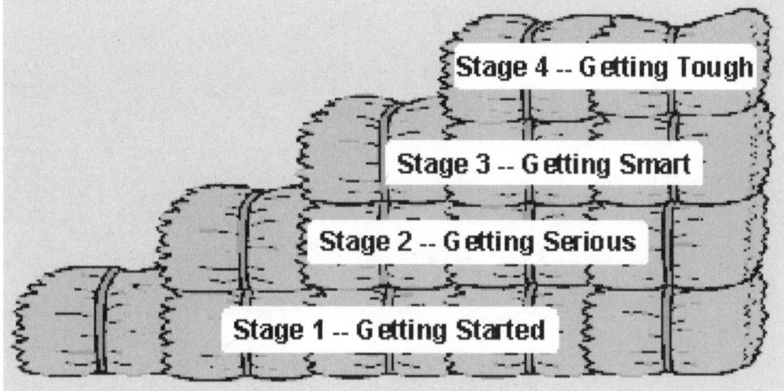

Figure 15-12 The four-stage Web Farming Methodology. *Source*: [WebFarming] Web site.

plans, as we discussed in Chapter 2. This stage formulates a systematic discovery plan, identifies important content providers, disseminates initial information to interested staff, and prepares a business case for Web farming. The business case is based on the objectives and business environment of the enterprise.

Stage 2: Getting Serious in Figure 15-12 establishes a foundation on which to build an infrastructure for Web farming. The role of Web farming is legitimized within the enterprise, a stable infrastructure is built for long-term growth, the critical external factors from Stage 1 are refined, a historical context for all collected content is maintained, and an intranet site is established for information dissemination and production operations.

These two stages are shown as Levels 1 and 2 in Figure 15-13. Initial content extracted from the Web is packaged and distributed to interested parties based on their identified interest in the information that is gathered.

Stage 3: Getting Smart in Figure 15-12 extends the foundation and infrastructure established in the previous two stages. It builds the required selection and extraction filters, constructs pipelines into primary content providers, then analyzes, structures, and publishes content by exploiting relevant technology.

Stage 4: Getting Tough embeds Web farming into an organization's culture. Hackathorn describes this stage by saying: *as an activity of intelligence gathering and synthesis, Web farming is an enabling technology, requiring (never replacing) the unique skill and hard work of domain experts* [Hackathorn 1999].

Figure 15-14 shows that Levels 3 and 4 integrate Web-based knowledge with the Data Warehouse. Stages 3 and 4 of Figure 15-12 extend the

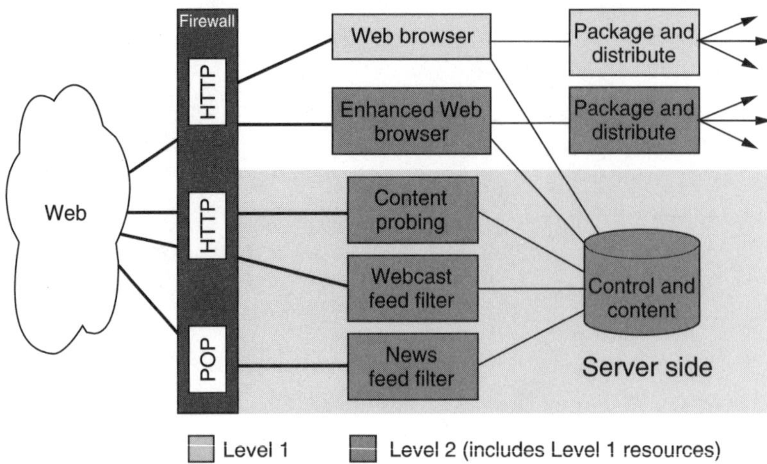

Figure 15-13 Result of the first two stages of the Web Farming Methodology. *Source*: [WebFarming] Web site.

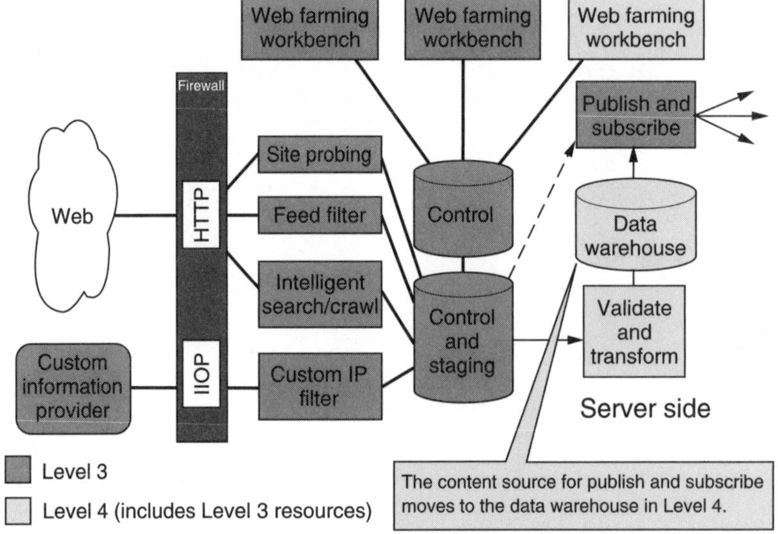

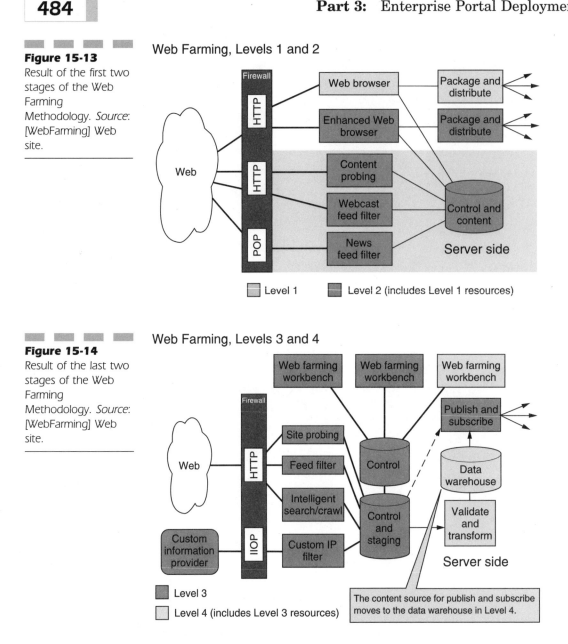

Figure 15-14 Result of the last two stages of the Web Farming Methodology. *Source*: [WebFarming] Web site.

warehouse schema and load content, establish links to other enterprise-level systems, resolve entity mapping through matching of key values, and establish credibility through various data checks. The business objectives and business case are revisited in light of the warehouse schema.

We now see an important important focus emerging:

> The Web Farming methodology enables a Data Warehouse to evolve into an Enterprise Portal.

When content is discovered, acquired, structured, and disseminated as described above, it is progressively refined as illustrated in Figure 15-15. From this refined content comes refined control; the results of earlier refinement are used to identify and locate new content which then moves through the same cycle. This information refinement is described as *converting data into information and then into knowledge* [Hackathorn 1999].

The benefits of Web farming become apparent when its impact on data warehousing or data marts is considered. For example, Figure 15-16 illustrates a warehouse schema used for a Sales Data Mart. This is similar to the Data Mart that was built by XYZ Corporation based on the Sales Analysis example discussed in Chapters 10, 12, and 13.

Figure 15-16 shows that sales data can be analyzed by Customer, Product, Store, and Month. But without Store Demographics, the Sales Department and Marketing Department will be reactive—as seen in Chapter 2, when we defined the *Market Share* and *Product Pricing* strategies together with the *Unit Market Share KPI*. Through Web farming, Store Demographics have been obtained from Census and other data sources on the Internet. This knowledge resource is now available for Online Analytical Processing and Data Mining in the Data Mart. It is

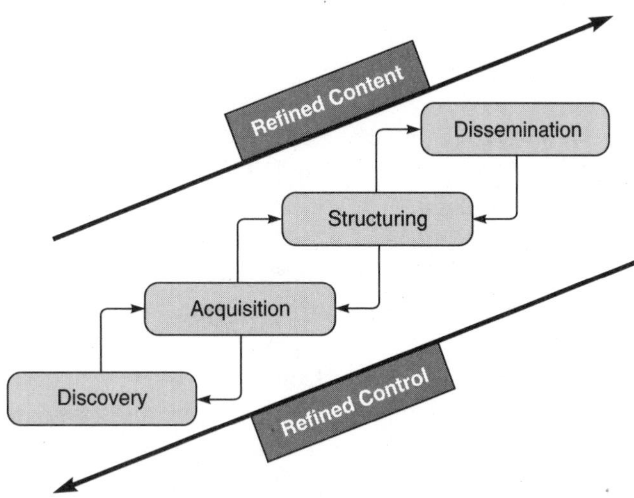

Figure 15-15 Refined Content leads to Refined Control. *Source*: [WebFarming] Web site.

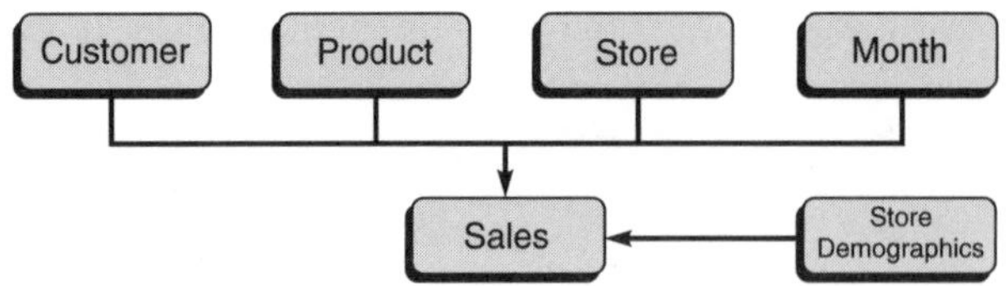

Figure 15-16 A Sales Data Mart has access to Store Demographics through Web Farming. *Source:* [WebFarming] Web site.

also available as an added resource for Decision Early Warning as we discussed in Chapter 5.

The [WebFarming] Web site is an excellent resource to keep abreast of developments in this field. This Web site is maintained by Richard Hackathorn, who produces a free monthly newsletter. Visit and register to receive this newsletter; it is invaluable—with links to many other relevant resources on the Internet. The Web site also makes it easy to purchase his book [Hackathorn 1999].

From the perspective of Web Farming, we will revisit the Data Warehouse. We will then examine its evolution to an Enterprise Portal. The following sections will bring together material covered in earlier chapters. They serve as a summary of Data Warehouse and Enterprise Portal concepts.

Data Warehouse Summary

Chapter 1 introduced the importance of metadata for effective communication between systems both within and outside the enterprise. Parts 1 and 2 provided methods to identify and capture metadata. We saw in Chapter 11 how XML uses metadata to integrate dissimilar systems, with a number of XML applications discussed earlier in this chapter.

The [Decision Processing] Web site provides a good summary of the Data Warehousing concepts covered in this book. Figure 15-17 illustrates that many databases and legacy files are sources of metadata for a Data Warehouse and for the Data Marts that are based on that warehouse. This metadata identifies the content, format, and meaning of those data sources.

Many benefits result from integrated metadata. Figure 15-17 shows that metadata is used to capture and transform source data into a format suitable for the data warehouse and data marts. This *Extract, Transform, and Load* (ETL) stage uses various ETL tools and applications to assist.

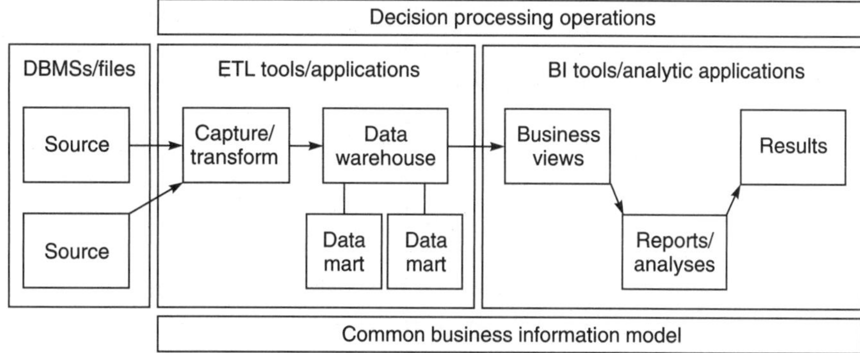

Figure 15-17 The Metadata Value Chain. *Source*: [Decision Processing] Web site.

Business users need to have a good understanding of what information exists in a data warehouse [Decision Processing]. The metadata is used to define business views for production of reports and analyses to deliver results to the business users, based on the use of Business Intelligence (BI) tools and analytic applications. The metadata results in the production of a *Common Business Information Model* in Figure 15-17 that assists the business users in carrying out *Decision Processing Operations*.

Transaction processing systems are used to maintain an organization's operational data, while decision processing systems *analyze and distribute business information captured from transaction processing systems to corporate decision makers.* The [Decision Processing] Web site further states that: *Decision processing uses a Web-based distributed computing architecture to integrate the various components of a decision processing system, and to manage and distribute information to business users.* Figure 15-18 illustrates the Business Information Value Chain that results.

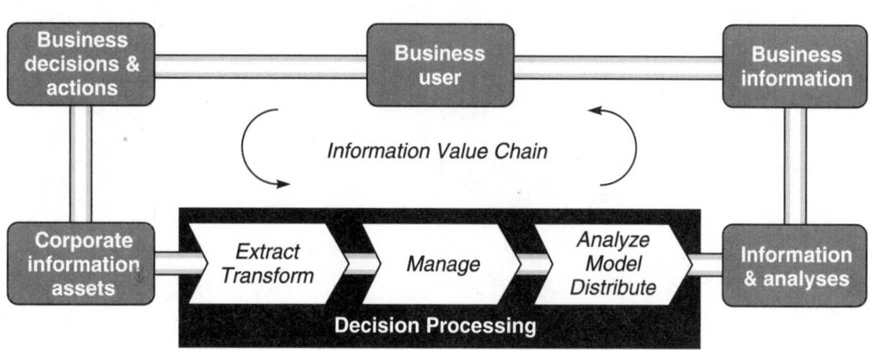

Figure 15-18 The Business Information Value Chain. *Source*: [Decision Processing] Web site.

In this book we have emphasized the importance of building an *Enterprise Data Warehouse* based on strategic and tactical business plans that identify the information needs of management, using methods such as described in Chapter 2. By applying strategic modeling as described in Chapter 4, the strategic data model that is produced—and the metadata that is captured at the same time—enable an enterprise-wide perspective to be taken. From this can be extracted Data Marts that address priority areas of the enterprise. We discussed a Sales Data Mart as one focus.

Figure 15-19 illustrates the central role that an Enterprise Data Warehouse takes, with dependent data marts fed from it, and with independent data marts separately present. This diagram summarizes our treatment of Data Warehouses in this book. The sections roughly correspond to the structure of the book.

The section labeled *DESIGN and DEVELOP* in Figure 15-19 refers to Parts 1 and 2. The *user information requirements* are defined in Chapters 2 and 4. *Business area templates* are developed also in Chapter 4 from other business areas, and to greater tactical detail. The result of this data modeling is a *common business model*, developed using Forward Engineering as we saw in Part 1.

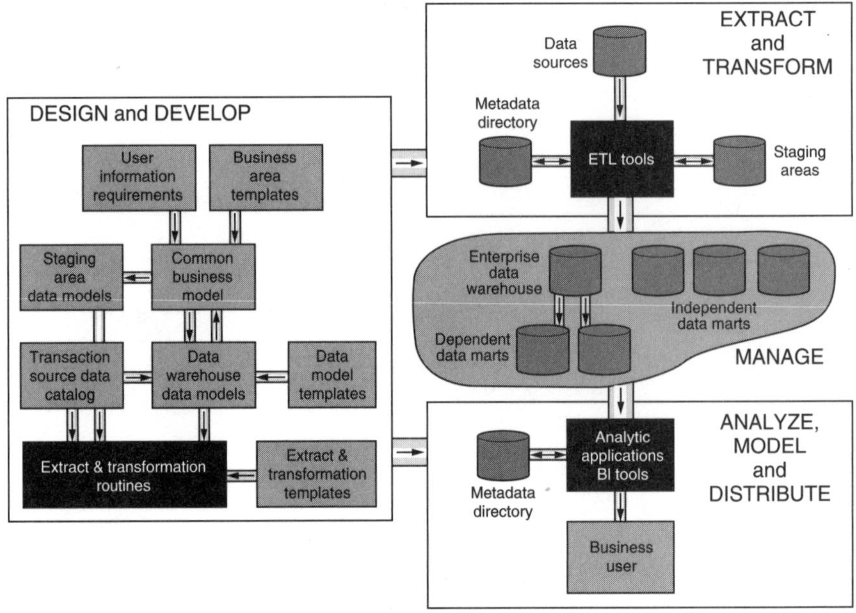

Figure 15-19 Example of an Enterprise Data Warehouse. *Source*: [Decision Processing] Web site.

The *common business model* is used to produce *staging area data models* for data sources that will feed the data warehouse, based also on Reverse Engineering as discussed in Part 2. *Transaction source data catalogs* from relational and other databases, and *data model templates* that are reverse engineered from legacy systems as well as packages, are used with the *common business model* to define *data warehouse data models*. *Extract and transformation templates* from ETL tools are used with *extract and transformation routines* to define the extraction, transformation, and loading of source data into the warehouse.

From this design and development, the *EXTRACT and TRANSFORM* section of Figure 15-19 refers to the periodic extraction from *data sources* using the *metadata directory* by *ETL tools* into *staging areas* for loading into the Data Warehouse and Data Marts, which *MANAGE* the information.

The *ANALYZE, MODEL, and DISTRIBUTE* section uses the *metadata directory* with *analytic applications* and *BI tools* such as EIS, DSS, and OLAP Business Intelligence packages—and also DEW systems as discussed in Chapter 5—to deliver requested information to the *business user*.

Enterprise Portal Architecture

In Chapter 1 we introduced the Enterprise Portal concept, based on the Enterprise Information Portal (EIP) report first published by Merrill Lynch on November 16, 1998—reported by *InfoWorld* on January 25, 1999. These are accessible from the [WebFarming] Web site or the [InfoWorld] Web site. Figure 15-20 repeats Figure 1-2 which is the diagram used in the *InfoWorld* article. We will review this figure now as a summary of Enterprise (Information) Portal concepts.

The focus of Data Warehouses has been *Structured Data*, as shown in the top part of Figure 15-20. Source data drawn from *online transactional databases* such as *ERP applications*, legacy or other relational databases, as well as *point of sale data*, is first extracted, transformed, and loaded by *ETL and data quality* tools into *Relational OLAP* databases and/or the *Data Warehouse*.

Data marts take subject area subsets from the *Data Warehouse* for *query and reporting*. *Analytical applications* carry out *OLAP analysis* using OLAP tools. Business Intelligence tools also provide analytical

Figure 15-20 Enterprise Information Portal Concepts (from Figure 1-2). *Source*: [InfoWorld] Web site and Merrill Lynch.

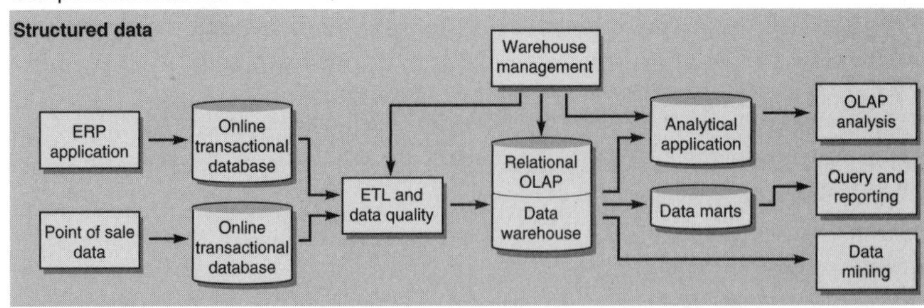

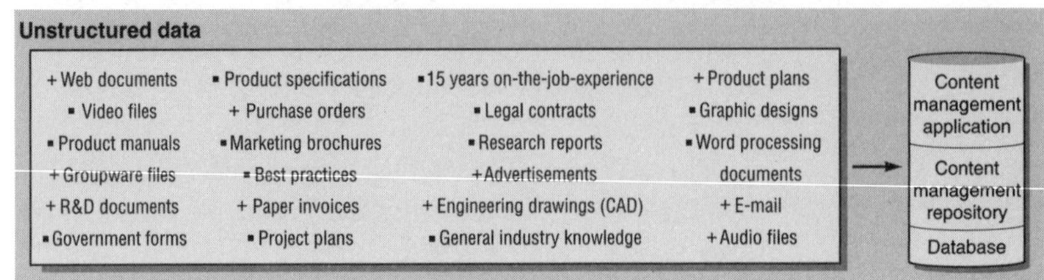

processing, such as EIS and DSS products. *Data mining* tools are used to drill down and analyze data in the warehouse. *Warehouse management* operates to manage the *ETL and data quality* stage, the *Relational OLAP* databases and *Data Warehouse*, and the *analytical applications*.

The bottom part of Figure 15-20 lists *Unstructured Data* sources that are used by Enterprise Portals. We discussed in Chapter 11 how XML uses metadata tags to integrate these data sources with the *Structured Data* sources above. The XML examples we discussed in Chapter 12 and earlier this chapter demonstrated how this is achieved. These unstructured data sources are managed by a *Content Management Repository* as *Content Management Applications* and *Database*. While they are conceptual in Figure 15-20, we saw them referenced as XML databases in the applications discussed earlier in this chapter.

We will now discuss the architecture of Enterprise Portals in Figure 15-21. We will then introduce typical products in the following pages.

Figure 15-21 shows the main components of Enterprise Portal Architecture. *Decision Processing Systems* and Data Warehouses were discussed in Figures 15-17 to 15-19; these are two data sources for Enterprise Portals. Other data sources are *Collaborative Processing Systems* and *Other Corporate/External Systems*, such as from the Internet, intranets, or extranets using Web Farming techniques.

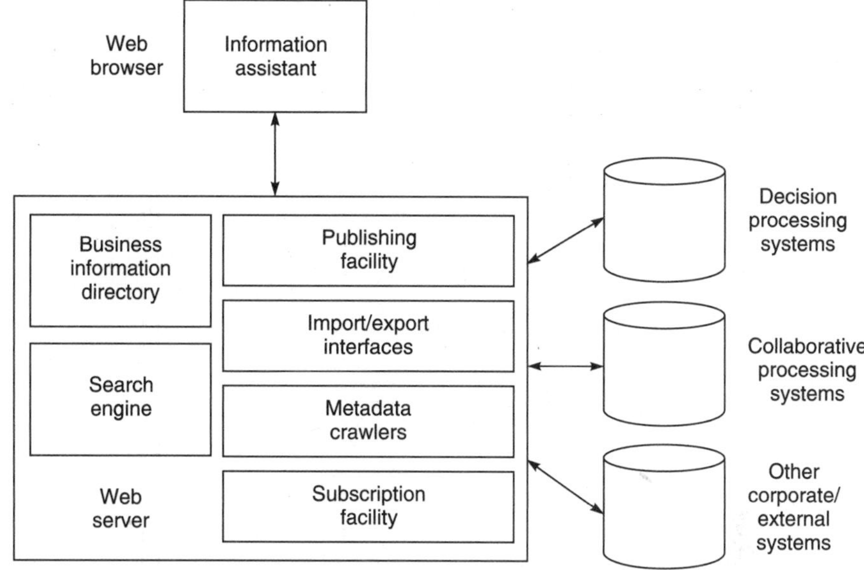

Figure 15-21 The Main Components of Enterprise Portal Architecture. *Source:* [Decision Processing] Web site.

The Enterprise Portal includes a *Business Information Directory*, described by Colin White—founder of DataBase Associates and the [Decision Processing] Web site—as *a server-based index of an organization's business information. This index is maintained via a web-based publishing facility by so-called* metadata crawlers *that regularly scan selected servers for new business information or by an* import interface *that enables users and third-party vendors to maintain directory information via flat files or a programmatic interface* [White 1999], available from the [DM Review] Web site.

The *Business Information Directory* has access to metadata for Data Warehouse databases, for word processing documents, Web pages and legacy files via XML, and access also to decision processing objects such as queries or analyses that are used to produce the business information. It has access to central corporate directories that contain active details of human resources (email, phone, fax, location), equipment resources (physical location and/or Internet/intranet address—URL or URI), and of data, information, and knowledge resources (Internet/intranet URL or URI address). As noted in [White 1999], the directory also *allows business users to annotate directory entries with additional metadata about the meaning and context of business information—and about the business actions that have been taken based on the information.*

A *Search Engine* locates resources for the *Business Information Directory. Metadata Crawlers* periodically—or on demand from the

Information Assistant (implemented through Web browsers)—locate and identify relevant data, information, and knowledge using Web Farming techniques. *Import/export interfaces* extract required information to be stored as data sources to satisfy current and future information requests. This Enterprise Portal functionality is managed and physically delivered by a *Web Server*.

Interested staff subscribe for information via the *Information Assistant* using the *Subscription Facility*. The *Information Assistant* is a fully customizable Web interface that operates with the *Search Engine* to enter and process user requests for information. The *Subscription Facility* defines how results are distributed and viewed through the Enterprise Portal.

A Publishing Facility notifies and delivers relevant information to interested staff, or runs decision processing objects. These can be initiated immediately, on certain events occurring, or at regular time-intervals. This information can be delivered automatically to interested staff using the Decision Early Warning concepts that we discussed in Chapter 5, based on upper and lower performance bounds defined in association with target values and decision early warning periods.

The result is a highly effective and responsive delivery environment for tailored information, using the Enterprise Portal as the central information dissemination vehicle. We will now discuss typical products that can be utilized for this purpose.

Evolution of Data Warehouses to Enterprise Portals

The Data Warehouse and Enterprise Portal concepts are now summarized together in Figure 15-22. Representing the evolution of Data Warehouses to the Internet and intranets, this diagram is from the [Decision Processing] Web site—where it is called the *Decision Processing Blueprint*. It is useful for our purposes as a vehicle to discuss the evolution of Data Warehouses to Enterprise Portals.

In the following discussion of Figure 15-22, we will use italics to refer to components in the diagram, with references or equivalent terms that we have used in this book also shown in brackets. For example, the term *Federated Data Warehouse* in this diagram has been referred to as an

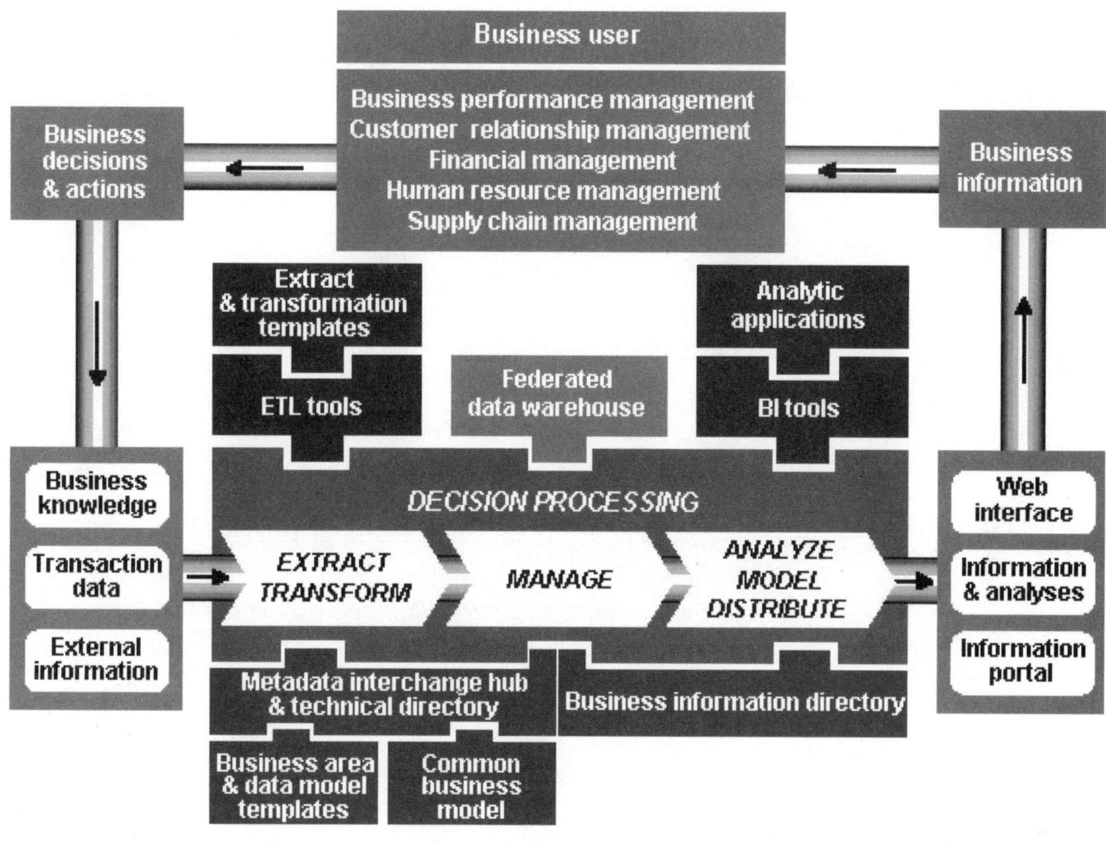

Figure 15-22
Evolution of Data Warehouses to Enterprise Portals. *Source*: [Decision Processing] Web site.

(Enterprise Data Warehouse) in this book. The following discussion is numbered for reference purposes.

1. The Business Information Value Chain for *Decision Processing* in Figure 15-18 is expanded in Figure 15-22.
2. *Transaction data* is *extracted* and *transformed* from structured data sources such as operational databases and transactions from batch and online systems. *Business knowledge* resources may be *extracted* and *transformed* from unstructured data sources on the corporate intranet. *External information* may be source data from the Internet or extranets.

3. *ETL tools* using metadata defined in the *metadata interchange hub and technical directory* (repository) use *extract and transformation templates*. This metadata was defined in the *common business model* (strategic model) *plus business area and data model templates* (tactical and operational models, plus reverse engineered data models).
4. The central role of the *Federated Data Warehouse* (Enterprise Data Warehouse) is to *Manage* this information.
5. The Data Warehouse is used by *Analytic Applications* and *BI tools* (EIS, DSS, OLAP, and DEW) to *Analyze, Model, and Distribute* this information based on the *Business Information Directory*.
6. Distribution of *information and analyses* is via a *Web interface* and *Information portal* (Enterprise Portal).
7. The *Business information* is distributed to *Business users* and is used for many purposes. These include *business performance management, customer relationship management, financial management, human resource management, and supply chain management*—to name some uses.
8. Based on *Business decisions and actions*, changes may result in *Business knowledge, Transaction data*, or *External information* and the Business Information Value Chain begins again.

The Business Information Value Chain in point (1) above is a central focus of both Data Warehouses and Enterprise Portals. Clearly, the techniques of Web Farming discussed earlier in this chapter provide great assistance to (2) above. We will discuss representative products that can be useful for this source data acquisition. CASE tools (in Chapter 4) as well as extract and transformation tools and migration products (in Chapter 14) relate to (3).

Data Warehouse products for (4) and Business Intelligence tools for (5) are available from companies such as IBM, Platinum, Pine Cone Systems, NCR, Unisys, Oracle, Cognos, Gentia, Hyperion, Pilot, Prism, and SAS, to name a few. Many of these organizations are actively extending their existing products to also support the needs of the emerging Enterprise Portal market. It is not the purpose of this book to discuss the detail of these companies' products. Many excellent Data Warehousing books provide this information. The latest product details and information for each of these companies is available from their respective Web sites.

The publish and subscribe components of an Enterprise Portal are used for (6). We will soon discuss representative products that assist in this information dissemination.

The applications listed in (7) and (8) will be greatly extended as Enterprise Portal applications are developed and business processes are reengineered. New applications and business opportunities will also arise from the central role that will be taken by Corporate Portals in most enterprises in the years ahead. These opportunities are discussed in the concluding pages of this chapter.

To illustrate the directions that Enterprise Portals will take in the coming years, we have selected four representative products—not as an endorsement of those products, but to indicate directions. We have chosen an Enterprise Portal product, an XML data server, a text acquisition product, and an information dissemination product.

Enterprise Portal Products

As we saw in Figure 15-21, an Enterprise Portal draws on *Data Warehouses, Decision Processing Systems, Collaborative Processing Systems*, and *Other Corporate/External Systems* for source data to be included in the Portal through *import interfaces*. In Part 2 we saw how reverse engineering and other metadata methods are used to identify the metadata from these various sources for use in the *Business Information Directory*.

A number of products are becoming available for Enterprise Portals. They support workgroup data in a *collaborative processing* environment, or decision support data in a *decision processing* environment. The following product summary is of necessity brief. Only a few product announcements have been made in this developing field at the time of writing. More information and product details can be obtained from the Web sites, or by Web searches, for the companies that are mentioned below.

Products that support a collaborative processing environment include Lotus *Domino* and *Notes*, Microsoft *Exchange* and *Office 2000*. Other third-party vendors provide products that interface with Lotus Notes and Microsoft Exchange to provide some Enterprise Portal capabilities. One example is Cipher Systems *Knowledge Works*. Because of their dependence on other mainstream products, we will refer to these as *Dependent Collaborative Processing Products*.

There are several *Independent Collaborative Processing Products* announced with an integrated business information directory. These include 2Bridge Software *2Share*, Plumtree Software *Plumtree Server*, and IBM *KnowledgeX for Workgroups*. These products focus on supporting workgroup information, but both 2Bridge and Plumtree support relational databases and Plumtree also supports Cognos *PowerPlay* and Informix *MetaCube*. IBM will expand its *KnowledgeX* product for enterprise-level knowledge management which also includes an information portal and a knowledge catalog of business information [White 1999].

Decision processing Enterprise Portal products are similarly grouped: as *dependent* products integrated with business intelligence (BI) tools; or as *independent* products.

Dependent Decision Processing Products typically include a BI tool for building decision processing objects—such as reports or analyses—and an Enterprise Portal to execute objects and distribute the results to users. These products include Viador (previously called Infospace) *E-Portal Suite*, Information Advantage *MyEureka!*, and SQRIBE *ReportMart Enterprise Information Portal* [White 1999].

Each of the above products is also available as an *Independent Decision Processing Product* with an integrated BI tool, but this is not their main marketing focus. Another independent product is VIT *deliveryMANAGER*. This supports business information managed by relational DBMS products, business intelligence tools, office, and Web products. VIT is also developing analytic applications that use its portal technology.

Of these two Enterprise Portal categories, Decision Processing products offer the greater potential payback for organizations. But Collaborative Processing products can be expected to add decision processing capabilities so that the differences between the product categories will blur over time [White 1999].

We will also see suppliers of Internet Portals offer Enterprise Portal products. An obvious example is Netscape, who see the enterprise as their real market. By earlier delivering Web servers and intranet products to run on many platforms and environments, Netscape differentiated themselves from Microsoft whose products run anywhere "provided it is on Windows." But unable to compete head-to-head with Microsoft, they were taken over by AOL. Distinct from most Internet companies, once AOL moved to New York Stock Exchange from NASDAQ it was regarded as a "blue-chip" Internet company. Like IBM, Microsoft, and Oracle, it now has the financial credibility to attract capital that will enable it to support Netscape as it develops Enterprise Portal and other products for this new market.

To illustrate the functionality and capability of Enterprise Portal products, we will examine one product above in greater detail. Being one of the first products in this new market, the *Viador E-Portal Suite* was referenced in the *InfoWorld* January 25, 1999 article on the [*InfoWorld* Electric] Web site, as shown in Figure 15-23.

The following product summary was extracted from the [Viador] Web site. The Viador E-Portal Suite Architecture is summarized in Figure 15-24. Each of these components is discussed briefly below.

The central component of the E-Portal Suite is the *Viador Information Center*. A high-performance Java server-based information backbone that provides data access, content delivery, session management, and user security, it coordinates Web Server capabilities as discussed in

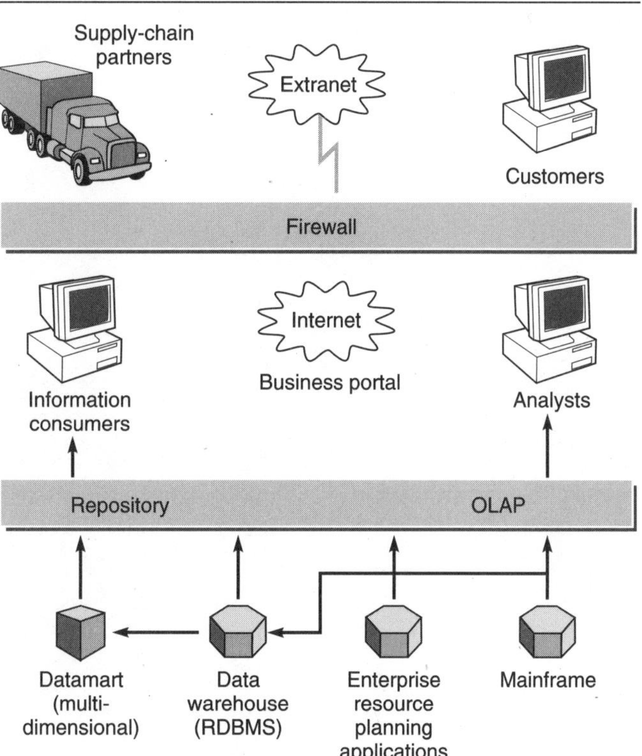

Figure 15-23 Viador E-Portal Suite Infrastructure. *Source*: [InfoWorld] Web site.

Figure 15-21. It supports additional CPUs and load balancing, which enable multiple servers throughout an enterprise to work together in servicing information requests.

Viador Sage is a browser-like portal interface that gives users the ability to access, analyze, and share information. It supports many of the Information Assistant capabilities that we discussed in relation to Figure 15-21. It is available in several server editions, ranging from: a *standard edition*—for static HTML and third-party information viewing; a *professional edition*—which adds Java chart viewing, parameterized reports, and the ability to publish to Viador and third-party environments; an *analyst edition*—which further adds a Business Semantic Query Wizard for metadata-based report generation and capability to view OLAP reports via an OLAP gateway; and a *designer edition*—which still further adds the capability to design enterprise or OLAP reports using relational or multidimensional data sources, to "create any type of report that is needed using virtually any data source" [Viador]. Version 6.0 of Viador E-Portal Suite also includes Infoseek Ultraseek Server. This integrates searches of unstructured data from Microsoft Office, Lotus Notes, intranet are other documents with structural data searches also carried out by Viador's other BI tools.

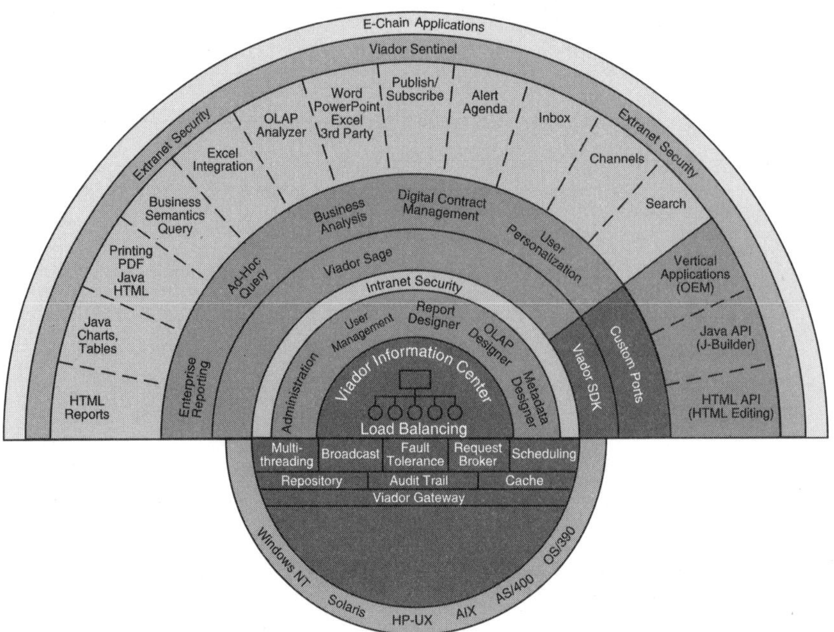

Figure 15-24
The Viador E-Portal Architecture. *Source*: [Viador] Web site.

Viador Sentinel is an integrated security server to extend secure, Web-based extranet access to partners, customers, and suppliers via the Internet. It operates with existing security services such as firewalls and proxy servers to identify and authenticate users, process requests, and deliver encrypted results.

Viador Gateway allows enterprises to choose from a range of native drivers for the data sources to be accessed with the Viador Information Center. These include: Oracle, Sybase, Informix, DB2, SQL Server, Hyperion, Essbase, Oracle Express, Microsoft Plato, WhiteLight, ODBC, and others.

Viador Administrator facilitates the management of large environments with thousands of users. Role-based user administration enables the administrator to define granular access privileges to reports and databases for individual users and groups. Server management facilities audit server usage and monitor user access in real time. It also includes the *Information Designer*, which allows developers to dynamically define semantic sources used for ad-hoc reports.

Finally, the *Viador SDK* is a software development kit for creating custom portals to meet unique needs of individual enterprises.

More product and company information is available from the Viador Corporate Brochure, which can be downloaded as an Adobe Acrobat PDF document from the [Viador] Web site. A self-running demonstration of the E-Portal Suite is also available for download and execution, as well as several articles, a white paper, and customer project descriptions and references. For example, links to articles in *InformationWeek* (describing how the IRS uses the E-Portal Suite) and to ZDNet (describing its use by Xerox) are provided. The latter article, *The Pitch for Portals*, provides references and links to some of the other Enterprise Portal products discussed above.

XML Database Products

We saw a number of references to XML databases earlier in this chapter. This is an area where many new products will emerge over the next few years. Some early announcements have already been made, with some innovative XML database products and XML data servers already released. We will discuss some announcements, and then examine one XML Data Server that is now available.

Microsoft has announced plans to build a *BizTalk Server*. This sits above an application server to support XML applications and data.

BizTalk will provide a framework to help businesses establish connections with each other, together with tracking and analysis tools to monitor transactions. It is similar in scope to the Bluestone *XML Server* and webMethods *B2B Server* used by some of the XML applications discussed earlier in this chapter.

The Microsoft and Bluestone products are designed to allow XML documents and applications to communicate across the Internet. In contrast, Software AG is developing an XML database, currently code-named *Tamino*, for storing and caching XML documents. This is designed to process information from existing databases and applications and convert it to XML.

Oracle supports a hybrid object-relational capability in *Oracle8i*, which is now available. It includes facilities that support XML. Oracle also offers an XML parser for Java, which allows applications written in Java to parse XML data.

The *Content Management Suite* from Poet is a Web-based server for technical and other complex documentation. This works with its Object Server product to manage the transfer of XML objects around a network.

At the time of writing, two major XML products had been released. These are Bluestone *XML Server* and Object Design *Excelon XML Data Server*. We will examine the latter product in more detail.

Object Design is well known for its *ObjectStore* Object Data Base Management System (ODBMS). An XML database is called an *XMLStore* by Object Design, as it is based on ObjectStore technology. Product details for the *eXcelon XML Data Server* are available from the [Object Design] Web site. This product is summarized briefly below in terms of its separate components.

The *eXcelon XML Data Engine* is a data management engine that supports the storage and retrieval of XML data and content. It supports industry standards such as Java, XML, and DOM (Document Object Model—see Chapter 11). An XML parser is used to parse XML data and store it as individual objects in XMLStore, for performance and reuse of XML elements. Any data can be stored, including text, multimedia, and HTML.

XML data is cached in memory for fast XML access and queries across multiple servers as required. Data is indexed at directory and document levels as XML files, documents, queries, Java objects, and Java server extensions in folders with security control. Query data is stored and accessed using XQL, the standard XSL Query Language. XQL adds an analogous SQL "WHERE" capability to XSL logic. Back-end connectivity to existing data for import is provided through ODBC and OLE DB.

The *eXcelon Server* distributes XML data across synchronized caches for scalability. Load balancing directs requests to the server most likely to have the requested data cached in memory, to support scalable XML-based multi-tier applications.

The *eXcelon Toolset* is an integrated set of tools: to administer the eXcelon server; to import, browse, manipulate, and organize data and content inside XMLStores; and to design, produce, and manipulate XML schemas and content. It includes the *eXcelon Explorer* browser to view, import, organize, modify, and query data. The *eXcelon Management Console* administers and configures eXcelon by setting server parameters. The *eXcelon Studio* is used to define XML schemas and generate XML forms and data-driven Web pages for rapid application development. A screenshot of the *eXcelon Studio* from the [Object Design] Web site is shown as Figure 15-25.

The *eXcelon XML Data Server* has been built by Object Design to support open industry standards such as XML, Java, and DOM. They claim that it can be easily extended to support other XML tools, Java objects, and other DOM-compliant languages. It provides standard interfaces that enable any programming or scripting language to be used, such as ASP, VBScript, or JavaScript. They also argue that XML data and applications built to use the *eXcelon XML Data Server* can be extended or changed more readily—owing to the use of the ObjectStore ODBMS—than if a relational DBMS was used to store XML data, multimedia, objects, and queries.

Object Design further claim that eXcelon can store and manipulate any XML data: from legacy data sources; enterprise databases and systems; Microsoft Office 2000; and even PowerPoint. They emphasize its ability to integrate all of these data sources easily with other data from sources such as ERP and other packages—including those from SAP, PeopleSoft, Oracle, and Baan.

Object Design and the *eXcelon XML Data Server* is one of the first XML database products to be released in this emerging market. Its capability is impressive, built as it is on the excellent ObjectStore technology. ODBMS products have found it difficult to compete against relational DBMS products up until now, because of their dependence also on complex object-oriented languages such as C++. But the ease of use and simplicity of XML, together with its hierarchical structure and object-orientation, make the *eXcelon XML Data Server* and its ODBMS technology a very attractive and powerful XML database product for the new XML applications that will be built.

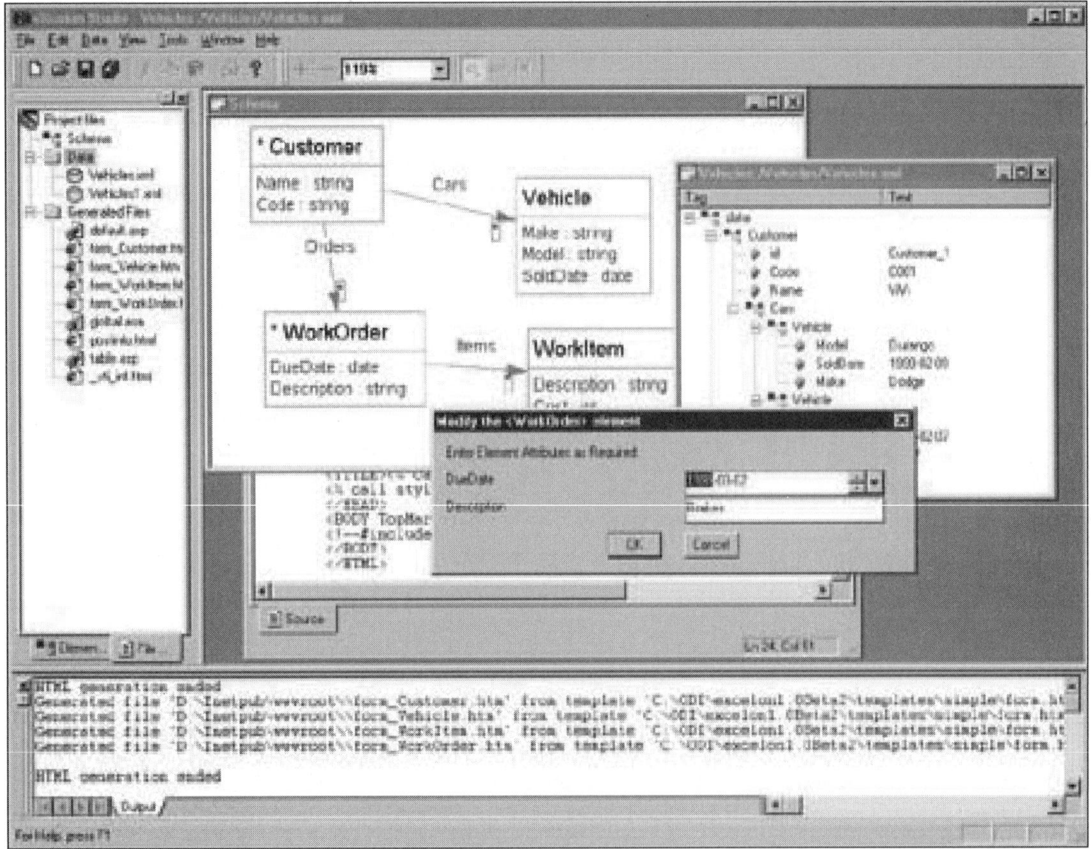

Figure 15-25
eXcelon Studio, for rapid application development of forms and XML applications. *Source*: [Object Design] Web site.

Text Acquisition Products

We earlier discussed the capability of XML to integrate unstructured and structured data and make it available to Enterprise Portals. This provides access to documents, reports, email, graphics, images, audio, and video resources that can represent more than 90 percent of the knowledge resources that exist as unstructured data in some organizations. It opens up another class of products that are now relevant: text retrieval and text mining products.

Text mining takes unstructured information and examines it to discover structure and implicit meanings buried in the text. It goes hand in hand with search technology. By identifying structure and meaning, text mining can impose relevant indexing on textual data. Once a compact useful index is built, information can be retrieved through search technology [Soto 1998].

Text mining software products should exhibit the following features:

- A development environment that makes it easy to build an application
- The ability to scale to distributed, multi-server environments
- Heterogeneous support for a variety of environments and search technologies
- Database integration for unstructured and structured data integration
- Internationalization, to support many languages in a global environment
- Analysis tools for categorization and clustering, as an additional capability and aid for indexing

One text mining poduct that is useful for Enterprise Portals is the IBM *Intelligent Miner for Text* [IBM Text Miner]. A brief summary of the product capabilities follows. The *Intelligent Miner for Text* includes:

Text Analysis Tools for: language identification—to automatically identify the language of a document; clustering—to group related documents based on their content; categorization—to assign documents to one or more user-defined categories; summarization—to extract sentences to create a document summary; and feature extraction—to recognize significant terms in text, such as names, technical terms, and abbreviations.

Full-Text Search Engine for advanced query enhancement and result preparation. This performs an in-depth document analysis during indexing, together with an online update capability for searching—even while the index is being updated. The search engine can be integrated with any document management system and can use third-party tools to support various document input formats. It supports linguistic analysis for many languages—with advanced search paradigms, including Boolean queries, free-text queries, fuzzy searches and synonym searches. For Chinese, Japanese, and Korean it supports Boolean queries, precise term searches, and fuzzy searches [IBM Text Miner].

Web-Crawler Tools monitor a user-defined set of URLs for Internet and intranet information. A ready-to-run generic Web crawler is supplied as an example. The Web crawler toolkit enables a tailored Web crawler to be developed and bound to specific applications.

The *Intelligent Miner for Text* combines the functions of the search engine and the Web crawler. The area to be searched is first specified, whether on the Internet, intranet or extranet. The Web crawler gathers pages and the search engine indexes them, enabling subsequent searches on those pages. A search form and associated Common Gateway Interface (CGI) script enables queries to be defined through a Web browser and the presentation of the results to be specified.

The [IBM Text Miner] Web site provides further product detail, as well as a number of customer references and technical articles.

Information Dissemination Products

We have selected an innovative product to illustrate the information dissemination potential afforded by Enterprise Portals. This is the *DSS Broadcaster* product from MicroStrategy. A developer and vendor of Decision Support Systems, Executive Information Systems, and Relational Online Analytical Processing (ROLAP) systems, MicroStrategy offers an integrated DSS Suite for implementation and deployment of Data Warehouses and Data Marts.

DSS Broadcaster is marketed as an "Active Information Portal Platform." It is described by the [MicroStrategy] Web site as *a platform for developing second-generation e-commerce solutions and enterprise-wide information broadcasting applications. It allows organizations to develop active information portals that harness both relational and non-relational data sources to target the right audience with the right information at the right time*, as illustrated in Figure 15-26.

Distinct from other Data Warehousing solutions that first require users to logon for information, DSS Broadcaster uses a publish and subscribe capability. Reports or other notification (such as alert messages) can be automatically triggered by business events, using an approach similar to what we discussed in Chapter 5 in relation to Decision Early Warning (DEW) systems. Users subscribe to receive specific information that is tailored uniquely to each person's particular needs. The tailored report or message can be sent to the user via many devices as shown in

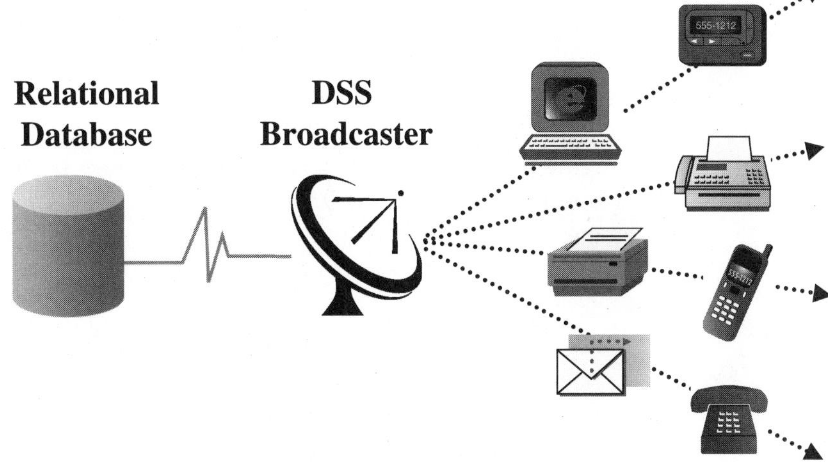

Figure 15-26 MicroStrategy DSS Broadcaster Communication Support. *Source*: [MicroStrategy].

Figure 15-26: by Web, email, fax, printer, phone, alphanumeric pager, personal digital assistant (PDA), mobile phone, or voice mail.

The MicroStrategy *DSS Suite* comprises several other products, illustrated in Figure 15-27 and discussed below. Greater product detail, customer references, demonstrations, and education courses can be found on the [MicroStrategy] Web site.

DSS Server is a scalable, multi-user server for the MicroStrategy DSS platform. It enables users to access the full analysis capabilities of the DSS Suite products and provides maximum performance from the Data Warehouse. *DSS Agent* is the Decision Support client for the DSS platform. This provides "integrated query and reporting, powerful analytics and decision support workflow to analysts, power users, and end users" [MicroStrategy]. DSS Broadcaster requires DSS Server and DSS Agent be installed, for correct operation.

DSS Web provides a Web-enabled interface and management toolset so that both casual and power users can access the full range of analysis capabilities of the DSS platform. *DSS Executive* is an object-based EIS design environment for the DSS platform, which enables application designers to produce an EIS solution in hours, with a high level of customization. *DSS Administrator* is a management and monitoring tool set, enabling administrators to manage performance and applications built with the DSS Suite. *DSS Objects* is a high-level object-oriented application program interface for building customized DSS solutions. Finally, *DSS Architect* is a graphical design tool that allows developers

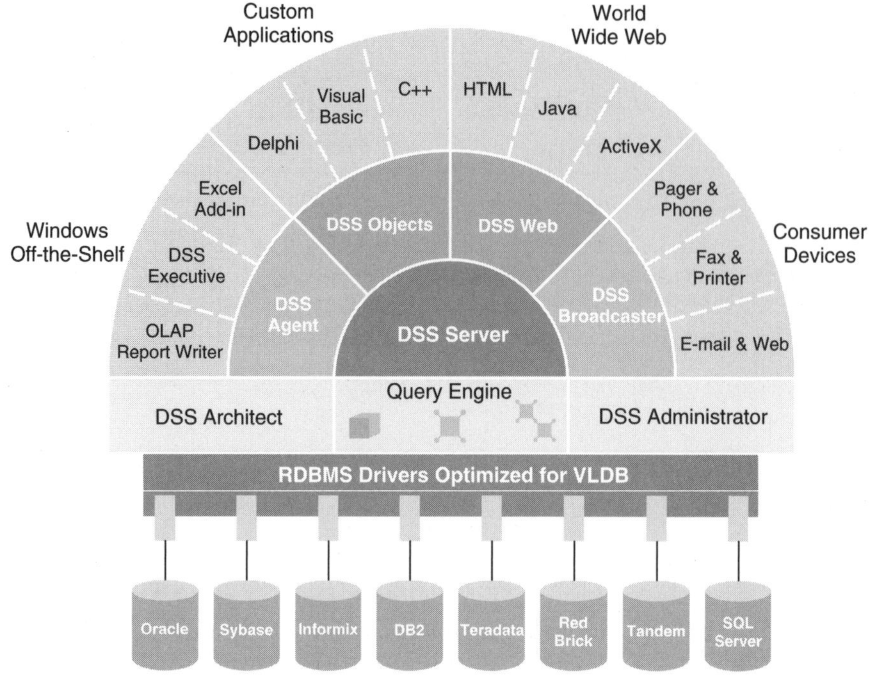

Figure 15-27 DSS Broadcaster Architecture. *Source*: [MicroStrategy] Web site.

to create a logical model of the Data Warehouse, based on business terms that are familiar to the end users.

Using DSS Broadcaster, all content can be personalized to an individual, or to a group of individuals with similar interests. Only information of specific relevance to the group or person is sent, meeting security requirements of the enterprise as defined during the subscription process. Because of the wide range of devices supported, DSS Broadcaster provides intelligent information delivery within the enterprise and also to vendors, partners, business customers, and consumers. It therefore presents opportunities for innovative new applications.

An example of an automatic email message is shown in Figure 15-28. This message has been tailored to the recipient. Highlighted alert results have been expressed in natural English, summary sales results can be in tabular (or graphical) format, an embedded Excel spreadsheet is provided for detailed examination, and a clickable link to other DSS Suite products allows further interactive analysis.

To demonstrate the capability of DSS Broadcaster, the [MicroStrategy] Web site provides a free, online subscription capability to *DSS StockMarket* for the novice or seasoned investor. This offers 11

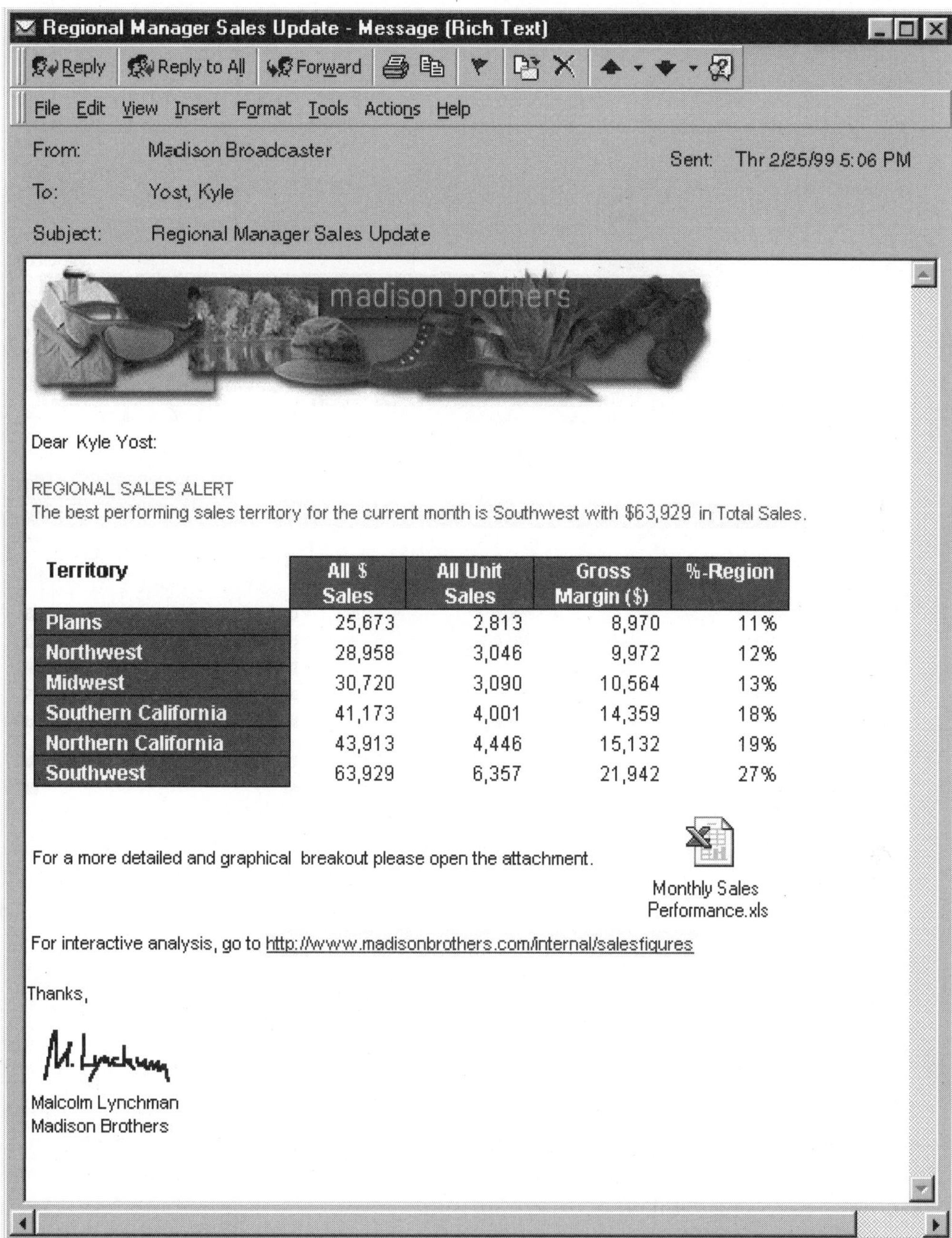

Figure 15-28
Example of a Personalized Email message from DSS Broadcaster, with sales summaries, an embedded Excel spreadsheet, and a clickable link for further interactive analysis using other DSS Suite products. *Source*: [MicroStrategy] Web site.

portfolio and research services including daily stock updates, weekly portfolio summaries, sector winners and losers, Price-Earnings ratios by industry, and stock-to-industry growth rates. After your subscription has been completed, the selected details are automatically sent to you via your nominated delivery mechanism, such as email, fax, pager, mobile phone, or telephone—based and triggered on your individual investment criteria, tailored to your own portfolio and notification preferences.

In a further example, daily store sales results can be automatically sent to all store managers, tailored uniquely to the actual results of each store. Emergency notification of critical stock levels can also be sent as exception reports, based on input from online point-of-sale devices and real-time inventory management. While the daily sales results would be sent by email, emergency notification may be sent by pager. Many other applications also come to mind.

DSS Broadcaster uses both XML and XSL to tailor reports and other information to the unique characteristics of each delivery device, using the data capabilities of XML and the formatting capabilities of XSL. It offers potential for interactive applications. For example, with the ability of PDAs now to support wireless communication, new interactive applications involving (say) subscription, purchasing, and searching can be built based on DSS Broadcaster. Instead of passive reports that are explicitly requested by logging on to a Data Warehousing terminal or via a browser, notification is automatic via a nominated wireless device. Action following that notification is then also immediate, using the wireless communication capabilities of the PDA to respond and react.

The Future of Enterprise Portals

We finish this chapter by discussing some typical Enterprise Portal applications and the impact they will have on many organizations. Enterprise Portals are the next stage of evolution beyond Data Warehouses and Data Marts. They offer an easy to use, integrated, central point of access to information from both structured and unstructured data sources. They present an opportunity to reengineer many business processes, applications, and systems for significant competitive advantage.

We conclude the book by highlighting the major task that still remains. To achieve the true flexibility and information support that is offered by Enterprise Portals, organizations must integrate and use their information and knowledge resources more effectively than they do today. This knowledge integration depends on the establishment of an Enterprise Architecture, and organizational structures, that can truly benefit from the information access capabilities and the technologies represented by Enterprise Portals.

Enterprise Portal Applications

With the XML applications discussed in Chapter 12 and earlier in this chapter, other business opportunities also come to mind. For example, how many families would use a service similar to the Online Shopping Guide for books, if they could use it for comparison shopping of needed products from many supermarkets at once? The earlier problems of proximity and traffic delays that affect physical trips to supermarkets no longer exist. Now many supermarkets can be visited from the comfort of your own home. The most suitable products can be selected based on many more criteria—not just close proximity—for delivery direct to the home.

Customers can subscribe and register interest in particular products or product categories. Using DSS Broadcaster, for example, the supermarket can notify relevant customers automatically of any special sales for products in which they have registered an interest. This notification can be via phone or voice mail, fax, pager, email, or any other supported device.

How many supermarkets would be happy to participate in such an online shopping experience? What does this say about an ability to personalize sales to customers' unique interests—quite apart from marketing information obtained by using subscriptions as an active customer-driven survey. And as the volume of online sales grows, deliveries can be made not from a physical supermarket, but from a central warehouse that exists only to ship for orders received online. Large supermarkets will benefit most from the economies of scale of this online selling environment.

But small "mom and pop" stores, who in an earlier era were forced out of business by large supermarkets, will participate—but now they will be on-line. For they will again have an opportunity to sell their products to local customers. They can offer a localized and personalized online experience to their customers, with delivery, that also distinguished these stores in an earlier era. And they can grow, without the staffing and bricks and mortar costs of that earlier time. They may not even carry much inventory. For if they can negotiate with their suppliers to deliver direct to their customers, they can act as a sales arm for those suppliers. Orders received from their customers are then forwarded to the relevant suppliers for direct delivery to the customer-call "drop-shipping".

Here we see yet another business opportunity. A growth industry will be home delivery. Courier companies can offer a service to "mom and pop" stores: to collect orders from different suppliers, consolidate them, and deliver directly to the end customer. Other Enterprise Portal applications are a catalyst for radical process transformations, as discussed next.

Enterprise Portals for Business Reengineering

The Information Age that we are entering indeed holds enormous promise. The Internet presents many business opportunities. It offers new, innovative business reengineering examples as we have seen above. Let us examine some other XML applications that present reengineering opportunities.

We saw that applications used in an Enterprise Portal are Web-enabled. The user interface is simplified. It is a common point-and-click browser interface, with online forms for data input. Tables, reports, and other results are dynamically generated. These replace the different interfaces used by legacy systems, relational databases, client/server products, and offline reference documents. Instead of a multitude of input formats and user instructions, with significant operator training overheads, we see a simple, well-understood interface that can be used with any application.

Staff are easier to train. People can provide input related to their job, often as a normal part of that job. For example, consider the *Time and Attendance System* discussed earlier. Previously, staff had to fill out Time and Attendance forms, which were forwarded to the Payroll Department. These forms were keyed into terminals used with legacy applications by data entry staff. Any errors had to be returned to the relevant employee for correction, then resubmitted. The result was high staff costs, high potential for errors, and significant delays.

Contrast this now with the reengineered Web-enabled application. Each employee has a personal Web page in the Enterprise Portal. This has links to all online resources needed by that employee to carry out the current assigned job. Time and attendance details are entered online by the individual, using a Web browser. Information about holiday entitlements are clearly shown. The manager can review and submit all employee timecards for payroll processing. But the manager also has a convenient central facility for dynamic rescheduling of staff if required.

The *Personal Investment System* that we discussed earlier has similar potential as a service offered to employees. It can provide up-to-date details of each employee's retirement benefits and investments. Linked to relevant stock exchange Web sites, it can provide real-time information in relation to Employee Share Plans. Other employee services can also be delivered through each employee's Enterprise Portal Web page.

The difficulty of providing ready access to unstructured data in text documents and reports, with graphics and images, is also resolved. Consider the earlier *Integrated Maintenance and Ordering* system used by the airline, or the *Automated Customer Help Desk* system. In each case, offline resources as unstructured data in Word, PDF, or other document formats were seamlessly integrated by XML with structured data in databases and reengineered processes.

Audio and video resources can also be easily included, accessible from a browser at the click of a mouse. Not only would these resources be associated with the repair and maintenance of specific parts or products, but also for other purposes. For example, for enterprises that provide day-care facilities to look after the children of employees, a button can be placed on the Web page of these parents. With a digital still or video camera in the day-care center, parents can view the current activities of their children. This camera view from the employee's desk into the day-care center may be designed to stay open in the employee's browser only for 30 seconds (say), to avoid affecting job productivity.

The *Online Shopping* system that we saw earlier, with the other applications also discussed, suggest other selling opportunities with clickable buttons for video sales demonstrations. The Purchasing process is the first that comes to mind. We discussed one such eaxmple in Chapter 12, with the *Multiple Supplier System* obtaining regular quotes from the many suppliers of specific parts. Other purchasing applications are also candidates for reengineering. These and many other business processes can be rengineered using XML and Enterprise Portals, with a potentially useful result:

> Enterprise Portals can present Business Reengineering implementation opportunities

We have seen that legacy processes can be transformed by XML, when used in this way. In some cases, radical transformation is the result: a major characteristic of Business Reengineering. This is achieved by application of XML and Internet/intranet technologies. Once the constraints of legacy systems and the limitations of offline or batch processes can be overcome, information flows can be changed. Processes can be fundamentally altered. More efficient workflows can be used as we saw in Chapter 12 and in this chapter.

The process and change constraints that were difficult to overcome with Business Reengineering may be somewhat reduced with XML. Instead of requiring complete redevelopment of applications and systems to implement reengineered processes, some systems and process transformations can be eased by using XML front-ends. With XML, some legacy systems may still be able to be used in part or in whole without requiring complete replacement, as was the only approach before the advent of XML.

In discussing the move towards Corporate Portals over the coming years in *The Portal is the Desktop*, the Director of Knowledge Technologies research at International Data Corporation (IDC) [Murray 1999] says:

> 'Corporate portals must connect us not only with everything we need, but (also) with everyone we need, and provide all the tools we need to work together. This means that groupware, e-mail, workflow, and desktop applications—even critical business applications—must all be accessible through the portal. Thus, the portal is the desktop, and your commute (to work) is just a phone call away.
>
> This is a radical new way of computing. It's much more effective for companies than traditional approaches, since they can outsource the entire infrastructure as a monthly service.' He makes the point that: 'Corporate Portals will provide access to everything from infrastructure to the desktop, so portal vendors will be the Microsofts of the future.'

He discusses four stages in the evolution of Corporate Portals:

1. Enterprise information portals, which connect people with information.
2. Enterprise collaborative portals, which provide collaborative computing capabilities of all kinds.
3. Enterprise expertise portals, which connect people with other people based on their abilities, expertise, and interests.

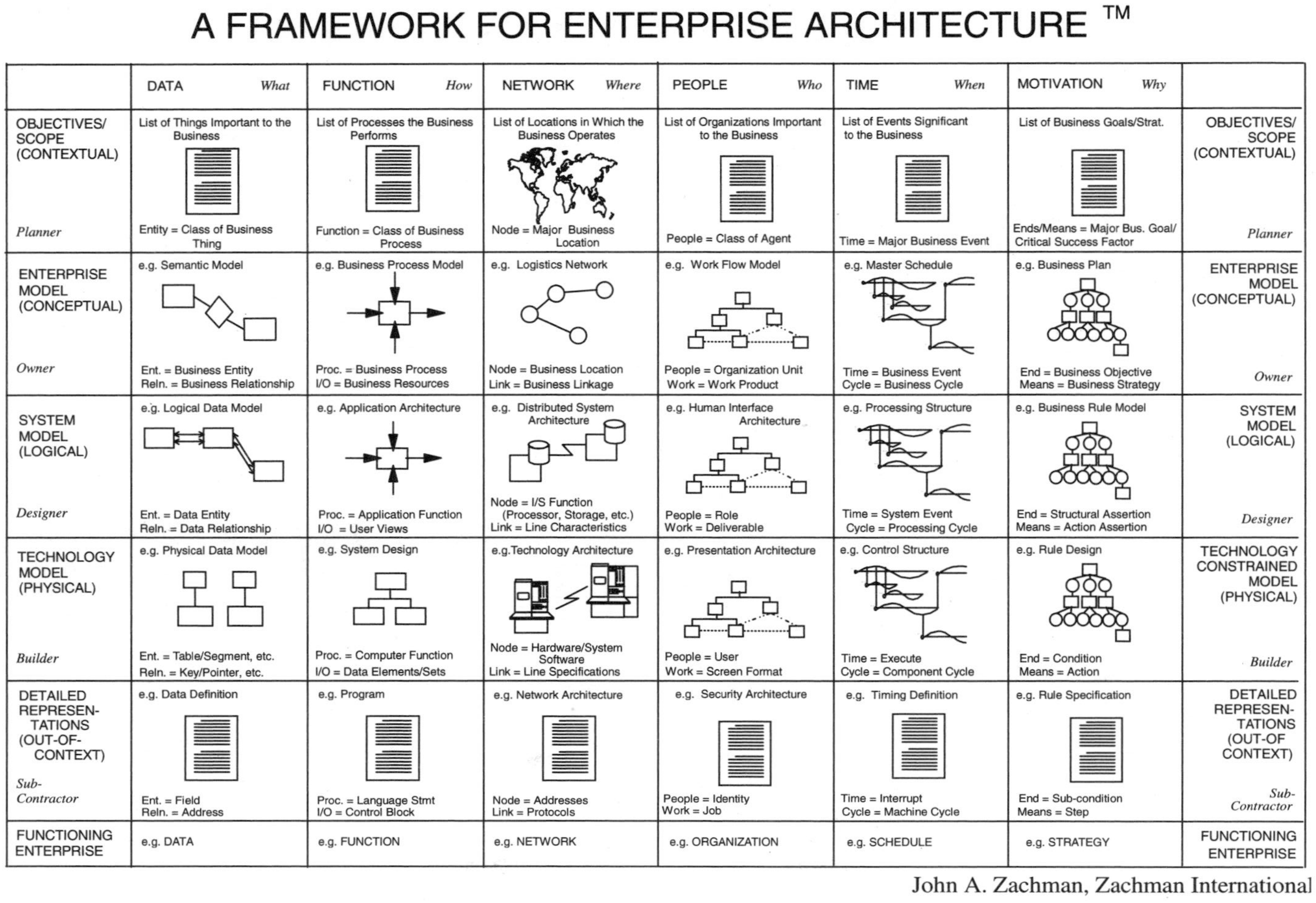

A FRAMEWORK FOR ENTERPRISE ARCHITECTURE ™

	DATA *What*	FUNCTION *How*	NETWORK *Where*	PEOPLE *Who*	TIME *When*	MOTIVATION *Why*	
OBJECTIVES/ SCOPE (CONTEXTUAL) *Planner*	List of Things Important to the Business Entity = Class of Business Thing	List of Processes the Business Performs Function = Class of Business Process	List of Locations in Which the Business Operates Node = Major Business Location	List of Organizations Important to the Business People = Class of Agent	List of Events Significant to the Business Time = Major Business Event	List of Business Goals/Strat. Ends/Means = Major Bus. Goal/ Critical Success Factor	OBJECTIVES/ SCOPE (CONTEXTUAL) *Planner*
ENTERPRISE MODEL (CONCEPTUAL) *Owner*	e.g. Semantic Model Ent. = Business Entity Reln. = Business Relationship	e.g. Business Process Model Proc. = Business Process I/O = Business Resources	e.g. Logistics Network Node = Business Location Link = Business Linkage	e.g. Work Flow Model People = Organization Unit Work = Work Product	e.g. Master Schedule Time = Business Event Cycle = Business Cycle	e.g. Business Plan End = Business Objective Means = Business Strategy	ENTERPRISE MODEL (CONCEPTUAL) *Owner*
SYSTEM MODEL (LOGICAL) *Designer*	e.g. Logical Data Model Ent. = Data Entity Reln. = Data Relationship	e.g. Application Architecture Proc. = Application Function I/O = User Views	e.g. Distributed System Architecture Node = I/S Function (Processor, Storage, etc.) Link = Line Characteristics	e.g. Human Interface Architecture People = Role Work = Deliverable	e.g. Processing Structure Time = System Event Cycle = Processing Cycle	e.g. Business Rule Model End = Structural Assertion Means = Action Assertion	SYSTEM MODEL (LOGICAL) *Designer*
TECHNOLOGY MODEL (PHYSICAL) *Builder*	e.g. Physical Data Model Ent. = Table/Segment, etc. Reln. = Key/Pointer, etc.	e.g. System Design Proc. = Computer Function I/O = Data Elements/Sets	e.g.Technology Architecture Node = Hardware/System Software Link = Line Specifications	e.g. Presentation Architecture People = User Work = Screen Format	e.g. Control Structure Time = Execute Cycle = Component Cycle	e.g. Rule Design End = Condition Means = Action	TECHNOLOGY CONSTRAINED MODEL (PHYSICAL) *Builder*
DETAILED REPRESEN-TATIONS (OUT-OF-CONTEXT) *Sub-Contractor*	e.g. Data Definition Ent. = Field Reln. = Address	e.g. Program Proc. = Language Stmt I/O = Control Block	e.g. Network Architecture Node = Addresses Link = Protocols	e.g. Security Architecture People = Identity Work = Job	e.g. Timing Definition Time = Interrupt Cycle = Machine Cycle	e.g. Rule Specification End = Sub-condition Means = Step	DETAILED REPRESEN-TATIONS (OUT-OF CONTEXT) *Sub-Contractor*
FUNCTIONING ENTERPRISE	e.g. DATA	e.g. FUNCTION	e.g. NETWORK	e.g. ORGANIZATION	e.g. SCHEDULE	e.g. STRATEGY	FUNCTIONING ENTERPRISE

John A. Zachman, Zachman International

Figure 15-29
The Zachman Framework for Enterprise Architecture (from Figure 8-18).

4. Enterprise knowledge portals, which combine all of the above to deliver personalized content based on what each user is actually doing.

He then goes on to describe a number of products that are starting to appear in each of these Corporate Portal evolution stages. His complete article is available on the Internet [Murray 1999].

Application Service Providers

We are beginning to see the early moves into the portal environment described above by Gerry Murray, with the emergence of Application Service Providers (ASPs). Early ASPs will typically also be Internet Service Providers (ISPs). They will not only provide ready access to the Internet, but also offer access to much of the software that you need from your desktop, as well as to other products such as Enterprise Resource Planning (ERP) systems from SAP and others.

This will be the true realization of Network Computing. Not by using Java as a portable language as promoted by Sun and Oracle, but by outsourcing hardware, servers, networks and network management, software and software management, help desk, maintenance and other Total Costs of Ownership (TCO) to ASPs. This is a radical move that will transform desktop computing as we know it. It will provide ubiquitous computing through the Internet and the intranet. And with a move to wider bandwidths on the Internet—with higher data rates available also through wireless computing via PDAs or mobile phones that access the Internet for email and browsing—we will soon be able to work not just from the office, but from anywhere. On a few short years, these ASPs will become Information Utilities for the future.

Seeing the potential threat to its desktop monopoly that is presented by Corporate Portals and by ASPs, Microsoft has decided that it will adopt a win–win strategy by also becoming part of this ultimate move to Network Computing. The release of Internet Explorer 5.0 and Microsoft Office 2000 provided some support for this capability. With Office 2000, Microsoft Office Web Server extensions for intranet servers within the enterprise support collaboration and other groupware applications. But Microsoft will also make these extensions available to ISPs to help them become ASPs. In the future, any of these ASPs will enter into license agreements with Microsoft; two initial ASP licencees were announced with the release of Office 2000. ASPs will be able to offer rental access to their customers so they can use Microsoft and other applications. These will be rented for a fixed monthly or annual fee, or on a pay-for-use basis. So Microsoft will benefit both ways—not just from new product sales and upgrade sales as we have today, but also from license fees that are paid by ASPs to Microsoft.

With the emergence of Corporate Portals (Enterprise Portals) over the next few years, we will see radical changes in the way we use computers. The Internet and intranet will become more and more a part of our daily work lives. Instead of commuting by road, rail or bus to work, increasingly we will be able to telecommute from wherever we are via the Internet or intranet. The Corporate Portal will be our desktop, available anywhere we log-on to our personalized portal page. From there we will have access to all of the software, systems and other knowledge resources that we need to do our job.

Enterprise Portals and Enterprise Architecture

The benefits of the Zachman Framework for Enterprise Architecture [Zachman 1987, 1991, 1992, 1996] that we discussed in Chapters 1 and 8 are difficult for enterprises to achieve. This has largely been due to the enormous legacy of systems and databases that were built early in the Information Age, in a non-architected, non-integrated fashion up until the late 1990s. The Zachman Framework for Enterprise Architecture from Figure 8-18 has been repeated as Figure 15-29, for easy reference and discussion.

Referring to the Zachman Framework, we see that Data Warehouses largely address the *Data* column—focusing on *what* information is required. XML applications, in contrast, use metadata of the *Data* column to focus also on the *Process* (*how*) column and the *when* and *who* columns of the six-column Zachman Framework in Figure 15-28. When Data Warehouses evolve to Enterprise Portals using XML, most cells of the Zachman Framework are addressed.

We discussed in Chapter 1 that manual processes have evolved over many years based on the approach taken by Adam Smith early in the Industrial Age [Smith 1910]. This was innovative when introduced by him in the late eighteenth century. But manual processes became increasingly chaotic with the rapid pace of change from the mid-twentieth century. With the introduction of the computer in the second half of the twentieth century, these manual processes were automated. But the automated systems generally implemented the same manual processes without significant change. And what has been the result?

> Instead of manual chaos, many enterprises now operate in a continual state of automated chaos!

Now with the pace of change and the competitive Armageddon of the Internet, customers can visit the front door of an enterprise—its Web site—with the click of a mouse. But if they do not find what they need, they will leave just as fast, also with the click of a mouse, and visit a competitor. For the chaos that previously existed in the back office is now on the front doorstep for the world to see. Not by what can be done, but rather by what cannot be done because of the legacy of the past.

Imagine how long large buildings or bridges would remain standing, or planes would continue to fly, if they were built without an architecture. Yet most enterprises have not been designed and built based on an Enterprise Architecture. Instead they have evolved. In an earlier era with less competition, there was time available to make required changes. There was time to reorganize. And if a new organization structure did not have the desired effect, the enterprise could be reorganized again, and again. It only cost money!

Yet today there is no time to reorganize. Enterprises must be designed to change, and to change often. No amount of money can be thrown at this problem. Bureaucratic or Regional organizational structures that served enterprises well in the past [Rowe et al 1990] are no longer effective or responsive enough for the rapid change environment of today. Matrix organization structures may be more flexible and responsive to corporate change for some industries and enterprises [Finkelstein 1992].

But an ability merely to change an organization structure quickly is no longer sufficient. Today, most enterprises totally depend on computers. Information systems must be closely aligned with an enterprise's corporate goals and strategic plans as we saw in Chapters 2 and 4. And systems must be built so that they can easily and rapidly change when the enterprise changes. The technology is now available: this book has been your guide. But the inhibiting factor now is the enterprise itself. No software can do this for you; it requires time, people, and therefore money. An ability to change is imperative, for enterprises and systems that cannot change rapidly—and often—will not survive in the competitive environment of the Information Age.

There is a ray of light; a glimmer of hope. John Zachman has defined an architecture for information systems and for enterprises which (when implemented) brings with it the stability, control, and flexibility that is missing from most organizations. But it is *not* a silver bullet. It is difficult to achieve. It requires work, it takes time, and it costs money. Except that now, it is no longer optional. It cannot be placed in the "too-hard" basket. It is a mandatory undertaking—if an enterprise wants to achieve the flexibility and rapid competitive response capability that is vital for success in the twenty-first century. For it closely aligns and integrates the information systems of an enterprise with its strategic plans and corporate goals.

In some enterprises the implementation of an Enterprise Architecture may be much more difficult than the design of a new airplane or a new building. Yet in the airplane and construction industries there is an enormous body of knowledge and countless years of experience that help these industries achieve success in new endeavors.

The IT industry has also learned well, and fast. We now have many years of experience behind us. But with the construction and the airplane industries, their early implementation failures are no longer standing, or flying. They have long since collapsed or crashed. In contrast, many of the early systems designed and built by the IT industry are still running. They are our legacy. And we are now paying the enormous price of designing and building those systems without first defining an architecture.

Enterprise Architecture is imperative for success and survival in the Information Age

Time is running out. Enterprises and the IT industry no longer have any other alternatives. An Enterprise Architecture is imperative for success and survival in the Information Age. This task has been delayed in most organizations for too long. It cannot be deferred any longer. The Zachman Framework for Enterprise Architecture provides the blueprint; the Internet, intranet, and extranet, together with XML, provide some of the technologies. Enterprise Portals provide effective deployment capability for these technologies. They remove many constraints and limitations of the past. They evolve from Enterprise Data Warehouses. With XML they provide ready access to structured and unstructured data and information within, and outside, the enterprise.

The technologies are available, the methods have been developed. Enterprises are applying these technologies and methods to their own environment to develop solutions that present significant competitive advantages. These organizations want to ensure that they are counted among the survivors—who will grow and prosper in the turbulent years ahead. Contact your authors and John Zachman to find out how you too can join their ranks [see references].

Visit the [IES] Web site for links, resources, papers, inhouse seminars, and self-study courses. This Web site is maintained as an up-to-date extension of this book, with the latest information on Enterprise Portals, XML, and related technologies and methods.

Enterprise Portals present process reengineering opportunities, with transformed processes or new processes that bring competitive advantage. They offer the promise of casting aside the shackles of past legacy systems and databases, producing enterprises that have been designed to change and compete more nimbly and aggressively than ever before. In the Information Age of the twenty-first century only strong, rapid-response organizations have the best potential for success. The law of the jungle will decide the winners.

REFERENCES

Clive Finkelstein, Peter Aiken and John Zachman can be contacted directly by emailing <cfink@ies.aust.com>.

DataBase Associates Decision Processing Web site—http://www.decisionprocessing.com

DM Review Web site—http://www.dmreview.com/

Finkelstein, C. (1989) *An Introduction to Information Engineering*, Reading, MA: Addison-Wesley [ISBN 0-201-41654-9]

Finkelstein, C. (1992) *Information Engineering: Strategic Systems Development*, Reading, MA: Addison-Wesley [ISBN 0-201-50988-1].

Finkelstein, C. (1996) *The Competitive Armageddon: Survival and Prosperity in the Connected World of the Internet.* Download from the "Papers" section of the IES Web Site located at—http://www.ies.aust.com/~ieinfo/

Hackathorn, R. (1999) *Web Farming for the Data Warehouse*, Morgan Kaufman, ISBN: Holzner, S. (1998), *XML Complete*, McGraw-Hill, ISBN: 0-07-913702-4. Covers XML with focus on Java (516 pages + CD-ROM).

IBM Web site—http://www.software.ibm.com/data/iminer/fortext/

IES Web site—http://www.ies.aust.com/~ieinfo/ for links, resources, papers, inhouse seminars and self-study courses. Clive Finkelstein maintains this with the latest information on Enterprise Portals, XML and related technologies and methods, as an extension of this book.

InfoWorld Web site—http://www.infoworld.com/cgi-bin/displayStory.pl?/features/990125eip.htm

MicroStrategy Web site—http://www.strategey.com/

Murray, G. (1999) *The Portal is the Desktop*, Framingham, MA. International Data Corporation. This article is also available from the Intraspect Web site—http://www.intraspect.com/news_press_a24.htm

Object Design Web site—http://www.objectdesign.com/

Rowe, A.J, Mason, R.O, Dickel, K.E. and Snyder, N.H. (1990) *Strategic Management and Business Policy: A Methodological Approach,* 3rd edn, Reading, MA: Addison-Wesley.

Smith, A. (1910) *The Wealth of Nations*, London: Dent.

Soto, P. (1998) "Text Mining: Beyond Search Technology," *DB2 Magazine Online*—http://www.db2mag.com/98fsoto.html

Viador E-Portal Suite Web site—http://www.viador.com/

WWW Consortium: XML, XSL, and XLL specifications—http://www.w3.org/

White, C. (1999) "Using Information Portals in the Enterprise," *DM Review* (April).

Web Farming Web site—http://www.webfarming.com/

James Tauber's XMLINFO Web site—http://www.xmlinfo.com/

Microsoft XML Scenarios Web site—http://microsoft.com/xml/scenario/intro.asp

Zachman, J.A. (1987) "A Framework for Information Systems Architecture," *IBM Systems Journal* 26(3):76–292, IBM Publication G321–5298.

Zachman, J.A. (1991) "Zachman Framework Extensions: An Update," *Data Base Newsletter*, July/August, 19(4): 1–16.

Zachman, J.A and Sowa, J.F. (1992) "Extending and Formalizing the Framework for Information Systems Architecture," *IBM Systems Journal*, 31(3), IBM Publication G321–5488.

Zachman, J.A. (1996) *Concepts of the Framework for Enterprise Architecture*, Los Angeles, CA: Zachman International.

INDEX

D

E

J

K

L

M

P

Q

R

S

T

U

V

W

X

Z

ABOUT THE AUTHORS

Clive Finkelstein is the acknowledged creator of the Information Engineering methodology. He is a distinguished International Advisory Board member of the Data Management Association (DAMA) International.

Peter H. Aiken is a professor at Virginia Commonwealth University and also an International Advisory Board Member of DAMA International. He is the author of Data Reverse Engineering (McGraw-Hill, 1995).